Philosophic Classics
Volume VI

ASIAN PHILOSOPHY

FORREST E. BAIRD
Whitworth College

RAEBURNE S. HEIMBECK
Central Washington University

PEARSON
Prentice
Hall

Upper Saddle River, New Jersey 07458

Library of Congress Cataloging-in-Publication Data

Philosophic classics, Volume VI: ASIAN PHIL. / Editors: Forrest E. Baird and Raeburne S. Heimbeck
 p. cm.
 "Walter Kaufmann, late, of Princeton University."
 Includes bibliographical references.
 Contents: v. 1. Ancient philosophy—v. 2. Medieval philosophy—v. 3. Modern philosophy—
v. 4. Nineteenth-century philosophy. 3rd ed.—v. 5. Twentieth-century philosophy. 3rd ed.—v. 6. Asian
philosophy. 1st ed.
 ISBN 0–13–048556–X (v. 1).—ISBN 0–13–048557–8 (v. 2).—ISBN 0–13–048558–6
(v. 3).—ISBN 0–13–048550–0 (v. 4).—ISBN 0–13–048563–2 (v. 5)—ISBN 0–13–352329–2 (v. 6)
 1. Philosophy.   I. Baird, Forrest E.   II. Kaufmann, Walter Arnold.   III. Heimbeck, Raeburne S.
B21.P39 2000
100—dc21   98–32332
                                                                                                    CIP

VP/Editorial Director: Charlyce Jones Owen
Assistant Editor: Wendy Yurash
Editorial Assistant: Carla Worner
Marketing Manager: Kara Kindstrom
Marketing Assistant: Jennifer Lang
Production Liaison: Fran Russello
Manufacturing Buyer: Christina Helder
Cover Art Director: Jayne Conte
Cover Design: Bruce Kenselaar
Manager, Cover Visual Research & Permissions: Karen Sanatar
Cover Photo: Krishna, acting as Arjuna's charioteer, Janet Peckam/Dorling Kindersley Media
 Library
Composition/Full-Service Project Management: Bruce Hobart/Pine Tree Composition, Inc.

This volume is dedicated to our dear friend,
F. DALE BRUNER

Credits and acknowledgments borrowed from other sources and reproduced, with permission, in this textbook appear on appropriate page within text.

Pearson Education LTD.   Pearson Education Australia PTY, Limited
Pearson Education Singapore, Pte. Ltd   Pearson Education North Asia Ltd
Pearson Education, Canada, Ltd   Pearson Educación de Mexico, S.A. de C.V.
Pearson Education–Japan   Pearson Education Malaysia, Pte. Ltd

ISBN 0-13-352329-2

Contents

CHINESE THOUGHT   279

Preface

Since 1961, *Philosophic Classics* has provided a generation of students with an anthology of quality in the history of Western philosophy. This latest edition extends the late Professor Kaufmann's work by adding a volume on Asian Thought.

In choosing texts for this volume we have tried wherever possible to follow three principles: (1) to use complete works or, where more appropriate, complete sections of works (2) in clear translations (3) of texts central to Asian philosophy. To make the works more accessible to students, most footnotes treating textual matters (variant readings, etc.) are omitted. In addition, each section is introduced by a brief essay giving a brief overview of the ideas and context of the readings along with suggestions for further reading.

Our spelling of Sanskrit and Chinese terms calls for a brief explanation. Both Sanskrit and Chinese have their own writing systems. Transliterating these languages into the Roman alphabet poses challenges that can be effectively met in various ways. Highly technical or advanced works on Indian philosophy in English usually employ a battery of diacritical marks to convey the precise pronunciation of Sanskrit words. Such an approach is unnecessarily cumbersome for the purposes of this book. Instead, we offer a simple, reasonably phonetic spelling of Sanskrit terms, a spelling found in many beginning and intermediate studies in the field. A number of methods for Romanizing Chinese have been devised. Either the older Wade-Giles or the more recent Pinyin are the preferred styles today. Pinyin, invented by the Chinese themselves and the more straightforward, will likely prevail in the future. We, however, have elected to use the Wade-Giles throughout this volume, because all the readings presented here still hold to it.

But we give the Pinyin equivalent after the first occurrence of each Chinese word written in Wade-Giles, to facilitate recognition of both styles.

*   *   *

We would like to thank the many people who assisted us in this volume including the library staff of Whitworth College, especially Hans Bynagle, Gail Fielding, and Jeanette Langston; Chenyang Li, Chairman of the Central Washington University Philosophy Department, who read and made astute comments on the Chinese sections; our acquisitions editor, Ross Miller of Prentice Hall, our copy editor, Linda Benson, and our production editor, Bruce Hobart; and the following reviewers: Paul Reasoner, Bethel College; Claudia Close, Cabrillo College; Richard F. Sherburne, Seattle University; David J. Kalupahana, University of Hawaii; and Elizabeth F. Collins, Ohio University.

We are especially thankful to our wives, Joy Lynn Fulton Baird and Cynthia Krieble, who have supported us in this process.

Finally, we would like to dedicate this volume to our dear friend F. Dale Bruner.

Forrest E. Baird
Professor of Philosophy
Whitworth College

Raeburne S. Heimbeck
Emeritus Professor of Philosophy
Central Washington University

Invitation to Asian Thought

Asian thought encompasses the leading ideas found in masterworks of Asian philosophy and religion. Since Asian philosophy and religion commingle extensively, Asian thought and Asian philosophy may be taken as virtually equivalent. This book is a reader in Asian philosophical classics. Most selections are given complete. Translations have been chosen for clarity, accuracy, and appeal. The readings are arranged in sections featuring major movements in their historical progression. Each section begins with an introduction that provides background information and an analysis of each reading, as well as bibliographical suggestions for further study. The sections are organized under two larger groupings that reflect the major traditions in the field—Indian thought and Chinese thought.

Asian thought holds a prominent place in world or global philosophy—the comparative investigation of philosophical traditions worldwide. The study of global philosophies is relatively new in the West. Only since the beginning of the twentieth century have Westerners, in increasing number, begun to pay close attention to Asian thought. And as a serious specialization among professional philosophers in Western countries, comparative philosophy dates back only to the middle of the last century. Asian philosophers, for their part, have been involved in the enterprise since the colonial era dawned in their part of the globe four centuries ago. Western culture impacted the East long before the East came west. World philosophy is composed of three major and several minor traditions. The European (Western), the Indian, and the Chinese are the majors, equally ancient, developed, and profound. Their origins are independent and go back 2,600 years. Almost all world-famous philosophers belong to one of these three. The minor traditions stem from the majors: Jewish, Arabic, North American, and Latin American philosophy from the European; Tibetan and Southeast Asian from the Indian; Japanese from both the Indian and the Chinese; and Korean from the Chinese alone.

When the philosophies of Europe, India, and China are compared, three findings emerge. The first has to do with time and place. Philosophical activity burst onto the scene of world history about the sixth century B.C.E. (the so-called Axial Age) in three civilizations geographically and culturally remote from one another. Why then and why there? No easy answers to these questions are available. The second finding concerns the central problems that make philosophy a distinct intellectual activity. Those problems are known in philosophical circles as metaphysics, epistemology, and ethics. *Metaphysics* deals with what is real, *epistemology* with how we know, and *ethics* with what has value. The centrality of just these problems in all three major traditions is what makes them the primary problems of philosophy. Other philosophical problems play lesser roles. Logic, for example, has received considerable attention in Europe and India but little in China, politics in Europe and China but much less in India, aesthetics in Europe but not in either India or China. The Greek terms *metaphysics, epistemology,* and *ethics* are used throughout European philosophy. Indian philosophy has its own technical terms, in Sanskrit, for the same problems. Chinese philosophy, historically, has dealt with the problems but has no technical terms for them. The tendency in recent times has been for Indian and Chinese philosophers to adopt the Greek terms. A third discovery from the comparison of the three major traditions is that practically the same spectrum of positions on the central problems appears in Asia as in Europe, with varying emphases. For example, idealism and materialism exist as world explanations in both Asian and European thought, but, whereas Asian thinkers prefer idealism, the picture in Europe is mixed. Again, Asia values intuition over sense perception and logic as a method of inquiry; Europe reverses those priorities. This third finding dispels the misconception, still current, that the philosophies of Europe, India, and China are mutually exclusive. Western oversimplifications of Asian philosophy are gradually disappearing, as comparative work shows that for centuries philosophy in India and China has been as diverse as that in Europe.

The sections that follow, while introducing the readings, also outline the history of Indian and Chinese philosophy. Indian philosophy surfaced in a body of sacred Hindu writings known as the Vedas between 1200 and 100 B.C.E. This early Hindu orthodoxy was challenged by heterodox alternatives, Buddhism especially, between 600 B.C.E. and 400 C.E. Later Hindu orthodoxy answered those challenges by creating forceful new perspectives between 400 and 1600 C.E. The orthodox tradition has undergone revision through encounters with Western thought from 1600 to the present.

Chinese philosophy has unfolded historically in three great periods—ancient (later Chou/Zhou and Ch'in/Qin dynasties, 600 to 200 B.C.E.), middle (Han through Ming dynasties, 200 B.C.E. to 1650 C.E.), and modern (Ch'ing/Qing Dynasty through the People's Republic of China, 1650 to the present). In the ancient period, the six classical schools emerged, of which the two most important were Confucianism and Taoism. In the middle period, Buddhist innovations arrived from India, and the three major traditions of Confucianism, Taoism, and Buddhism interacted to produce Neo-Confucian syntheses. The modern period, finally, has seen Chinese philosophy respond to its own encounters with the West.

*   *   *

Should the reader wish to pursue further the study of Asian thought, a number of excellent works are available, listed here in four sections and in order of publication.

WORLD PHILOSOPHY

Sarvepali Radhakrishnan, ed., *History of Philosophy, Eastern and Western*, 2 vols. (London: George Allen & Unwin, 1952).

P.T. Raju, *Introduction to Comparative Philosophy* (Lincoln: University of Nebraska Press, 1962).

John C. Plott, et al., *Global History of Philosophy*, 5 vols. (Delhi: Motilal Banarsidass, 1963–1989).

Robert C. Solomon and Kathleen M. Higgins, eds., *From Africa to Zen: An Invitation to World Philosophy* (Lanham, MD: Rowman & Littlefield, 1993).

David E. Cooper, *World Philosophies: An Historical Introduction* (Oxford: Blackwell, 1995).

Robert C. Solomon and Kathleen M. Higgins, *World Philosophy: A Text with Readings* (New York: McGraw-Hill, 1995).

Eliot Deutsch and Ron Bontekoe, eds., *A Companion to World Philosophies* (Oxford: Blackwell, 1997).

Ben-Ami Scharfstein, *A Comparative History of World Philosophy* (Albany: SUNY Press, 1998).

Chenyang Li, *The Tao Encounters the West: Explorations in Comparative Philosophy* (Albany: SUNY Press, 1999).

ASIAN PHILOSOPHY

Hajime Nakamura, *Ways of Thinking of Eastern Peoples: India, China, Tibet, Japan*, rev. English translation, ed. Philip P. Wiener (Honolulu: The University Press of Hawaii, 1964).

Michael C. Brannigan, *The Pulse of Wisdom: The Philosophies of India, China, and Japan* (Belmont, CA: Wadsworth, 1995).

Brian Carr and Indira Mahalingam, eds., *Companion Encyclopedia of Asian Philosophy* (London and New York: Routledge, 1997).

Patrick S. Bresnan, *Awakening: An Introduction to the History of Eastern Thought* (Upper Saddle River, NJ: Prentice Hall, 1999).

Joel J. Kupperman, *Learning from Asian Philosophy* (New York and Oxford: Oxford University Press, 1999).

Joel J. Kupperman, *Classic Asian Philosophy: A Guide to the Essential Texts* (New York and Oxford: Oxford University Press, 2000).

John M. Koller, *Asian Philosophies*, 4th ed. (Upper Saddle River, NJ: Prentice Hall, 2002).

INDIAN PHILOSOPHY

Surendranath Dasgupta, *A History of Indian Philosophy,* 5 vols. (Cambridge, Eng.: Cambridge University Press, 1922).

Sarvepalli Radhakrishnan, *Indian Philosophy,* 2 vols., rev. ed. (Oxford: Oxford University Press, 1929).

M. Hiriyanna, *Outlines of Indian Philosophy* (London: George Allen & Unwin, 1932).

Heinrich Zimmer, *Philosophies of India,* ed. Joseph Campbell (Princeton, NJ: Princeton University Press, 1951).

Sarvepalli Radhakrishnan and Charles A. Moore, eds., *A Source Book in Indian Philosophy* (Princeton, NJ: Princeton University Press, 1957).

Chandradhar Sharma, *Indian Philosophy: A Critical Survey* (London: Rider and Co., 1960).

Karl H. Potter, *Presuppositions of India's Philosophies* (Westport, CT: Greenwood Press, 1963).

Charles A. Moore, ed., *The Indian Mind: Essentials of Indian Philosophy and Culture* (Honolulu: East-West Center Press, 1967).

Satischandra Chatterjee and Dhirendramohan Datta, *An Introduction to Indian Philosophy,* 7th ed. (Calcutta: Calcutta University Press, 1968).

Karl H. Potter, gen. ed., *Encyclopedia of Indian Philosophies,* 8 vols., 15 total promised (Delhi: Motilal Banarsidass, 1970–1999).

P.T. Raju, *The Philosophical Traditions of India* (London: George Allen & Unwin, 1971).

P.T. Raju, *Structural Depths of Indian Thought* (Albany: SUNY Press, 1985).

Karl H. Potter, *Guide to Indian Philosophy* (Boston: G.K. Hall, 1988).

CHINESE PHILOSOPHY

Fung Yu-lan, *The Spirit of Chinese Philosophy,* tr. E.R. Hughes (London: Kegan Paul, Trench, Trubner and Co., 1947).

Fung Yu-lan, *A Short History of Chinese Philosophy,* ed. Derk Bodde (New York: The Free Press, 1948).

Fung Yu-lan, *A History of Chinese Philosophy,* 2 vols., tr. Derk Bodde (Princeton, NJ: Princeton University Press, 1952).

H.G. Creel, *Chinese Thought: From Confucius to Mao Tse-tung* (Chicago: University of Chicago Press, 1953).

Wing-tsit Chan, tr. and ed., *A Source Book in Chinese Philosophy* (Princeton, NJ: Princeton University Press, 1963).

Charles A. Moore, ed., *The Chinese Mind: Essentials of Chinese Philosophy and Culture* (Honolulu: East-West Center Press, 1967).

Colin A. Ronan, *The Shorter Science and Civilisation in China: An Abridgement of Joseph Needham's Original Text,* Vol. 1 (Cambridge, Eng.: Cambridge University Press, 1978).

Robert E. Allinson, *Understanding the Chinese Mind: The Philosophical Roots* (Oxford: Oxford University Press, 1989).

Antonio Cua, ed., *Encyclopedia of Chinese Philosophy* (New York and London: Routledge, 2003).

Thinkers/Works in This Volume

<500 B.C.E. 400	200	0	200 C.E.	400	600	800

Indian

Abhidhamma (at 200 B.C.E.)

Upanishads

Siddhartha Gautama, The Buddha

Dhammapada

Diamond Sutra
Bhagavad Gita

Patanjali

Nagarjuna

Vasubandhu

Shankara

Chinese

Confucius (Kongfuzi)

Mencius (Mengzi)
Lao Tzu (Laozi)
Chuang Tzu (Zhuangzi)

Awakening of Faith   Hui-neng (Huineng)
Fa-tsang (Fazang)

A Sampling of Major Indian and Chinese Events

Indian

Mauryan Empire
Alexander the Great Invades India

Guptan Empire

Arab Conquests Reach Indus River

Chinese

Great Wall begun

Chou (Zhou) Dynasty (1111–249)

Ch'in (Qin) Dynasty (221–206)

Han Dynasty (206 BCE–220CE)

Chin (Jin) Dynasty (265–420)

Sui Dynasty (581–618)

T'ang (Tang) Dynasty (618–907)

Other Major World Events

Death of Socrates

Punic Wars and Rise of Roman Empire

Jerusalem Temple Destroyed

Furthest Extent of the Roman Empire

Roman Empire Divided

Fall of Rome

Buddhism Introduced in Japan

Great Dharma Assembly

Peak of Mayan Civilization in Central America

Muslim Conquest of Northern Africa and Spain

1000	1200	1400	1600	1800	2000

Ramanuja   Madhva

Mohandas Gandhi
Aurobindo Ghose

Mao Tse-tung
(Mao Zedong)

Chu Hsi (Zhu Xi)   Wang Yang-ming
(Wang Yangming)

Lin Yu-t'ang
(Lin Yutang)

Mughal Empire

British Rule
Established

Independence and
Partition of
India-Pakistan

Explosives used in battle

Opium
wars

Boxer Rebellion

Sung (Song) Dynasty (960–1279)	Yuan Dynasty (1279–1368)	Ming Dynasty (1368–1644)	Ch'ing (Qing) Dynasty (1644–1911)	Republic (1912–1949)	People's Republic (1949–)

First Crusade
Paris University Founded
Magna Carta

Columbus Sails to America
Luther Begins
Protestant Reformation
English Defeat Spanish Armada
U.S. Declaration of Independence
French Revolution
Chaka Founds
Zulu Empire
American Civil War
Suez Canal
World War I
Russian Revolution
World War II
Korean War
Vietnam War
Soviet Union
Crumbles

1000	1200	1400	1600	1800	2000

INDIAN THOUGHT

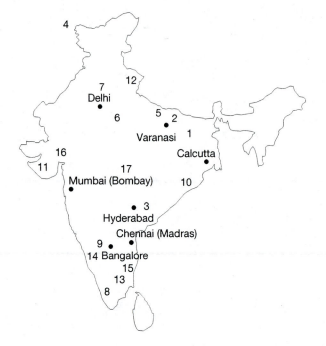

- Major cities today

1   Bodhgaya (Buddha's enlightenment)
2   Sarnath (Buddha's first sermon)
3   Nagarjunakanda (Nagarjuna's temple)
4   Peshawar (Vasubandhu's birthplace)
5   Ayodhya (Vasubandhu's deathplace)
6   Mathura (Krishna's birthplace)
7   Kurukshetra (*Gita's* battlefield)
8   Kaladi (Shankara's birthplace)
9   Sringeri (Shankara's southern monastery)
10 Puri (Shankara's eastern monastery)
11 Dwarka (Shankara's western monastery)
12 Badrinath (Shankara's northern monastery)
13 Srirangam (Ramanuja's temple)
14 Udipi (Madhva's temple)
15 Pondicherry (Sri Aurobindo's Ashram)
16 Ahmadabad (Gandhi's Sabarmati Ashram, 1915–1933)
17 Wardha (Gandhi's Sevagram Ashram, 1933–1948)

VEDIC ORIGINS

Indian thought emerged from sacred Hindu writings called the Vedas (meaning "knowledge"). They are among the oldest religious texts in the world. There are four Vedas—Rig, Sama, Yajur, and Atharva. The Rig is the earliest, largest, and most important. The Sama and Yajur draw heavily on the Rig, while the Atharva follows its own course. The four Vedas began as collections (Samhitas) of hymns praising and petitioning a host of deities believed to control the elements of nature. In time, other types of scriptures were added to these four Samhitas. Brahmanas were added first, then Aranyakas, and finally Upanishads. The Brahmanas are manuals used by priests while conducting elaborate fire sacrifices to the deities; the Aranyakas contain allegorical interpretations of the fire sacrifice; and the Upanishads are mystical texts often cast as dialogues. Once finished, each of the four Vedas was a compilation of four types of material.

Of all their many sacred texts, Hindus accord supernatural origin only to the Vedas. These four books exclusively are trusted to reveal the essential knowledge of life. Such knowledge, Hindus hold, has existed eternally in the form of vibrations sounding throughout the universe. These elusive vibrations remained undetected until certain Indian sages equipped with spiritual hearing finally heard and formulated them in the Sanskrit language, beginning about 3,200 years ago. Composition and transmission of the Vedas were strictly oral for centuries, until they were written down around the beginning of the Common Era. This literature, therefore, is uniquely "that which was heard" *(shruti),* indicating its absolute authority. All later orthodox Hindu scriptures—law books, epics, philosophical texts, mythologies, and others—are merely "that which was remembered" *(smriti),* signifying their lesser, dependent status. The Vedas, like the Bible and

Statue of Brahma the Creator. (*Geoff Dann © Dorling Kindersley, Courtesy of the Ashmolean Museum, Oxford England, U.K.*)

the Koran, are said to contain the supreme message to humankind but, unlike these others, to lack a divine sender. The message stands on its own, everlasting and omnipresent.

A shift in religious beliefs and practices can be discovered between the early and late portions of the Vedas. The Samhitas and Brahmanas, composed orally approximately 1200 to 700 B.C.E., feature a pantheon of gods and goddesses (polytheism) approached for this-worldly favors through fire sacrifice. The Upanishads, belonging to the period 700 to 100 B.C.E., conclude the Vedas and urge union with one mysterious force (monism) sought by meditation for other-worldly aims. The difference is sharp enough to justify speaking of early Vedic Hinduism in contrast to late Vedic Hinduism. Indian philosophy sprang from the Upanishads during the last half of the Vedic period.

*   *   *

The Upanishads are the glory of the Vedas. The name comes from Sanskrit roots originally designating a teaching situation in which students sat close enough to their guru to hear him whisper secret words of wisdom. The name was later applied to the secret wisdom itself in the form of brief sayings, and later yet to full texts explaining those sayings. These texts are what we today call the Upanishads. They often take the form of dialogues between teachers who know the sacred wisdom and disciples who wish to learn it. The traditional number of Upanishads is 108, but in fact, more than 200 exist. Of these only thirteen are Vedic (that is, appended to the ends of the four Vedas); the rest came later. About 750 C.E., the eminent philosopher Shankara collected these thirteen Vedic Upanishads and arranged them in the following order: Isha, Kena, Katha, Prashna, Mundaka, Mandukya, Taittiriya, Aitareya, Chandogya, Brihadaranyaka, Shvetashvatara, Kaushitaki, and Maitri. Chronologically, however, they were composed as follows: Brihadaranyaka, Chandogya, Taittiriya, Aitareya, Kaushitaki, and Kena preceded the Buddha (563–483 B.C.E.); Katha, Isha, Shvetashvatara, Mundaka, Prashna, Maitri, and Mandukya succeeded him. Scholars today agree on the chronology of the first eight and argue about that of the last five.

The Vedic Upanishads present a mystical vision of the universe at once evolved from, immersed in, and permeated by its divine ground. The divine ground is the very substance from which the universe is made. It is also perceived as a vast sea encompassing the tiny universe. The divine ground further appears to suffuse and fill everything in the universe. The mystic, by definition, professes consciousness of something more than nonmystics behold, something wondrous and life transforming; the mystic claims awareness of the infinite spirit projecting, enveloping, and dwelling in the finite universe. With such a vision, these ancient Vedic Upanishads take an honored place in the great mystical literature of the world. The mysticism in the Upanishads inspired the rise of Indian philosophy, because it had implications for the main problems of philosophy—metaphysics, epistemology, and ethics.

Metaphysics addresses the question of ultimate reality. According to the Upanishads, only one such reality (monism), not two (dualism) or more (pluralism), exists. That single reality, however, is indicated by two key terms. *Brahman* designates the divine ground of the entire universe, while *Atman* is the divine ground deep inside individual persons—one reality looked at from two perspectives. Brahman is usually represented as completely mysterious and hence beyond thought or language. But occasionally Brahman is minimally described as being-consciousness-bliss; some of the later Upanishads even suggest it is a person. Because of this ambiguity, Indian philosophers over the centuries have debated whether Brahman has intelligible properties, is personal, or is totally abstract.

Brahman the divine ground, as representative of mysticism generally, at once projects, engulfs, and suffuses the universe. These three ascriptions are found together in certain passages. The Chandogya Upanishad (Chapter III.14.1–4), for example, attests that all is Brahman, that Brahman enfolds and contains all, and that Brahman pervades all. The Mundaka Upanishad likewise interweaves all three throughout in elegant poetry. Other passages, however, usually for reasons specific to their context, highlight only one of the three. The Kena Upanishad makes only the third ascription, in its splendid allegory (Kena III and IV) of Brahman securing the gods' victory over the demons and thereby emerging as the secret power within everything. Yet the very meaning of *Brahman* ("to blossom" or "to burst forth") underscores just the first ascription, as does the second verse of the Mandukya, which proclaims Brahman is all.

Atman ("breath"), the other key term for ultimate reality in the Upanishads, is the divine ground deep within persons—their true Self or Soul. One important passage on this theme is from the Mundaka Upanishad (Part III.1; see also Shvetashvatara IV.6–7). It posits two souls in a human being, the ego and the Self (Atman), like two birds in the same tree. Identification with the individual ego, the surface but recognizable soul, leads to alienation and sorrow, whereas union with the covert, universal, innermost Self brings joyful solidarity with the universe. Another such passage, in the Kena Upanishad (I), makes the Self the empowering agent within thought, speech, perception, and life, always the subject operating behind these functions and never their overt object. In yet another—the brief Mandukya Upanishad—the Self links the four states of consciousness. The first, the waking state, is consciousness that includes both the perceiving subject and the external world as object perceived. In dreaming, the second state, subject awareness is retained, but the internal dream world replaces the external world as object perceived. The third is deep dreamless sleep. Awareness of both subject and object vanishes, and the sleeper unknowingly enjoys the peace of undivided wholeness. The fourth and supreme state of consciousness, unlike the familiar first three, is a sublime rarity exceeding the others in peace, unity, and especially knowledge. It is achieved only in meditation and brings experiential knowledge of the Self by abiding directly in it—knowledge by identity. Since ultimate reality is nondual, awareness of it is also nondual; the subject-object, inner-outer, waking-sleeping distinctions binding the lower three states are transcended in the fourth. The Self is secretly present in the lower three as their invisible ground but totally monopolizes the fourth state. It is the Self, therefore, that unites the separate episodes of waking, dreaming, deep sleep, and (for those who attain it) supreme consciousness, providing a sense of continuous identity.

The crowning insight of the entire Upanishadic literature is the equation of Brahman and Atman; the divine ground as cosmic energy (Brahman) and as innermost Self (Atman) is one and the same. Variations on this theme consolidate the Upanishads as a literary body. The Mandukya unambiguously declares "the Self is Brahman" (verse 2). Other Upanishads, to press the mysteriousness of Brahman, employ demonstrative pronouns (which denote without connoting), as in the justly famous "You are that" of the Chandogya (VI). The Kena (IV) culminates with the claim that it is the same divine power in a flash of lightning (Brahman) as in a flash of vision (Atman). The Isha Upanishad climaxes (verse 16) with an invocation to the sun to show its secret truth (Brahman), then affirms "Even that very Self am I" (Atman). These are among the "great sayings" (mahavakya) of the Upanishads.

The epistemological implications of the Upanishads are no less significant. Epistemology inquires into the nature and sources of knowledge. Questions relevant to the Upanishads include the following: What is the nature of the knowledge of Brahman-Atman? How can that knowledge be achieved? The Mundaka Upanishad opens with a distinction between lower knowledge (apara vidya) and higher knowledge (para vidya). Theoretical mastery of school subjects (including the Vedas) is the lower knowledge; experiential knowledge of ultimate reality is the higher. The latter is knowledge of Brahman-Atman by becoming one with it in ecstatic awareness of sublime unity beyond subject-object duality. If such knowledge is by nature exceptional, the means of acquiring it follow suit. Sense perception and inference do not work, because Brahman-Atman is not an object of perception or thought. It is known only as the power behind the senses and the mind, never as their object. It comes to the thought of those who realize it is beyond thought. According to the Kena Upanishad (II), such knowledge is extraordinary in what it is knowledge of (a nonobject), in how it is gained (through a flash of awakening), and in its result (permanent liberation). The higher state of consciousness here is, of course, the same as the fourth or supreme state in the Mandukya (explained earlier), hence attainable only by meditation.

Meditation in the Upanishads is called *yoga,* an Indian word now familiar the world round. What would over time grow into several different yogas or systems of practice is in the Upanishads the single practice of meditation. Found first in the Katha, Shvetashvatara, and Taittiriya Upanishads, yoga ("union") refers both to the goal of uniting with Brahman-Atman and to the method for accomplishing that goal. These Upanishads make mention of five yoga-meditation techniques, later supplemented and systematized by Patanjali in his *Yoga Sutras* (see "Orthodox Perspectives"). These techniques are sitting in the lotus posture, quieting the breath, withdrawing attention from the external world, concentrating attention on a single point (repetition of the mantra or sacred word of power OM), and sustaining attention on that one point indefinitely (contemplation). As a result of this practice, metabolic rate slows, trance is induced, subject and object disappear, and the meditator enters into knowledge by identity of Brahman-Atman, the nondual ultimate reality. OM is the vibration that puts one on Brahman-Atman's wavelength and opens the doors of awareness to ultimate knowledge.

The ethics of the Upanishads stems from the Indian view of life that is common and unique to all Indian religions except early Vedic Hinduism. It seems to have been absorbed into later Upanishadic thought from Jainism and Buddhism after the sixth century B.C.E. The Indian life view combines beliefs about suffering, karma, rebirth, ignorance, bondage, and liberation. Ethics is specifically concerned with good and evil. According to the Indian life view, the greatest evil is bondage through ignorance to suffering, karma, and rebirth; the greatest good, on the other hand, is liberation from such bondage. The major obstacle to fulfillment in life is suffering. Suffering is caused by karma ("action"). The Law of Karma mandates that all thoughts, words, and deeds have repercussions for the actor; whatever we sow, we must eventually reap. Present suffering is determined by past choices and is therefore deserved. This is neither determinism (because we choose) nor fatalism (because the future is open to new choices). Present conditions that are not determined by past choices in this life are the result of choices made in previous lifetimes. The Indian belief in rebirth postulates that we live not once but repeatedly, so long as we carry undischarged karma. We may be reborn in a higher or a lower form. Either way, something vital to the old being is reborn in the new. But what that something is differs from one Indian religion to another. It may be an eternal Soul (as in the Upanishads) or simply karmic residues (as in early Buddhism). Whatever it is, in India rebirth is considered a disaster not a victory, because the world into which one is reborn lies under the curse of suffering. Ignoring suffering, karma, and rebirth dooms one to bondage to them, a bondage that is virtually universal among living beings. Opposite the evil of bondage stands the prospect of liberation. In the Upanishads, liberation comes through reunion with Brahman-Atman, the spirit divine. Rebirth stops, karma is canceled, suffering is overcome, separation through individuality from perfect unity is bridged, and at death one's Atman is reabsorbed into the cosmic Brahman. That is the ethical goal of the Upanishads.

* * *

For further reading, start with single chapters on the Upanishads in the standard introductions to Indian philosophy: M. Hiriyanna, *Outlines of Indian Philosophy* (London: George Allen & Unwin, 1932), Chap. II; S. Radhakrishnan, *Indian Philosophy,* 2nd ed. (Delhi: Oxford University Press, 1929), Vol. I, Chap. IV; P.T. Raju, *The Philosophical Traditions of India* (London: George Allen & Unwin, 1971), Chap. III, and *Structural Depths of Indian Thought* (Albany: SUNY Press, 1985), Chap. I; and Chandradhar Sharma, Chap. I *Indian Philosophy: A Critical Survey* (London: Rider and Co., 1960). Also of value are introductions to translations of the Upanishads: R.E. Hume, tr., *The Thirteen Principal Upanishads* (Oxford: Oxford University Press, 1931); S. Radhakrishnan, tr., *The Principal Upanishads* (London: George Allen & Unwin, 1953); and the most up-to-date, Patrick Olivelle, tr., *Upanishads* (Oxford: Oxford University Press, 1996).

For advanced studies, two older authorities are highly recommended: Paul Deussen, *The Philosophy of the Upanishads,* tr. by A.S. Geden (London: T.&T. Clark, 1906); and Arthur Berriedale Keith, *The Religion and Philosophy of the Veda and Upanishads,* 2 vols. (Cambridge, MA: Harvard University Press, 1925).

More recent works of note include Franklin Edgerton, *The Beginnings of Indian Philosophy* (Cambridge, MA: Harvard University Press, 1965); A.L. Herman, *An Introduction to Indian Thought* (Englewood Cliffs, NJ: Prentice Hall, 1976), pp. 83–141; N.S. Subrahmanian, *Encyclopedia of the Upanishads* (Flushing, NY: Apt Books, 1990); and Richard Gotshalk, *The Beginnings of Philosophy in India* (Lanham, MD: University Press of America, 1998).

THE UPANISHADS (IN PART)

THE BRIHADARANYAKA UPANISHAD

CHAPTER 2

The Path to Immortality

"Maitreyi," Yajnavalkya said to his wife one day, "the time has come for me to go   4.1
forth from the worldly life. Come, my dear, let me divide my property between you and
Katyayani."

MAITREYI

My lord, if I could get all the wealth in the world, would it help me to go beyond death?   4.2

YAJNAVALKYA

Not at all. You would live and die like any other rich person. No one can buy immortality with money.

MAITREYI

Of what use then are money and material possessions to me? Please tell me, my lord,   4.3
of the way that leads to immortality.

YAJNAVALKYA

You have always been dear to me, Maitreyi, and I love you even more now that you have   4.4
asked me about immortality. Sit here by my side and reflect deeply on what I say.

A wife loves her husband not for his own sake, dear, but because the Self lives in him.   4.5

A husband loves his wife not for her own sake, dear, but because the Self lives in her.

Children are loved not for their own sake, but because the Self lives in them.

Wealth is loved not for its own sake, but because the Self lives in it.

Upanishads: Portions of Brihadaranyaka, Chandogya, and Taittiriya, and the complete text of Aitareya, Kena,
Katha, Isha, Shvetashvatara, Mundaka, Prashna, and Mandukya. From *The Upanishads,* translated by Eknath
Easwaran, founder of the Blue Mountain Center of Meditation, copyright 1987; reprinted by permission of
Nilgiri Press, P. O. Box 256, Tomales, CA 94971, www.nilgiri.org.

Brahmins are loved not for their own sake, but because the Self lives in them.

Kshatriyas* are loved not for their own sake, but because the Self lives in them.

The universe is loved not for its own sake, but because the Self lives in it.

The gods are loved not for their own sake, but because the Self lives in them.

Creatures are loved not for their own sake, but because the Self lives in them.

Everything is loved not for its own sake, but because the Self lives in it.

This Self has to be realized. Hear about this Self and meditate upon him, Maitreyi. When you hear about the Self, meditate upon the Self, and finally realize the Self, you come to understand everything in life.

4.6   For brahmins confuse those who regard them as separate from the Self. Kshatriyas confuse those who regard them as separate from the Self. The universe confuses those who regard it as separate from the Self. Gods and creatures confuse those who regard them as separate from the Self. Everything confuses those who regard things as separate from the Self

Brahmins, kshatriyas, creatures, the universe, the gods, everything: these are the Self.

4.7　　No one can understand the sounds of a drum without understanding both drum
4.8　and drummer; nor the sounds of a conch without understanding both the conch and its
4.9　blower; nor the sounds of a vina without understanding both vina and musician. As
4.10　clouds of smoke arise from a fire laid with damp fuel, even so from the Supreme have issued forth all the Vedas, history, arts, sciences, poetry, aphorisms, and commentaries. All these are the breath of the Supreme.

4.11   As there can be no water without the sea, no touch without the skin, no smell without the nose, no taste without the tongue, no form without the eye, no sound without the ear, no thought without the mind, no wisdom without the heart, no work without hands, no walking without feet, no scriptures without the word, so there can be nothing without the Self.

4.12   As a lump of salt thrown in water dissolves and cannot be taken out again, though wherever we taste the water it is salty, even so, beloved, the separate self dissolves in the sea of pure consciousness, infinite and immortal. Separateness arises from identifying the Self with the body, which is made up of the elements; when this physical identification dissolves, there can be no more separate self. This is what I want to tell you, beloved.

MAITREYI

4.13   I am bewildered, Blessed One, when you say there is then no separate self.

*Ruler-warrior caste in ancient India.

YAJNAVALKYA

Reflect on what I have said, beloved, and you will not be confused.

As long as there is separateness, one sees another as separate from oneself, hears   4.14
another as separate from oneself, smells another as separate from oneself, speaks to
another as separate from oneself, thinks of another as separate from oneself, knows
another as separate from oneself. But when the Self is realized as the indivisible unity
of life, who can be seen by whom, who can be heard by whom, who can be smelled by
whom, who can be spoken to by whom, who can be thought of by whom, who can be
known by whom? Maitreyi, my beloved, how can the knower ever be known?

CHAPTER 3

The Imperishable

King Janaka of Videha once performed a lavish sacrifice and distributed many gifts.   1
Many wise men from Kuru and Panchala attended the ceremony, and Janaka wanted to
know who was the wisest among them. So he drove a thousand cows into a pen, and   2
between the horns of each cow he fastened ten gold coins. Then he said: "Venerable brahmins, these cows are for the wisest one among you. "Let him take them away."

None of the other brahmins dared to speak, but Yajnavalkya said to his pupil
Samashrava: "Son, you can drive these cows home." "Hero of seers!" his pupil
exclaimed joyfully, and he drove them home.

The other brahmins were furious. "How presumptuous!" they shouted. And
Ashvala, the royal priest, asked: "Yajnavalkya, do you really believe you are the wisest
of those assembled here?"

Yajnavalkya replied: "I salute the wisest, but I want those cows."

Then Gargi, daughter of Vachaknu, said: "Venerable brahmins, I shall ask   1
Yajnavalkya only two questions. If he answers them well, no one here can defeat him
in a spiritual debate."

"Ask, Gargi," the sage replied.

GARGI

Yajnavalkya, as a warrior from Kashi or Videha rises with bow and arrow to fell his   2
opponent, I rise to fell you with two questions.

YAJNAVALKYA

Ask them, Gargi.

GARGI

3   That which is above heaven and below the earth, which is also between heaven and earth, which is the same through past, present, and future, in what is that woven, warp and woof? Tell me, Yajnavalkya.

YAJNAVALKYA

4   That which is above heaven and below earth, which is also between heaven and earth, which is the same through the past, present, and future—that is woven, warp and woof, in space.

GARGI

5   My first question is answered well. Now for my second question.

YAJNAVALKYA

Ask, Gargi.

GARGI

6   In what is space itself woven, warp and woof? Tell me, Yajnavalkya.

YAJNAVALKYA

7–8   The sages call it Akshara, the Imperishable. It is neither big nor small, neither long nor short, neither hot nor cold, neither bright nor dark, neither air nor space. It is without attachment, without taste, smell, or touch, without eyes, ears, tongue, mouth, breath, or mind, without movement, without limitation, without inside or outside. It consumes nothing, and nothing consumes it.

9   In perfect accord with the will of the Imperishable, sun and moon make their orbits; heaven and earth remain in place; moments, hours, days, nights, fortnights, months and seasons become years; rivers starting from the snow-clad mountains flow east and west, north and south, to the sea.

10   Without knowing the Imperishable, Gargi, whoever performs rites and ceremonies and undergoes austerities, even for many years, reaps little benefit, because rites, ceremonies, and austerities are all perishable. Whosoever dies without knowing the Imperishable dies in a pitiable state; but those who know the Imperishable attain immortality when the body is shed at death.

11   The Imperishable is the seer, Gargi, though unseen; the hearer, though unheard; the thinker, though unthought; the knower, though unknown. Nothing other than the

Imperishable can see, hear, think, or know. It is in the Imperishable that space is woven,   12
warp and woof.

GARGI

Venerable brahmins, count yourselves fortunate if you get away with merely paying this
man homage. No one can defeat Yajnavalkya in debate about Brahman.

With these words Gargi ended her questions.

CHAPTER 4

The States of Consciousness

Yajnavalkya came to Janaka, king of Videha, saying to himself, "I will not talk   1
today." But earlier, while they were discussing the fire ceremony, Yajnavalkya had promised him any boon he wanted. Now the king asked the sage permission to question him.

JANAKA

Yajnavalkya, what is the light of man?   2

YAJNAVALKYA

The sun is our light, for by that light we sit, work, go out, and come back.

JANAKA

When the sun sets, what is the light of man?   3

YAJNAVALKYA

The moon is our light, for by that light we sit, work, go out, and come back.

JANAKA

When the sun sets, Yajnavalkya, and the moon sets, what is the light of man?   4

YAJNAVALKYA

Fire is our light, for by that we sit, work, go out, and come back.

JANAKA

When the sun sets, Yajnavalkya, and the Moon sets, and the fire goes out, what is the   5
light of man?

YAJNAVALKYA

Then speech is our light, for by that we sit, work, go out, and come back. Even though we cannot see our own hand in the dark, we can hear what is said and move toward the person speaking.

JANAKA

6   When the sun sets, Yajnavalkya, and the moon sets, and the fire goes out, and no one speaks, what is the light of man?

YAJNAVALKYA

The Self indeed is the light of man, your majesty, for by that we sit, work, go out, and come back.

JANAKA

7   Who is that Self?

YAJNAVALKYA

The Self, pure awareness, shines as the light within the heart, surrounded by the senses. Only seeming to think, seeming to move, the Self neither sleeps nor wakes nor dreams.

8   When the Self takes on a body, he seems to assume the body's frailties and limitations; but when he sheds the body at the time of death, the Self leaves all these behind.

9   The human being has two states of consciousness: one in this world, the other in the next. But there is a third state between them, not unlike the world of dreams, in which we are aware of both worlds, with their sorrows and joys. When a person dies, it is only the physical body that dies; that person lives on in a nonphysical body, which carries the impressions of his past life. It is these impressions that determine his next life. In this intermediate state he makes and dissolves impressions by the light of the Self.

10   In that third state of consciousness there are no chariots, no horses drawing them or roads on which to travel, but he makes up his own chariots, horses, and roads. In that state there are no joys or pleasures, but he makes up his own joys and pleasures. In that state there are no lotus ponds, no lakes, no rivers, but he makes up his own lotus ponds, lakes, and rivers. It is he who makes up all these from the impressions of his past or waking life.

11–13   It is said of these states of consciousness that in the dreaming state, when one is sleeping, the shining Self, who never dreams, who is ever awake, watches by his own light the dreams woven out of past deeds and present desires. In the dreaming state, when one is sleeping, the shining Self keeps the body alive with the vital force of prana, and wanders wherever he wills. In the dreaming state, when one is sleeping, the shining Self assumes many forms, eats with friends, indulges in sex, sees fearsome spectacles. But he is not affected by anything because he is detached and free; and after wandering here and there in the state of dreaming, enjoying pleasures and seeing good and evil, he returns to the state from which he began.   16–17

As a great fish swims between the banks of a river as it likes, so does the shining Self move between the states of dreaming and waking.   18

As an eagle, weary after soaring in the sky, folds its wings and flies down to rest in its nest, so does the shining Self enter the state of dreamless sleep, where one is freed from all desires.   19

The Self is free from desire, free from evil, free from fear.   21

As a man in the arms of his beloved is not aware of what is without and what is within, so a person in union with the Self is not aware of what is without and what is within, for in that unitive state all desires find their perfect fulfillment. There is no other desire that needs to be fulfilled, and one goes beyond sorrow.

In that unitive state there is neither father nor mother, neither worlds nor gods nor even scriptures. In that state there is neither thief nor slayer, neither low caste nor high, neither monk nor ascetic. The Self is beyond good and evil, beyond all the suffering of the human heart.   22

In that unitive state one sees without seeing, for there is nothing separate from him; smells without smelling, for there is nothing separate from him; tastes without tasting, for there is nothing separate from him; speaks without speaking, for there is nothing separate from him; hears without hearing, for there is nothing separate from him; touches without touching, for there is nothing separate from him; thinks without thinking, for there is nothing separate from him; knows without knowing, for there is nothing separate from him.   23–30

Where there is separateness, one sees another, smells another, tastes another, speaks to another, hears another, touches another, thinks of another, knows another. But where there is unity, one without a second, that is the world of Brahman. This is the supreme goal of life, the supreme treasure, the supreme joy. Those who do not seek this supreme goal live on but a fraction of this joy.   31   32

JANAKA

I give you another thousand cows! Please teach me more of the way to Self-realization.   33

YAJNAVALKYA

As a heavily laden cart creaks as it moves along, the body groans under its burden when a person is about to die. When the body grows weak through old age or illness, the Self separates himself as a mango or fig or banyan fruit frees itself from the stalk, and returns the way he came to begin another life.   35   36

37   Just as when a king is expected to visit a village, the mayor and all the other officials turn out to welcome him with food and drink, all creation awaits the person who sheds his body having realized Brahman. "Here he comes!" they say. "Here comes

38   Brahman himself!" But the senses, while that man lies dying, gather around and mourn the Self's departure, as courtiers mourn when their king is about to leave.

1   When body and mind grow weak, the Self gathers in all the powers of life and

2   descends with them into the heart. As prana leaves the eye, it ceases to see. "He is becoming one," say the wise; "he does not see. He is becoming one; he no longer hears. He is becoming one; he no longer speaks, or tastes, or smells, or thinks, or knows." By the light of the heart the Self leaves the body by one of its gates; and when he leaves, prana follows, and with it all the vital powers of the body. He who is dying merges in consciousness, and thus consciousness accompanies him when he departs, along with the impressions of all that he has done, experienced, and known.

3   As a caterpillar, having come to the end of one blade of grass, draws itself together and reaches out for the next, so the Self, having come to the end of one life and dispelled all ignorance, gathers in his faculties and reaches out from the old body to a new.

4   As a goldsmith fashions an old ornament into a new and more beautiful one, so the Self, having reached the end of the last life and dispelled all ignorance, makes for himself a new, more beautiful shape, like that of the devas or other celestial beings.

5   The Self is indeed Brahman, but through ignorance people identify it with intellect, mind, senses, passions, and the elements of earth, water, air, space, and fire. This is why the Self is said to consist of this and that, and appears to be everything.

As a person acts, so he becomes in life. Those who do good become good; those who do harm become bad. Good deeds make one pure; bad deeds make one impure. So we are said to be what our desire is. As our desire is, so is our will. As our will is, so are our acts. As we act, so we become.

6   We live in accordance with our deep, driving desire. It is this desire at the time of death that determines what our next life is to be. We will come back to earth to work out the satisfaction of that desire.

But not those who are free from desire; they are free because all their desires have found fulfillment in the Self. They do not die like the others; but realizing Brahman,

7   they merge in Brahmin. So it is said:

When all the desires that surge in the heart
Are renounced, the mortal becomes immortal.
When all the knots that strangle the heart
Are loosened, the mortal becomes immortal,
Here in this very life.

As the skin of a snake is sloughed onto an anthill, so does the mortal body fall; but the Self, freed from the body, merges in Brahman, infinite life, eternal light.

JANAKA

I give you another thousand cows! Please teach me more of the way to Self-realization.

YAJNAVALKYA

Those who realize the Self enter into the peace that brings complete self-control and perfect patience. They see themselves in everyone and everyone in themselves. Evil cannot overcome them because they overcome all evil. Sin cannot consume them because they consume all sin. Free from evil, free from sin and doubt, they live in the kingdom of Brahman. Your majesty, this kingdom is yours! 23

JANAKA

Venerable One, I offer myself and my kingdom in your service.

CHAPTER 5

What the Thunder Said

The children of Prajapati, the Creator—gods, human beings, and asuras, the godless—lived with their father as students. When they had completed the allotted period the gods said, "Venerable One, please teach us." Prajapati answered with one syllable: *"Da."*

"Have you understood?" he asked.

"Yes," they said. "You have told us *damyata*, be self-controlled."

"You have understood," he said.

Then the human beings approached. "Venerable One, please teach us." 2

Prajapati answered with one syllable: *"Da."*

"Have you understood?" he asked.

"Yes," they said. "You have told us *datta*, give."

"You have understood," he said.

Then the godless approached. "Venerable One, please teach us."

Prajapati answered with the same syllable: *"Da."*

"Have you understood?" he asked.

"Yes," they said. "You have told us *dayadhvam*, be compassionate."

"You have understood," he said.

The heavenly voice of the thunder repeats this teaching. *Da-da-da!* Be self-controlled! Give! Be compassionate!

OM shanti shanti shanti

THE CHANDOGYA UPANISHAD

CHAPTER 1

The Word

1.1   Let us meditate on OM the imperishable, the beginning of prayer.

2   For as the earth comes from the waters, plants from earth, and man from plants, so man is speech, and speech is OM. Of all speech the essence is the Rig Veda; but Sama is the essence of Rig, and of Sama the essence is OM, the Udgitha.

3   This is the essence of essences, the highest, the eighth rung, venerated above all that human beings hold holy. OM is the Self of all.

4   What is *rig*, what is *sama*, at the heart of prayer? As rig is speech, so prana is
5   song, and the imperishable OM is the Udgitha. Speech and breath, Sama and Rig, are
6   couples, and in the imperishable OM they come together to fulfill each other's desire.
7   For those who, knowing this, meditate on the imperishable OM, all desires are fulfilled.

8   With the word OM we say, "I agree," and fulfill desires. With OM we recite, we give
9   direction, we sing aloud the honor of that Word, the key to the three kinds of knowledge.

10   Side by side, those who know the Self and those who know it not do the same thing; but it is not the same: the act done with knowledge, with inner awareness and faith, grows in power. That, in a word, tells the significance of OM, the indivisible.

CHAPTER 3

The Wisdom of Shandilya

14.1   This universe comes forth from Brahman and will return to Brahman. Verily, all is Brahman.

A person is what his deep desire is. It is our deepest desire in this life that shapes the life to come. So let us direct our deepest desires to realize the Self.

The Self, who can be realized by the pure in heart, who is life, light, truth, space, who gives rise to all works, all desires, all odors, all tastes, who is beyond words, who is joy abiding—this is the Self dwelling in my heart.   14.2

14.3

Smaller than a grain of rice, smaller than a grain of barley, smaller than a mustard seed, smaller than a grain of millet, smaller even than the kernel of a grain of millet is the Self. This is the Self dwelling in my heart, greater than the earth, greater than the sky, greater than all the worlds.

This Self who gives rise to all works, all desires, all odors, all tastes, who pervades the universe, who is beyond words, who is joy abiding, who is ever present in my heart, is Brahman indeed. To him I shall attain when my ego dies.   14.4

So said Shandilya; so said Shandilya.

CHAPTER 4

The Story of Satyakama

"Mother," Satyakama said, "I feel the time has come for me to go to the home of a spiritual teacher. From whom does our family come, so that I may tell him when he asks my lineage?"   4.1

"I do not know, dear," she replied. "You were born when I was young and going from place to place as a servant. Your name is Satyakama and my name is Jabala; why not call yourself Satyakama Jabala?"   4.2

Satyakama went to Haridrumata Gautama and said to him, "Sir, I want to become your disciple."   4.3

"What family are you from, bright one?"   4.4

"Sir, I don't know. My mother says she bore me in her youth and doesn't know my ancestry. She says that since my name is Satyakama and hers is Jabala I should call myself Satyakama Jabala."

"None but a true brahmin could have said that. Fetch the firewood, my boy; I will initiate you. You have not flinched from the truth."   4.5

He selected four hundred lean and sickly cows and gave them to Satyakama to care for. "I shall not return," the boy said to himself, "until they become a thousand."

For years Satyakama dwelt in the forest, tending the herd. Then one day the bull of the herd said to him: "Satyakama!"   5.1

"Sir?" he replied.

"We have become a thousand. Let us now rejoin our teacher's family, and I will tell you one of the four feet of Brahman."   5.2

"Please tell me, revered sir," the boy said.

6.1   "There are four quarters: east, west, south, and north. This is one foot of Brahman, called the Shining. To meditate on these four is to become full of light and master the resplendent regions of the cosmos, knowing this portion of the truth. Agni, fire, will tell you more.

6.2   The next day Satyakama set out for his teacher's house with the herd. Toward evening he made a fire, penned the cows, and sat by the fire facing east. The fire spoke: "Satyakama!"

"Sir?"

"Friend, I can teach you another foot of Brahman."

"Please do, revered sir."

7.1   "There are four quarters: earth, sky, heaven, and ocean. This is one foot of Brahman, called Without End. Know this, meditate on this reality, and your life will be without end on this earth. A swan will tell you more."

7.2   The next day Satyakama drove the cows onward. Toward evening he lit a fire, penned the cows, and sat by the fire facing east. Then a swan flew near and said: "Satyakama!"

"Sir?"

7.3   "Friend, I can teach you another foot of Brahman."

"Please do, revered sir."

7.4
8.1   "There are four quarters: fire, the sun, the moon, and lightning. These make one foot of Brahman, called Full of Light. To meditate on this fourfold foot of truth is to be filled with light in this world and master the world of light. A diver bird will tell you more."

8.2   The next day Satyakama drove the cows onward. Toward evening he lit a fire, penned the cows, and sat by the fire facing east. Then a diver bird flew near and spoke to him: "Satyakama!"

"Sir?"

8.3   "Friend, I can teach you another foot of Brahman."

"Please do, revered sir."

8.4   "There are four parts: breath, eye, ear, and mind. This is one foot of Brahman, called Established. To meditate on this fourfold foot of Brahman is to be at home in this world and master space. Whoever knows this fourfold foot of Brahman is called established."

So Satyakama returned to his teacher's home. "Satyakama," his teacher called,   9.1
"you glow like one who has known the truth. Tell me, who has taught you?"   9.2

Satyakama replied, "No human, sir. But I wish to hear the truth from you alone.   9.3
For I have heard that only the teacher's wisdom comes to fruition for us."

Then his teacher taught Satyakama that same wisdom. Nothing was left out from
it; nothing was left out.

CHAPTER 6

The Story of Shvetaketu

Shvetaketu was Uddalaka's son.   1.1
When he was twelve, his father said to him:
"It is time for you to find a teacher,
Dear one, for no one in our family
Is a stranger to the spiritual life."

So Shvetaketu went to a teacher   1.2
And studied all the Vedas for twelve years.
At the end of this time he returned home,
Proud of his intellectual knowledge.

"You seem to be proud of all this learning,"
Said Uddalaka. "But did you ask
Your teacher for that spiritual wisdom
Which enables you to hear the unheard,   1.3
Think the unthought, and know the unknown?"

"What is that wisdom, Father?" asked the son.

Uddalaka said to Shvetaketu:
"As by knowing one lump of clay, dear one,   1.4
We come to know all things made out of clay:
That they differ only in name and form,
While the stuff of which all are made is clay;
As by knowing one gold nugget, dear one,   1.5
We come to know all things made out of gold:
That they differ only in name and form,
While the stuff of which all are made is gold;
As by knowing one tool of iron, dear one,   1.6
We come to know all things made out of iron:
That they differ only in name and form,
While the stuff of which all are made is iron—
So through that spiritual wisdom, dear one,
We come to know that all of life is one."

"My teachers must not have known this wisdom,"   1.7
Said Shvetaketu, "for if they had known,
How could they have failed to teach it to me?
Father, please instruct me in this wisdom."

"Yes, dear one, I will," replied his father.

2.2

"In the beginning was only Being,
One without a second.

2.3   Out of himself he brought forth the cosmos
And entered into everything in it.
There is nothing that does not come from him.
Of everything he is the inmost Self.
He is the truth; he is the Self supreme.
You are that, Shvetaketu; you are that."

"Please, Father, tell me more about this Self."

"Yes, dear one, I will," Uddalaka said.

8.1   "Let us start with sleep. What happens in it?
When a man is absorbed in dreamless sleep,
He is one with the Self, though he knows it not.
We say he sleeps, but he sleeps in the Self.

8.2   As a tethered bird grows tired of flying
About in vain to find a place of rest
And settles down at last on its own perch,
So the mind, tired of wandering about
Hither and thither, settles down at last
In the Self, dear one, to which it is bound.

8.4   All creatures, dear one, have their source in him.
He is their home, he is their strength.

8.6   "When a man departs from this world, dear one,
Speech merges in mind, mind in prana,
Prana in fire, and fire in pure Being.

8.7   There is nothing that does not come from him.
Of everything he is the inmost Self.
He is the truth; he is the Self supreme.
You are that, Shvetaketu; You are that."

"Please, Father, tell me more about this Self."

"Yes, dear one, I will," Uddalaka said.

9.1   "As bees suck nectar from many a flower
9.2   And make their honey one, so that no drop
Can say, 'I am from this flower or that,'
All creatures, though one, know not they are that One.

9.3   There is nothing that does not come from him.
Of everything he is the inmost Self.
He is the truth; he is the Self supreme.
You are that, Shvetaketu; you are that."

"Please tell me, Father, more about this Self."

10.1   "Yes, dear one, I will," Uddalaka said.
"As the rivers flowing east and west
Merge in the sea and become one with it,
Forgetting they were ever separate rivers,

10.2   So do all creatures lose their separateness

When they merge at last into pure Being.
There is nothing that does not come from him.   10.3
Of everything he is the inmost Self.
He is the truth; he is the Self supreme.
You are that, Shvetaketu; You are that."

"Please, Father, tell me more about this Self."

"Yes, dear one, I will," Uddalaka said.
"Strike at the root of a tree; it would bleed   11.1
But still live. Strike at the trunk; it would bleed
But still live. Strike again at the top;
It would bleed but still live. The Self as life
Supports the tree, which stands firm and enjoys
The nourishment it receives.
If the Self leaves one branch, that branch withers.   11.2
If it leaves a second, that too withers.
If it leaves a third, that again withers.
Let it leave the whole tree, the whole tree dies.
Just so, dear one, when death comes and the Self   11.3
Departs from the body, the body dies.
But the Self dies not.

"There is nothing that does not come from him.
Of everything he is the inmost Self.
He is the truth; he is the Self supreme.
You are that, Shvetaketu; you are that."

"Please, Father, tell me more about this Self."

"Yes, dear one, I will," Uddalaka said.
"Bring me a fruit from the nyagrodha tree."   12.1

"Here it is, Sir."

"Break it. What do you see?"

"These seeds, Father, all exceedingly small."

"Break one. What do you see?"

"Nothing at all."

"That hidden essence you do not see, dear one,   12.2
From that a whole nyagrodha tree will grow.
There is nothing that does not come from him.   12.3
Of everything he is the inmost Self.
He is the truth; he is the Self supreme.
You are that, Shvetaketu; you are that."

"Please, Father, tell me more about this Self."

"Yes, dear one, I will," Uddalaka said.
"Place this salt in water and bring it here   13.1
Tomorrow morning." The boy did.

"Where is that salt?" his father asked.

"I do not see it."

13.2   "Sip here. How does it taste?"

"Salty, Father."

"And here? And there?"

"I taste salt everywhere."

"It Is everywhere, though we see it not.
Just so, dear one, the Self is everywhere,
Within all things, although we see him not.
13.3   There is nothing that does not come from him.
Of everything he is the inmost Self.
He is the truth; he is the Self supreme
You are that, Shvetaketu; you are that."

"Please, Father, tell me more about this Self."

"Yes, dear one, I will," Uddalaka said.

14.1   "As a man from Gandhara, blindfolded,
Led away and left in a lonely place,
Turns to the east and west and north and south
And shouts, 'I am left here and cannot see!'
14.2   Until one removes his blindfold and says,
'There lies Gandhara; follow that path,'
And thus informed, able to see for himself,
The man inquires from village to village
And reaches his homeland at last—just so,
My son, one who finds an illumined teacher
Attains to spiritual wisdom in the Self.
14.3   There is nothing that does not come from him.
Of everything he is the inmost Self.
He is the truth; he is the Self supreme.
You are that, Shvetaketu; you are that."

"Please Father tell me more about this Self."

"Yes, dear one, I will," Uddalaka said.

15.1   "When a man is dying, his family
All gather round and ask, 'Do you know me?
Do you know me?' And so long as his speech
Has not merged in mind, his mind in prana,
Prana in fire, and fire in pure Being,
15.2   He knows them all. But there is no more knowing
When speech merges in mind, mind in prana,
Prana in fire, and fire in pure Being.
15.3   There is nothing that does not come from him.
Of everything he is the inmost Self.
He is the truth; he is the Self supreme.

You are that, Shvetaketu; you are that."

Then Shvetaketu understood this teaching;   16.3
Truly he understood it all.

CHAPTER 7

Narada's Education

Narada approached the sage Sanatkumara and said, "Please teach me,   1.1
Venerable One."

"Tell me what you know," replied the sage, "and then I will teach you what is
beyond that."

"I know the four Vedas—Rig, Yajur, Sama, Atharva—and the epics, called the   1.2
fifth. I have studied grammar, rituals, mathematics, astronomy, logic, economics,
physics, psychology, the fine arts, and even snake-charming. But all this knowledge has   1.3
not helped me to know the Self. I have heard from spiritual teachers like you that one
who realizes the Self goes beyond sorrow. I am lost in sorrow. Please teach me how to
go beyond."

"Whatever you know is just words," said Sanatkumara, "names of finite phenomena. It is the Infinite that is the source of abiding joy because it is not subject to   23.1
change. Therefore seek to know the Infinite."

"I seek to know the Infinite, Venerable One."

"Where one realizes the indivisible unity of life, sees nothing else, hears nothing   24.1
else, knows nothing else, that is the Infinite. Where one sees separateness, hears separateness, knows separateness, that is the finite. The Infinite is beyond death, but the
finite cannot escape death."

"On what does the Infinite depend, Venerable One?"

"On its own glory—no, not even on that. In the world people think they can attain   24.2
glory by having cows and horses, elephants and gold, family and servants, fields and
mansions. But I do not call that glory, for here one thing depends on another. Utterly
independent is the Infinite.

"The Infinite is above and below, before and behind, to the right and to the left. I   25.1
am all this. The Self is above and below, before and behind, to the right and to the left.   25.2
I am all this. One who meditates upon the Self and realizes the Self sees the Self everywhere, and rejoices in the Self. Such a one lives in freedom and is at home wherever he
goes. But those who pursue the finite are blind to the Self and live in bondage.

"One who meditates upon and realizes the Self discovers that everything in the   26.1
cosmos—energy and space, fire and water, name and form, birth and death, mind and
will, word and deed, mantram and meditation—all come from the Self.

26.2   "The Self is one, though it appears to be many. Those who meditate upon the Self and realize the Self go beyond decay and death, beyond separateness and sorrow. They see the Self in everyone and obtain all things.

"Control the senses and purify the mind. In a pure mind there is constant awareness of the Self. Where there is constant awareness of the Self, freedom ends bondage and joy ends sorrow."

Thus the sage Sanatkumara taught the pure Narada to go beyond bondage, beyond sorrow, beyond darkness, to the light of the Self.

CHAPTER 8

The City of Brahman

1.1   In the city of Brahman is a secret dwelling, the lotus of the heart. Within this dwelling is a space, and within that space is the fulfillment of our desires. What is within that space should be longed for and realized.

1.3   As great as the infinite space beyond is the space within the lotus of the heart. Both heaven and earth are contained in that inner space, both fire and air, sun and moon, lightning and stars. Whether we know it in this world or know it not, everything is contained in that inner space.

1.5   Never fear that old age will invade that city; never fear that this inner treasure of all reality will wither and decay. This knows no age when the body ages; this knows no dying when the body dies. This is the real city of Brahman; this is the Self, free from old age, from death and grief, hunger and thirst. In the Self all desires are fulfilled.

The Self desires only what is real, thinks nothing but what is true. Here people do what they are told, becoming dependent on their country, or their piece of land, or the

1.6   desires of another, so their desires are not fulfilled and their works come to nothing, both in this world and in the next. Those who depart from this world without knowing who they are or what they truly desire have no freedom here or hereafter.

But those who leave here knowing who they are and what they truly desire have freedom everywhere, both in this world and in the next.

1.1–2   Would they see their departed mother or father? Lo, they see them and are happy.
1.3–6   Would they see their family and friends? Lo, they see them and are happy. Would they enjoy the world of music, of spring flowers, of elegance? Lo, by their mere will they
1.10   enjoy these things. Whatever they desire, the object of that desire arises from the power of their own thoughts; they have it and are happy.

3.1   Here our selfless desires are hidden by selfish ones. They are real, but they are covered by what is false. Therefore whoever of our own departs from this life, not one
3.2   can ever be brought back before our eyes. But all those we love, alive or departed, and all things we desire but do not have, are found when we enter that space within the heart; for there abide all desires that are true, though covered by what is false.

Like strangers in an unfamiliar country walking over a hidden treasure, day by day we enter the world of Brahman while in deep sleep but never find it, carried away by what is false.

The Self is hidden in the lotus of the heart. Those who see themselves in all crea-   3.3
tures go day by day into the world of Brahman hidden in the heart. Established in peace, they rise above body-consciousness to the supreme light of the Self. Immortal, free from fear, this Self is Brahman, called the True. Beyond the mortal and the immortal, he binds both worlds together. Those who know this live day after day in heaven in this very life.

The Self is a bulwark against the confounding of these worlds and a bridge   4.1
between them. Day and night cannot cross that bridge, nor old age, nor death, nor grief, nor evil nor good deeds. All evils turn back there, unable to cross; evil comes not into this world of Brahman.

One who crosses by this bridge, therefore, if blind, is blind no more; if hurt,   4.2
ceases to be hurt; if in sorrow, ceases sorrowing. At this boundary night itself becomes day: night comes not into this world of Brahman.

Only those who are pure and self-controlled can find this world of Brahman. That   4.3
world is theirs alone. In that world, in all the worlds, they live in perfect freedom.

The Gods and the Godless

The great teacher Prajapati said: "The Self is pure, free from decay and death, free   7.1
from hunger and thirst, and free from sorrow. The Self desires nothing that is not good, wills nothing that is not good. Seek and realize the Self! Those who seek and realize the Self fulfill all their desires and attain the goal supreme."

The devas and the asuras, the gods and the godless, heard this truth and said: "Let   7.2
us seek and realize the Self so that we may fulfill all our desires." So Indra from among the gods and Virochana from among the godless approached Prajapati, carrying fuel in their hands as a sign that they wanted to become his disciples. They dwelt with him for   7.3
thirty-two years, and at the end of that time Prajapati asked why they had stayed with him so long.

Indra and Virochana replied, "We have heard of your inspiring words: 'The Self is pure, free from decay and death, free from hunger and thirst, and free from sorrow. The Self desires nothing that is not good, wills nothing that is not good. Seek and realize the Self! Those who seek and realize the Self fulfill all their desires and attain the goal supreme.' We have been living here as your disciples because we want to realize the Self."

Prajapati said to them: "When you look into another's eyes, what you see is the   7.4
Self, fearless and deathless. That is Brahman, the supreme."

"Venerable One," asked the two disciples, "what is it we see reflected in the water or in a mirror?"

"It is the Self you see in all these," he said to them. "Now look at yourselves in a   8.1
bowl of water, and ask me anything you want to learn about the Self."

They looked at themselves in a bowl of water.

"What did you see in the water?"

"We have seen the Self, even the hair and the nails."

8.2   "Put on your best clothes, adorn your body, and look again in the water."

They did so, and came back to Prajapati.

"What did you see in the water?" he asked.

"We have seen the Self, well dressed and well adorned," they replied.

"That is the Self, fearless and deathless. That is Brahman, the supreme."

8.4   Indra and Virochana went away satisfied. But Prajapati said to himself, "They have seen the Self, but they have not recognized the Self. They mistake the Self to be the body. Those who think the Self is the body will lose their way in life."

8.5   Virochana, quite sure that the Self is the body, went back to the godless and began to teach them that the body alone is to be saved, the body alone is to be adored. He taught them that whoever lives for indulging the senses will find joy in this world and the next. Even today people are called godless when they lack faith, love, and charity, because that is the way of the godless. They dress even dead bodies in fine clothes and adorn them with ornaments so that they may enjoy their life in the next world.

9.1   But Indra, as he was on his way home to the gathering of the gods, began to question this knowledge. "If the Self is the same as the body, well dressed when the body is well dressed, well adorned when the body is well adorned, then the Self will be blind when the body is blind, lame when the body is lame, paralyzed when the body is paralyzed. And when the body dies, the Self too will die. In such knowledge I see no value."

9.2   Again Indra went back to Prajapati with fuel in hand.

"Why have you returned, Indra?" his teacher asked. "Did you not go away quite satisfied?"

"Venerable One," replied India, "if the Self is well dressed when the body is well dressed, well adorned when the body is well adorned, then the Self will be blind when the body is blind, lame when the body is lame, paralyzed when the body is paralyzed. And when the body dies, the Self too will die. In such knowledge I see no value."

9.3   "You are thinking clearly, Indra," said Prajapati. "Live with me for another thirty-two years and I will teach you more of the Self."

10.1   So Indra lived with Prajapati for another thirty-two years. Then Prajapati said to him: "That which moves about in joy in the dreaming state is the Self, fearless and deathless. That is Brahman, the supreme."

Indra went away satisfied, but on his way home to the gathering of the gods he began to question this knowledge. "In the dreaming state, it is true, the Self is not blind when the body is blind, nor lame when the body is lame, nor paralyzed when the body

is paralyzed, nor slain when the body is slain. Yet in dreams the Self may appear to suf-   10.2
fer and to be slain; it may become conscious of pain and even weep. In such knowledge
I see no value."

Again Indra went back to Prajapati with fuel in hand.   10.3

"Why have you returned, Indra?" his teacher asked. "Did you not go away quite
satisfied?"

"Venerable One," replied Indra, "in the dreaming state, it is true, the Self is not
blind when the body is blind, nor lame when the body is lame; yet in this state the Self
may still suffer and even weep. In such knowledge I see no value."

"You are thinking clearly, Indra," said Prajapati. "Live with me for another   10.4
thirty-two years and I will teach you more of the Self."

Indra lived with Prajapati for another thirty-two years. Then his teacher said:

"When a person is sleeping soundly, free from dreams, with a still mind, that is   11.1
the Self, fearless and deathless. That is Brahman, the supreme."

Indra went away satisfied, but on his way home to the gathering of the gods he
began to question this knowledge. "In the state of dreamless sleep one is not aware of
oneself or any other. The state of dreamless sleep is very close to extinction. In this
knowledge I see no value."

Again Indra went back to Prajapati with fuel in hand.   11.2

"Why have you returned, Indra?" his teacher asked. "Did you not go away quite
satisfied?"

"Venerable One," replied Indra, "in the state of dreamless sleep one is not aware
of oneself or of any other. The state of dreamless sleep is very close to extinction. In
this knowledge I see no value."

"You are thinking clearly, Indra." said Prajapati. "Live with me for another five   11.3
years and I will teach you to realize the Self."

Indra lived with Prajapati for another five years. Altogether he lived with his
teacher for one hundred and one years, which is why people say, "Even Indra had to
live with his teacher for one hundred and one years." After that time, Prajapati revealed
the highest truth of the Self to Indra:

"It is true the body is perishable, but within it dwells the imperishable Self. This   12.1
body is subject to pleasure and pain; no one who identifies with the body can escape
from pleasure and pain. But those who know they are not the body pass beyond pleasure and pain to live in abiding joy.

"Like the wind, like clouds, like thunder and lightning, which rise from space   12.2
without physical shape and reach the transcendent light in their own form, those who rise
above body-consciousness ascend to the transcendent light in their real form, the Self.

"In that state, free from attachment, they move at will, laughing, playing, and rejoicing. They know the Self is not this body, but only tied to it for a time as an ox is tied to its cart. Whenever one sees, smells, speaks, hears, or thinks, they know it is the Self that sees, smells, speaks, hears, and thinks; the senses are but his instruments.

"Worshipping this Self in the world of Brahman, the gods obtained all worlds and all desires. Those who know this Self and realize this Self obtain all worlds and all desires." So said Prajapati; so taught Prajapati.

A Paean of Illumination

13.1
From the Divine Dark to the manifest
To the Divine Dark I pass again.
As a horse shakes free its mane, I have
Shaken off all evil. Freeing myself
From the bonds of birth and death as the moon
Escapes from Rahu's mouth, I have attained
The pure realm of Brahman; I have attained
The pure realm of Brahman.

15.1
Brahman is my home. I shall not lose it.
Truly I shall not be lost again.

OM shanti shanti shanti

THE TAITTIRIYA UPANISHAD

PART I

[1]

1
May the Lord of day grant us peace.
May the Lord of night grant us peace.
May the Lord of sight grant us peace.
May the Lord of might grant us peace.
May the Lord of speech grant us peace.
May the Lord of space grant us peace.
I bow down to Brahman, source of all power.
I will speak the truth and follow the law.
Guard me and my teacher against all harm.
Guard me and my teacher against all harm.

[2]

2
Let us learn the art of recitation,
Which calls for knowledge of letters, accent,
Measure, emphasis, sequence, and rhythm.

[3]

1
May the light of wisdom illumine us.
May we become united with the Lord.
Let us contemplate five categories:

This world and luminous worlds in the sky,
Education, progeny, and speech.
What is this world? Earth below, sky above,
Air between, and space connecting them.
What are the luminous worlds in the sky?   2
Fire on one side and sun on the other,
Water between, lightning connecting them.
What is education? Teacher speaking   3
To the disciple seated by his side,
Wisdom between, discourse connecting them.
What is progeny? Mother on one side,   4
Father on the other, the child between,
The sexual organ connecting them.

What is speech? The lower jaw and the upper,   5
Words between, and the tongue connecting them.
Those who contemplate these categories   6
Will have children, cattle, food, and wisdom.

[4]

O Lord of Love, revealed in the scriptures,   1
Who have assumed the forms of all creatures,
Grant me wisdom to choose the path
That can lead me to immortality.
May my body be strong, my tongue be sweet;
May my ears hear always the sound of OM,
The supreme symbol of the Lord of Love,
And may my love for him grow more and more.

Lord, may I grow in spiritual wisdom,   2
And may I have food and clothes and cattle.
May students come to me from far and near,
Like a flowing river all the year;
May I be enabled to guide them all
To train their senses and still their minds;
May this be my wealth, may this be my fame.   3
O Lord of Love, may I enter into you,
And may you reveal yourself unto me,
The pure One masquerading as many.
You are the refuge of all devotees.
I am your devotee. Make me your own.

[5]

Bhur, bhuvas, suvar are three vibrations.   1
Mahachamasya taught a fourth, *maha,*
To stand for the Self. The rest are his limbs.

When *bhur* is the earth, *bhuvas* space between,
And *suvar* the world above, *maha* is the sun
That nourishes life everywhere.
When *bhur* is fire, *bhuvas* air, and *suvar*   2
The sun, *maha* is the moon that supports
All the planets and celestial bodies.

3   When *bhur* is the Rig, *bhuvas* the Sama,
And *suvar* the Yajur, *maha* is Brahman,
Wisdom that nourishes all the four Vedas.

4   When *bhur* is prana upward, *bhuvas*
Downward, and *suvar* is prana widespread,
Maha is food that nourishes vital forces

5   In everyone. Thus these vibrations
Are four times four. Those who understand them
Realize the Self and are loved by all.

[6]

1   The Lord of Love dwells in the hearts of all.
To realize him is to go beyond death.
Between the parietal bones of the skull
Swings the sagittal door, as the lobe swings
Behind the palate. Through that one goes out
Chanting *bhur,* to become one with fire;
Chanting *bhuvas,* to become one with air;
Chanting *suvar,* to be one with the sun;
Chanting *maha,* to be one with the Lord.
Thus one becomes king of his own life, ruler
Of his passions, senses, and intellect.
He is united with the Lord of Love,
Who is truth, peace, and immortality,
The source of joy, the supreme goal of life.
Meditate always on the Lord of Love.

[7]

1   Earth, sky, worlds above, quarters and their halves;
Fire, air, sun, moon, and stars; water, herbs, trees,
Space, and entity are the elements.
Eye, ear, mind, tongue, and touch; skin, flesh, muscle,
Marrow, and skeleton; and the five
Vital forces constitute the body.
The sage, contemplating these sets of five,
Discovered that everything is holy.
Man can complete the inner with the outer.

[8]

1   OM is the supreme symbol of the Lord.
OM is the whole. OM affirms; OM signals
The chanting of the hymns from the Vedas.
The priest begins with OM; spiritual teachers
And their students commence with OM.
The student who is established in OM
Becomes united with the Lord of Love.

[9]

To the Householder

1   Practice right conduct, learning and teaching;
Be truthful always, learning and teaching;
Master the passions, learning and teaching;

Control the senses, learning and teaching;
Strive for peace always, learning and teaching;
Rouse kundalini, learning and teaching;
Serve humanity, learning and teaching;
Beget progeny, learning and teaching.
Satyavacha says: "Be truthful always."
Taponitya says: "Master the passions."
Naka declares: "Learning and teaching are
Necessary for spiritual progress."

[10]

"I have become one with the tree of life.   1
My glory rises like the mountain peak.
I have realized the Self, who is ever
Pure, all-knowing, radiant, and immortal."
Thus spoke sage Trishanku when he became
United with the Lord of Love.

[11]

Having taught the Vedas, the teacher says: 1
"Speak the truth. Do your duty. Neglect not
The scriptures. Give your best to your teacher.
Do not cut off the line of progeny. Swerve not
From the truth. Swerve not from the good.
Protect your spiritual progress always.
Give your best in learning and teaching.
Never fail in respect to the sages.   2
See the divine in your mother, father,
Teacher, and guest. Never do what is wrong.
Honor those who are worthy of honor.   3
Give with faith. Give with love. Give with joy.
If you are in doubt about right conduct,   4
Follow the example of the sages,
Who know what is best for spiritual growth.
This is the instruction of the Vedas;   5
This is the secret; this is the message.

PART II

They have attained the goal who realize   1.1
Brahman as the supreme reality,
The source of truth, wisdom, and boundless joy.
They see the Lord in the cave of the heart
And are granted all the blessings of life.

From Brahman came space; from space, air;
From air, fire; from fire, water; from water,
Earth; from earth, plants; from plants, food; and from food,
The human body, head, arms, legs, and heart.

From food are made all bodies, which become   2.1
Food again for others after their death.

Food is the most important of all things
For the body; therefore it is the best
Medicine for all the body's ailments.
They who look upon food as the Lord's gift
Shall never lack life's physical comforts.
From food are made all bodies. All bodies
Feed on food, and it feeds on all bodies.

The physical sheath is made up of food.
Within it is contained the vital sheath,
Which has the same form, with prana as head,
Vyana as right arm, apana as left,
Space as heart, and earth as foundation.

3.1   Man and woman, beast and bird live by breath.
Breath is therefore called the true sign of life.
It is the vital force in everyone
That determines how long we are to live.
Those who look upon breath as the Lord's gift
Shall live to complete the full span of life.
The vital sheath is made of living breath.
Within it is contained the mental sheath,
Which has the same form, with Yajur as head,
Rig as right arm, Sama as left. The heart
Is the wisdom of the Upanishads,
And the Atharva is the foundation.

4.1   Realizing That from which all words turn back
And thoughts can never reach, one knows
The bliss of Brahman and fears no more.

Within the mental sheath, made up of waves
Of thought, there is contained the sheath of wisdom.
It has the same form, with faith as the head,
Righteousness as right arm and truth as left.
Practice of meditation is its heart,
And discrimination its foundation.

5.1   Wisdom means a life of selfless service.
Even the gods seek spiritual wisdom.
Those who attain wisdom are freed from sin,
And find all their selfless desires granted.

The wisdom sheath is made of detachment.
Within it is contained the sheath of bliss,
Which has the same form, with joy as the head,
Contentment as right arm, and delight the left.
Bliss is the heart, and Brahman the foundation.

6.1   Those who deny the Lord deny themselves;
Those who affirm the Lord affirm themselves.
The wise, not the unwise, realize the Lord.

The Lord of Love willed: "Let me be many!"
And in the depths of his meditation
He created everything that exists.
Meditating, he entered into everything.

He who has no form assumed many forms;
He who is infinite appeared finite;
He who is everywhere assumed a place;
He who is all wisdom caused ignorance;
He who is real caused unreality.
It is he who has become everything.
It is he who gives reality to all.
Before the universe was created,   7.1
Brahman existed as unmanifest.
Brahman brought the Lord out of himself;
Therefore he is called the Self-existent.

The Self is the source of abiding joy.
Our hearts are filled with joy in seeing him
Enshrined in the depths of our consciousness.
If he were not there, who would breathe, who live?
He it is who fills every heart with joy.

When one realizes the Self, in whom
All life is one, changeless, nameless, formless,
Then one fears no more. Until we realize
The unity of life, we live in fear.
For the mere scholar who knows not the Self,
His separateness becomes fear itself.
Through fear of Brahman the wind blows, sun shines,   8.1
Fire burns, rain falls, and death snatches all away.

What is the joy of realizing the Self?
Take a young man, healthy, strong, good, and cultured,
Who has all the wealth that earth can offer;
Let us take this as one measure of joy.

One hundred times that joy is one measure
Of the gandharvas' joy; but no less joy
Has one illumined, free from self-will.
One hundred times that joy is one measure
Of the joy of pitris; but no less joy
Has one illumined, free from self-will.
One hundred times that joy is one measure
Of the joy of devas; but no less joy
Has one illumined, free from self-will.
One hundred times that joy is one measure
Of the karmadevas' joy; but no less joy
Has one illumined, free from self-will.
One hundred times that joy is one measure
Of the joy of Indra; but no less joy
Has one illumined, free from self-will.
One hundred times that joy is one measure
Of Brihaspati's joy; but no less joy
Has one illumined, free from self-will.
One hundred times that joy is one measure
Of the joy of Virat; but no less joy
Has one illumined, free from self-will.
One hundred times that joy is one measure
Of Prajapati's joy; but no less joy

Has one illumined, free from self-will.

The Self in man and in the sun are one.
Those who understand this see through the world
And go beyond the various sheaths of being
To realize the unity of life.

9.1 Realizing That from which all words turn back
And thoughts can never reach, they know
The bliss of Brahman and fear no more.
No more are they oppressed by the question,
"How did I fail to perform what is right?
And how did I perform what is not right?"
Those who realize the joy of Brahman,
Having known what is right and what is wrong,
Are delivered forever from this duality.

PART III

1.1 Bhrigu went to his father, Varuna,
And asked respectfully: "What is Brahman?"

Varuna replied: "First learn about food,
Breath, eye, ear, speech, and mind; then seek to know
That from which these are born, by which they live,
For which they search, and to which they return.
That is Brahman."

2.1 Bhrigu meditated and found that food
Is Brahman. From food are born all creatures,
By food they grow, and to food they return.
Not fully satisfied with his knowledge,
Bhrigu went to his father, Varuna,
And appealed: "Please teach me more of Brahman."

"Seek it through meditation," replied Varuna,
"For meditation is Brahman."

3.1 Bhrigu meditated and found that life
Is Brahman. From life are born all creatures,
By life they grow, and to life they return.
Not fully satisfied with his knowledge,
Bhrigu went to his father, Varuna,
And appealed: "Please teach me more of Brahman."

"Seek it through meditation," replied Varuna,
"For meditation is Brahman."

4.1 Bhrigu meditated and found that mind
Is Brahman. From mind are born all creatures,
By mind they grow, and to mind they return.
Not fully satisfied with his knowledge,
Bhrigu went to his father, Varuna,
And appealed: "Please teach me more of Brahman."

"Seek it through meditation," replied Varuna,
"For meditation is Brahman."

Bhrigu meditated and found that wisdom   5.1
Is Brahman. From wisdom come all creatures,
By wisdom they grow, to wisdom return.
Not fully satisfied with his knowledge,
Bhrigu went to his father, Varuna,
And appealed: "Please teach me more of Brahman."

"Seek it through meditation," replied Varuna,
"For meditation is Brahman."

Bhrigu meditated and found that joy   6.1
Is Brahman. From joy are born all creatures,
By joy they grow, and to joy they return.

Bhrigu, Varuna's son, realized this Self
In the very depths of meditation.
Those who realize the Self within the heart
Stand firm, grow rich, gather a family
Around them, and receive the love of all.

Respect food: the body is made of food;   7.1
Food and body exist to serve the Self.
Those who realize the Self within the heart
Stand firm, grow rich, gather a family
Around them, and receive the love of all.

Waste not food, waste not water, waste not fire;   8.1
Fire and water exist to serve the Self.
Those who realize the Self within the heart
Stand firm, grow rich, gather a family
Around them, and receive the love of all.

Increase food. The earth can yield much more.   9.1
Earth and space exist to serve the Self.
Those who realize the Self within the heart
Stand firm, grow rich, gather a family
Around them, and receive the love of all.

Refuse not food to those who are hungry.   10.1
When you feed the hungry, you serve the Lord,
From whom is born every living creature.
Those who realize the Self within the heart
Stand firm, grow rich, gather a family
Around them, and receive the love of all.

Realizing this makes our words pleasing,   10.2
Our breathing deep, our arms ready to serve
The Lord in all around, our feet ready
To go to the help of everyone in need.
Realizing this we see the Lord of Love   10.3–
In beast and bird, in starlight and in joy,   4
In sex energy and in the grateful rain,

In everything the universe contains.
Drawing on the Lord's resources within,
Security, wisdom, and love in action,
We conquer every enemy within
To be united with the Lord of Love.

10.5
The Self in man and in the sun are one.
Those who understand this see through the world
And go beyond the various sheaths
Of being to realize the unity of life.
Those who realize that all life is one
Are at home everywhere and see themselves
In all beings. They sing in wonder:
"I am the food of life, I am, I am;
I eat the food of life, I eat, I eat.
I link food and water, I link, I link.
I am the first-born in the universe;
Older than the gods, I am immortal.
Who shares food with the hungry protects me;
Who shares not with them is consumed by me.
I am this world and I consume this world.
They who understand this understand life."

This is the Upanishad, the secret teaching.

OM shanti shanti shanti

THE AITAREYA UPANISHAD

May my word be one with my thought, and my thought
Be one with my word. O Lord of Love,
Let me realize you in my consciousness.
May I realize the truth of the scriptures
And translate it into my daily life.
May I proclaim the truth of the scriptures.
May I speak the truth. May it protect me,
And may it protect my teacher.

OM shanti shanti shanti

PART I

[1]

1
Before the world was created, the Self
Alone existed; nothing whatever stirred.
Then the Self thought: "Let me create the world."

2
He brought forth all the worlds out of himself:
Ambhas, high above the sky; Marichi,
The sky; Mara, the middle region that is earth;
And Apa, the realm of waters below.

The Self thought: "I have created these worlds.   3
Let me now create guardians for these worlds."
From the waters he drew forth Purusha
And gave him a form. As the Self brooded   4
Over the form, a mouth opened, as does
An egg, giving forth speech and fire; nostrils
Opened with the power of breathing the air;
Eyes opened, giving rise to sight and sun;
And ears opened to hear the sound in space.
Skin appeared and from it hair; from hair came
Plants and trees. The heart gushed forth; from the heart
Came the mind, and from the mind came the moon.
The navel opened with the downward force,
Apana, which gave rise to death. The sex organ rose
With living water which gave rise to birth.

[2]

Thus came these guardians into the mighty   1
Ocean of existence. The Self caused them
To hunger and thirst. They said to the Self:
"Give us a place where we can live and eat."
He brought them the form of a cow. They said: 2
"This is not what we desire." He brought them
The form of a horse. But they said again:
"This is not what we desire." He brought them   3
A human form. They said in joy: "Just right!
The human body is just right for us."
The Self asked them to enter the body
And take up their places. Fire, becoming   4
Speech, entered the mouth; air, becoming smell,
Entered the nose; the sun, becoming sight,
Entered the eyes; sounds in space, becoming
Hearing, entered the ears; plants, herbs, and trees,
Becoming hair, entered the skin; the moon,
Becoming mind, entered the heart. The god
Of death, becoming downward force, entered
The navel; the god of living water,
Becoming sperm, entered the sex organ.
Hunger and thirst said to the Self: "Give us   5
A place." He told them: "Enter into these
Guardians and share their life with them."
Thus hunger and thirst for food, drink, and pleasure
Attend us, whatever we do in life.

[3]

The Self, Creator, thought: "Here are the worlds   1
And their guardians. Let me now bring forth food
For them." He brooded over the waters,   2
And food appeared in the form of matter.
It tried to run away in fear, and man,   3
The first embodied being, tried to catch
It with his speech. But he could not catch it
With words. Merely by repeating the name
Of food one cannot satisfy hunger.

4   He tried to catch it with his breath, but he
     Could not. Just by smelling food one cannot
5   Satisfy hunger. He tried to catch it
     With his eyes, but he could not. By looking
     At food one cannot satisfy hunger.
6   He tried to catch it with his ears, but he
     Could not. By merely hearing about food
7   One cannot satisfy hunger. He tried
     To catch it with his skin, but he could not.
     By touching food one cannot satisfy
8   Hunger. He tried to catch it with his mind,
     But he could not. By thinking about food
9   One cannot satisfy hunger. He tried
     To catch it with his genital organ,
     But he could not. By sexual union
10   One cannot satisfy hunger. He tried
     To catch it with apana, the downward prana
     Of digestion, and at last he caught it.
     Thus it is apana that takes in food;
     Thus it is apana that lives on food.

11   The Self thought, "How can this be without me?
     If speaking is done by speech, breathing by
     Breath, seeing by eyes, hearing by ears, smelling
     By nose, and meditation by the mind,
12   Then who am I?" Entering the body
     Through the gateway at the crown of the head,
     He passed into the three states of consciousness
     In which the Self resides.

13   Filled with wonder, we sing: "I see the Lord."
14   So his name is Idamdra, "He who sees."
     The name Indra stands for Idamdra.
     The gods do like to sit behind a veil;
     Indeed they like to sit behind a veil.

PART II

[1]

1   Life begins in man as sexual fluid,
     Which has the strength gathered from all his limbs.
     Man holds this quintessence in his body,
     And it becomes child in woman. This is
2   The first birth. Child and mother are one.
     She protects the child, and needs protection.
3   The mother carries the child in her womb,
     And the father bestows his loving care
     Before and after birth. The child is their
     Atman, their very Self, and continues
     Their line without break as the second birth.
4   He discharges all their holy duties
     And sheds his body, too, when it grows old,
     To be born again. This is the third birth.

The sage Vamadeva declared of old:
"While dwelling in the womb I understood   5
The birth of all the gods. A hundred forms,
Strong as steel, held me prisoner. But I
Broke loose from them, like a hawk from the cage,
And came out swiftly." While still in the womb,
Vamadeva made this declaration.
He emerged from his mother's womb, fully   6
Illumined, to live in abiding joy,
And went beyond death. Indeed
He went beyond death.

PART III

[1]

Who is this Self on whom we meditate?   1
Is it the Self by which we see, hear, smell, and taste,
Through which we speak in words? Is Self the mind   2
By which we perceive, direct, understand,
Know, remember, think, will, desire, and love?

These are but the servants of the Self, who is
Pure consciousness.
This self is all in all.
He is all the gods, the five elements,
Earth, air, fire, water, and space; all creatures,   3
Great or small, born of eggs, of wombs, of heat,
Of shoots; horses, cows, elephants, men, and women;
All beings that walk, all beings that fly,
And all that neither walk nor fly. Prajna
Is pure consciousness, guiding all. The world
Rests on prajna, and prajna is Brahman.

Those who realize Brahman live joy   4
And go beyond death. Indeed
They go beyond death.

OM shanti shanti shanti

THE KENA UPANISHAD

[1]

The student inquires: 1
"Who makes my mind think?
Who fills my body with vitality?
Who causes my tongue to speak? Who is that
Invisible one who sees through my eyes
And hears through my ears?"

2   *The teacher replies:*
"The Self is the ear of the ear,
The eye of the eye, the mind of the mind,
The word of words, and the life of life.
Rising above the senses and the mind
And renouncing separate existence,
The wise realize the deathless Self.

3   "Him our eyes cannot see, nor words express;
He cannot be grasped even by the mind.
We do not know, we cannot understand,
4   Because he is different from the known
And he is different from the unknown.
Thus have we heard from the illumined ones.

5   "That which makes the tongue speak but cannot be
Spoken by the tongue, know that as the Self.
This Self is not someone other than you.

6   "That which makes the mind think but cannot be
Thought by the mind, that is the Self indeed.
This Self is not someone other than you.

7   "That which makes the eye see but cannot be
Seen by the eye, that is the Self indeed.
This Self is not someone other than you.

8   "That which makes the ear hear but cannot be
Heard by the ear, that is the Self indeed.
This Self is not someone other than you.

9   "That which makes you draw breath but cannot be
Drawn by your breath, that is the Self indeed.
This Self is not someone other than you."

[2]

THE TEACHER

1   If you think, "I know the Self," you know not.
All you can see is his external form.
Continue, therefore, your meditation.

THE STUDENT

2   I do not think I know the Self, nor can
I say I know him not.

THE TEACHER

There is only one way to know the Self,
And that is to realize him yourself.

3   The ignorant think the Self can be known
By the intellect, but the illumined

Know he is beyond the duality
Of the knower and the known.

The Self is realized in a higher state   4
Of consciousness when you have broken through
The wrong identification that you are
The body, subject to birth and death.
To be the Self is to go beyond death.

Realize the Self, the shining goal of life!   5
If you do not, there is only darkness.
See the Self in all, and go beyond death.

[3]

Once upon a time the gods defeated   1
The demons; and though the victory
Was brought about through the power of Brahman,
The gods boasted, "Ours is the victory,
And ours the power and glory."

Brahman saw their foolish pride and appeared   2
Before them. But they recognized him not.
They said to Agni, god of fire, "Find out   3
Who this mysterious being is." "I will,"
Promised Agni, and approached the being.   4

"Who are you?" asked the mysterious one.
"I am Agni, god of fire, known to all."
"Are you powerful?" "I can burn all on earth."   5
"Burn this:" and Brahman placed a straw in front.   6
The god of fire attacked the straw, but failed
To burn it. Then he ran back to the gods
And confessed, "I have failed to discover
Who this mysterious being is."
They said to Vayu, god of air, "Find out   7
Who this mysterious being is." "I will,"
Promised Vayu and approached the being.   8
"Who are you?" asked the mysterious one.
"I am Vayu, god of air, king of space."
"Are you powerful?" "I can blow all away."   9
"Blow this away." Brahman placed a straw in front.   10
The god of air attacked the straw, but failed
To move it. Then he ran back to the gods
And confessed, "I have failed to discover
Who this mysterious being is."

They begged Indra, leader of gods, "Find out   11
Who this mysterious being is." "I will,"
Promised Indra and approached the being,
Who disappeared instantly. In his place   12
Appeared the lovely goddess of wisdom,
Uma, daughter of the Himalayas;
And Indra asked her, "Who was that being?"

[4]

1   Uma replied, "That was Brahman, from whom
Comes all your power and glory." The gods
Realized at last the Self is Brahman.

2–3   Agni, Vayu, Indra—these three excel
Among the gods because they realized Brahman.

4   The light of Brahman flashes in lightning;
The light of Brahman flashes in our eyes.

5   It is the power of Brahman that makes

6   The mind to think, desire, and will.
Therefore
Use this power to meditate on Brahman.

He is the inmost Self of everyone;
He alone is worthy of all our love.
Meditate upon him in all. Those who
Meditate upon him are dear to all.

THE STUDENT

7   Teach me more of this spiritual wisdom.

THE TEACHER

8   I shall share with you fully what I know.
Meditation, control of the senses
And passions, and selfless service of all
Are the body, the scriptures are the limbs,
And truth is the heart of this wisdom.

9   Those who realize Brahman shall conquer
All evil and attain the supreme state.
Truly they shall attain the supreme state!

OM shanti shanti shanti

THE KATHA UPANISHAD

PART I

[1]

1   Once, long ago, Vajasravasa gave away his possessions to gain religious merit. He
2 had a son named Nachiketa who, though only a boy, was full of faith in the scriptures.
3 Nachiketa thought when the offerings were made: "What merit can one obtain by giv-
4 ing away cows that are too old to give milk?" To help his father understand this,
Nachiketa said: "To whom will you offer me?" He asked this again and again. "To death
I give you!" said his father in anger.

The son thought: "I go, the first of many who will die, in the midst of many who   5
are dying, on a mission to Yama, king of death.

> See how it was with those who came before,   6
> How it will be with those who are living.
> Like corn mortals ripen and fall; like corn
> They come up again."

Nachiketa went to Yama's abode, but the king of death was not there. He waited
three days. When Yama returned, he heard a voice say:

> "When a spiritual guest enters the house,   7
> Like a bright flame, he must be received well,
> With water to wash his feet. Far from wise   8
> Are those who are not hospitable
> To such a guest. They will lose all their hopes,
> The religious merit they have acquired,
> Their sons and their cattle."

YAMA

> O spiritual guest, I grant you three boons   9
> To atone for the three inhospitable nights
> You have spent in my abode.
> Ask for three boons, one for each night.

NACHIKETA

> O king of death, as the first of these boons   10
> Grant that my father's anger be appeased,
> So he may recognize me when I return
> And receive me with love.

YAMA

> I grant that your father, The son of Uddalaka and Aruna,   11
> Will love you as in the past. When he sees you
> Released from the jaws of death, he will sleep
> Again with a mind at peace.

NACHIKETA

> There is no fear at all in heaven; for you   12
> Are not there, neither old age nor death.
> Passing beyond hunger and thirst and pain,
> All rejoice in the kingdom of heaven.
> You know the fire sacrifice that leads to heaven,   13
> O king of death. I have full faith

In you and ask for instruction. Let this
Be your second boon to me.

YAMA

14   Yes, I do know, Nachiketa, and shall
Teach you the fire sacrifice that leads
To heaven and sustains the world, that knowledge
Concealed in the heart. Now listen.

THE NARRATOR

15   Then the king of death taught Nachiketa how to perform the fire sacrifice, how to erect
the altar for worshipping the fire from which the universe evolves. When the boy repeated his instruction, the dread king of death was well pleased and said:

YAMA

16   Let me give you a special boon: this sacrifice
Shall be called by your name, Nachiketa.
Accept from me this many-hued chain too.

17   Those who have thrice performed this sacrifice,
Realized their unity with father, mother,
And teacher, and discharged the three duties
Of studying the scriptures, ritual worship,
And giving alms to those in need, rise above
Birth and death. Knowing the god of fire
Born of Brahman, they attain perfect peace.

18   Those who carry out this triple duty
Conscious of its full meaning will shake off
The dread noose of death and transcend sorrow
To enjoy the world of heaven.

19   Thus have I granted you the second boon,
Nachiketa, the secret of the fire
That leads to heaven. It will have your name.
Ask now, Nachiketa, for the third boon.

NACHIKETA

20   When a person dies, there arises this doubt:
"He still exists," say some; "he does not,"
Say others. I want you to teach me the truth.
This is my third boon.

YAMA

21   This doubt haunted even the gods of old;
For the secret of death is hard to know.
Nachiketa, ask for some other boon
And release me from my promise.

NACHIKETA

This doubt haunted even the gods of old;   22
For it is hard to know, O Death, as you say.
I can have no greater teacher than you,
And there is no boon equal to this.

YAMA

Ask for sons and grandsons who will live   23
A hundred years. Ask for herds of cattle,
Elephants and horses, gold and vast land,
And ask to live as long as you desire.
Or, if you can think of anything more   24
Desirable, ask for that, with wealth and
Long life as well. Nachiketa, be the ruler
Of a great kingdom, and I will give you
The utmost capacity to enjoy
The pleasures of life. Ask for beautiful   25
Women of loveliness rarely seen on earth,
Riding in chariots, skilled in music,
To attend on you. But Nachiketa,
Don't ask me about the secret of death.

NACHIKETA

These pleasures last but until tomorrow,   26
And they wear out the vital powers of life.
How fleeting is all life on earth! Therefore
Keep your horses and chariots, dancing
And music, for yourself. Never can mortals   27
Be made happy by wealth. How can we be
Desirous of wealth when we see your face
And know we cannot live while you are here?
This is the boon I choose and ask you for.

Having approached an immortal like you,   28
How can I, subject to old age and death,
Ever try to rejoice in a long life
For the sake of the senses' fleeting pleasures?
Dispel this doubt of mine, O king of death: 29
Does a person live after death or does he not?
Nachiketa asks for no other boon
Than the secret of this great mystery.

[2]

Having tested young Nachiketa and found him fit to receive spiritual instruction,
Yama, king of death, said:

YAMA

1   The joy of the Atman ever abides,
But not what seems pleasant to the senses.
Both these, differing in their purpose, prompt
Man to action. All is well for those who choose
The joy of the Atman, but they miss
The goal of life who prefer the pleasant.

2   Perennial joy or passing pleasure?
This is the choice one is to make always.
The wise recognize these two, but not
The ignorant. The first welcome what leads
To abiding joy, though painful at the time.
The latter run, goaded by their senses,
After what seems immediate pleasure.

3   Well have you renounced these passing pleasures
So dear to the senses, Nachiketa,
And turned your back on the way of the world
Which makes mankind forget the goal of life.

4   Far apart are wisdom and ignorance.
The first leads one to Self-realization;
The second makes one more and more
Estranged from his real Self. I regard you,
Nachiketa, worthy of instruction,
For passing pleasures tempt you not at all.

5   Ignorant of the ignorance, yet wise
In their own esteem, these deluded men
Proud of their vain learning go round and round

6   Like the blind led by the blind. Far beyond
Their eyes, hypnotized by the world of sense,
Opens the way to immortality.
"I am my body; when my body dies,
I die." Living in this superstition
They fall life after life under my sway.

7   It is but few who hear about the Self.
Fewer still dedicate their lives to its
Realization. Wonderful is the one
Who speaks about the Self; rare are they
Who make it the supreme goal of their lives.
Blessed are they who, through an illumined
Teacher, attain to Self-realization.

8   The truth of the Self cannot come through one
Who has not realized that he is the Self.
The intellect cannot reveal the Self,
Beyond its duality of subject
And object. They who see themselves in all
And all in them help others through spiritual
Osmosis to realize the Self themselves.

9   This awakening you have known comes not
Through logic and scholarship, but from

Close association with a realized teacher.
Wise are you, Nachiketa, because you seek
The Self eternal. May we have more
Seekers like you!

NACHIKETA

I know that earthly treasures are transient,   10
And never can I reach the eternal through them.
Hence have I renounced all my desires for earthly treasures
To win the eternal through your instruction.

YAMA

I spread before your eyes, Nachiketa,   11
The fulfillment of all worldly desires:
Power to dominate the earth, delights
Celestial gained through religious rites,
Miraculous powers beyond time and space.
These with will and wisdom have you renounced.

The wise, realizing through meditation   12
The timeless Self, beyond all perception,
Hidden in the cave of the heart,
Leave pain and pleasure far behind.
Those who know they are neither body nor mind   13
But the immemorial Self, the divine
Principle of existence, find the source
Of all joy and live in joy abiding.
I see the gates of joy are opening
For you, Nachiketa.

NACHIKETA

Teach me of That you see as beyond right   14
And wrong, cause and effect, past and future.

YAMA

I will give you the Word all the scriptures   15
Glorify, all spiritual disciplines
Express, to attain which aspirants lead
A life of sense-restraint and self-naughting.
It is OM. This symbol of the Godhead   16
Is the highest. Realizing it one finds
Complete fulfillment of all one's longings.
It is of the greatest support to all seekers.   17
Those in whose hearts OM reverberates

Unceasingly are indeed blessed
And deeply loved as one who is the Self.

18   The all-knowing Self was never born,
Nor will it die. Beyond cause and effect,
This Self is eternal and immutable.
When the body dies, the Self does not die.

19   If the slayer believes that he can slay
Or the slain believes that he can be slain,
Neither knows the truth. The eternal Self
Slays not, nor is ever slain.

20   Hidden in the heart of every creature
Exists the Self, subtler than the subtlest,
Greater than the greatest. They go beyond
Sorrow who extinguish their self-will
And behold the glory of the Self
Through the grace of the Lord of Love.

21   Though one sits in meditation in a
Particular place, the Self within
Can exercise his influence far away.
Though still, he moves everything everywhere.

22   When the wise realize the Self,
Formless in the midst of forms, changeless
In the midst of change, omnipresent
And supreme, they go beyond sorrow.

23   The Self cannot be known through study
Of the scriptures, nor through the intellect,
Nor through hearing learned discourses.
The Self can be attained only by those
Whom the Self chooses. Verily unto them
Does the Self reveal himself.

24   The Self cannot be known by anyone
Who desists not from unrighteous ways,
Controls not his senses, stills not his mind,
And practices not meditation.

25   None else can know the omnipresent Self,
Whose glory sweeps away the rituals
Of the priest and the prowess of the warrior
And puts death itself to death.

[3]

1   In the secret cave of the heart, two are seated
By life's fountain. The separate ego
Drinks of the sweet and bitter stuff,
Liking the sweet, disliking the bitter,
While the supreme Self drinks sweet and bitter
Neither liking this nor disliking that.
The ego gropes in darkness, while the Self
Lives in light. So declare the illumined sages
And the householders who worship

The sacred fire in the name of the Lord.

May we light the fire of Nachiketa   2
That burns out the ego and enables us
To pass from fearful fragmentation
To fearless fullness in the changeless whole.

Know the Self as lord of the chariot,   3
The body as the chariot itself,
The discriminating intellect as charioteer,
And the mind as reins.
The senses, say the wise, are the horses;   4
Selfish desires are the roads they travel.
When the Self is confused with the body,
Mind, and senses, they point out, he seems
To enjoy pleasure and suffer sorrow.

When one lacks discrimination   5
And his mind is undisciplined, the senses
Run hither and thither like wild horses.
But they obey the rein like trained horses   6
When one has discrimination and has made
The mind one-pointed. Those who lack   7
Discrimination, with little control
Over their thoughts and far from pure,
Reach not the pure state of immortality
But wander from death to death; but those   8
Who have discrimination, with a still mind
And a pure heart, reach journey's end,
Never again to fall into the jaws of death.
With a discriminating intellect   9
As charioteer and a trained mind as reins,
They attain the supreme goal of life
To be united with the Lord of Love.

The senses derive from objects of sense-perception,   10
Sense objects from mind, mind from intellect,
And intellect from ego;
Ego from undifferentiated consciousness,   11
And consciousness from Brahman.
Brahman is the first cause and last refuge.
Brahman, the hidden Self in everyone,   12
Does not shine forth. He is revealed only
To those who keep their mind one-pointed
On the Lord of Love and thus develop
A superconscious manner of knowing.
Meditation enables them to go   13
Deeper and deeper into consciousness,
From the world of words to the world of thoughts,
Then beyond thoughts to wisdom in the Self.

Get up! Wake up! Seek the guidance of an   14
Illumined teacher and realize the Self.
Sharp like a razor's edge, the sages say,
Is the path, difficult to traverse.

15   The supreme Self is beyond name and form,
      Beyond the senses, inexhaustible,
      Without beginning, without end, beyond
      Time, space, and causality, eternal,
      Immutable. Those who realize the Self
      Are forever free from the jaws of death.

16   The wise, who gain experiential knowledge
      Of this timeless tale of Nachiketa,
      Narrated by Death, attain the glory
      Of living in spiritual awareness.
      Those who, full of devotion, recite this
      Supreme mystery at a spiritual
      Gathering, are fit for eternal life.
      They are indeed fit for eternal life.

PART II

[1]

1   The self-existent Lord pierced the senses
      To turn outward. Thus we look to the world
      Outside and see not the Self within us.
      A sage withdrew his senses from the world
      Of change and, seeking immortality,
      Looked within and beheld the deathless Self.

2   The immature run after sense pleasures
      And fall into the widespread net of death.
      But the wise, knowing the Self as deathless,
      Seek not the changeless in the world of change.

3   That through which one enjoys form, taste, smell, sound,
      Touch, and sexual union is the Self.
      Can there be anything not known to That
      Who is the One in all? Know One, know all.

4   That through which one enjoys the waking
      And sleeping states is the Self. To know That
      As consciousness is to go beyond sorrow.

5   Those who know the Self as enjoyer
      Of the honey from the flowers of the senses,
      Ever present within, ruler of time,
      Go beyond fear. For this Self is supreme!

6   The god of creation, Brahma,
      Born of the Godhead through meditation
      Before the waters of life were created,
      Who stands in the heart of every creature,
      Is the Self indeed. For this Self is supreme!

7   The goddess of energy, Aditi,
      Born of the Godhead through vitality,
      Mother of all the cosmic forces
      Who stands in the heart of every creature,

Is the Self indeed. For this Self is supreme!

The god of fire, Agni, hidden between   8
Two firesticks like a child well protected
In the mother's womb, whom we adore
Every day in meditation,
Is the Self indeed. For this Self is supreme!

That which is the source of the sun   9
And of every power in the cosmos, beyond which
There is neither going nor coming,
Is the Self indeed. For this Self is supreme!

What is here is also there; what is there,   10
Also here. Who sees multiplicity
But not the one indivisible Self
Must wander on and on from death to death.

Only the one-pointed mind attains   11
This state of unity. There is no one
But the Self. Who sees multiplicity
But not the one indivisible Self
Must wander on and on from death to death.

That thumb-sized being enshrined in the heart,   12
Ruler of time, past and future,
To see whom is to go beyond all fear,
Is the Self indeed. For this Self is supreme!

That thumb-sized being, a flame without smoke,   13
Ruler of time, past and future,
The same on this day as on tomorrow,
Is the Self indeed. For this Self is supreme!

As the rain on a mountain peak runs off   14
The slopes on all sides, so those who see
Only the seeming multiplicity of life
Run after things on every side.

As pure water poured into pure water   15
Becomes the very same, so does the Self
Of the illumined man or woman, Nachiketa,
Verily become one with the Godhead.

[2]

There is a city with eleven gates   1
Of which the ruler is the unborn Self,
Whose light forever shines. They go beyond
Sorrow who meditate on the Self
And are freed from the cycle of birth and death.
For this Self is supreme!

The Self is the sun shining in the sky,   2
The wind blowing in space; he is the fire

At the altar and in the home the guest;
He dwells in human beings, in gods, in truth,
And in the vast firmament; he is the fish
Born in water, the plant growing in the earth,
The river flowing down from the mountain.
For this Self is supreme!

3   The adorable one who is seated
In the heart rules the breath of life.
Unto him all the senses pay their homage.
4   When the dweller in the body breaks out
In freedom from the bonds of flesh, what remains?
For this Self is supreme!

5   We live not by the breath that flows in
And flows out, but by him who causes the breath
To flow in and flow out.

6   Now, O Nachiketa, I will tell you
Of this unseen, eternal Brahman, and
7   What befalls the Self after death. Of those
Unaware of the Self, some are born as
Embodied creatures while others remain
In a lower stage of evolution,
As determined by their own need for growth.

8   That which is awake even in our sleep,
Giving form in dreams to the objects of
Sense craving, that indeed is pure light,
Brahman the immortal, who contains all
The cosmos, and beyond whom none can go.
For this Self is supreme!

9   As the same fire assumes different shapes
When it consumes objects differing in shape,
So does the one Self take the shape
Of every creature in whom he is present.
10   As the same air assumes different shapes
When it enters objects differing in shape,
So does the one Self take the shape
Of every creature in whom he is present.

11   As the sun, who is the eye of the world,
Cannot be tainted by the defects in our eyes
Or by the objects it looks on,
So the one Self, dwelling in all, cannot
Be tainted by the evils of the world.
For this Self transcends all!

12   The ruler supreme, inner Self of all,
Multiplies his oneness into many.
Eternal joy is theirs who see the Self
In their own hearts. To none else does it come!

13   Changeless amidst the things that pass away,

Pure consciousness in all who are conscious
The One answers the prayers of many.
Eternal peace is theirs who see the Self
In their own hearts. To none else does it come!

NACHIKETA

How can I know that blissful Self, supreme,   14
Inexpressible, realized by the wise?
Is he the light, or does he reflect light?

YAMA

There shines not the sun, neither the moon nor star,   15
Nor flash of lightning, nor fire lit on earth.
The Self is the light reflected by all.
He shining, everything shines after him.

[3]

The Tree of Eternity has its roots above   1
And its branches on earth below.
Its pure root is Brahman the immortal
From whom all the worlds draw their life, and whom
None can transcend. For this Self is supreme!

The cosmos comes forth from Brahman and moves   2
In him. With his power it reverberates,
Like thunder crashing in the sky. Those who realize him
Pass beyond the sway of death.

In fear of him fire burns; in fear of him   3
The sun shines, the clouds rain, and the winds blow.
In fear of him death stalks about to kill.

If one fails to realize Brahman in this life   4
Before the physical sheath is shed,
He must again put on a body
In the world of embodied creatures.

Brahman can be seen, as in a mirror,   5
In a pure heart; in the world of the ancestors
As in a dream; in the gandharva world
As the reflections in trembling waters;
And clear as light in the realm of Brahma.

Knowing the senses to be separate   6
From the Self, and the sense experience
To be fleeting, the wise grieve no more.

Above the senses is the mind,   7
Above the mind is the intellect,

Above that is the ego, and above the ego
Is the unmanifested Cause.

8   And beyond is Brahman, omnipresent,
Attributeless. Realizing him one is released
From the cycle of birth and death.

9   He is formless, and can never be seen
With these two eyes. But he reveals himself
in the heart made pure through meditation
And sense-restraint. Realizing him one is released
From the cycle of birth and death.

10   When the five senses are stilled, when the mind
Is stilled, when the intellect is stilled,
That is called the highest state by the wise.

11   They say yoga is this complete stillness
In which one enters the unitive state,
Never to become separate again.
If one is not established in this state,
The sense of unity will come and go.

12   The unitive state cannot be attained
Through words or thoughts or through the eye.
How can it be attained except through one
Who is established in this state himself?

13   There are two selves, the separate ego
And the indivisible Atman. When
One rises above *I* and *me* and *mine*,
The Atman is revealed as one's real Self.

14   When all desires that surge in the heart
Are renounced, the mortal becomes immortal.

15   When all the knots that strangle the heart
Are loosened, the mortal becomes immortal.
This sums up the teaching of the scriptures.

16   From the heart there radiate a hundred
And one vital tracks. One of them rises
To the crown of the head. This way leads
To immortality, the others to death.

17   The Lord of Love, not larger than the thumb,
Is ever enshrined in the hearts of all.
Draw him clear out of the physical sheath,
As one draws the stalk from the munja grass.
Know thyself to be pure and immortal!
Know thyself to be pure and immortal!

THE NARRATOR

Nachiketa learned from the king of death
The whole discipline of meditation.

Freeing himself from all separateness,
He won immortality in Brahman.
So blessed is everyone who knows the Self!

OM shanti shanti shanti

THE ISHA UPANISHAD

All this is full. All that is full.
From fullness, fullness comes.
When fullness is taken from fullness,
Fullness still remains

OM shanti shanti shanti

The Lord is enshrined in the hearts of all.   1
The Lord is the supreme Reality.
Rejoice in him through renunciation.
Covet nothing. All belongs to the Lord.
Thus working may you live a hundred years.   2
Thus alone will you work in real freedom.

Those who deny the Self are born again   3
Blind to the Self, enveloped in darkness,
Utterly devoid of love for the Lord.

The Self is one. Ever still, the Self is   4
Swifter than thought, swifter than the senses.
Though motionless, he outruns all pursuit.
Without the Self, never could life exist.

The Self seems to move, but is ever still.   5
He seems far away, but is ever near.
He is within all, and he transcends all.

Those who see all creatures in themselves   6
And themselves in all creatures know no fear.
Those who see all creatures in themselves   7
And themselves in all creatures know no grief.
How can the multiplicity of life
Delude the one who sees its unity?

The Self is everywhere. Bright is the Self,   8
Indivisible, untouched by sin, wise,
Immanent and transcendent. He it is
Who holds the cosmos together.

In dark night live those for whom   9–
The world without alone is real; in night   11
Darker still, for whom the world within
Alone is real. The first leads to a life
Of action, the second to a life of meditation.
But those who combine action with meditation

Cross the sea of death through action
And enter into immortality
Through the practice of meditation.
So have we heard from the wise.

12–
14

In dark night live those for whom the Lord
Is transcendent only; in night darker still,
For whom he is immanent only.
But those for whom he is transcendent
And immanent cross the sea of death
With the immanent and enter into
Immortality with the transcendent.
So have we heard from the wise.

15

The face of truth is hidden by your orb
Of gold, O sun. May you remove your orb
So that I, who adore the true, may see

16

The glory of truth. O nourishing sun,
Solitary traveler, controller,
Source of life for all creatures, spread your light
And subdue your dazzling splendor
So that I may see your blessed Self.
Even that very Self am I!

17

May my life merge in the Immortal
When my body is reduced to ashes.
O mind, meditate on the eternal Brahman.
Remember the deeds of the past.
Remember, O mind, remember.

18

O god of fire, lead us by the good path
To eternal joy. You know all our deeds.
Deliver us from evil, we who bow
And pray again and again.

OM shanti shanti shanti

THE SHVETASHVATARA UPANISHAD

I

1

What is the cause of the cosmos? Is it Brahman?
From where do we come? By what live?
Where shall we find peace at last?
What power governs the duality
Of pleasure and pain by which we are driven?

2

Time, nature, necessity, accident,
Elements, energy, intelligence—
None of these can be the First Cause.
They are effects, whose only purpose is
To help the self rise above pleasure and pain.

In the depths of meditation, sages   3
Saw within themselves the Lord of Love,
Who dwells in the heart of every creature.
Deep in the hearts of all he dwells, hidden
Behind the gunas of law, energy,
And inertia. He is One. He it is
Who rules over time, space, and causality.

The world is the wheel of God, turning round   4
And round with all living creatures upon its rim.
The world is the river of God,   5
Flowing from him and flowing back to him.
On this ever-revolving wheel of being   6
The individual self goes round and round
Through life after life, believing itself
To be a separate creature, until
It sees its identity with the Lord of Love
And attains immortality in the indivisible whole.
He is the eternal Reality, sing the scriptures,   7
And the ground of existence.
Those who perceive him in every creature
Merge in him and are released from the wheel
Of birth and death.

The Lord of Love holds in his hand the world,   8
Composed of the changing and the changeless,
The manifest and the unmanifest.
The separate self, not yet aware of the Lord,
Goes after pleasure, only to become
Bound more and more. When it sees the Lord,
There comes an end to its bondage.

Conscious spirit and unconscious matter   9
Both have existed since the dawn of time,
With maya appearing to connect them,
Misrepresenting joy as outside us.

When all these three are seen as one, the Self
Reveals his universal form and serves
As an instrument of the divine will.

All is change in the world of the senses,   10
But changeless is the supreme Lord of Love.
Meditate on him, be absorbed in him,
Wake up from this dream of separateness.

Know God and all fetters will fall away.   11
No longer identifying yourself
With the body, go beyond birth and death.
All your desires will be fulfilled in him
Who is One without a second.

Know him to be enshrined in your heart always.   12
Truly there is nothing more in life to know.

Meditate and realize this world
Is filled with the presence of God.

13   Fire is not seen until one firestick rubs
Against another, though fire is still there,
Hidden in the firestick. So does the Lord
Remain hidden in the body until
He is revealed through the mystic mantram.

14   Let your body be the lower firestick;
Let the mantram be the upper. Rub them
Against each other in meditation
And realize the Lord.

15   Like oil in sesame seeds, like butter
In cream, like water in springs, like fire
In firesticks, so dwells the Lord of Love,
The Self, in the very depths of consciousness.
Realize him through truth and meditation.

16   The Self is hidden in the hearts of all,
As butter lies hidden in cream. Realize
The Self in the depths of meditation—
The Lord of Love, supreme Reality,
Who is the goal of all knowledge.

This is the highest mystical teaching;
This is the highest mystical teaching.

II

1   May we harness body and mind to see
The Lord of Life, who dwells in everyone.
2   May we ever with one-pointed mind
Strive for blissful union with the Lord.
3   May we train our senses to serve the Lord
Through the practice of meditation.

4   Great is the glory of the Lord of Life,
Infinite, omnipresent, all-knowing.
He is known by the wise who meditate
And conserve their vital energy.

5   Hear, O children of immortal bliss,
You are born to be united with the Lord.
Follow the path of the illumined ones
And be united with the Lord of Life.

6   Kindle the fire of kundalini deep
In meditation. Bring your mind and breath
Under control. Drink deep of divine love,
And you will attain the unitive state.

7   Dedicate yourself to the Lord of Life,
Who is the cause of the cosmos. He will

Remove the cause of all your suffering
And free you from the bondage of karma.

Be seated with spinal column erect   8
And turn your senses and mind deep within.
With the mantram echoing in your heart,
Cross over the dread sea of birth and death.

Train your senses to be obedient.   9
Regulate your activities to lead you
To the goal. Hold the reins of your mind
As you hold the reins of restive horses.

Choose a place for meditation that is   10
Clean, quiet, and cool, a cave with a smooth floor
Without stones and dust, protected against
Wind and rain and pleasing to the eye.

In deep meditation aspirants may   11
See forms like snow or smoke. They may feel
A strong wind blowing or a wave of heat.
They may see within them more and more light:
Fireflies, lightning, sun, or moon. These are signs
That one is far on the path to Brahman.

Health, a light body, freedom from cravings,   12–
A glowing skin, sonorous voice, fragrance   13
Of body: these signs indicate progress
In the practice of meditation.

Those who attain the supreme goal of life,   14
Realizing the Self and passing beyond
All sorrow, shine bright as a mirror
Which has been cleansed of dust.

In the supreme climax of samadhi   15
They realize the presence of the Lord
Within their heart. Freed from impurities,
They pass forever beyond birth and death.

The Lord dwells in the womb of the cosmos,   16
The creator who is in all creatures.
He is that which is born and to be born;
His face is everywhere.

Let us adore the Lord of Life, who is   17
Present in fire and water, plants and trees.
Let us adore the Lord of Life!
Let us adore the Lord of Life!

III

Brahman, attributeless Reality,   1
Becomes the Lord of Love who casts his net
Of appearance over the cosmos and rules

It from within through his divine power.
He was before creation; he will be
After dissolution. He alone is.
Those who know him become immortal.

2 The Lord of Love is one. There is indeed
No other. He is the inner ruler
In all beings. He projects the cosmos
From himself, maintains and withdraws it
Back into himself at the end of time.

3 His eyes, mouths, arms, and feet are everywhere.
Projecting the cosmos out of himself,
He holds it together.

4 He is the source of all the powers of life.
He is the lord of all, the great seer
Who dwells forever in the cosmic womb.
May he purify our consciousness!

5 O Lord, in whom alone we can find peace,
May we see your divine Self and be freed
From all impure thoughts and all fear.

6 O Lord, from whom we receive the mantram
As a weapon to destroy our self-will,
Reveal yourself, protector of all.

7 You are the supreme Brahman, infinite,
Yet hidden in the hearts of all creatures.
You pervade everything. Realizing you,
We attain immortality.

8 I have realized the Lord of Love,
Who is the sun that dispels our darkness.
Those who realize him go beyond death;
No other way is there to immortality.

9 There is nothing higher than him, nothing other
Than him. His infinity is beyond great
And small. In his own glory rooted,
He stands and fills the cosmos.

10 He fills the cosmos, yet he transcends it.
Those who know him leave all separateness,
Sorrow, and death behind. Those who know him not
Live but to suffer.

11 The Lord of Love, omnipresent, dwelling
In the heart of every living creature,
All mercy, turns every face to himself.

12 He is the supreme Lord, who through his grace
Moves us to seek him in our own hearts.
He is the light that shines forever.

13 He is the inner Self of all,
Hidden like a little flame in the heart.

Only by the stilled mind can he be known.
Those who realize him become immortal.

He has thousands of heads, thousands of eyes,   14
Thousands of feet; he surrounds the cosmos
On every side. This infinite being   15
Is ever present in the hearts of all.
He has become the cosmos. He is what was
And what will be. Yet he is unchanging,
The lord of immortality.

His hands and feet are everywhere; his heads   16
And mouths everywhere. He sees everything,
Hears everything, and pervades everything.

Without organs of sense, he shines through them.   17
He is the lord of all, inner ruler,
Protector and friend of all.

He resides in the city with nine gates,   18
Which is the body. He moves in the world
Enjoying the play of his countless forms.
He is the master of the universe,
Of animate and inanimate.

He runs without feet and holds without hands.   19
He sees without eyes and hears without ears.
He knows everyone, but no one knows him.
He is called the First, the Great, the Supreme.

The Lord of Love is hidden in the heart   20
Of every creature, subtler than the subtlest,
Greater than the greatest. Through his grace
One sheds all selfish desires and sorrow
And becomes united with the Self.

I know this Self, sage Shvetashvatara said,   21
To be immortal and infinite. I know this
Self who is the Self of all,
Whom the sages call the Eternal One.

IV

May the Lord of Love, who projects himself   1
Into this universe of myriad forms,
From whom all beings come and to whom all
Return, grant us the grace of wisdom.

He is fire and the sun, and the moon   2
And the stars. He is the air and the sea,
And the Creator, Prajapati.
He is this boy, he is that girl, he is   3
This man, he is that woman, and he is

This old man, too, tottering on his staff.
His face is everywhere.

4   He is the blue bird, he is the green bird
With red eyes; he is the thundercloud,
And he is the seasons and the seas.
He has no beginning, he has no end.
He is the source from which the worlds evolve.

5   From his divine power comes forth all this
Magical show of name and form, of you
And me, which casts the spell of pain and pleasure.
Only when we pierce through this magic veil
Do we see the One who appears as many.

6   Two birds of beautiful plumage, comrades
Inseparable, live on the selfsame tree.
One bird eats the fruit of pleasure and pain;
The other looks on without eating.

7   Forgetting our divine origin,
We become ensnared in the world of change.
And bewail our helplessness. But when
We see the Lord of Love in all his glory,
Adored by all, we go beyond sorrow.

8   What use are the scriptures to anyone
Who knows not the one source from whom they come,
In whom all gods and worlds abide?
Only those who realize him as ever present
Within the heart attain abiding joy.

9   The Lord, who is the supreme magician,
Brings forth out of himself all the scriptures,
Oblations, sacrifices, spiritual disciplines,
The past and present, the whole universe.
Invisible through the magic of maya,
He remains hidden in the hearts of all.

10   Know him to be the supreme magician
Whose maya brought all the worlds out of himself.
Know that all beings in the universe
Partake of his divine splendor.

11   Know him to be the supreme magician
Who has become boy and girl, bird and beast.
He is the bestower of all blessings,
And his grace fills the heart with profound peace.

12   Know him to be the supreme source of all
The gods, sole support of the universe,
The sower of the golden seed of life.
May he grant us the grace of wisdom.

13   Know him to be the supreme God of gods,
From whom all the worlds draw their breath of life

And who rules every creature from within.
May he be worshipped by everyone!

Know him to be the supreme pervader,   14
In whom the whole universe is smaller
Than the smallest atom. May he, Shiva,
Fill our hearts with infinite peace.

Know him to be the supreme guardian   15
Of the cosmos, protecting all creatures

Figurine of Shiva as "Lord of the Dance." Shiva functions as the destroyer of
ignorance, one of the three primary Hindu deities (together with Brahma and
Vishnu) and, for members of the influential Shaivite sect, the supreme deity
(*Ellen Howdon/Dorling Kindersley © St Mungo, Glasgow City Council Museums*)

From within. May he, Shiva, in whom all
Are one, free us from the bonds of death.

16   Know him to be the One supreme, hidden
Within the hearts of all as cream in milk
And yet encompassing the universe.
May he, Shiva, free us from all bondage.

17   Know him to be the supreme architect,
He who is enshrined in the hearts of all.
Know him in the depths of meditation.
May he grant us immortality!

18   Know him to be the supreme source of all
Religions, ruler of the world of light,
Where there is neither day nor night,
Neither what is nor what is not, but only Shiva.

19   He is far beyond the reach of the mind.
He alone is. His glory fills all worlds.

20   He is far beyond the reach of the eye.
He alone is. May he, Shiva, reveal
Himself in the depths of meditation
And grant us immortality.

21–   I live in fear of death, O Lord of Love;
22   I seek refuge at your feet. Protect me;
Protect us man and woman, cow and horse.
May the brave ones who seek you be released
From the bondage of death.

V

1   To know the unity of all life leads
To deathlessness; to know not leads to death.
Both are hidden in the infinity
Of Brahman, who is beyond both.

2   He is the One who presides over all
And rules over everyone from within.
He sows the golden seed of life when time begins
And helps us know its unity.

3   He is the Lord who casts the net of birth
And death and withdraws it again,
The supreme Self who governs the forces of life.

4   Even as the sun shines and fills all space
With light, above, below, across, so shines
The Lord of Love and fills the hearts of all created beings.

5   From him the cosmos comes, he who teaches
Each living creature to attain perfection
According to its own nature. He is
The Lord of Love who reigns over all life.

He is the supreme creator, hidden
Deep in the mystery of the scriptures.   6
By realizing him the gods and sages
Attained immortality.

Under the hypnotic spell of pleasure   7
And pain, we live for ourselves and are bound.
Though master of ourselves, we roam about
From birth to birth, driven by our own deeds.

The Self, small as the thumb, dwelling in the heart,   8
Is like the sun shining in the sky.
But when identified with the ego,
The Self appears other than what it is.
It may appear smaller than a hair's breadth.   9
But know the Self to be infinite.

Not female, male, nor neuter is the Self.   10
As is the body, so is the gender.
The Self takes on a body, with desires,   11
Attachments, and delusions. The Self is
Born again and again in new bodies
To work out the karma of former lives.

The embodied self assumes many forms,   12
Heavy or light, according to its needs
For growth and the deeds of previous lives.
This evolution is a divine law.

Love the Lord and be free. He is the One   13
Who appears as many, enveloping
The cosmos, without beginning or end.
None but the pure in heart can realize him.

May Lord Shiva, creator, destroyer,   14
The abode of all beauty and wisdom,
Free us from the cycle of birth and death.

VI

The learned say life is self-created;   1
Others say that life has evolved from time.
It is the Lord who has brought the cosmos
Out of himself.

He is pure consciousness, omnipresent,   2
Omnipotent, omniscient, creator
Of time and master of the three gunas.
Evolution takes place at his command.

Those who act without thought of personal   3
Profit and lead a well-disciplined life
Discover in course of time the divine principle
That all forms of life are one.

4   Those who work in the service of the Lord
     Are freed from the law of karma.

5   Know him to be the primal source of life,
     Whose glory permeates the universe:
     Who is beyond time and space, and is seen
     Within the heart in meditation.

6   Know that he is beyond the tree of life,
     He whose power makes the planets revolve:
     Who is both law and mercy, and is seen
     Within the heart in meditation.

7   Know him to be the supreme Lord of lords,
     King of kings, God of gods, ruler of all,
8   Without action or organs of action,
     Whose power is seen in myriad ways.

9   Know him to be the cause without a cause,
     Without a second, parent or master.
10   May he, Lord of Love, who conceals himself
     In creatures as a spider in its web,
     Grant us illumination.

11   The Lord is hidden in every heart.
     He is the eternal witness, beyond
     The gunas, watching our work from within
     As pure consciousness.

12   The Lord is the operator; we are
     But his innumerable instruments.
     May we, in our consciousness, realize
     The bliss he alone can give us.

13   Changeless amidst the changing, consciousness
     Of the conscious, he grants all our prayers.
     May we, in our consciousness, realize
     The freedom he alone can give us.

14   Neither sun nor moon nor star nor fire shines;
     Everything reflects the light of the Lord.
15   May we realize him in our consciousness;
     There is no other way to conquer death.

16– He is the maker of the universe,
17   Self-existent, omniscient, destroyer
     Of death, the source and inmost Self of all,
     Ruler of the cycle of birth and death.
     May we realize him in our consciousness;
     There is no other way to conquer death.

18– Lord Shiva is my refuge: he who grants
19   Freedom from the cycle of birth and death.
     Lord Shiva is my refuge: he who gave

The sacred scriptures at the dawn of time.
Lord Shiva is my refuge: he who is
The source of purity and perfection.
Lord Shiva is my refuge: he who is
The bridge from death to immortality.
Lord Shiva is my refuge: he whose grace
Has made me long for his lotus feet.

How can we roll up the sky like a piece   20
Of deerskin? How can we end our misery
Without realizing that the Lord of Love
Is enshrined in our heart of hearts?

Sage Shvetashvatara realized the Lord   21
In meditation through His infinite grace
And imparted this highest wisdom
To devoted disciples.

This highest mystical experience,   22
Revealed at the dawn of time, must be shared
Only with one whose heart is pure
Or with a disciple or one's own child.
If you have deep love for the Lord of Love   23
And for your teacher, the light of this teaching
Will shine in your heart. It will shine indeed!

OM shanti shanti shanti

THE MUNDAKA UPANISHAD

PART I

[1]

From infinite Godhead came forth Brahma,   1
First among gods, from whom sprang the cosmos.
Brahma gave the vision of the Godhead,
The true source of wisdom that life demands,
To his eldest son, Atharva, who gave it   2
To Angi. In turn Angi gave it
To Satyavaha. In this tradition
Satyavaha gave it to Angiras.

A great householder named Shaunaka once came   3
To Angiras and reverently asked:
"What is that by knowing which all is known?"
He replied: "The illumined sages say   4
Knowledge is twofold, higher and lower.
The study of the Vedas, linguistics,   5
Rituals, astronomy, and all the arts
Can be called lower knowledge. The higher
Is that which leads to Self-realization.

6   "The eye cannot see it; mind cannot grasp it.
The deathless Self has neither caste nor race,
Neither eyes nor ears nor hands nor feet.
Sages say this Self is infinite in the great
And in the small, everlasting and changeless,
The source of life.

7   "As the web issues out of the spider
And is withdrawn, as plants sprout from the earth,
As hair grows from the body, even so,
The sages say, this universe springs from
The deathless Self, the source of life.

8   "The deathless Self meditated upon
Himself and projected the universe
As evolutionary energy.
From this energy developed life, mind,
The elements, and the world of karma,
Which is enchained by cause and effect.

9   "The deathless Self sees all, knows all. From him
Springs Brahma, who embodies the process
Of evolution into name and form
By which the One appears to be many."

[2]

1   The rituals and the sacrifices described
In the Vedas deal with lower knowledge.
The sages ignored these rituals
And went in search of higher knowledge.

2–
5   Look at these rituals: "When the fire is lit,
Pour butter into the fire in two spots;
Then place the offering between these two.
These obligations will take the worshipper
6   On the sun's rays to the world of Brahma,
Where he can have his fill of enjoyment."

7   Such rituals are unsafe rafts for crossing
The sea of samsara, of birth and death.
Doomed to shipwreck are those who try to cross
The sea of samsara on these poor rafts.
8   Ignorant of their ignorance, yet wise
In their own esteem, these deluded men
Proud of their vain learning go round and round
Like the blind led by the blind.

9–
10   Living in darkness, immature, unaware
Of any higher good or goal, they fall
Again and again into the sea.

11   But those who are pure in heart, who practice
Meditation and conquer their senses
And passions, shall attain the immortal Self,
Source of all light and source of all life.

Action prompted by pleasure or profit   12
Cannot help anyone to cross this sea.
Seek a teacher who has realized the Self.
To a student whose heart is full of love,   13
Who has conquered his senses and passions,
The teacher will reveal the Lord of Love.

PART II

[1]

Imperishable is the Lord of Love.   1
As from a blazing fire thousands of sparks
Leap forth, so millions of beings arise
From the Lord of Love and return to him.

The Lord of Love is above name and form.   2
He is present in all and transcends all.
Unborn, without body and without mind,
From him comes every body and mind.
He is the source of space, air, fire, water,   3
And the earth that holds us all.

Fire is his head, the sun and moon his eyes,   4
The heavens his ears, the scriptures his voice,
The air his breath, the universe his heart,
And the earth his footrest. The Lord of Love
Is the innermost Self of all.

From him comes the fire that burns in the sun;   5
From the sky lit by sun and moon comes rain;
From rain comes food, from food the sexual seed;
All finally come from the Lord of Love.

From him come the scriptures, chants, and prayers,   6
Religious rites and sacrificial gifts;
From him come work, time, and givers of gifts,
And all things under the sun and moon.

From him come the gods of the natural world,   7
Men, beasts, and birds, and food to nourish them;
From him come all spiritual disciplines,
Meditation, truth, faith, and purity.

From him come the seven organs of sense,   8
Seven hot desires and their sevenfold objects,
And the seven levels of consciousness
In the cavern of the heart.

From him come all the seas and the mountains,   9
The rivers and the plants that support life.
As the innermost Self of all, he dwells
Within the cavern of the heart.

10   The Lord of Love is the one Self of all.
He is detached work, spiritual wisdom,
And immortality. Realize the Self
Hidden in the heart, and cut asunder
The knot of ignorance here and now.

[2]

1   Bright but hidden, the Self dwells in the heart.
Everything that moves, breathes, opens, and closes
Lives in the Self. He is the source of love
And may be known through love but not through thought.
He is the goal of life. Attain this goal!

2   The shining Self dwells hidden in the heart.
Everything in the cosmos, great and small,
Lives in the Self. He is the source of life,
Truth beyond the transience of this world.
He is the goal of life. Attain this goal!

3   Take the great bow of the sacred scriptures,
Place on it the arrow of devotion;
Then draw the bowstring of meditation
And aim at the target, the Lord of Love.

4   The mantram is the bow, the aspirant
Is the arrow, and the Lord the target.
Now draw the bowstring of meditation,
And hitting the target be one with him.

5   In his robe are woven heaven and earth,
Mind and body. Realize him as the One
Behind the many and stop all vain talk.
He is the bridge from death to deathless life.

6   Where all the nerves meet like spokes in a wheel,
There he dwells, the One behind the many.
Meditate upon him in the mantram.
May he guide us from death to deathless life!

7   He knows everyone and sees everything.
It is his glory that fills the cosmos.
He resides in the city of the heart.

8   It is his power that moves body and mind.
May he guide us from death to deathless life!

9   When he is seen within us and without,
He sets right all doubts and dispels the pain
Of wrong actions committed in the past.

10   In the golden city of the heart dwells
The Lord of Love, without parts, without stain,
Know him as the radiant light of lights.

11   There shines not the sun, neither moon nor star,
Nor flash of lightning, nor fire lit on earth.
The Lord is the light reflected by all.
He shining, everything shines after him.

The Lord of Love is before and behind.   12
He extends to the right and to the left.
He extends above; he extends below.
There is no one here but the Lord of Love.
He alone is; in truth, he alone is.

PART III

[1]

Like two golden birds perched on the selfsame tree,   1
Intimate friends, the ego and the Self
Dwell in the same body. The former eats
The sweet and sour fruits of the tree of life
While the latter looks on in detachment.

As long as we think we are the ego,   2
We feel attached and fall into sorrow.
But realize that you are the Self, the Lord
Of life, and you will be freed from sorrow.
When you realize that you are the Self,   3
Supreme source of light, supreme source of love,
You transcend the duality of life
And enter into the unitive state.

The Lord of Love shines in the hearts of all.   4
Seeing him in all creatures, the wise
Forget themselves in the service of all.
The Lord is their joy, the Lord is their rest;
Such as they are the lovers of the Lord.

By truth, meditation, and self-control   5
One can enter into this state of joy
And see the Self shining in a pure heart.

Truth is victorious, never untruth.   6
Truth is the way; truth is the goal of life,
Reached by sages who are free from self-will.

The effulgent Self, who is beyond thought,   7
Shines in the greatest, shines in the smallest,
Shines in the farthest, shines in the nearest,
Shines in the secret chamber of the heart.

Beyond the reach of the senses is he,   8
But not beyond the reach of a mind stilled
Through the practice of deep meditation.
Beyond the reach of words and works is he,   9
But not beyond the reach of a pure heart
Freed from the sway of the senses.

Sages are granted all the help they need   10
In everything they do to serve the Lord.

Let all those who seek their own fulfillment
Love and honor the illumined sage.

[2]

1   The wise have attained the unitive state,
And see only the resplendent Lord of Love.
Desiring nothing in the physical world,
They have become one with the Lord of Love.

2   Those who dwell on and long for sense-pleasure
Are born in a world of separateness.
But let them realize they are the Self
And all separateness will fall away.

3   Not through discourse, not through the intellect,
Not even through study of the scriptures
Can the Self be realized. The Self reveals
Himself to the one who longs for the Self.
Those who long for the Self with all their heart
Are chosen by the Self as his own.

4   Not by the weak, not by the unearnest,
Not by those who practice wrong disciplines
Can the Self be realized. The Self reveals
Himself as the Lord of Love to the one
Who practices right disciplines.

5   What the sages sought they have found at last.
No more questions have they to ask of life.
With self-will extinguished, they are at peace.
Seeing the Lord of Love in all around,
Serving the Lord of Love in all around,
They are united with him forever.

6   They have attained the summit of wisdom
By the steep path of renunciation.
They have attained to immortality
And are united with the Lord of Love.

7   When they leave the body, the vital force
Returns to the cosmic womb, but their work
Becomes a beneficial force in life
To bring others together in the Self.

8   The flowing river is lost in the sea;
The illumined sage is lost in the Self.
The flowing river has become the sea;
The illumined sage has become the Self.

9   Those who know the Self become the Self.
None in their family forgets the Self.
Freed from the fetters of separateness,
They attain to immortality.

10   Let this wisdom be taught only to those
Who obey the law of life's unity.

Let this wisdom be taught only to those
Who offer their lives to the Lord of Love.

This is the great truth taught in ancient times   11
By the sage Angiras to Shaunaka.
Let us adore the illumined sages!
Let us adore the illumined sages!

OM shanti shanti shanti

THE PRASHNA UPANISHAD

May we hear only what is good for all.
May we see only what is good for all.
May we serve you, Lord of Love, all our life.
May we be used to spread your peace on earth.

OM shanti shanti shanti

QUESTION 1

Sukesha, Satyakama, and Gargya,   1
Kausalya, Bhargava, and Kabandhi,
Who were all seeking Self-realization,
Approached with love sage Pippalada
For his guidance on the spiritual path.

The sage told them: "Live with me for one year,   2
Practicing sense-restraint and complete trust.
Ask me questions at the end of the year,
And I will answer them if I can."

After a year Kabandhi asked the sage: 3
"Master, who created the universe?"

The sage replied: 4
"The Lord meditated and brought forth prana
With rayi, the giver of name and form:
Male and female, so that they would bring forth
Innumerable creatures for him.

"Prana is the sun; rayi is the moon.   5
Matter is solid, matter is subtle;
Rayi therefore is present everywhere.

"The sun gives light and life to all who live,   6
East and west, north and south, above, below;   7
It is the prana of the universe.

"The wise see the Lord of Love in the sun,   8
Rising in all its golden radiance
To give its warmth and light and life to all.

"The wise see the Lord of Love in the year,   9
Which has two paths, the northern and the southern.

Those who observe outward forms of worship
And are content with personal pleasures
Travel after death by the southern path,
The path of the ancestors and of rayi,
To the lunar world, and are born again.

10   "But those who seek the Self through meditation,
Self-discipline, wisdom, and faith in God
Travel after death by the northern path,
The path of prana, to the solar world,
Supreme refuge, beyond the reach of fear
And free from the cycle of birth and death.

11   "Some look upon the sun as our father
Who makes life possible with heat and rain
And divides time into months and seasons.
Others have seen him riding in wisdom
On his chariot, with seven colors
As horses and six wheels to represent
The whirling spokes of time.

12   "The wise see the Lord of Love in the month,
Rayi is the dark half, prana the bright.
The wise worship in the light of wisdom,
Others in the darkness of ignorance.

13   "The wise see the Lord of Love in the day;
Rayi is the dark night, prana daylight.
Those who use their days for sexual pleasure
Consume prana, the very stuff of life;
But mastered, sex becomes a spiritual force.

14   "The wise see the Lord of Love in all food;
From food comes seed, and from seed all creatures.
15   They take the lunar path who live for sex;
But those who are self-controlled and truthful
Will go to the bright regions of the sun.

16   "The bright world of Brahman can be attained
Only by those who are pure and true,
Only by those who are pure and true."

QUESTION 2

1   Then Bhargava approached the sage and asked:
"Master, what powers support this body?
Which of them are manifested in it?
And among them all, which is the greatest?"
2   The sage replied: "The powers are space, air, fire,
Water, earth, speech, mind, vision, and hearing.
All these boasted, 'We support this body.'
3   But prana, vital energy, supreme
Over them all, said, 'Don't deceive yourselves.

It is I, dividing myself fourfold,
Who hold this body together.'

"But they would not believe these words of prana.   4
To demonstrate the truth, prana arose
And left the body, and all the powers
Knew they had to leave as well. When prana
Returned to the body, they too were back.
As when the queen bee goes out, all the bees
Go out, and when she returns all return,
So returned speech, mind, vision, and hearing.
Then the powers understood and sang this song:

"'Prana burns as fire; he shines as the sun;   5
He rains as the cloud; he blows as the wind;
He crashes as the thunder in the sky.
He is the earth; he has form and no form;
Prana is immortality.

"'Everything rests in prana, as spokes rest   6
In the hub of the wheel: all the Vedas,
All the rituals, all the warriors and kings.

"'O prana, you move in the mother's womb   7
As life to be manifested again.
All creatures pay their homage to you.

"'You carry offerings to gods and ancestors   8
And help sages to master their senses,
Which depend upon you for their function.

"'You are the creator and destroyer,   9
And our protector. You shine as the sun
In the sky; you are the source of all light.

"'When you pour yourself down as rain on earth,   10
Every living creature is filled with joy
And knows food will be abundant for all.

"'You are pure and master of everything.   11
As fire you receive our oblations;
It is you who gives us the breath of life.

"'Be kind to us with your invisible form,   12
Which dwells in the voice, the eye, and the ear,
And pervades the mind. Abandon us not.

"'O prana, all the world depends on you.   13
As a mother looks after her children,
Look after us. Grant us wealth and wisdom.'"

QUESTION 3

Then Kausalya approached the sage and asked: 1
"Master, from what source does this prana come?

How does he enter the body, how live
After dividing himself into five,
How leave the body at the time of death?
How does he support all that is without
And all that is within?"

2   The sage replied: "You ask searching questions.
Since you are a devoted aspirant
Seeking Brahman, I shall answer them.

3   "Prana is born of the Self. As a man
Casts a shadow, the Self casts prana
Into the body at the time of birth
So that the mind's desires may be fulfilled.

4   "As a king appoints officers
To do his work in all the villages,
So prana works with four other pranas,
Each a part of himself, to carry out
Different functions in the body.

5   "The main prana dwells in eye, ear, mouth, and nose;
Apana, the downward force, in the organs
Of sex and of excretion. Samana,
The equalizing force in the middle,
Digests food and kindles the seven fires.

6   "Vyana, distributor of energy,
Moves through the myriad vital currents
Radiating from the heart, where lives the Self.
7   At the time of death, through the subtle track
That runs upward through the spinal channel,
Udana, the fifth force, leads the selfless
Up the long ladder of evolution,
And the selfish down. But those who are both
Selfless and selfish come back to this earth.

8   "The sun is the prana of the universe,
And it rises to bring light to our eyes.
The earth draws the lower fire of apana;
The space between sun and earth is samana,
And the moving air is vyana.

9   "Fire is udana. When that fire goes out,
The senses are drawn back into the mind
And the person is ready for rebirth.

10   "Whatever the content of consciousness
At the time of death, that is what unites us
To prana, udana, and the Self,
To be reborn in the plane we have earned.

11   "Those who realize this go beyond death.
Their children too follow in their footsteps.
12   Those who perceive how prana rises,

Enters the body, and becomes fivefold
To serve the Self, they die not; they die not."

QUESTION 4

Then Gargya approached the sage and asked him: 1
"Sir, when a man is sleeping, who is it
That sleeps in him? Who sees the dreams he sees?
When he wakes up, who in him is awake?
When he enjoys, who is enjoying?
In whom do all these faculties rest?"

The sage replied: "As the rays of the sun,   2
When night comes, become all one in his disk
Until they spread out again at sunrise,
Even so the senses are gathered up
In the mind, which is master of them all.
Therefore when a person neither hears, sees, smells,
Tastes, touches, speaks, nor enjoys, we say he sleeps.

"Only the fires of prana are burning.   3
Apana is like the holy hearth-fire
Ever burning in the householder's shrine;
Vyana is like the fire that faces south
For carrying offerings to our ancestors;
And prana is the fire that faces eastward.
Samana is the equalizing fire   4
That balances inward and outward breath,
The offerings made by the mind.
Udana is the fruit of dreamless sleep,
In which the mind is led close to the Self.

"The dreaming mind recalls past impressions.   5
It sees again what has been seen; it hears
Again what has been heard, enjoys again
What has been enjoyed in many places.
Seen and unseen, heard and unheard, enjoyed
And unenjoyed, the real and the unreal,
The mind sees all; the mind sees all.

"When the mind is stilled in dreamless sleep,   6
It brings rest and repose to the body.
Just as birds fly to the tree for rest,   7
All things in life find their rest in the Self.
Earth, water, fire, air, space, and their subtle   8
Elements, the eyes and what can be seen,
The ears and what can be heard, the nostrils
And what can be smelled, the palate and what
Can be tasted, the skin and what can be touched,
The tongue and what can be spoken,
The hands and what can be held, the organ
Of sex and its object of enjoyment,

The organ of excretion and what is
Excreted, the feet and what they walk on,
The mind and what it thinks, the intellect
And what it knows, the ego and what
It grasps, the heart and what it loves, the light
And what it reveals: all things in life
Find their rest in the Self in dreamless sleep.

9   "It is the Self who sees, hears, smells, touches,
And tastes, who thinks, acts, and is pure consciousness.
The Self is Brahman, changeless and supreme.

10   "Those who know the supreme Self as formless,
Without shadow, without impurity,
Know all, gentle friend, and live in all.

11   Those who know the Self, the seat of consciousness,
In whom the breath and all the senses live,
Know all, gentle friend, and live in all.

QUESTION 5

1   Satyakama approached the sage and asked:
"Those who have become established in AUM,
What happens to them after death?"

2   The sage replied: " AUM is both immanent
And transcendent. Through it one can attain
The personal and the impersonal.

3   "AUM has three sounds. Those who meditate on *a*
Come back to earth, led by the Rig Veda,
To lead a pure life, full of faith and love.

4   Those who meditate on the first two sounds,
A and *u,* led by the Yajur Veda,
Go to the lunar world, full of pleasure,
From which they come back cloyed to earth again.

5   But those who meditate on *a, u,* and *m*
Are led by the Sama chants to the sun,
Where freed from sin, as a snake sheds its skin,
They see the supreme Lord, who lives in all.

6   "These three sounds when they are separated
Cannot lead one beyond mortality;
But when the whole mantram, A, U, and M,
Indivisible, interdependent,
Goes on reverberating in the mind,
One is freed from fear, awake or asleep.

7   "The Rig Veda brings one to earth; the Yajur
Escorts one to the region of the moon;
The Sama leads one to the solar world,
To which the sage attains through the mantram.
Established in this cosmic vibration,

The sage goes beyond fear, decay, and death
To enter into infinite peace."

QUESTION 6

Then Sukesha approached the sage and said: 1
"Master, the prince of Kosala asked me
This question once: 'Sukesha, do you know the Self
With his sixteen forms?' 'I don't,' I replied.
'If I did, I would certainly tell you;
For he who speaks an untruth perishes
Like a tree without roots.' The prince mounted
His chariot and went away silent.
Now may I ask you, where is that Self?"

The sage replied: "Within this body dwells   2
The Self with his sixteen forms, gentle friend.
The Self asked himself, 'What is it that makes   3
Me go if it goes and stay if it stays?'
So he created prana, and from it   4
Desire; and from desire he made space, air,
Fire, water, the earth, the senses, the mind,
And food; from food came strength, austerity,
The scriptures, sacrifice, and all the worlds;
And everything was given name and form.
"As rivers lose their private name and form   5
When they reach the sea, so that people speak
Of the sea alone, so all these sixteen
Forms disappear when the Self is realized.
Then there is no more name and form for us,
And we attain immortality.

"The Self is the hub of the wheel of life,   6
And the sixteen forms are only the spokes.
The Self is the paramount goal of life.
Attain this goal and go beyond death!"

The sage concluded: "There is nothing more   7
To be said of the Self, nothing more."

The students adored their teacher and said: 8
"You are our father; you have taken us
Across the sea to the other shore."
Let us adore the illumined sages!
Let us adore the illumined sages!

THE MANDUKYA UPANISHAD

AUM stands for the supreme Reality.   1
It is a symbol for what was, what is,

And what shall be. AUM represents also
What lies beyond past, present, and future.

2   Brahman is all, and the Self is Brahman.
This Self has four states of consciousness.

3   The first is called Vaishvanara, in which
One lives with all the senses turned outward,
Aware only of the external world.

4   Taijasa is the name of the second,
The dreaming state in which, with the senses
Turned inward, one enacts the impressions
Of past deeds and present desires.

5   The third state is called Prajna, of deep sleep,
In which one neither dreams nor desires.
There is no mind in Prajna, there is no
Separateness; but the sleeper is not
Conscious of this. Let him become conscious
In Prajna and it will open the door
To the state of abiding joy.

6   Prajna, all-powerful and all-knowing,
Dwells in the hearts of all as the ruler.
Prajna is the source and end of all.

7   The fourth is the superconscious state called
Turiya, neither inward nor outward,
Beyond the senses and the intellect,
In which there is none other than the Lord.
He is the supreme goal of life. He is
Infinite peace and love. Realize him!

8   Turiya is represented by AUM.
Though indivisible, it has three sounds.

9   *A* stands for Vaishvanara. Those who know this,
Through mastery of the senses, obtain
The fruit of their desires and attain greatness.

10   *U* indicates Taijasa. Those who know this,
By mastering even their dreams, become
Established in wisdom. In their family
Everyone leads the spiritual life.

11   M corresponds to Prajna. Those who know this,
By stilling the mind, find their true stature
And inspire everyone around to grow.

12   The mantram AUM stands for the supreme state
Of Turiya, without parts, beyond birth
And death, symbol of everlasting joy.
Those who know AUM as the Self becoming the Self,
Truly they become the Self.

OM shanti shanti shanti

HETERODOX ALTERNATIVES

The first stage in the development of Indian philosophy is based on its Vedic origins; the second addresses the heterodox alternatives that arose to challenge both the ritualism of the early Vedas and the mysticism of the later ones. Vedism had become the entrenched *orthodoxy* ("correct doctrine") of ancient India. Several *heterodox* ("other than orthodox") movements denying the authority of the Vedas developed in the eastern Ganges valley before spreading throughout the land. They had their greatest influence between 600 B.C.E. and 400 C.E. These movements had a negative effect on Vedic orthodoxy and are called collectively the Nastika ("dissenting") Tradition. This label, however, partially obscures their intent, which was not only to oppose orthodoxy but also to open positive alternatives to it. In so doing, they produced the first genuinely philosophical systems in India—Charvaka, Jainism, and Buddhism. We look at each in turn, the first two briefly, the third for the remainder of this section.

*   *   *

Charvaka is Indian materialism. Its other name, Lokayata, implies that just the material world exists; there is no other reality beyond or within it. The point of departure for Charvaka is epistemology. Charvaka argues that ordinary perception is the only valid source of knowledge, once the remaining candidates (including inference and testimony) are discredited. Charvaka's criticism of inductive inference constitutes its most stimulating contribution and anticipates much later discussions of the topic in the West. From its empiricist base, Charvaka derives its materialist metaphysics: Matter alone is real, for it is all we perceive. Matter consists of the four elements of earth, water, fire, and air perceived through the five external senses. Physical objects are composed of and on destruction reduced to these four elements. Mind, monitored through the internal sense, is also material. It is a property of the living material body rather than an independent substance of another order. Rejected as unreal because not perceivable are atoms, ether, causality, a spiritual soul, an afterlife in another world, and God. Charvaka's ethics relies on sensory experience exclusively and affirms tangible values (pleasure and wealth) while denying intangible ones (duty and liberation). Such opinions ran counter to the mainstream of Indian thought. But the persistence of the Charvakan viewpoint for many centuries indicates the breadth of Indian philosophy.

*   *   *

Jainism played a much larger role than Charvaka in shaping the Indian heritage. Jain thought flows from its ethical axioms that the greatest good is liberation of the spiritual soul from material embodiment and the greatest evil is perpetuation of embodiment for the soul. No part in liberation is assigned to divinity; the soul is on its own. Jains believe that every material form contains a soul that is bound by its body to pain, karma, and rebirth. Soul and matter are two of the six substances (ultimate reals) acknowledged by Jain metaphysics. The other four are space, time, motion, and rest, which set the stage for the drama of souls in combat with matter for their freedom. Souls are innumerable, eternal and uncreated, inherently alive and conscious. Matter is composed of the atoms of earth, water, fire, and air. Atoms are imperceptible but amass into objects that can be perceived. Foolish choices and actions (karma) cause the embodied soul to be invaded by material atoms that form a "karma body" inside itself, obstructing its natural purity, bliss, and omniscience. This karma body accompanies the soul in rebirth, determining the circumstances of its next existence. In final liberation, the soul distances itself from the material realm altogether. Preliminary liberation, however, can be achieved during embodiment, through asceticism (self-punishment), moral actions, and meditation. Asceticism burns up the existing karma body. Moral actions, especially avoidance of injury to any life form (ahimsa), prevents new karma body growth. And meditation restores the soul's natural perfections.

Jain epistemology meshes neatly with its ethics of bondage (evil) and liberation (good). The conscious soul in bondage is restricted to (1) ordinary knowledge (gained through perception, inference, memory, etc.) and (2) scriptural knowledge (the Jain scriptures, not the Vedas). Liberated, the conscious soul recovers (3) extraordinary knowledge (extrasensory perception), (4) mental knowledge (telepathy), and (5) perfect knowledge. Ordinary knowledge is necessarily incomplete, since it is obtained from only one of many perspectives, each perspective addressing only one of many aspects of an object or situation. Perfect knowledge, on the other hand, embraces the total object or situation all at once, free of perspective. Jain epistemology recommends that debaters qualify their ordinary knowledge claims by declaring the limited perspectives from which those claims are made. Conflicts that arise when partial claims are overstated could thus be avoided. This aspect of Jain epistemology is well illustrated by the familiar story of the elephant and the blind men who mistake for the whole the isolated part of the beast each happens to be touching.

* * *

Of the three heterodox systems of Indian philosophy, Buddhism towers over the other two in importance and profundity. Its founder was Siddhartha Gautama (563–483 B.C.E.). According to standard accounts, he was born a prince in northeastern India and as a youth prepared for a regal career while indulging in princely pleasures. But in early manhood, his life was permanently redirected by a spiritual crisis. Encounters with the sick, the aged, and the dead and dying so affected him that he became preoccupied with questions about the causes of and solutions to suffering. He renounced his position in society and became a spiritual seeker. He started by training under meditation masters; then he followed extreme ascetic practices. Neither path led to the answers he sought. Finally, he resolved to sit in meditation under a tree until his search bore fruit. After surviving fierce temptations, he achieved enlightenment, drawing on resources inherent in human nature and available to all.

Buddhists think of Siddhartha's enlightenment as occurring in three stages. First, he descended through a series of "trance states" (attention inwardly withdrawn) to the deepest trance possible. Then six "superknowledges" (amazing physical and psychical abilities) blossomed in him. The experience culminated

Siddhartha Gautama the Buddha in serene meditation. The top-knot signifies his enlightenment, the elongated ears his unique status in history. (*The National Museum of India, New Delhi, India. Courtesy of The Bridgeman Art Library International Ltd.*)

with three "cognitions" (realizations) that satisfied his questioning. Through enlightenment Siddhartha became a Buddha or fully awakened one, the latest of an elite few who existed across history. These Buddhas are human beings perfected by self-effort, not gods with creative or saving powers; they rediscover the same ancient truth once it is forgotten.

After his experience, the Buddha launched a forty-five-year public ministry of preaching, awakening others, and organizing a religious community called the Sangha, the heart of which has always been its monks and nuns. He died at the age of eighty, leaving behind a dynamic movement that soon became international. Today it is the fourth largest religion in the world.

Buddhist philosophy became highly diversified as it developed but is anchored in the simple teaching (Dharma) the Buddha distilled from his enlightenment experience. At the center of this Dharma shine the famous Four Noble Truths, which present Buddhist core values (ethics) on a medical model. The first truth diagnoses the fundamental human disorder. It is suffering, the focus of Siddhartha's quest. Suffering includes conscious pain and, of greater concern, subconscious negative states, which are more damaging because undetected. The second truth traces the root causes of the disorder to craving and ignorance. Craving is compulsive desire for or attachment to something. Its extreme form is addiction. Mild or acute, it is detrimental; it both sets up suffering and, like other forms of hunger, is itself subtly painful. Ignorance compounds the problem by turning a blind eye to the folly of "having to have" in a world where nothing keeps for long. The third truth prescribes the cure for the disease—Nirvana ("snuffing out"). Nirvana has both positive and negative sides. Enlightenment, freedom, and joy (the positives) extinguish ignorance, craving, and sorrow (the negatives). Nirvana is not a place but a condition humans can attain in the here and now. What happens after death to those who reach Nirvana in this life is unimaginable and can be indicated only as neither rebirth nor annihilation. The fourth truth maps the path to the cure, the Noble Eightfold Path. Nirvana can be achieved by mastering (1) right views, (2) right intent, (3) right speech, (4) right conduct, (5) right vocation, (6) right effort, (7) right mindfulness, and (8) right concentration. This Noble Eightfold Path is also called the Middle Way—the path between indulgence in pleasure and harsh asceticism. Siddhartha had tried both, and both had failed him. He found success instead by clearing the path between those extremes.

In addition to the ethically oriented Four Noble Truths, the early Dharma includes several points in metaphysics. First, the Principle of Dependent Origination asserts that everything arises in orderly fashion from prior causes and conditions. The oak tree, for example, arises from the acorn (cause) plus soil, water, and sunlight (conditions). It follows that nothing is without a cause, nor is it its own cause, nor is it randomly related to its cause (e.g., apple seeds do not produce orange trees and cats do not give birth to dogs). This principle grounds Buddhist beliefs in karma (actions affect the actor) and the Four Noble Truths (treating causes cures the disease). It also conflicts with the explanation of creation as a primal act by a divine Creator, opting instead for a universe of endless process with no absolute beginning or deity.

Second, impermanence complements Dependent Origination in the Buddha's vision of the real world. Even as everything arises from prior causes and conditions, everything also eventually fades away. Decaying is as universal as arising through causation; indeed, it is the other side of the coin. Ignorance of impermanence combined with clinging to what must pass yields suffering. But realizing that all things are transitory stops clinging and averts suffering—the formula for Nirvana.

Finally, amidst relentless becoming there is no eternal spiritual soul or self, no secret agent hiding within the psychophysical organism, no inner core with stable identity that transmigrates in rebirth and ultimately gains Nirvana. The idea of such a soul—the Atman of the Upanishads—is a figment of the imagination with no basis in reality. What is ultimately real in a human being are "the five aggregates" (body, feeling, perception, impulse, and consciousness) of the psychophysical organism, components not further reducible though dependently originated and temporary. This reductive analysis of the self into five basic constituents set a precedent employed with different conclusions in later Indian Buddhist thought. The radical No-soul (Pali: *anatta;* Sanskrit: *anatman*) doctrine of early Buddhism aimed to sever attachment to a fictitious self and thus relieve suffering. But it is questionable whether it explained satisfactorily what transmigrates in rebirth, what achieves Nirvana, and what survives death after Nirvana. Hence, it left unfinished business for Buddhist thinkers yet to come.

The ethical and metaphysical ideas just reviewed epitomize the initial stage in the evolution of Buddhist philosophy in India. They inform the oldest extant body of Buddhist scriptures, known both as the *Pali Canon* ("officially sanctioned texts written in the Pali language"; Pali is related to Sanskrit) and as the *Tripitaka* ("three baskets") because of its three-part organization. The *Pali Canon* is the only authoritative scripture acknowledged by the Theravada sect of Buddhism. Theravada ("teaching of the elders") ultimately prevailed with the help of imperial backing among a score of early schools in the third century B.C.E. Other early sects had their own canons, but of these the *Pali Canon* alone survives complete in its original language. Composed and transmitted orally for several centuries, the *Tripitaka* was probably written down late in the first century B.C.E. Its three divisions, all together several times the length of the Bible, are the *Vinaya* (monastic rules), the *Sutta* (sermons and discourses of the Buddha), and the *Abhidhamma* (commentaries on the *Sutta*). Primitive Buddhist philosophy pervades the *Sutta* (Sanskrit: *Sutra*) section specifically. The *Dhammapada,* first of the three readings presented in this section, as translated by Eknath Easwaran, is one of fifteen texts contained in the last of five subdivisions of the *Sutta.* Its doctrines are of the Theravada school and differ in part from those of later schools, especially the Mahayana ("great vehicle") school. Mahayana Buddhism honors the *Pali Canon* but favors later and longer collections written in Sanskrit, Chinese, and Tibetan. These other collections together with the *Pali Canon* complete the immense library of Buddhist sacred literature. Theravada and Mahayana represent the major paths in the Buddhist world today. Both originated in India but spread to different areas of Asia, Theravada to Southeast Asia and Mahayana to China, Korea, Japan, and Tibet, where they continue to thrive.

The *Dhammapada* is a great favorite among Buddhists, who believe it contains the gist of the original Dharma in the Buddha's own words. It has also earned a high place in world literature. Its charms include simplicity, clarity, poetic beauty, and relevance to life. The title means the path (*pada*) set by the Buddha's teaching (Pali: *dhamma;* Sanskrit: *dharma*). The central theme is the choice between Samsara and Nirvana, antithetical modes of living, figuratively spoken of in the text as alternative paths to travel and shores to inhabit. Samsara is life diminished by ignorance, craving, suffering, and rebirth. Nirvana, its opposite, is life enhanced by enlightenment, freedom from craving, supreme joy, and at death final liberation from rebirth. The choice is determined by karma, by actions that rebound upon the actor. Wrong thoughts, words, and deeds result in Samsara, right ones in Nirvana. The key to karma is the mind. A mind untrained and out of control dooms its owner to Samsara; a trained mind under firm control lifts its owner into Nirvana. Switching from a lower to a higher path and crossing the river from wasteland to paradise are encouraged throughout. The shift can be accomplished by meditation, which rouses the mind to full and pure awareness. Chapters 14 (The Awakened One) and 20 (The Path) stand out, since both offer summaries of doctrines crucial to the early Dharma as taught by Theravada. Chapter 14 makes explicit mention of the Buddha as the awakened one, Nirvana as the highest goal in life, the Three Refuges (Buddha, Dharma, Sangha), the Four Noble Truths, the Noble Eightfold Path, and the images of Samsara and Nirvana as two shores separated by a river. Chapter 20 designates the Eightfold as the best of paths, the Noble Four as the best of truths, detachment (freedom from worldly desire) as the best of mental states, and the illumined person as the best of human beings. It also speaks of the Three Marks of Existence (impermanence, sorrow, no self) and the Nirvana path as an awakening of the mind that terminates ignorance, selfish desire, and suffering.

*   *   *

The *Abhidhamma* (Sanskrit: *Abhidharma*) division of the *Pali Canon*, later and longer than the *Sutta* section upon which it comments, ushers in the second major phase of Indian Buddhist thought. The theory of dharmas advanced there became a rallying point for otherwise rival schools, such as Theravada, Sarvastivada, and Sautrantika. The word *dharma* bears various meanings in Indian thought. In Hinduism, it means "duty" and in early Buddhism "the teaching of the Buddha." But in the *Abhidhamma,* it acquires the technical meaning of "a basic unit of reality not divisible into anything simpler." *Dharma* theory turns on the metaphysical distinction between primary and secondary existence, between the way things really are and the way they mistakenly appear to be. Within that framework, the theory proposes a two-step reductive analysis to get from deceptive appearance to ultimate reality. Objects normally regarded as solid wholes are first broken down into bundles of perceivable properties (color, weight, shape, etc.) without support from anything under or within them. Each property is then further resolved into a chain reaction of momentary events, like a string of firecrackers rapidly igniting one another. Each event in the chain reaction arises from its predecessor, lasts only a moment, and expires giving rise to its successor. Color, in this analysis, is really a causal series of color flashes, weight a sequence of fluctuating weights, shape a succession of fleeting shapes, and so on. These short-lived units are the *dharmas,* the irreducible building blocks of reality. They are judged real not because they endure (the usual criterion of reality) but because they produce effects and are partless (hence bedrock). The mind unconsciously assembles them into "solid wholes," just as it configures the dots on a TV screen into a consolidated image or the separate frames of a movie film into a steady picture. *Dharma* theory, therefore, defines secondary existence as an illusory construction by the mind of a whole object out of *dharmas* and primary existence as what remains after the secondary is reduced to these basic bits. The *Sutta* texts originated the trend in Buddhist thought toward reductive analysis by dissecting the human being into the five aggregates. The *Abhidhamma* section, however, extends reductive analysis beyond the five aggregates to everything except *dharmas,* which alone are deemed real. Physical objects as well as the five aggregates are declared "empty" of primary existence though qualified for secondary existence. The point of calling these objects empty is to discourage attachment to them in order to defeat suffering. What right-minded person would continue craving anything exposed as a false appearance? *Dharma* theory prepares the way for discussion of the third major development in Indian Buddhist philosophy.

*   *   *

In the first century B.C.E., about the time the *Pali Canon* of the Theravada school was finally recorded after decades of oral transmission, a new corpus of Buddhist literature written in the Sanskrit language began to appear. This *Sanskrit Canon* took many centuries to complete, far exceeds the *Pali Canon* in length, and reflects the Mahayana version of the faith. It boasts superiority and rationalizes its doctrinal innovations on the ground that it propounds the Buddha's private teaching to advanced students; the *Pali Canon* is merely his public teaching to novices. Mahayana belief departs radically from the standard Theravada view on a number of important issues, none more notable than Buddhas and bodhisattvas. For Theravada, Buddhas are those rare human beings in earthly history perfected by self-effort, not gods in heaven who create or save. And a bodhisattva is simply a Buddha designate, the next human destined to become such a Buddha by breaking through to enlightenment. For Mahayana, in contrast, Buddhas are gods; by transferring divine merit, they save people with bad karmic debts. They comprise a great host, with a select few spotlighted. Some Buddhas are extraterrestrial, ruling their respective Buddha-lands populated by earthlings they have saved. Others are terrestrial, disguised as humans but actually apparitions on earth of the cosmic Buddha-essence. A bodhisattva, in the Mahayana view, is a human being who hears an inner call and responds to it with a vow. The call is to become a celestial Buddha in order to use divine power thus gained for the benefit of all sentient creatures. The vow is to work tirelessly for universal salvation. During many rebirths, this Buddha-in-the-making achieves six perfections: charity, morality, patience, zeal, meditative calm, and wisdom. A bodhisattva's merit, like that of a Buddha, can be imputed to needy humans for salvation into a celestial Buddha-land. Bodhisattvas are also numerous and either heavenly or earthly. First among the Mahayana scriptures, preaching such interpretations of Buddhas and bodhisattvas, are the *Perfection of Wisdom Sutras* (Sanskrit: *Prajnaparamitasutras*). About several dozen of these texts exist. They were composed over a span of more than a millennium (first century B.C.E. on), some of them quite long (between 8,000 and 100,000 verses), others compact summaries of the essential teaching. Favored by the faithful for their power are the short compendia—the *Diamond Sutra* of 300 verses and the *Heart Sutra* of just 30. All these *Perfection of Wisdom Sutras* emphasize the bodhisattva ideal, wisdom as the pinnacle of perfection, and emptiness as the supreme wisdom.

The *Diamond Sutra,* the second selection in this section, translated by A.F. Price, concisely sums up the entire genre it represents. For that reason, it holds an honored place in Mahayana monastery chanting services and study sessions. The original title of the work was the *Diamond Cutter Perfection of Wisdom Sutra*

(Sanskrit: *Vajrachchedikaprajnaparmitasutra*), suggesting the incisiveness of the perfect wisdom it offers. An early Chinese translator referred to the text simply as the *Diamond Sutra,* and so it has been called ever since. The date of composition is uncertain. An older generation of scholars placed it in the fourth or fifth century C.E., but more recent scholars place it in the first century B.C.E. as the very source of the *Perfection of Wisdom* literature. It purports to be a dialogue between Gautama Buddha and his disciple Subhuti, a bodhisattva. Here this Buddha is frequently designated as the "Tathagata," a title literally meaning "he who has thus come" or "he who has there gone," the intent of which is obscure. By means of a volley of denials and disclaimers throughout its thirty-two sections, the *Diamond Sutra* plies its underlying point—emptiness. In general, the pattern of negation in passage after passage is this: Though the reality of *X* is commonly assumed, there is in reality no *X,* "*X*" being merely a name; to take *X* as fact is to accept the "idea of an ego-entity, a personality, a being, or a separated individuality," whereas all things are "devoid" of these fictions. In sum, the text denies the commonsense view of the world as enduring subjects confronting concrete objects. It denies also the Buddhist plan of salvation with Buddhas and bodhisattvas providing for the faithful a glorious afterlife in a celestial Buddha-land. Repudiating virtually all accepted truths, this sutra leaves the reader with absolutely nothing to cling to, which is precisely its purpose. For what is Nirvana if not the cessation of all clinging and craving? To surrender all empty attachments, beliefs as well as things, is to awaken the "Consummation of Incomparable Enlightenment"; it is to attain "Unbounded Liberation Nirvana" and the "Perfection of Transcendental Wisdom." Even these are only vain words, to be relinquished with everything else, since words never capture truth. Nothing escapes the rejection process, not even the process itself, lest anything remain to clasp onto for security.

Emptiness is widely acknowledged to be the most elusive and controversial concept in the vast web of Buddhist thought. It is the controlling idea behind not only the *Perfection of Wisdom* books but also the most influential sect of Indian Buddhist philosophy, the Madhyamika ("middle doctrine") or Shunyavada ("emptiness teaching") school. Founded in the second century C.E. by Nagarjuna, one of the true geniuses of Indian philosophy, it underwent elaborate development in India before spreading to China, Japan, and Tibet. The reductive analysis trend in Indian Buddhist philosophy climaxes in Madhyamika. As discussed earlier, the *Sutta* division of the *Pali Canon* pronounces the self or soul empty and the five aggregates, to which the soul is reduced, real instead. The *Abhidhamma* division goes a step further, reducing the five aggregates (empty) to *dharmas* (real). Madhyamika extends the reduction maximally, declaring everything empty and nothing real, including *dharmas.* The temptation to misunderstand this position can be avoided by clarifying how Madhyamika defines emptiness in terms of its opposite. Reality or full existence (Sanskrit: *svabhava,* literally "self-existence" or "inherent existence") must first be defined by specifying three interrelated criteria. Something has full existence only if it is (1) independent of originating causes and supporting conditions (i.e., beyond the Principle of Dependent Origination), (2) everlasting, and (3) immutable. Emptiness (Sanskrit: *shunyata*) can then properly be defined as absence or lack of full existence. Something is empty, consequently, only if it is dependent upon originating causes and supporting conditions (i.e., subject to the Principle of Dependent Origination), temporal, and mutable.

Emptiness has been misinterpreted on the one hand as nihilism and on the other as absolutism. Nihilism contends that nothing at all exists. Emptiness admits that the world exists but insists that it lacks full existence (*svabhava*) as just defined. Absolutism finds within or behind the empty world a mysterious ground or power providing the sufficient reason for the world's qualified existence. Such a ground or power would have full existence and hence is contradicted by emptiness. Emptiness, therefore, is neither nihilism nor absolutism but something intermediate, as the name of the school that champions it implies. Madhyamika, the Middle Doctrine school, construes emptiness as neither total nonexistence nor full existence but conditioned, temporal, mutable existence in between. That this school views everything in the world as empty gains feasibility in light of the doctrine's ultimate purpose—to relieve suffering by extinguishing craving and attachments. What sane person would cling for survival to something tenuous, insubstantial, and itself already sinking? Contrary to common assumption, salvation is in not clinging to anything whatsoever.

Thus far the discussion of emptiness has been metaphysical. Nagarjuna carries the discussion into epistemology with his distinction between two levels of truth—conventional and ultimate. Conventional truth is what appears to be the case to the unenlightened mind. It applies to the commonsense worldview of subjects confronting objects and also to the Buddhist plan of salvation wherein Buddhas and bodhisattvas liberate karma-laden creatures to a glorious afterlife in a celestial Buddha-land. Ultimate truth, on the other hand, refers to what is really the case, perceived only by the enlightened mind. At this superior level, the commonsense worldview and Buddhist plan of salvation are found wanting, both being neither true nor false but once again in the uncharted middle. They have conventional truth and so are not categorically false. But they are not categorically true either, because the situations they envision lack full existence. What is ultimately true is the emptiness of all things. But that truth must be held in enlightened silence. Once formulated as a proposition and asserted, it lapses from ultimate to conventional truth, falls under its own ban, and must be given up. Even emptiness, asserted as a truth, is empty. There is a delicate difference between Nagarjuna and the *Diamond Sutra* with its chorus of denials and disclaimers. Denial, like assertion, is a rational position requiring defense. Nagarjuna neither asserts nor denies and consequently has no commitment he must defend. Rather, by means of subtle dialectics unexcelled in Indian philosophy, he strips away the reasons for either asserting or denying. In the twenty-seven chapters of his masterwork, the *Mulamadhyamakakarika,* he subjects that same number of essential Buddhist doctrines (including dependent origination, the five aggregates, desire, suffering, bondage, karma, the Four Noble Truths, nirvana, and causality) to intense cross-examination and concludes they cannot be rationally sustained as either true or false. His intent in undercutting everything while asserting/denying nothing is to rise above rationality itself to a state of mind free from clinging and pain because it is empty of true/false claims altogether, even the claim of emptiness to truth. Nagarjuna's Madhyamika, together with the *Perfection of Wisdom Sutras,* caps the third phase of Indian Buddhist thought.

*   *   *

The fourth phase surpasses emptiness while still endorsing it. Two movements—one a major school and the other a set of scriptures unattached to any specific sect—manage to integrate emptiness with the conviction that there really is something with full existence (*svabhava*) after all. The school is an outstanding instance in Indian philosophy of metaphysical idealism. Metaphysical idealism provides yet another way to cancel ignorance, craving, and pain by challenging the reality of self and world, the objective all Buddhist schools share. This school trims primary reality down to mental phenomena (consciousness) alone. There is no enduring self behind consciousness, nor is there a solid world outside consciousness. The commonsense assumption of real subjects and objects is empty *(shunya)*, an illusion constructed out of and reducible to consciousness, while consciousness alone remains fully real. Two of the three names for this school confirm its identification with the idealist viewpoint—Chittamatra ("mind-only") and Vijnanavada ("consciousness doctrine"). Its third and most common name—Yogachara ("yoga practitioner")—refers to meditation as the method for realizing the idealist insight. It is generally accepted that the brothers Asanga and Vasubandhu founded Yogachara in the fourth century C.E. The appealing story from an early reputable biography that Asanga converted his younger brother from Sarvastivada (a rival of Theravada) to his own original perspective has been questioned in recent scholarship. Vasubandhu's *Thirty Verses on the Mind-Only Doctrine* (Sanskrit: *Trimshika*) offers a handy synopsis of Yogachara's essential teaching. This short text, translated by Wing-tsit Chan, is the third reading included in the present section.

The *Thirty Verses*, Vasubandhu's seminal work, makes a case for Buddhist idealism that is plausible but so compact as to invite clarification. Mind-only is the basic premise: Consciousness alone exists, there being no other reality behind or outside it. Feelings of love may abound, for example, but on this theory no lover or beloved—despite impressions to the contrary. To believe in a lover behind or beloved outside the bare feelings of love is to swallow illusion, which also exists in consciousness, since it has no other place to be. How do the illusions of self and world ("false ideas of the ego and *dharmas*," verse I) arise in consciousness ("ideation")? The answer is through a series of sudden changes ("revulsions," I), prompted by latent tendencies ("revulsion-energy," XVIII), whereby an initial core is progressively augmented with additional dimensions. A model for this might be the development in motion pictures from the old black-and-white silent films, to "talkies," to Technicolor and stereo, then finally to virtual reality. Through three sudden transformations, consciousness acquires eight supplemental layers (I–XIX). The process begins with "pure consciousness" (III–IV), the initial core. This core is a stream of mental phenomena that includes perception ("touch" broadly construed), volition, feeling, thought, and cognition without self-awareness or memory. Hence it has no illusion ("darkness of ignorance") about a self behind or an external world corresponding to those phenomena. The first transformation adds the *alaya* or "ideation-store consciousness" to the core (II). With it, memory comes into play and with memory a sense of karma ("fruition of seeds," i.e., past mental events) and rebirth ("ripening in a different life"). The second transformation ushers in "mind-consiousness," which through reflection on itself ("intellection") is self-conscious and introduces the illusion of a separate stable self behind the flow of consciousness (V–VII). The many functions of this layer are catalogued under six heads (IX–XIV). The third transformation brings forth the "last six categories of discrimination" (VIII, XV–XVI), namely, the five "external" senses and the "internal" sense ("sense-center consciousness"), though there is, of course, nothing literally external or internal to consciousness. Those six together cast the spell of an external world. The text is silent about whether this evolution of consciousness occurs within the long history of the species or within the short lifetime of each specimen. Further, the text indeed says that in enlightenment the *arhat* (a person awakened by the Buddha's Dharma) "abandons" the eight incremental layers of consciousness. This could mean no more than that the illusions foisted by the additional eight lose credibility. A nightmare ceases to be nightmarish if the dreamer senses it is only a dream. Perhaps the *arhat* awakens within the illusion rather than from it.

The other major item addressed in this text is the perfecting of consciousness as bodhisattva wisdom disillusions it (XX–XXX). The "dependent" aspect is primary. In dependence upon normal conscious processes, a self behind and a world outside of consciousness arise as constructs within consciousness, but are not yet accorded existence independent of consciousness. The "falsely discriminated" aspect is secondary. The unenlightened consciousness mistakes for reality the illusions of a self behind and a world outside of consciousness and accords them independent existence. The "Absolute" (perfect wisdom) aspect is ultimate. The enlightened consciousness sees through the falsely discriminated aspect and stands eternally free and clear of its illusions. These aspects are in different ways both existent ("the three aspects of entity") and empty ("have no entity"), combining the emptiness principle with the belief that something really exists after all (XXIII–XXIV). The dependent aspect as the initial core is bedrock reality but empty because it fails Madhyamika's three criteria of full existence ("the nonentity of self-existence"). The self-world fictions of the falsely discriminated aspect are both actual as illusions and empty because the phenomena they refer to are nonexistent ("the non-entity of phenomena"). The Absolute aspect both clears the bar of full existence and is empty of all illusions ("the non-entity of the ultimate existence of the falsely discriminative ego and *dharmas* now to be eliminated"). The text peaks with the translation of the Absolute aspect into explicitly Buddhist terms (XXV–XXX). With the repealing of the six sense organs and the external world illusion they project, nothing real is left to grasp after. Consciousness passes suddenly (the final revulsion) beyond "its unawakened state" to enlightenment ("the true nature of mind-only"), from "relative knowledge to perfect wisdom." The promise of "the law [Dharma] of the Great Buddha" is fullfilled—Nirvana, "the realm of passionlessness or purity, which is beyond description, is good, and is eternal, where one is in the state of emancipation, peace, and joy." In short, Yogachara philosophy cuts craving by negating the reality of the self that craves and of the world that is craved.

Discounting Tantrism, whose real significance falls outside philosophy per se, Buddhist thought in India culminates with a few scriptures united in proclaiming the Buddha-nature or Buddha-essence in every sentient creature. The texts in question appeared after the advent of Madhyamika in the second century C.E. and before that of Yogachara in the fourth. Examination of the Sanskrit word glossed as "Buddha-essence" *(tathagatagarbha)* is illuminating. *Tathagata,* as in the *Diamond Sutra,* denotes the Buddha, and *garbha* means "womb" or "embryo." This suggests that inside every conscious being there is a divine embryo gestating that will eventually be born as a full-blown Buddha. The Buddha-essence endows every conscious creature with a divine nature in addition to its earthly nature and the guarantee of future Buddhahood. Several ideas from different sources, all of them affirming an ultimate reality with full existence *(svabhava)*, are equated with the Buddha-essence in these texts. The Atman idea of the Upanishads (see the introduction to the previous section) is one of them. The Buddha-essence doctrine never produced a school of its own in India. What force it generated there seems anticlimactic after Madhyamika and Yogachara. But that doctrine did erect a solid bridge between Indian Buddhism and the Chinese schools, where its influence is pervasive and powerful. So much so that one of the great figures of Chinese Buddhism spoke in retrospect of the Buddha-essence teaching in India as the "fourth turning of the Dharma Wheel," elevating that teaching to the level of the early Dharma, Madhyamika, and Yogachara. The rest of the story on the Buddha-essence concept awaits the section on Chinese Buddhism.

* * *

For further reading on the three major heterodox schools—Charvaka, Jainism, and Buddhism—see any of the following standard introductions to Indian philosophy, all of them by Indians of high scholarly reputation: Satischandra Chatterjee and Dhirendramohan Datta, *An Introduction to Indian Philosophy,* 7th ed. (Calcutta: University of Calcutta Press, 1968), chaps. 2, 3, 4; M. Hiriyanna, *Outlines of Indian Philosophy* (London: George Allen & Unwin, 1967), chaps. 5, 6, 8, 9; S. Radhakrishnan, *Indian Philosophy* (Delhi: Oxford University Press, 1989), Vol. I, chaps. 5, 6, 7, 10, 11; P.T. Raju, *Structural Depths of Indian Thought* (Albany: SUNY Press, 1985), chaps. 3, 4, 5; and Chandradhar Sharma, *Indian Philosophy: A Critical Survey* (N.P.: Barnes & Noble, 1962), chaps. 3–8, 17.

Readers with a special interest in Buddhist philosophy have available a number of reliable works. Three pioneers in the field are Edward J. Thomas, *The History of Buddhist Thought,* 2nd ed. (London: Routledge & Kegan Paul, 1951); Edward Conze, *Buddhist Thought in India: Three Phases of Buddhist Philosophy* (Ann Arbor: University of Michigan Press, 1967); and D.T. Suzuki, *On Indian Mahayana Buddhism,* ed. by Edward Conze (New York: Harper & Row, 1968). Also useful and more recent are David J. Kalupahana, *Buddhist Philosophy: A Historical Analysis* (Honolulu: University of Hawaii Press, 1976); Arthur L. Herman, *An Introduction to Buddhist Thought: A Philosophic History of Indian Buddhism* (Lanham, MD: University Press of America, 1983); and David J. Kalupahana, *A History of Buddhist Philosophy: Continuities and Discontinuities* (Honolulu: University of Hawaii Press, 1992). But for clarity, depth, and command of both original sources and current scholarship, perhaps nothing tops two books by Paul Williams: *Mahayana Buddhism: The Doctrinal Foundations* (London and New York: Routledge, 1989), and (with Anthony Tribe) *Buddhist Thought: A Complete Introduction to the Indian Tradition* (London and New York: Routledge, 2000).

For advanced studies of the Madhyamika school in particular, see T.V.R. Murti, *The Central Philosophy of Buddhism,* 2nd ed. (London: George Allen & Unwin, 1970) and Richard H. Robinson, *Early Madhyamika in India and China* (Madison: University of Wisconsin Press, 1967). Both Madhyamika and Yogachara are explored in Jay L. Garfield, *Empty Words: Buddhist Philosophy and Cross-Cultural Interpretation* (Oxford: Oxford University Press, 2001).

THE DHAMMAPADA

1: TWIN VERSES

Our life is shaped by our mind; we become what we think. Suffering follows an evil thought as the wheels of a cart follow the oxen that draw it.   1

Our life is shaped by our mind; we become what we think. Joy follows a pure thought like a shadow that never leaves.   2

"He was angry with me, he attacked me, he defeated me, he robbed me"—those who dwell on such thoughts will never be free from hatred.   3

"He was angry with me, he attacked me, he defeated me, he robbed me"—those who do not dwell on such thoughts will surely become free from hatred.   4

For hatred can never put an end to hatred; love alone can. This is an unalterable law.   5
People forget that their lives will end soon. For those who remember, quarrels come to an end.   6

As a strong wind blows down a weak tree, Mara the Tempter overwhelms weak people who, eating too much and working too little, are caught in the frantic pursuit of pleasure. As the strongest wind cannot shake a mountain, Mara cannot shake those who are self-disciplined and full of faith.   7   8

Those who put on the saffron robe without purifying the mind, who lack truthfulness and self-control, are not fit to wear the saffron robe. But those who have purified their minds, who are endowed with truth and self-control, are truly fit to wear the saffron robe.   9   10

The deluded, imagining trivial things to be vital to life, follow their vain fancies and never attain the highest knowledge. But the wise, knowing what is trivial and what is vital, set their thoughts on the supreme goal and attain the highest knowledge.   11   12

As rain seeps through an ill-thatched hut, passion will seep through an untrained mind.   13
As rain cannot seep through a well-thatched hut, passion cannot seep through a well-trained mind.   14

Those who are selfish suffer here and hereafter; they suffer in both worlds from the results of their own actions. But those who are selfless rejoice here and rejoice hereafter. They rejoice in both worlds from the results of their own actions.   15   16

From *The Dhammapada*, translated by Eknath Easwaran, founder of the Blue Mountain Center of Meditation, copyright 1985; reprinted by permission of Nilgiri Press, P. O. Box 256, Tomales, CA 94971, www.nilgiri.org.

17
18
Those who are selfish suffer in this life and in the next. They suffer seeing the results of the evil they have done, and more suffering awaits them in the next life. But those who are selfless rejoice in this life and in the next. They rejoice seeing the good that they have done, and more joy awaits them in the next life.

19
20
Those who recite many scriptures but fail to practice their teachings are like a cowherd counting another's cows. They do not share in the joys of the spiritual life. But those who know few scriptures yet practice their teachings, overcoming all lust, hatred, and delusion, live with a pure mind in the highest wisdom. They stand without external supports and share in the joys of the spiritual life.

2: VIGILANCE

21
22
23
Be vigilant and go beyond death. If you lack vigilance, you cannot escape death. Those who strive earnestly will go beyond death; those who do not can never come to life. The wise understand this, and rejoice in the wisdom of the noble ones. Meditating earnestly and striving for nirvana, they attain the highest joy and freedom.

24
25
If you meditate earnestly, pure in mind and kind in deeds, leading a disciplined life in harmony with the dharma, you will grow in glory. If you meditate earnestly, through spiritual disciplines you can make an island for yourself that no flood can overwhelm.

26
27
The immature lose their vigilance, but the wise guard it as their greatest treasure. Do not fall into ways of sloth and lust. Those who meditate earnestly attain the highest happiness.

28
Overcoming sloth through earnestness, the wise climb beyond suffering to the peaks of wisdom. They look upon the suffering multitude as one from a mountaintop looks on the plains below.

29
30
Earnest among those who are indolent, awake among those who slumber, the wise advance like a race horse, leaving others behind. It was through earnest effort that Indra became lord of the gods. The earnest are always respected, the indolent never.

31
32
The earnest spiritual aspirant, fearing sloth, advances like a fire, burning all his fetters. He will never fall back: he is nearing nirvana.

3: THOUGHT

33
As an archer aims his arrow, the wise aim their restless thoughts, hard to aim, hard to restrain.

34
As a fish hooked and left on the sand thrashes about in agony, the mind being trained in meditation trembles all over, desperate to escape the hand of Mara.

Hard it is to train the mind, which goes where it likes and does what it wants. But a trained mind brings health and happiness. The wise can direct their thoughts, subtle and elusive, wherever they choose: a trained mind brings health and happiness. 35 36

Those who can direct thoughts, which are unsubstantial and wander so aimlessly, are freed from the bonds of Mara. 37

They are not wise whose thoughts are not steady and minds not serene, who do not know dharma, the law of life. They are wise whose thoughts are steady and minds serene, unaffected by good and bad. They are awake and free from fear. Remember, this body is like a fragile clay pot. Make your mind a fortress and conquer Mara with the weapon of wisdom. Guard your conquest always. Remember that this body will soon lie in the earth without life, without value, useless as a burned log. 38 39 40 41

More than those who hate you, more than all your enemies, an undisciplined mind does greater harm. More than your mother, more than your father, more than all your family, a well-disciplined mind does greater good. 42 43

4: FLOWERS

As a garland-maker chooses the right flowers, choose the well-taught path of dharma and go beyond the realms of death and of the gods. As a garland-maker chooses the right flowers, those who choose the well-taught path of dharma will go beyond the realms of death and of the gods. 44 45

Remembering that this body is like froth, of the nature of a mirage, break the flower–tipped arrows of Mara. Never again will death touch you. 46

As a flood sweeps away a slumbering village, death sweeps away those who spend their lives gathering flowers. Death sweeps them away while they are still gathering, caught in the pursuit of pleasure. But the wise live without injuring nature, as the bee drinks honey without harming the flower. 47 48 49

Do not give your attention to what others do or fail to do; give it to what you do or fail to do. 50

Like a lovely flower, full of color but lacking in fragrance, are the words of those who do not practice what they preach. Like a lovely flower full of color and fragrance are the words of those who practice what they preach. 51 52

Many garlands can be made from a heap of flowers. Many good deeds can be done in this life. 53

The scent of flowers or sandalwood cannot travel against the wind; but the fragrance of the good spreads everywhere. Neither sandalwood nor the tagara flower, neither lotus nor jasmine, can come near the fragrance of the good. 54 55

56   Faint is the scent of sandalwood or the tagara, but the fragrance of the good rises high
57   to reach the gods. Good, earnest, and enlightened, never can Mara come near them.

58   A true follower of the Buddha shines among blind mortals as the fragrant lotus, grow-
59   ing in the garbage by the roadside, brings joy to all who pass by.

5: THE IMMATURE

60   Long is the night to those who are awake; long is the road to those who are weary. Long
     is the cycle of birth and death to those who know not the dharma.

61   If you find no one to support you on the spiritual path, walk alone. There is no com-
62   panionship with the immature. They think, "These sons are mine; this wealth is mine."
     They cannot even call themselves their own, much less their sons or wealth.

63   The immature who know they are immature have a little wisdom. But the immature
64   who look on themselves as wise are utterly foolish. They cannot understand the dhar-
     ma even if they spend their whole life with the wise. How can the spoon know the taste
65   of soup? If the mature spend even a short time with the wise, they will understand dhar-
     ma, just as the tongue knows the taste of soup.

66   The immature are their own enemies, doing selfish deeds which will bring them sorrow.
67   That deed is selfish which brings remorse and suffering in its wake. But good is that
68   deed which brings no remorse, only happiness in its wake.

69   Sweet are selfish deeds to the immature until they see the results; when they see the
70   results, they suffer. Even if they fast month after month, eating with only the tip of a
     blade of grass, they are not worth a sixteenth part of one who truly understands dharma.

71   As fresh milk needs time to curdle, a selfish deed takes time to bring sorrow in its wake.
     Like fire smoldering under the ashes, slowly does it burn the immature.

72   Even if they pick up a little knowledge, the immature misuse it and break their heads
     instead of benefiting from it.

73   The immature go after false prestige—precedence of fellow monks, power in the
74   monasteries, and praise from all. "Listen, monks and householders, I can do this; I can
     do that. I am right and you are wrong." Thus their pride and passion increase.

75   Choose the path that leads to nirvana; avoid the road to profit and pleasure. Remember
     this always, O disciples of the Buddha, and strive for wisdom.

6: THE WISE

76   If you see a wise man who steers you away from the wrong path, follow him as you
     would one who can reveal hidden treasures. Only good can come out of it.

Let him admonish or instruct or restrain you from what is wrong. He will be loved by   77
the good but disliked by the bad.

Make friends with those who are good and true, not with those who are bad and false.   78

To follow the dharma revealed by the noble ones is to live in joy with a serene mind.   79

As irrigators lead water where they want, as archers make their arrows straight, as car-   80
penters carve wood, the wise shape their minds.

As a solid rock cannot be moved by the wind, the wise are not shaken by praise or   81
blame. When they listen to the words of the dharma, their minds become calm and clear   82
like the waters of a still lake.

Good people keep on walking whatever happens. They do not speak vain words and are   83
the same in good fortune and bad. If a person desires neither children nor wealth nor   84
power nor success by unfair means, know him to be good, wise, and virtuous.

Few are those who reach the other shore; most people keep running up and down this   85
shore. But those who follow the dharma, when it has been well taught, will reach the   86
other shore, hard to reach, beyond the power of death.

They leave darkness behind and follow the light. They give up home and leave pleas-   87
ure behind. Calling nothing their own, they purify their hearts and rejoice. Well trained   88
in the seven fields of enlightenment, their senses disciplined and free from attachments,   89
they live in freedom, full of light.

7: THE SAINT

He has completed his voyage; he has gone beyond sorrow. The fetters of life have fallen   90
from him, and he lives in full freedom.

The thoughtful strive always. They have no fixed abode, but leave home like swans   91
from their lake.

Like the flight of birds in the sky, it is hard to follow the path of the selfless. They have   92
no possessions, but live on alms in a world of freedom. Like the flight of birds in the   93
sky, it is hard to follow their path. With their senses under control, temperate in eating,
they know the meaning of freedom.

Even the gods envy the saints, whose senses obey them like well-trained horses and   94
who are free from pride. Patient like the earth, they stand like a threshold. They are pure   95
like a lake without mud, and free from the cycle of birth and death.

Wisdom has stilled their minds, and their thoughts, words, and deeds are filled with   96
peace. Freed from illusion and from personal ties, they have renounced the world of   97
appearance to find reality. Thus have they reached the highest.

98 They make holy wherever they dwell, in village or forest, on land or at sea. With their
99 senses at peace and minds full of joy, they make the forests holy.

8: THOUSANDS

100 Better than a speech of a thousand vain words is one thoughtful word which brings
101 peace to the mind. Better than a poem of a thousand vain verses is one thoughtful line
102 which brings peace to the mind. Better than a hundred poems of vain stanzas is one
word of the dharma that brings peace to the mind.

103 One who conquers himself is greater than another who conquers a thousand times a
104 thousand men on the battlefield. Be victorious over yourself and not over others. When
105 you attain victory over yourself, not even the gods can turn it into defeat.

106 Better than performing a thousand rituals month by month for a hundred years is a
107 moment's homage to one living in wisdom. Better than tending the sacrificial fire in the
forest for a thousand years is a moment's homage to one living in wisdom.

108 Making gifts and offerings for a whole year to earn merit is not worth a quarter of the
109 honor paid to the wise. To those who honor the wise and follow them, four gifts will
come in increasing measure: health, happiness, beauty, and long life.

110 Better to live in virtue and wisdom for one day than to live a hundred years with an evil
111 and undisciplined mind. Better to live in goodness and wisdom for one day than to lead
112 an ignorant and undisciplined life for a hundred years. Better to live in strength and wis-
113 dom for one day than to lead a weak and idle life for a hundred years. Better to live in
freedom and wisdom for one day than to lead a conditioned life of bondage for a hundred years.

114 One day's glimpse of the deathless state is better than a hundred years of life without
115 it. One day's glimpse of dharma is better than a hundred years of life without it.

9: EVIL CONDUCT

116 Hasten to do good; refrain from evil. If you neglect the good, evil can enter your mind.

117 If you do what is evil, do not repeat it or take pleasure in making it a habit. An evil habit
118 will cause nothing but suffering. If you do what is good, keep repeating it and take
pleasure in making it a habit. A good habit will cause nothing but joy.

119 The evil-doer may be happy as long as he does not reap what he has sown, but when he
120 does, sorrow overcomes him. The good man may suffer as long as he does not reap what
he has sown, but when he does, joy overcomes him.

Let no one think lightly of evil and say to himself, "Sorrow will not come to me." Little   121
by little a person becomes evil, as a water pot is filled by drops of water. Let no one   122
think lightly of good and say to himself, "Joy will not come to me." Little by little a person becomes good, as a water pot is filled by drops of water.

As a rich merchant traveling alone avoids dangerous roads, as a lover of life avoids poison, let everyone avoid dangerous deeds.   123

If you have no wound on your hand, you can touch poison without being harmed. No   124
harm comes to him who does no harm. If you harm a pure and innocent person, you   125
harm yourself, as dust thrown against the wind comes back to the thrower.

Some are born again; those caught in evil ways go to a state of intense suffering; those   126
who have done good go to a state of joy. But the pure in heart enter nirvana.

Not in the sky, not in the ocean, not in mountain canyons, is there a place anywhere in   127
the world where a person can hide from his evil deeds. Not in the sky, not in the ocean,   128
not in mountain canyons, is there a place where one can hide from death.

10: PUNISHMENT

Everyone fears punishment; everyone fears death, just as you do. Therefore do not kill   129
or cause to kill. Everyone fears punishment; everyone loves life, as you do. Therefore   130
do not kill or cause to kill.

If, hoping to be happy, you strike at others who also seek happiness, you will be happy   131
neither here nor hereafter. If, hoping to be happy, you do not strike at others who are   132
also seeking happiness, you will be happy here and hereafter.

Speak quietly to everyone, and they too will be gentle in their speech. Harsh words hurt,   133
and come back to the speaker. If your mind is still, like a broken gong, you have entered   134
nirvana, leaving all quarrels behind you.

As a cowherd with his staff drives cows to fresh fields, old age and death lead all crea-   135
tures to new lives. The selfish, doing harm, do not know what is in store for them. They   136
are burned as if by fire by the results of their own deeds.

If one harms the innocent, suffering will come in these ten ways. He may suffer grief,   137
infirmity, painful accident, serious illness, loss of mind, legal prosecution, fearful accu-   138
sation, family bereavement, or financial loss; or his house may burn down, and after   139
death he may be thrown into the fire of suffering.

Going about with matted hair, without food or bath, sleeping on the ground smeared with   141
dust, or sitting motionless—no amount of penance can help a person whose mind is not   142
purified. But one whose mind is serene and chaste, whose senses are controlled and whose
life is nonviolent—such a one is a true brahmin, a true monk, even if he wears fine clothes.

143   As a well-trained horse needs no whip, a well-trained mind needs no prodding from the
144   world to be good. Be like a well-trained horse, swift and spirited, and go beyond sorrow through faith, meditation, and energetic practice of the dharma.

145   As an irrigator guides water to his fields, as an archer aims an arrow, as a carpenter
carves wood, the wise shape their lives.

11: AGE

146   Why is there laughter, why merriment, when this world is on fire? When you are living
in darkness, why don't you look for light?

147   This body is a painted image, subject to disease, decay and death, activated by thoughts
148   that come and go. What joy can there be for him who sees that his white bones will be
149   cast away like gourds in the autumn?

150   Around the bones is built a house, plastered over with flesh and blood, in which dwell
151   pride and pretence, old age and death. Even the chariot of a king loses its glitter in the
course of time; so too the body loses its health and strength. But goodness does not
grow old with the passage of time.

152   A man who does not learn from life grows old like an ox: his body grows, but not his
wisdom.

153   I have gone through many rounds of birth and death, looking in vain for the builder of
154   this body. Heavy indeed is birth and death again and again! But now I have seen you,
housebuilder, you shall not build this house again. Its beams are broken; its dome is
shattered: self-will is extinguished; nirvana is attained.

155   Those who have not practiced spiritual disciplines in their youth pine away like old cranes
156   in a lake without fish. Like worn-out bows they lie in old age, sighing over the past.

12: SELF

157   If you hold yourself dear, guard yourself diligently. Keep vigil during one of the three
watches of the night.

158   Learn what is right; then teach others, as the wise do.

159   Before trying to guide others, be your own guide first. It is hard to learn to guide oneself.

160   Your own self is your master; who else could be? With yourself well controlled, you
gain a master very hard to find.

161   The evil done by the selfish crushes them as a diamond breaks a hard gem. As a vine
162   overpowers a tree, evil overpowers the evil-doer, trapping him in a situation only his

enemies would wish him to be in. Evil deeds, which harm oneself, are easy to do; good deeds are not so easy. 163

Foolish people who scoff at the teachings of the wise, the noble, and the good, following false doctrines, bring about their own downfall like the khattaka tree, which dies after bearing fruit. 164

By oneself is evil done; by oneself one is injured. Do not do evil, and suffering will not come. Everyone has the choice to be pure or impure. No one can purify another. 165

Don't neglect your own duty for another, however great. Know your own duty and perform it. 166

13: THE WORLD

Don't follow wrong laws; don't be thoughtless; don't believe false doctrines. Don't follow the way of the world. 167

Wake up! Don't be lazy. Follow the right path, avoid the wrong. You will be happy here as well as hereafter. 168 169

Look on the world as a bubble, look on it as a mirage; then the King of Death cannot even see you. Come look at this world! Is it not like a painted royal chariot? The wise see through it, but not the foolish. 170 171

When a foolish man becomes wise, he gives light to the world like the moon breaking free from behind the clouds. When his good deeds overcome his bad, a man gives light to the world like the moon breaking free from behind the clouds. 172 173

In this dark world, few can see. Like birds that free themselves from the net, only a few find their way to heaven. Swans fly on the path of the sun by their wonderful power; the wise rise above the world, after conquering Mara and his train. 174 175

He who transgresses the central law of life, who speaks falsely or scoffs at the life to come, is capable of any evil. 176

Misers do not go to the world of the gods; they do not want to give. The wise are generous, and go to a happier world. 177

Better than ruling this world, better than attaining the realm of the gods, better than being lord of all the worlds, is one step taken on the path to nirvana. 178

14: THE AWAKENED ONE

He is the conqueror who can never be conquered, into whose conquest no other can ever enter. By what track can you reach him, the Buddha, the awakened one, free of all conditioning? How can you describe him in human language—the Buddha, the 179 180 awakened one, free from the net of desires and the pollution of passions, free from all conditioning?

181   Even the gods emulate those who are awakened. Established in meditation, they live in freedom, at peace.

182   It is hard to obtain human birth, harder to live like a human being, harder still to understand the dharma, but hardest of all to attain nirvana.

183   Avoid all evil, cultivate the good, purify your mind: this sums up the teaching of the Buddhas.

184   Cultivate the patience that endures, and attain nirvana, the highest goal in life. Do not
185   oppress others or cause them pain; that is not the way of the spiritual aspirant. Do not find fault with others, do not injure others, but live in accordance with the dharma. Be moderate in eating and sleeping, and meditate on the highest. This sums up the teaching of the Buddhas.

186   Even a shower of gold cannot quench the passions. They are wise who know that passions are passing, and bring pain in their wake.

187   Even celestial pleasures cannot quench the passions. They are true followers of the Buddha who rejoice in the conquest of desires.

188   Driven by fear, people run for security to mountains and forests, to sacred spots and shrines.
189   But none of these can be a safe refuge, because they cannot free the mind from fear.

190   Take refuge in the Buddha, the dharma, and the sangha, and you will grasp the Four
191   Noble Truths: suffering, the cause of suffering, the end of suffering, and the Noble
192   Eightfold Path that takes you beyond suffering. That is your best refuge, your only refuge. When you reach it, all sorrow falls away.

193   One like the Buddha is hard to find; such a one is not born everywhere. Where those established in wisdom are born, the community flourishes.

194   Blessed is the birth of the Buddha; blessed is the teaching of the dharma; blessed is the
195   sangha, where all live in harmony. Blessed beyond measure are they who pay homage

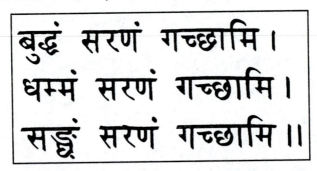

In Pali, this text says "I take my refuge in the Buddha. I take my refuge in the Dhamma. I take my refuge in the Sangha." (*Dorling Kindersley Media Library*, © *The British Library*.)

to those worthy of homage: to the Buddha and his disciples, who have gone beyond   196
evil, shed all fear, and crossed the river of sorrow to the other shore.

15: Joy

Let us live in joy, never hating those who hate us. Let us live in freedom, without hatred   197
even among those who hate.

Let us live in joy, never falling sick like those who are sick. Let us live in freedom, with-   198
out disease even among those who are ill.

Let us live in joy, never attached among those who are selfishly attached. Let us live in   199
freedom, even among those who are bound by selfish attachments.

Let us live in joy, never hoarding things among those who hoard. Let us live in grow-   200
ing joy like the bright gods.

Conquest breeds hatred, for the conquered live in sorrow. Let us be neither conqueror   201
nor conquered, and live in peace and joy.

There is no fire like lust, no sickness like hatred, no sorrow like separateness, no joy   202
like peace. No disease is worse than greed, no suffering worse than selfish passion.   203
Know this, and seek nirvana as the highest joy.

Health is the best gift, contentment the best wealth, trust the best kinsman, nirvana the   204
greatest joy. Drink the nectar of the dharma in the depths of meditation, and become   205
free from fear and sin.

It is good to meet the wise, even better to live with them. But avoid the company of the   206
immature if you want joy.

Keeping company with the immature is like going on a long journey with an enemy.   207
The company of the wise is joyful, like reunion with one's family. Therefore, live   208
among the wise, who are understanding, patient, responsible, and noble. Keep their
company like the moon moving among the stars.

16: On Pleasure

Don't run after pleasure and neglect the practice of meditation. If you forget the goal of   209
life and get caught in the pleasures of the world, you will come to envy those who put
meditation first.

Not seeing what is pleasant brings pain; seeing what is unpleasant brings pain.   210
Therefore go beyond both pleasure and pain.

Don't get selfishly attached to anything, for trying to hold on to it will bring you pain.   211
When you have neither likes nor dislikes, you will be free.

212   Selfish attachment brings suffering; selfish attachment brings fear. Be detached, and you will be free from suffering and fear.

213   Selfish bonds cause grief; selfish bonds cause fear. Be unselfish, and you will be free from grief and fear.

214   Selfish enjoyments lead to frustration; selfish enjoyments lead to fear. Be unselfish, and you will be free from frustration and fear.

215   Selfish desires give rise to anxiety; selfish desires give rise to fear. Be unselfish, and you will be free from anxiety and fear.

216   Craving brings pain; craving brings fear. Don't yield to cravings, and you will be free from pain and fear.

217   Those who have character and discrimination, who are honest and good and follow the dharma with devotion, win the respect of all the world.

218   If you long to know what is hard to know and can resist the temptations of the world, you will cross the river of life.

219   As your family and friends receive you with joy when you return from a long journey,
220   so will your good deeds receive you when you go from this life to the next, where they will be waiting for you with joy like your kinsmen.

17: ON ANGER

221   Give up anger, give up pride, and free yourself from worldly bondage. No sorrow can befall those who never try to possess people and things as their own.

222   Those who hold back rising anger like a rolling chariot are real charioteers. Others merely hold the reins.

223   Conquer anger through gentleness, unkindness through kindness, greed through gen-
224   erosity, and falsehood by truth. Be truthful; do not yield to anger. Give freely, even if you have but little. The gods will bless you.

225   Injuring no one, self-controlled, the wise enter the state of peace beyond all sorrow.
226   Those who are vigilant, who train their minds day and night and strive continually for nirvana, enter the state of peace beyond all selfish passions.

227   There is an old saying: "People will blame you if you say too much; they will blame you if you say too little; they will blame you if you say just enough." No one in this world escapes blame.

228   There never was and never will be anyone who receives all praise or all blame. But who
229   can blame those who are pure, wise, good, and meditative? They shine like a coin of
230   pure gold. Even the gods praise them, even Brahma the Creator.

Use your body for doing good, not for harm. Train it to follow the dharma. Use your   231
tongue for doing good, not for harm. Train it to speak kindly. Use your mind for doing   232
good, not for harm. Train your mind in love. The wise are disciplined in body, speech,   233
and mind. They are well controlled indeed.   234

18: On Impurity

You are like a withered leaf, waiting for the messenger of death. You are about to go on   235
a long journey, but you are so unprepared. Light the lamp within; strive hard to attain   236
wisdom. Become pure and innocent, and live in the world of light.

Your life has come to an end, and you are in the presence of death. There is no place to   237
rest on this journey, and you are so unprepared. Light the lamp within; strive hard to   238
attain wisdom. Become pure and innocent, and you will be free from birth and death.

Make your mind pure as a silversmith blows away the impurities of silver, little by lit-   239
tle, instant by instant. As rust consumes the iron which breeds it, evil deeds consume   240
those who do them.

The mantram is weak when not repeated; a house falls into ruin when not repaired; the   241
body loses health when it is not exercised; the watchman falls when vigilance is lost.

Lack of modesty is a drawback in women; lack of generosity taints those who give.   242
Selfish deeds are without merit here and hereafter. But there is no impurity greater than   243
ignorance. Remove that through wisdom and you will be pure.

Life seems easy for one without shame, no better than a crow, a mischief-maker who is   244
insolent and dissolute. Life is hard for one who is humble, gentle, and detached, who   245
tries to live in purity.

They dig their own graves who kill, lie, get drunk, or covet the wealth or spouse of   246
another. Those who drink to intoxication are digging up their own roots. Any indisci-   247
pline brings evil in its wake. Know this, and do not let greed and vice bring you lin-   248
gering pain.

Some give out of faith, others out of friendship. Do not envy others for the gifts they   249
receive, or you will have no peace of mind by day or night. Those who have destroyed   250
the roots of jealousy have peace of mind always.

There is no fire like lust, no jailor like hate, no snare like infatuation, no torrent like   251
greed.

It is easy to see the faults of others; we winnow them like chaff. It is hard to see our own;   252
we hide them as a gambler hides a losing draw. But when one keeps dwelling on the faults   253
of others, his own compulsions grow worse, making it harder to overcome them.

There is no path in the sky; there is no refuge in the world for those driven by their   254
desires. But the disciples of the Buddha live in freedom. There is no path in the sky;   255

there is no refuge in the world for those who are driven by their desires. All is change in the world, but the disciples of the Buddha are never shaken.

19: THE PERSON ESTABLISHED IN DHARMA

256   They are not following dharma who resort to violence to achieve their purpose. But
257   those who lead others through nonviolent means, knowing right and wrong, may be called guardians of the dharma.

258   One is not wise because he talks a good deal. They are wise who are patient, and free from hate and fear.

259   Dharma is not upheld by talking about it. Dharma is upheld by living in harmony with it, even if one is not learned.

260   Gray hair does not make an elder; one can grow old and still be immature. A true elder
261   is truthful, virtuous, gentle, self-controlled, and pure in mind.

262   Neither pleasant words nor a pretty face can make beautiful a person who is jealous,
263   selfish, or deceitful. Only those who have uprooted such impurities from their mind are fit to be called beautiful.

264   Shaving one's head cannot make a monk of one who is undisciplined, untruthful, and
265   driven by selfish desires. He is a real monk who has extinguished all selfish desires, large and small.

266   Begging alms does not make a bhikshu; one must follow the dharma completely. He is
267   a true bhikshu who is chaste and beyond the reach of good and evil, who passes through the world with detachment.

268   Observing silence cannot make a sage of one who is ignorant and immature. He is wise
269   who, holding the scales, chooses the good and avoids the bad.

270   One is not noble who injures living creatures. They are noble who hurt no one.

271   Not by rituals and resolutions, nor by much learning, nor by celibacy, nor even by med-
272   itation can you find the supreme, immortal joy of nirvana until you have extinguished your self-will.

20: THE PATH

273   Of paths the Eightfold is the best; of truths the Noble Four are best; of mental states, detachment is the best; of human beings the illumined one is best.

274   This is the path; there is no other that leads to the purification of the mind. Follow this
275   path and conquer Mara. This path will lead to the end of suffering. This is the path I made known after the arrows of sorrow fell away.

All the effort must be made by you; Buddhas only show the way. Follow this path and practice meditation; go beyond the power of Mara.   276

All created things are transitory; those who realize this are freed from suffering. This is the path that leads to pure wisdom.   277

All created beings are involved in sorrow; those who realize this are freed from suffering. This is the path that leads to pure wisdom.   278

All states are without self; those who realize this are freed from suffering. This is the path that leads to pure wisdom.   279

Now is the time to wake up, when you are young and strong. Those who wait and waver, with a weak will and a divided mind, will never find the way to pure wisdom.   280

Guard your thoughts, words, and deeds. These three disciplines will speed you along the path to pure wisdom.   281

Meditation brings wisdom; lack of meditation leaves ignorance. Know well what leads you forward and what holds you back, and choose the path that leads to wisdom.   282

Cut down the whole forest of selfish desires, not just one tree only. Cut down the whole forest and you will be on your way to liberation.   283

If there is any trace of lust in your mind, you are bound to life like a suckling calf to its mother. Pull out every selfish desire as you would an autumn lotus with your hand. Follow the path to nirvana with a guide who knows the way.   284 285

"I will make this my winter home, have another house for the monsoon, and dwell in a third during the summer"—lost in such fancies one forgets his final destination.   286

Death comes and carries off a man absorbed in his family and possessions as the monsoon flood sweeps away a sleeping village.   287

Neither children nor parents can rescue one whom death has seized. Remember this, and follow without delay the path that leads to nirvana.   288 289

21: Varied Verses

If a man who enjoys a lesser happiness beholds a greater one, let him leave aside the lesser to gain the greater.   290

Don't try to build your happiness on the unhappiness of others. You will be enmeshed in a net of hatred.   291

Do not fail to do what ought to be done, and do not do what ought not to be done. Otherwise your burden of suffering will grow heavier. Those who meditate and keep their senses under control never fail to do what ought to be done, and never do what ought not to be done. Their suffering will come to an end.   292 293

294   Kill mother lust and father self-will, kill the kings of carnal passions, and you will be
295   freed from sin. The true brahmin has killed mother lust and father self-will; he has
       killed the kings of carnal passions, and the ego that obstructs him on the path. He is
       freed from sin.

296   The disciples of Gautama are wide-awake and vigilant, with their thoughts focused on
       the Buddha day and night.

297   The disciples of Gautama are wide-awake and vigilant, absorbed in the dharma day and
       night.

298   The disciples of Gautama are wide-awake and vigilant, with their thoughts focused on
       the sangha day and night.

299   The disciples of Gautama are wide-awake and vigilant, with their thoughts focused on
       sense-training day and night.

300   The disciples of Gautama are wide-awake and vigilant, rejoicing in compassion day and
       night.

301   The disciples of Gautama are wide-awake and vigilant, rejoicing in meditation day and
       night.

302   It is hard to leave the world and hard to live in it, painful to live with the worldly and
       painful to be a wanderer. Reach the goal; you will wander and suffer no more.

303   Those who are good and pure in conduct are honored wherever they go. The good shine
304   like the Himalayas, whose peaks glisten above the rest of the world even when seen
       from a distance. Others pass unseen, like an arrow shot at night.

305   Sitting alone, sleeping alone, going about alone, vanquish the ego by yourself alone.
       Abiding joy will be yours when all selfish desires end.

22: THE DOWNWARD COURSE

306   He who says what is not true, he who denies what he has done, both choose the down-
       ward course. After death these two become partners in falsehood.

307   Those who put on the saffron robe but remain ill-mannered and undisciplined are
308   dragged down by their evil deeds. It is better for all undisciplined monks to swallow a
       red-hot ball of iron than to live on the charity of the devout.

309   Adultery leads to loss of merit, loss of sleep, condemnation, and increasing suffering.
310   On this downward course, what pleasure can there be for the frightened lying in the
       arms of the frightened, both going in fear of punishment? Therefore do not commit
       adultery.

311   As a blade of kusha grass can cut the finger when it is wrongly held, asceticism prac-
       ticed without discrimination can send one on the downward course.

An act performed carelessly, a vow not kept, a code of chastity not strictly observed: 312
these things bring little reward. If anything is worth doing, do it with all your heart. A 313
half-hearted ascetic covers himself with more and more dust.

Refrain from evil deeds, which cause suffering later. Perform good deeds, which can 314
cause no suffering. Guard yourself well, both within and without, like a well-defended 315
fort. Don't waste a moment, for wasted moments send you on the downward course.

Those who are ashamed of deeds they should not be ashamed of, and not ashamed of 316
deeds they should be ashamed of, follow false doctrines on the downward course.

Those who fear what they ought not to fear, and do not fear what they ought to fear, fol- 317
low false doctrines on the downward course.

Those who see wrong where there is none, and do not see wrong where there is, follow 318
false doctrines on the downward course.

But those who see wrong where there is wrong, and see no wrong where there is none, 319
follow true doctrines on the upward course.

23: THE ELEPHANT

Patiently I shall bear harsh words as the elephant bears arrows on the battlefield. People 320
are often inconsiderate.

Only a trained elephant goes to the battlefield; only a trained elephant carries the king. 321
Best among men are those who have trained their mind to endure harsh words patiently.

Mules are good animals when trained; even better are well-trained Sind horses and 322
great elephants. Best among men is one with a well-trained mind. No animal can take 323
you to nirvana; only a well-trained mind can lead you to this untrodden land.

The elephant Dhanapalaka in heat will not eat at all when he is bound; he pines for his 324
mate in the elephant grove.

Eating too much, sleeping too much, like an overfed hog, those too lazy to exert effort 325
are born again and again.

Long ago my mind used to wander as it liked and do what it wanted. Now I can rule my 326
mind as the mahout controls the elephant with his hooked staff.

Be vigilant; guard your mind against negative thoughts. Pull yourself out of bad ways 327
as an elephant raises itself out of the mud.

If you find a friend who is good, wise, and loving, walk with him all the way and over- 328
come all dangers.

329   If you cannot find a friend who is good, wise, and loving, walk alone, like a king who
330   has renounced his kingdom or an elephant roaming at will in the forest. It is better to
be alone than to live with the immature. Be contented, and walk alone like an elephant
roaming in the forest. Turn away from evil.

331   It is good to have friends when friendship is mutual. Good deeds are friends at the time
of death. But best of all is going beyond sorrow.

332   It is good to be a mother, good to be a father, good to be one who follows the dharma.
But best of all is to be an illumined sage.

333   It is good to live in virtue, good to have faith, good to attain the highest wisdom, good
to be pure in heart and mind. This will bring you lasting joy.

24: ON COMPULSIVE URGES

334   The compulsive urges of the thoughtless grow like a creeper. They jump like a monkey
from one life to another, looking for fruit in the forest.

335   When these urges drive us, sorrow spreads like wild grass. Conquer these fierce crav-
336   ings and sorrow will fall away from your life like drops of water from a lotus leaf.

Therefore I say, dig up craving root and all, as you would uproot birana grass, if you
337   don't want Mara to crush you as the stream crushes reeds on its banks. As a tree, though
338   cut down, recovers and grows if its roots are not destroyed, suffering will come to you
more and more if these compulsive urges are not extinguished.

339   Wherever the thirty-six streams flow from the mind toward pleasure, the currents will
340   sweep that unfortunate person away. The currents flow everywhere. Creepers of passion
grow everywhere. Whenever you see one growing in your mind, uproot it with wisdom.

341   All human beings are subject to attachment and thirst for pleasure. Hankering after
342   these, they are caught in the cycle of birth and death. Driven by this thirst, they run
343   about frightened like a hunted hare, suffering more and more. Driven by this thirst, they
run about frightened like a hunted hare. Overcome this thirst and be free.

344   Look at those who manage to come out of one forest of cravings, only to be driven into
another. Though free, they run into bondage again.

345   Fetters of wood, rope, or even iron, say the wise, are not as strong as selfish attachment
346   to wealth and family. Such fetters drag us down and are hard to break. Break them by
overcoming selfish desires, and turn from the world of sensory pleasure without a
backward glance.

347   Like a spider caught in its own web is a person driven by fierce cravings. Break out of
the web, and turn away from the world of sensory pleasure and sorrow.

If you want to reach the other shore of existence, give up what is before, behind, and in between. Set your mind free, and go beyond birth and death.   348

If you want to reach the other shore, don't let doubts, passions, and cravings strengthen your fetters. Meditate deeply, discriminate between the pleasant and the permanent, and break the fetters of Mara.   349
350

One who is free from fear, thirst, and sin has removed all the thorns from his life. This body is his last.   351

He is supremely wise who is free from compulsive urges and attachments, and who understands what words really stand for. This body is his last.   352

I have conquered myself and live in purity. I know all. I have left everything behind, and live in freedom. Having taught myself, to whom shall I point as teacher?   353

There is no gift better than the gift of the dharma, no gift more sweet, no gift more joyful. It puts an end to cravings and the sorrow they bring.   354

Wealth harms the greedy, but not those who seek nirvana. Of little understanding, the greedy harm themselves and those around them.   355

Greed ruins the mind as weeds ruin fields. Therefore honor those who are free from greed.   356

Lust ruins the mind as weeds ruin fields. Therefore honor those who are free from lust.   357

Hatred ruins the mind as weeds ruin fields. Therefore honor those who are free from hatred.
358

Selfish desires ruin the mind as weeds ruin fields. Therefore honor those who are free from selfish desire.
359

25: THE BHIKSHU

Train your eyes and ears; train your nose and tongue. The senses are good friends when they are trained. Train your body in deeds, train your tongue in words, train your mind in thoughts. This training will take you beyond sorrow.   360
361

He is a true bhikshu who has trained his hands, feet, and speech to serve others. He meditates deeply, is at peace with himself, and lives in joy.   362

He is a true bhikshu who keeps repeating his mantram, lives simply, and explains the dharma in sweet words.   363

He is a true bhikshu who follows the dharma, meditates on the dharma, rejoices in the dharma, and therefore never falls away from the dharma.   364

365   He is a bhikshu who is content with what he receives and is never jealous of others. Those who are jealous cannot do well in meditation.

366   Even the gods praise the bhikshu who is contented and lives a pure life of selfless serv-
367   ice. Free from the desire to possess people and things, he does not grieve over what is
368   not. With friendship toward all and faith in the Buddha's teachings, he will reach the holy state where all is peace.

369   Bhikshu, empty your boat! It will go faster. Cast out greed and hatred and reach nirvana.

370   Overcome the five obstacles, rise above the five selfish attachments, and you will cross the river of life.

371   Meditate, bhikshu, meditate! Do not run after sense pleasures. Do not swallow a red-hot iron ball and then cry, "I am in great pain!"

372   There can be no meditation for those who are not wise, and no wisdom for those who do not meditate. Growing in wisdom through meditation, you will surely be close to nirvana.

373   When a bhikshu stills his mind, he enters an empty house; his heart is full of the divine
374   joy of the dharma. Understanding the rise and fall of the elements that make up the body, he gains the joy of immortality.

375   Learn to be wise, O bhikshu! Train your senses; be contented. Follow the teachings of
376   the dharma and keep pure and noble friends. Be a friend of all. Perform your duties well. Then, with your joy ever growing, you will put an end to sorrow.

377   As the varsika plant sheds its faded flowers, O bhikshu, shed all greed and hatred. He
378   is a bhikshu who is calm in thought, word, and deed, and has turned his back upon the allurements of the world.

379   Raise yourself by your own efforts, O bhikshu; be your own critic. Thus self-reliant and
380   vigilant you will live in joy. Be your own master and protector. Train your mind as a merchant trains his horse.

381   Full of peace and joy is the bhikshu who follows the dharma and reaches the other
382   shore, beyond the flux of mortal life. Full of light is the young bhikshu who follows the dharma. He lights up the world as the moon lights a cloudless sky.

26: THE BRAHMIN

383   Cross the river bravely; conquer all your passions. Go beyond the world of fragments, and know the deathless ground of life.

384   Cross the river bravely; conquer all your passions. Go beyond your likes and dislikes and all fetters will fall away.

Who is a true brahmin? Him I call a brahmin who has neither likes nor dislikes, and is free from the chains of fear.   385

Who is a true brahmin? Him I call a brahmin who has trained his mind to be still and reached the supreme goal of life.   386

The sun shines in the day; the moon shines in the night. The warrior shines in battle, the brahmin in meditation. But day and night the Buddha shines in radiance of love for all.   387

Him I call a brahmin who has shed all evil. I call him a recluse whose mind is serene; a wanderer, him whose heart is pure.   388

Him I call a brahmin who is never angry, never causes harm to others even when he is harmed by them.   389

Him I call a brahmin who clings not to pleasure. Do not cause sorrow to others; no more sorrow will come to you.   390

Him I call a brahmin who does not hurt others with unkind acts, words, or thoughts. His body and mind obey him.   391

Him I call a brahmin who walks in the footsteps of the Buddha. Light your torch from the fire of his sacrifice.   392

It is not matted hair nor birth that makes a brahmin, but truth and the love for all of life with which one's heart is full. What use is matted hair? What use is a deerskin on which to sit for meditation, if your mind still seethes with lust?   393 394

Saffron robe and outward show do not make a brahmin, but training of the mind and senses through practice of meditation. Neither riches nor high caste make a brahmin. Free yourself from selfish desires, and you will become a brahmin.   395 396

He has thrown off his chains; he trembles not in fear. No selfish bonds can ensnare him, no impure thoughts pollute his mind.   397

Him I call a brahmin who has cut through the strap and thong and chain of karma. He has got up from sleep, fully awake.   398

Him I call a brahmin who fears neither prison nor death. He has the power of love no army can defeat.   399

Him I call a brahmin who is never angry, never goes astray from the path. He is pure and self-controlled. He has received his last body.   400

Him I call a brahmin who clings not to pleasure, no more than water to a lotus leaf or mustard seed to the tip of a needle. For him no more sorrow will come. On him no more burden will fall.   401 402

Him I call a brahmin whose wisdom is profound and whose understanding deep, who by following the right path and avoiding the wrong has reached the highest goal.   403

404   Him I call a brahmin whose wants are few who is detached from householders and homeless mendicants alike.

405   Him I call a brahmin who has put aside weapons and renounced violence toward all creatures. He neither kills nor helps others to kill.

406   Him I call a brahmin who is never hostile to those who are hostile toward him, who is detached among those who are selfish, and at peace among those at war.

407   Him I call a brahmin from whom passion and hatred, arrogance and deceit, have fallen away like mustard seed from the point of a needle.

408   Him I call a brahmin who is ever true, ever kind. He never asks what life can give, only
409   what he can give to life.

410   Him I call a brahmin who has found his heaven, free from every selfish desire, free from
411   every impurity. Wanting nothing at all, doubting nothing at all, master of his body and mind, he has gone beyond time and death.

412   Him I call a brahmin who has gone beyond good and evil and is free from sorrow, passion, and impurity.

413   Him I call a brahmin who has risen above the duality of this world, free from sorrow and free from sin. He shines like the full moon with no cloud in the sky.

414   Him I call a brahmin who has crossed the river difficult and dangerous to cross, and safely reached the other shore.

415   Him I call a brahmin who has turned his back upon himself. Homeless, he is ever at home; egoless, he is ever full.

416   Self-will has left his mind; it will never return. Sorrow has left his life; it will never return.

417   Him I call a brahmin who has overcome the urge to possess even heavenly things, and is free from all selfish attachments.

418   Him I call a brahmin who is free from bondage to human beings and to nature alike, the hero who has conquered the world.

419   Him I call a brahmin who is free from *I, me*, and *mine*, who knows the rise and fall of life. He is awake: he will not fall asleep again.

420   Him I call a brahmin whose way no one can know. He lives free from past and future; he lives free from decay and death.

421   Possessing nothing, desiring nothing for his own pleasure or his own profit, he has become a force for good, working for the freedom of all.

422   Him I call a brahmin who is fearless, heroic, unshakable, a great sage who has conquered death and attained life's goal.

He has reached the end of the way; he has crossed the river of life. All that he had to do   423
is done: he has become one with all life.

THE DIAMOND SUTRA

SECTION 1: THE CONVOCATION OF THE ASSEMBLY

Thus have I heard. Upon a time Buddha sojourned in Anathapindika's Park by Shravasti with a great company of bhikshus, even twelve hundred and fifty.

One day, at the time for breaking fast, the World-honoured enrobed, and carrying His bowl made His way into the great city of Shravasti to beg for His food. In the midst of the city He begged from door to door according to rule. This done, He returned to His retreat and took His meal. When He had finished He put away His robe and begging bowl, washed His feet, arranged His seat, and sat down.

SECTION 2: SUBHUTI MAKES A REQUEST

Now in the midst of the assembly was the Venerable Subhuti. Forthwith he arose, uncovered his right shoulder, knelt upon his right knee, and, respectfully raising his hands with palms joined, addressed Buddha thus: World-honoured One, it is most precious how mindful the Tathagata is of all the Bodhisattvas, protecting and instructing them so well! World-honoured One, if good men and good women seek the Consummation of Incomparable Enlightenment, by what criteria should they abide and how should they control their thoughts?

Buddha said: Very good, Subhuti! Just as you say, the Tathagata is ever-mindful of all the Bodhisattvas, protecting and instructing them well. Now listen and take my words to heart: I will declare to you by what criteria good men and good women seeking the Consummation of Incomparable Enlightenment should abide, and how they should control their thoughts.

Said Subhuti: Pray, do, World-honoured One. With joyful anticipation we long to hear.

SECTION 3: THE REAL TEACHING OF THE GREAT WAY

Buddha said: Subhuti, all the Bodhisattva-Heroes should discipline their thoughts as follows: All living creatures of whatever class, born from eggs, from wombs, from moisture, or by transformation, whether with form or without form, whether in a state

From *The Diamond Sutra and The Sutra of Hui Neng,* tr. by A.F. Price and Wong Mou-Lam (Berkeley, CA: Shambala, 1969). Reprinted by arrangement with Shambala Publications, Inc., Boston, www.shambala.com.

of thinking or exempt from thought-necessity, or wholly beyond all thought realms—all these are caused by Me to attain Unbounded Liberation Nirvana. Yet when vast, uncountable, immeasurable numbers of beings have thus been liberated, verily no being has been liberated. Why is this, Subhuti? It is because no Bodhisattva who is a real Bodhisattva cherishes the idea of an ego-entity, a personality, a being, or a separated individuality.

SECTION 4: EVEN THE MOST BENEFICENT PRACTICES ARE RELATIVE

Furthermore, Subhuti, in the practice of charity a Bodhisattva should be detached. That is to say, he should practise charity without regard to appearances; without regard to sound, odour, touch, flavour or any quality. Subhuti, thus should the Bodhisattva practise charity without attachment. Wherefore? In such a case his merit is incalculable.

Subhuti, what do you think? Can you measure all the space extending eastward?

No, World-honoured One, I cannot.

Then can you, Subhuti, measure all the space extending southward, westward, northward, or in any other direction, including nadir and zenith?

No, World-honoured One, I cannot.

Well, Subhuti, equally incalculable is the merit of the Bodhisattva who practises charity without any attachment to appearances. Subhuti, Bodhisattvas should persevere one-pointedly in this instruction.

SECTION 5: UNDERSTANDING THE ULTIMATE PRINCIPLE OF REALITY

Subhuti, what do you think? Is the Tathagata to be recognized by some material characteristic?

No, World-honoured One; the Tathagata cannot be recognized by any material characteristic. Wherefore? Because the Tathagata has said that material characteristics are not, in fact, material characteristics.

Buddha said: Subhuti, wheresoever are material characteristics there is delusion; but whoso perceives that all characteristics are in fact no-characteristics, perceives the Tathagata.

SECTION 6: RARE IS TRUE FAITH

Subhuti said to Buddha: World-honoured One, will there always be men who will truly believe after coming to hear these teachings?

Buddha answered: Subhuti, do not utter such words! At the end of the last five-hundred-year period following the passing of the Tathagata, there will be self-controlled men, rooted in merit, coming to hear these teachings, who will be inspired with belief. But you should realize that such men have not strengthened their root of merit under just one Buddha, or two Buddhas, or three, or four, or five Buddhas but under countless Buddhas; and their merit is of every kind. Such men, coming to hear these teachings, will have an immediate uprising of pure faith, Subhuti; and the Tathagata will recognize them. Yes, He will clearly perceive all these of pure heart, and the magnitude of their moral excellences. Wherefore? It is because such men will not fall back to cherishing the idea of an ego-entity, a personality, a being, or a separated individuality. They will neither fall back to cherishing the idea of things as having intrinsic qualities, nor even of things as devoid of intrinsic qualities.

Wherefore? Because if such men allowed their minds to grasp and hold on to anything they would be cherishing the idea of an ego-entity, a personality, a being, or a separated individuality; and if they grasped and held on to the notion of things as having intrinsic qualities they would be cherishing the idea of an ego-entity, a personality, a being, or a separated individuality. Likewise, if they grasped and held on to the notion of things as devoid of intrinsic qualities they would be cherishing the idea of an ego-entity, a personality, a being, or a separated individuality. So you should not be attached to things as being possessed of, or devoid of, intrinsic qualities.

This is the reason why the Tathagata always teaches this saying: My teaching of the Good Law is to be likened unto a raft. The Buddha-teaching must be relinquished; how much more so misteaching!

SECTION 7: GREAT ONES, PERFECT BEYOND LEARNING, UTTER NO WORDS OF TEACHING

Subhuti, what do you think? Has the Tathagata attained the Consummation of Incomparable Enlightenment? Has the Tathagata a teaching to enunciate?

Subhuti answered: As I understand Buddha's meaning there is no formulation of truth called Consummation of Incomparable Enlightenment. Moreover, the Tathagata has no formulated teaching to enunciate. Wherefore? Because the Tathagata has said that truth is uncontainable and inexpressible. It neither *is* nor is it *not*.

Thus it is that this unformulated Principle is the foundation of the different systems of all the sages.

SECTION 8: THE FRUITS OF MERITORIOUS ACTION

Subhuti, what do you think? If anyone filled three thousand galaxies of worlds with the seven treasures and gave all away in gifts of alms, would he gain great merit?

Subhuti said: Great indeed, World-honoured One! Wherefore? Because merit partakes of the character of no-merit, the Tathagata characterized the merit as great.

Then Buddha said: On the other hand, if anyone received and retained even only four lines of this Discourse and taught and explained them to others, his merit would be the greater. Wherefore? Because, Subhuti, from this Discourse issue forth all the Buddhas and the Consummation of Incomparable Enlightenment teachings of all the Buddhas.

Subhuti, what is called "the Religion given by Buddha" is not, in fact, Buddha-Religion.

SECTION 9: REAL DESIGNATION IS UNDESIGNATE

Subhuti, what do you think? Does a disciple who has entered the Stream of the Holy Life say within himself: I obtain the fruit of a Stream-entrant?

Subhuti said: No, World-honoured One. Wherefore? Because "Stream-entrant" is merely a name. There is no stream-entering. The disciple who pays no regard to form, sound, odour, taste, touch, or any quality, is called a Stream-entrant.

Subhuti, what do you think? Does an adept who is subject to only one more rebirth say within himself: I obtain the fruit of a Once-to-be-reborn?

Subhuti said: No, World-honoured One. Wherefore? Because "Once-to-be-reborn" is merely a name. There is no passing away nor coming into existence. [The adept who realizes]—this is called "Once-to-be-reborn."

Subhuti, what do you think? Does a venerable one who will never more be reborn as a mortal say within himself: I obtain the fruit of a Non-returner?

Subhuti said: No, World-honoured One. Wherefore? Because "Non-returner" is merely a name. There is no non-returning; hence the designation "Non-returner."

Subhuti, what do you think? Does a holy one say within himself: I have obtained Perfective Enlightenment?

Subhuti said: No, World-honoured One. Wherefore? Because there is no such condition as that called "Perfective Enlightenment." World-honoured One, if a holy one of Perfective Enlightenment said to himself "such am I," he would necessarily partake of the idea of an ego-entity, a personality, a being, or a separated individuality. World-honoured One, when the Buddha declares that I excel amongst holy men in the Yoga of perfect quiescence, in dwelling in seclusion, and in freedom from passions, I do not say within myself: I am a holy one of Perfective Enlightenment, free from passions. World-honoured One, if I said within myself: Such am I; you would not declare: Subhuti finds happiness abiding in peace, in seclusion in the midst of the forest. This is because Subhuti abides no where: therefore he is called, "Subhuti, Joyful-Abider-in-Peace, Dweller-in-Seclusion-in-the-Forest."

SECTION 10: SETTING FORTH PURE LANDS

Buddha said: Subhuti, what do you think? In the remote past when the Tathagata was with Dipankara Buddha, did he have any degree of attainment in the Good Law?

No, World-honoured One. When the Tathagata was with Dipankara Buddha he had no degree of attainment in the Good Law.

Subhuti, what do you think? Does a Bodhisattva set forth any majestic Buddha-lands?

No, World-honoured One. Wherefore? Because setting forth majestic Buddha-lands is not a majestic setting forth; this is merely a name.

[Then Buddha continued:] Therefore, Subhuti all Bodhisattvas, lesser and great, should develop a pure, lucid mind, not depending upon sound, flavour, touch, odour or any quality. A Bodhisattva should develop a mind which alights upon no thing whatsoever; and so should he establish it.

Subhuti, this may be likened to a human frame as large as the mighty Mount Sumeru. What do you think? Would such a body be great?

Subhuti replied: Great indeed, World-honoured One. This is because Buddha has explained that no body is called a great body.

SECTION 11: THE SUPERIORITY OF UNFORMULATED TRUTH

Subhuti, if there were as many Ganges rivers as the sand-grains of the Ganges, would the sand-grains of them all be many?

Subhuti said: Many indeed, World-honoured One! Even the Ganges rivers would be innumerable; how much more so would be their sand-grains?

Subhuti, I will declare a truth to you. If a good man or good woman filled three thousand galaxies of worlds with the seven treasures for each sand-grain in all those Ganges rivers, and gave all away in gifts of alms, would he gain great merit?

Subhuti answered: Great indeed, World-honoured One!

Then Buddha declared: Nevertheless, Subhuti, if a good man or good woman studies this Discourse only so far as to receive and retain four lines, and teaches and explains them to others, the consequent merit would be far greater.

SECTION 12: VENERATION OF THE TRUE DOCTRINE

Furthermore, Subhuti, you should know that wheresoever this Discourse is proclaimed, by even so little as four lines, that place should be venerated by the whole realms of Gods, Men and Titans, as though it were a Buddha-Shrine. How much more is this so in the case of one who is able to receive and retain the whole and read and recite it throughout!

Subhuti, you should know that such an one attains the highest and most wonderful truth. Wheresoever this sacred Discourse may be found there should you comport yourself as though in the presence of Buddha and disciples worthy of honour.

SECTION 13: HOW THIS TEACHING SHOULD BE RECEIVED AND RETAINED

At that time Subhuti addressed Buddha, saying:

World-honoured One, by what name should this Discourse be known, and how should we receive and retain it?

Buddha answered: Subhuti, this Discourse should be known as "The Diamond of the Perfection of Transcendental Wisdom"—thus should you receive and retain it.

Subhuti, what is the reason herein? According to the Buddha-teaching the Perfection of Transcendental Wisdom is not really such. "Perfection of Transcendental Wisdom" is just the name given to it. Subhuti, what do you think? Has the Tathagata a teaching to enunciate?

Subhuti replied to Buddha: World-honoured One, the Tathagata has nothing to teach.

Subhuti, what do you think? Would there be many molecules in [the composition of] three thousand galaxies of worlds?

Subhuti said: Many, indeed, World-honoured One!

Subhuti, the Tathagata declares that all these molecules are not really such; they are called "molecules." [Furthermore,] the Tathagata declares that a world is not really a world; it is called "a world."

Subhuti, what do you think? May the Tathagata be perceived by the thirty-two physical peculiarities [of an outstanding sage]?

No, World-honoured One, the Tathagata may not be perceived by these thirty-two marks. Wherefore? Because the Tathagata has explained that the thirty-two marks are not really such; they are called "the thirty-two marks."

Subhuti, if on the one hand a good man or a good woman sacrifices as many lives as the sand-grains of the Ganges, and on the other hand anyone receives and retains even only four lines of this Discourse, and teaches and explains them to others, the merit of the latter will be the greater.

SECTION 14: PERFECT PEACE LIES IN FREEDOM FROM CHARACTERISTIC DISTINCTIONS

Upon the occasion of hearing this Discourse Subhuti had an interior realization of its meaning and was moved to tears. Whereupon he addressed Buddha thus: It is a most precious thing, World-honoured One, that you should deliver this supremely profound Discourse. Never have I heard such an exposition since of old my eye of wisdom first opened. World-honoured One, if anyone listens to this Discourse in faith with a pure, lucid mind, he will thereupon conceive an idea of Fundamental Reality. We should know that such an one establishes the most remarkable virtue. World-honoured One, such an idea of Fundamental Reality is not, in fact, a distinctive idea; therefore the Tathagata teaches: "Idea of Fundamental Reality" is merely a name.

World-honoured One, having listened to this Discourse, I receive and retain it with faith and understanding. This is not difficult for me, but in ages to come—in the last five hundred years, if there be men coming to hear this Discourse who receive and retain it with faith and understanding, they will be persons of most remarkable achievement. Wherefore? Because they will be free from the idea of an ego-entity, free from the idea of a personality, free from the idea of a being, and free from the idea of a separated individuality. And why? Because the distinguishing of an ego-entity is erroneous. Likewise the distinguishing of a personality, or a being, or a separated individuality is erroneous. Consequently those who have left behind every phenomenal distinction are called Buddhas all.

Buddha said to Subhuti: Just as you say! If anyone listens to this Discourse and is neither filled with alarm nor awe nor dread, be it known that such an one is of remarkable achievement. Wherefore? Because, Subhuti, the Tathagata teaches that the

First Perfection [the Perfection of Charity] is not, in fact, the First Perfection: such is merely a name.

Subhuti, the Tathagata teaches likewise that the Perfection of Patience is not the Perfection of Patience: such is merely a name. Why so? It is shown thus, Subhuti: When the Rajah of Kalinga mutilated my body, I was at that time free from the idea of an ego-entity, a personality, a being, and a separated individuality. Wherefore? Because then when my limbs were cut away piece by piece, had I been bound by the distinctions aforesaid, feelings of anger and hatred would have been aroused within me. Subhuti, I remember that long ago, sometime during my last past five hundred mortal lives, I was an ascetic practising patience. Even then was I free from those distinctions of separated selfhood. Therefore, Subhuti, Bodhisattvas should leave behind all phenomenal distinctions and awaken the thought of the Consummation of Incomparable Enlightenment by not allowing the mind to depend upon notions evoked by the sensible world—by not allowing the mind to depend upon notions evoked by sounds, odours, flavours, touch–contacts or any qualities. The mind should be kept independent of any thoughts which arise within it. If the mind depends upon anything it has no sure haven. This is why Buddha teaches that the mind of a Bodhisattva should not accept the appearances of things as a basis when exercising charity. Subhuti, as Bodhisattvas practise charity for the welfare of all living beings they should do it in this manner. Just as the Tathagata declares that characteristics are not characteristics, so He declares that all living beings are not, in fact, living beings.

Subhuti, the Tathagata is He who declares that which is true; He who declares that which is fundamental; He who declares that which is ultimate. He does not declare that which is deceitful, nor that which is monstrous. Subhuti, that Truth to which the Tathagata has attained is neither real nor unreal.

Subhuti, if a Bodhisattva practises charity with mind attached to formal notions he is like unto a man groping sightless in the gloom; but a Bodhisattva who practises charity with mind detached from any formal notions is like unto a man with open eyes in the radiant glory of the morning, to whom all kinds of objects are clearly visible.

Subhuti, if there be good men and good women in future ages, able to receive, read and recite this Discourse in its entirety, the Tathagata will clearly perceive and recognise them by means of His Buddha-knowledge; and each one of them will bring immeasurable and incalculable merit to fruition.

SECTION 15: THE INCOMPARABLE VALUE OF THIS TEACHING

Subhuti, if on the one hand, a good man or a good woman performs in the morning as many charitable acts of self-denial as the sand-grains of the Ganges, and performs as many again in the noonday and as many again in the evening, and continues so doing throughout numberless ages, and, on the other hand, anyone listens to this Discourse with heart of faith and without contention, the latter would be the more blessed. But how can any comparison be made with one who writes it down, receives it, retains it, and explains it to others!

Subhuti, we can summarise the matter by saying that the full value of this Discourse can neither be conceived nor estimated, nor can any limit be set to it. The Tathagata has declared this teaching for the benefit of initiates of the Great Way; he has declared it for the benefit of initiates of the Supreme Way. Whosoever can receive and retain this teaching, study it, recite it and spread it abroad will be clearly perceived and recognized by the Tathagata and will achieve a perfection of merit beyond measurement or calculation—a perfection of merit unlimited and inconceivable. In every case such an one will exemplify the Tathagata-Consummation of the Incomparable Enlightenment. Wherefore? Because, Subhuti, those who find consolation in limited doctrines involving the conception of an ego-entity, a personality, a being, or a separated individuality are unable to accept, receive, study, recite and openly explain this Discourse.

Subhuti, in every place where this Discourse is to be found the whole realms of Gods, Men and Titans should offer worship; for you must know that such a place is sanctified like a shrine, and should properly be venerated by all with ceremonial obeisance and circumambulation and with offerings of flowers and incense.

SECTION 16: PURGATION THROUGH SUFFERING THE RETRIBUTION FOR PAST SINS

Furthermore, Subhuti, if it be that good men and good women, who receive and retain this Discourse, are downtrodden, their evil destiny is the inevitable retributive result of sins committed in their past mortal lives. By virtue of their present misfortunes the reacting effects of their past will be thereby worked out, and they will be in a position to attain the Consummation of Incomparable Enlightenment.

Subhuti, I remember the infinitely remote past before Dipankara Buddha. There were 84,000 myriads of multi-millions of Buddhas and to all these I made offerings; yes, all these I served without the least trace of fault. Nevertheless, if anyone is able to receive, retain, study, and recite this Discourse at the end of the last [500-year] period he will gain such a merit that mine in the service of all the Buddhas could not be reckoned as one-hundredth part of it, not even one-thousandth part of it, not even one thousand myriad multi-millionth part of it—indeed, no such comparison is possible.

Subhuti, if I fully detailed the merit gained by good men and good women coming to receive, retain, study, and recite this Discourse in the last period, my hearers would be filled with doubt and might become disordered in mind, suspicious and unbelieving. You should know; Subhuti, that the significance of this Discourse is beyond conception, likewise the fruit of its rewards is beyond conception.

SECTION 17: NO ONE ATTAINS TRANSCENDENTAL WISDOM

At that time Subhuti addressed Buddha, saying: World-honoured One, if good men and good women seek the Consummation of Incomparable Enlightenment, by what criteria should they abide and how should they control their thoughts?

Buddha replied to Subhuti: Good men and good women seeking the Consummation of Incomparable Enlightenment must create this resolved attitude of mind: I must liberate all living beings, yet when all have been liberated, verily not any one is liberated. Wherefore? If a Bodhisattva cherishes the idea of an ego-entity, a personality, a being, or a separated individuality, he is consequently *not* a Bodhisattva, Subhuti. This is because in reality there is no formula which gives rise to the Consummation of Incomparable Enlightenment.

Subhuti, what do you think? When the Tathagata was with Dipankara Buddha was there any formula for the attainment of the Consummation of Incomparable Enlightenment?

No, World-honoured One, as I understand Buddha's meaning, there was no formula by which the Tathagata attained the Consummation of Incomparable Enlightenment.

Buddha said: You are right, Subhuti! Verily there was no formula by which the Tathagata attained the Consummation of Incomparable Enlightenment. Subhuti, had there been any such formula, Dipankara Buddha would not have predicted concerning me: "In the ages of the future you will come to be a Buddha called Shakyamuni"; but Dipankara Buddha made that prediction concerning me because there is actually no formula for the attainment of the Consummation of Incomparable Enlightenment. The reason herein is that Tathagata is a signification implying all formulas. In case anyone says that the Tathagata attained the Consummation of Incomparable Enlightenment, I tell you truly, Subhuti, that there is no formula by which the Buddha attained it. Subhuti, the basis of Tathagata's attainment of the Consummation of Incomparable Enlightenment is wholly *beyond;* it is neither real nor unreal. Hence I say that the whole realm of formulations is not really such, therefore it is called "Realm of formulations."

Subhuti, a comparison may be made with [the idea of] a gigantic human frame.

Then Subhuti said: The World-honoured One has declared that such is not a great body; "a great body" is just the name given to it.

Subhuti, it is the same concerning Bodhisattvas. If a Bodhisattva announces: I will liberate all living creatures, he is not rightly called a Bodhisattva. Wherefore? Because, Subhuti, there is really no such condition as that called Bodhisattvaship, because Buddha teaches that all things are devoid of selfhood, devoid of personality, devoid of entity, and devoid of separate individuality. Subhuti, if a Bodhisattva announces: I will set forth majestic Buddha-lands one does not call him a Bodhisattva, because the Tathagata has declared that the setting forth of majestic Buddha-lands is not really such: "a majestic setting forth" is just the name given to it.

Subhuti, Bodhisattvas who are wholly devoid of any conception of separate selfhood are truthfully called Bodhisattvas.

SECTION 18: ALL MODES OF MIND ARE REALLY ONLY MIND

Subhuti, what do you think? Does the Tathagata possess the human eye?

Yes, World-honoured One, He does.

Well, do you think the Tathagata possesses the divine eve?

Yes, World-honoured One, He does.

And do you think the Tathagata possesses the gnostic eye?

Yes, World-honoured One, He does.

And do you think the Tathagata possesses the eye of transcendent wisdom?

Yes, World-honoured One, He does.

And do you think the Tathagata possesses the Buddha-eye of omniscience?

Yes, World-honoured One, He does.

Subhuti, what do you think? Concerning the sand-grains of the Ganges, has the Buddha taught about them?

Yes, World-honoured One, the Tathagata has taught concerning these grains.

Well, Subhuti, if there were as many Ganges rivers as the sand-grains of the Ganges and there was a Buddha-land for each sand-grain in all those Ganges rivers, would those Buddha-lands be many?

[Subhuti replied]: Many indeed, World-honoured One!

Then Buddha said: Subhuti, however many living beings there are in all those Buddha-lands, though they have manifold modes of mind, the Tathagata understands them all. Wherefore? Because the Tathagata teaches that all these are not Mind; they are merely called "mind." Subhuti, it is impossible to retain past mind, impossible to hold on to present mind, and impossible to grasp future mind.

SECTION 19: ABSOLUTE REALITY IS THE ONLY FOUNDATION

Subhuti, what do you think? If anyone filled three thousand galaxies of worlds with the seven treasures and gave all away in gifts of alms, would he gain great merit?

Yes, indeed, World-honoured One, he would gain great merit.

Subhuti, if such merit was Real, the Tathagata would not have declared it to be great, but because it is without a foundation the Tathagata characterised it as "great."

SECTION 20: THE UNREALITY OF PHENOMENAL DISTINCTIONS

Subhuti, what do you think? Can the Buddha be perceived by His perfectly-formed body?

No, World-honoured One, the Tathagata cannot be perceived by His perfectly-formed body, because the Tathagata teaches that a perfectly-formed body is not really such; it is merely called "a perfectly-formed body."

Subhuti, what do you think? Can the Tathagata be perceived by means of any phenomenal characteristic?

No, World-honoured One, the Tathagata may not be perceived by any phenomenal characteristic, because the Tathagata teaches that phenomenal characteristics are not really such; they are merely termed "phenomenal characteristics."

SECTION 21: WORDS CANNOT EXPRESS TRUTH. THAT WHICH WORDS EXPRESS IS NOT TRUTH

Subhuti, do not say that the Tathagata conceives the idea: I must set forth a Teaching. For if anyone says that the Tathagata sets forth a Teaching he really slanders Buddha and is unable to explain what I teach. As to any Truth-declaring system, Truth is undeclarable; so "an enunciation of Truth" is just the name given to it.

Thereupon, Subhuti spoke these words to Buddha: World-honoured One, in the ages of the future will there be men coming to hear a declaration of this Teaching who will be inspired with belief?

And Buddha answered: Subhuti, those to whom you refer are neither living beings nor not-living beings. Wherefore? Because "living beings," Subhuti, these "living beings" are not really such; they are just called by that name.

SECTION 22: IT CANNOT BE SAID THAT ANYTHING IS ATTAINABLE

Then Subhuti asked Buddha: World-honoured One, in the attainment of the Consummation of Incomparable Enlightenment did Buddha make no acquisition whatsoever?

Buddha replied: Just so, Subhuti. Through the Consummation of Incomparable Enlightenment I acquired not even the least thing; wherefore it is called "Consummation of Incomparable Enlightenment."

SECTION 23: THE PRACTICE OF GOOD WORKS PURIFIES THE MIND

Furthermore, Subhuti, *This* is altogether everywhere, without differentiation or degree; wherefore it is called "Consummation of Incomparable Enlightenment." It is straightly attained by freedom from separate personal selfhood and by cultivating all kinds of goodness.

Subhuti, though we speak of "goodness" the Tathagata declares that there is no goodness; such is merely a name.

SECTION 24: THE INCOMPARABLE MERIT OF THIS TEACHING

Subhuti, if there be one who gives away in gifts of alms a mass of the seven treasures equal in extent to as many mighty Mount Sumerus as there would be in three thousand galaxies of worlds, and if there be another who selects even only four lines from this Discourse upon the Perfection of Transcendental Wisdom, receiving and retaining them, and clearly expounding them to others, the merit of the latter will be so far greater than that of the former that no conceivable comparison can be made between them.

SECTION 25: THE ILLUSION OF EGO

Subhuti, what do you think? Let no one say the Tathagata cherishes the idea: I must liberate all living beings. Allow no such thought, Subhuti. Wherefore? Because in reality there are no living beings to be liberated by the Tathagata. If there were living beings for the Tathagata to liberate, He would partake in the idea of selfhood, personality, entity, and separate individuality.

Subhuti, though the common people accept egoity as real, the Tathagata declares that ego is not different from non-ego. Subhuti, whom the Tathagata referred to as "common people" are not really common people; such is merely a name.

SECTION 26: THE BODY OF TRUTH HAS NO MARKS

Subhuti, what do you think? May the Tathagata be perceived by the thirty-two marks [of a great man]?

Subhuti answered: Yes, certainly the Tathagata may be perceived thereby.

Then Buddha said: Subhuti, if the Tathagata may be perceived by such marks, any great imperial ruler is the same as the Tathagata.

Subhuti then said to Buddha: World-honoured One, as I understand the meaning of Buddha's words the Tathagata may not be perceived by the thirty-two marks.

Whereupon the World-honoured One uttered this verse:

Who sees Me by form,
Who seeks Me in sound,
Perverted are his footsteps upon the Way;
For he cannot perceive the Tathagata.

SECTION 27: IT IS ERRONEOUS TO AFFIRM THAT ALL THINGS ARE EVER EXTINGUISHED

Subhuti, if you should conceive the idea that the Tathagata attained the Consummation of Incomparable Enlightenment by reason of His perfect form, do not countenance such thoughts. The Tathagata's attainment was not by reason of His perfect form. [On the other hand] Subhuti, if you should conceive the idea that anyone in whom dawns the Consummation of Incomparable Enlightenment declares that all manifest standards are ended and extinguished, do not countenance such thoughts. Wherefore? Because the man in whom the Consummation of Incomparable Enlightenment dawns does not affirm concerning any formula that it is finally extinguished.

SECTION 28: ATTACHMENT TO REWARDS OF MERIT

Subhuti, if one Bodhisattva bestows in charity sufficient of the seven treasures to fill as many worlds as there be sand-grains in the river Ganges, and another, realizing that all things are egoless, attains perfection through patient forbearance, the merit of the latter will far exceed that of the former. Why is this, Subhuti? It is because all Bodhisattvas are insentient as to the rewards of merit.

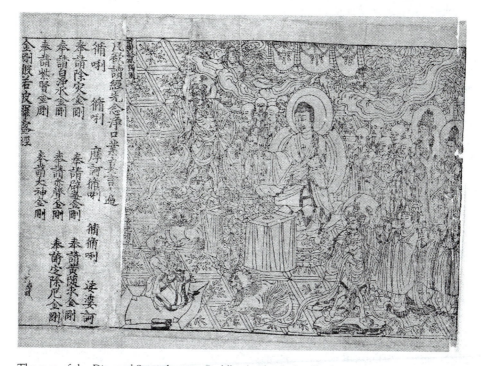

The text of the *Diamond Sutra* showing Buddha (with a halo effect) preaching to his aged disciple Subhuti. This is the earliest known printed work (868 C.E.). (*Dorling Kindersley Media Library, © The British Library.*)

Then Subhuti said to Buddha: What is this saying, World-honoured One, that Bodhisattvas are insentient as to rewards of merit?

[And Buddha answered]: Subhuti, Bodhisattvas who achieve merit should not be fettered with desire for rewards. Thus it is said that the rewards of merit are not received.

SECTION 29: PERFECT TRANQUILITY

Subhuti, if anyone should say that the Tathagata comes or goes or sits or reclines, he fails to understand my teaching. Why? Because TATHAGATA has neither whence nor whither, therefore is He called "Tathagata."

SECTION 30: THE INTEGRAL PRINCIPLE

Subhuti, if a good man or a good woman ground an infinite number of galaxies of worlds to dust, would the resulting minute particles be many?

Subhuti replied: Many indeed, World-honoured One! Wherefore? Because if such were really minute particles, Buddha would not have spoken of them as minute particles. For as to this, Buddha has declared that they are not really such. "Minute particles" is just the name given to them. Also, World-honoured One, when the Tathagata speaks of galaxies of worlds these are not worlds; for if reality could be predicated of a world it would be a self-existent cosmos and the Tathagata teaches that there is really no such thing. "Cosmos" is merely a figure of speech.

[Then Buddha said]: Subhuti, words cannot explain the real nature of a cosmos. Only common people fettered with desire make use of this arbitrary method.

SECTION 31: CONVENTIONAL TRUTH SHOULD BE CUT OFF

Subhuti, if anyone should say that Buddha declares any conception of egoity do you consider he would understand my teaching aright?

No, World-honoured One, such a man would not have any sound understanding of the Tathagata's teaching, because the World-honoured One declares that notions of selfhood, personality, entity, and separate individuality, as really existing, are erroneous—these terms are merely figures of speech.

[Thereupon Buddha said]: Subhuti, those who aspire to the Consummation of Incomparable Enlightenment should recognize and understand all varieties of things in the same way and cut off the arising of [views which are mere] aspects. Subhuti, as regards aspects, the Tathagata declares that in reality they are not such. They are called "aspects."

SECTION 32: THE DELUSION OF APPEARANCES

Subhuti, someone might fill innumerable worlds with the seven treasures and give all away in gifts of alms, but if any good man or any good woman awakens the thought of Enlightenment and takes even only four lines from this Discourse, reciting, using, receiving, retaining and spreading them abroad and explaining them for the benefit of others, it will be far more meritorious.

Now in what manner may he explain them to others? By detachment from appearances—abiding in Real Truth.—So I tell you—

Thus shall ye think of all this fleeting world:
A star at dawn, a bubble in a stream;
A flash of lightning in a summer cloud,
A flickering lamp, a phantom, and a dream.

When Buddha finished this Discourse the venerable Subhuti, together with the bhikshus, bhikshunis, lay-brothers and sisters, and the whole realms of Gods, Men and Titans, were filled with joy by His teaching, and, taking it sincerely to heart they went their ways.

VASUBANDHU, THE THIRTY VERSES ON THE MIND-ONLY DOCTRINE

Because our ideation gives rise to the false ideas of the ego and *dharmas* (elements of existence),
There are various revulsions of appearances.
This ideation, depending on the mind, goes through certain transformations.
These transformations are of three kinds.

I.

They are the consciousness of "ripening in a different life,"
The consciousness of intellection, and the consciousness of the discrimination of the objective world.
First of all, the *alaya* (ideation-store) consciousness,
Which brings into fruition all seeds [or effects of good and evil deeds].

II.

[In its state of pure consciousness], it is not conscious of its clingings and impressions.
In both its objective and subjective functions, it is always associated with touch,
Volition, feeling, thought, and cognition.
But it is always indifferent to its associations.

III.

It is not affected by the darkness of ignorance or by the memory [of the distinction of good and evil].
The same is true in the case of touch, etc.
It is always flowing like a torrent,
And is abandoned in the state of the *arhat*.

IV.

The second transformation
Is called the mind-consciousness,
Which, while it depends on the ideation-store consciousness, in turn conditions it.
Its nature and characteristic consist of intellection.

V.

It is always accompanied by the four evil desires,
Namely, ignorance of the self, view of the self [as being real and permanent],
Self-pride, and self-love,
And by touch, etc. [volition, feeling, thought, and cognition].

VI.

It is free from the memory [of the distinction of good and evil] but not from the darkness of ignorance.
It follows its objects in their emergence and dependence.
It is abandoned by the *arhat* when he arrives at the state of complete extinction of sensation and thought,
And transcends this mundane world.

VII.

Next comes the third transformation,
Which consists of the last six categories of discrimination [the consciousness of touch, sight, hearing, smell, taste, and the sense-center consciousness].

VIII.

The *Trimshika* of Vasubandhu, translated from the Chinese version of Hsuan Tsang (CE 596–664) by Wing-tsit Chan. Reprinted with permission from Sarvepalli Radhakrishnan and Charles A. Moore, *A Source Book on Indian Philosophy* (Princeton, NJ: Princeton University Press, 1957). Copyright 1957, renewed 1985 by PUP. Reprinted by permission of Princeton University Press.

Its nature and characteristic consist of the discrimination of objects.
It is neither good nor evil.

IX. Mental functions consist of general mental functions,
Particular mental functions, good functions, evil functions,
Minor evil functions, and indeterminate mental functions.
They all impress the mind in three ways [of joy, of suffering, and of indifference].

X. General mental functions are touch, etc. [volition, feeling, thought, cognition].
Particular mental functions are desire,
Resolve, remembrance, concentration, and wisdom,
Each depending on different conditions.

XI. Good mental functions are belief, sense of shame, bashfulness,
The three roots of the absence of covetousness, etc. [the absence of hatred and the absence
of attachment],
Energy, repose of mind, vigilance,
Equanimity, and non-injury.

XII. Evil mental functions are covetousness, hatred,
Attachment, arrogance, doubt, and false view.
Minor evil mental functions are anger,
Enmity, concealment, affliction, envy, parsimony,

XIII. Deception, fraudulence, injury, pride,
Absence of the sense of shame, absence of bashfulness,
High-mindedness, low-mindedness,
Unbelief, indolence,

XIV. Idleness, forgetfulness,
Distraction, and non-discernment.
Indeterminate mental functions are repentance, drowsiness,
Reflection, and investigation, the former two composing a different class from the latter.

XV. Based on the mind-consciousness
The five consciousnesses [of the senses] manifest themselves in concomitance with the
objective world.
Sometimes the senses manifest themselves together, and sometimes not,
Just as waves are dependent on the water.

XVI. The sense-center consciousness always arises and manifests itself,
Except when born in the realm of the absence of thought,
In the state of unconsciousness, in the two forms of concentration,
In sleep, and in that state where the spirit is depressed or absent.

XVII. Thus the various consciousnesses are but transformations.
That which discriminates and that which is discriminated
Are, because of this, both unreal.
For this reason, everything is mind only.

XVIII. As the result of various ideations which serve as seeds,
Different transformations take place.
The revulsion-energy of these ideations
Gives rise to all sorts of discrimination.

Due to the habit-energy of various *karmas*   XIX.
The habit-energy of both the six organs and their objects is influenced.
As the previous "ripening in a different life" is completed,
Succeeding "ripenings in a different life" are produced.

Because of false discriminations,   XX.
Various things are falsely discriminated.
What is grasped by such false discrimination
Has no self-nature whatsoever.

The self-nature which results from dependence on others   XXI.
Is produced by the condition of discrimination.
The difference between the Absolute (perfect wisdom) and the dependent
Is that the former is eternally free from what is grasped by false discrimination.

Thus the Absolute and the dependent   XXII.
Are neither the same nor different;
As in the case of impermanence and permanence,
The one can be seen only in the other.

From the three aspects of entity,   XXIII.
The three aspects of non-entity are established.
Therefore the Enlightened One abstrusely preached
That all *dharmas* have no entity.

The first is the non-entity of phenomenon.   XXIV.
The second is the non-entity of self-existence.
The last is the non-entity of the ultimate existence
Of the falsely discriminative ego and *dharmas* now to be eliminated.

The supreme truth of all *dharmas*   XXV.
Is nothing other than the True Norm [suchness].
It is forever true to its nature,
Which is the true nature of mind-only.

Inasmuch as consciousness in its unawakened state   XXVI.
Is not in the abode of the reality of mind-only,
The six sense-organs, their objects, and the seeds of evil desires
Cannot be controlled and extirpated.

To hold something before oneself,   XXVII.
And to say that it is the reality of mind-only,
Is not the state of mind-only,
Because it is the result of grasping.

But when [the objective world which is] the basis of conditioning as well as the wisdom   XXVIII.
   [which does the conditioning]
Are both eliminated,
The state of mind-only is realized,
Since the six sense-organs and their objects are no longer present.

Without any grasping and beyond thought   XXIX.
Is the supra-mundane wisdom [of *bodhisattva*hood].

Because of the abandonment of the habit-energy of various *karmas* and the six sense-
    organs as well as their objects,
The revulsion from relative knowledge to perfect wisdom is attained.

XXX.   This is the realm of passionlessness or purity,
Which is beyond description, is good, and is eternal,
Where one is in the state of emancipation, peace, and joy.
This is the law of the Great Buddha.

ORTHODOX PERSPECTIVES

The revolution in Indian thought spearheaded by heterodox alternatives to Vedism endured for a millennium, roughly from 600 B.C.E. until 400 C.E. Concurrently, a counterrevolution was taking shape. A post-Vedic, reconstituted orthodox tradition was gathering force. Once firmly established, it prevailed during the next phase of Indian intellectual history, recapturing for orthodoxy the lead taken away by the major heterodox movements (Buddhism, Jainism, Charvaka). Philosophically, the period from 400 to 1600 C.E. was marked by the dominance of six great orthodox systems or perspectives *(darshanas)*. They had their roots in the heterodox period and eventually overtook their unorthodox rivals.

The counterrevolutionary orthodox tradition stemmed from an outpouring of new literature called *smriti* ("remembered"). The *smriti* literature, though written after the Vedas, was very much in their spirit. Only the Vedas have been accepted by orthodox Hindus as revealed *(shruti,* "heard"). Still, the new *smriti* literature gained approval because it resonated with *shruti* in much the same way that what is remembered recalls what was earlier heard. Several types of *smritis* structured the new literature. The Shastras codified the fundamental principles of the Hindu social system, such as caste *(varnas),* life stages *(ashramas),* and legitimate aims *(purusharthas).* Two monumental epics entitled *Ramayana* and *Mahabharata* celebrated the heroes and battles of ancient Hindu civilization. The Puranas recounted the exploits of Brahma, Vishnu, and Shiva, the presiding trinity of a revised Hindu pantheon. But of chief importance for our purposes were the Sutras ("threads") and their respective Bhashyas ("commentaries"). These were the seminal texts for the six outstanding philosophical systems or *darshanas* of the age.

The six orthodox schools were Nyaya, Vaisheshika, Sankhya, Yoga, Mimamsa, and Vedanta. Each school produced a single sutra book composed of brief statements or aphorisms setting forth the philosophical views of that school. It is impossible to date with precision specific sutra books. They took form sometime during 400 B.C.E. to 600 C.E. Each sutra book was associated with the name of its supposed author and school founder: the *Nyayasutra* with Gautama (not the Buddha), the *Vaisheshikasutra* with Kanada, the *Sankhyasutra* (lost) with Kapila (legendary?), the *Yogasutra* with Patanjali, the *Mimamsasutra* with Jaimini, and the *Brahmasutra* or *Vedantasutra* with Badarayana. Because the aphorisms of the sutra books were exceedingly compact and not infrequently obscure, this primary literature of the *darshanas* generated the need for a secondary literature of commentaries (Bhashyas) to elucidate the meaning of the Sutras. Specific Bhashyas can be accurately dated between 600 and 1600 C.E. Different commentaries on a single sutra book sometimes yielded radically divergent interpretations. But the contribution of the commentaries to the formulation of their respective *darshanas* was not slight. In the case of one of the perspectives—the Vedanta—its greatest commentaries overshadowed the basic sutra book in originality, systematic sweep, and lasting influence. The six schools exhibit considerable philosophical variety. No one doctrine is shared by all six, except endorsement of the Vedas as revealed truth. Metaphysically, five prefer realism (the external world is real and independent of mind), but one holds to idealism (the external world is an illusion of the mind). Theologically, monotheism (one personal God), monism (one mysterious Absolute), and even agnosticism (doubt about any divinity) can be found among them. They all believe in an eternal soul but name and define it variously. One of them even fails to follow the Indian life view (discussed at end of the section on Vedic Origins, pages 3–7), commonly accepted throughout Indian philosophy since the time of the Upanishads.

After several centuries on separate tracks, the Nyaya and Vaisheshika systems formed an alliance to which Nyaya contributed methodology and Vaisheshika metaphysics. Nyaya developed epistemology and logic to a high degree. Its discussion of the valid means of knowledge *(pramanas)* was the accepted point of departure on that question for other systems of Indian philosophy. The four reliable sources of knowledge are perception, inference, testimony, and comparison. Perception is both ordinary and extraordinary. Inference involves terms, propositions, and five-part arguments; logical fallacies were identified and exposed. Charvaka's strictures against induction, which focused on the problem of justifying any claim to invariable concomitance *(vyapti)* between sign and signified, was countered effectively by Nyaya for the first time, using criteria predictive of nineteenth-century British philosopher John Stuart Mill's agreement of presence and absence. This contribution alone was enough to secure Nyaya's preeminence in the field of logic.

Vaisheshika depended on Nyaya for logic and epistemology but replaced Nyaya's account of the objects of knowledge *(prameyas)* with its more solid treatment of seven metaphysical categories: substance, quality, action, generality, particularity, inherence, and nonexistence. Inherence supplies the key to understanding the inner connections among the others. It explains how substances support qualities, participate in actions, belong to classes, and enjoy uniqueness. Nine kinds of substances exist: the atoms of earth, water, fire, and air; the all-pervasive ether, which is a fifth, nonatomic material substance and the most subtle of all; space and time; and minds and souls. Vaisheshika alone among the orthodox schools offered an atomic theory of matter with a vision of recurrent divine creation from and dissolution into those fundamental particles. It interpreted the cosmic creation-dissolution process as a divine plan promoting the liberation of souls trapped by karma in the material world. Its theory of soul *(atman)* as the hidden ground or matrix of the complete psychophysical organism (body as well as mind) became one of several standard views on the subject in Indian philosophy. Its most distinctive contribution to metaphysics, however, was its belief in the particularity of atoms and souls (the basic reals), no two of which are exactly alike. This special doctrine gave the school its name—*vishesha* is the Sanskrit word for particularity or uniqueness.

The Sankhya and Yoga schools turned to each other for theory and practice respectively. Sankhya's metaphysical theory was dualistic: The two orders of reality are a single material substance *(prakriti)* and many spiritual souls *(purusha)*. The world we experience evolves in stages from singular *prakriti* into twenty-three mental and physical elements as three forces *(gunas)* inherent within *prakriti* interact and combine once their original equilibrium is disturbed. The manifold evolved world eventually devolves back into unitive *prakriti* when its *gunas* become quiescent again. The evolution-devolution cycle repeats itself, but not under divine stimulation or guidance. The process is self-sufficient. The manifold evolved world as effect pre-exists in its cause—*prakriti* with its component *gunas*. *Prakriti* itself is the material cause of that world, the characteristics of the *gunas* its formal cause (what determines its nature), and the interaction of the *gunas* its efficient cause (causal force or agency). Its final cause (purpose) is the emancipation of souls ensnared in the life of the most evolved of all creatures—the psychophysical organism, a human being.

The concept of soul *(purusha)* in Sankhya philosophy is unique. Unlike the Vaisheshika *atman,* the soul, according to this school, is not the metaphysical ground supporting the psychophysical organism; that organism evolves from, and hence is grounded in, *prakriti* alone. *Purusha* has nothing to do with any faculty such as intellect, will, or personality, or with any activity such as animating the body or organizing and interpreting sensations. Mental faculties and activities, in the Sankhya view, belong on the *prakriti* side of the metaphysical divide, not the *purusha* side. The Sankhya *purusha,* in contrast, is pure consciousness, passive, simply a witness, and never a participant in any mental or physical process of the world evolved from *prakriti.* Its incarceration within the psychophysical organism, a human, is a case of mistaken identity. Intellect *(buddhi),* the first and most subtle product of *prakriti,* is erroneously credited with innate consciousness; so long as that misconception remains in force, the true source of consciousness, the *purusha,* is doomed to imprisonment within the material domain. In order for the soul to be released from the psychophysical organism and to escape from the vortex of matter altogether, the soul must be distinguished from the intellect with which it is mistakenly identified. This may be accomplished either through philosophy or through meditation. The former was Sankhya's province, the latter the specialty of the Yoga school (discussed later in this section).

Consider how Sankhya proposed, through philosophical argumentation alone, to dispel the mistaken identity by distinguishing consciousness from intellect. The argument turns on the premise that knowledge has two necessary conditions—modification of the intellect and awareness of that modification. Modification of the intellect can be fully and accurately accounted for by *prakritic* events alone: Contact with objects of the world modifies the sense organs *(jnanendriyas);* that modification stimulates modification in the mind *(manas),* where sensory information is organized and interpreted; that modification is forwarded to the ego-sense *(ahamkara)*, the organ that owns interpreted perceptions as "mine"; and that modification finally advances to the intellect *(buddhi)*, which is modified by assuming the shape of the worldly object originally contacted. This chain of command is clear and thoroughly *prakritic*, since all of the organs involved issue from *prakriti*. But whence comes the consciousness that is essential to the completion of the knowledge transaction? The causal chain that leads from modification of the sense organs to modification of the intellect is purely mechanical, and a machine is unconscious of what it accomplishes. Knowing is like watching a motion picture: The projector may be turning and the film moving (the intellect may be undergoing modifications), but unless the bulb is switched on (unless consciousness is shining), nothing is seen on the screen. Sankhya concluded that since consciousness (the illumination required for knowing) cannot be accounted for by *prakritic* organs and their activities, it must come from a metaphysical principle completely independent of *prakriti*. That principle, *purusha*, was considered by Sankhya to be proven by philosophical reasoning such as this.

The last pair of philosophical allies were Mimamsa and Vedanta. The other schools acquired their tenets from reason and then squared them with revelation (the Vedas). Mimamsa and Vedanta took the opposite approach. They claimed that their tenets came from revelation but were also susceptible to proof by reason. Each looked to a different division of revelation, however, and hence espoused very different beliefs. Mimamsa focused on the early Vedas, Vedanta on the later (Upanishads). The mission of Mimamsa was to provide a philosophical rationale for the ancient Vedic ritual of fire sacrifice, commanded in the early Vedas and promising paradise for the soul. To fulfill that mission, Mimamsa needed to invent three proofs. First, it needed to prove that the imperatives contained in the Vedas were binding and obligatory. This it argued on the ground that scriptural testimony is a valid source of knowledge of duty as well as fact. Second, Mimamsa needed to prove the immortality of the soul, for without it the prospect of paradise would collapse. Third, it had to prove that performance of the fire sacrifice could generate the causality to send the soul to paradise for eternity. Here it appealed to a special metaphysical concept of causal power *(shakti)*, knowable not by perception, inference, testimony, or comparison, but by one of Mimamsa's two additional *pramanas*—postulation. Causal force cannot be detected by the normal means; it is properly assumed as the only rational explanation of how one event can bring forth another.

The last and greatest of the six orthodox perspectives was Vedanta ("end of the Vedas"). Appropriately named, its central intent was to systematize the philosophy implicit in the Upanishads, the last part of the Vedas. The philosophical implications of the Upanishads, unfortunately, are not entirely consistent. This problem was reflected also in the *Brahmasutra* or *Vedantasutra* of Badarayana. Ambivalence on major issues in both the scriptural and sutra sources of the system accounted for wide variations of interpretation among the principal commentaries. During the bhashya period, therefore, Vedanta split into several subsystems. The main three are the Advaita of Shankara (eighth century), the Vishishtadvaita of Ramanuja (eleventh to twelfth centuries), and the Dvaita of Madhva (thirteenth century).

Shankara's Advaita Vedanta has over the centuries distinguished itself as the dominant influence in all of Indian philosophy. *Advaita* means "nondual," and Advaita Vedanta is the philosophy of the Upanishads constructed on the nonduality principle. The principle states that there is only one reality—Brahman. No second reality exists outside Brahman, and no parts or attributes divide Brahman internally. Shankara resolved the problem of Upanishadic inconsistencies by means of his ingenius bifocal vision of reality. Reality is indeed one but can be viewed from two different standpoints, one inferior and one superior. Shankara took this distinction from the *Mundaka Upanishad,* which speaks of lower knowledge (*apara vidya*) and higher knowledge (*para vidya*). By using this distinction, Shankara sought to reconcile the disparities in the Upanishads and Badarayana concerning God, World, and Soul. The Inferior Viewpoint includes a creator-god, Ishvara, as the few theistic Upanishads teach. Ishvara is the supreme personality, possessed of all excellent attributes, known and worshipped as an object separate from the human knower-worshipper. The world is the creation of Ishvara, metaphysically real apart from human knowers and the divine creator and composed of many real objects with real parts and attributes. The soul is the individualized ego, of which there are many, each separate from its fellows, the world, and God the creator. In the Superior Viewpoint, found in the majority of the Upanishads, however, the picture is radically altered. Brahman alone is real, has no parts or attributes, is known by identity (becoming one with the One), and is neither knowable as an object nor appropriately worshipped. In this viewpoint, the world is unmasked as a distorted perception *(maya)* of the one reality Brahman, neither exactly real (because not what it appears to be) nor exactly unreal (because the reality *is* there, underneath the superimposed distortion). Better described as "surreal" (reality distorted) than as "illusory" (misleadingly suggesting complete unreality), the world's apparent reality, its multiplicity, and its separation from the knower as well as from its divine ground are all part of the distortion. Lastly, the soul is not the individualized ego, of which there are many, but the universal Atman, identical with Brahman.

The quandary facing each Vedantin was how to manage two incompatible precepts taught by both the Upanishads and Badarayana. Those incompatible precepts were the doctrine of creation and the nonduality principle. The creation doctrine implies a theistic view of God as supreme personality, a realistic view of the world as separate from the creator and from the human knower, and a pluralistic view of the soul as individualized egos. The nonduality principle, on the other hand, coheres with a suprapersonal Absolute (Brahman), a world surreal rather than real or unreal, and one universal Soul (Atman) in place of many individualized egos. What distinguished each Vedantin was his method of coping with this quandary. Shankara took the nonduality principle at full face value while relegating creation to the Inferior Viewpoint. Ramanuja's solution was just the opposite. A devout Vaishnavite committed to the worship of God as the supreme personality Lord Vishnu, the creation doctrine was his priority, leaving him no alternative but to modify (or surrender, which he was unwilling to do) the nonduality principle. Madhva, another Vaishnava devotee, went even further, denying the nonduality principle altogether and basing his Vedanta entirely on the creation doctrine.

Ramanuja's Vishishtadvaita Vedanta, as its name implies, was predicated on a modification of the nonduality principle. Reality is indeed divine and one without a second (nondual) but has parts and attributes (the modification). Ramanuja rejected Shankara's two-truths theory; truth is and must be one. He accepted as absolute truth the theistic view of God, the realistic view of the world, and the pluralistic view of the soul. God is none other than Lord Vishnu, known and worshipped as the supreme personality, possessed of all superlative qualities and no imperfections. Contained as parts within the unity of God are unconscious matter *(prakriti)* and eternal souls. During the causal-state of God, those parts remain internalized but become externalized during God's effect-state. God creates by transforming the unconscious material part of himself into a real external world of manifold objects and then consigns eternal souls according to their karma to a life within psychophysical organisms. In due time, God withdraws the external world and souls back into himself, alternating repeatedly between causal-state and effect-state. The purpose of cyclical creation and dissolution of the world is the progress of souls toward liberation. Souls participate in liberation through the practice of various yogas, especially *bhakti,* the yoga of devotion. But in the last analysis, liberation is the work of God's grace. The creation doctrine has been preserved intact in Ramanuja's Vedanta; the nonduality principle, while affirmed, has been trimmed to fit.

Madhva's Dvaita (dualistic) Vedanta, paradoxically, dispensed with the nonduality principle of the Upanishads altogether and adhered without compromise to the creation doctrine. Throughout the realms of being, it claimed, difference is real, similarity less so, and identity nonexistent. To consider matter and souls to be parts of God, as Ramanuja did, was in Madhva's view to diminish the holiness of God. God, the matter from which the manifold external world evolves, and souls are, to the contrary, essentially different from one another, though the latter two are eternally dependent on the first. In fact, Madhva affirmed a fivefold metaphysical difference—between God (creator) and souls (creatures), between God (creator) and material world (creature), between souls (spiritual) and world (material), between any two souls, and between any two material objects in the world. Madhva's extreme duality reflects an influence from the Vaisheshika doctrine of particularity, which likewise discovered uniqueness and difference at the very heart of reality. In Vaishnava devotionalism, such as Madhva's, the higher Lord Vishnu the Creator is exalted over the creature, the deeper the creature's feelings of worship for its maker and savior.

These sketches of the leading orthodox systems suggest the range of philosophical options that developed before and during 400 to 1600 C.E. They also provide a backdrop for introducing the three texts included as readings in this chapter: the *Bhagavad Gita,* the *Yogasutra* of Patanjali, and Shankara's *A Thousand Teachings.* All three belong to the *smriti* literature on which the orthodox counterrevolution was launched. The *Bhagavad Gita,* part of one of the great Indian epics rather than the *darshana* literature proper, contains ideas of philosophical importance upon which the orthodox perspectives drew. The second, the *Yogasutra,* as its title indicates, is one of the six seminal sutra books from which the major schools of the period sprang. And the third, *A Thousand Teachings,* though not a commentary in the usual sense, can be placed with the bhashya literature, since it was written by the most commanding figure of the bhashya phase of orthodox Indian philosophy. All three, furthermore, are prominent among the Hindu texts that have attracted the most attention in the West.

*   *   *

The *Bhagavad Gita* has received more acclaim from readers in India and more attention from commentators abroad than any other Indian classic. It has been translated into dozens of languages, into English alone scores of times with fresh efforts appearing regularly as its readership expands. Its title means "Song of

God," for in it Krishna delivers a rhapsodic revelation of himself as the Supreme Deity. The word of God straight from God himself concerning God's true essence is more than ordinary speech; it is song! A slender text of 700 verses in eighteen short chapters, it became incorporated more than two millennia ago into that colossal Indian epic, the *Mahabharata*. The *Gita* has been likened to an Upanishad, because it assumes the form of a dialogue between a knower and a seeker of the sacred wisdom, and because it brings the reader to the very portal of direct mystical experience. Though technically a *smriti* text, it is believed by many to share with the Vedas the full stature of *shruti*, the only *smriti* warranting that high honor.

The context of the *Bhagavad Gita* cannot be fully grasped apart from the larger work into which it was grafted. The name of that larger work, the *Mahabharata*, means "the great narrative of the battle of the Bharatas," and it comes from *Bharata* (an ancient name for India) and *maha* ("great"). The story, of exceptional length, culminates in a disastrous battle fought between two branches of one extended family, the Kurus, over the right of succession to the throne. The king, Pandu, has died, and his blind brother, Dhritarashtra, though unfit, has assumed control of the realm. Yudhishthira, the eldest of the five Pandavas (sons of Pandu) and the legitimate claimant to the throne, has gambled away his birthright in a rigged dice game, condemning himself and his brothers and their common wife to fourteen years of exile in the forest, where they miraculously survive fantastic trials and tribulations. On their return to Hastinapura, the capital, Yudhishthira's renewed claim to the throne is rejected by his corrupt cousin, Duryodhana, the senior of Dhritarashtra's hundred sons (the Kauravas), who has usurped the rule of the kingdom. The war that ensues pits the army of the Pandavas against that of the Kauravas in a conflict among combatants related by blood and the bonds of affection and loyalty. The result of the war is the destruction of the royal house. As with Homer's *Iliad*, there is evidence that some such battle was actually fought at Kurukshetra ("field of the Kurus") about sixty miles north of the modern Delhi, perhaps sometime during 1000 to 700 B.C.E.

The complete action of the *Bhagavad Gita* transpires on the battlefield at Kurukshetra in the early hours of the day the terrible war commenced. The scene is charged with epic grandeur. The time is a glorious age in the distant past, when events were more momentous than they are today. The fate of a mighty kingdom, and of the noble Pandavas with whom the reader has come to sympathize, hangs in the balance. The major characters are of heroic proportions, possess powers superior to ours, and deal with forces and situations that make ours pale by comparison. The action begins when Arjuna directs Krishna to drive their war chariot into the middle of the battlefield between the armies amassed on either side. Arjuna is the mightiest warrior of the five Pandavas, and his brothers are counting on him to make their cause prevail. Krishna is thought by all present to be Arjuna's uncle and charioteer, and so he is from the limited human point of view. The intent of the *Gita*, however, is to privilege the reader with a deeper insight into the identity of Krishna as the Deity Supreme, incarnate but incognito. From his central position, Arjuna surveys the opposing warrior hosts and sees on both sides kinsmen and friends. Appalled by the prospect of family catastrophe, he decides in a twinkling that he wants no part of it and throws down his famous bow, refusing to fight. The spiritual message Krishna brings as the substance of the *Gita* is addressed to the anguished Arjuna in the throes of his darkest hour. Its intent, however, is universal. The entire story of the *Gita*, we are told at the outset, is being reported to the blind Dhritarashtra back in the capital by Sanjaya, a man equipped with the psychic power of clairvoyance.

Krishna's teaching to Arjuna in the *Bhagavad Gita* has won a paramount place in orthodox Hindu faith. It has even become something of a normative creed, though a flexible one. Hinduism generally resists precise theological formulations imposed as dogma. Its tendency instead is to be permissive and inclusive. Many Hindus, nevertheless, if asked to specify a single source in which the essence of their diverse faith comes most clearly to expression, would single out the *Gita.* Its teaching can be summarized in three simple points: (1) The true aim of life is release from the world and union with God. (2) Krishna is the Deity Supreme with whom union should be sought. (3) There are four ways of achieving union with Krishna.

The first point is embedded in context rather than explicitly stated. Yet there is no doubt that the *Gita* proposes that release *(moksha)* and union *(yoga)* are the keys to human existence. Since the Upanishads, religions native to India have generally agreed that liberation from bondage to suffering, karma, and rebirth is the true quest of life. Further, on the authority of their Shastras, Hindus over the centuries have acknowledged four legitimate aims of life *(purusharthas)*—pleasure *(kama),* wealth *(artha),* duty *(dharma),* and liberation or release, the fourth being their primary concern. In the *Gita,* the ideal of union completes that of release. This text does not directly address the question of the nature of the human soul, except to affirm its immortality. Nor does it specify what kind of union with the divine the human soul can expect. From the fact that God in the *Gita* is the supreme personality, however, we may reasonably infer that union with God is communion in which both God and the human soul retain their separate identities.

Arjuna's problem, when Krishna begins to instruct him, is precisely that the liberation-union ideal is not uppermost in his thinking and has not shaped his decision. His motive for refusing participation in the military campaign about to commence makes perfectly good human sense. He wants to avoid an action he foresees will bring dire consequences on his family (ruination) and himself (the guilt of killing relatives and friends). But it makes very bad divine sense, as Krishna is quick to inform him. Actions based on anticipated consequences of personal reward or penalty in this world are karmic and bind the soul to suffering and rebirth. Krishna urges Arjuna to take a superior view and reverse his decision. He, Arjuna, is by divine design a member of the warrior caste *(kshatriya);* it is therefore his holy duty *(dharma)* to fight with all his might in the war effort. Performance of sacred duty, without regard for earthly reward or penalty, is obedient service to God and a pathway to union with God *(yoga).* In order to embrace the way of Krishna, Arjuna must disengage his mind from thoughts that seem perfectly right to the majority of humankind. To sort through the confusion between lower motives and higher motives is the real battle confronting him at the moment. His responsibility is to surrender to the higher Self symbolized by Krishna; this is the real victory for Arjuna, the allegorical representation of humanity in the *Gita.* It takes Krishna eighteen chapters to convince Arjuna. But at the end, Arjuna assures Krishna that his teaching has been life changing.

The second point is the crux of the *Gita,* argued in an unconventional fashion. Krishna builds his claim to divine supremacy on top of alternative theologies he first identifies with and then surpasses. Since the alternative theologies are mutually exclusive from a logical standpoint, the result is a composite theology that looks something like a patchwork quilt. Four commonly accepted Hindu theologies meet in the *Bhagavad Gita.* The first is Upanishadic monism. Throughout the

Gita, Krishna equates himself with the Brahman or Atman of the Upanishads. But he also extols himself above Brahman, as the ground and support of that which grounds and supports the universe. The second theology is Bhagavata theism, the precursor of Vaishnavism. In Bhagavata theism, Lord Vishnu is lifted up as creator-preserver-destroyer of the universe. He is also the loving father-God who mercifully rescues his human children on earth when danger threatens, by incarnating himself in animal or human form. There are ten incarnations (*avatara*) of Lord Vishnu on earth, Krishna being one of them. In the *Gita,* however, Krishna is more than an earthly incarnation of Lord Vishnu; he is one with Vishnu, superior even. The third theology is early Vedic polytheism. Krishna associates himself with a number of important gods of the Rig Veda while also setting himself above them. The most curious component in the composite theology of the *Gita* is Sankhya dualism. Considerable plastic surgery is required to transform Sankhya into a theology Krishna can both affirm and trump. Initially, Sankhya philosophy was agnostic, lacking any theology. To employ Sankhya as a theology necessitates converting *purusha* into a God-concept, which it is not in Sankhya. It also involves imputing activity to *purusha* as the Knower, whereas in Sankhya *purusha* is passive witnessing consciousness and unknowing, knowledge being an activity of the *prakritic* intellect. Finally, *prakriti* and *purusha* need to be linked in the creative process as co-producers of the evolved universe; *prakriti* alone in the Sankhya philosophy provides all the causality (material, formal, and efficient) needed for evolution.

The climax of Krishna's divine self-revelation in the *Gita* comes in chapters 10 and 11, premier passages in mystical literature. Chapter 10 is the most extensive and intensive declaration by Krishna of his godliness in the entire work. In it, Krishna compiles a stunning catalogue of his innumerable divine powers and attributes. He identifies with Atman the true Self (Upanishadic monism), with Lord Vishnu (Bhagavata theism), with Indra the chief of the Rig Vedic gods (early Vedic polytheism), and with consciousness (the *purusha* of Sankhya dualism). He then proclaims himself the best in a wide assortment of categories—mountains, bodies of water, trees, rivers, animals, birds, priests, warriors, seers. The list goes on and on, and its cumulative effect is compelling. Chapter 11 is even more evocative. It recounts a private epiphany that takes place in that lone chariot mid-battlefield as the two armies, primed for action, threaten each other with brandishing of weapons and battle cries. Arjuna is given the spiritual eyes to see Krishna transfigured into full divinity. Arjuna sees the universe divinized and subsumed within the body of Krishna, with Krishna's face in every form. He sees Krishna merge with Vishnu, holding Vishnu's insignia, the mace and the discus, and wearing his crown. He also sees Krishna change into time the destroyer, consuming not only worlds but also the warriors present on the battlefield that morning. In this final form, Krishna overpoweringly commands Arjuna to join in the battle. Arjuna, shocked and terrified by the abundance of his vision, breaks out into impassioned speech, praising Krishna as Brahman the all-inclusive divine ground of the cosmos, as the knower and known (*purusha* and *prakriti*), as Vayu, Yama, Agni, Varuna, and Prajapati (all major Vedic deities), and as "the shining God of gods . . . carrying the mace and discus and wearing a crown" (Vishnu). The theology of the *Gita* may not be logically tidy, but it is highly imaginative and leaves no doubt that it elevates Krishna as the Deity Supreme.

The third main point of the *Gita* is the one for which it is best known. There are four ways to union with Krishna—Karma Yoga, Jnana Yoga, Raja Yoga, and

Bhakti Yoga. Karma Yoga is the way of action or, as the text says, "selfless service." Krishna reverses the common assumption, that all action in this world binds the actor to suffering and rebirth, by making a certain kind of action a way of release from suffering and rebirth and to union with God. Performance of sacred duties to caste and stage in life, undertaken as service to God without concern for earthly consequences to oneself, is Karma Yoga. It is the first yoga that Krishna urges on Arjuna, because of the four it impinges most directly on Arjuna's decision regarding participation in the war. Jnana Yoga is the way of knowledge or, in the words of the text, "spiritual wisdom." Precise exposition of this yoga is not undertaken in the text. By implication, it is the yoga that approaches enlightenment or higher consciousness through the perceptive study of scripture (*shruti* and *smriti*). What was later dubbed Raja Yoga (the term itself does not appear in this text), the "royal" yoga, is the way of meditation. It involves mental mastery of concentration, contemplation, and absorption, and through them of exalted states of consciousness. Bhakti Yoga is the pathway of loving devotion to a personal god. Adoring a deity with affection exceeding that between family members, friends, or lovers is the meaning of Bhakti Yoga. Its inclusion in this text is indicative of the highly popular devotional movement (*bhakti*) that was sweeping India at the time the *Gita* was written. Jnana and Raja yogas were known prior to the *Gita*, but Karma and Bhakti are its very own innovations. Hindus through the ages have turned to this text for authoritative instruction and inspiration on Yoga—how to achieve union with God.

*   *   *

Patanjali's *Yogasutra* is another major milestone in the development of Indian yoga. It is the sutra sourcebook for the Yoga School and the all-time definitive text on Raja Yoga, the yoga of meditation. Nothing of historical certainty is known about Patanjali the man. Nor can his *Yogasutra* be dated accurately; estimates range from the third century B.C.E. to the fifth century C.E. Patanjali divided the almost 200 aphorisms of his *Yogasutra* into four chapters dealing with yogic consciousness (*samadhi*), practices (*sadhana*), powers (*vibhuti*), and liberation (*kaivalya*). Patanjali's originality is to be found mostly in the masterful way he assembled and shaped materials borrowed from older texts. He took his theory of yogic consciousness from the Upanishads. Most of the meditative practices he advocated came from that same source, though Patanjali must be credited with giving them their permanent strategic order (posture, breath restraint, sense withdrawal, concentration, and contemplation). His discussion of supernormal powers parallels that offered in earlier Buddhist and Jain literature. His belief in liberation from bondage through ignorance to suffering, karma, and rebirth (the Indian life view) was already widespread in Indian religion, both orthodox and heterodox. He molded to his purposes the philosophical perspective of the Sankhya school, supplemented by a minimal theism. Since Shankara (eighth century C.E.), however, it has become the preference of many commentators to construe Patanjali from the Vedanta rather than the Sankhya perspective. Sankhya then began to decline and Vedanta ascend over all other systems. As the discussion of Patanjali proceeds, it will be helpful to note differences between the Sankhya and Vedanta interpretations of some key points. Both are relevant to the historical understanding of this text.

Yogic consciousness *(samadhi)* is the topic of Chapter One. Patanjali's discussion includes four points. First, *samadhi* is engrossment. It is the state in which consciousness is totally involved, engaged, absorbed, entranced, like that of a child in play, an athlete at peak effort, a thinker lost in thought, or a lover in the presence of the beloved. Second, *samadhi* is progressive. It passes through stages, from coarse to fine and from shallow to deep. Third, *samadhi* is the objective of yoga. Yoga aims at "stopping all thought-waves in the mind" *(chittavritt-inirodha)*, thereby disengaging consciousness from the psychophysical organism where thought-waves are produced. Yoga thus speeds consciousness toward its goal of optimal engrossment. Finally, *samadhi* brings forth the true self or soul. When thought-waves are present, the inclination is to mistake the psychophysical organism for the seat of consciousness. When thought-waves are suppressed by yogic practices, it becomes clear that pure consciousness, still shining brightly, is the true self or soul, not any aspect of the psychophysical organism. In Sankhya philosophy, that soul (of which there are many) is *purusha*—pure, passive, witnessing consciousness discriminated from the psychophysical organism evolved from *prakriti*. In Vedanta philosophy, the soul (one and universal) is Atman—the ground and power of the psychophysical organism.

Patanjali's detailed analysis of the progression of stages in *samadhi* is an original contribution. He breaks down that progression into two main stages with four substages under the first. The first main stage is engrossment "with seed" *(savikalpa samadhi)*, in which consciousness is so preoccupied with whatever object it is concentrating on that self-awareness ceases. The first substage begins with consciousness of the object together with its name and concept *(savitarka)*. Then name and concept vanish and just the object remains *(nirvitarka)*. Then consciousness penetrates into the gross object to perceive its component particles *(savichara)*. And finally consciousness beholds pure matter *(prakriti)* behind the component particles *(nirvichara)*. This first main stage ends when consciousness penetrates to the deepest level of truth about the material world.

The second main stage, flowing smoothly from the first, is "seedless" engrossment *(nirvikalpa samadhi)*. Pure matter also now totally disappears from conscious view, but consciousness is all the more engrossed. With what? With nothing, for awareness of both subject and object has been left behind. Consciousness now abides totally within itself and, because self-luminous, shines with undiminished brilliance, there being no subject or object to draw off its light. This is the omega point of consciousness, the point at which consciousness is most engrossed and luminous but with no content present to it; the point at which consciousness has finally fully found itself and is perfectly at home; the point, paradoxically, of both plenitude and emptiness. Sankhya philosophy interprets the experience of *nirvikalpa samadhi* as the emancipation (separation) of the soul or *purusha* from the psychophysical organism evolved from *prakriti,* the undoing of an unfortunate union caused by mistaken identity. Vedanta philosophy, in contrast, interprets the same experience as the reunion of the individual Atman with the universal Brahman, the undoing of an unfortunate separation caused by mistaken disidentification. These interpretations stand diametrically opposed.

Discussion of yogic practices *(sadhana)* overlaps the second half of Chapter Two and the first half of Chapter Three of the *Yogasutra*. The eight practices that gave Patanjali's yoga the name Ashtanga ("eight limbs") Yoga and for which the *Yogasutra* is most renown are abstentions *(yamas)*, observances *(niyamas)*, posture *(asana)*, breath restraint *(pranayama)*, sense withdrawal *(pratyahara)*, concentration *(dharana),* contemplation *(dhyana),* and absorption *(samadhi).* Patanjali deliberately set the eight in this strategic order (permanently fixed in the yoga tradition) to suggest that they build on one another from foot to head. The entire sequence functions in two ways—deactivation and activation. First, these practices deactivate the psychophysical organism in which thought-waves are produced, leading to *nirvikalpa samadhi* (Chapter One). Abstentions (injury, falsehood, theft, incontinence, and greed) prevent bad karmic formations in the social domain. Observances (purity, contentment, self-control, self-study, and holding to the ideal of God as the eternally free *purusha*) remove the harmful influence of latent tendencies in the subconscious *(samskaras).* Posture (the lotus position) puts to rest the organs of action. Breath restraint tranquilizes the nerves and inner organs. Sense withdrawal enervates the sense organs. Concentration (gathering consciousness into one-pointed focus), contemplation (dwelling on that one point), and absorption (progressive deepening of engrossment) curtail thought-waves in the mind *(manas),* ego-sense *(ahamkara),* and intellect *(buddhi),* the three components of the psychophysical organism where thought-wave are generated. Once all the centers in the chain of command that produces thought-waves have been deactivated from bottom to top, consciousness is emancipated from the psychophysical organism and shines alone, empty of content but with its luminosity at full strength.

The second function of the eight limbs is to activate yogic powers *(vibhuti),* more than thirty of which are listed in the second half of Chapter Three. Concentration, Contemplation, and Absorption team up as a triple force *(samyama)* capable of releasing a broad range of supernormal abilities *(siddhis,* "accomplishments"). Some of the more sensational are knowledge of past lives, invisibility, extrasensory perception, walking on water, flying, omnipotence, and omniscience. Similar claims are encountered in other religions. Understood as occult powers, they evoke a spectrum of positive and negative reactions from readers. A few of the powers are subject to nonoccult interpretations. Using *samyama* to cultivate friendliness and compassion or to control hunger and thirst seems feasible. Patanjali himself had reservations about the importance, not the actuality, of the *siddhis.* Questing after magical powers could distract from the pursuit of *nirvikalpa samadhi,* which remained uppermost in Patanjali's thinking.

Chapter Four concludes the *Yogasutra* with a summary of the role of yoga in achieving liberation *(kaivalya).* The yogi (masc.) or yogini (fem.) whose mind has been purified by attaining *samadhi* is released from craving and karma. The subconscious tendencies through which much of karma works are themselves thought-waves; those tendencies are overcome once thought-waves are suppressed by the practice of Ashtanga Yoga. When consciousness shines on after yoga has terminated thought-waves in the mind *(chitta),* the yogi/yogini discriminates consciousness from mind, no longer mistakes the mind for the true self (the Atman of Vedanta, the *purusha* of Sankhya), and discovers liberation from bondage through ignorance to suffering, karma, and rebirth. The Sanskrit term Patanjali used for liberation is *kaivalya* ("isolation") rather than the standard term *moksha. Kaivalya* supports the Sankhya interpretation of liberation better than the Vedantic. Sankhya thinks of liberation as the eternal *purusha* retreating to a place completely isolated from the material world *(prakriti)* as well as from other souls, enjoying perpetual *nirvikalpa samadhi* and hence, though conscious of nothing (nescient), magnificently engrossed. Vedanta's idea, however, is anything but isolationistic: The individual Atman, shedding its temporary separateness and reuniting with the universal Brahman, merges with everything and hence knows everything (is omniscient) through identity with it.

*   *   *

A brief sketch of Shankara's Advaita Vedanta philosophy was given earlier in the introduction to this section. Shankara (700–750 C.E.) has been proclaimed the foremost of the Vedantins. From its origin until now, his Advaita has remained the most popular version of Vedanta and the ranking school of Indian philosophy. Since Vedanta is primarily an exegetical philosophy, growing out of scriptural interpretation rather than logical reflection on experience of the world, Shankara's favorite literary form was commentary *(bhashya)*. The major sources behind Vedanta are the Upanishads, the *Bhagavad Gita,* and Badarayana's *Brahmasutra.* Shankara, accordingly, worked out his system of thought largely by writing commentaries on ten of the principal Upanishads, on the *Gita,* and on the *Brahmasutra.* The last is considered his masterpiece. In addition to his many commentaries, a number of philosophical treatises have been attributed to Shankara. The only one of unquestionable authenticity is *A Thousand Teachings.* Better than his commentaries, despite their greater fame, this work offers the beginner a clear impression of Shankara's subtle ideas.

A Thousand Teachings has two parts. Part One is metrical and falls into nineteen chapters of increasing length, depth, and intricacy. Part Two (the third reading included in this chapter, translated by Mayeda Sengaku) is in prose; its three chapters apply Shankara's threefold method of guiding the student to final release through scriptural exposition, philosophical dialogue, and meditation. All but four of the twenty-two chapters took their names, as did many ancient writings, either from the first word in the text or from a prominent word in the opening verse. The title of the work reflects its length—787 verses in all, rounded off to 1,000. Chapter 18 in Part One ("Thou Art That") and Chapter 2 of Part Two ("Awareness") deserve recognition as the philosophically meatiest chapters in the book. They underscore the priority Shankara placed on two "great sayings" *(mahavakyas)* of the Upanishads, "Thou art That" (*Chandogya Upanishad* VI, 8–16) and "I am Brahman" (*Brihadaranyaka Upanishad* I, 4, 10). It is widely recognized that Upanishadic teaching climaxes in the identity of Brahman and Atman. The *mahavakyas* provide the chief medium for expressing that equation (see the introduction to the first section in this text, page 6).

Shankara made those two great sayings the center of his philosophy of nonduality. Advaita (nondual) Vedanta takes identity as the key to understanding God, World, and Soul. These three are ultimately one and the same; apparent differences among them are a distortion imposed on that seamless Reality by ignorance *(avidya)*. Shankara was more of an apologist than a philosopher in the usual sense. His mission was to give a rational defense of a faith based on revelation (the Upanishads). There are two truths, a higher and a lower. The correct method of knowing the higher truth is revelation. Revelation neither requires nor permits rational proof. Reason is useful only at the lower level of truth. The proper role for reason is to demonstrate at the lower level the coherence, consistency, and cogency of revelation at the higher. The three chapters of Part Two suggest this role for reason relative to revelation. In guiding the pupil to enlightenment and final release, the teacher first expounds the essential teaching of the revealed Upanishads—the nonduality or identity of Brahman (God) and Atman (Soul). Then the teacher engages the pupil in rational discussion of the teaching, exploring its implications at the lower level. Finally, the teacher has the pupil meditate on the issues discussed until enlightenment is achieved. For Shankara, revelation is master, reason servant.

A Thousand Teachings, like the Buddha's Four Noble Truths (see the introduction to the second section in this text, page 86), sets forth a problem, its cause, the solution, and a method for gaining the solution. First, transmigratory existence is the human predicament. Transmigratory existence is a string of lifetimes connected by karma and (for Shankara but not the Buddha) an eternal Soul (Atman). The karma left over at the end of one lifetime determines the conditions of the next. The transmigrating Soul carries residual karma with it across lifetimes. Each lifetime involves birth, actions creating karma, experiences of suffering resulting from karma, death, and eventually rebirth. Transmigratory existence refers also to the systematic misunderstanding of the situation that prevails throughout each rebirth. A host of individualized egos or psychophysical organisms living out their lives in an objectively real and ever changing world seems to be the situation. That, unfortunately, is not reality; it is a delusion. The heart of the predicament is that humans live totally within this delusion without realizing it, never glimpsing what reality is. Consequently, the eternal Soul is doomed to continue its transmigratory career.

Second, ignorance *(avidya)* is the cause of transmigratory existence. Ignorance casts a mirage across reality, hides it under a deceptive veneer, and wraps it up in false pretenses. Shankara defined ignorance as the mutual superimposition of distortion, of non-Atman on Atman and of Atman on non-Atman. We ignorantly project on Atman (one universal Soul) the distortion of non-Atman (many individualized egos or psychophysical organisms). And we ignorantly project on non-Atman the illusion of Atman, imputing the consciousness of Atman to the unconscious psychophysical organism. In the knowing process at the lower level, Atman reflects its consciousness on the unconscious intellect *(buddhi),* the highest part of the psychophysical organism. But even as the image of a face in a mirror does not truly belong to the mirror, so also the reflection of consciousness in the intellect does not actually belong to the intellect. This is one of several points Shankara borrowed from Sankhya philosophy, substituting the standard Vedanta word for soul *(atman)* for the standard Sankhya term *(purusha).* Through his notion of mutual superimposition of distortion, Shankara explained what ignorance is and how it works. The cause of ignorance, however, he never explained. He left that problem as a legacy to later Advaitins, who struggle with it still.

Third, discriminating knowledge (Jnana Yoga) alone brings final release from transmigratory existence; action (Karma Yoga) is of no avail. Knowledge alone is effective, because knowledge shares the nature of the Soul (Atman). Action does not share that nature. The deception that the Soul acts is part of the superimposition of non-Atman upon Atman. The psychophysical organism, not Atman, acts. The knowledge that brings final release is discriminating knowledge, knowledge that distinguishes Atman from non-Atman. Such knowledge works by denying to Atman everything falsely attributed to it as part of the superimposition. Discriminating knowledge, therefore, is knowledge by negation, "Not this, not so" *(neti neti)*. The knowledge that Atman is pure consciousness (the passive witness, beholder, observer) alone survives the process of distinguishing what Atman is by denying what Atman is not. Pure consciousness cannot be known as an object, for it is always witnessing and never being witnessed. When it looks for itself, all it catches is an image of itself, which, like the face reflected in the mirror, is not the original. Pure consciousness "catches" but is never "caught."

Finally, the identification of Atman (the innermost Self) with Brahman (the Absolute) is the way to discriminate Atman from non-Atman, the reality from the distortion. Identity between any two elements entails that whatever is true of one must also be true of the other. Brahman, according to revelation (the Upanishads), is the Ultimate Reality, hence one, nondual, eternal, unborn, unchanging, unknowable as object, and so on. Since Atman is identical with Brahman ("Thou art That," "I am Brahman"), Atman must also be one, nondual, eternal, unborn, unchanging, unknowable as object, and so on. It follows that everything else we normally impute to Atman is really non-Atman and must be denied, "Not this, not so." Non-Atman may pass as lower truth, but from the vantage point of absolute truth, non-Atman is a deception cast by ignorance. Once this is realized, once Atman is clearly discriminated from non-Atman, misidentification with non-Atman vanishes, identification with the real Atman dawns, transmigratory existence terminates, and final release ensues. The shadow of transmigratory existence may linger, but the lie has been exposed. Reality cannot be fooled by appearances.

*   *   *

For further reading in the six schools of orthodox Indian philosophy, see Chatterjee and Datta, *An Introduction to Indian Philosophy;* M. Hiriyanna, *Outlines of Indian Philosophy;* C. Sharma, *Indian Philosophy: A Critical Survey;* S. Radhakrishnan, *Indian Philosophy,* 2 vols.; P.T. Raju, *The Philosophical Traditions of India;* and P.T. Raju, *Structural Depths of Indian Thought.* For more information on the *Bhagavad Gita,* consult Franklin Edgerton, tr., *The Bhagavad Gita* (New York: Harper & Row, 1964); A.L. Herman, *An Introduction to Indian Thought* (Englewood Cliffs, NJ: Prentice Hall, 1976); Eric Sharpe, *The Universal Gita: Western Images of the Bhagavad Gita, A Bicentenary Survey* (La Salle, IL: Open Court, 1985); Robert Minor, ed., *Modern Indian Interpreters of the Bhagavad Gita* (Albany: SUNY Press, 1986); and Arvind Sharma, *The Hindu Gita: Ancient and Classical Interpretations of the Bhagavadgita* (La Salle, IL: Open Court, 1986). For studies on Patanjali, refer to Aranya Hariharananda, *The Yoga Philosophy of Patanjali,* tr. P.N. Mukerji (Calcutta: University of Calcutta Press, 1963); Mircea Eliade, *Patanjali and Yoga,* tr. Charles Lam Markham (New York: Schocken Books, 1975); Ian Whicher, *The Integrity of the Yoga Darsana: A Reconsideration of Classical Yoga* (Albany: SUNY Press, 1998); and Georg Feuerstein, *The Yoga Tradition: Its History, Literature, Philosophy, and Practice* (Albany: SUNY Press, 1998). Finally, for discussions about Shankara, see Paul Deussen, *The System of the Vedanta,* tr. Charles Johnston (Chicago: Open Court, 1912); Eliot Deutsch, *Advaita Vedanta: A Philosophical Reconstruction* (Honolulu: East-West Center Press, 1969); and Natalia Isayeva, *Shankara and Indian Philosophy* (Albany: SUNY Press, 1992).

THE BHAGAVAD GITA

CHAPTER 1: THE WAR WITHIN

DHRITARASHTRA:

1   O Sanjaya, tell me what happened at Kurukshetra, the field of dharma, where my family and the Pandavas gathered to fight.

SANJAYA:

2   Having surveyed the forces of the Pandavas arrayed for battle, prince Duryodhana
3   approached his teacher, Drona, and spoke. "O my teacher, look at this mighty army of the
4   Pandavas, assembled by your own gifted disciple, Yudhishthira. There are heroic warriors
5   and great archers who are the equals of Bhima and Arjuna: Yuyudhana, Virata, the mighty
6   Drupada, Dhrishtaketu, Chekitana, the valiant king of Kashi, Purujit, Kuntibhoja, the
    great leader Shaibya, the powerful Yudhanianyu, the valiant Uttamaujas, and the son of
    Subhadra, in addition to the sons of Draupadi. All these command mighty chariots.

7   "O best of brahmins, listen to the names of those who are distinguished among our own
8   forces: Bhishma, Karna, and the victorious Kripa; Ashvatthama, Vikarna, and the son
9   of Somadatta. There are many others, too, heroes giving up their lives for my sake, all
10 proficient in war and armed with a variety of weapons. Our army is unlimited and com-
11 manded by Bhishma; theirs is small and commanded by Bhima. Let everyone take his
    proper place and stand firm supporting Bhishma!"

12 Then the powerful Bhishma, the grandsire, oldest of all the Kurus, in order to cheer
13 Duryodhana, roared like a lion and blew his conch horn. And after Bhishma, a tremen-
    dous noise arose of conchs and cowhorns and pounding on drums.

14 Then Sri Krishna and Arjuna, who were standing in a mighty chariot yoked with white
15 horses, blew their divine conchs. Sri Krishna blew the conch named Panchajanya, and
16 Arjuna blew that called Devadatta. The mighty Bhima blew the huge conch Paundra.
17 Yudhishthira, the king, the son of Kunti, blew the conch Anantavijaya; Nakula and
18 Sahadeva blew their conchs as well. Then the king of Kashi, the leading bowman, the
19 great warrior Shikhandi, Dhrishtadyumna, Virata, the invincible Satyaki, Drupada, all
    the sons of Draupadi, and the strong-armed son of Subhadra joined in, and the noise
    tore through the heart of Duryodhana's army. Indeed, the sound was tumultuous, echo-
    ing throughout heaven and earth.

20 Then, O Dhritarashtra, lord of the earth, having seen your son's forces set in their places
    and the fighting about to begin, Arjuna spoke these words to Sri Krishna:

From *The Bhagavad Gita*, translated by Eknath Easwaran, founder of the Blue Mountain Center of Meditation, copyright 1985; reprinted by permission of Nilgiri Press, P.O. Box 256, Tomales, CA 94971, www.nilgiri.org.

ARJUNA:

O Krishna, drive my chariot between the two armies. I want to see those who desire to   21–22
fight with me. With whom will this battle be fought? I want to see those assembled to   23
fight for Duryodhana, those who seek to please the evil-minded son of Dhritarashtra by
engaging in war.

SANJAYA:

Thus Arjuna spoke, and Sri Krishna, driving his splendid chariot between the two   24
armies, facing Bhishma and Drona and all the kings of the earth, said: "Arjuna, behold   25
all the Kurus gathered together."

And Arjuna, standing between the two armies, saw fathers and grandfathers, teachers,   26
uncles, and brothers, sons and grandsons, in-laws and friends. Seeing his kinsmen   27
established in opposition, Arjuna was overcome by sorrow. Despairing, he spoke these
words:

ARJUNA:

O Krishna, I see my own relations here anxious to fight, and my limbs grow weak; my   28–29
mouth is dry, my body shakes, and my hair is standing on end. My skin burns, and the   30
bow Gandiva has slipped from my hand. I am unable to stand; my mind seems to be
whirling. These signs bode evil for us. I do not see that any good can come from killing   31
our relations in battle. O Krishna, I have no desire for victory, or for a kingdom or pleas-   32
ures. Of what use is a kingdom or pleasure or even life, if those for whose sake we   33
desire these things—teachers, fathers, sons, grandfathers, uncles, in-laws, grandsons,   34
and others with family ties—are engaging in this battle, renouncing their wealth and
their lives? Even if they were to kill me, I would not want to kill them, not even to   35
become ruler of the three worlds. How much less for the earth alone?

O Krishna, what satisfaction could we find in killing Dhritarashtra's sons? We would   36
become sinners by slaying these men, even though they are evil. The sons of   37
Dhritarashtra are related to us; therefore, we should not kill them. How can we gain
happiness by killing members of our own family?

Though they are overpowered by greed and see no evil in destroying families or injur-   38
ing friends, *we* see these evils. Why shouldn't we turn away from this sin? When a fam-   39
ily declines, ancient traditions are destroyed. With them are lost the spiritual   40
foundations for life, and the family loses its sense of unity. Where there is no sense of   41
unity, the women of the family become corrupt; and with the corruption of its women,
society is plunged into chaos. Social chaos is hell for the family and for those who have   42
destroyed the family as well. It disrupts the process of spiritual evolution begun by our   43
ancestors. The timeless spiritual foundations of family and society would be destroyed
by these terrible deeds, which violate the unity of life.

It is said that those whose family dharma has been destroyed dwell in hell. This is a   44
great sin! We are prepared to kill our own relations out of greed for the pleasures of a   45

46 kingdom. Better for me if the sons of Dhritarashtra, weapons in hand, were to attack me in battle and kill me unarmed and unresisting.

SANJAYA:

47 Overwhelmed by sorrow, Arjuna spoke these words. And casting away his bow and his arrows, he sat down in his chariot in the middle of the battlefield.

CHAPTER 2: THE ILLUMINED MAN

SANJAYA:

1 These are the words that Sri Krishna spoke to the despairing Arjuna, whose eyes were burning with tears of pity and confusion.

SRI KRISHNA:

2 This despair and weakness in a time of crisis are mean and unworthy of you, Arjuna.
3 How have you fallen into a state so far from the path to liberation? It does not become you to yield to this weakness. Arise with a brave heart and destroy the enemy.

ARJUNA:

4 How can I ever bring myself to fight against Bhishma and Drona, who are worthy of
5 reverence? How can I, Krishna? Surely it would be better to spend my life begging than to kill these great and worthy souls! If I killed them, every pleasure I found would be
6 tainted. I don't even know which would be better, for us to conquer them or for them to conquer us. The sons of Dhritarashtra have confronted us; but why would we care to live if we killed them?

7 My will is paralyzed, and I am utterly confused. Tell me which is the better path for me.
8 Let me be your disciple. I have fallen at your feet; give me instruction. What can overcome a sorrow that saps all my vitality? Even power over men and gods or the wealth of an empire seems empty.

SANJAYA:

9 This is how Arjuna, the great warrior, spoke to Sri Krishna. With the words, "O Krishna, I will not fight," he fell silent.

10 As they stood between the two armies, Sri Krishna smiled and replied to Arjuna, who had sunk into despair.

SRI KRISHNA:

You speak sincerely, but your sorrow has no cause. The wise grieve neither for the liv-   11
ing nor for the dead. There has never been a time when you and I and the kings gath-   12
ered here have not existed, nor will there be a time when we will cease to exist. As the   13
same person inhabits the body through childhood, youth, and old age, so too at the time
of death he attains another body. The wise are not deluded by these changes.

When the senses contact sense objects, a person experiences cold or heat, pleasure or   14
pain. These experiences are fleeting; they come and go. Bear them patiently, Arjuna.
Those who are not affected by these changes, who are the same in pleasure and pain,   15
are truly wise and fit for immortality. Assert your strength and realize this!

The impermanent has no reality; reality lies in the eternal. Those who have seen the   16
boundary between these two have attained the end of all knowledge. Realize that which   17
pervades the universe and is indestructible; no power can affect this unchanging, imperishable reality. The body is mortal, but he who dwells in the body is immortal and   18
immeasurable. Therefore, Arjuna, fight in this battle.

One man believes he is the slayer; another believes he is the slain. Both are ignorant;   19
there is neither slayer nor slain. You were never born; you will never die. You have never   20
changed; you can never change. Unborn, eternal, immutable, immemorial, you do not
die when the body dies. Realizing that which is indestructible, eternal, unborn, and   21
unchanging, how can you slay or cause another to slay?

As a man abandons worn-out clothes and acquires new ones, so when the body is worn   22
out a new one is acquired by the Self, who lives within.

The Self cannot be pierced by weapons or burned by fire; water cannot wet it, nor can the   23
wind dry it. The Self cannot be pierced or burned, made wet or dry. It is everlasting and   24
infinite, standing on the motionless foundations of eternity. The Self is unmanifested,   25
beyond all thought, beyond all change. Knowing this, you should not grieve.

O mighty Arjuna, even if you believe the Self to be subject to birth and death, you   26
should not grieve. Death is inevitable for the living; birth is inevitable for the dead.   27
Since these are unavoidable, you should not sorrow. Every creature is unmanifested at   28
first and then attains manifestation. When its end has come, it once again becomes
unmanifested. What is there to lament in this?

The glory of the Self is beheld by a few, and a few describe it; a few listen but many   29
without understanding. The Self of all beings, living within the body, is eternal and can-   30
not be harmed. Therefore, do not grieve.

Considering your dharma, you should not vacillate. For a warrior, nothing is higher than   31
a war against evil. The warrior confronted with such a war should be pleased, Arjuna,   32
for it comes as an open gate to heaven. But if you do not participate in this battle against   33
evil, you will incur sin, violating your dharma and your honor.

The story of your dishonor will be repeated endlessly: and for a man of honor, dishonor   34
is worse than death. These brave warriors will think you have withdrawn from battle out   35

36   of fear, and those who formerly esteemed you will treat you with disrespect. Your enemies will ridicule your strength and say things that should not be said. What could be
more painful than this?

37   Death means the attainment of heaven; victory means the enjoyment of the earth.
38   Therefore rise up, Arjuna, resolved to fight! Having made yourself alike in pain and
pleasure, profit and loss, victory and defeat, engage in this great battle and you will be
freed from sin.

39   You have heard the intellectual explanation of Sankhya, Arjuna; now listen to the prin-
40   ciples of yoga. By practicing these you can break through the bonds of karma. On this
path effort never goes to waste, and there is no failure. Even a little effort toward spiritual awareness will protect you from the greatest fear.

41   Those who follow this path, resolving deep within themselves to seek Me alone, attain
singleness of purpose. For those who lack resolution, the decisions of life are many-
branched and endless.

42   There are ignorant people who speak flowery words and take delight in the letter of the
43   law, saying that there is nothing else. Their hearts are full of selfish desires, Arjuna.
Their idea of heaven is their own enjoyment, and the aim of all their activities is pleas-
44   ure and power. The fruit of their actions is continual rebirth. Those whose minds are
swept away by the pursuit of pleasure and power are incapable of following the
supreme goal and will not attain samadhi.

45   The scriptures describe the three gunas. But you should be free from the action of the
gunas, established in eternal truth, self-controlled, without any sense of duality or the
desire to acquire and hoard.

46   Just as a reservoir is of little use when the whole countryside is flooded, scriptures are
of little use to the illumined man or woman, who sees the Lord everywhere.

47   You have the right to work, but never to the fruit of work. You should never engage in
48   action for the sake of reward, nor should you long for inaction. Perform work in this
world, Arjuna, as a man established within himself—without selfish attachments, and
alike in success and defeat. For yoga is perfect evenness of mind.

49   Seek refuge in the attitude of detachment and you will amass the wealth of spiritual
awareness. Those who are motivated only by desire for the fruits of action are miser-
50   able, for they are constantly anxious about the results of what they do. When consciousness is unified, however, all vain anxiety is left behind. There is no cause for
worry, whether things go well or ill. Therefore, devote yourself to the disciplines of
yoga, for yoga is skill in action.

51   The wise unify their consciousness and abandon attachment to the fruits of action,
which binds a person to continual rebirth. Thus they attain a state beyond all evil.

52   When your mind has overcome the confusion of duality, you will attain the state of holy
53   indifference to things you hear and things you have heard. When you are unmoved by

the confusion of ideas and your mind is completely united in deep samadhi, you will attain the state of perfect yoga.

ARJUNA:

Tell me of those who live established in wisdom, ever aware of the Self, O Krishna. How do they talk? How sit? How move about?   54

SRI KRISHNA:

They live in wisdom who see themselves in all and all in them, who have renounced every selfish desire and sense craving tormenting the heart.   55

Neither agitated by grief nor hankering after pleasure, they live free from lust and fear and anger. Established in meditation, they are truly wise. Fettered no more by selfish attachments, they are neither elated by good fortune nor depressed by bad. Such are the seers. Even as a tortoise draws in its limbs, the wise can draw in their senses at will. Aspirants abstain from sense pleasures, but they still crave for them. These cravings all disappear when they see the highest goal. Even of those who tread the path, the stormy senses can sweep off the mind. They live in wisdom who subdue their senses and keep their minds ever absorbed in me.   56 57 58 59 60 61

When you keep thinking about sense objects, attachment comes. Attachment breeds desire, the lust of possession that burns to anger. Anger clouds the judgment; you can no longer learn from past mistakes. Lost is the power to choose between what is wise and what is unwise, and your life is utter waste. But when you move amidst the world of sense, free from attachment and aversion alike, there comes the peace in which all sorrows end, and you live in the wisdom of the Self.   62 63 64 65

The disunited mind is far from wise; how can it meditate? How be at peace? When you know no peace, how can you know joy? When you let your mind follow the call of the senses, they carry away your better judgment as storms drive a boat off its charted course on the sea.   66 67

Use all your power to free the senses from attachment and aversion alike, and live in the full wisdom of the Self. Such a sage awakes to light in the night of all creatures. That which the world calls day is the night of ignorance to the wise.   68 69

As rivers flow into the ocean but cannot make the vast ocean overflow, so flow the streams of the sense-world into the sea of peace that is the sage. But this is not so with the desirer of desires.   70

They are forever free who renounce all selfish desires and break away from the ego-cage of "I," "me," and "mine" to be united with the Lord. This is the supreme state. Attain to this, and pass from death to immortality.   71

CHAPTER 3: SELFLESS SERVICE

ARJUNA:

1 O Krishna, you have said that knowledge is greater than action; why then do you ask
2 me to wage this terrible war? Your advice seems inconsistent. Give me one path to follow to the supreme good.

SRI KRISHNA:

3 At the beginning of time I declared two paths for the pure heart: *jnana yoga*, the con-
templative path of spiritual wisdom, and *karma yoga*, the active path of selfless service.

4 He who shirks action does not attain freedom; no one can gain perfection by abstaining
5 from work. Indeed, there is no one who rests for even an instant; every creature is driv-
en to action by his own nature.

6 Those who abstain from action while allowing the mind to dwell on sensual pleasure
7 cannot be called sincere spiritual aspirants. But they excel who control their senses
through the mind, using them for selfless service.

8 Fulfill all your duties; action is better than inaction. Even to maintain your body,
9 Arjuna, you are obliged to act. Selfish action imprisons the world. Act selflessly, without any thought of personal profit.

10 At the beginning, mankind and the obligation of selfless service were created together.
"Through selfless service, you will always be fruitful and find the fulfillment of your
desires": this is the promise of the Creator.

11 Honor and cherish the devas as they honor and cherish you; through this honor and love
12 you will attain the supreme good. All human desires are fulfilled by the devas, who are
pleased by selfless service. But anyone who enjoys the things given by the devas without offering selfless acts in return is a thief.

13 The spiritually minded, who eat in the spirit of service, are freed from all their sins; but
14 the selfish, who prepare food for their own satisfaction, eat sin. Living creatures are
nourished by food, and food is nourished by rain; rain itself is the water of life, which
comes from selfless worship and service.

15 Every selfless act, Arjuna, is born from Brahman, the eternal, infinite Godhead. He is
16 present in every act of service. All life turns on this law, O Arjuna. Whoever violates it,
indulging his senses for his own pleasure and ignoring the needs of others, has wasted
17 his life. But those who realize the Self are always satisfied. Having found the source of
18 joy and fulfillment, they no longer seek happiness from the external world. They have
nothing to gain or lose by any action; neither people nor things can affect their security.

19 Strive constantly to serve the welfare of the world; by devotion to selfless work one
20 attains the supreme goal of life. Do your work with the welfare of others always in

mind. It was by such work that Janaka attained perfection; others, too, have followed this path.

What the outstanding person does, others will try to do. The standards such people create will be followed by the whole world. There is nothing in the three worlds for me to gain, Arjuna, nor is there anything I do not have; I continue to act, but I am not driven by any need of my own. If I ever refrained from continuous work, everyone would immediately follow my example. If I stopped working, I would be the cause of cosmic chaos, and finally of the destruction of this world and these people. 21 22 23 24

The ignorant work for their own profit, Arjuna; the wise work for the welfare of the world, without thought for themselves. By abstaining from work you will confuse the ignorant, who are engrossed in their actions. Perform all work carefully, guided by compassion. 25 26

All actions are performed by the gunas of prakriti. Deluded by his identification with the ego, a person thinks, "*I* am the doer." But the illumined man or woman understands the domain of the gunas and is not attached. Such people know that the gunas interact with each other; they do not claim to be the doer. 27 28

Those who are deluded by the operation of the gunas become attached to the results of their action. Those who understand these truths should not unsettle the ignorant. Performing all actions for my sake, completely absorbed in the Self, and without expectations, fight!—but stay free from the fever of the ego. 29 30

Those who live in accordance with these divine laws without complaining, firmly established in faith, are released from karma. Those who violate these laws, criticizing and complaining, are utterly deluded, and are the cause of their own suffering. 31 32

Even a wise man acts within the limitations of his own nature. Every creature is subject to prakriti; what is the use of repression? The senses have been conditioned by attraction to the pleasant and aversion to the unpleasant. Do not be ruled by them; they are obstacles in your path. 33 34

It is better to strive in one's own dharma than to succeed in the dharma of another. Nothing is ever lost in following one's own dharma, but competition in another's dharma breeds fear and insecurity. 35

ARJUNA:

What is the force that binds us to selfish deeds, O Krishna? What power moves us, even against our will, as if forcing us? 36

SRI KRISHNA:

It is selfish desire and anger, arising from the guna of rajas; these are the appetites and evils which threaten a person in this life. 37

38
39   Just as a fire is covered by smoke and a mirror is obscured by dust, just as the embryo rests deep within the womb, knowledge is hidden by selfish desire—hidden, Arjuna, by this unquenchable fire for self-satisfaction, the inveterate enemy of the wise.

40
41   Selfish desire is found in the senses, mind, and intellect, misleading them and burying the understanding in delusion. Fight with all your strength, Arjuna! Controlling your senses, conquer your enemy, the destroyer of knowledge and realization.

42
43   The senses are higher than the body, the mind higher than the senses; above the mind is the intellect, and above the intellect is the Atman. Thus, knowing that which is supreme, let the Atman rule the ego. Use your mighty arms to slay the fierce enemy that is selfish desire.

Chapter 4: Wisdom in Action

Sri Krishna:

1   I told this eternal secret to Vivasvat. Vivasvat taught Manu, and Manu taught Ikshvaku.
2   Thus, Arjuna, eminent sages received knowledge of yoga in a continuous tradition. But through time the practice of yoga was lost in the world.

3   The secret of these teachings is profound. I have explained them to you today because you are my friend and devotee.

Arjuna:

4   You were born much after Vivasvat; he lived very long ago. Why do you say that you taught this yoga in the beginning?

Sri Krishna:

5   You and I have passed through many births, Arjuna. You have forgotten, but I remember them all.

6   My true being is unborn and changeless. I am the Lord who dwells in every creature. Through the power of my own maya, I manifest myself in a finite form.

7
8   Whenever dharma declines and the purpose of life is forgotten, I manifest myself on earth. I am born in every age to protect the good, to destroy evil, and to re-establish dharma.

9
10   He who knows me as his own divine Self breaks through the belief that he is the body and is not reborn as a separate creature. Such a one, Arjuna, is united with me. Delivered from selfish attachment, fear, and anger, filled with me, surrendering themselves to me, purified in the fire of my being, many have reached the state of unity in me.

As men approach me, so I receive them. All paths, Arjuna, lead to me. Those desiring   11
success in their actions worship the gods; through action in the world of mortals, their   12
desires are quickly fulfilled.

The distinctions of caste, guna, and karma have come from me. I am their cause, but I   13
myself am changeless and beyond all action. Actions do not cling to me because I am   14
not attached to their results. Those who understand this and practice it live in freedom.
Knowing this truth, aspirants desiring liberation in ancient times engaged in action. You   15
too can do the same, pursuing an active life in the manner of those ancient sages.

What is action and what is inaction? This question has confused the greatest sages. I   16
will give you the secret of action, with which you can free yourself from bondage. The   17
true nature of action is difficult to grasp. You must understand what is action and what
is inaction, and what kind of action should be avoided.

The wise see that there is action in the midst of inaction and inaction in the midst of   18
action. Their consciousness is unified, and every act is done with complete awareness.

The awakened sages call a person wise when all his undertakings are free from anxiety   19
about results; all his selfish desires have been consumed in the fire of knowledge. The   20
wise, ever satisfied, have abandoned all external supports. Their security is unaffected
by the results of their action; even while acting, they really do nothing at all. Free from   21
expectations and from all sense of possession, with mind and body firmly controlled by
the Self, they do not incur sin by the performance of physical action.

They live in freedom who have gone beyond the dualities of life. Competing with no   22
one, they are alike in success and failure and content with whatever comes to them.
They are free, without selfish attachments; their minds are fixed in knowledge. They   23
perform all work in the spirit of service, and their karma is dissolved.

The process of offering is Brahman; that which is offered is Brahman. Brahman offers   24
the sacrifice in the fire of Brahman. Brahman is attained by those who see Brahman in
every action.

Some aspirants offer material sacrifices to the gods. Others offer selfless service as sac-   25
rifice in the fire of Brahman. Some renounce all enjoyment of the senses, sacrificing   26
them in the fire of sense restraint. Others partake of sense objects but offer them in service through the fire of the senses. Some offer the workings of the senses and the vital   27
forces through the fire of self-control, kindled in the path of knowledge.

Some offer wealth; others offer sense restraint and suffering. Some take vows and offer   28
knowledge and study of the scriptures; and some make the offering of meditation.
Some offer the forces of vitality, regulating their inhalation and exhalation, and thus   29
gain control over these forces. Others offer the forces of vitality through restraint of   30
their senses. All these understand the meaning of service and will be cleansed of their
impurities.

True sustenance is in service, and through it a man or woman reaches the eternal   31
Brahman. But those who do not seek to serve are without a home in this world. Arjuna,
how can they be at home in any world to come?

32   These offerings are born of work, and each guides mankind along a path to Brahman.
33   Understanding this, you will attain liberation. The offering of wisdom is better than any material offering, Arjuna; for the goal of all work is spiritual wisdom.

34   Approach someone who has realized the purpose of life and question him with rever-
35   ence and devotion; he will instruct you in this wisdom. Once you attain it, you will never again be deluded. You will see all creatures in the Self, and all in me.

36   Even if you were the most sinful of sinners, Arjuna, you could cross beyond all sin by
37   the raft of spiritual wisdom. As the heat of a fire reduces wood to ashes, the fire of
38   knowledge burns to ashes all karma. Nothing in this world purifies like spiritual wis- dom. It is the perfection achieved in time through the path of yoga, the path which leads to the Self within.

39   Those who take wisdom as their highest goal, whose faith is deep and whose senses are
40   trained, attain wisdom quickly and enter into perfect peace. But the ignorant, indecisive and lacking in faith, waste their lives. They can never be happy in this world or any other.

41   Those established in the Self have renounced selfish attachments to their actions and cut through doubts with spiritual wisdom. They act in freedom. Arjuna, cut through this doubt in your heart with the sword of spiritual wisdom. Arise; take up the path of yoga!

CHAPTER 5: RENOUNCE & REJOICE

ARJUNA:

1   O Krishna, you have recommended both the path of selfless action and *sannyasa*, the path of renunciation of action. Tell me definitely which is better.

SRI KRISHNA:

2   Both renunciation of action and the selfless performance of action lead to the supreme goal. But the path of action is better than renunciation.

3   Those who have attained perfect renunciation are free from any sense of duality; they are unaffected by likes and dislikes, Arjuna, and are free from the bondage of self-will.
4   The immature think that knowledge and action are different, but the wise see them as the same. The person who is established in one path will attain the rewards of both.
5   The goal of knowledge and the goal of service are the same; those who fail to see this are blind.

6   Perfect renunciation is difficult to attain without performing action. But the wise, fol- lowing the path of selfless service, quickly reach Brahman.

Those who follow the path of service, who have completely purified themselves and conquered their senses and self-will, see the Self in all creatures and are untouched by any action they perform. 7

Those who know this truth, whose consciousness is unified, think always, "I am not the doer." While seeing or hearing, touching or smelling; eating, moving about, or sleeping; breathing or speaking, letting go or holding on, even opening or closing the eyes, they understand that these are only the movements of the senses among sense objects. 8 9

Those who surrender to Brahman all selfish attachments are like the leaf of a lotus floating clean and dry in water. Sin cannot touch them. Renouncing their selfish attachments, those who follow the path of service work with body, senses, and mind for the sake of self-purification. 10 11

Those whose consciousness is unified abandon all attachment to the results of action and attain supreme peace. But those whose desires are fragmented, who are selfishly attached to the results of their work, are bound in everything they do. 12

Those who renounce attachment in all their deeds live content in the "city of nine gates," the body, as its master. They are not driven to act, nor do they involve others in action. 13

Neither the sense of acting, nor actions, nor the connection of cause and effect comes from the Lord of this world. These three arise from nature. 14

The Lord does not partake in the good and evil deeds of any person; judgment is clouded when wisdom is obscured by ignorance. But ignorance is destroyed by knowledge of the Self within. The light of this knowledge shines like the sun, revealing the supreme Brahman. Those who cast off sin through this knowledge, absorbed in the Lord and established in him as their one goal and refuge, are not reborn as separate creatures. 15 16 17

Those who possess this wisdom have equal regard for all. They see the same Self in a spiritual aspirant and an outcaste, in an elephant, a cow, and a dog. Such people have mastered life. With even mind they rest in Brahman, who is perfect and is everywhere the same. They are not elated by good fortune nor depressed by bad. With mind established in Brahman, they are free from delusion. Not dependent on any external support, they realize the joy of spiritual awareness. With consciousness unified through meditation, they live in abiding joy. 18 19 20 21

Pleasures conceived in the world of the senses have a beginning and an end and give birth to misery, Arjuna. The wise do not look for happiness in them. But those who overcome the impulses of lust and anger which arise in the body are made whole and live in joy. They find their joy, their rest, and their light completely within themselves. United with the Lord, they attain nirvana in Brahman. 22 23 24

Healed of their sins and conflicts, working for the good of all beings, the holy sages attain nirvana in Brahman. Free from anger and selfish desire, unified in mind, those who follow the path of yoga and realize the Self are established forever in that supreme state. 25 26

27 Closing their eyes, steadying their breathing, and focusing their attention on the center of
28 spiritual consciousness, the wise master their senses, mind, and intellect through medita-
    tion. Self-realization is their only goal. Freed from selfish desire, fear, and anger, they live
29 in freedom always. Knowing me as the friend of all creatures, the Lord of the universe,
    the end of all offerings and all spiritual disciplines, they attain eternal peace.

CHAPTER 6: THE PRACTICE OF MEDITATION

SRI KRISHNA:

1   It is not those who lack energy or refrain from action, but those who work without
    expectation of reward who attain the goal of meditation. Theirs is true renunciation.
2   Therefore, Arjuna, you should understand that renunciation and the performance of
    selfless service are the same. Those who cannot renounce attachment to the results of
    their work are far from the path.

3   For aspirants who want to climb the mountain of spiritual awareness, the path is self-
4   less work; for those who have ascended to yoga the path is stillness and peace. When a
    person has freed himself from attachment to the results of work, and from desires for
    the enjoyment of sense objects, he ascends to the unitive state.

5   Reshape yourself through the power of your will; never let yourself be degraded by self-
    will. The will is the only friend of the Self, and the will is the only enemy of the Self.

6   To those who have conquered themselves, the will is a friend. But it is the enemy of
    those who have not found the Self within them.

7   The supreme Reality stands revealed in the consciousness of those who have con-
    quered themselves. They live in peace, alike in cold and heat, pleasure and pain, praise
    and blame.

8   They are completely fulfilled by spiritual wisdom and Self-realization. Having con-
    quered their senses, they have climbed to the summit of human consciousness. To such
9   people a clod of dirt, a stone, and gold are the same. They are equally disposed to fam-
    ily, enemies, and friends, to those who support them and those who are hostile, to the
    good and the evil alike. Because they are impartial, they rise to great heights.

10 Those who aspire to the state of yoga should seek the Self in inner solitude through
    meditation. With body and mind controlled they should constantly practice one-
    pointedness, free from expectations and attachment to material possessions.

11 Select a clean spot, neither too high nor too low, and seat yourself firmly on a cloth, a
12 deerskin, and kusha grass. Then, once seated, strive to still your thoughts. Make your
13 mind one-pointed in meditation, and your heart will be purified. Hold your body, head,
14 and neck firmly in a straight line, and keep your eyes from wandering. With all fears
    dissolved in the peace of the Self and all desires dedicated to Brahman, controlling the
15 mind and fixing it on me, sit in meditation with me as your only goal. With senses and
    mind constantly controlled through meditation, united with the Self within, an aspirant
    attains nirvana, the state of abiding joy and peace in me.

Arjuna, those who eat too much or eat too little, who sleep too much or sleep too little,   16
will not succeed in meditation. But those who are temperate in eating and sleeping,   17
work and recreation, will come to the end of sorrow through meditation. Through con-   18
stant effort they learn to withdraw the mind from selfish cravings and absorb it in the
Self. Thus they attain the state of union.

When meditation is mastered, the mind is unwavering like the flame of a lamp in a   19
windless place. In the still mind, in the depths of meditation, the Self reveals itself.   20
Beholding the Self by means of the Self, an aspirant knows the joy and peace of complete fulfillment. Having attained that abiding joy beyond the senses, revealed in the   21
stilled mind, he never swerves from the eternal truth. He desires nothing else, and can-   22
not be shaken by the heaviest burden of sorrow.

The practice of meditation frees one from all affliction. This is the path of yoga. Follow   23
it with determination and sustained enthusiasm. Renouncing wholeheartedly all selfish   24
desires and expectations, use your will to control the senses. Little by little, through   25
patience and repeated effort, the mind will become stilled in the Self.

Wherever the mind wanders, restless and diffuse in its search for satisfaction without,   26
lead it within; train it to rest in the Self. Abiding joy comes to those who still the mind.   27
Freeing themselves from the taint of self-will, with their consciousness unified, they
become one with Brahman.

The infinite joy of touching Brahman is easily attained by those who are free from the   28
burden of evil and established within themselves. They see the Self in every creature   29
and all creation in the Self. With consciousness unified through meditation, they see
everything with an equal eye.

I am ever present to those who have realized me in every creature. Seeing all life as   30
my manifestation, they are never separated from me. They worship me in the hearts of   31
all, and all their actions proceed from me. Wherever they may live, they abide
in me.

When a person responds to the joys and sorrows of others as if they were his own, he   32
has attained the highest state of spiritual union.

ARJUNA:

O Krishna, the stillness of divine union which you describe is beyond my comprehen-   33
sion. How can the mind, which is so restless, attain lasting peace? Krishna, the mind is   34
restless, turbulent, powerful, violent; trying to control it is like trying to tame the wind.

SRI KRISHNA:

It is true that the mind is restless and difficult to control. But it can be conquered,   35
Arjuna, through regular practice and detachment. Those who lack self-control will find   36
it difficult to progress in meditation; but those who are self-controlled, striving earnestly through the right means, will attain the goal.

ARJUNA:

37 Krishna, what happens to the man who has faith but who lacks self-control and wan-
38 ders from the path, not attaining success in yoga? If a man becomes deluded on the spiritual path, will he lose the support of both worlds, like a cloud scattered in the sky?
39 Krishna, you can dispel all doubts; remove this doubt which binds me.

SRI KRISHNA:

40 Arjuna, my son, such a person will not be destroyed. No one who does good work will
ever come to a bad end, either here or in the world to come.

41 When such people die, they go to other realms where the righteous live. They dwell
there for countless years and then are reborn into a home which is pure and prosperous.
42 Or they may be born into a family where meditation is practiced; to be born into such
43 a family is extremely rare. The wisdom they have acquired in previous lives will be
44 reawakened, Arjuna, and they will strive even harder for Self-realization. Indeed, they
will be driven on by the strength of their past disciplines. Even one who inquires after
the practice of meditation rises above those who simply perform rituals.

45 Through constant effort over many lifetimes, a person becomes purified of all selfish
desires and attains the supreme goal of life.

46 Meditation is superior to severe asceticism and the path of knowledge. It is also supe-
47 rior to selfless service. May you attain the goal of meditation, Arjuna! Even among
those who meditate, that man or woman who worships me with perfect faith, completely absorbed in me, is the most firmly established in yoga.

CHAPTER 7: WISDOM FROM REALIZATION

SRI KRISHNA:

1 With your mind intent on me, Arjuna, discipline yourself with the practice of yoga.
Depend on me completely. Listen, and I will dispel all your doubts; you will come to
know me fully and be united with me.

2 I will give you both jnana and vijnana. When both these are realized, there is nothing
more you need to know.

3 One person in many thousands may seek perfection, yet of these only a few reach the
4 goal and come to realize me. Earth, water, fire, air, *akasha,* mind, intellect, and ego—
5 these are the eight divisions of my prakriti. But beyond this I have another, higher
nature, Arjuna; it supports the whole universe and is the source of life in all beings.

6 In these two aspects of my nature is the womb of all creation. The birth and dissolution
7 of the cosmos itself take place in me. There is nothing that exists separate from me,
Arjuna. The entire universe is suspended from me as my necklace of jewels.

Arjuna, I am the taste of pure water and the radiance of the sun and moon. I am the 8
sacred word and the sound heard in air, and the courage of human beings. I am the 9
sweet fragrance in the earth and the radiance of fire; I am the life in every creature and
the striving of the spiritual aspirant.

My eternal seed, Arjuna, is to be found in every creature. I am the power of discrimi- 10
nation in those who are intelligent, and the glory of the noble. In those who are strong, 11
I am strength, free from passion and selfish attachment. I am desire itself, if that desire
is in harmony with the purpose of life.

The states of sattva, rajas, and tamas come from me, but I am not in them. These three 12
gunas deceive the world: people fail to look beyond them to me, supreme and imper- 13
ishable. The three gunas make up my divine maya, difficult to overcome. But they cross 14
over this maya who take refuge in me. Others are deluded by maya; performing evil 15
deeds, they have no devotion to me. Having lost all discrimination, they follow the way
of their lower nature.

Good people come to worship me for different reasons. Some come to the spiritual life 16
because of suffering, some in order to understand life; some come through a desire to
achieve life's purpose, and some come who are men and women of wisdom. Unwavering
in devotion, always united with me, the man or woman of wisdom surpasses all the oth- 17
ers. To them I am the dearest beloved, and they are very dear to me. All those who follow the spiritual path are blessed. But the wise who are always established in union, for 18
whom there is no higher goal than me, may be regarded as my very Self. After many
births the wise seek refuge in me, seeing me everywhere and in everything. 19

Such great souls are very rare. There are others whose discrimination is misled by many 20
desires. Following their own nature, they worship lower gods, practicing various rites.

When a person is devoted to something with complete faith, I unify his faith in that. 21
Then, when his faith is completely unified, he gains the object of his devotion. In this 22
way, every desire is fulfilled by me. Those whose understanding is small attain only 23
transient satisfaction: those who worship the gods go to the gods. But my devotees
come to me.

Through lack of understanding, people believe that I, the Unmanifest, have entered into 24
some form. They fail to realize my true nature, which transcends birth and death. Few 25
see through the veil of maya. The world, deluded, does not know that I am without birth
and changeless. I know everything about the past, the present, and the future, Arjuna; 26
but there is no one who knows me completely.

Delusion arises from the duality of attraction and aversion, Arjuna; every creature is 27
deluded by these from birth. But those who have freed themselves from all wrongdoing 28
are firmly established in worship of me. Their actions are pure, and they are free from
the delusion caused by the pairs of opposites.

Those who take refuge in me, striving for liberation from old age and death, come to 29
know Brahman, the Self, and the nature of all action. Those who see me ruling the cos- 30
mos, who see me in the *adhibhuta*, the *adhidaiva*, and the *adhiyajna*, are conscious of
me even at the time of death.

CHAPTER 8: THE ETERNAL GODHEAD

ARJUNA:

1   O Krishna, what is Brahman, and what is the nature of action? What is the *adhyatma,* the *adhibhuta,* the *adhidaiva?*

2   What is the *adhiyajna,* the supreme sacrifice, and how is it to be offered? How are the self-controlled united with you at the time of death?

SRI KRISHNA:

3   My highest nature, the imperishable Brahman, gives every creature its existence and lives in every creature as adhyatma. My action is creation and the bringing forth of crea-
4   tures. The adhibhuta is perishable body; the adhidaiva is Purusha, eternal spirit. The adhiyajna, the supreme sacrifice, is made to me as the Lord within you.

5   Those who remember me at the time of death will come to me. Do not doubt this.
6   Whatever occupies the mind at the time of death determines the destination of the
7   dying; always they will tend toward that state of being. Therefore, remember me at all times and fight on. With your heart and mind intent on me, you will surely come to me.
8   When you make your mind one-pointed through regular practice of meditation, you will find the supreme glory of the Lord.

9   The Lord is the supreme poet, the first cause, the sovereign ruler, subtler than the tini-est particle, the support of all, inconceivable, bright as the sun, beyond darkness.
10   Remembering him in this way at the time of death, through devotion and the power of meditation, with your mind completely stilled and your concentration fixed in the center of spiritual awareness between the eyebrows, you will realize the supreme Lord.

11   I will tell you briefly of the eternal state all scriptures affirm, which can be entered only by those who are self-controlled and free from selfish passions. Those whose lives are dedicated to Brahman attain this supreme goal.

12   Remembering me at the time of death, close down the doors of the senses and place the mind in the heart, Then, while absorbed in meditation, focus all energy upwards to the
13   head, Repeating in this state the divine Name, the syllable *Om* that represents the change-less Brahman, you will go forth from the body and attain the supreme goal.

14   I am easily attained by the person who always remembers me and is attached to nothing
15   else. Such a person is a true yogi, Arjuna. Great souls make their lives perfect and dis-
16   cover me; they are freed from mortality and the suffering of this separate existence. Every creature in the universe is subject to rebirth, Arjuna, except the one who is united with me.

17   Those who understand the cosmic laws know that the Day of Brahma ends after a thou-
18   sand yugas and the Night of Brahma ends after a thousand yugas. When the day of Brahma dawns, forms are brought forth from the Unmanifest; when the night of

Brahma comes, these forms merge in the Formless again. This multitude of beings is   19
created and destroyed again and again in the succeeding days and nights of Brahma.
But beyond this formless state there is another, unmanifested reality, which is eternal   20
and is not dissolved when the cosmos is destroyed. Those who realize life's supreme
goal know that I am unmanifested and unchanging. Having come home to me, they   21
never return to separate existence.

This supreme Lord who pervades all existence, the true Self of all creatures, may be   22
realized through undivided love.

There are two paths, Arjuna, which the soul may follow at the time of death. One leads   23
to rebirth and the other to liberation.

The six months of the northern path of the sun, the path of light, of fire, of day, of the   24
bright fortnight, leads knowers of Brahman to the supreme goal. The six months of the   25
southern path of the sun, the path of smoke, of night, of the dark fortnight, leads other
souls to the light of the moon and to rebirth.

These two paths, the light and the dark, are said to be eternal, leading some to libera-   26
tion and others to rebirth. Once you have known these two paths, Arjuna, you can never   27
be deluded again, Attain this knowledge through perseverance in yoga. There is merit   28
in studying the scriptures, in selfless service, austerity, and giving, but the practice of
meditation carries you beyond all these to the supreme abode of the highest Lord.

CHAPTER 9: THE ROYAL PATH

SRI KRISHNA:

Because of your faith, I shall tell you the most profound secrets: obtaining both jnana   1
and vijnana you will be free from all evil.

This royal knowledge, this royal secret, is the greatest purifier. Righteous and imper-   2
ishable, it is a joy to practice and can be directly experienced. But those who have no   3
faith in the supreme law of life do not find me, Arjuna. They return to the world, passing from death to death.

I pervade the entire universe in my unmanifested form. All creatures find their existence   4
in me, but I am not limited by them. Behold my divine mystery! These creatures do not   5
really dwell in me, and though I bring them forth and support them, I am not confined
within them. They move in me as the winds move in every direction in space.   6

At the end of the eon these creatures return to unmanifested matter; at the beginning of   7
the next cycle I send them forth again. Controlling my prakriti, again and again I bring   8
forth these myriad forms and subject them to the laws of prakriti. None of these actions   9
bind me, Arjuna. I am unattached to them, so they do not disturb my nature.

10   Under my watchful eye the laws of nature take their course. Thus is the world set in motion; thus the animate and the inanimate are created.

11   The foolish do not look beyond physical appearances to see my true nature as the Lord
12   of all creation. The knowledge of such deluded people is empty; their lives are fraught with disaster and evil and their work and hopes are all in vain.

13   But truly great souls seek my divine nature. They worship me with a one-pointed mind,
14   having realized that I am the eternal source of all. Constantly striving, they make firm their resolve and worship me without wavering. Full of devotion, they sing of my divine glory.

15   Others follow the path of jnana, spiritual wisdom. They see that where there is One, that One is me; where there are many, all are me; they see my face everywhere.

16   I am the ritual and the sacrifice; I am true medicine and the mantram. I am the offering and the fire which consumes it, and he to whom it is offered.

17   I am the father and mother of this universe, and its grandfather too; I am its entire support. I am the sum of all knowledge, the purifier, the syllable *Om;* I am the sacred scriptures, the Rik, Yajur, and Sama Vedas.

18   I am the goal of life, the Lord and support of all, the inner witness, the abode of all. I am the only refuge, the one true friend; I am the beginning, the staying, and the end of creation; I am the womb and the eternal seed.

19   I am heat; I give and withhold the rain. I am immortality and I am death; I am what is and what is not.

20   Those who follow the rituals given in the Vedas, who offer sacrifices and take soma, free themselves from evil and attain the vast heaven of the gods, where they enjoy celes-
21   tial pleasures. When they have enjoyed these fully, their merit is exhausted and they return to this land of death. Thus observing Vedic rituals but caught in an endless chain of desires, they come and go.

22   Those who worship me and meditate on me constantly, without any other thought, I will provide for all their needs.

23   Those who worship other gods with faith and devotion also worship me, Arjuna, even
24   if they do not observe the usual forms. I am the object of all worship, its enjoyer and
25   Lord. But those who fail to realize my true nature must be reborn. Those who worship the devas will go to the realm of the devas; those who worship their ancestors will be united with them after death. Those who worship phantoms will become phantoms; but my devotees will come to me.

26   Whatever I am offered in devotion with a pure heart—a leaf, a flower, fruit, or water—
27   I partake of that love offering. Whatever you do, make it an offering to me—the food
28   you eat, the sacrifices you make, the help you give, even your suffering. In this way you will be freed from the bondage of karma, and from its results both pleasant and painful. Then, firm in renunciation and yoga, with your heart free, you will come to me.

I look upon all creatures equally; none are less dear to me and none more dear. But   29
those who worship me with love live in me, and I come to life in them.

Even a sinner becomes holy when he worships me alone with firm resolve. Quickly his   30
soul conforms to dharma and he attains to boundless peace. Never forget this, Arjuna: 31
no one who is devoted to me will ever come to harm.

All those who take refuge in me, whatever their birth, race, sex, or caste, will attain the   32
supreme goal; this realization can be attained even by those whom society scorns. Kings   33
and sages too seek this goal with devotion. Therefore, having been born in this transient
and forlorn world, give all your love to me. Fill your mind with me; love me; serve me;   34
worship me always. Seeking me in your heart, you will at last be united with me.

CHAPTER 10: DIVINE SPLENDOR

SRI KRISHNA:

Listen further, Arjuna, to my supreme teaching, which gives you such joy. Desiring   1
your welfare, O strong-armed warrior, I will tell you more.

Neither gods nor sages know my origin, for I am the source from which the gods and   2
sages come. Whoever knows me as the Lord of all creation, without birth or beginning,   3
knows the truth and frees himself from all evil.

Discrimination, wisdom, understanding, forgiveness, truth, self-control, and peace of   4
mind; pleasure and pain, birth and death, fear and courage, honor and infamy; nonvio-   5
lence, charity, equanimity, contentment, and perseverance in spiritual disciplines—all
the different qualities found in living creatures have their source in me.

The seven great sages and the four ancient ancestors were born from my mind and   6
received my power. From them came all the creatures of this world. Whoever under-   7
stands my power and the mystery of my manifestations comes without doubt to be united with me.

I am the source from which all creatures evolve. The wise remember this and worship   8
me with loving devotion. Their thoughts are all absorbed in me, and all their vitality   9
flows to me. Teaching one another, talking about me always, they are happy and fulfilled.

To those steadfast in love and devotion I give spiritual wisdom, so that they may come   10
to me. Out of compassion I destroy the darkness of their ignorance. From within them   11
I light the lamp of wisdom and dispel all darkness from their lives.

ARJUNA:

You are Brahman supreme, the highest abode, the supreme purifier, the divine, eternal   12
spirit, first among the gods, unborn and infinite. The great sages and seers—Narada,   13

Asita, Devala, and Vyasa too—have acclaimed you thus; now you have declared it to me yourself.

14   Now, O Krishna, I believe that everything you have told me is divine truth. O Lord, nei-
15   ther gods nor demons know your real nature. Indeed, you alone know yourself, O supreme spirit. You are the source of being and the master of every creature, God of gods, the Lord of the universe.

16   Tell me all your divine attributes, leaving nothing unsaid. Tell me of the glories with
17   which you fill the cosmos. Krishna, you are a supreme master of yoga. Tell me how I should meditate to gain constant awareness of you. In what things and in what ways
18   should I meditate on you? O Krishna, you who stir up people's hearts, tell me in detail your attributes and your powers; I can never tire of hearing your immortal words.

SRI KRISHNA:

19   All right, Arjuna, I will tell you of my divine powers. I will mention only the most glorious; for there is no end to them.

20   I am the true Self in the heart of every creature, Arjuna, and the beginning, middle, and end of their existence.

21   Among the shining gods I am Vishnu; of luminaries I am the sun; among the storm gods I am Marichi, and in the night sky I am the moon.

22   Among scriptures I am the Sama Veda, and among the lesser gods I am Indra. Among the senses I am the mind, and in living beings I am consciousness.

23   Among the Rudras I am Shankara. Among the spirits of the natural world I am Kubera, god of wealth, and Pavaka, the purifying fire. Among mountains I am Meru.

24   Among priests I am Brihaspati, and among military leaders I am Skanda. Among bodies of water I am the ocean.

25   Among the great seers I am Bhrigu, and among words, the syllable *Om;* I am the repetition of the Holy Name, and among mountains I am the Himalayas.

26   Among trees I am the *ashvattha,* the sacred fig; among the *gandharvas* or heavenly musicians I am Chitraratha. Among divine seers I am Narada, and among sages I am Kapila.

27   I was born from the nectar of immortality as the primordial horse and as Indra's noble elephant. Among men, I am the king.

28   Among weapons I am the thunderbolt. I am Kamadhuk, the cow that fulfills all desires; I am Kandarpa, the power of sex, and Vasuki, the king of snakes.

29   I am Ananta, the cosmic serpent, and Varuna, the god of water; I am Aryaman among the noble ancestors. Among the forces which restrain I am Yama, the god of death.

Among animals I am the lion; among birds, the eagle Garuda. I am Prahlada, born
among the demons, and of all that measures, I am time. 30

Among purifying forces I am the wind; among warriors, Rama. Of water creatures I am
the crocodile, and of rivers I am the Ganges. 31

I am the beginning, middle, and end of creation. Of all the sciences I am the science of 32
Self-knowledge, and I am logic in those who debate. Among letters I am *A;* among 33
grammatical compounds I am the dvandva. I am infinite time, and the sustainer whose
face is seen everywhere.

I am death, which overcomes all, and the source of all beings still to be born. I am the 34
feminine qualities: fame, beauty, perfect speech, memory, intelligence, loyalty, and forgiveness.

Among the hymns of the Sama Veda I am the Brihat; among poetic meters, the Gayatri. 35
Among months I am Margashirsha, first of the year; among seasons I am spring, that
brings forth flowers.

I am the gambling of the gambler and the radiance in all that shines. I am effort, I am 36
victory, and I am the goodness of the virtuous.

Among the Vrishnis I am Krishna, and among the Pandavas I am Arjuna. Among sages 37
I am Vyasa, and among poets, Ushanas.

I am the scepter which metes out punishment, and the art of statesmanship in those who 38
lead. I am the silence of the unknown and the wisdom of the wise.

I am the seed that can be found in every creature, Arjuna; for without me nothing can 39
exist, neither animate nor inanimate.

But there is no end to my divine attributes, Arjuna; these I have mentioned are only a 40
few. Wherever you find strength, or beauty, or spiritual power, you may be sure that 41
these have sprung from a spark of my essence.

But of what use is it to you to know all this, Arjuna? Just remember that I am, and that 42
I support the entire cosmos with only a fragment of my being.

CHAPTER 11: THE COSMIC VISION

ARJUNA:

Out of compassion you have taught me the supreme mystery of the Self. Through your 1
words my delusion is gone. You have explained the origin and end of every creature, O 2
lotus-eyed one, and told me of your own supreme, limitless existence.

3   Just as you have described your infinite glory, O Lord, now I long to see it. I want to
4   see you as the supreme ruler of creation. O Lord, master of yoga, if you think me strong
enough to behold it, show me your immortal Self.

SRI KRISHNA:

5   Behold, Arjuna, a million divine forms, with an infinite variety of color and shape. Behold
6   the gods of the natural world, and many more wonders never revealed before. Behold
7   the entire cosmos turning within my body, and the other things you desire to see.

8   But these things cannot be seen with your physical eyes; therefore I give you spiritual
vision to perceive my majestic power.

SANJAYA:

9   Having spoken these words, Krishna, the master of yoga, revealed to Arjuna his most
exalted, lordly form.

10   He appeared with an infinite number of faces, ornamented by heavenly jewels, dis-
11   playing unending miracles and the countless weapons of his power. Clothed in celestial garments and covered with garlands, sweet-smelling with heavenly fragrances, he
showed himself as the infinite Lord, the source of all wonders, whose face is everywhere.

12   If a thousand suns were to rise in the heavens at the same time, the blaze of their light
would resemble the splendor of that supreme spirit.

13   There, within the body of the God of gods, Arjuna saw all the manifold forms of the
14   universe united as one. Filled with amazement, his hair standing on end in ecstasy, he
bowed before the Lord with joined palms and spoke these words.

ARJUNA:

15   O Lord, I see within your body all the gods and every kind of living creature. I see
Brahma, the Creator, seated on a lotus; I see the ancient sages and the celestial serpents.

16   I see infinite mouths and arms, stomachs and eyes, and you are embodied in every form.
I see you everywhere, without beginning, middle, or end. You are the Lord of all creation, and the cosmos is your body.

17   You wear a crown and carry a mace and discus; your radiance is blinding and immeasurable. I see you, who are so difficult to behold, shining like a fiery sun blazing in every
direction.

18   You are the supreme, changeless Reality, the one thing to be known. You are the refuge
of all creation, the immortal spirit, the eternal guardian of eternal dharma.

You are without beginning, middle, or end; you touch everything with your infinite   19
power. The sun and moon are your eyes, and your mouth is fire; your radiance warms
the cosmos.

O Lord, your presence fills the heavens and the earth and reaches in every direction.   20
I see the three worlds trembling before this vision of your wonderful and terrible
form.

The gods enter your being, some calling out and greeting you in fear. Great saints sing   21
your glory, praying, "May all be well!"

The multitudes of gods, demigods, and demons are all overwhelmed by the sight of you.   22
O mighty Lord, at the sight of your myriad eyes and mouths, arms and legs, stomachs   23
and fearful teeth, I and the entire universe shake in terror.

O Vishnu, I can see your eyes shining; with open mouth, you glitter in an array of col-   24
ors, and your body touches the sky. I look at you and my heart trembles; I have lost all
courage and all peace of mind.

When I see your mouths with their fearful teeth, mouths burning like the fires at the end   25
of time, I forget where I am and I have no place to go. O Lord, you are the support of
the universe; have mercy on me!

I see all the sons of Dhritarashtra; I see Bhishma, Drona, and Karna; I see our warriors   26
and all the kings who are here to fight. All are rushing into your awful jaws; I see some   27
of them crushed by your teeth. As rivers flow into the ocean, all the warriors of this   28
world are passing into your fiery jaws; all creatures rush to their destruction like moths   29
into a flame.

You lap the worlds into your burning mouths and swallow them. Filled with your terri-   30
ble radiance, O Vishnu, the whole of creation bursts into flames.

Tell me who you are, O Lord of terrible form. I bow before you; have mercy! I want to   31
know who you are, you who existed before all creation. Your nature and workings con-
found me.

SRI KRISHNA:

I am time, the destroyer of all; I have come to consume the world. Even without your   32
participation, all the warriors gathered here will die.

Therefore arise, Arjuna; conquer your enemies and enjoy the glory of sovereignty. I   33
have already slain all these warriors; you will only be my instrument.

Bhishma, Drona, Jayadratha, Karna, and many others are already slain. Kill those   34
whom I have killed. Do not hesitate. Fight in this battle and you will conquer your enemies.

SANJAYA:

35 Having heard these words, Arjuna trembled in fear. With joined palms he bowed before Krishna and addressed him stammering.

ARJUNA:

36 O Krishna, it is right that the world delights and rejoices in your praise, that all the saints and sages bow down to you and all evil flees before you to the far corners of the universe.

37 How could they not worship you, O Lord? You are the eternal spirit, who existed before Brahma the Creator and who will never cease to be. Lord of the gods, you are the abode of the universe. Changeless, you are what is and what is not, and beyond the duality of existence and nonexistence.

38 You are the first among the gods, the timeless spirit, the resting place of all beings. You are the knower and the thing which is known. You are the final home; with your infinite form you pervade the cosmos.

39 You are Vayu, god of wind; Yama, god of death; Agni, god of fire; Varuna, god of water. You are the moon and the creator Prajapati, and the great-grandfather of all creatures. I bow before you and salute you again and again.

40 You are behind me and in front of me; I bow to you on every side. Your power is immeasurable. You pervade everything; you are everything.

41 Sometimes, because we were friends, I rashly said, "Oh, Krishna!" "Say, friend!"—
42 casual, careless remarks. Whatever I may have said lightly, whether we were playing or resting, alone or in company, sitting together or eating, if it was disrespectful, forgive me for it, O Krishna. I did not know the greatness of your nature, unchanging and imperishable.

43 You are the father of the universe, of the animate and the inanimate; you are the object of all worship, the greatest guru. There is none to equal you in the three worlds. Who
44 can match your power? O gracious Lord, I prostrate myself before you and ask for your blessing. As a father forgives his son, or a friend a friend, or a lover his beloved, so should you forgive me.

45 I rejoice in seeing you as you have never been seen before, yet I am filled with fear by this vision of you as the abode of the universe. Please let me see you again as the shining
46 God of gods. Though you are the embodiment of all creation, let me see you again not with a thousand arms but with four, carrying the mace and discus and wearing a crown.

SRI KRISHNA:

47 Arjuna, through my grace you have been united with me and received this vision of my radiant, universal form, without beginning or end, which no one else has ever seen.

Not by knowledge of the Vedas, nor sacrifice, nor charity, nor rituals, nor even by severe asceticism has any other mortal seen what you have seen, O heroic Arjuna. 48

Do not be troubled; do not fear my terrible form. Let your heart be satisfied and your fears dispelled in looking at me as I was before. 49

SANJAYA:

Having spoken these words, the Lord once again assumed the gentle form of Krishna and consoled his devotee, who had been so afraid. 50

ARJUNA:

O Krishna, now that I have seen your gentle human form my mind is again composed and returned to normal. 51

SRI KRISHNA:

It is extremely difficult to obtain the vision you have had; even the gods long always to 52
see me in this aspect. Neither knowledge of the Vedas, nor austerity, nor charity, nor 53
sacrifice can bring the vision you have seen. But through unfailing devotion, Arjuna, 54
you can know me, see me, and attain union with me. Whoever makes me the supreme 55
goal of all his work and acts without selfish attachment, who devotes himself to me completely and is free from ill will for any creature, enters into me.

CHAPTER 12: THE WAY OF LOVE

ARJUNA:

Of those steadfast devotees who love you and those who seek you as the eternal form- 1
less Reality, who are the more established in yoga?

SRI KRISHNA:

Those who set their hearts on me and worship me with unfailing devotion and faith are 2
more established in yoga.

As for those who seek the transcendental Reality, without name, without form, con- 3
templating the Unmanifested, beyond the reach of thought and of feeling, with their 4
senses subdued and mind serene and striving for the good of all beings, they too will verily come unto me.

5   Yet hazardous and slow is the path to the Unrevealed, difficult for physical man to tread.
6   But they for whom I am the supreme goal, who do all work renouncing self for me and
7   meditate on me with single-hearted devotion, these I will swiftly rescue from the frag-
     ment's cycle of birth and death, for their consciousness has entered into me.

8   Still your mind in me, still your intellect in me, and without doubt you will be united
9   with me forever. If you cannot still your mind in me, learn to do so through the regular
10   practice of meditation. If you lack the will for such self-discipline, engage yourself in
11   my work, for selfless service can lead you at last to complete fulfillment. If you are
     unable to do even this, surrender yourself to me, disciplining yourself and renouncing
     the results of all your actions.

12   Better indeed is knowledge than mechanical practice. Better than knowledge is medita-
     tion. But better still is surrender of attachment to results, because there follows imme-
     diate peace.

13   That one I love who is incapable of ill will, who is friendly and compassionate. Living
14   beyond the reach of *I* and *mine* and of pleasure and pain, patient, contented, self-
     controlled, firm in faith, with all his heart and all his mind given to me—with such a
     one I am in love.

15   Not agitating the world or by it agitated, he stands above the sway of elation, competi-
     tion, and fear: he is my beloved.

16   He is detached, pure, efficient, impartial, never anxious, selfless in all his undertakings;
     he is my devotee, very dear to me.

17   He is dear to me who runs not after the pleasant or away from the painful, grieves not,
     lusts not, but lets things come and go as they happen.

18   That devotee who looks upon friend and foe with equal regard, who is not buoyed up
     by praise nor cast down by blame, alike in heat and cold, pleasure and pain, free from
19   selfish attachments, the same in honor and dishonor, quiet, ever full, in harmony every-
     where, firm in faith—such a one is dear to me.

20   Those who meditate upon this immortal dharma as I have declared it, full of faith and
     seeking me as life's supreme goal, are truly my devotees, and my love for them is very
     great.

CHAPTER 13: THE FIELD AND THE KNOWER

SRI KRISHNA:

1   The body is called a field, Arjuna; he who knows it is called the Knower of the field.
2   This is the knowledge of those who know. I am the Knower of the field in everyone,
     Arjuna. Knowledge of the field and its Knower is true knowledge.

Listen and I will explain the nature of the field and how change takes place within it. I will also describe the Knower of the field and his power. These truths have been sung by great sages in a variety of ways, and expounded in precise arguments concerning Brahman.   3
4

The field, Arjuna, is made up of the following: the five areas of sense perception; the five elements; the five sense organs and the five organs of action; the three components of the mind: *manas, buddhi,* and *ahamkara;* and the undifferentiated energy from which all these evolved. In this field arise desire and aversion, pleasure and pain, the body, intelligence, and will.   5
6

Those who know truly are free from pride and deceit. They are gentle, forgiving, upright, and pure, devoted to their spiritual teacher, filled with inner strength, and self-controlled. Detached from sense objects and self-will, they have learned the painful lesson of separate birth and suffering, old age, disease, and death.   7
8

Free from selfish attachment, they do not get compulsively entangled even in home and family. They are even-minded through good fortune and bad. Their devotion to me is undivided. Enjoying solitude and not following the crowd, they seek only me. This is true knowledge, to seek the Self as the true end of wisdom always. To seek anything else is ignorance.   9
10
11

I will tell you of the wisdom that leads to immortality: the beginningless Brahman, which can be called neither being nor nonbeing.   12

It dwells in all, in every hand and foot and head, in every mouth and eye and ear in the universe. Without senses itself, it shines through the functioning of the senses. Completely independent, it supports all things. Beyond the gunas, it enjoys their play.   13
14

It is both near and far, both within and without every creature; it moves and is unmoving. In its subtlety it is beyond comprehension. It is indivisible, yet appears divided in separate creatures. Know it to be the creator, the preserver, and the destroyer.   15
16

Dwelling in every heart, it is beyond darkness. It is called the light of lights, the object and goal of knowledge, and knowledge itself.   17

I have revealed to you the nature of the field and the meaning and object of true knowledge. Those who are devoted to me, knowing these things, are united with me.   18

Know that prakriti and Purusha are both without beginning, and that from prakriti come the gunas and all that changes. Prakriti is the agent, cause, and effect of every action, but it is Purusha that seems to experience pleasure and pain.   19
20

Purusha, resting in prakriti, witnesses the play of the gunas born of prakriti. But attachment to the gunas leads a person to be born for good or evil.   21

Within the body the supreme Purusha is called the witness, approver, supporter, enjoyer, the supreme Lord, the highest Self.   22

23   Whoever realizes the true nature of Purusha, prakriti, and the gunas, whatever path he
or she may follow, is not born separate again.

24   Some realize the Self within them through the practice of meditation, some by the path
25   of wisdom, and others by selfless service. Others may not know these paths; but hearing and following the instructions of an illumined teacher, they too go beyond death.

26   Whatever exists, Arjuna, animate or inanimate, is born through the union of the field
and its Knower.

27   He alone sees truly who sees the Lord the same in every creature, who sees the
28   Deathless in the hearts of all that die. Seeing the same Lord everywhere, he does not
harm himself or others. Thus he attains the supreme goal.

29   They alone see truly who see that all actions are performed by prakriti, while the Self
30   remains unmoved. When they see the variety of creation rooted in that unity and growing out of it, they attain fulfillment in Brahman.

31   This supreme Self is without a beginning, undifferentiated, deathless. Though it dwells
32   in the body, Arjuna, it neither acts nor is touched by action. As akasha pervades the cosmos but remains unstained, the Self can never be tainted though it dwells in every creature.

33   As the sun lights up the world, the Self dwelling in the field is the source of all light in
34   the field. Those who, with the eye of wisdom, distinguish the field from its Knower and
the way to freedom from the bondage of prakriti, attain the supreme goal.

CHAPTER 14: THE FORCES OF EVOLUTION

SRI KRISHNA:

1   Let me tell you more about the wisdom that transcends all knowledge, through which
2   the saints and sages attained perfection. Those who rely on this wisdom will be united
with me. For them there is neither rebirth nor fear of death.

3   My womb is prakriti; in that I place the seed. Thus all created things are born. Everything
4   born, Arjuna, comes from the womb of prakriti, and I am the seed-giving father.

5   It is the three gunas born of prakriti—sattva, rajas, and tamas—that bind the immortal
6   Self to the body. Sattva—pure, luminous, and free from sorrow—binds us with attach-
7   ment to happiness and wisdom. Rajas is passion, arising from selfish desire and attach-
8   ment. These bind the Self with compulsive action. Tamas, born of ignorance, deludes
all creatures through heedlessness, indolence, and sleep.

9   Sattva binds us to happiness; rajas binds us to action. Tamas, distorting our understanding, binds us to delusion.

Sattva predominates when rajas and tamas are transformed. Rajas prevails when sattva   10
is weak and tamas overcome. Tamas prevails when rajas and sattva are dormant.

When sattva predominates, the light of wisdom shines through every gate of the body.   11
When rajas predominates, a person runs about pursuing selfish and greedy ends, driven   12
by restlessness and desire. When tamas is dominant a person lives in darkness—sloth-   13
ful, confused, and easily infatuated.

Those dying in the state of sattva attain the pure worlds of the wise. Those dying in rajas   14
are reborn among people driven by work. But those who die in tamas are conceived in   15
the wombs of the ignorant.

The fruit of good deeds is pure and sattvic. The fruit of rajas is suffering. The fruit of   16
tamas is ignorance and insensitivity.

From sattva comes understanding; from rajas, greed. But the outcome of tamas is con-   17
fusion, infatuation, and ignorance.

Those who live in sattva go upwards; those in rajas remain where they are. But those   18
immersed in tamas sink downwards.

The wise see clearly that all action is the work of the gunas. Knowing that which is   19
above the gunas, they enter into union with me.

Going beyond the three gunas which form the body, they leave behind the cycle of birth   20
and death, decrepitude and sorrow, and attain to immortality.

ARJUNA:

What are the characteristics of those who have gone beyond the gunas, O Lord? How   21
do they act? How have they passed beyond the gunas' hold?

SRI KRISHNA:

They are unmoved by the harmony of sattva, the activity of rajas, or the delusion of   22
tamas. They feel no aversion when these forces are active, nor do they crave for them
when these forces subside.

They remain impartial, undisturbed by the actions of the gunas. Knowing that it is the   23
gunas which act, they abide within themselves and do not vacillate.

Established within themselves, they are equal in pleasure and pain, praise and blame,   24
kindness and unkindness. Clay, a rock, and gold are the same to them. Alike in honor   25
and dishonor, alike to friend and foe, they have given up every selfish pursuit. Such are
those who have gone beyond the gunas.

26   By serving me with steadfast love, a man or woman goes beyond the gunas. Such a one is fit for union with Brahman. For I am the support of Brahman, the eternal, the unchanging, the deathless, the everlasting dharma, the source of all joy.

CHAPTER 15: THE SUPREME SELF

SRI KRISHNA:

1   Sages speak of the immutable ashvattha tree, with its taproot above and its branches below. On this tree grow the scriptures; seeing their source, one knows their essence.

2   Nourished by the gunas, the limbs of this tree spread above and below. Sense objects grow on the limbs as buds; the roots hanging down bind us to action in this world.

3   The true form of this tree—its essence, beginning, and end—is not perceived on this
4   earth. Cut down this strong-rooted tree with the sharp axe of detachment; then find the path which does not come back again. Seek That, the First Cause, from which the universe came long ago.

5   Not deluded by pride, free from selfish attachment and selfish desire, beyond the duality of pleasure and pain, ever aware of the Self, the wise go forward to that eternal goal.
6   Neither the sun nor the moon nor fire can add to that light. This is my supreme abode, and those who enter there do not return to separate existence.

7   An eternal part of me enters into the world, assuming the powers of action and percep-
8   tion and a mind made of prakriti. When the divine Self enters and leaves a body, it takes
9   these along as the wind carries a scent from place to place. Using the mind, ears, eyes, nose, and the senses of taste and touch, the Self enjoys sense objects.

10   The deluded do not see the Self when it leaves the body or when it dwells within it. They do not see the Self enjoying sense objects or acting through the gunas. But they who have the eye of wisdom see.

11   Those who strive resolutely on the path of yoga see the Self within. The thoughtless, who strive imperfectly, do not.

12   The brightness of the sun, which lights up the world, the brightness of the moon and of
13   fire—these are my glory. With a drop of my energy I enter the earth and support all
14   creatures. Through the moon, the vessel of life-giving fluid, I nourish all plants. I enter breathing creatures and dwell within as the life-giving breath. I am the fire in the stomach which digests all food.

15   Entering into every heart, I give the power to remember and understand; it is I again who take that power away. All the scriptures lead to me; I am their author and their wisdom.

16   In this world there are two orders of being: the perishable, separate creature and the
17   changeless spirit. But beyond these there is another, the supreme Self, the eternal Lord, who enters into the entire cosmos and supports it from within.

I am that supreme Self, praised by the scriptures as beyond the changing and the   18
changeless. Those who see in me that supreme Self see truly. They have found the   19
source of all wisdom, Arjuna, and they worship me with all their heart.

I have shared this profound truth with you, Arjuna. Those who understand it will attain   20
wisdom; they will have done that which has to be done.

CHAPTER 16: TWO PATHS

SRI KRISHNA:

Be fearless and pure; never waver in your determination or your dedication to the spir-   1
itual life. Give freely. Be self-controlled, sincere, truthful, loving, and full of the desire
to serve. Realize the truth of the scriptures; learn to be detached and to take joy in
renunciation. Do not get angry or harm any living creature, but be compassionate and   2
gentle; show good will to all. Cultivate vigor, patience, will, purity; avoid malice and   3
pride. Then, Arjuna, you will achieve your divine destiny.

Other qualities, Arjuna, make a person more and more inhuman: hypocrisy, arrogance,   4
conceit, anger, cruelty, ignorance.

The divine qualities lead to freedom; the demonic, to bondage. But do not grieve,   5
Arjuna; you were born with divine attributes.

Some people have divine tendencies, others demonic. I have described the divine at   6
length, Arjuna; now listen while I describe the demonic.

The demonic do things they should avoid and avoid the things they should do. They   7
have no sense of uprightness, purity, or truth.

"There is no God," they say, "no truth, no spiritual law, no moral order. The basis of life   8
is sex; what else can it be?" Holding such distorted views, possessing scant discrimi-   9
nation, they become enemies of the world, causing suffering and destruction.

Hypocritical, proud, and arrogant, living in delusion and clinging to deluded ideas, insa-   10
tiable in their desires, they pursue their unclean ends. Although burdened with fears that   11
end only with death, they still maintain with complete assurance, "Gratification of lust
is the highest that life can offer."

Bound on all sides by scheming and anxiety, driven by anger and greed, they amass by   12
any means they can a hoard of money for the satisfaction of their cravings.

"I got this today," they say; "tomorrow I shall get that. This wealth is mine, and that will   13
be mine too. I have destroyed my enemies. I shall destroy others too! Am I not like   14
God? I enjoy what I want. I am successful. I am powerful. I am happy. I am rich and   15
wellborn. Who is equal to me? I will perform sacrifices and give gifts, and rejoice in
my own generosity." This is how they go on, deluded by ignorance. Bound by their   16

greed and entangled in a web of delusion, whirled about by a fragmented mind, they fall into a dark hell.

17
18
Self-important, obstinate, swept away by the pride of wealth, they ostentatiously perform sacrifices without any regard for their purpose. Egotistical, violent, arrogant, lustful, angry, envious of everyone, they abuse my presence within their own bodies and in the bodies of others.

19
20
Life after life I cast those who are malicious, hateful, cruel, and degraded into the wombs of those with similar demonic natures. Birth after birth they find themselves with demonic tendencies. Degraded in this way, Arjuna, they fail to reach me and fall lower still.

21
22
23
There are three gates to this self-destructive hell: lust, anger, and greed. Renounce these three. Those who escape from these three gates of darkness, Arjuna, seek what is best and attain life's supreme goal. Others disregard the teachings of the scriptures. Driven by selfish desire, they miss the goal of life, miss even happiness and success.

24
Therefore let the scriptures be your guide in what to do and what not to do. Understand their teachings; then act in accordance with them.

CHAPTER 17: THE POWER OF FAITH

ARJUNA:

1
O Krishna, what is the state of those who disregard the scriptures but still worship with faith? Do they act from sattva, rajas, or tamas?

SRI KRISHNA:

2
Every creature is born with faith of some kind, either sattvic, rajasic, or tamasic. Listen, and I will describe each to you.

3
Our faith conforms to our nature, Arjuna. Human nature is made of faith. Indeed, a person is his faith.

4
5
6
Those who are sattvic worship the forms of God; those who are rajasic worship power and wealth. Those who are tamasic worship spirits and ghosts. Some invent harsh penances. Motivated by hypocrisy and egotism, they torture their innocent bodies and me who dwells within. Blinded by their strength and passion, they act and think like demons.

7
The three kinds of faith express themselves in the habits of those who hold them: in the food they like, the work they do, the disciplines they practice, the gifts they give. Listen, and I will describe their different ways.

Sattvic people enjoy food that is mild, tasty, substantial, agreeable, and nourishing, food   8
that promotes health, strength, cheerfulness, and longevity. Rajasic people like food that   9
is salty or bitter, hot, sour, or spicy—food that promotes pain, discomfort, and disease.
Tamasic people like overcooked, stale, leftover, and impure food, food that has lost its   10
taste and nutritional value.

The sattvic perform sacrifices with their entire mind fixed on the purpose of the sacri-   11
fice. Without thought of reward, they follow the teachings of the scriptures. The rajasic   12
perform sacrifices for the sake of show and the good it will bring them. The tamasic   13
perform sacrifices ignoring both the letter and the spirit. They omit the proper prayers,
the proper offerings, the proper food, and the proper faith.

To offer service to the gods, to the good, to the wise, and to your spiritual teacher; puri-   14
ty, honesty, continence, and nonviolence: these are the disciplines of the body. To offer   15
soothing words, to speak truly, kindly, and helpfully, and to study the scriptures: these
are the disciplines of speech. Calmness, gentleness, silence, self-restraint, and purity: 16
these are the disciplines of the mind.

When these three levels of self-discipline are practiced without attachment to the   17
results, but in a spirit of great faith, the sages call this practice sattvic. Disciplines prac-   18
ticed in order to gain respect, honor, or admiration are rajasic; they are undependable
and transitory in their effects. Disciplines practiced to gain power over others, or in the   19
confused belief that to torture oneself is spiritual, are tamasic.

Giving simply because it is right to give, without thought of return, at a proper time, in   20
proper circumstances, and to a worthy person, is sattvic giving. Giving with regrets or   21
in the expectation of receiving some favor or of getting something in return is rajasic.
Giving at an inappropriate time, in inappropriate circumstances, and to an unworthy   22
person, without affection or respect, is tamasic.

Om Tat Sat: these three words represent Brahman, from which come priests and scrip-   23
tures and sacrifice. Those who follow the Vedas, therefore, always repeat the word *Om*   24
when offering sacrifices, performing spiritual disciplines, or giving gifts. Those seek-   25
ing liberation and not any personal benefit add the word *Tat* when performing these acts
of worship, discipline, and charity. *Sat* means "that which is"; it also indicates good-   26
ness. Therefore it is used to describe a worthy deed.

To be steadfast in self-sacrifice, self-discipline, and giving is *sat*. To act in accordance   27
with these three is *sat* as well. But to engage in sacrifice, self-discipline, and giving with-   28
out good faith is *asat,* without worth or goodness, either in this life or in the next.

CHAPTER 18: FREEDOM & RENUNCIATION

ARJUNA:

O Krishna, destroyer of evil, please explain to me sannyasa and tyaga and how one kind   1
of renunciation differs from another.

SRI KRISHNA:

2   To refrain from selfish acts is one kind of renunciation, called sannyasa; to renounce the fruit of action is another, called tyaga.

3   Among the wise, some say that all action should be renounced as evil. Others say that certain kinds of action—self-sacrifice, giving, and self-discipline—should be continued.
4   Listen, Arjuna, and I will explain three kinds of tyaga and my conclusions concerning them.

5   Self-sacrifice, giving, and self-discipline should not be renounced, for they purify the
6   thoughtful. Yet even these, Arjuna, should be performed without desire for selfish rewards. This is essential.

7   To renounce one's responsibilities is not fitting. The wise call such deluded renuncia-
8   tion tamasic. To avoid action from fear of difficulty or physical discomfort is rajasic.
9   There is no reward in such renunciation. But to fulfill your responsibilities knowing that they are obligatory, while at the same time desiring nothing for yourself—this is sattvic
10   renunciation. Those endowed with sattva clearly understand the meaning of renuncia-tion and do not waver. They are not intimidated by unpleasant work, nor do they seek a job because it is pleasant.

11   As long as one has a body, one cannot renounce action altogether. True renunciation is
12   giving up all desire for personal reward. Those who are attached to personal reward will reap the consequences of their actions: some pleasant, some unpleasant, some mixed. But those who renounce every desire for personal reward go beyond the reach of karma.

13   Listen, Arjuna, and I will explain the five elements necessary for the accomplishment
14   of every action, as taught by the wisdom of Sankhya. The body, the means, the ego, the
15   performance of the act, and the divine will: these are the five factors in all actions, right or wrong, in thought, word, or deed.

16   Those who do not understand this think of themselves as separate agents. With their
17   crude intellects they fail to see the truth. The person who is free from ego, who has attained purity of heart, though he slays these people, he does not slay and is not bound
18   by his action.

19   Knowledge, the thing to be known, and the knower: these three promote action. The means, the act itself, and the doer: these three are the totality of action. Knowledge, action, and the doer can be described according to the gunas. Listen, and I will explain their distinctions to you.

20   Sattvic knowledge sees the one indestructible Being in all beings, the unity underlying
21   the multiplicity of creation. Rajasic knowledge sees all things and creatures as separate
22   and distinct. Tamasic knowledge, lacking any sense of perspective, sees one small part and mistakes it for the whole.

23   Work performed to fulfill one's obligations, without thought of personal reward or of
24   whether the job is pleasant or unpleasant, is sattvic. Work prompted by selfish desire or
25   self-will, full of stress, is rajasic. Work that is undertaken blindly, without any consid-eration of consequences, waste, injury to others, or one's own capacities, is tamasic.

A sattvic worker is free from egotism and selfish attachments, full of enthusiasm and 26
fortitude in success and failure alike. A rajasic worker has strong personal desires and 27
craves rewards for his actions. Covetous, impure, and destructive, he is easily swept
away by fortune, good or bad. The tamasic worker is undisciplined, vulgar, stubborn, 28
deceitful, dishonest, and lazy. He is easily depressed and prone to procrastination.

Listen, Arjuna, as I describe the three types of understanding and will. 29

To know when to act and when to refrain from action, what is right action and what is 30
wrong, what brings security and what insecurity, what brings freedom and what
bondage: these are the signs of a sattvic intellect.

The rajasic intellect confuses right and wrong actions, and cannot distinguish what is to 31
be done from what should not be done. The tamasic intellect is shrouded in darkness, 32
utterly reversing right and wrong wherever it turns.

The sattvic will, developed through meditation, keeps prana, mind, and senses in vital 33
harmony. The rajasic will, conditioned by selfish desire, pursues wealth, pleasure, and 34
respectability. The tamasic will shows itself in obstinate ignorance, sloth, fear, grief, 35
depression, and conceit.

Now listen, Arjuna: there are also three kinds of happiness. By sustained effort, one 36
comes to the end of sorrow.

That which seems like poison at first, but tastes like nectar in the end—this is the joy 37
of sattva, born of a mind at peace with itself. Pleasure from the senses seems like nec- 38
tar at first, but it is bitter as poison in the end. This is the kind of happiness that comes
to the rajasic. Those who are tamasic draw their pleasures from sleep, indolence, and 39
intoxication. Both in the beginning and in the end, this happiness is a delusion.

No creature, whether born on earth or among the gods in heaven, is free from the con- 40
ditioning of the three gunas. The different responsibilities found in the social order— 41
distinguishing brahmin, kshatriya, vaishya, and shudra—have their roots in this
conditioning.

The responsibilities to which a brahmin is born, based on his nature, are self-control, 42
tranquility, purity of heart, patience, humility, learning, austerity, wisdom, and faith.
The qualities of a kshatriya, based on his nature, are courage, strength, fortitude, dex- 43
terity, generosity, leadership, and the firm resolve never to retreat from battle. The occu- 44
pations suitable for a vaishya are agriculture, dairying, and trade. The proper work of a
shudra is service.

By devotion to one's own particular duty, everyone can attain perfection. Let me tell 45
you how. By performing his own work, one worships the Creator who dwells in every 46
creature. Such worship brings that person to fulfillment.

It is better to perform one's own duties imperfectly than to master the duties of another. 47
By fulfilling the obligations he is born with, a person never comes to grief. No one 48
should abandon duties because he sees defects in them. Every action, every activity, is
surrounded by defects as a fire is surrounded by smoke.

49
50 He who is free from selfish attachments, who has mastered himself and his passions, attains the supreme perfection of freedom from action. Listen and I shall explain now, Arjuna, how one who has attained perfection also attains Brahman, the supreme consummation of wisdom.

51
52 Unerring in his discrimination, sovereign of his senses and passions, free from the clamor of likes and dislikes, he leads a simple, self-reliant life based on meditation, controlling his speech, body, and mind.

53
54
55
56 Free from self-will, aggressiveness, arrogance, anger, and the lust to possess people or things, he is at peace with himself and others and enters into the unitive state. United with Brahman, ever joyful, beyond the reach of desire and sorrow, he has equal regard for every living creature and attains supreme devotion to me. By loving me he comes to know me truly; then he knows my glory and enters into my boundless being. All his acts are performed in my service, and through my grace he wins eternal life.

57
58 Make every act an offering to me; regard me as your only protector. Relying on interior discipline, meditate on me always. Remembering me, you shall overcome all difficulties through my grace. But if you will not heed me in your self-will, nothing will avail you.

59
60 If you egotistically say, "I will not fight this battle," your resolve will be useless; your own nature will drive you into it. Your own karma, born of your own nature, will drive you to do even that which you do not wish to do, because of your delusion.

61
62 The Lord dwells in the hearts of all creatures and whirls them round upon the wheel of maya. Run to him for refuge with all your strength, and peace profound will be yours through his grace.

63
64 I give you these precious words of wisdom; reflect on them and then do as you choose. These are the last words I shall speak to you, dear one, for your spiritual fulfillment. You are very dear to me.

65
66 Be aware of me always, adore me, make every act an offering to me, and you shall come to me; this I promise; for you are dear to me. Abandon all supports and look to me for protection. I shall purify you from the sins of the past; do not grieve.

67
68
69 Do not share this wisdom with anyone who lacks in devotion or self-control, lacks the desire to learn, or scoffs at me. Those who teach this supreme mystery of the Gita to all who love me perform the greatest act of love; they will come to me without doubt. No one can render me more devoted service; no one on earth can be more dear to me.

70
71 Those who meditate on these holy words worship me with wisdom and devotion. Even those who listen to them with faith, free from doubts, will find a happier world where good people dwell.

72 Have you listened with attention? Are you now free from your doubts and confusion?

ARJUNA:

You have dispelled my doubts and delusions, and I understand through your grace. My   73
faith is firm now, and I will do your will.

SANJAYA:

This is the dialogue I heard between Krishna, the son of Vasudeva, and Arjuna, the   74
great-hearted son of Pritha. The wonder of it makes my hair stand on end! Through   75
Vyasa's grace, I have heard the supreme secret of spiritual union directly from the Lord
of Yoga, Krishna himself.

Whenever I remember these wonderful, holy words between Krishna and Arjuna, I am   76
filled with joy And when I remember the breathtaking form of Krishna, I am filled with   77
wonder and my joy overflows.

Wherever the divine Krishna and the mighty Arjuna are, there will be prosperity, vic-   78
tory, happiness, and sound judgment. Of this I am sure!

PATANJALI, THE YOGA SUTRAS

I. YOGA AND ITS AIMS

1. This is the beginning of instruction in yoga.

2. Yoga is the control of thought-waves in the mind.

3. Then man abides in his real nature.

4. At other times, when he is not in the state of yoga, man remains identified with the thought-waves in the mind.

5. There are five kinds of thought-waves—some painful, others not painful.

6. These five kinds of thought-waves are: right knowledge, wrong knowledge, verbal delusion, sleep and memory.

7. The right kinds of knowledge are: direct perception, inference and scriptural testimony.

8. Wrong knowledge is knowledge which is false and not based upon the true nature of its object.

9. Verbal delusion arises when words do not correspond to reality.

10. Sleep is a wave of thought about nothingness.

11. Memory is when perceived objects are not forgotten, but come back to consciousness.

12. They are controlled by means of practice and non-attachment.

13. Practice is the repeated effort to follow the disciplines which give permanent control of the thought-waves of the mind.

14. Practice becomes firmly grounded when it has been cultivated for a long time, uninterruptedly, with earnest devotion.

15. Non-attachment is self-mastery; it is freedom from desire for what is seen or heard.

16. When, through knowledge of the Atman, one ceases to desire any manifestation of Nature, then that is the highest kind of non-attachment.

From *How to Know God: The Yoga Aphorisms of Patanjali*, tr. by Swami Prabhavananda and Christopher Isherwood (New York: Harper & Brothers, 1953), copyright by the Vedanta Society of Southern California.

17. Concentration upon a single object may reach four stages: examination, discrimination, joyful peace and simple awareness of individuality.

18. The other kind of concentration is that in which the consciousness contains no object—only sub-conscious impressions, which are like burnt seeds. It is attained by constantly checking the thought-waves through the practice of non-attachment.

19. When such concentration is not accompanied by non-attachment, and ignorance therefore remains, the aspirant will reach the state of the disincarnate gods or become merged in the forces of Nature.

20. The concentration of the true spiritual aspirant is attained through faith, energy, recollectedness, absorption and illumination.

21. Success in yoga comes quickly to those who are intensely energetic.

22. Success varies according to the means adopted to obtain it—mild, medium or intense.

23. Concentration may also be attained through devotion to Ishwara.

24. Ishwara is a special kind of Being, untouched by ignorance and the products of ignorance, not subject to karmas or samskaras or the results of action.

25. In Him, knowledge is infinite; in others it is only a germ.

26. He was the teacher even of the earliest teachers, since He is not limited by time.

27. The word which expresses Him is OM.

28. This word must be repeated with meditation upon its meaning.

29. Hence comes knowledge of the Atman and destruction of the obstacles to that knowledge.

30. Sickness, mental laziness, doubt, lack of enthusiasm, sloth, craving for sense-pleasure, false perception, despair caused by failure to concentrate and unsteadiness in concentration: these distractions are the obstacles to knowledge.

31. These distractions are accompanied by grief, despondency, trembling of the body and irregular breathing.

32. They can be removed by the practice of concentration upon a single truth.

33. Undisturbed calmness of mind is attained by cultivating friendliness toward the happy, compassion for the unhappy, delight in the virtuous, and indifference toward the wicked.

34. The mind may also be calmed by expulsion and retention of the breath.

35. Those forms of concentration which result in extraordinary perceptions encourage perseverance of the mind.

36. Concentration may also be attained by fixing the mind upon the Inner Light, which is beyond sorrow.

37. Or by meditating on the heart of an illumined soul, that is free from passion.

38. Or by fixing the mind upon a dream experience, or the experience of deep sleep.

39. Or by fixing the mind upon any divine form or symbol that appeals to one as good.

40. The mind of a yogi can concentrate upon any object of any size, from the atomic to the infinitely great.

41. Just as the pure crystal takes color from the object which is nearest to it, so the mind, when it is cleared of thought-waves, achieves sameness or identity with the object of its concentration. This may be either a gross object, or the organ of perception, or the sense of ego. This achievement of sameness or identity with the object of concentration is known as *samadhi*.

42. When the mind achieves identity with a gross object of concentration, mixed with awareness of name, quality and knowledge, this is called *savitarka samadhi*.

43. When the mind achieves identity with a gross object of concentration, unmixed with awareness of name, quality and knowledge, so that the object alone remains, this is called *nirvitarka samadhi*.

44. When the object of concentration is a subtle object, two kinds of *samadhi*, called *savichara* and *nirvichara*, may be distinguished in the same manner.

45. Behind all subtle objects is *Prakriti*, the primal cause.

46. These kinds of *samadhi* are said to be "with seed."

47. In reaching *nirvichara samadhi* the mind becomes pure.

48. In that *samadhi*, knowledge is said to be "filled with truth."

49. The knowledge which is gained from inference and the study of scriptures is knowledge of one kind. But the knowledge which is gained from *samadhi* is of a much higher order. It goes beyond inference and scriptures.

50. The impression which is made upon the mind by that *samadhi* wipes out all other past impressions.

51. When the impression made by that *samadhi* is also wiped out, so that there are no more thought-waves at all in the mind, then one enters the *samadhi* which is called "seedless."

II. YOGA AND ITS PRACTICE

1. Austerity, study, and the dedication of the fruits of one's work to God: these are the preliminary steps toward yoga.

2. Thus we may cultivate the power of concentration and remove the obstacles to enlightenment which cause all our sufferings.

3. These obstacles—the causes of man's sufferings—are ignorance, egoism, attachment, aversion, and the desire to cling to life.

4. Ignorance creates all the other obstacles. They may exist either in a potential or a vestigial form, or they may have been temporarily overcome or fully developed.

5. To regard the noneternal as eternal, the impure as pure, the painful as pleasant and the non-Atman as the Atman—this is ignorance.

6. To identify consciousness with that which merely reflects consciousness—this is egoism.

7. Attachment is that which dwells upon pleasure.

8. Aversion is that which dwells upon pain.

9. The desire to cling to life is inherent both in the ignorant and in the learned. This is because the mind retains impressions of the death experience from many previous incarnations.

10. When these obstacles have been reduced to a vestigial form, they can be destroyed by resolving the mind back into its primal cause.

11. In their fully developed form, they can be overcome through meditation.

12. A man's latent tendencies have been created by his past thoughts and actions. These tendencies will bear fruits, both in this life and in lives to come.

13. So long as the cause exists, it will bear fruits—such as rebirth, a long or a short life, and the experiences of pleasure and of pain.

14. Experiences of pleasure and of pain are the fruits of merit and demerit, respectively.

15. But the man of spiritual discrimination regards all these experiences as painful. For even the enjoyment of present pleasure is painful, since we already fear its loss. Past pleasure is painful because renewed cravings arise from the impressions it has left upon the mind. And how can any happiness be lasting if it depends only upon our moods? For these moods are constantly changing, as one or another of the ever-warring *gunas* seizes control of the mind.

16. The pain which is yet to come may be avoided.

17. This pain is caused by false identification of the experiencer with the object of experience. It may be avoided.

18. The object of experience is composed of the three *gunas*—the principles of illumination *(sattwa)*, activity *(rajas)* and inertia *(tamas)*. From these, the whole universe has evolved, together with the instruments of knowledge—such as the mind, senses, etc.—and the objects perceived—such as the physical elements. The universe exists in order that the experiencer may experience it, and thus become liberated.

19. The *gunas* pass through four states—gross, subtle, primal and unevolved.

20. The Atman—the experiencer—is pure consciousness. It appears to take on the changing colors of the mind. In reality, it is unchangeable.

21. The object of experience exists only to serve the purpose of the Atman.

22. Though the object of experience becomes unreal to him who has reached the state of liberation, it remains real to all other beings.

23. The Atman—the experiencer—is identified with *Prakriti*—the object of experience—in order that the true nature of both *Prakriti* and Atman may be known.

24. This identification is caused by ignorance.

25. When ignorance has been destroyed, this identification ceases. Then bondage is at an end and the experiencer is independent and free.

26. Ignorance is destroyed by awakening to knowledge of the Atman, until no trace of illusion remains.

27. The experiencer gains this knowledge in seven stages, advancing toward the highest.

28. As soon as all impurities have been removed by the practice of spiritual disciplines—the "limbs" of yoga—a man's spiritual vision opens to the light-giving knowledge of the Atman.

29. The eight limbs of yoga are: the various forms of abstention from evil-doing *(yama)*, the various observances *(niyamas)*, posture *(asana)*, control of the *prana (pranayama)*, withdrawal of the mind from sense objects *(pratyahara)*, concentration *(dharana)*, meditation *(dhyana)* and absorption in the Atman *(samadhi)*.

30. *Yama* is abstention from harming others, from falsehood, from theft, from incontinence, and from greed.

31. These forms of abstention are basic rules of conduct. They must be practiced without any reservations as to time, place, purpose, or caste rules.

32. The *niyamas* (observances) are purity, contentment, mortification, study and devotion to God.

33. To be free from thoughts that distract one from yoga, thoughts of an opposite kind must be cultivated.

34. The obstacles to yoga—such as acts of violence and untruth—may be directly created or indirectly caused or approved, they may be motivated by greed, anger or self-interest, they may be small or moderate or great, but they never cease to result in pain and ignorance. One should overcome distracting thoughts by remembering this.

35. When a man becomes steadfast in his abstention from harming others, then all living creatures will cease to feel enmity in his presence.

36. When a man becomes steadfast in his abstention from falsehood, he gets the power of obtaining for himself and others the fruits of good deeds, without having to perform the deeds themselves.

37. When a man becomes steadfast in his abstention from theft, all wealth comes to him.

38. When a man becomes steadfast in his abstention from incontinence, he acquires spiritual energy.

39. When a man becomes steadfast in his abstention from greed, he gains knowledge of his past, present and future existences.

40. As the result of purity, there arises indifference toward the body and disgust for physical intercourse with others.

41. Moreover, one achieves purification of the heart, cheerfulness of mind, the power of concentration, control of the passions and fitness for vision of the Atman.

42. As the result of contentment, one gains supreme happiness.

43. As the result of mortification, impurities are removed. Then special powers come to the body and the sense-organs.

44. As the result of study, one obtains the vision of that aspect of God which one has chosen to worship.

45. As the result of devotion to God, one achieves *samadhi*.

46. Posture (*asana*) is to be seated in a position which is firm but relaxed.

47. Posture becomes firm and relaxed through control of the natural tendencies of the body, and through meditation on the Infinite.

48. Thereafter, one is no longer troubled by the dualities of sense-experience.

49. After mastering posture, one must practice control of the *prana (pranayama)* by stopping the motions of inhalation and exhalation.

50. The breath may be stopped externally, or internally, or checked in mid-motion, and regulated according to place, time and a fixed number of moments, so that the stoppage is either protracted or brief.

51. The fourth kind of *pranayama* is the stoppage of the breath which is caused by concentration upon external or internal objects.

52. As the result of this, the covering of the Inner Light is removed.

53. The mind gains the power of concentration *(dharana)*.

54. When the mind is withdrawn from sense-objects, the sense-organs also withdraw themselves from their respective objects and thus are said to imitate the mind. This is known as *pratyahara*.

55. Thence arises complete mastery over the senses.

III. POWERS

1. Concentration *(dharana)* is holding the mind within a center of spiritual consciousness in the body, or fixing it on some divine form, either within the body or outside it.

2. Meditation *(dhyana)* is an unbroken flow of thought toward the object of concentration.

3. When, in meditation, the true nature of the object shines forth, not distorted by the mind of the perceiver, that is absorption *(samadhi)*.

4. When these three—concentration, meditation and absorption—are brought to bear upon one subject, they are called *samyama*.

5. Through mastery of *samyama* comes the light of knowledge.

6. It must be applied stage by stage.

7. These three are more direct aids to experience than the five limbs previously described.

8. But even these are not direct aids to the seedless *samadhi*.

9. When the vision of the lower *samadhi* is suppressed by an act of conscious control, so that there are no longer any thoughts or visions in the mind, that is the achievement of control of the thought-waves of the mind.

10. When this suppression of thought-waves becomes continuous, the mind's flow is calm.

11. When all mental distractions disappear and the mind becomes one-pointed, it enters the state called *samadhi*.

12. The mind becomes one-pointed when similar thought-waves arise in succession without any gaps between them.

13. In this state, it passes beyond the three kinds of changes which take place in subtle or gross matter, and in the organs: change of form, change of time and change of condition.

14. A compound object has attributes and is subject to change, either past, present or yet to be manifested.

15. The succession of these changes is the cause of manifold evolution.

16. By making *samyama* on the three kinds of changes, one obtains knowledge of the past and the future.

17. By making *samyama* on the sound of a word, one's perception of its meaning, and one's reaction to it—three things which are ordinarily confused—one obtains understanding of all sounds uttered by living beings.

18. By making *samyama* on previous thought-waves, one obtains knowledge of one's past lives.

19. By making *samyama* on the distinguishing marks of another man's body, one obtains knowledge of the nature of his mind.

20. But not of its contents, because that is not the object of the *samyama*.

21. If one makes *samyama* on the form of one's body, obstructing its perceptibility and separating its power of manifestation from the eyes of the beholder, then one's body becomes invisible.

22. Thus, also, its sounds cease to be heard.

23. By making *samyama* on two kinds of karma—that which will soon bear fruit and that which will not bear fruit until later—or by recognizing the portents of death, a yogi may know the exact time of his separation from the body.

24. By making *samyama* on friendliness, compassion, etc., one develops the powers of these qualities.

25. By making *samyama* on any kind of strength, such as that of the elephant, one obtains that strength.

26. By making *samyama* on the Inner Light, one obtains knowledge of what is subtle, hidden, or far distant.

27. By making *samyama* on the sun, one gains knowledge of the cosmic spaces.

28. By making *samyama* on the moon, one gains knowledge of the arrangement of the stars.

29. By making *samyama* on the polestar, one gains knowledge of the motions of the stars.

30. By making *samyama* on the navel, one gains knowledge of the constitution of the body.

31. By making *samyama* on the hollow of the throat, one stills hungers and thirsts.

32. By making *samyama* on the tube within the chest, one acquires absolute motionlessness.

33. By making *samyama* on the radiance within the back of the head, one becomes able to see the celestial beings.

34. All these powers of knowledge may also come to one whose mind is spontaneously enlightened through purity.

35. By making *samyama* on the heart, one gains knowledge of the contents of the mind.

36. The power of enjoyment arises from a failure to discriminate between the Atman and the *sattwa guna,* which are totally different. The *sattwa guna* is merely the agent of the Atman, which is independent, existing only for its own sake. By making *samyama* on the independence of the Atman, one gains knowledge of the Atman.

37. Hence, one gains the knowledge due to spontaneous enlightenment, and obtains supernatural powers of hearing, touch, sight, taste and smell.

38. They are powers in the worldly state, but they are obstacles to *samadhi.*

39. When the bonds of the mind caused by karma have been loosened, the yogi can enter into the body of another by knowledge of the operation of its nerve-currents.

40. By controlling the nerve-currents that govern the lungs and the upper part of the body, the yogi can walk on water and swamps, or on thorns and similar objects, and he can die at will.

41. By controlling the force which governs the *prana,* he can surround himself with a blaze of light.

42. By making *samyama* on the relation between the ear and the ether, one obtains supernatural powers of hearing.

43. By making *samyama* on the relation between the body and the ether, or by acquiring through meditation the lightness of cotton fiber, the yogi can fly through the air.

44. By making *samyama* on the thought-waves of the mind when it is separated from the body—the state known as the Great Disincarnation—all coverings can be removed from the light of knowledge.

45. By making *samyama* on the gross and subtle forms of the elements, on their essential characteristics and the inherence of the *gunas* in them, and on the experiences they provide for the individual, one gains mastery of the elements.

46. Hence one gains the power of becoming as tiny as an atom and all similar powers; also perfection of the body, which is no longer subject to the obstructions of the elements.

47. Perfection of the body includes beauty, grace, strength and the hardness of a thunderbolt.

48. By making *samyama* on the transformation that the sense-organs undergo when they contact objects, on the power of illumination of the sense-organs, on the ego-sense, on the *gunas* which constitute the organs, and on the experiences they provide for the individual, one gains mastery of the organs.

49. Hence the body gains the power of movement as rapid as that of the mind, the power of using the sense-organs outside the confines of the body, and the mastery of *Prakriti*.

50. By making *samyama* on the discrimination between the *sattwa guna* and the Atman, one gains omnipotence and omniscience.

51. By giving up even these powers, the seed of evil is destroyed and liberation follows.

52. When tempted by the invisible beings in high places, let the yogi feel neither allured nor flattered; for he is in danger of being caught once more by ignorance.

53. By making *samyama* on single moments and on their sequence in time, one gains discriminative knowledge.

54. Thus one is able to distinguish between two exactly similar objects, which cannot be distinguished by their species, characteristic marks, or positions in space.

55. This discriminative knowledge delivers a man from the bondage of ignorance. It comprehends all objects simultaneously, at every moment of their existence and in all their modifications.

56. Perfection is attained when the mind becomes as pure as the Atman itself.

IV. LIBERATION

1. The psychic powers may be obtained either by birth, or by means of drugs, or by the power of words, or by the practice of austerities, or by concentration.

2. The transformation of one species into another is caused by the inflowing of nature.

3. Good or bad deeds are not the direct causes of the transformation. They only act as breakers of the obstacles to natural evolution; just as a farmer breaks down the obstacles in a water course, so that water flows through by its own nature.

4. The ego-sense alone can create minds.

5. Though the activities of the different created minds are various, the one original mind controls them all.

6. Of the various types of mind, only that which is purified by *samadhi* is freed from all latent impressions of karma and from all cravings.

7. The karma of the yogi is neither white nor black. The karma of others is of three kinds: white, black, or mixed.

8. Of the tendencies produced by these three kinds of karma, only those are manifested for which the conditions are favorable.

9. Because of our memory of past tendencies, the chain of cause and effect is not broken by change of species, space or time.

10. Since the desire to exist has always been present, our tendencies cannot have had any beginning.

11. Our subconscious tendencies depend upon cause and effect. They have their basis in the mind, and they are stimulated by the sense-objects. If all these are removed, the tendencies are destroyed.

12. There is the form and expression we call "past," and the form and expression we call "future"; both exist within the object, at all times. Form and expression vary according to time—past, present or future.

13. They are either manifest or subtle, according to the nature of the *gunas.*

14. Since the *gunas* work together within every change of form and expression, there is a unity in all things.

15. The same object is perceived in different ways by different minds. Therefore the mind must be other than the object.

16. The object cannot be said to be dependent on the perception of a single mind. For, if this were the case, the object could be said to be non-existent when that single mind was not perceiving it.

17. An object is known or unknown, depending upon the moods of the mind.

18. Because the Atman, the Lord of the mind, is unchangeable, the mind's fluctuations are always known to it.

19. The mind is not self–luminous, since it is an object of perception.

20. And since it cannot perceive both subject and object simultaneously.

21. If one postulates a second mind to perceive the first, then one would have to postulate an infinite number of minds; and this would cause confusion of memory.

22. The pure consciousness of the Atman is unchangeable. As the reflection of its consciousness falls upon the mind, the mind takes the form of the Atman and appears to be conscious.

23. The mind is able to perceive because it reflects both the Atman and the objects of perception.

24. Though the mind has innumerable impressions and desires, it acts only to serve another, the Atman; for, being a compound substance, it cannot act independently, and for its own sake.

25. The man of discrimination ceases to regard the mind as the Atman.

26. When the mind is bent on the practice of discrimination, it moves toward liberation.

27. Distractions due to past impressions may arise if the mind relaxes its discrimination, even a little.

28. They may be overcome in the same manner as the obstacles to enlightenment.

29. He who remains undistracted even when he is in possession of all the psychic powers, achieves, as the result of perfect discrimination, that *samadhi* which is called the "cloud of virtue."

30. Thence come cessation of ignorance, the cause of suffering, and freedom from the power of karma.

31. Then the whole universe, with all its objects of sense-knowledge, becomes as nothing in comparison to that infinite knowledge which is free from all obstructions and impurities.

32. Then the sequence of mutations of the *gunas* comes to an end, for they have fulfilled their purpose.

33. This is the sequence of the mutations which take place at every moment, but which are only perceived at the end of a series.

34. Since the *gunas* no longer have any purpose to serve for the Atman, they resolve themselves into *Prakriti*. This is liberation. The Atman shines forth in its own pristine nature, as pure consciousness.

SHANKARA, A THOUSAND TEACHINGS

CHAPTER 1: HOW TO ENLIGHTEN THE PUPIL

1. Now we shall explain how to teach the means to final release for the benefit of seekers thereafter with faith and desire.

2. The means to final release is knowledge [of *Brahman*]. It should be repeatedly related to the pupil until it is firmly grasped, if he is dispassionate toward all things non-eternal which are attained by means [other than knowledge]; if he has abandoned the desire for sons, wealth, and worlds and reached the state of a *paramahamsa* wandering ascetic; if he is endowed with tranquility, self-control, compassion, and so forth; if he is possessed of the qualities of a pupil which are well known from the scriptures; if he is a Brahmin who is [internally and externally] pure; if he approaches his teacher in the prescribed manner; if his caste, profession, behavior, knowledge [of the Veda], and family have been examined.

3. The *Shruti* also says:

"Having scrutinized [the worlds that are built up by action, a Brahmin should arrive at indifference. . . . For the sake of this knowledge let him go, with fuel in hand, to a spiritual teacher who is learned in the scriptures and established in *Brahman*. To him who has approached properly, whose thought is calm, who has reached tranquility, the man of knowledge teaches] in its very truth that knowledge of *Brahman* [by which he knows the Imperishable]" (Mund. Up. I,2,12–13);

for when knowledge [of *Brahman*] is firmly grasped, it is conducive to one's own beatitude and to the continuity [of knowledge of *Brahman*]. And the continuity of knowledge [*of Brahman*] is helpful to people, as a boat [is helpful] to one wishing to get across a river. The scripture also says:

"[Verily, a father may teach this *Brahman* to his eldest son or to a worthy pupil, but to no one else at all.] Even if one should offer him this [earth] that is encompassed by water and filled with treasure, [he should say,] 'This, truly, is more than that'" (Chand. Up. III,ll,[5–]6),

since knowledge [*of Brahman*] is not obtained in any other way [than from a teacher] according to passages from the *Shruti* and the *Smrti* such as:

"One who has a teacher knows . . ." (Chand. Up. VI,14,2);

"The knowledge which has been learned from a teacher [best helps to attain his end" (Chand. Up. IV,9,3);

"A teacher is a boatman; his [right] knowledge is called a boat here."

Shankara, *A Thousand Teachings:* Part II (Prose Part), complete. Reprinted by permission from *A Thousand Teachings: The Upadesasahasri of Sankara* edited and translated by Sengaku Mayeda, the State University of New York Press. © 1992 State University of New York. All rights reserved.

4. When [the teacher] finds from some indications that the pupil has not grasped [this] knowledge, he should remove the causes which hinder his grasping it—demerit, worldly laxity, absence of firm preliminary learning concerning the discrimination between things eternal and non-eternal, care about what other people think, pride of caste and the like—by the means contrary to those causes and enjoined by the *Shruti* and the *Smrti*, that is to say, non-anger, etc., non-injury and other abstentions, and the observances which are not contradictory to knowledge.

5. He should also let [him] properly achieve the virtues such as modesty which are the means to attain knowledge.

6. And the teacher is able to consider the pros and cons [of an argument], is endowed with understanding, memory, tranquility, self-control, compassion, favor and the like; he is versed in the traditional doctrine; not attached to any enjoyments, visible or invisible, he has abandoned all the rituals and their requisites; a knower of *Brahman*, he is established in *Brahman*; he leads a blameless life, free from faults such as deceit, pride, trickery, wickedness, fraud, jealousy, falsehood, egotism, self-interest, and so forth; with the only purpose of helping others he wishes to make use of knowledge.

First of all, he should teach the *Shrutis* which are concerned primarily with the oneness of *Atman* [with *Brahman*], for example:

"In the beginning, my dear, this universe was the Existent only, one alone, without a second" (Chand. Up. VI,2,1);

"Where one sees nothing else, [hears nothing else, understands nothing else—that is the Fullness]" (Chand. Up. VII,24,1);

"*Atman*, indeed, is this all" (Chand. Up. VII,25,2);

"*Brahman*, indeed, is this all" (Brh. Up. II,5,1?);

"*Atman*, verily, was this universe, one alone, in the beginning" (Ait. Up. I,1,1);

"Verily, this all is *Brahman*" (Chand. Up. III,14,1).

7. And after teaching [these *Shrutis*], he should help [him] by means of the *Shrutis* to grasp the marks indicative *of Brahman*, for example:

"*Atman*, which is free from evil . . ." (Chand. Up. VIII,7,1);

"[Explain to me] what the manifest, unconcealed *Brahman* is" (Brh. Up. III,4,1; 5,1);

"That which transcends hunger and thirst" (Brh. Up. III,5,1);

"Not Thus! Not so!" (Brh. Up. II,3,6);

"[It is] not coarse, not fine" (Brh. Up. III,8,8);

"This *Atman* is [described as] 'not, not'" (Brh. Up. III,9,26; IV,2,4; 4,22; 5,15);

"[Verily, O Gargi, that Imperishable is] the unseen Seer" (Brh. Up. III,8,1); "[*Brahman* is] knowledge, bliss" (Brh. Up. III,9,28);

"[He who knows *Brahman* as the real,] as knowledge, as the infinite" (Taitt. Up. II,1);

"[For truly, when one finds fearlessness as a foundation] in That (= Brahman) which is invisible, bodiless, [. . . then he has reached fearlessness]" (Taitt. Up. II,7);

"This, verily, is [the great, unborn *Atman*]" (Brh. Up. IV,4,22);

"[This *Brahman* is . . .] breathless, mindless" (Mund. Up. II, 1,2);

"[This *Brahman* is] without and within, unborn" (Mund. Up. II,1,2,);

"[This great Being . . .] is just a mass of knowledge" (Brh. Up. II,4,12);

"[This *Brahman* is . . .] without an inside and without an outside" (Brh. Up. II,5,19);

"It is, indeed, other than the known and than the unknown" *(Kena Up.* I, 4);

"Verily, what is called 'Space' [is the accomplisher of name-and-form]" (Chand. Up. VIII,14,1).

8. [He should] also [help him grasp the marks indicative of *Brahman*] by means of the *Smrtis,* if they are not incompatible with the marks indicative [*of Brahman*] described by the *Shrutis* and concerned primarily with teaching that the highest *Atman* is not subject to transmigration and that It is identical with all—for example:

"He is not born, nor does he ever die" (BhG II,20; Kath. Up. II,18);

"He does not receive [the effect of] any one's evil" (BhG V, 15);

"As [the great Wind] constantly abides in space [. . . so all beings abide in Me]" (BhG IX, 6);

"Know also that I am the Field-Knower (= Atman)" (BhG XIII,2);

"It is called neither existent nor non-existent" (BhG XIII, 12);

"Because [He] is beginningless and attributeless" (BhG XIII, 31);

"[The supreme Lord, abiding] alike in all beings" (BhG XIII, 27);

"But there is the highest *Purusha* (= Atman)" (BhG XV, 17).

9. If the pupil who has thus grasped the marks indicative of the highest *Atman* according to the *Shrutis* and the *Smrtis* wishes to get out of the ocean of transmigratory existence, [the teacher] should ask him: "Who are you, my dear?"

10. If he answers: "I am a Brahmin's son belonging to such and such a family. I was a student—or, I was a householder—[but] now I am a *paramahamsa* wandering ascetic. I wish to get out of the ocean of transmigratory existence infested with great sharks of birth and death";

11. [then] the teacher should say: "My dear, when you are dead your body will be eaten by birds or will turn into earth right here. How then do you wish to get out of the ocean of transmigratory existence? Because if you turn into ashes on this bank of the river you cannot get across to the other side of the river."

12. If he answers: "I am different from the body. The body is born, dies, is eaten by birds, turns into earth, is destroyed by weapons, fire and so forth, and suffers from disease and so on. I have entered this body as a bird enters a nest, by force of the merit and demerit accumulated by myself. Again and again by force of the merit and demerit, when this body perishes, I shall enter another body as a bird enters another nest when its previous one has been destroyed. Thus I am in beginningless transmigratory existence. I have been abandoning [old] bodies which have been obtained one after another in the spheres of gods, animals, men, and hells by force of my own *karman* and I have been getting other new bodies over and over again. I am forced by my own *karman* to rotate in the incessant cycle of birth and death as in a water-wheel. I have obtained this body in the course of time. I am tired of this rotation in the wheel of transmigratory existence, so I have come to you, Your Holiness, in order to end the rotation in the wheel of transmigratory existence. Therefore I am eternal and different from the body. The bodies come and go like a person's garments";

13. [then] the teacher should say: "You are right. Your view is correct. [Then] why did you say incorrectly, 'I am a Brahmin's son belonging to such and such a family. I was a student—or, I was a householder—[but] now I am a *paramahamsa* wandering ascetic'?"

14. If he says: "Your Holiness, how have I spoken wrongly?"

15. [then] the teacher should reply to him: "Because, through such statements as 'I am a Brahmin's son belonging to such and such a family,' you have identified the *Atman,* which is free from caste, family, and purifying ceremonies, with the body, which has different caste, family, and purifying ceremonies."

16. If he asks: "How does the body have different caste, family, and purifying ceremonies?" or, "How am I (= Atman) free from caste, family, and purifying ceremonies?"

17. [then] the teacher should reply: "Listen, my dear, [this is] how this body, different from you (= Atman), has different caste, family and purifying ceremonies and how you (= Atman) are free from caste, family, and purifying ceremonies."
Thereupon [the teacher] should remind him: "You should remember, my dear, that you have been taught that the highest *Atman,* the *Atman* of all, is endowed with the marks described above according to such *Shruti* and *Smrti* passages as:

'[In the beginning,] my dear, this universe was the Existent only, [one alone, without a second]' (Chand. Up. VI,2,1)

and [that you have also been taught] the marks indicative of the highest *Atman* according to *Shruti* and *Smrti* passages."

18. When [the pupil] has recalled to mind the marks indicative of the highest *Atman,* [the teacher] should tell him [in answer to his first question]: "This [highest

Atman] which is called 'Space' is something different from name-and-form, bodiless, characterized as 'not coarse,' etc., and as 'free from evil,' etc. It is not afflicted with any attributes of transmigratory existence;

'[Explain to me] what the manifest, unconcealed *Brahman* is, . . . It is your *Atman*, which is within everything' (Brh. Up. III,4,1).

It is

'the unseen Seer, the unheard Hearer, the unthought Thinker, the unknown Knower' (Brh. Up. III,7,23).

It is of the nature of eternal knowledge,

'without an inside and without an outside' (Brh. Up. II,5,19),

'just a mass of knowledge' (Brh. Up. II,4,12).

It is all-pervading like ether, possessed of infinite power, the *Atman* of all, free from hunger, etc., and free from appearance and disappearance. This [highest *Atman*] is the Evolver of the unevolved name-and-form merely by being existent since It is possessed of inconceivable power. The unevolved name-and-form is different in essence from this [*Atman*] and it is the seed of the world, abiding in It, indescribable as this or something else, and known to It.

19. "[Originally] unevolved, this name-and-form took the name-and-form of 'ether' in the course of its evolution from this very *Atman*. And in this manner this element named 'ether' arose from the highest *Atman* as dirty foam from clear water. Foam is neither [identical with] water nor absolutely different from water since it is not seen without water. But water is clear and different from foam which is of the nature of dirt. Likewise, the highest *Atman* is different from name-and-form which corresponds to foam; *Atman* is pure, clear, and different in essence from it. This name-and-form, [originally] unevolved, took the name-and-form of 'ether,' which corresponds to foam, in the course of its evolution.

20. "Becoming grosser in the course of evolution, the name-and-form becomes air from ether, fire from air, water from fire, earth from water. In this order each preceding [element] entered each succeeding one and the five gross elements, [ether, air, fire, water, and] earth, came into existence. Consequently earth is characterized by the qualities of the five gross elements. And from earth, rice, barley, and other plants consisting of the five elements are produced; from them, when they are eaten, blood and sperm are produced, related respectively to the bodies of women and men. Both blood and sperm, produced by churning with the churning stick of sexual passion driven by nescience and sanctified with sacred formulas, are poured into the womb at the proper time. Through the penetration of fluid from the womb, they become an embryo and it is delivered in the ninth or tenth month.

21. "When it is born it obtains its name-and-form, sanctified with sacred formulas by means of a birth ceremony and other [purifying ceremonies]. Again it obtains the name of a student through the performance of the purifying ceremony for initiation.

This same body obtains the name of a householder through the performance of the purifying ceremony for union with a wife. This same body obtains the name of an ascetic through the purifying ceremony of becoming a forest-dweller. This same body obtains the name of a wandering ascetic through the purifying ceremony which ends the ritual actions. Thus the body is different from you (= Atman) and is possessed of different caste, family, and purifying ceremonies.

22. "The mind and the sense organs consist only of name-and-form according to the *Shrutis* such as:

'For, my dear, the mind consists of food' (Chand. Up. VI,5,4; 6,5; 7,6).

23. "[The second question you asked me earlier was,] 'How am I (= Atman) free from caste, family, and purifying ceremonies?' Listen to what [I am going to say]. The Evolver (= the highest *Atman*) of name-and-form, by nature different in essence from name-and-form, created this body in the course of evolving name-and-form. And [the Evolver] entered the name-and-form [of the body], Itself being free from the duties of purifying ceremonies. Itself unseen by others, [the Evolver] is seeing; unheard, It is hearing; unthought, It is thinking; unknown, It is knowing.

'The wise one who having distinguished all forms and having created [their] names, sits calling' (Taitt. A. III,12,7).

There are thousands of *Shruti* passages which have this same meaning, for example:

'Having created it, It, indeed, entered into it' (Taitt. Up. II,6,l);

'The Ruler of the creatures entered into [them]' (Taitt. A. III, 11,1);

'It entered here, [even to the fingertips]' (Brh. Up. I,4,7);

'It is your *Atman*, [which is in everything]' (Brh. Up. III,4,1; 5,1);

'So, cleaving asunder this very top of the skull, It entered by that door' (Ait. Up. I,3,12);

'Though It is hidden in all things, that *Atman* [does not shine forth]' (Kath. Up. III,12);

'That divinity thought, "Come! Let me [enter] these three divinities [(*i.e.*, heat, water, and food) with this living *Atman* and evolve name-and-form]"' (Chand. Up. VI, 3, 2);

'[*Atman* which is] the bodiless among bodies' (Kath. Up. II,22).

24. "There are also *Smrti* passages [which have this same meaning], for example:

'*Atman* is truly all gods' (Manu XII,119);

'The embodied *Atman* in the city of nine gates' (BhG V,13);

'Know also that I am the Field-Knower' (= *Atman*) (BhG XIII,2);

'[The supreme Lord abiding] alike in all beings' (BhG XIII,27);

'The onlooker and consenter, [the highest *Atman* . . . is also declared to be the highest *Purusha,* in this body]' (BhG XIII,22);

'But there is the highest *Purusha,* different [from this]' (BhG XV, 17).

It is, therefore, established that you (= *Atman*) are free from caste, family, and purifying ceremonies."

25. If he says: "I am one [and] He is another; I am ignorant, I experience pleasure and pain, am bound and a transmigrator [whereas] He is essentially different from me, the god not subject to transmigration. By worshipping Him with oblations, offerings, homage, and the like and through the [performance of] the actions prescribed for [my] class and stage of life, I wish to get out of the ocean of transmigratory existence. How am I He?"

26. [then] the teacher should reply: "My dear, you should not hold such a view since it is prohibited to understand that [*Atman*] is different [from *Brahman*]."
[The pupil may say:] "How is it prohibited to understand that [*Atman*] is different [from *Brahman*]?" Then the teacher replies:

" 'So whoever worships another divinity [than his *Atman*], thinking that He is one and I another, he does not know' (Brh. Up. I,4,10);

'Brahmanhood has deserted him who knows Brahmanhood as different from *Atman*' (Brh. Up. II,4,6);

'He who thinks he sees manifoldness in this world attains death after death' (Brh. Up. IV,4,19).

27. "These *Shruti* passages indeed reveal that transmigratory existence results from the understanding that [*Atman*] is different [from *Brahman*].

28. "And thousands [of *Shruti* passages] reveal that final release results from the realization of the identity [of *Atman* and *Brahman*]. [For example, through the statement,]

'That is *Atman,* Thou art That' (Chand. Up. VI, 8,7, etc.),

[the *Shrutis*] establish that [*Atman*] is the highest *Atman* (= Brahman). Then [they] state,

'One who has a teacher knows' (Chand. Up. VI, 14,2),

and [they] show final release with the words,

'He is delayed only until [he is freed from bondage of ignorance; then he will arrive at his final goal]' (Chand. Up. VI, 14,2).

With the simile about the [man] who was not a thief and [therefore] not burned [in the ordeal of the heated axe, the *Shrutis*] teach that he who covers himself with truth does not undergo transmigratory existence since he knows that [*Atman*] is identical [with *Brahman*]; [on the other hand], with the simile about the [man] who was a thief and was [therefore] burned, [the *Shrutis*] teach that he who covers himself with the untruth undergoes transmigratory existence since [he holds] the view that [*Atman*] is different [from *Brahman*].

29. "And with such [similes] as,

'Whatever they are in this world, whether tiger or [lion . . . mosquito, they become That Existent]' (Chand. Up. VI,9,3),

[the *Shrutis*] say that because of the view of the identity [of *Atman* with *Brahman*]

'[he] rules himself' (Chand. Up. VII,25,2).

And with the words,

'But they who know otherwise than this are ruled by another; theirs are perishable worlds' (Chand. Up. VII, 25, 2),

the *Shrutis* [continue to] teach that on account of the contrary view, *viz.* the view that [*Atman*] is different [from *Brahman*], he undergoes transmigratory existence. This is what is taught in every school of the *Veda*. So you were indeed wrong in saying, '[I (= *Atman*) am] a Brahmin's son belonging to such and such a family; [I (= *Atman*) am] a transmigrator, essentially different from the highest *Atman*.'

30. "For the above reason it is prohibited [by the *Shrutis*] to hold the view that [*Atman*] is different [from *Brahman*]; use of the rituals is [made] in the sphere of [the view] that [*Atman*] is different [from *Brahman*]; and the sacred thread and the like are requisites for the rituals. Therefore, it should be known that the use of rituals and their requisites is prohibited, if the identity [of *Atman*] with the highest *Atman* is realized, since [the use of] rituals and their requisites such as the sacred thread is contradictory to the realization of the identity [of *Atman*] with the highest *Atman*. [The use of] rituals and their requisites such as the sacred thread is indeed enjoined upon a transmigrator [but] not upon one who holds the view of the identity [of *Atman*] with the highest *Atman;* and the difference [of *Atman*] from It is merely due to the view that [*Atman*] is different [from *Brahman*].

31. "If rituals were to be performed and it were not desirable to abandon them, [the *Shrutis*] would not declare in such unambiguous sentence as,

'That is *Atman*, Thou art That' (Chand. Up. VI, 8,7, etc.),

that the highest *Atman,* unrelated to the rituals, their requisites, and such factors of the rituals as castes and stages of life, should be realized to be identical with [the inner] *Atman;* nor would [the *Shrutis*] condemn the realization that [*Atman*] is different [from *Brahman*], [in passages] such as,

'This is the constant greatness of the knower of *Brahman;* [it does not increase nor decrease by action]' (Brh. Up. IV,4,23);

'[He] is unaffected by good, unaffected by evil, [for then he has transcended all sorrows of the heart]' (Brh. Up. IV,3,22);

'In this state a thief is no thief [. . . a mendicant no mendicant, an ascetic no ascetic]' (Brh. Up. IV,3,22).

32. "[The *Shrutis*] would not declare that [*Atman*] is by nature unrelated to the rituals, by nature unconnected with the class and other factors of the rituals, if it were not desirable that the rituals and such requisites of the rituals as the sacred thread be abandoned completely. Therefore, the seeker after final release should abandon the ritual together with its requisites since [they] are contradictory to the view of the identity [of *Atman*] with the highest *Atman*. And [he] should realize that [his] *Atman* is the highest [*Atman*] since It has characteristics stated [about *Brahman*] by the *Shrutis*."

33. If [the pupil] says: "Your Holiness, when the body is burned or cut, I (= Atman) evidently perceive pain and I evidently experience suffering from hunger, etc. But in all the *Shrutis* and the *Smrtis* the highest *Atman* is said to be

'free from evil, ageless, deathless, sorrowless, hungerless, thirstless' (Chand. Up. VIII,1,5),

free from all attributes of transmigratory existence. I (= *Atman*) am different in essence from It and bound up with many attributes of transmigratory existence. How then can I realize that the highest *Atman* is [my] *Atman* and that I, a transmigrator, am the highest *Atman?*—it is as if I were to hold that fire is cold! Though I am [now] a transmigrator, I am entitled to the means of [attaining] all prosperity and beatitude. How then should I abandon the rituals and their requisites such as the sacred thread which lead [me] to prosperity and beatitude?"

34. [then the teacher] should answer him: "Your statement, 'When the body is burned or cut, I (= *Atman*) evidently perceive pain,' is not correct."
"Why?"
"The body, like a tree which is burned [or] cut, is the object [which is perceived by the perceiver]. The pain of burning or cutting is perceived in the body, which is the object; so the pain has the same locus as the burning [or cutting], since people point out the pain of burning [or cutting] right there where [the body] is burned or cut and not in the perceiver of burning [or cutting]."
"How?"
"When a man is asked, 'Where do you have pain?', he points to the locus where [the body] is burned [or cut] and not to the perceiver, saying, 'I have pain in the head' or 'In the chest' or 'In the stomach.' If pain or the cause of pain such as burning and cutting were located in the perceiver, he would point to [the perceiver] as the locus of pain just as [he points to a part of the body as] the locus of burning and so forth.

35. "And [pain] itself would not be perceived as the form-and-color in the eye [are not perceived by the eye]. Therefore, pain is perceived as having the same locus as burning, cutting, and so on; so pain is merely an object like burning and the like.
"As [pain] is of the nature of 'becoming,' [it] has its substratum like the cooking of rice. The impression of pain [also] has exactly the same substratum as the pain, since [the impression of pain] is perceived only simultaneously with the recollection [of

pain]. The aversion to pain and its causes also has precisely the same substratum as the impression. So it is said,

> 'Passion and aversion have, and the latent impression of form-and-color, a common substratum [the intellect], and what is perceived as fear has the intellect as its substratum; therefore, the Knower is always pure and free from fear' (Upad I,15,13)."

36. [The student may ask:] "What locus do then the impressions of form-and-color and the like have?"
[Then the teacher] answers: "[The locus] where there are desire and so forth."
"Where are there these desire and the like?"
"Right in the intellect according to such *Shruti* passages as,

> 'Desire, volition, doubt, [faith, lack of faith, steadfastness, lack of steadfastness, shame, meditation, fear—all this is truly mind]' (Brh. Up. I,5,3).

Right there are also the impressions of form-and-color and the like according to the *Shruti*,

> 'And on what are the colors and forms based?—On the heart' (Brh. Up. III,9,20).

Impurity [such as desire and aversion] is in the object and not in *Atman* [which is the subject] according to hundreds of *Shruti* passages such as,

> 'The desires that are based on heart' (Brh. Up. IV,4,7; Kath. Up. VI, 14);

> 'For [then] he has passed beyond [all sorrows of the heart]' (Brh. Up. IV,3,22);

> 'This [person] is without attachments' (Brh. Up. IV,3,16);

> 'Even this is His form that is beyond desire' (Brh. Up. IV,3,21),

and according to *Smrti* passages such as,

> 'He is declared to be unchangeable' (BhG II, 25);

> 'Because [He] is beginningless and attributeless' (BhG XIII, 31);

moreover,

> 'Desire, aversion' and so on are the attributes of 'the Field,' *i.e.*, the object, and not those of *Atman* (BhG XIII, 6).

37. "For this reason you (= *Atman*) have no relation with the impressions of form-and-color and the like; so you (= *Atman*) are not different in essence from the highest *Atman*. As there is no contradiction to sense-perception and other [means of knowledge], it is reasonable to realize that I (= *Atman*) am the highest *Atman* according to such *Shruti* passages as,

> 'It knew only Itself, ["I am Brahman!"] (Brh. Up. I,4,10);

> 'As a unity only is It to be looked upon' (Brh. Up. IV, 4,20);

'I, indeed, am below. [I am above. . . .]' (Chand. Up. VII,25, 1);

'*Atman,* indeed, is below. [*Atman* is behind. . . .]' (Chand. Up. VII, 25,2);

'One should see everything as *Atman*' (Brh. Up. IV,4,23);

'Where truly everything [has become] one's own *Atman,* [then whereby and whom does] one smell?' (Brh. Up. II,4,14);

'This all is what this *Atman* is' (Brh. Up. II,4,6);

'That one [is without parts, immortal]' (Pras. Up. VI,5);

[This *Brahman* is . . .] without an inside and without an outside' (Brh. Up. II,5,19);

'[This is] without and within, unborn' (Mund. Up. II,1,2);

'*Brahman* indeed is this [whole] world' (Mund. Up. II,2,12);

'[So, cleaving asunder this very top of the skull,] He entered by that door' (Ait. Up. I,3,12);

'[All these, indeed, are] names of intelligence' (Ait. Up. III,1,2);

'[He who knows *Brahman* as the real,] as knowledge, as the infinite' (Taitt. Up. II, 1);

'[Space] arose indeed from this [*Atman*]' (Taitt. Up. II, 1);

'Having created it, It indeed entered into it' (Taitt. Up. II,6,1);

'The one God, hidden in all things, [all-pervading]' (Svet. Up. VI, 11);

'[*Atman* which is] the bodiless among bodies' (Kath. Up. II,22);

'[The wise one] is not born, nor dies' (Kath. Up. II, 18);

'[Thinking on the great all-pervading *Atman,* by which one contemplates both] the dreaming state and the waking state, [the wise man is not grieved]' (Kath. Up. IV,4);

'One should know that It is my *Atman*' (Kaus. Up. III,8);

'Now, he who on all beings [looks as indeed in *Atman* and on *Atman* as in all beings—he does not shrink away from It]' (*Isha Up. VI*);

'It moves. It does not move' (*Isha Up.* V);

'Vena (the longing one?), seeing It, [knows all creatures, where all have the same nest]' (M.N.Up. II,3);

'It is, indeed, Agni, [It is Aditya, It is Vayu . . .]' (Taitt. A. X,l,2);

'I was Manu and the Sun' (Brh. Up. I,4,10; *Rgveda* IV,26,1);

'The Ruler of the creatures entered into [them]' (Taitt. A III, 11,1);

'[In the beginning,] my dear, [this universe was] the Existent only, [one alone, without a second]' (Chand. Up. VI,2,1);

'That is the Real, That is *Atman*, Thou art That' (Chand. Up. VI,8,7, etc.).

38. "From *Smrti* passages as well it is established that, being one alone, you, *Atman*, are the highest *Atman* [and] free from all the attributes of transmigratory existence—for example:

'[All] beings are the bodies of Him who lives in the hearts' *(Apastamba Dharmasutra* I,8,22,4);

'*Atman* is indeed [all] gods' (Manu, XII, 119);

'[The embodied *Atman*,] in the city of nine gates' (BhGV,13);

'[The supreme Lord abiding] alike in all beings' (BhG XIII,27);

'[The wise see the same thing] in a learned and well-behaved *Brahman*, [in a cow, in an elephant, and in a mere dog, and in an outcaste]' (BhG V,18);

'Unmanifold in the manifold' (BhG XVIII,20; cf. BhG XIII,16);

'Vasudeva (= Krsna) is all' (BhG VII,19)."

39. If [the pupil] says: "If, your Holiness, *Atman* is

'without an inside and without an outside' (Brh. Up. IV,5,13),

'without and within, unborn' (Mund. Up. II,1,2),

'entirely a mass of knowledge' (Brh. Up. IV,5,13),

like a mass of salt, devoid of all the varieties of forms, and homogeneous like ether, then how is it that the object, means, and agent of actions are [either actually] experienced or stated in *the Shrutis?* This is well-known in the *Shrutis* and *Smrtis* and among common people, and is a matter which causes differences of opinion among hundreds of disputants";

40. [then] the teacher should reply, "It is the effect of nescience that the object, means, and agent of actions are [either actually] experienced or stated in the *Shrutis;* but from the standpoint of the highest truth *Atman* is one alone and [only] appears as many through the vision [affected] by nescience just as the moon [appears] as many to sight [affected] by *timira* eye-disease. Duality is the effect of nescience, since it is reasonable [for the *Shrutis*] to condemn the view that [*Atman*] is different [from *Brahman*] by saying,

'Verily, where there seems to be another, [there the one might see the other]' (Brh. Up. IV,3,31);

'For where there is a duality, as it were, there one sees another' (Brh. Up. II,4,14);

'Death after death attains he [who thinks he sees manifoldness in this world]' (Brh. Up. IV,4,19);

'But where one sees something else, hears something else, understands something else—that is the small. . . . but the small is the same as the mortal' (Chand. Up. VII,24,1);

'[As, my dear, by one clod of clay everything made of clay may be understood;] the modification is a verbal distinction, a name' (Chand. Up. VI,1,4), [untrue];

'[So whoever worships another divinity than his *Atman*, thinking that] He is one and I another, [he does not know]' (Brh. Up. I,4,10).

And [the same conclusion is reached] from *Shruti* passages which establish oneness, for example:

'[In the beginning, my dear, this universe was the Existent only,] one alone, without a second' (Chand. Up. VI,2,1);

'Where, verily, [everything has become] one's own [*Atman*, then whereby and whom would one smell?]' (Brh. Up. II,4,14; cf. Brh. Up. IV,5,15);

'[Then] what delusion, what sorrow is there [for him who perceives the oneness!]' (*Isha Up.* 7)."

41. [The pupil may ask:] "If this be so, Your Holiness, for what purpose is difference in object, means, etc., of actions as well as origination and dissolution [of the world] stated in the *Shrutis?*"

42. Then [the teacher] replies: "A man possessed of nescience, being differentiated by the body, etc., thinks that his *Atman* is connected with things desirable and undesirable; [and] he does not know how to distinguish the means of attaining things desirable from that of abandoning things undesirable, although he desires to attain things desirable and to abandon things undesirable by some means. The scripture gradually removes his ignorance concerning this matter, but it does not establish the difference in object, means, etc., of actions, since the difference [constitutes] transmigratory existence which is undesirable by nature. Thus [the scripture] uproots nescience which is the view that [*Atman*] is different [from *Brahman*], the root of transmigratory existence, by showing the reasonableness of the oneness of the origination, dissolution, etc. [of the world].

43. "When nescience has been uprooted by means of the *Shrutis*, *Smrtis*, and reasoning, the only knowledge of one who sees the highest truth is established right in this [*Atman*] that is described as follows:

'Without an inside and without an outside' (Brh. Up. II, 5, 19);

'Without and within, unborn' (Mund. Up. II,1,2);

like a mass of salt;

'[Entirely] a mass of knowledge' (Brh. Up. IV,5,13);

and the homogeneous *Atman* which is all-pervading like ether. It is not reasonable that [in *Atman*] even a trace of impurity should arise from the difference in object and means of actions, origination and dissolution [of the world], and so forth.

44. "A man who wishes to attain this very view of the highest truth should abandon the fivefold form of desire, *viz.*, desires for a son, wealth, and worlds, which result from the misconception that [his] caste, stage of life, etc., [belong to his *Atman*]. And as this misconception is contradictory to the right conception, the reasoning for negating the view that [*Atman*] is different [from *Brahman*] is possible; for, when the conception that the sole *Atman* is not subject to transmigratory existence has occurred by means of the scripture and reasoning, no contradictory conception persists [any more]; for a conception that fire is cold, or that the body is not subject to old age and death, does not exist. Therefore, since all the rituals and their requisites such as the sacred thread are the effects of nescience, they should be abandoned by him who is established in the view of the highest truth."

CHAPTER 2: AWARENESS

1. A certain student, who was tired of transmigratory existence characterized by birth and death and was seeking after final release, approached in the prescribed manner a knower of *Brahman* who was established in *Brahman* and sitting at his ease, and asked him, "Your Holiness, how can I be released from transmigratory existence? I am aware of the body, the senses and [their] objects; I experience pain in the waking state, and I experience it in the dreaming state after getting relief again and again by entering into the state of deep sleep again and again. Is it indeed my own nature or [is it] due to some cause, my own nature being different? If [this is] my own nature, there is no hope for me to attain final release, since one cannot avoid one's own nature. If [it is] due to some cause, final release is possible after the cause has been removed."

2. The teacher replied to him, "Listen, my child, this is not your own nature but is due to a cause."

3. When he was told this the pupil said, "What is the cause? And what will remove it? And what is my own nature? When the cause is removed, the effect due to the cause no [longer] exists; I will attain to my own nature like a sick person [who recovers his health] when the cause of his disease has been removed."

4. The teacher replied, "The cause is nescience; it is removed by knowledge. When nescience has been removed, you will be released from transmigratory existence which is characterized by birth and death, since its cause will be gone and you will no [longer] experience pain in the dreaming and waking states."

5. The pupil said, "What is that nescience? And what is its object? And what is knowledge, remover of nescience, by which I can realize my own nature?"

6. The teacher replied, "Though you are the highest *Atman* and not a transmigrator, you hold the inverted view, 'I am a transmigrator.' Though you are neither an agent nor an experiencer, and exist [eternally], [you hold the inverted view, 'I am] an agent, an experiencer, and do not exist [eternally]'—this is nescience."

7. The pupil said, "Even though I exist [eternally], still I am not the highest *Atman*. My nature is transmigratory existence which is characterized by agency and experiencership, since it is known by sense-perception and other means of knowledge. [Transmigratory existence] has not nescience as its cause, since nescience cannot have one's own *Atman* as its object.

"Nescience is [defined as] the superimposition of the qualities of one [thing] upon another. For example, fully known silver is superimposed upon fully known mother-of-pearl, a fully known person upon a [fully known] tree trunk, or a fully known trunk upon a [fully known] person; but not an unknown [thing] upon [one that is] fully known nor a fully known [thing] upon one that is unknown. Nor is non-*Atman* superimposed upon *Atman* because *Atman* is not fully known, nor *Atman* [superimposed] upon non-*Atman*, [again] because *Atman* is not fully known."

8. The teacher said to him, "That is not right, since there is an exception. My child, it is not possible to make a general rule that a fully known [thing] is superimposed only upon a fully known [thing], since it is a matter of experience that [a fully known thing] is superimposed upon *Atman*. [For example,] if one says, 'I am white,' 'I am dark,' this is [the superimposition] of qualities of the body upon *Atman* which is the object of the 'I'-notion. And if one says, 'I am this,' this is [the superimposition of *Atman*,] which is the object of the 'I'-notion, upon the body."

9. The pupil said, "In that case *Atman* is indeed fully known as the object of the 'I'-notion; so is the body as 'this.' If so, [it is only a case of] the mutual superimposition of body and *Atman*, both fully known, just like [the mutual superimposition] of tree-trunk and person, and of mother-of-pearl and silver. So, is there a particular reason why Your Holiness said that it is not possible to make a general rule that two fully known [things] are mutually superimposed?"

10. The teacher replied, "Listen. It is true that the body and *Atman* are fully known; but they are not fully known to all people as the objects of distinct notions like a tree-trunk and a person."

"How [are they known] then?"

"[They are] always [known] as the objects of constantly non-distinct notions. Since nobody grasps the body and *Atman* as two distinct notions, saying, 'This is the body, that is *Atman*,' people are deluded with regard to *Atman* and non-*Atman*, thinking, '*Atman* is thus' or '*Atman* is not thus.' This is the particular reason why I said that it is impossible to make a general rule."

11. [The pupil raised another objection:] "Is it not experienced that the thing which is superimposed [upon something] else through nescience does not exist [in the latter]? For example, silver [does not exist] in a mother-of-pearl nor a person in a tree-trunk nor a snake in a rope; nor the dark color of the earth's surface in the sky. Likewise, if the body and *Atman* are always mutually superimposed in the form of constantly non-distinct notions, then they cannot exist in each other at anytime. Silver, etc., which are superimposed through nescience upon mother-of-pearl, etc., do not exist [in the latter] at any time in any way and *vice versa;* likewise the body and *Atman* are mutually superimposed through nescience; this being the case, it would follow as the result that neither the body nor *Atman* exists. And it is not acceptable, since it is the theory of the Nihilists.

"If, instead of mutual superimposition, [only] the body is superimposed upon *Atman* through nescience, it would follow as the result that the body does not exist in

Atman while the latter exists. This is not acceptable either since it is contradictory to sense-perception and other [means of knowledge]. For this reason the body and *Atman* are not superimposed upon each other through nescience."

"How then?"

"They are permanently connected with each other like bamboo and pillars [which are interlaced in the structure of a house]."

12. [The teacher said,] "No; because it would follow as the result that [*Atman* is] non-eternal and exists for another's sake; since [in your opinion *Atman*] is composite, [*Atman* exists for another's sake and is non-eternal] just like bamboo, pillars, and so forth. Moreover, the *Atman* which is assumed by some others to be connected with the body exists for another's sake since it is composite. [Therefore,] it has been first established that the highest [*Atman*] is not connected with the body, is different [from it], and is eternal.

13. [The pupil objected:] "Although [the *Atman*] is not composite, It is [regarded] merely as the body and superimposed upon the body; from this follow the results that [the *Atman*] does not exist and that [It] is non-eternal and so on. Then there would arise the fault that [you will] arrive at the Nihilists' position that the body has no *Atman*."

14. [The teacher replied,] "Not so; because it is accepted that *Atman*, like space, is by nature not composite. Although *Atman* exists as connected with nothing, it does not follow that the body and other things are without *Atman*, just as, although space is connected with nothing, it does not follow that nothing has space. Therefore, there would not arise the fault that [I shall] arrive at the Nihilists' position.

15. "Your further objection—namely that, if the body does not exist in *Atman* [although *Atman* exists], this would contradict sense-perception and the other [means of knowledge]: this is not right, because the existence of the body in *Atman* is not cognized by sense-perception and the other [means of knowledge]; in *Atman*—like a jujube-fruit in a pot, ghee in milk, oil in sesame and a picture on a wall—the body is not cognized by sense-perception and the other [means of knowledge]. Therefore there is no contradiction with sense-perception and the other [means of knowledge]."

16. [The pupil objected,] "How is the body then superimposed upon *Atman* which is not established by sense-perception and the other [means of knowledge], and how is *Atman* superimposed upon the body?"

17. [The teacher said,] "That is not a fault, because *Atman* is established by Its own nature. A general rule cannot be made that superimposition is made only on that which is adventitiously established and not on that which is permanently established, for the dark color and other things on the surface of the earth are seen to be superimposed upon the sky [which is permanently established]."

18. [The pupil asked,] "Your Holiness, is the mutual superimposition of the body and *Atman* made by the composite of the body and so on or by *Atman?*"

19. The teacher said, "What would happen to you, if [the mutual superimposition] is made by the composite of the body and so on, or if [it] is made by *Atman?*"

20. Then the pupil answered, "If I am merely the composite of the body and so on, then I am non-conscious, so I exist for another's sake; consequently, the mutual superimposition of body and *Atman* is not effected by me. If I am the highest *Atman* different from the composite [of the body and so on], then I am conscious, so I exist for my own sake; consequently, the superimposition [of body] which is the seed of every calamity is effected upon *Atman* by me who am conscious."

21. To this the teacher responded, "If you know that the false superimposition is the seed of [every] calamity, then do not make it!"

22. "Your Holiness, I cannot help [it]. I am driven [to do it] by another; I am not independent."

23. [The teacher said,] "Then you are non-conscious, so you do not exist for your own sake. That by which you who are not self-dependent are driven to act is conscious and exists for its own sake; you are only a composite thing [of the body, etc.]."

24. [The pupil objected,] "If I am non-conscious, how do I perceive feelings of pleasure and pain, and [the words] you have spoken?"

25. The teacher said, "Are you different from feelings of pleasure and pain and from [the words] I have spoken, or are you identical [with them]?"

26. The pupil answered, "I am indeed not identical."
"Why?"
"Because I perceive both of them as objects just as [I perceive] a jar and other things [as objects]. If I were identical [with them] I could not perceive either of them; but I do perceive them, so I am different [from both of them]. If [I were] identical [with them] it would follow that the modifications of the feelings of pleasure and pain exist for their own sake and so do [the words] you have spoken; but it is not reasonable that any of them exists for their own sake, for the pleasure and pain produced by a sandal and a thorn are not for the sake of the sandal and the thorn, nor is use made of a jar for the sake of the jar. So, the sandal and other things serve my purpose, *i.e.,* the purpose of their perceiver, since I who am different from them perceive all the objects seated in the intellect."

27. The teacher said to him, "So, then, you exist for your own sake since you are conscious. You are not driven [to act] by another. A conscious being is neither dependent on another nor driven [to act] by another, for it is not reasonable that a conscious being should exist for the sake of another conscious being since they are equal like two lights. Nor does a conscious being exist for the sake of a non-conscious being since it is not reasonable that a non-conscious being should have any connection with its own object precisely because it is non-conscious. Nor does experience show that two non-conscious beings exist for each other, as for example a stick of wood and a wall do not fulfill each other's purposes."

28. [The pupil objected,] "Is it not experienced that a servant and his master, though they are equal in the sense of being conscious, exist for each other?"

29. [The teacher said,] "It is not so, for what [I] meant was that you have consciousness just as fire has heat and light. And [in this meaning I] cited the example, 'like two lights.' This being the case, you perceive everything seated in your intellect through

your own nature, *i.e.*, the transcendentally changeless, eternal, pure consciousness which is equivalent to the heat and light of fire. And if you admit that *Atman* is always without distinctions, why did you say, 'After getting relief again and again in the state of deep sleep, I perceive pain in the waking and dreaming states. Is this indeed my own nature or [is it] due to some cause?' Has this delusion left [you now] or not?"

30. To this the pupil replied, "Your Holiness, the delusion has gone thanks to your gracious assistance; but I am in doubt as to how I am transcendentally changeless."
"How?"
"Sound and other [external objects] are not self-established, since they are not conscious. But they [are established] through the rise of notions which take the forms of sound and other [external objects]. It is impossible for notions to be self-established, since they have mutually exclusive attributes and the forms [of external objects] such as blue and yellow. It is, therefore, understood that [notions] are caused by the forms of the external objects; so, [notions] are established as possessing the forms of external objects, *i.e.*, the forms of sound, etc. Likewise, notions, which are the modifications of a thing (= the intellect), the substratum of the 'I'-notion, are also composite, so it is reasonable that they are non-conscious; therefore, as it is impossible that they exist for their own sake, they, like sound and other [external objects], are established as objects to be perceived by a perceiver different in nature [from them]. If I am not composite, I have pure consciousness as my nature; so I exist for my own sake. Nevertheless, I am a perceiver of notions which have the forms [of the external objects] such as blue and yellow [and] so I am indeed subject to change. [For the above reason, I am] in doubt as to how [I am] transcendentally changeless."

31. The teacher said to him, "Your doubt is not reasonable. [Your] perception of those notions is necessary and entire; for this very reason [you] are not subject to transformation. It is, therefore, established that [you] are transcendentally changeless. But you have said that precisely the reason for the above positive conclusion—namely, that [you] perceive the entire movement of the mind—is the reason for [your] doubt [concerning your transcendental changelessness]. This is why [your doubt is not reasonable].
"If indeed you were subject to transformation, you would not perceive the entire movement of the mind which is your object, just as the mind [does not perceive] its [entire] object and just as the senses [do not perceive] their [entire] objects, and similarly you as *Atman* would not perceive even a part of your object. Therefore, you are transcendentally changeless."

32. Then [the pupil] said, "Perception is what is meant by the verbal root, that is, nothing but change; it is contradictory [to this fact] to say that [the nature of] the perceiver is transcendentally changeless."

33. [The teacher said,] "That is not right, for [the term] 'perception' is used figuratively in the sense of a change which is meant by the verbal root; whatever the notion of the intellect may be, that is what is meant by the verbal root; [the notion of the intellect] has change as its nature and end, with the result that the perception of *Atman* falsely appears [as perceiver]; thus the notion of the intellect is figuratively indicated by the term, 'perception.' For example, the cutting action results [in the static state] that [the object to be cut] is separated in two parts; thus [the term, 'cutting,' in the sense of an object to be cut being separated in two parts,] is used figuratively as [the cutting action] which is meant by the verbal root."

34. To this the pupil objected, "Your Holiness, the example cannot explain my transcendental changelessness."

"Why not?"

"'Cutting' which results in a change in the object to be cut is used figuratively as [the cutting action] which is meant by the verbal root; in the same manner, if the notion of the intellect, which is figuratively indicated by the term 'perception' and is meant by the verbal root, results also in a change in the perception of *Atman,* [the example] cannot explain *Atman's* transcendental changelessness."

35. The teacher said, "It would be true, if there were a distinction between perception and perceiver. The perceiver is indeed nothing but eternal perception. And it is not [right] that perception and perceiver are different as in the doctrine of the logicians."

36. [The pupil said,] "How does that [action] which is meant by the verbal root result in perception?"

37. [The teacher] answered, "Listen, [I] said that [it] ends with the result that the perception [of *Atman*] falsely appears [as perceiver]. Did you not hear? I did not say that [it] results in the production of any change in *Atman.*"

38. The pupil said, "Why then did you say that if I am transcendentally changeless I am the perceiver of the entire movement of the mind which is my object?"

39. The teacher said to him, "I told [you] only the truth. Precisely because [you are the perceiver of the entire movement of the mind], I said, you are transcendentally changeless."

40. "If so, Your Holiness, I am of the nature of transcendentally changeless and eternal perception whereas the notions of the intellect, which have the forms of [external objects] such as sound, arise and end with the result that my own nature which is perception falsely appears [as perceiver]. Then what is my fault?"

41. [The teacher replied,] "You are right. [You] have no fault. The fault is only nescience as I have said before."

42. [The pupil said,] "If, Your Holiness, as in the state of deep sleep I undergo no change, how [do I experience] the dreaming and waking states?"

43. The teacher said to him, "But do you experience [these states] continuously?"

44. [The pupil answered,] "Certainly I do experience [them], but intermittently and not continuously."

45. The teacher said [to him,] "Both of them are adventitious [and] not your nature. If [they] were your nature [they] would be self-established and continuous like your nature, which is Pure Consciousness. Moreover, the dreaming and waking states are not your nature, for [they] depart [from you] like clothes and so on. It is certainly not experienced that the nature of anything, whatever it may be, departs from it. But the dreaming and waking states depart from the state of Pure Consciousness-only. If one's own nature were to depart [from oneself] in the state of deep sleep, it would be negat-

ed by saying, 'It has perished,' 'It does not exist,' since the adventitious attributes which are not one's own nature are seen to consist in both [perishableness and non-existence]; for example, wealth, clothes, and the like are seen to perish and things which have been obtained in dream or delusion are seen to be non-existent."

46. [The pupil objected,] "[If] so, Your Holiness, it follows [either] that my own nature, *i.e.,* Pure Consciousness, is also adventitious, since [I] perceive in the dreaming and waking states but not in the state of deep sleep; or that I am not of the nature of Pure Consciousness."

47. [The teacher replied,] "No, Look. Because that is not reasonable. If you [insist on] looking your own nature, *i.e.* Pure Consciousness, as adventitious, do so! We cannot establish it logically even in a hundred years, nor can any other *(i.e.* non-conscious) being do so. As [that adventitious consciousness] is composite, nobody can logically deny that [it] exists for another's sake, is manifold and perishable; for what does not exist for its own sake is not self-established, as we have said before. Nobody can, however, deny that *Atman,* which is of the nature of Pure Consciousness, is self-established; so It does not depend upon anything else, since It does not depart [from anybody]."

48. [The pupil objected,] "Did I not point out that [It] does depart [from me] when I said that in the state of deep sleep I do not see?"

49. [The teacher replied,] "That is not right, for it is contradictory."
"How is it a contradiction?"
"Although you are [in truth] seeing, you say, 'I do not see.' This is contradictory."
"But at no time in the state of deep sleep, Your Holiness, have I ever seen Pure Consciousness or anything else."
"Then you are seeing in the state of deep sleep; for you deny only the seen object, not the seeing. I said that your seeing is Pure Consciousness. That [eternally] existing one by which you deny [the existence of the seen object] when you say that nothing has been seen, [that precisely is the seeing] that is Pure Consciousness. Thus as [It] does not ever depart [from you] [Its] transcendental changelessness and eternity are established solely by Itself without depending upon any means of knowledge. The knower, though self-established, requires means of knowledge for the discernment of an object to be known other [than itself]. And that eternal Discernment, which is required for discerning something else (= non-*Atman*) which does not have Discernment as its nature—that is certainly eternal, transcendentally changeless, and of a self-effulgent nature. The eternal Discernment does not require any means of knowledge in order to be Itself the means of knowledge or the knower since the eternal Discernment is by nature the means of knowledge or the knower. [This is illustrated by the following] example: iron or water requires fire or sun [to obtain] light and heat since light and heat are not their nature; but fire and sun do not require [anything else] for light and heat since [these] are always their nature.

50. "If [you object,] 'There is empirical knowledge in so far as it is not eternal and [there is] no [empirical knowledge], if it is eternal,'

51. "[then I reply,] 'Not so; because it is impossible to make a distinction between eternal apprehension and non-eternal apprehension; when apprehension is empirical knowledge, such distinction is not apprehended that empirical knowledge is non-eternal apprehension and not eternal one.'

52. "If [you object,] 'When [empirical knowledge] is eternal [apprehension, it] does not require the knower, but when [empirical knowledge] is non-eternal [apprehension], apprehension requires [the knower], since it is mediated by [the knower's] effort. There would be the above distinction,'

53. "then, it is established that the knower itself is self-established, since [it] does not require any means of knowledge.

54. "If [you object,] 'Even when [apprehension or empirical knowledge] does not exist, [the knower] does not require [any means of knowledge], since [the knower] is eternal,' [my reply is,] 'No; because apprehension exists only in [the knower] itself. Thus your opinion is refuted.

55. "If the knower is dependent upon the means of knowledge for its establishment, where does the desire to know belong? It is admitted that that to which the desire to know belongs is indeed the knower. And the object of this desire to know is the object to be known, not the knower, since if the object [of the desire to know] were the knower, a *regressus ad infinitum* with regard to the knower and the desire to know would result: there would be a second knower for the first one, a third knower for the second, and so on. Such would be the case if the desire to know had the knower as its object. And the knower itself cannot be the object to be known, since it is never mediated [by anything]; what in this world is called the object to be known is established, when it is mediated by the rise of desire, remembrance, effort, and means of knowledge which belong to the knower. In no other way is apprehension experienced with regard to the object to be known. And it cannot be assumed that the knower itself is mediated by any of the knower's own desire and the like. And remembrance has as its object the object to be remembered and not the subject of remembrance. Likewise, desire has as its object only the object desired and not the one who desires. If remembrance and desire had as their object the subject of remembrance and the one who desires respectively, a *regressus ad infinitum* would be inevitable as before.

56. "If [you say,] 'If apprehension which has the knower as its object is impossible, the knower would not be apprehended,'

57. "not so; because the apprehension of the apprehender has as its object the object to be apprehended. If [it] were to have the apprehender as its object, a *regressus ad infinitum* would result as before. And it has been proved before that apprehension, *i.e.*, the transcendentally changeless and eternal light of *Atman*, is established in *Atman* without depending upon anything else as heat and light are in fire, the sun, and so on. If apprehension, *i.e.*, the light of *Atman* which is Pure Consciousness, were not eternal in one's own *Atman*, it would be impossible for *Atman* to exist for Its own sake; as It would be composite like the aggregate of the body and senses, It would exist for another's sake and be possessed of faults as we have already said."

"How?"

"If the light of *Atman* which is Pure Consciousness were not eternal in one's own *Atman*, it would be mediated by remembrance and the like and so it would be composite. And as this light of Pure Consciousness would therefore not exist in *Atman* before Its origination and after Its destruction, It would exist for another's sake, since It would be composite like the eye and so on. And if the light of Pure Consciousness exists in *Atman* as something which has arisen, then *Atman* does not exist for Its own sake, since it is established according to the existence and absence of that light of Pure Consciousness that *Atman* exists for Its own sake and non-*Atman* exists for another's sake. It is therefore established that *Atman* is the eternal light of Pure Consciousness without depending upon anything else."

58. [The pupil objected,] "If so, [and] if the knower is not the subject of empirical knowledge, how is it a knower?"

59. [The teacher] answered, "Because there is no distinction in the nature of empirical knowledge, whether it is eternal or non-eternal, since empirical knowledge is apprehension. There is no distinction in the nature of this [empirical knowledge] whether it be non-eternal, preceded by remembrance, desire, and the like, or transcendentally changeless and eternal, just as there is no distinction in the nature of what is meant by verbal root such as *stha* (stand), whether it is a non-eternal result preceded by 'going' and other [forms of actions], or an eternal result not preceded [by 'going' or any other forms of actions]; so the same expression is found [in both cases]: 'People stand,' 'The mountains stand,' and so forth. Likewise, although the knower is of the nature of eternal apprehension, it is not contradictory to designate [It] as 'knower,' since the result is the same."

60. Here the pupil said, "*Atman*, which is of the nature of eternal apprehension, is changeless, so it is impossible for *Atman* to be an agent without being connected with the body and the senses, just as a carpenter and other [agents are connected] with an axe and so on. And if that which is by nature not composite were to use the body and the senses, a *regressus ad infinitum* would result. But the carpenter and the other [agents] are constantly connected with the body and the senses; so, when [they] use an axe and the like, no *regressus ad infinitum* occurs."

61. [The teacher said,] "But in that case [*Atman*], which is by nature not composite, cannot be an agent when It makes no use of instruments; [It] would have to use an instrument [to be an agent]. [But] the use [of an instrument] would be a change; so in becoming an agent which causes that [change], [It] should use another instrument, [and] in using this instrument, [It] should also use another one. Thus if the knower is independent, a *regressus ad infinitum* is inevitable.

"And no action causes *Atman* to act, since [the action] which has not been performed does not have its own nature. If [you object,] 'Something other [than *Atman*] approaches *Atman* and causes It to perform an action', [I reply,] 'No; because it is impossible for anything other [than *Atman*] to be self-established, a non-object, and so forth; it is not experienced that anything else but *Atman*, being non-conscious, is self-evident. Sound and all other [objects] are established when they are known by a notion which ends with the result of apprehension.

"If apprehension were to belong to anything else but *Atman*, It would also be *Atman*, not composite, existing for Its own sake, and not for another. And we cannot apprehend that the body, the senses, and their objects exist for their own sake, since it is experienced that they depend for their establishment upon the notions which result in apprehension."

62. [The pupil objected,] "In apprehending the body nobody depends upon any other notions due to sense-perception and other [means of knowledge]."

63. [The teacher said,] "Certainly in the waking state it would be so. But in the states of death and deep sleep the body also depends upon sense-perception and other

means of knowledge for its establishment. This is true of the senses. Sound and other [external objects] are indeed transformed into the form of the body and senses; so, [the body and the senses] depend upon sense-perception and other means of knowledge for [their] establishment. And 'establishment' (*siddhi*) is Apprehension, *i.e.,* the result of the means of knowledge as we have already said, and this Apprehension is transcendentally changeless, self-established, and by nature the light of *Atman.*"

64. Here [the pupil] objected, saying, "It is contradictory to say that Apprehension is the result of the means of knowledge and that It is by nature the transcendentally changeless and eternal light *of Atman.*"

To this [the teacher] said, "It is not contradictory."

"How then [is it not contradictory]?"

"Although [Apprehension] is transcendentally changeless and eternal, [It] appears at the end of the notion [forming process] due to sense-perception and other [means of knowledge] since [the notion-forming process] aims at It. If the notion due to sense-perception and other [means of knowledge] is non-eternal, [Apprehension, though eternal,] appears as if it were non-eternal. Therefore, [Apprehension] is figuratively called the result of the means of knowledge."

65. [The pupil said,] "If so, Your Holiness, Apprehension is transcendentally changeless, eternal, indeed of the nature of the light *of Atman,* and self-established, since It does not depend upon any means of knowledge with regard to Itself; everything other than This is non-conscious and exists for another's sake, since it acts together [with others].

"And because of this nature of being apprehended as notion causing pleasure, pain, and delusion, [non-*Atman*] exists for another's sake; on account of this very nature non-*Atman* exists and not on account of any other nature. It is therefore merely non-existent from the standpoint of the highest truth. Just as it is experienced in this world that a snake [superimposed] upon a rope does not exist, nor water in a mirage, and the like, unless they are apprehended [as a notion], so it is reasonable that duality in the waking and dreaming states also does not exist unless it is apprehended [as a notion]. In this manner, Your Holiness, Apprehension, *i.e.,* the light of *Atman,* is uninterrupted; so It is transcendentally changeless, eternal and non-dual, since It is never absent from any of the various notions. But various notions are absent from Apprehension. Just as in the dreaming state the notions in different forms such as blue and yellow, which are absent from that Apprehension, are said to be non-existent from the standpoint of the highest truth, so in the waking state also, the various notions such as blue and yellow, which are absent from this very Apprehension, must by nature be untrue. And there is no apprehender different from this Apprehension to apprehend It; therefore It can Itself neither be accepted nor rejected by Its own nature, since there is nothing else."

66. [The teacher said,] "Exactly so it is. It is nescience that is the cause of transmigratory existence which is characterized by the waking and dreaming states. The remover of this nescience is knowledge. And so you have reached fearlessness. From now on you will not perceive any pain in the waking and dreaming states. You are released from the sufferings of transmigratory existence."

67. [The pupil said,] "Om."

CHAPTER 3: *PARISAMKHYANA* MEDITATION

1. This *parisamkhyana* meditation is described for seekers after final release, who are devoting themselves to destroying their acquired merit and demerit and do not wish to accumulate new ones. Nescience causes faults (= passion and aversion); they cause the activities of speech, mind, and body; and from these activities are accumulated *karmans* of which [in turn] the results are desirable, undesirable, and mixed. For the sake of final release from those *karmans* [this *parisamkhyana* meditation is described].

2. Now, sound, touch, form-and-color, taste, and odor are the objects of the senses; they are to be perceived by the ear and other [senses]. Therefore, they do not have any knowledge of themselves nor of others, since they are merely things evolved [from the unevolved name-and-form] like clay and the like. And they are perceived through the ear and other [senses].

And that by which they are perceived is of a different nature since it is a perceiver. Because they are connected with one another, sound and other [objects of the senses] are possessed of many attributes such as birth, growth, change of state, decay, and destruction; connection and separation; appearance and disappearance; effect of change and cause of change; field (= female?) and seed (= male?). They are also commonly possessed of many [other] attributes such as pleasure and pain. Their perceiver is different in its nature from all the attributes of sound and the other [objects of the senses], precisely because it is their perceiver.

3. So the wise man who is tormented by sound and the other [objects of the senses] which are being perceived should perform *parisamkhyana* meditation as follows:

4. I (= *Atman*) am of the nature of Seeing, non-object (= subject) unconnected [with anything], changeless, motionless, endless, fearless, and absolutely subtle. So sound cannot make me its object and touch me, whether as mere noise in general or as [sound] of particular qualities—pleasant [sounds] such as the first note of music or the desirable words of praise and the like, or the undesirable words of untruth, disgust, humiliation, abuse, and the like—since I am unconnected [with sound]. For this very reason neither loss nor gain is caused [in me] by sound. Therefore, what can the pleasant sound of praise, the unpleasant sound of blame, and so on do to me? Indeed a pleasant sound may produce gain, and an unpleasant one destruction, for a man lacking in discriminating knowledge, who regards sound as [connected with his] *Atman* since he has no discriminating knowledge. But for me who am endowed with discriminating knowledge, [sound] cannot produce even a hair's breadth [of gain or loss].

In the very same manner [touch] does not produce for me any change of gain and loss, whether as touch in general or as touch in particular forms—the unpleasant [touch] of cold, heat, softness, hardness, etc., and of fever, stomachache, etc., and any pleasant [touch] either inherent in the body or caused by external and adventitious [objects]—since I am devoid of touch, just as a blow with the fist and the like [does not produce any change] in the sky.

Likewise [form-and-color] produces neither loss nor gain for me, whether as form-and-color in general or as form-and-color in particular, pleasant or unpleasant, such as the female characteristics of a woman and the like, since I am devoid of form-and-color.

Similarly, [taste] produces neither loss nor gain for me who am by nature devoid of taste, whether as taste in general or as taste in particular forms [, pleasant or unpleasant,] such as sweetness, sourness, saltiness, pungency, bitterness, astringency which are perceived by the dull-witted.

In like manner [odor] produces neither loss nor gain for me who am by nature devoid of odor, whether as odor in general or as odor in particular forms, pleasant or unpleasant, such as [the odor] of flowers, etc., and ointment, etc. That is because the *Shruti* says:

"That which is soundless, touchless, formless, imperishable, also tasteless, constant, odorless,
. . . [—having perceived that, one is freed from the jaws of death]" (Kath. Up. III,15).

5. Moreover, whatever sound and the other external [objects of the senses] may be, they are changed into the form of the body, and into the form of the ear and the other [senses] which perceive them, and into the form of the two internal organs and their objects [such as pleasure and pain], since they are mutually connected and composite in all cases of actions. This being the case, to me, a man of knowledge, nobody is foe, friend or neutral.

In this context, if [anybody,] through a misconception [about *Atman*] due to false knowledge, were to wish to connect [me] with [anything], pleasant or unpleasant, which is characteristic of the result of action, he wishes in vain to connect [me] with it, since I am not its object according to the *Smrti* passage:

"Unmanifest he, unthinkable he, [unchangeable he is declared to be]" (BhG II,25).

Likewise, I am not to be changed by [any of] the five elements, since I am not their object according to the *Smrti* passage:

"Not to be cut is he, not to be burnt is he, [not to be wet nor yet dried]" (BhG II,24).

Furthermore, paying attention only to the aggregate of the body and the senses, [people, both] devoted and adverse to me, have the desire to connect [me] with things, pleasant, unpleasant, etc., and therefrom results the acquisition of merit, demerit, and the like. It belongs only to them and does not occur in me who am free from old age, death, and fear, since the *Shrutis* and the *Smrtis* say:

"Neither what has been done nor what has been left undone affects It" (Brh. Up. IV, 4,22);

"[This is the constant greatness of the knower of *Brahman*]; he does not increase nor become less by action" (Brh. Up. IV,4,23);

"[This is] without and within, unborn" (Mund. Up. II,1,2);

"[So the one inner *Atman* of all beings] is not afflicted with the suffering of the world, being outside of it" (Kath. Up. V,11); etc.

That is because anything other than *Atman* does not exist,—this is the highest reason.

As duality does not exist, all the sentences of the *Upanishads* concerning non-duality of *Atman* should be fully contemplated, should be contemplated.

WESTERN ENCOUNTERS—INDIA

One of the major influences shaping Indian civilization in recent centuries has been the Western presence. From the arrival of Vasco da Gama in 1497 to the departure of the British in 1947, India was obliged to host foreign explorers, merchants, soldiers, missionaries, and colonial administrators. Few aspects of Indian life remained unaffected. Most (caste, marriage customs, untouchability) were at least challenged, and some (technology, education, government) revolutionized. Indian philosophy could not escape the impact of the West. In fact, during the nineteenth and twentieth centuries, that encounter catalyzed Indian thought. Responses among Indian thinkers were fundamentally the same as those in other societies exposed to the shock of cultural invasion. Some abandoned their own traditions and espoused Western styles, considering them superior. Others rejected Western ideas, deeming them inferior, while retrenching into their native traditions. Yet others, appreciative of both, attempted to combine Indian and Western thought into some kind of higher synthesis. From the last group have come the innovators of modern Indian philosophy. This section centers on two representatives of the synthetic tendency—Sri Aurobindo and Mahatma Gandhi.

* * *

Aurobindo Ghose (1872–1950), known respectfully as Sri Aurobindo, is a prime example of the meeting of East and West. Born into the family of an anglophile Bengali physician, one of the first Indians to be educated in England, Sri Aurobindo received his formal training at St. Paul's School, London, and King's College, Cambridge. His academic career in British schools lasted fourteen years,

225

during which he mastered Latin, Greek, English, French, German, Italian, and the great literatures written in those languages. In England his creative imagination was awakened, his habit of large and original thought established, and his keen rhetorical skills honed. There also he witnessed the debate unleashed by the biggest scientific breakthrough of the nineteenth century—the evolutionary hypothesis of Charles Darwin and A.R. Wallace.

On his return to India at age twenty-one, Sri Aurobindo immersed himself in a second education, a self-education in Indian culture, from which he had been shielded in youth by his father. While teaching Indian schoolboys French and English in Baroda (western India), he taught himself Sanskrit (plus several modern Indian languages) and read the masterworks of Indian literature, philosophy, and religion. In the last decade of the nineteenth century and the first of the twentieth, he embarked on two new pursuits—politics and yoga. His forceful journalism on behalf of Indian independence terminated with a year of pretrial detention in Calcutta's Alipore Jail, on charges of sedition against the British government. While in solitary confinement, he had two life-changing mystical experiences. Soon after release, he sought permanent refuge in Pondicherry, French India. During his last forty years, he gave himself to yoga, writing, and directing the practice of a growing number of yoga aspirants who formed what became the Sri Aurobindo Ashram. That institution expanded and still flourishes, attracting members and visitors from around the world. Sri Aurobindo is believed by many to be the greatest Indian philosopher of modern times and the most accomplished yogi of the twentieth century.

Sri Aurobindo's literary output reflects the depth of his dual education, yogic practice, and mystical experience. His collected works, in the current revised edition, fill thirty-five volumes. Included are poetry, drama, short stories, literary criticism, political journalism, exegetical studies of Sanskrit classics, cultural essays, writings on yoga, and philosophy. Three works are looked upon as his masterpieces. *The Life Divine* (1,100 pages) is the articulation of his full philosophy. *Savitri* (800 pages) is the transposition of that philosophy into epic poetry. And *The Synthesis of Yoga* (900 pages) is the application of that philosophy to the practice of yoga. He wrote mostly in English, and his works have been translated into numerous foreign languages.

Where does his philosophy stand vis-à-vis the philosophical traditions of India and the West? In the context of Indian philosophy, Sri Aurobindo's position is fully aligned with Vedanta while calling little attention to that fact. Among the great Vedantins, his closest counterpart is Ramanuja (see the introduction to the third section of this text, pages 139–140), an association unacknowledged in his writings. He did not philosophize like a Vedantin. He bypassed commentary on Badarayana and dialogue with other Vedantins, except to attack Shankara's "illusionism." He founded his system instead on a fresh reading of the *Rig Veda*, the Upanishads, and the *Bhagavad Gita*, rethinking the whole project from scratch. He spoke as a modern to the modern situation rather than as a Vedantin building on that historic tradition. His grasp of the modern milieu was at once thoroughly Indian and Western, accounting for his appeal to both cultures. From the standpoint of Western philosophy, monographs have been written comparing him to such twentieth-century thinkers as Henri Bergson, Alfred North Whitehead, and Pierre Teilhard de Chardin. His blend of theology and evolution resonated with theirs, for it issued from a common intellectual background. His matter-life-mind-spirit schema can be traced to the Upanishads but smacks also of famous European debates on those subjects that occurred during his formative years. Sri

Aurobindo's philosophy deserves the name "integral" (*purna*), not only because of its nondual view of reality but also because of its pioneering East-West nexus.

A synopsis of *The Life Divine* provides a digest of Sri Aurobindo's integral philosophy. The overarching theme is the evolution of the Divine. This work is divided into two books. Book One deals with the evolution of the Divine into the cosmos. There is one all-inclusive reality—the Divine, Brahman. Brahman encompasses within its unity seven latent forms: Pure Being, Pure Consciousness, Pure Delight, Supermind, Mind, Life, and Matter. Cosmic evolution is the progressive manifestation in the overt universe of Brahman's seven covert forms. The Divine commences its evolutionary journey by overtly taking the form of Matter, within which Life, Mind, and Supermind are covertly telescoped. Life then evolves from Matter, Mind from Life, and finally (in the future) Supermind from Mind. When Supermind ascends out of Mind, the other three latent forms of Brahman (Pure Being, Pure Consciousness, and Pure Delight) will simultaneously descend. At that moment in history and on earth, a species of beings will appear that overtly embraces all seven of the divine forms. The evolution of such a species is the divine purpose of the entire process.

Book Two of *The Life Divine,* triple the length of the first, contains a detailed analysis of the future and final phase of cosmic evolution—the evolution of the human species into a divine superhuman species, of Mind into Supermind, and of Ignorance into Knowledge. Accordingly, the two parts into which Book Two divides deal with Ignorance and Knowledge. Humans live under the shadow of Ignorance because the information we possess is learned, incomplete, subject to revision, at best probable, not universally agreed upon, and sometimes ignored in seeking sound action. Superhumans, on the other hand, will bask in the light of Knowledge; the information they possess will be innate, complete, beyond revision, certain, universally agreed upon, and necessarily linked to sound action. It will be perfect in every respect.

What is the present status of divine evolution? Matter and Life are fully evolved, Mind partly evolved but partly latent, and Supermind completely latent. Mind, therefore, is the locus of present evolution. The cutting edge of evolution can be plotted precisely by analyzing Mind into its five components. They are Physical Mind (sense perception), Vital Mind (desire for personal gratification), Mental Mind (thought limited to true-or-false), Psychic Mind, and Spiritual Mind. Psychic Mind includes inner sense-mind (extrasensory perception), inner desire-mind (for universal welfare), and inner thought-mind (not limited to true or false). Spiritual Mind covers Higher Mind (grasping the idea of the unity of everything), Illumined Mind (actually perceiving unity in everything), Intuitive Mind (feeling incorporated into that unity), and Overmind (living in unity with everything). Physical Mind, Vital Mind, and Mental Mind are already evolved; Psychic Mind and Spiritual Mind are still latent, waiting their turn to evolve. The future evolution of humans and superhumans, of Mind and Supermind, will result from a Triple Transformation. The Psychic Transformation and the Spiritual Transformation will facilitate the evolution of the Psychic Mind and the Spiritual Mind, completing the evolution of Mind and of the human species. The Supramental Transformation, climaxing the series, will fulfill the whole scheme of cosmic evolution by bringing into existence on earth in future history a species manifesting all seven forms of the Divine. This will be the "Divine Life on Earth." Though Supermind will indeed ascend out of Mind by divine action from within, it must also be "brought down" from above and established on earth—the ultimate task and purpose of humankind. Accomplishment of the entire Triple

Transformation is fundamentally the work of the Divine evolving. It can, however, be accelerated by humans practicing Sri Aurobindo's Integral (*purna*) Yoga, laid out in *The Synthesis of Yoga* and designed to enhance divine evolution—a sweeping enlargement of yoga's mission.

The Supramental Manifestation Upon Earth is the work by Sri Aurobindo chosen for inclusion in this volume. It is his final prose writing, penned during the last year of his life, and it conveniently recapitulates *The Life Divine*. The reader of both books learns that the Divine is one without a second (nondual) and all-inclusive and encompasses the seven latent forms—listed earlier. The Divine evolves into the cosmos by progressively externalizing the forms implicit within its own unity, producing finally on earth the divine life in a divine body. Human Ignorance will phase into superhuman Knowledge when the Divine evolving brings forth, as it is presently poised to do, Psychic Mind, Spiritual Mind, and Supermind through the Triple Transformation. The work included here is, however, more specific than *The Life Divine* in its speculations about the Supramental Transformation. Supramental beings will enjoy freedom from human limitations with respect to sleep, fatigue, illness, food, sex, and reproduction. They will have at their disposal new channels of communication, additional and more powerful senses, and higher cognitive abilities. Their presence on earth will enrich the quality of life for humans cohabiting with such superior creatures. There is no mention in this work of the ascent of Supermind out of Mind, only of its descent from above. Humans are to "bring it down" from on high, rather than extricate it from its involvement in Mind. An intriguing feature of the book is a new concept advanced in it—the concept of the Mind of Light. The Mind of Light belongs to the range of dimensions included within Spiritual Mind and is hence the potential possession of humans. It contains more of the influence of Supermind than any other dimension of Spiritual Mind, including Overmind. The difference between Overmind and the Mind of Light does not emerge clearly in *The Supramental Manifestation*. Had Sri Aurobindo lived to rethink and revise his last book, this shortcoming might have been remedied.

* * *

Mohandas K. Gandhi (1869–1948) and Sri Aurobindo were contemporaries. The lives of both had roots in two cultures, Indian and Western. Sri Aurobindo's academic career was brilliant, Gandhi's mediocre. In fact, given the dynamic leader he became, Gandhi's youth was remarkable for its lack of distinction. During the first decade of the twentieth century, both men experienced a spiritual awakening that led them to yoga. Sri Aurobindo took up the practice of Integral Yoga in seclusion, disavowing further participation in politics. Gandhi reinvented a Karma Yoga that thrust him into a storm of intense political activism. A turning point came for Gandhi in South Africa when he was twenty-five (1894). After receiving a law degree in London (1888–1891) and finding the job market at home in India unfriendly, he was lucky to land a position in an Indian law firm in Natal, South Africa. There he endured all the indignities afflicting the Indian community in that racist society. Something galvanized within him—a sense of his own dignity as an Indian and a man, and an iron will to resist injustice actively wherever he encountered it. He began to organize his fellow Indians and use legal tools to relieve their plight. In 1906, after the Boer War, he reached another turning point. His Satyagraha principle crystallized. Around this principle he rebuilt his religious faith, his personal life, and his political career. The Indian cause in South Africa now had a regenerated leader and an inspiring ideal. Gains that attracted world attention were scored, but no permanent solution achieved. Gandhi's last seven years in South Africa (1906–1913) proved to be an apprenticeship for something much larger. After returning to India in 1914, he gradually rose to leadership of his country's struggle to acquire self-rule (*svaraj*) and independence from colonial domination. That victory was won in 1947. The following year, Gandhi was assassinated by religious extremists. The whole world mourned the loss of the Mahatma or "great souled" one. His idealism and courage had made him a global hero, a saint.

Satyagraha was for Gandhi an ethical and religious principle. It grew out of exposure to a broad spectrum of influences. The unadorned Vaishnava Hinduism of his mother, rejecting idols, temples, priests, and rituals, inclined him toward a religion of the heart in which an all-encompassing and indefinable God is approached directly. His Muslim childhood playmates confirmed his repugnance of idolatry, and Jains taught him the importance of self-discipline and noninjury (*ahimsa*). Frequenting a vegetarian restaurant in London during law school days, he associated with Theosophists, Fabian Socialists, and religious followers of Tolstoy. They helped imbue his social conscience with altruistic values, such as universal dignity, equality, due process, and sympathy for the oppressed. In South Africa, Quakers bolstered his belief in nonviolence, Trappist monks impressed him with their austere communal life (Gandhi himself founded communes in both South Africa and India), and friendship with an Anglican missionary fired in him zeal for socially and politically responsible religion. In South Africa, his study of the *Bhagavad Gita*, begun in London, intensified. This text became his spiritual handbook and its Karma Yoga the impetus for his political activism. He also relished reading the New Testament (the Sermon on the Mount especially), the Koran, and the religious writings of Tolstoy, with whom he engaged in correspondence. Remaining attuned to universalism in religion, he returned ultimately to identification with Hinduism, where he sparked a movement of liberal reform.

The result of all this was in Gandhi's mature years a profound faith in a God best suggested by the symbols of Truth, Love, and Law. These symbols meant for Gandhi that the immense universe as well as tiny human society are ruled by the force of Law, that such Law is in fact the Law of Love, and that this Law of Love is not arbitrary but absolute Truth. Love he understood as noninjury; forgiveness; and utter respect for the dignity and value of humans, animals, and the elements. Love also entailed fighting injustice with the courage of a soldier willing to accept the ordeals of combat and death if necessary. The only way to fight the oppressor while respecting even that person's human dignity was through nonviolent action shorn of malice. Do frail humans have the strength to live by the Truth of the Law of Love? Gandhi believed they did. There is in everyone a soul to be met. When that soul is encountered, the soul affirms the Truth that Love must be the Law of one's personal and social existence. By faithfully living that Law, a person unleashes the Force of its Truth inwardly and outwardly. Inwardly, new resources of will power and moral courage are uncovered. Outwardly, one's efforts in the struggle for justice and equality pack an unexpected effectiveness. That is Gandhi's philosophy of Satyagraha—literally "Truth Force" but commonly glossed as "Soul Force."

Gandhi regarded Soul Force as the only political strategy offering a moral and effective alternative to the immoral and counterproductive body force (violence) blindly favored by history. Soul Force is legitimated by Truth, by the Law of Love that rules the universe and speaks in the soul. It is nonviolent action applied to the immediate political situation. Such action champions the cause of human dignity, social justice, and equality. It opposes injustice, oppression, and exploitation of human or beast. It criticizes those who accept intolerable conditions out of timidity or cowardice. It demands of its followers humility, discipline, self-criticism, respect for the adversary, and above all the courage of a soldier. There will be suffering to bear for provoking established authority; there will be brutality, imprisonment, maybe even death. Gandhi's message proved to be immensely popular among the common people and of keen interest to the press. Armed with this idealism, Gandhi launched his campaigns against racial discrimination in South Africa and colonial exploitation in India, advocating nonviolent resistance, active noncooperation, and civil disobedience. His work swayed world opinion, and it brought results. In later life he spoke out against untouchability and the abuse of cows. He also endeavored to lift his people up by promoting education, cottage industries such as cotton spinning, and Hindu-Muslim reconciliation. His commitment to Truth (his God) remained steadfast to the end.

Gandhi's collected works fill eighty-nine volumes and consist mostly of letters and journalistic pieces. No single essay comprehensively covers his thought, but the selections included here give some idea of the range of his work.

*   *   *

For further reading about recent Indian philosophy in general, a standard source is Sarvepalli Radhakrishnan and J.H. Muirhead, eds., *Contemporary Indian Philosophy,* 2nd ed. (London: George Allen & Unwin, 1952).

A number of reputable studies have been written about Sri Aurobindo and his philosophy. The most detailed of the standard biographies is K.R. Srinivasa Iyengar, *Sri Aurobindo: A Biography and a History,* 2 vols. (Pondicherry, India: Sri Aurobindo Ashram Press, 1972). Among good expository studies of his philosophy are Robert A. McDermott, *Six Pillars: An Introduction to the Major Works of Sri Aurobindo* (Chambersburg, PA: Wilson Books, 1974); S.K. Maitra, *An Introduction to the Philosophy of Sri Aurobindo* (Pondicherry, India: Sri Aurobindo Ashram Press, 1965) is the briefest coverage, and his *The Meeting of East and West in Sri Aurobindo's Philosophy* (Pondicherry, India: Sri Aurobindo Ashram Press, 1956) provides comparisons with Bergson, Plotinus, Hegel, Plato, Goethe, Whitehead, and others. Satprem, *Sri Aurobindo or The Adventure of Consciousness,* tr. Tehmi (Pondicherry, India: Sri Aurobindo Ashram Press, 1968) and Haridas Chaudhuri and Frederic Spiegelberg, eds., *The Integral Philosophy of Sri Aurobindo: A Commemorative Symposium* (London: George Allen & Unwin, 1960) are also useful. The best critical study to date is Stephen H. Phillips, *Aurobindo's Philosophy of Brahman* (Leiden: E.J. Brill, 1986).

The serious student of Gandhi's life and thought will find M.K. Gandhi, *An Autobiography or The Story of My Experiments with Truth,* tr. Mahadev Desai, 2nd ed. (Ahmedabad, India: Navajivan Press, 1940) valuable. Among the reliable biographies is Louis Fischer, *Gandhi: His Life and Message for the World* (New York: Mentor Books, 1954). General studies of Gandhi thought include Margaret Chatterji, *Gandhi's Religious Thought* (London: Macmillan, 1983); Dhirendra Mohan Datta, *The Philosophy of Mahatma Gandhi* (Madison: University of Wisconsin Press, 1953); Gopinath Dhawan, *The Political Philosophy of Mahatma Gandhi,* 2nd rev. ed. (Ahmedabad, India: Navajivan Publishing House, 1962); and Raghavan N. Iyer, *The Moral and Political Thought of Mahatma Gandhi* (Oxford, Eng.: Oxford University Press, 1973).

AUROBINDO, THE SUPRAMENTAL MANIFESTATION UPON EARTH

PERFECTION OF THE BODY

The perfection of the body, as great a perfection as we can bring about by the means at our disposal, must be the ultimate aim of physical culture. Perfection is the true aim of all culture, the spiritual and psychic, the mental, the vital, and it must be the aim of our physical culture also. If our seeking is for a total perfection of the being, the physical part of it cannot be left aside; for the body is the material basis, the body is the instrument that we have to use. *Shariram khalu dharmasadhanam,* says the old Sanskrit adage—the body is the means of fulfillment of dharma, and dharma means every ideal that we can propose to ourselves and the law of its working out and its action. A total perfection is the ultimate aim that we set before us, for our ideal is the Divine Life that we wish to create here, the life of the Spirit fulfilled on earth, life accomplishing its own spiritual transformation even here on earth in the conditions of the material universe. That cannot be unless the body, too, undergoes a transformation, unless its action and functioning attain to a supreme capacity and the perfection that is possible to it or that can be made possible.

I have already indicated in a previous message a relative perfection of the physical consciousness in the body and of the mind, the life, the character that it houses as, no less than an awakening and development of the body's own native capacities, a desirable outcome of the exercises and practices of the physical culture to which we have commenced to give in this Ashram a special attention and scope. A development of the physical consciousness must always be a considerable part of our aim, but for that the right development of the body itself is an essential element; health, strength, fitness are the first needs, but the physical frame itself must be the best possible. A divine life in a material world implies necessarily a union of the two ends of existence, the spiritual summit and the material base. The soul with the basis of its life established in Matter ascends to the heights of the Spirit but does not cast away its base, it joins the heights and the depths together. The Spirit descends into Matter and the material world with all its lights and glories and powers and with them fills and transforms life in the material world so that it becomes more and more divine. The transformation is not a change into something purely subtle and spiritual to which Matter is in its nature repugnant and by which it is felt as an obstacle or as a shackle binding the Spirit; it takes up Matter as a form of the Spirit though now a form that conceals, and turns it into a revealing instrument, it does not cast away the energies of Matter, its capacities, its methods; it brings out their hidden possibilities, uplifts, sublimates, discloses their innate divinity. The divine life will reject nothing that is capable of divinization; all is to be seized, exalted, made utterly perfect. The mind now still ignorant, though struggling toward knowledge, has to rise toward and into the supramental light and truth and bring it down so that it shall suffuse our thinking and perception and insight and all our means of knowing till they become radiant with the highest truth in their inmost and outermost movements. Our life, still full of obscurity and confusion and occupied with so many dull and lower

From Aurobindo, *The Supramental Manifestation Upon Earth* (Pondicherry, India: Sri Aurobindo Ashram, 1952). Reprinted by permission.

aims, must feel all its urges and instincts exalted and irradiated and become a glorious counterpart of the supramental super-life above. The physical consciousness and physical being, the body itself, must reach a perfection in all that it is and does, which now we can hardly conceive. It may even in the end be suffused with a light and beauty and bliss from the Beyond and the life divine assume a body divine.

But first the evolution of the nature must have reached a point at which it can meet the Spirit direct, feel the aspiration toward the spiritual change, and open itself to the workings of the Power that shall transform it. A supreme perfection, a total perfection, is possible only by a transformation of our lower or human nature, a transformation of the mind into a thing of light, our life into a thing of power, an instrument of right action, right use for all its forces, of a happy elevation of its being lifting it beyond its present comparatively narrow potentiality for a self-fulfilling force of action and joy of life. There must be equally a transforming change of the body by a conversion of its action, its functioning, its capacities as an instrument beyond the limitations by which it is clogged and hampered even in its greatest present human attainment. In the totality of the change we have to achieve, human means and forces too have to be taken up, not dropped but used and magnified to their utmost possibility as part of the new life. Such a sublimation of our present human powers of mind and life into elements of a divine life on earth can be conceived without much difficulty; but in what figure shall we conceive the perfection of the body?

In the past the body has been regarded by spiritual seekers rather as an obstacle, as something to be overcome and discarded, than as an instrument of spiritual perfection and a field of the spiritual change. It has been condemned as a grossness of Matter, as an insuperable impediment, and the limitations of the body as something unchange-

Sri Aurobindo Ghose (1872–1950) (*Akhil Bahkshi © Dorling Kindersley*)

able making transformation impossible. This is because the human body even at its best seems only to be driven by an energy of life that has its own limits and is debased in its smaller physical activities by much that is petty or coarse or evil, the body in itself is burdened with the inertia and inconscience of Matter, only partly awake and, although quickened and animated by a nervous activity, subconscient in the fundamental action of its constituent cells and tissues and their secret workings. Even in its fullest strength and force and greatest glory of beauty, it is still a flower of the material Inconscience; the inconscient is the soil from which it has grown and at every point opposes a narrow boundary to the extension of its powers and to any effort of radical self-exceeding. But if a divine life is possible on earth, then this self-exceeding must also be possible.

In the pursuit of perfection we can start at either end of our range of being and we have then to use, initially at least, the means and processes proper to our choice. In Yoga the process is spiritual and psychic; even its vital and physical processes are given a spiritual or psychic turn and raised to a higher motion than belongs properly to the ordinary life and Matter, as for instance in the Hathayogic and Rajayogic use of the breathing or the use of Asana. Ordinarily a previous preparation of the mind and life and body is necessary to make them fit for the reception of the spiritual energy and the organization of psychic forces and methods, but this too is given a special turn proper to the Yoga. On the other hand, if we start in any field at the lower end, we have to employ the means and processes that Life and Matter offer to us and respect the conditions and what we may call the technique imposed by the vital and the material energy. We may extend the activity, the achievement, the perfection attained beyond the initial, even beyond the normal, possibilities but still we have to stand on the same base with which we started and within the boundaries it gives to us. It is not that the action from the two ends cannot meet and the higher take into itself and uplift the lower perfection; but this can usually be done only by a transition from the lower to a higher outlook, aspiration, and motive: this we shall have to do if our aim is to transform the human into the divine life. But here there comes in the necessity of taking up the activities of human life and sublimating them by the power of the spirit. Here the lower perfection will not disappear; it will remain but will be enlarged and transformed by the higher perfection that only the power of the spirit can give. This will be evident if we consider poetry and art, philosophic thought, the perfection of the written word, or the perfect organization of earthly life: these have to be taken up and the possibilities already achieved or whatever perfection has already been attained included in a new and greater perfection but with the larger vision and inspiration of a spiritual consciousness and with new forms and powers. It must be the same with the perfection of the body.

The taking up of life and Matter into what is essentially a spiritual seeking, instead of the rejection and ultimate exclusion of them, which was the attitude of a spirituality that shunned or turned away from life in the world, involves certain developments that a spiritual institution of the older kind could regard as foreign to its purpose. A divine life in the world or an institution having that for its aim and purpose cannot be or cannot remain something outside or entirely shut away from the life of ordinary men in the world or unconcerned with the mundane existence; it has to do the work of the Divine in the world and not a work outside or separate from it. The life of the ancient Rishis in their Ashramas had such a connection; they were creators, educators, guides of men and the life of the Indian people in ancient time was largely developed and directed by their shaping influence. The life and activities involved in the new endeavor are not identical, but they too must be an action upon the world and a new creation in it. It must have contacts and connections with it and activities that take their place in the general life and whose initial or primary objects may not seem to differ from those of the same activities in the outside world. In our Ashram here we have found it necessary to establish a school for the education of the children of the resident *sadhaks,* teaching upon familiar lines though with certain modifications and taking as part and an important part of their development an intensive physical training that has given form to the sports and athletics practiced by the Jeunesse Sportive of the Ashram and of which this Bulletin is the expression. It has been questioned by some what place sports can have in an Ashram created for spiritual seekers and what connection there can be between spirituality and sports. The first answer lies in what I have already written about the connections of an institution of this kind with the activities of the general life of men and what I have indicated in the previous number as to the utility such a training can have for the life of a nation and its benefit for the international life. Another answer can occur to us if we look beyond first objects and turn to the aspiration for a total perfection including the perfection of the body.

In the admission of an activity such as sports and physical exercises into the life of the Ashram it is evident that the methods and the first objects to be attained must belong to what we have called the lower end of the being. Originally they had been introduced for the physical education and bodily development of the children of the Ashram school and these are too young for a strictly spiritual aim or practice to enter into their activities and it is not certain that any great number of them will enter the spiritual life when they are of an age to choose what shall be the direction of their future. The object must be the training of the body and the development of certain parts of mind and character so far as this can be done by or in connection with this training and I have already indicated in a previous number how and in what directions this can be done. It is a relative and human perfection that can be attained within these limits; anything greater can be reached only by the intervention of higher powers, psychic powers, the power of the spirit. Yet what can be attained within the human boundaries can be something very considerable and sometimes immense: what we call genius is part of the development of the human range of being and its achievements, especially in things of the mind and will, can carry us halfway to the divine. Even what the mind and will can do with the body in the field proper to the body and its life, in the way of physical achievement, bodily endurance, feats of prowess of all kinds, a lasting activity refusing fatigue or collapse and continuing beyond what seems at first to be possible, courage, and refusal to succumb under an endless and murderous physical suffering, these and other victories of many kinds sometimes approaching or reaching the miraculous are seen in the human field and must be reckoned as a part of our concept of a total perfection. The unflinching and persistent reply that can be made by the body as well as the mind of man and by his life-energy to whatever call can be imposed on it in the most difficult and discouraging circumstances by the necessities of war and travel and adventure is of the same kind and their endurance can reach astounding proportions and even the inconscient in the body seems to be able to return a surprising response.

The body, we have said, is a creation of the Inconscient and itself inconscient or at least subconscient in parts of its self and much of its hidden action; but what we call the Inconscient is an appearance, a dwelling place, an instrument of a secret Consciousness or a Superconscient that has created the miracle we call the universe. Matter is the field and the creation of the Inconscient and the perfection of the operations of inconscient Matter, their perfect adaptation of means to an aim and end, the wonders they perform and the marvels of beauty they create, testify, in spite of all the ignorant denial we can oppose, to the presence and power of consciousness of this Superconscience in every part and movement of the material universe. It is there in the body, has made it, and its emergence in our consciousness is the secret aim of evolution and the key to the mystery of our existence.

In the use of such activities as sports and physical exercises for the education of the individual in childhood and first youth, which should mean the bringing out of his actual and latent possibilities to their fullest development, the means and methods we must use are limited by the nature of the body and its aim must be such relative human perfection of the body's powers and capacities and those of the powers of mind, will, character, action of which it is at once the residence and the instrument so far as these methods can help to develop them. I have written sufficiently about the mental and moral parts of perfection to which these pursuits can contribute and this I need not repeat here. For the body itself the perfections that can be developed by these means are those of its natural qualities and capacities and, secondly, the training of its general fitness, as an instrument for all the activities that may be demanded from it by the mind and the will, by the life-energy or by the dynamic perceptions, impulses, and instincts of our subtle physical being, which is an unrecognized but very important element and agent in our nature. Health and strength are the first conditions for the natural perfection of the body, not only muscular strength and the solid strength of the limbs and physical stamina, but the finer, alert and plastic and adaptable force which our nervous and subtle physical parts can put into the activities of the frame. There is also the still more dynamic force that a call upon the life-energies can bring into the body and stir it to greater activities, even feats of extraordinary character, of which in its normal state it would not be capable. There is also the strength that the mind and the will by their demands and stimulus and by their secret powers, which we use or by which we are used without knowing clearly the source of their action, can impart to the body or impose upon it as masters and inspirers. Among the natural qualities and powers of the body that can thus be awakened, stimulated, and trained to a normal activity, we must reckon dexterity and stability in all kinds of physical action, such as swiftness in the race, dexterity in combat, skill and endurance of the mountaineer, the constant and often extraordinary response to all that can be demanded from the body of the soldier, sailor, traveler, or explorer to which I have already made reference or in adventure of all kinds and all the wide range of physical attainment to which man has accustomed himself or to which he is exceptionally pushed by his own will or by the compulsion of circumstance. It is a general fitness of the body for all that can be asked from it that is the common formula of all this action, a fitness attained by a few or by many, that could be generalized by an extended and many-sided physical education and discipline. Some of these activities can be included under the name of sports; there are others for which sport and physical exercises can be an effective preparation. In some of them a training for common action, combined movement, discipline are needed, and for that our physical exercises can make us ready; in others a developed individual will, skill of mind, quick perception, forcefulness of life-energy, and subtle physical impulse are more prominently needed and may even be the one sufficient trainer. All must be included in our conception of the natural powers of the body and its capacity and instrumental fitness in the service of the human mind and will and therefore in our concept of the total perfection of the body.

There are two conditions for this perfection: an awakening in as great an entirety as possible of the body consciousness; and an education, an evocation of its potentialities, also as entire and fully developed and, it may be, as many-sided as possible. The form or body is, no doubt, in its origin a creation of the Inconscient and limited by it on all sides, but still of the Inconscient developing the secret consciousness concealed within it and growing the light of knowledge, power, and *Ananda*. We have to take it at the point it has reached in its human evolution in these things, make as full a use of them as may be and, as much as we can, further this evolution to as high a degree as is permitted by the force of the individual temperament and nature. In all forms in the world there is a force at work, unconsciously active or oppressed by inertia in its lower formulations, but in the human being conscious from the first, with its potentialities partly awake, partly asleep, or latent: what is awake in it we have to make fully conscious; what is asleep we have to arouse and set to its work; what is latent we have to evoke and educate. Here there are two aspects of the body consciousness, one that seems to be a kind of automatism carrying on its work in the physical plane without any intervention of the mind and in parts even beyond any possibility of direct observation by the mind or, if conscious or observable, still proceeding or capable of continuing, when once started, by an apparently mechanical action not needing direction by the mind and continuing so long as the mind does not intervene.

There are other movements taught and trained by the mind that can yet go on operating automatically but faultlessly even when not attended to by the thought or will; there are others that can operate in sleep and produce results of value to the waking intelligence. But more important is what may be described as a trained and developed automatism, a perfected skill and capacity of eyes and ears and hands and all the members prompt to respond to any call made on them, a developed spontaneous operation as an instrument, a complete fitness for any demand that the mind and life-energy can make upon it. This is ordinarily the best we can achieve at the lower end, when we start from that end and limit ourselves to the means and methods that are proper to it. For more, we have to turn to the mind and life-energy themselves or to the energy of the spirit and to what they can do for a greater perfection of the body. The most we can do in the physical field by physical means is necessarily insecure as well as bound by limits; even what seems a perfect health and strength of the body is precarious and can be broken down at any moment by fluctuations from within or by a strong attack or shock from outside. Only by the breaking of our limitations can a higher and more enduring perfection come. One direction in which our consciousness must grow is an increasing hold from within or from above on the body and its powers and its more conscious response to the higher parts of our being. The mind preeminently is man; he is a mental being and his human perfection grows the more he fulfills the description of the Upanishad, a mental being, Purusha, leader of the life and the body. If the mind can take up and control the instincts and automatisms of the life-energy and the subtle physical consciousness and the body, if it can enter into them, consciously use and, as we may say, fully mentalize their instinctive or spontaneous action, the perfection of these energies, their action, too, becomes more conscious and more aware of itself and more perfect. But it is necessary for the mind, too, to grow in perfection and this it can do best when it depends less on the fallible intellect of physical mind, when it is not limited even by the more orderly and accurate working of the reason, and can grow in intuition and acquire a wider, deeper, and closer seeing and the more luminous drive of energy of a higher intuitive will. Even within the limits of its present evolution it is difficult to measure the degree to which the mind is able to extend its control or its use of the body's powers and capacities, and when the mind rises to higher powers still and pushes back its human boundaries, it becomes impossible to fix any limits: even, in certain realizations, an intervention by the will in the automatic working of the bodily organs seems to become possible. Wherever limitations recede and in proportion as they recede, the body becomes a more plastic and responsive and, in that measure, a more fit and perfect instrument of the action of the spirit. In all effective and expressive activities here in the material world the cooperation of the two ends of our being is indispensable. If the body is unable, whether by fatigue or by natural incapacity or any other cause, to second the thought or will or is in any way irresponsive or insufficiently responsive, to that extent, the action fails or falls short or becomes in some degree unsatisfying or incomplete. In what seems to be an exploit of the spirit so purely mental as the outpouring of poetic inspiration, there must be a responsive vibration of the brain and its openness as a channel for the power of the thought and vision and the light of the word that is making or breaking its way through or seeking for its perfect expression. If the brain is fatigued or dulled by any clog, either the inspiration cannot come and nothing is written or it fails and something inferior is all that can come out; or else a lower inspiration takes the place of the more luminous formulation that was striving to shape itself or the brain finds it more easy to lend itself to a less radiant stimulus or else it labors and constructs or responds to poetic artifice. Even in the most purely mental activities the fitness, readiness, or perfect training of the bodily instrument is a condition indispensable. That readiness, that response, too, is part of the total perfection of the body.

The essential purpose and sign of the growing evolution here is the emergence of consciousness in an apparently inconscient universe, the growth of the consciousness, and with it growth of the light and power of the being; the development of the form and its functioning or its fitness to survive, although indispensable, is not the whole meaning or the central motive. The greater and greater awakening of consciousness and its climb to a higher and higher level and a wider extent of its vision and action is the condition of our progress toward that supreme and total perfection that is the aim of our existence. It is the condition also of the total perfection of the body. There are higher levels of the mind than any we now conceive and to these we must one day reach and rise beyond them to the heights of a greater, a spiritual existence. As we rise we have to open to them our lower members and fill these with those superior and supreme dynamisms of light and power; the body we have to make a more and more and even entirely conscious frame and instrument, a conscious sign and seal and power of the spirit. As it grows in this perfection, the force and extent of its dynamic action and its response and service to the spirit must increase, the control of the spirit over it also must grow, and the plasticity of its functioning both in its developed and acquired parts of power and in its automatic responses down to those that are now purely organic and seem to be the movements of a mechanic inconscience. This cannot happen without a veritable transformation and a transformation of the mind and life and very body is indeed the change to which our evolution is secretly moving and without this transformation the entire fullness of a divine life on earth cannot emerge. In this transformation the body itself can become an agent and a partner. It might indeed be possible for the spirit to achieve a considerable manifestation with only a passive and imperfectly conscious body as its last or bottommost means of material functioning, but this could not be anything perfect or complete. A fully conscious body might even discover and work out the right material method and process of a material transformation. For this, no doubt, the spirit's supreme light and power and creative joy must have manifested on the summit of the individual consciousness and sent down their fiat into the body, but still the body may take in the working out its spontaneous part of self-discovery and achievement. It would be thus a participator and agent in its own transformation and the integral transformation of the whole being; this too would be a part and a sign and evidence of the total perfection of the body.

If the emergence and growth of consciousness is the central motive of the evolution and the key to its secret purpose, then by the very nature of that evolution this growth must involve not only a wider and wider extent of its capacities but also an ascent to a higher and higher level till it reaches the highest possible. For it starts from a nethermost level of involution in the Inconscience that we see at work in Matter creating the material universe; it proceeds by an Ignorance that is yet ever developing knowledge and reaching out to an ever greater light and ever greater organization and efficacy of the will and harmonization of all its own inherent and emerging powers; it must at last reach a point where it develops or acquires the complete fullness of its capacity and that must be a state or action in which there is no longer an ignorance seeking for knowledge, but Knowledge self-possessed, inherent in the being, master of its own truths and working them out with a natural vision and force that is not afflicted by limitation or error. Or if there is a limitation, it must be a self-imposed veil behind which it would keep truth back for a manifestation in Time but draw it out at will and without any need of search or acquisition in the order of a right perception of things or in the just succession of that which has to be manifested in obedience to the call of Time. This would mean an entry or approach into what might be called a Truth-Consciousness self-existent in which the being would be aware of its own realities and would have the inherent power to manifest them in a Time-creation in which all would be Truth following out its own unerring steps and combining its own harmonies; every thought and will and feeling and act would be spontaneously right, inspired or intuitive, moving by the light of Truth and therefore perfect. All would express inherent realities of the spirit; some fullness of the power of the spirit would be there. One would have overpassed the present limitations of mind: mind would become a seeing of the light of Truth, will a force and power of the Truth, Life a progressive fulfillment of the Truth, the body itself a conscious vessel of the Truth and part of the means of its self-effectuation and a form of its self-aware existence. It would be at least some initiation of this Truth-Consciousness, some first figure and action of it, that must be reached and enter into a first operation if there is to be a divine life or any full manifestation of a spiritualized consciousness in the world of Matter. Or, at the very least, such a Truth-Consciousness must be in communication with our own mind and life and body, descend into touch with it, control its seeing and action, impel its motives, take hold of its forces, and shape their direction and purpose. All touched by it might not be able to embody it fully, but each would give some form to it according to his spiritual temperament, inner capacity, the line of his evolution in Nature: he would reach securely the perfection of which he was immediately capable and he would be on the road to the full possession of the truth of the Spirit and of the truth of Nature.

In the workings of such a Truth-Consciousness there would be a certain conscious seeing and willing automatism of the steps of its truth that would replace the infallible automatism of the inconscient or seemingly inconscient Force that has brought out of an apparent Void the miracle of an ordered universe and this could create a new order of the manifestation of the Being in which a perfect perfection would become possible, even a supreme and total perfection would appear in the vistas of an ultimate possibility. If we could draw down this power into the material world, our agelong dreams of human perfectibility, individual perfection, the perfectibility of the race, of society, inner mastery over self, and a complete mastery, governance, and utilization of the forces of Nature could see at long last a prospect of total achievement. This complete human self-fulfillment might well pass beyond limitations and be transformed into the character of a divine life. Matter, after taking into itself and manifesting the power of life and the light of mind, would draw down into it the superior or supreme power and light of the spirit and in an earthly body shed its parts of inconscience and become a perfectly conscious frame of the spirit. A secure completeness and stability of the health and strength of its physical tenement could be maintained by the will and force of this inhabitant; all the natural capacities of the physical frame, all powers of the physical consciousness would reach their utmost extension and be there at command and sure of their flawless action. As an instrument the body would acquire a fullness of capacity, a totality of fitness for all uses that the inhabitant would demand of it far beyond anything now possible. Even it could become a revealing vessel of a supreme beauty and bliss,—casting the beauty of the light of the spirit suffusing and radiating from it as a lamp reflects and diffuses the luminosity of its indwelling flame, carrying in itself the beatitude of the spirit, its joy of the seeing mind, its joy of life and spiritual happiness, the joy of Matter released into a spiritual consciousness and thrilled with a constant ecstasy. This would be the total perfection of the spiritualized body.

All this might not come all at once, though such a sudden illumination might be possible if a divine Power and Light and *Ananda* could take their stand on the summit of our being and send down their force into the mind and life and body illumining and remolding the cells, awakening consciousness in all the frame. But the way would be open and the consummation of all that is possible in the individual could progressively take place. The physical also would have its share in that consummation of the whole.

There would always remain vistas beyond as the infinite Spirit took up toward higher heights and larger breadths the evolving Nature, in the movement of the liberated being toward the possession of the supreme Reality, the supreme existence, consciousness, beatitude. But of this it would be premature to speak: what has been written is perhaps as much as the human mind as it is now constituted can venture to look forward to and the enlightened thought understand in some measure. These consequences of the Truth-Consciousness descending and laying its hold upon Matter would be a sufficient justification of the evolutionary labor. In this upward, all-uplifting sweep of the Spirit there could be a simultaneous or consecutive downward sweep of the triumph of a spiritualized Nature all-including, all-transmuting, and in it there could occur a glorifying change of Matter and the physical consciousness and physical form and functioning of which we could speak as not only the total but the supreme perfection of the body.

THE DIVINE BODY

A divine life in a divine body is the formula of the ideal that we envisage. But what will be the divine body? What will be the nature of this body, its structure, the principle of its activity, the perfection that distinguishes it from the limited and imperfect physicality within which we are now bound? What will be the conditions and operations of its life still physical in its base upon the earth by which it can be known as divine?

If it is to be the product of an evolution, and it is so that we must envisage it, an evolution out of our human imperfection and ignorance into a greater truth of spirit and nature, by what process or stages can it grow into manifestation or rapidly arrive? The process of the evolution upon earth has been slow and tardy—what principle must intervene if there is to be a transformation, a progressive or sudden change?

It is indeed as a result of our evolution that we arrive at the possibility of this transformation. As Nature has evolved beyond Matter and manifested Life, beyond Life and manifested Mind, so she must evolve beyond Mind and manifest a consciousness and power of our existence free from the imperfection and limitation of our mental existence, a supramental or Truth-Consciousness and able to develop the power and perfection of the spirit. Here a slow and tardy change need no longer be the law or manner of our evolution; it will be only so to a greater or less extent so long as a mental ignorance clings and hampers our ascent; but once we have grown into the Truth-Consciousness its power of spiritual truth of being will determine all. Into that truth we shall be freed and it will transform mind and life and body. Light and bliss and beauty and a perfection of the spontaneous right action of all the being are there as native powers of the supramental Truth-Consciousness and these will in their very nature transform mind and life and body even here upon earth into a manifestation of the Truth-Conscious spirit. The obscurations of earth will not prevail against the supramental Truth-Consciousness, for even into the earth it can bring enough of the omniscient light and omnipotent force of the spirit to conquer. All may not open to the fullness of its light and power, but whatever does open must to that extent undergo the change. That will be the principle of transformation.

It might be that a psychological change, a mastery of the nature by the soul, a transformation of the mind into a principle of light, of the life-force into power and purity would be the first approach, the first attempt to solve the problem, to escape beyond the merely human formula and establish something that could be called a divine life upon earth, a first sketch of supermanhood, of a supramental living in the circumstances of the earth-nature. But this could not be the complete and radical change needed; it would not be the total transformation, the fullness of a divine life in a divine body. There would be a body still human and indeed animal in its origin and fundamental character and this would impose its own inevitable limitations on the higher parts of the embodied being. As limitation by ignorance and error is the fundamental defect of an untransformed mind, as limitation by the imperfect impulses and strainings and wants of desire are the defects of an untransformed life-force, so also imperfection of the potentialities of the physical action, an imperfection, a limitation in the response of its half-consciousness to the demands made upon it and the grossness and stains of its original animality would be the defects of an untransformed or an imperfectly transformed body. These could not but hamper and even pull down toward themselves the action of the higher parts of the nature. A transformation of the body must be the condition for a total transformation of the nature.

It might be also that the transformation might take place by stages; there are powers of the nature still belonging to the mental region that are yet potentialities of a growing gnosis lifted beyond our human mentality and partaking of the light and power of the Divine and an ascent through these planes, a descent of them into the mental being might seem to be the natural evolutionary course. But in practice it might be found that these intermediate levels would not be sufficient for the total transformation since, being themselves illumined potentialities of mental being not yet supramental in the full sense of the word, they could bring down to the mind only a partial divinity or raise the mind toward that but not effectuate its elevation into the complete supramentality of the Truth-Consciousness. Still these levels might become stages of the ascent that some would reach and pause there while others went higher and could reach and live on superior strata of a semidivine existence. It is not to be supposed that all humanity would rise in a block into the Supermind; at first those only might attain to the highest or some intermediate height of the ascent whose inner evolution has fitted them for so great a change or who are raised by the direct touch of the Divine into its perfect light and power and bliss. The large mass of human beings might still remain for long content with a normal or only a partially illumined and uplifted human nature. But this would be itself a sufficiently radical change and initial transformation of earth-life; for the way would be open to all who have the will to rise, the supramental influence of the Truth-Consciousness would touch the earth-life and influence even its untransformed mass and a hope would be there and a promise eventually available to all, which now only the few can share in or realize.

In any case these would be beginnings only and could not constitute the fullness of the divine life upon earth; it would be a new orientation of the earthly life but not the consummation of its change. For that there must be the sovereign reign of a supramental Truth-Consciousness to which all other forms of life would be subordinated and depend upon it as the master principle and supreme power to which they could look up as the goal, profit by its influences, be moved and upraised by something of its illumination and penetrating force. Especially, as the human body had to come into existence with its modification of the previous animal form and its erect figure of a new power of life and its expressive movements and activities serviceable and necessary to the principle of mind and the life of a mental being, so too a body must be developed with new powers, activities, or degrees of a divine action expressive of a Truth-Conscious being and proper to a supramental consciousness and manifesting a conscious spirit. While the capacity for taking up and sublimating all the activities of the earth-life capable of being spiritualized must be there, a transcendence of the original animality and the actions incurably tainted by it or at least some saving transformation of them, some spiritualizing or psychicizing of the consciousness and motives animating them, and the shedding of whatever could not be so transformed, even a change of what might be called its instrumental structure, its functioning, and organization, a complete and hitherto unprecedented control of these things must be the consequence or incidental to this total change. These things have already been to some extent illustrated in the lives of many who have become possessed of spiritual powers but as something exceptional and occasional, the casual or incomplete manifestation of an acquired capacity rather than the organization of a new consciousness, a new life, and a new nature. How far can such physical transformation be carried, what are the limits within which it must remain to be consistent with life upon earth and without carrying that life beyond the earthly sphere or pushing it toward the supraterrestrial existence? The supramental consciousness is not a fixed quantity but a power that passes to higher and higher levels of possibility until it reaches supreme consummations of spiritual existence fulfilling Supermind and Supermind fulfills the ranges of spiritual consciousness that are pushing toward it from the human or mental level. In this progression the body also may reach a more perfect form and a higher range of its expressive powers, become a more and more perfect vessel of divinity.

*　*　*

This destiny of the body has rarely been envisaged in the past or else not for the body here upon earth; such forms would rather be imagined or visioned as the privilege of celestial beings and not possible as the physical residence of a soul still bound to terrestrial nature. The Vaishnavas have spoken of a spiritualized conscious body, *chinmaya deha;* there has been the conception of a radiant or luminous body, which might be the Vedic *jyotirmaya deha.* A light has been seen by some radiating from the bodies of highly developed spiritual persons, even extending to the emission of an enveloping aura and there has been recorded an initial phenomenon of this kind in the life of so great a spiritual personality as Ramakrishna. But these things have been either conceptual only or rare and occasional and for the most part the body has not been regarded as possessed of spiritual possibility or capable of transformation. It has been spoken of as the means of effectuation of the dharma, and dharma here includes all high purposes, achievements, and ideals of life not excluding the spiritual change; but it is an instrument that must be dropped when its work is done and though there may be and must be spiritual realization while yet in the body, it can only come to its full fruition after the abandonment of the physical frame. More ordinarily in the spiritual tradition the body has been regarded as an obstacle, incapable of spiritualization or transmutation and a heavy weight holding the soul to earthly nature and preventing its ascent either to spiritual fulfillment in the Supreme or to the dissolution of its individual being in the Supreme. But while this conception of the role of the body in our destiny is suitable enough for a sadhana that sees earth only as a field of the ignorance and earth-life as a preparation for a saving withdrawal from life, which is the indispensable condition for spiritual liberation, it is insufficient for a sadhana that conceives of a divine life upon earth and liberation of earth-nature itself as part of a total purpose of the embodiment of the spirit here. If a total transformation of the being is our aim, a transformation of the body must be an indispensable part of it; without that no full divine life on earth is possible.

It is the past evolution of the body and especially its animal nature and animal history that seems to stand in the way of this consummation. The body, as we have seen, is an offspring and creation of the Inconscient, itself inconscient or only half-conscious; it began as a form of unconscious Matter, developed life and from a material object became a living growth, developed mind and from the subconsciousness of the plant and the initial rudimentary mind or incomplete intelligence of the animal developed the intellectual mind and more complete intelligence of man and now serves as the physical base, container, and instrumental means of our total spiritual endeavor. Its animal character and its gross limitations stand indeed as obstacles to our spiritual perfection; but the fact that it has developed a soul and is capable of serving it as a means may indicate that it is capable of further development and may become a shrine and expression of the spirit, reveal a secret spirituality of Matter, become entirely and not only half-conscious, reach a certain oneness with the spirit. This much it must do, so far at least it must transcend its original earth-nature, if it is to be the complete instrument of the divine life and no longer an obstacle.

*   *   *

Still the inconveniences of the animal body and its animal nature and impulses and the limitations of the human body at its best are there in the beginning and persist always so long as there is not the full and fundamental liberation, and its inconscience or half-conscience and its binding of the soul and mind and life-force to Matter, to materiality of all kinds, to the call of the unregenerated earth-nature are there and constantly oppose the call of the spirit and circumscribe the climb to higher things. To the physical being it brings a bondage to the material instruments, to the brain and heart and senses, wed to materiality and materialism of all kinds, to the bodily mechanism and its needs and obligations, to the imperative need of food and the preoccupation with the means of getting it and storing it as one of the besetting interests of life, to fatigue and sleep, to the satisfaction of bodily desire. The life-force in man also is tied down to these small things; it has to limit the scope of its larger ambitions and longings, its drive to rise beyond the pull of earth and follow the more heavenly intuitions of its psychic parts, the heart's ideal, and the soul's yearnings. On the mind the body imposes the boundaries of the physical being and the physical life and the sense of the sole complete reality of physical things with the rest as a sort of brilliant fireworks of the imagination, of lights and glories that can only have their full play in heavens beyond, on higher planes of existence, but not here; it afflicts the idea and aspiration with the burden of doubt, the evidence of the subtle senses and the intuition with uncertainty, and the vast field of supraphysical consciousness and experience with the imputation of unreality, and clamps down to its earth-roots the growth of the spirit from its original limiting humanity into the supramental truth and the divine nature. These obstacles can be overcome, the denials and resistance of the body surmounted, its transformation is possible. Even the inconscient and animal part of us can be illumined and made capable of manifesting the god-nature, even as our mental humanity can be made to manifest the superhumanity of the supramental Truth-Consciousness and the divinity of what is now superconscious to us and the total transformation made a reality here. But for this the obligations and compulsions of its animality must cease to be obligatory and a purification of its materiality effected by which that very materiality can be turned into a material solidity of the manifestation of the divine nature. For nothing essential must be left out in the totality of the earth-change; Matter itself can be turned into a means of revelation of the spiritual reality, the Divine.

The difficulty is dual, psychological and corporeal: the first is the effect of the unregenerated animality upon the life especially by the insistence of the body's gross instincts, impulses, desires; the second is the outcome of our corporeal structure and organic instrumentation imposing its restrictions on the dynamism of the higher divine nature. The first of these two difficulties is easier to deal with and conquer; for here the will can intervene and impose on the body the power of the higher nature. Certain of these impulses and instincts of the body have been found especially harmful by the spiritual aspirant and weighed considerably in favor of an ascetic rejection of the body. Sex and sexuality and all that springs from sex and testifies to its existence had to be banned and discarded from the spiritual life, and this, though difficult, is not at all impossible and can be made a cardinal condition for the spiritual seeker. This is natural and unescapable in all ascetic practice and the satisfaction of this condition, though not easy at first to fulfill, becomes after a time quite feasible; the overcoming of the sex-instinct and impulse is indeed binding on all who would attain to self-mastery and lead the spiritual life. A total mastery over it is essential for all spiritual seekers, the eradication of it for the complete ascetic. This much has to be recognized and not diminished in its obligatory importance and its principle.

But all recognition of the sex principle, as apart from the gross physical indulgence of the sex-impulse, could not be excluded from a divine life upon earth; it is there in life, plays a large part and has to be dealt with, it cannot simply be ignored, merely suppressed or held down or put away out of sight. In the first place, it is in one of its aspects a cosmic and even a divine principle: it takes the spiritual form of the Ishwara and the Shakti and without it there could be no world-creation or manifestation of the world-principle of Purusha and Prakriti, which are both necessary for the creation, necessary too in their association and interchange for the play of its psychological working and in their manifestation as soul and Nature fundamental to the whole process of the *Lila.** In the divine life itself an incarnation or at least in some form a presence of the two powers or their initiating influence through their embodiments or representatives would be indispensable for making the new creation possible. In its human action on the mental and vital level sex is not altogether an undivine principle; it has its nobler aspects and idealities and it has to be seen in what way and to what extent these can be admitted into the new and larger life. All gross animal indulgence of sex desire and impulse would have to be eliminated; it could only continue among those who are not ready for the higher life or not yet ready for a complete spiritual living. In all who aspired to it but could not yet take it up in its fullness sex will have to be refined, submit to the spiritual or psychic impulse and a control by the higher mind and the higher vital and shed all its lighter, frivolous, or degraded forms and feel the touch of the purity of the ideal. Love would remain, all forms of the pure truth of love in higher and higher steps till it realized its highest nature, widened into universal love, merged into the love of the Divine. The love of man and woman would also undergo that elevation and consummation; for all that can feel a touch of the ideal and the spiritual must follow the way of ascent till it reaches the divine Reality. The body and its activities must be accepted as part of the divine life and pass under this law; but, as in the other evolutionary transitions, what cannot accept the law of the divine life cannot be accepted and must fall away from the ascending nature.

---

*God creates for play, not for some purpose.

Another difficulty that the transformation of the body has to face is its dependence for its very existence upon food and here too are involved the gross physical instincts, impulses, desires that are associated with this difficult factor, the essential cravings of the palate, the greed of food and animal gluttony of the belly, the coarsening of the mind when it grovels in the mud of sense, obeys a servitude to its mere animal part, and hugs its bondage to Matter. The higher human in us seeks refuge in a temperate moderation, in abstemiousness and abstinence, or in carelessness about the body and its wants, and in an absorption in higher things. The spiritual seeker often, like the Jain ascetics, seeks refuge in long and frequent fasts that lift him temporarily at least out of the clutch of the body's demands and help him to feel in himself a pure vacancy of the wide rooms of the spirit. But all this is not liberation and the question may be raised whether, not only at first but always, the divine life also must submit to this necessity. But it could only deliver itself from it altogether if it could find out the way so to draw upon the universal energy that the energy would sustain not only the vital parts of our physicality but its constituent matter with no need of aid for sustenance from any outside substance of Matter. It is indeed possible even while fasting for very long periods to maintain the full energies and activities of the soul and mind and life, even those of the body, to remain wakeful but concentrated in Yoga all the time, or to think deeply and write day and night, to dispense with sleep, to walk eight hours a day, maintaining all these activities separately or together and not feel any loss of strength, any fatigue, any kind of failure or decadence. At the end of the fast one can even resume at once taking the normal or even a greater than the normal amount of nourishment without any transition or precaution such as medical science enjoins, as if both the complete fasting and the feasting were natural conditions, alternating by an immediate and easy passage from one to the other, of a body already trained by a sort of initial transformation to be an instrument of the powers and activities of Yoga. But one thing one does not escape and that is the wasting of the material tissues of the body, its flesh and substance. Conceivably, if a practicable way and means could only be found, this last invincible obstacle too might be overcome and the body maintained by an interchange of its forces with the forces of material Nature, giving to her her need from the individual and taking from her directly the sustaining energies of her universal existence. Conceivably, one might rediscover and reestablish at the summit of the evolution of life the phenomenon we see at its base, the power to draw from all around it the means of sustenance and self-renewal. Or else the evolved being might acquire the greater power to draw down those means from above rather than draw them up or pull them in from the environment around, all about it and below it. But until something like this is achieved or made possible we have to go back to food and the established material forces of Nature.

In fact we do, however unconsciously, draw constantly upon the universal energy, the force in Matter to replenish our material existence and the mental, vital, and other potencies in the body: we do it directly in the invisible processes of interchange constantly kept up by Nature, and by special means devised by her; breathing is one of these, sleep also, and repose. But as her basic means for maintaining and renewing the gross physical body and its workings and inner potencies Nature has selected the taking in of outside matter in the shape of food, its digestion, assimilation of what is assimilable, and elimination of what cannot or ought not to be assimilated, this by itself is sufficient for mere maintenance, but for assuring health and strength in the body so maintained it has added the impulse toward physical exercise and play of many kinds, ways for the expenditure and renewal of energy, the choice or the necessity of manifold action and labor. In the new life, in its beginnings at least, it would not be necessary or advisable to make any call for an extreme or precipitate rejection of the need of food or the established natural method for the maintenance of the still imperfectly transformed body. If or when these things have to be transcended, it must come as a result of the awakened will of the spirit, a will also in Matter itself, an imperative evolutionary urge, an act of the creative transmutations of Time or a descent from the Transcendence. Meanwhile the drawing in of the universal energy by a conscious action of the higher powers of the being from around or from above, by a call to what is still to us a transcending consciousness or by an invasion or descent from the Transcendence itself may well become an occasional, a frequent, or a constant phenomenon and even reduce the part played by food and its need to an incidence no longer preoccupying, a necessity minor and less and less imperative. Meanwhile food and the ordinary process of Nature can be accepted although its use has to be liberated from attachment and desire and the grosser undiscriminating appetites and clutch at the pleasures of the flesh, which is the way of the Ignorance; the physical processes have to be subtilized and the grossest may have to be eliminated and new processes found or new instrumentalities emerge. So long as it is accepted, a refined pleasure in it may be permitted and even a desireless *Ananda* of taste take the place of the physical relish and the human selection by likings and dislikings which is our present imperfect response to what is offered to us by Nature. It must be remembered that for the divine life on earth, earth and Matter have not to be and cannot be rejected but have only to be sublimated and to reveal in themselves the possibilities of the spirit, serve the spirit's highest uses, and be transformed into instruments of a greater living.

The divine life must always be actuated by the push toward perfection; a perfection of the joy of life is part and an essential part of it, the body's delight in things and the body's joy of life are not excluded from it; they too have to be made perfect. A large totality is the very nature of this new and growing way of existence, a fullness of the possibilities of the mind transmuted into a thing of light, of the life converted into a force of spiritual power and joy, of the body transformed into an instrument of a divine action, divine knowledge, divine bliss. All can be taken into its scope that is capable of transforming itself, all that can be an instrument, a vessel, an opportunity for the expression of this totality of the self-manifesting Spirit.

*   *   *

There is one problem raised by sex for those who would reject in toto the obligations imposed by the animality of the body and put forward by it as an insistent opposition in the way of the aspirant to a higher life: it is the necessity of the prolongation of the race for which the sex activity is the only means already provided by Nature for living beings and inevitably imposed upon the race. It is not indeed necessary for the individual seeker after a divine life to take up this problem or even for a group who do not seek after it for themselves alone, but desire a wide acceptance of it by mankind as at least an ideal. There will always be the multitude who do not concern themselves with it or are not ready for its complete practice and to these can be left the care for the prolongation of the race. The number of those who lead the divine life can be maintained and increased as the ideal extends itself, by the voluntary adhesion of those who are touched by the aspiration and there need be no resort to physical means for this purpose, no deviation from the rule of a strict sexual abstinence. But yet there may be circumstances in which, from another standpoint, a voluntary creation of bodies for souls that seek to enter the earth-life to help in the creation and extension of the divine life upon earth might be found to be desirable. Then the necessity of a physical procreation for this purpose could only be avoided if new means of a supraphysical kind were evolved and made available. A development of this kind must necessarily belong to what is now considered as the sphere of the occult and the use of concealed powers of action or creation not known or possessed by the common mind of the race. Occultism means rightly the use of the higher powers of our nature, soul, mind, life-force, and the faculties of the subtle physical consciousness to bring about results on their own or on the material plane by some pressure of their own secret law and its potentialities, for manifestation and result in human or earthly mind and life and body or in objects and events in the world of Matter. A discovery or an extension of these little-known or yet undeveloped powers is now envisaged by some well-known thinkers as a next step to be taken by mankind in its immediate evolution; the kind of creation spoken of has not been included among these developments, but it could well be considered as one of the new possibilities. Even physical science is trying to find physical means for passing beyond the ordinary instrumentation or procedure of Nature in this matter of propagation or the renewal of the physical life-force in human or animal beings; but the resort to occult means and the intervention of subtle physical processes, if it could be made possible, would be a greater way that could avoid the limitations, degradations, incompleteness, and heavy imperfection of the means and results solely available to the law of material force. In India there has always been from the earliest times a widely spread belief in the possibility and reality of the use of these powers by men with an advanced knowledge of these secret things or with a developed spiritual knowledge and experience and dynamic force and even, in the Tantras, an organized system of their method and practice. The intervention of the Yogi in bringing about a desired birth of offspring is also generally believed in and often appealed to and the bestowal on the child so obtained of a spiritual attainment or destiny by his will or his blessing is sometimes asked for and such a result is recorded not only in the tradition of the past, but maintained by the witness of the present. But there is here still the necessity of a resort to the normal means of propagation and the gross method of physical Nature. A purely occult method, a resort to supraphysical processes acting by supraphysical means for a physical result would have to be possible if we are to avoid this necessity: the resort to the sex impulse and its animal process could not be transcended otherwise. If there is some reality in the phenomenon of materialization and dematerialization, claimed to be possible by occultists and evidenced by occurrences many of us have witnessed, a method of this kind would not be out of the range of possibility. For in the theory of the occultists and in the gradation of the ranges and planes of our being that Yoga-knowledge outlines for us there is not only a subtle physical force but a subtle physical Matter intervening between life and gross Matter and to create in this subtle physical substance and precipitate the forms thus made into our grosser materiality is feasible. It should be possible and it is believed to be possible for an object formed in this subtle physical substance to make a transit from its subtlety into the state of gross Matter directly by the intervention of an occult force and process whether with or even without the assistance or intervention of some gross material procedure. A soul wishing to enter into a body or form for itself a body and take part in a divine life upon earth might be assisted to do so or even provided with such a form by this method of direct transmutation without passing through birth by the sex process or undergoing any degradation or any of the heavy limitations in the growth and development of its mind and material body inevitable to our present way of existence. It might then assume at once the structure and greater powers and functionings of the truly divine material body, which must one day emerge in a progressive evolution to a totally transformed existence both of the life and form in a divinized earth-nature.

But what would be the internal or external form and structure and what the instrumentation of this divine body? The material history of the development of the animal and human body has left it bound to a minutely constructed and elaborated system of organs and a precarious order of their functioning, which can easily become a disorder, open to a general or local disorganization, dependent on an easily disturbed nervous system and commanded by a brain whose vibrations are supposed to be mechanical and automatic and not under our conscious control. According to the materialist all this is a functioning of Matter alone whose fundamental reality is chemical. We have to suppose that the body is constructed by the agency of chemical elements building atoms and molecules and cells and these again are the agents and only conductors at the basis of a complicated physical structure and instrumentation that is the sole mechanical cause of all our actions, thoughts, feelings, the soul a fiction, and mind and life only a material and mechanical manifestation and appearance of this machine, which is worked out and automatically driven with a figment of consciousness in it by the forces inherent in inconscient Matter. If that were the truth, it is obvious that any divinization or divine transformation of the body or of anything else would be nothing but an illusion, an imagination, a senseless and impossible chimera. But even if we suppose a soul, a conscious will at work in this body, it could not arrive at a divine transformation if there were no radical change in the bodily instrument itself and in the organization of its material workings. The transforming agent will be bound and stopped in its work by the physical organism's unalterable limitations and held up by the unmodified or imperfectly modified original animal in us. The possibility of the disorders, derangements, maladies native to these physical arrangements would still be there and could only be shut out by a constant vigilance or perpetual control obligatory on the corporeal instrument's spiritual inhabitant and master. This could not be called a truly divine body, for in a divine body an inherent freedom from all these things would be natural and perpetual; this freedom would be a normal and native truth of its being and therefore inevitable and unalterable. A radical transformation of the functioning and, it may well be, of the structure and certainly of the too mechanical and material impulse and driving forces of the bodily system would be imperative. What agency could we find that we could make the means of this all-important liberation and change? Something there is in us or something has to be developed, perhaps a central and still occult part of our being containing forces whose powers in our actual and present makeup are only a fraction of what could be, but if they become complete and dominant would be truly able to bring about with the help of the light and force of the soul and the supramental Truth-Consciousness the necessary physical transformation and its consequences. This might be found in the system of Chakras revealed by Tantric knowledge and accepted in the systems of Yoga, conscious centers and sources of all the dynamic powers of our being organizing their action through the plexuses and arranged in an ascending series from the lowest physical to the highest mind center and spiritual center called the thousand-petaled lotus, where ascending Nature, the Serpent Power of the Tantrics, meets the Brahman and is liberated into the Divine Being. These centers are closed or half-closed within us and have to be opened before their full potentiality can be manifested in our physical nature; but once they are opened and completely active, no limit can easily be set to the development of their potencies and the total transformation to be possible.

But what would be the result of the emergence of these forces and their liberated and more divine action on the body itself, what would be their dynamic connection with it and their transforming operation on the still existing animal nature and its animal impulses and gross material procedure? It might be held that the first necessary change would be the liberation of the mind, the life-force, the subtle physical agencies, and the physical consciousness into a freer and a more divine activity, a many-dimensioned and unlimited operation of their consciousness, a large outbreak of higher powers, and the sublimation of the bodily consciousness itself, of its instrumentation, capacity, capability for the manifestation of the soul in the world of Matter. The subtle senses now concealed in us might come forward into a free action and the material senses themselves become means or channels for the vision of what is now invisible to us or the discovery of things surrounding us but at present unseizable and held back from our knowledge. A firm check might be put on the impulses of the animal nature or they might be purified and subtilized so as to become assets and not liabilities and so transformed as to be parts and processes of a more divine life. But even these changes would still leave a residue of material processes keeping the old way and not amenable to the higher control and, if this could not be changed, the rest of the transformation might itself be checked and incomplete. A total transformation of the body would demand a sufficient change of the most material part of the organism, its constitution, its processes, and its setup of nature.

Again, it might be thought that a full control would be sufficient, a knowledge and a vision of this organism and its unseen action and an effective control determining its operations according to the conscious will; this possibility has been affirmed as something already achieved and a part of the development of the inner powers in some. The cessation of the breathing while the life of the body still remained stable, the hermetic sealing up at will not only of the breath, but of all the vital manifestations for long periods, the stoppage of the heart similarly at will while thought and speech and other mental workings continued unabated, these and other phenomena of the power of the will over the body are known and well-attested examples of this kind of mastery. But these are occasional or sporadic successes and do not amount to transformation; a total control is necessary and an established and customary and, indeed, a natural mastery. Even with that achieved something more fundamental might have to be demanded for the complete liberation and change into a divine body.

Again, it might be urged that the organic structure of the body no less than its basic outer form would have to be retained as a necessary material foundation for the retention of the earth-nature, the connection of the divine life with the life of earth and a continuance of the evolutionary process so as to prevent a breaking upward out of and away from it into a state of being that would properly belong to a higher plane and not to a terrestrial divine fulfillment. The prolonged existence of the animal itself in our nature, if sufficiently transformed to be an instrument of manifestation and not an obstacle, would be necessary to preserve the continuity, the evolutionary total; it would be needed as the living vehicle, *vahana,* of the emergent god in the material world where he would have to act and achieve the works and wonders of the new life. It is certain that a form of body making this connection and a bodily action containing the earth-dynamism and its fundamental activities must be there, but the connection should not be a bond or a confining limitation or a contradiction of the totality of the change. The maintenance of the present organism without any transformation of it would not but act as such a bond and confinement within the old nature. There would be a material base but it would be of the earth earthy, an old and not a new earth with a more divine psychological structure; for with that structure the old system would be out of harmony and it would be unable to serve its further evolution or even to uphold it as a base in Matter. It would bind a part of the being, a lower part, to an untransformed humanity and unchanged animal functioning and prevent its liberation into the superhumanity of the supramental nature. A change is then necessary here too, a necessary part of the total bodily transformation, which would divinize the whole man, at least in the ultimate result and not leave his evolution incomplete.

This aim, it must be said, would be sufficiently served if the instrumentation of the centers and their forces reigned over all the activities of the nature with an entire domination of the body and made it, both in its structural form and in its organic workings, a free channel and means of communication and a plastic instrument of cognition and dynamic action for all that they had to do in the material life, in the world of Matter. There would have to be a change in the operative processes of the material organs themselves and, it may well be, in their very constitution and their importance; they could not be allowed to impose their limitations imperatively on the new physical life. To begin with, they might become more clearly outer ends of the channels of communication and action, more serviceable for the psychological purposes of the inhabitant, less blindly material in their responses, more conscious of the act and aim of the inner movements and powers which use them and which they are wrongly supposed by the material man in us to generate and to use. The brain would be a channel of communication of the form of the thoughts and a battery of their insistence on the body and the outside world where they could then become effective directly, communicating themselves without physical means from mind to mind, producing with a similar directness effects on the thoughts, actions, and lives of others or even upon material things. The heart would equally be a direct communicant and medium of interchange for the feelings and emotions thrown outward upon the world by the forces of the psychic center. Heart could reply directly to heart, the life-force come to the help of other lives and answer their call in spite of strangeness and distance, many beings without any external communication thrill with the message and meet in the secret light from one divine center. The will might control the organs that deal with food, safeguard automatically the health, eliminate greed and desire, substitute subtler processes or draw in strength and substance from the universal life-force so that the body could maintain for a long time its own strength and substance without loss or waste, remaining thus with no need of sustenance by material aliments, and yet continue a strenuous action with no fatigue or pause for sleep or repose. The soul's will or the mind's could act from higher sources upon the sex-center and the sex organs so as to check firmly or even banish the grosser sexual impulse or stimulus, and instead of serving an animal excitation or crude drive or desire turn their use to the storing, production, and direction toward brain and heart and life-force of the essential energy, *ojas,* of which this region is the factory so as to support the works of the mind and soul and spirit and the higher life-powers and limit the expenditure of the energy on lower things. The soul, the psychic being, could more easily fill all with the light and turn the very matter of the body to higher uses for its own greater purpose.

This would be a first potent change, but not by any means all that is possible or desirable. For it may well be that the evolutionary urge would proceed to a change of the organs themselves in their material working and use and diminish greatly the need of their instrumentation and even of their existence. The centers in the subtle body, *sukshma sharira,* of which one would become conscious and aware of all going on in it would pour their energies into material nerve and plexus and tissue and radiate them through the whole material body; all the physical life and its necessary activities in this new existence could be maintained and operated by these higher agencies in a freer and ampler way and by a less burdensome and restricting method. This might go so far that these organs might cease to be indispensable and even be felt as too obstructive: the central force might use them less and less and finally throw aside their use altogether. If that happened they might waste by atrophy, be reduced to an insignificant minimum, or even disappear.

The central force might substitute for them subtle organs of a very different character or, if anything material was needed, instruments that would be forms of dynamism or plastic transmitters rather than what we know as organs. This might well be part of a supreme total transformation of the body, though this too might not be final. To envisage such changes is to look far ahead and minds attached to the present form of things may be unable to give credence to their possibility. No such limits and no such impossibility of any necessary change can be imposed on the evolutionary urge. All has not to be fundamentally changed: on the contrary, all has to be preserved that is still needed in the totality, but all has to be perfected. Whatever is necessary for the evolutionary purpose for the increasing, enlarging, heightening of the consciousness, which seems to be its central will and aim here, or the progression of its enabling means and preserving environment, has to be kept and furthered; but what has to be overpassed, whatever has no longer a use or is degraded, what has become unhelpful or retarding, can be discarded and dropped on the way. That has been evident in the history of the evolution of the body from its beginning in elementary forms to its most developed type, the human. There is no reason why this process should not intervene in the transition from the human into the divine body. For the manifestation or building of a divine body on earth there must be an initial transformation, the appearance of a new, a greater and more developed type, not a continuance with little modifications of the present physical form and its limited possibilities. What has to be preserved must indeed be preserved and that means whatever is necessary or thoroughly serviceable for the uses of the new life on earth; whatever is still needed and will serve its purpose but is imperfect will have to be retained but developed and perfected; whatever is no longer of use for new aims or is a disability must be thrown aside. The necessary forms and instrumentations of Matter must remain since it is in a world of Matter that the divine life has to manifest, but their materiality must be refined, uplifted, ennobled, illumined, since Matter and the world of Matter have increasingly to manifest the indwelling Spirit.

The new type, the divine body, must continue the already developed evolutionary forms; there must be a continuation from the type Nature has all along been developing, a continuity from the human to the divine body, no breaking away to something unrecognizable, but a high sequel to what has already been achieved and in part perfected. The human body has in it parts and instruments that have been sufficiently evolved to serve the divine life; these have to survive in their form, though they must be still further perfected, their limitations of range and use removed, their liability to defect and malady and impairment eliminated, their capacities of cognition and dynamic action carried beyond the present limits. New powers have to be acquired by the body that our present humanity could not hope to realize, could not even dream of or could only imagine. Much that can now only be known, worked out, or created by the use of invented tools and machinery might be achieved by the new body in its own power or by the inhabitant spirit through its own direct spiritual force. The body itself might acquire new means and ranges of communication with other bodies, new processes of acquiring knowledge, a new aesthesis, new potencies of manipulation of itself and objects. It might not be impossible for it to possess or disclose means native to its own constitution, substance, or natural instrumentation for making the far near and annulling distance, cognizing what is now beyond the body's cognizance, acting where action is now out of its reach or its domain, developing subtleties and plasticities that could not be permitted under present conditions to the needed fixity of a material frame. These and other numerous potentialities might appear and the body become an instrument immeasurably superior to what we can now imagine as possible. There could be an evolution from a first apprehending Truth-Consciousness to the utmost heights of the ascending ranges of Supermind and it may pass the borders of the Supermind proper itself where it begins to shadow out, develop, delineate expressive forms of life touched by a supreme pure existence, consciousness, and bliss that constitute the worlds of a highest truth of existence, dynamism of *Tapas,* glory and sweetness of bliss, the absolute essence and pitch of the all-creating *Ananda.* The transformation of the physical being might follow this incessant line of progression and the divine body reflect or reproduce here in a divine life on the earth something of this highest greatness and glory of the self-manifesting Spirit.

SUPERMIND AND THE LIFE DIVINE

A divine life upon earth, the ideal we have placed before us, can only come about by a spiritual change of our being and a radical and fundamental change, an evolution or revolution of our nature. The embodied being upon earth would have to rise out of the domination over it of its veils of mind, life, and body into the full consciousness and possession of its spiritual reality and its nature also would have to be lifted out of the consciousness and power of consciousness proper to a mental, vital, and physical being into the greater consciousness and greater power of being and the larger and freer life of the spirit. It would not lose these former veils but they would no longer be veils or imperfect expressions but true manifestations; they would be changed into states of light, powers of spiritual life, vehicles of a spiritual existence. But this again could not be if mind, life, and body were not taken up and transformed by a state of being and a force of being superior to them, a power of Supermind as much above our incomplete mental nature as that is above the nature of animal life and animated Matter, as it is immeasurably above the mere material nature.

The Supermind is in its very essence a Truth-Consciousness, a consciousness always free from the Ignorance that is the foundation of our present natural or evolutionary existence and from which nature in us is trying to arrive at self-knowledge and world-knowledge and a right consciousness and the right use of our existence in the universe. The Supermind, because it is a Truth-Consciousness, has this knowledge inherent in it and this power of true existence; its course is straight and can go direct to its aim, its field is wide and can even be made illimitable. This is because its very nature is knowledge: it has not to acquire knowledge but possesses it in its own right; its steps are not from nescience or ignorance into some imperfect light, but from truth to greater truth, from right perception to deeper perception, from intuition to intuition, from illumination to utter and boundless luminousness, from growing widenesses to the utter vasts and to very infinite. On its summits it possesses the divine omniscience and omnipotence, but even in an evolutionary movement of its own graded self-manifestation by which it would eventually reveal its own highest heights it must be in its very nature essentially free from ignorance and error. It starts from truth and light and moves always in truth and light. As its knowledge is always true, so too its will is always true; it does not fumble in its handling of things or stumble in its paces. In the Supermind feeling and emotion do not depart from their truth, make no slips or mistakes, do not swerve from the right and the real, cannot misuse beauty and delight, or twist away from a divine rectitude. In the Supermind sense cannot mislead or deviate into the grossnesses that are here its natural imperfections and the cause of reproach, distrust, and misuse by our ignorance. Even an incomplete statement made by the Supermind is a truth leading to a further truth, its incomplete action a step toward completeness. All the life and action and leading of the Supermind is guarded in its very nature from the falsehoods and uncertainties that are our lot; it moves in safety toward its perfection. Once the Truth-Consciousness was established here on its own sure foundation, the evolution of divine life would be a progress in felicity, a march through light to *Ananda.*

Supermind is an eternal reality of the divine Being and the divine Nature. In its own plane it already and always exists and possesses its own essential law of being; it has not to be created or to emerge or evolve into existence out of involution in Matter or out of nonexistence, as it might seem to the view of mind, which itself seems to its own view to have so emerged from life and Matter or to have evolved out of an involution in life and Matter. The nature of Supermind is always the same, a being of knowledge, proceeding from truth to truth, creating or rather manifesting what has to be manifested by the power of a preexistent knowledge, not by hazard but by a self-existent destiny in the being itself, a necessity of the thing in itself and therefore inevitable. Its manifestation of the divine life will also be inevitable; its own life on its own plane is divine and, if Supermind descends upon the earth, it will necessarily bring the divine life with it and establish it here.

Supermind is the grade of existence beyond mind, life, and Matter and, as mind, life, and Matter have manifested on the earth, so too must Supermind in the inevitable course of things manifest in this world of Matter. In fact, a supermind is already here but it is involved, concealed behind this manifest mind, life, and Matter and not yet acting overtly or in its own power; if it acts, it is through these inferior powers and modified by their characters and so is not yet recognizable. It is only by the approach and arrival of the descending Supermind that it can be liberated upon earth and reveal itself in the action of our material, vital, and mental parts so that these lower powers can become portions of a total divinized activity of our whole being: it is that that will bring to us a completely realized divinity or the divine life. It is indeed so that life and mind involved in Matter have realized themselves here; for only what is involved can evolve, otherwise there could be no emergence.

The manifestation of a supramental Truth-Consciousness is therefore the capital reality that will make the divine life possible. It is when all the movements of thought, impulse, and action are governed and directed by a self-existent and luminously automatic Truth-Consciousness and our whole nature comes to be constituted by it and made of its stuff that the life divine will be complete and absolute. Even as it is, in reality though not in the appearance of things, it is a secret self-existent knowledge and truth that is working to manifest itself in the creation here. The Divine is already there immanent within us, ourselves are that in our inmost reality, and it is this reality that we have to manifest; it is that that constitutes the urge toward the divine living and makes necessary the creation of the life divine even in this material existence.

A manifestation of the Supermind and its Truth-Consciousness is then inevitable; it must happen in this world sooner or later. But it has two aspects, a descent from above, an ascent from below, a self-revelation of the Spirit, an evolution in Nature. The ascent is necessarily an effort, a working of Nature, an urge or nisus on her side to raise her lower parts by an evolutionary or revolutionary change, conversion, or transformation into the divine reality and it may happen by a process and progress or by a rapid miracle. The descent or self-revelation of the Spirit is an act of the supreme Reality from above that makes the realization possible and it can appear either as the divine aid that brings about the fulfillment of the progress and process or as the sanction of the miracle. Evolution, as we see it in this world, is a slow and difficult process and, indeed, usually needs ages to reach abiding results; but this is because it is in its nature an emergence from inconscient beginnings, a start from nescience and a working in the ignorance of natural beings by what seems to be an unconscious force. There can be, on the contrary, an evolution in the light and no longer in the darkness, in which the evolving being is a conscious participant and cooperator, and this is precisely what must take place here. Even in the effort and progress from the Ignorance to Knowledge this must be in part if not wholly the endeavor to be made on the heights of the nature and it must be wholly that in the final movement toward the spiritual change, realization, transformation. It must be still more so when there is a transition across the dividing line between the Ignorance and the Knowledge and the evolution is from knowledge to greater knowledge, from consciousness to greater consciousness, from being to greater being. There is then no longer any necessity for the slow pace of the ordinary evolution; there can be rapid conversion, quick transformation after transformation, what would seem to our normal present mind, a succession of miracles. An evolution on the supramental levels could well be of that nature; it could be equally, if the being so chose, a more leisurely passage of one supramental state or condition of things to something beyond but still supramental from level to divine level, a building up of divine gradations, a free growth to the supreme Supermind or beyond it to yet undreamed levels of being, consciousness, and *Ananda*.

The supramental knowledge, the Truth-Consciousness of the Supermind is in itself one and total. Even when there is a voluntary limitation of the knowledge or what might seem to be a partial manifestation, it is so voluntarily; the limitation does not proceed from or result in any kind of ignorance, it is not a denial or withholding of knowledge, for all the rest of the truth that is not brought into expression is implicit there. Above all, there are no contradictions: whatever would seem to be opposites to the mind, here carry in themselves their own right relation and reconciling agreement,—if indeed any reconciliation were needed, for the harmony of these apparent opposites is complete. The mind tends to put the personal and the impersonal in face of each other as if they were two contraries, but the Supermind sees and realizes them as, at the lowest, complements and mutually fulfilling powers of the single Reality and, more characteristically, as interfused and inseparable and themselves that single Reality. The Person has his aspect of impersonality inseparable from himself without which he could not be what he is or could not be his whole self: the Impersonal is in its truth not a state of existence, a state of consciousness and a state of bliss, but a Being self-existent, conscious of self, full of his own self-existent bliss, bliss the very substance of his being,—so, the one single and illimitable Person, Purusha. In the Supermind the finite does not cut up or limit the infinite, does not feel itself contrary to the infinite; but rather it feels its own infinity. The relative and temporal are not contradictions of eternity but a right relation of its aspects, a native working or an imperishable feature of the eternal. Time there is only the eternal in extension and the eternal can be felt in the momentary. Thus the integral Divine is there in the Supermind and no theory of illusion or self-contradictory Maya need be thrust in to justify its way of existence. It will be obvious that an escape from life is not necessary for the Divine to find itself or its reality; it possesses that always whether in cosmic life or in its transcendent existence. The divine life cannot be a contradiction of the Divine or of the supreme reality; it is part of that reality, an aspect or expression of it and it can be nothing else. In life on the supramental plane all the Divine is possessed, and when the Supermind descends on earth, it must bring the Divine with it and make that full possession possible here.

The divine life will give to those who enter into it and possess it an increasing and finally a complete possession of the Truth-Consciousness and all that it carries in it; it will bring with it the realization of the Divine in self and the Divine in Nature. All that is sought by the God-seeker will be fulfilled in his spirit and in his life as he moves toward spiritual perfection. He will become aware of the transcendent reality, possess in the self-experience the supreme existence, consciousness, bliss, be one with *Sachchidananda.* He will become one with cosmic being and universal Nature: he will contain the world in himself, in his own cosmic consciousness and feel himself one with all beings; he will see himself in all and all in himself, become united and identified with the Self that has become all existences. He will perceive the beauty of the All-Beautiful and the miracle of the All-Wonderful; he will enter in the end into the bliss of the Brahman and live abidingly in it and for all this he will not need to shun existence or plunge into the annihilation of the spiritual Person in some self-extinguishing Nirvana. As in the Self, so in Nature, he can realize the Divine. The nature of the Divine is Light and Power and Bliss; he can feel the divine Light and Power and Bliss above him and descending into him, filling every strand of his nature, every cell and atom of his being, flooding his soul and mind and life and body, surrounding him like an illimitable sea and filling the world, suffusing all his feeling and sense and experience, making all his life truly and utterly divine. This and all else that the spiritual consciousness can bring to him the divine life will give him when it reaches its utmost completeness and perfection and the supramental Truth-Consciousness is fulfilled in all himself; but even before that he can attain to something of it all, grow in it, live in it, once the Supermind has descended upon him and has the direction of his existence. All relations with the Divine will be his: the trinity of God-knowledge, divine works, and devotion to God will open within him and move toward an utter self-giving and surrender of his whole being and nature. He will live in God and with God, possess God, as it is said, even plunge in him forgetting all separate personality, but not losing it in self-extinction. The love of God and all the sweetness of love will remain his, the bliss of contact as well as the bliss of oneness, and the bliss of difference in oneness. All the infinite ranges of experience of the Infinite will be his and all the joy of the finite in the embrace of the Infinite.

The descent of the Supermind will bring to one who receives it and is fulfilled in the Truth-Consciousness all the possibilities of the divine life. It will take up not only the whole characteristic experience that we recognize already as constituting the spiritual life but also all that we now exclude from that category but which is capable of divinization, not excluding whatever of the earth-nature and the earth-life can be transformed by the touch of the Supermind and taken up into the manifested life of the Spirit. For a divine life on earth need not be a thing apart and exclusive having nothing to do with the common earthly existence: it will take up human being and human life, transform what can be transformed, spiritualize whatever can be spiritualized, cast its influence on the rest and effectuate either a radical or an uplifting change, bring about a deeper communion between the universal and the individual, invade the ideal with the spiritual truth of which it is a luminous shadow and help to uplift into or toward a greater and higher existence. Mind it will uplift toward a more divine light of thought and will, life toward deeper and truer emotion and action, toward a larger power of itself, toward high aims and motives. Whatever cannot yet be raised into its own full truth of being, it will bring nearer to that fullness; whatever is not ready even for that change, will still see the possibility open to it whenever its still incomplete evolution has made it ready for self-fulfillment. Even the body, if it can bear the touch of Supermind, will become more aware of its own truth,—for there is a body-consciousness that has its own instinctive truth and power of right condition and action, even a kind of unexpressed occult knowledge in the constitution of its cells and tissues that may one day become conscious and contribute to the transformation of the physical being. An awakening must come in the earth-nature and in the earth-consciousness, which will be, if not the actual beginning, at least the effective preparation and the first steps of its evolution toward a new and more divine world order.

This would be the fulfillment of the divine life that the descent of Supermind and the working of the Truth-Consciousness taking hold of the whole nature of the living being would bring about in all who could open themselves to its power or influence. Even its first immediate effect would be on all who are capable of the possibility of entering into the Truth-Consciousness and changing all the movements of the nature more and more into the movements of the supramental truth, truth of thought, truth of will, truth in the feelings, truth in the acts, true conditions of the whole being even to the body, eventually transformation, a divinizing change. For those who could so open themselves and remain open, there would be no limitation to this development and even no fundamental difficulty; for all difficulties would be dissolved by the pressure of the supramental light and power from above pouring itself into the mind and the life-force and the body. But the result of the supramental descent need not be limited to those who could thus open themselves entirely and it need not be limited to the supramental change; there could also be a minor or secondary transformation of the mental being within a freed and perfected scope of the mental nature. In place of the human mind as it now is, a mind limited, imperfect, open at every moment to all kinds of deviation from the truth or missing of the truth, all kinds of error and openness even to the persuasions of a complete falsehood and perversion of the nature, a mind blinded and pulled down toward inconscience and ignorance, hardly arriving at knowledge, an intellect prone to interpret the higher knowledge in abstractions and indirect figures seizing and holding even the messages of the higher intuition with an uncertain and disputed grasp, there could emerge a true mind liberated and capable of the free and utmost perfection of itself and its instruments, a life governed by the free and illumined mind, a body responsive to the light and able to carry out all that the free mind and will could demand of it. This change might happen not only in the few, but extend and generalize itself in the race. This possibility, if fulfilled, would mean that the human dream of perfection, perfection of itself, of its purified and enlightened nature, of all its ways of action and living, would be no longer a dream but a truth that could be made real and humanity lifted out of the hold on it of inconscience and ignorance. The life of the mental being could be harmonized with the life of the Supermind, which will then be the highest order above it, and become even an extension and annex of the Truth-Consciousness, a part and province of the divine life. It is obvious that if the Supermind is there and an order of supramental being is established as the leading principle in earth-nature, as mind is now the leading principle, but with a sureness, a complete government of the earthly existence, a capacity of transformation of all upon their level and within their natural boundaries of which the mind in its imperfection was not capable, an immense change of human life, even if it did not extend to transformation, would be inevitable.

It remains to consider what might be the obstacles in the way of this possibility, especially those offered by the nature of the earth-order and its function as a field of a graded evolution in which our humanity is a stage and, it might be argued, its very imperfection an evolutionary necessity. How far could or would Supermind by its presence and government of things overcome this difficulty, while respecting the principle of gradation, and whether it could not rectify the wrong and ignorant order imposed by the Ignorance and Inconscience, and substitute for it a right gradation in which the perfection and divinization would be possible? Certainly, the way for the individual would be open, whatever group of human beings aspire as united in an endeavor, at a perfect and individual collective living or aspire to the divine life, would be assisted toward the attainment of its aspiration: that at least the Supermind would make its minimum consequence. But the greater possibility is also there and might even be offered to the whole of humanity. This, then, we have to consider, what would the descent of the Supermind

mean for mankind and what would be its result or its promise for the whole life and evolutionary future and destiny of the human race?

SUPERMIND AND HUMANITY

What then would be the consequence for humanity of the descent of Supermind into our
earthly existence, its consequence for this race born into a world of ignorance and inconscience but capable of an upward evolution of its consciousness and an ascent into
the light and power and bliss of a spiritual being and spiritual nature? The descent into
the earth-life of so supreme a creative power as the Supermind and its Truth-
Consciousness could not be merely a new feature or factor added to that life or put in
its front but without any other importance or only a restricted importance carrying with
it no results profoundly affecting the rest of earth-nature. Especially it could not fail to
exercise an immense influence on mankind as a whole, even a radical change in the aspect and prospect of its existence here, even if this power had no other capital result on
the material world in which it had come down to intervene. One cannot but conclude
that the influence, the change made, would be far reaching, even enormous: it would
not only establish the Supermind and a supramental race of beings upon the earth, it
could bring about an uplifting and transforming change in mind itself and as an inevitable consequence in the consciousness of man, the mental being, and would equally
bring about a radical and transforming change in the principles and forms of his living,
his ways of action and the whole build and tenor of his life. It would certainly open to
man the access to the supramental consciousness and the supramental life; for we must
suppose that it is by such a transformation that a race of supramental beings would be
created, even as the human race itself has arisen by a less radical but still a considerable
uplifting and enlargement of consciousness and conversion of the body's instrumentation and its indwelling and evolving mental and spiritual capacities and powers out of
a first animal state. But even without any such complete transformation the truth-
principle might so far replace the principle we see here of an original ignorance seeking for knowledge and arriving only at a partial knowledge that the human mind could
become a power of light, of knowledge finding itself, not the denizen of a half-way twi-
light or a servant and helper of the ignorance, a purveyor of mingled truth and error.
Mind might even become in man what it is in its fundamental origin, a subordinate, limited, and special action of the Supermind, a sufficiently luminous receptacle of truth,
and at least all falsity in its works might cease.

It could at once be objected that this would alter the whole evolutionary order and
its balance and leave an incurable gap in its completeness: there would be an unbridged
gulf between man and the animal and no way for the evolutionary nisus to a journey
over it in the progress of the consciousness from animality to divinity; for, some kind
of divinity would be involved in the suggested metamorphosis. It might be contended
that the true process of evolution is to add a new principle, degree, or stage to the already existing order and not to make any alteration in any previously established feature. Man came into being but the animal remained the animal and made no progress
toward the half-humanity: all slight modifications of consciousness, capacities, or
habits in domestic animals produced by the association with man or by his training of
them are only slight alterations of the animal intelligence. Still less can the plants move
toward animal consciousness or brute Matter become in the slightest degree, even sub-

consciously or half-subconsciously, aware of itself or responsive or reactive. The fundamental distinctions remain and must remain unaltered in the cosmic order. But this objection presumes that the new humanity must be all of one level; there may well be gradations of consciousness in it which would bridge the distance between its least developed elements and the higher animals who, although they cannot pass into a semi-human kind, might still progress toward a higher animal intelligence, for, certain experiments show that these are not at all entirely unprogressive. These gradations would serve the purpose of the transition quite as well as the least developed humans in the present scale without leaving a gap so wide as to disturb the evolutionary order of the universe. A considerable saltus can, as it is, be observed separating the different orders, Matter and the plant, the plant and the lower animals, one species of animals and another, as well as that always existing and large enough between the highest animal and man. There would therefore be no incurable breach in the evolutionary order, no such distance between human mind and animal mind, between the new type of human being and the old animal level as could not be overleaped or would create an unbridgeable gulf for the most developed animal soul in its passage to the least developed type of the new humanity. A leap, a saltus, there would be, as there is now; but it would not be between animality and divinity, from animal mind to Supermind, it would be between a most highly developed animal mind turning toward human possibilities—for without that the passage from animal to man could not be achieved—and a human mind waking to the possibility, not yet the full achievement, of its own higher yet unattained capacities.

One result of the intervention of Supermind in the earth-nature, the descent of the supreme creative Truth-Power might well be a change in the law of evolution, its method and its arrangement: a larger element of the principle of evolution through knowledge might enter into the forces of the material universe. This might extend itself from a first beginning in the new creation and produce increasing effects in the order that is now wholly an evolution in the ignorance and indeed starts from the complete nescience of the Inconscient and proceeds toward what can be regarded even in its highest attainment of knowledge as a lesser ignorance, since it is more a representation than a direct and complete possession of knowledge. If man began to develop the powers and means of a higher knowledge in something like fullness, if the developing animal opened the door of his mentality to beginnings of conscious thought and even a rudimentary reason—at his highest he is not so irrevocably far from that even now—if the plant developed its first subconscient reactions and attained to some kind of primary nervous sensitiveness, if Matter, which is a blind form of the Spirit, were to become more alive with the hidden power within it and to offer more readily the secret sense of things, the occult realities it covers, as for instance, the record of the past it always preserves even in its dumb inconscience or the working of its involved forces and invisible movements revealing veiled powers in material nature to a subtler generalized perception of the new human intelligence, this would be an immense change promising greater changes in the future, but it would mean only an uplifting and not a disturbance of the universal order. Evolution would itself evolve, but it would not be perturbed or founder.

It is difficult for us to conceive in theory or admit as a practical possibility the transformation of the human mentality I have suggested as a change that would naturally take place under the lead of the supramental Truth-Consciousness, because our notions about mind are rooted in an experience of human mentality in a world that starts from inconscience and proceeds through a first almost complete nescience and a slowly lessening ignorance toward a high degree but always incomplete scope and imperfect method of only partially equipped knowledge that does not serve fully the needs of a consciousness always pushing toward its own still immeasurably distant absolute. The visible imperfections and limitations of mind in the present stage of its evolution here we take as part of its very nature; but in fact the boundaries in which it is still penned are only temporary limits and measures of its still incomplete evolutionary advance; its defects of methods and means are faults of its immaturity and not proper to the constitution of its being; its achievement although extraordinary under the hampering conditions of the mental being weighed down by its instrumentation in an earthly body is far below and not beyond what will be possible to it in its illumined future. For mind is not in its very nature an inventor of errors, a father of lies bound down to a capacity of falsehood, wedded to its own mistakes, and the leader of a stumbling life as it too largely is at present owing to our human shortcomings: it is in its origin a principle of light, an instrument put forth from the Supermind, and though set to work within limits and even set to create limits, yet the limits are luminous borders for a special working, voluntary and purposive bounds, a service of the finite ever extending itself under the eye of infinity. It is this character of Mind that will reveal itself under the touch of Supermind and make human mentality an adjunct and a minor instrumentation of the supramental knowledge. It will even be possible for the mind no longer limited by the intellect to become capable of a sort of mental gnosis, a luminous reproduction of the Truth in a diminished working extending the power of the Light not only to its own but to lower levels of consciousness in their climb toward self-transcendence. Overmind, Intuition, Illumined Mind, and what I have called Higher Mind, these and other levels of a spiritualized and liberated mentality, will be able to reflect in the uplifted human mind and its purified and exalted feeling and force of life and action something of their powers and prepare the ascent of the soul to their own plateaus and peaks of an ascending existence. This is essentially the change that can be contemplated as a result of the new evolutionary order and it would mean a considerable extension of the evolutionary field itself and will answer the question as to the result on humanity of the advent of Supermind into the earth-nature.

If mind in its origin from Supermind is itself a power of Supermind, a principle of Light and a power of Light or a force for Knowledge specialized in its action for a subordinate purpose, yet it assumes a different aspect when in the working out of this purpose it separates itself more and more from the supramental light, from the immediate power and supporting illumination of the supramental principle. It is as it departs more and more in this direction from its own highest truth that it becomes a creator or parent of ignorance and is or seems to be the highest power in a world of ignorance; it becomes itself subject to ignorance and seems only to arrive at a partial and imperfect knowledge. The reason for this decline is that it is used by the Supermind principally for the work of differentiation, which is necessary if there is to be a creation and a universe. In the Supermind itself, in all its creation there is this differentiating power, the manifestation of the One in the Many and the Many in the One; but the One is never forgotten or lost in its multiplicity, which always consciously depends upon and never takes precedence over the eternal oneness. In the mind, on the contrary, the differentiation, the multiplicity does take precedence and the conscious sense of the universal oneness is lost and the separated unit seems to exist for itself and by itself as a sufficient self-conscious integer or in inanimate objects as the inconscient integer. It should be noted, however, that a world or plane of mind need not be a reign of ignorance where falsity, error, or nescience must have a place; it may be only a voluntary self-limitation of knowledge. It could be a world where all possibilities capable of being determined by mind could manifest themselves in the successions of Time and find a true form and field of their action, the expressive figure of themselves, their capacity of self-development, self-realization of a kind, self-discovery. This is actually what we meet when we follow in psychic experience the line of descent by which the involution takes place, which ends in Matter and the creation of the material universe. What we see here is not the planes or worlds of the descent in which mind and life can keep something of their truth and something of the light of the spirit, something of their true and real being; here we see an original inconscience and a struggle of life and mind and spirit to evolve out of the material inconscience and in a resultant ignorance to find themselves and grow toward their full capacity and highest existence. If mind succeeds in that endeavor, there is no reason why it should not recover its true character and be once more a principle and power of Light and even in its own way aid in the workings of a true and complete knowledge. At its highest it might pass out of its limitations into the supramental truth and become part and function of the supramental knowledge or at the least serve for a minor work of differentiation in the consensus of that knowledge. In the lower degree below Supermind it might be a mental gnosis, a spiritual or spiritualized perception, feeling, activity, sense that could do the works of knowledge and not of ignorance. Even at a still lower level it could be an increasingly luminous passage leading from light to light, from truth to truth, and no longer a circling in the mazes of half-truth and half-nescience. This would not be possible in a world where untransformed mind or human mind burdened with its hampering disabilities, as it now is, will still be the leader or the evolution's highest achievement, but with Supermind for the leading and dominant power this might well happen, and might even be regarded as one result and an almost inevitable result of its descent into the human world and its touch on the mind of humanity.

How far this would go, whether the whole of humanity would be touched or only a part of it ready for the change, would depend on what was intended or possible in the continued order of the universe. If the old evolutionary principle and order must be preserved, then only a section of the race would pass onward, the rest would keep the old human position, level, and function in the ascending order. But even so there must be a passage or bridge between the two levels or orders of being by which the evolution would make its transition from one to the other; the mind would there be capable of contact with and modification by the supramental truth and thus would be the means of the soul's passing on upward. There must be a status of mind capable of receiving and growing in the Light toward Supermind though not reaching it; through that, as even now happens in a lesser degree through a dimmer medium, the luster of a greater truth would send down its rays for the liberation and uplift of the soul in the ignorance. Supermind is here veiled behind a curtain and, though not organized for its own characteristic action, it is the true cause of all creation here, the power for the growth of truth and knowledge and the ascension of the soul toward the hidden Reality. But in a world where Supermind has made its appearance, it could hardly be a separate factor isolated from the rest, it would inevitably not only create superman but change and uplift man. A total change of the mental principle, such as has been suggested, cannot be ruled out as impossible.

Mind, as we know it, has a power of consciousness quite distinct from Supermind, no longer a power devolved from it, connected with it, and dependent upon it, but practically divorced from its luminous origin, is marked by several characteristics that we conceive to be the very signs of its nature; but some of these belong to Supermind also and the difference is in the way and scope of their action, not in their stuff or in their principle. The difference is that mind is not a power of whole knowledge and only when it begins to pass beyond itself, a power of direct knowledge. It receives rays of the truth but does not live in the sun; it sees as through glasses and its knowledge is colored by its instruments, it cannot see with the naked eye or look straight at the sun. It is not possible for mind to take its stand in the solar center or anywhere in the radiant body or even on the shining circumference of the orb of perfect truth and acquire or share in its privilege of infallible or absolute knowledge. It would only be possible if it had already drawn near to the light of Supermind that it could live anywhere near this sun in the full splendor of its rays, in something of the full and direct blaze of Truth and the human mind even at its highest is far from that; it can only live at most in a limited circle, in some narrow beginnings of a pure insight, a direct vision, and it would take long for it, even in surpassing itself, to reach to an imitative and fragmentary reflection of a dream of the limited omniscience and omnipotence, that is the privilege of a delegated divinity, of the god, of a demiurge. It is a power for creation, but either tentative and uncertain and succeeding by good chance or the favor of circumstance or else, if assured by some force of practical ability or genius, subject to flaw or pent within unescapable limits. Its highest knowledge is often abstract, lacking in a concrete grasp; it has to use expedients and unsure means of arrival, to rely upon reasoning, argumentation and debate, inferences, divinations, set methods of inductive or deductive logic, succeeding only if it is given correct and complete data and even then liable to reach on the same data different results and varying consequences; it has to use means and accept results of a method that are hazardous even when making a claim to certitude and of which there would be no need if it had a direct or a supra-intellectual knowledge. It is not necessary to push the description further; all this is the very nature of our terrestrial ignorance and its shadow even hangs onto the thought and vision of the sage and the seer and can be escaped only if the principle of a Truth-Conscious supramental knowledge descends and takes up the governance of the earth-nature.

It should be noted, however, that even at the bottom of the involutionary descent, in the blind eclipse of consciousness in Matter, in the very field of the working of the Inconscient, there are signs of the labor of an infallible force, the drive of a secret consciousness and its promptings, as if the Inconscient itself were secretly informed or impelled by a Power with a direct and absolute knowledge; its acts of creation are infinitely surer than the workings of our human consciousness at its best or the normal workings of the life-power. Matter, or rather the Energy in Matter, seems to have a more certain knowledge, a more infallible operation of its own, and its mechanism once set going can be trusted for the most part to do its work accurately and well. It is so that man is able, taking hold of a material energy, to mechanize it for his own ends and trust it under proper conditions to do his work for him. The self-creating life-power, amazingly abundant in its invention and fantasy, yet seems to be more capable of flaw, aberration, and failure; it is as if its greater consciousness carried in it a greater capacity for error. Yet it is sure enough ordinarily in its workings: but as consciousness increases in the forms and operations of life, and most when mind enters in, disturbances also increase as if the increase of consciousness brought with it not only richer possibilities but more possibilities of stumbling, error, flaw, and failure. In mind, in man, we seem to reach the height of this antinomy, the greatest, highest, widest reach and achievements of consciousness, the greatest amount of uncertainty, defect, failure, and error. This, we may conjecture, may be because in inconscient Nature there is a truth of energy at work, which follows infallibly its own law, an energy that can walk blindfolded without stumbling because the automatic law of the truth is within it operating surely without swerving or mistake when there is no external intervention or interference. But in all normally automatic processes of existence there is this law: even the body has an unexpressed knowledge of its own, a just instinct in its action within certain limits and this when not interfered with by life's desires and mind's errors can work with a certain accuracy and sureness. But Supermind alone has the Truth-Consciousness in full and, if this comes down and intervenes, mind, life, and body too can attain to the full power of the truth in them and their full possibility of perfection, This, no doubt, would not take place at once, but an evolutionary progress toward it could begin and grow with increasing rapidity toward its fullness. All men might not reach that fullness till a later time, but still the human mind could come to stand perfected in the Light and a new humanity take its place as part of the new order.

This is the possibility we have to examine. If it is destined to fulfill itself, if man is not doomed to remain always as a vassal of the Ignorance, the disabilities of the human mind on which we have dwelt are not such as must remain irredeemably in possession and binding forever. It could develop higher means and instrumentalities, pass over the last borders of the Ignorance into a higher knowledge, grow too strong to be held back by the animal nature. There would be a liberated mind escaping from ignorance into light, aware of its affiliation to Supermind, a natural agent of Supermind and capable of bringing down the supramental influence into the lower reaches of being, a creator in the light, a discoverer in the depths, an illuminant in the darkness, helping perhaps to penetrate even the Inconscient with the rays of a secret Superconscience. There would be a new mental being not only capable of standing enlightened in the radiance of the Supermind but able to climb consciously toward it and into it, training life and body to reflect and hold something of the supramental light, power, and bliss, aspiring to release the secret divinity into self-finding and self-fulfillment and self-poise, aspiring toward the ascension to the divine consciousness, able to receive and bear the descent of the divine light and power, fitting itself to be a vessel of the divine Life.

SUPERMIND IN THE EVOLUTION

A new humanity would then be a race of mental beings on the earth and in the earthly body but delivered from its present conditions in the reign of the cosmic Ignorance so far as to be possessed of a perfected mind, a Mind of Light, which could even be a subordinate action of the Supermind or Truth-Consciousness, and in any case capable of the full possibilities of mind acting as a recipient of that truth and at least a secondary action of it in thought and life. It could even be a part of what could be described as a divine life upon earth and at least the beginnings of an evolution in the Knowledge and no longer entirely or predominantly in the Ignorance. How far this would go, whether it would eventually embrace the whole of humanity or only an advanced portion of it, would depend upon the intention in the evolution itself, on the intention in whatever cosmic or transcendent Will is guiding the movements of the universe. We have supposed not only the descent of the Supermind upon the earth but its embodiment in a supramental race with all its natural consequences and a new total action in which the new humanity would find its complete development and its assured place in the new order.

But it is clear that all this could only come as a result of the evolution that is already taking place upon earth extending far beyond its present bounds and passing into a radically new movement governed by a new principle in which mind and man would be subordinate elements and no longer mind the utmost achievement or man the head or leader. The evolution we see around us at present is not of that kind and, it might be said, shows few signs of such a possibility, so few that the reason, at present our only sure guide, has no right to hazard belief in it. Earth, the earth we see, with its life deeply immersed and founded in inconscience and ignorance, is not built for such a development or capable of holding such an advent; its materiality and limitations condemn it to be permanently the field of a far inferior order. It may be said, too, that for such an order there must be a place somewhere and even if Supermind is not a mere unwarranted speculation and is a concrete reality, there is no need and no place for its embodying itself here. Mind as marking the full play of the knowledge possible to the ignorance must have its field somewhere and to keep the earth as its natural field would best serve the economy of cosmic Nature. A materialistic philosophy would admit of no possibility of a divine life in Matter; but even a philosophy admitting a soul or spirit or a spiritual terminus of the evolutionary movement here could very well deny the capacity of earth for a divine life: a divine existence could only be achieved by a departure from earth and the body. Even if cosmic existence is not an illusion or Maya, a divine or a completely spiritual being is likely to be possible only in another less material world or only in the pure spirit. At any rate, to the normal human reason, the odds seem to be heavily against any early materialization on earth of anything divine.

Again, if too strong a stress is laid on the present or apparent character of the evolution here as it is presented to us by physical science, it might be urged that there is no warrant for expecting any emergence of a principle higher than human mind or of any such thing as superhuman beings in a world of Matter. Consciousness is itself dependent upon Matter and material agencies for its birth and its operations and an infallible Truth-Consciousness, such as we suppose Supermind to be, would be a contradiction of these conditions and must be dismissed as a chimera. Fundamentally, physical science regards evolution as a development of forms and vital activities; the development of a larger and more capable consciousness is a subordinate result of the development of life and form and not a major or essential characteristic or circumstance and it cannot go beyond limits determined by the material origin of mind and life. Mind has shown itself capable of many extraordinary achievements, but independence of the material organ or of physical conditions or a capability for any such thing as a power of direct and absolute knowledge not acquired by material means would be beyond the conditions imposed by Nature. At a certain point, therefore, the evolution of consciousness can go no further. Even if a something definite and independent, which we call a soul, exists, it is limited by its natural conditions here where Matter is the basis, physical life the condition, mind the highest possible instrument; there is no possibility of an action of consciousness apart from the body or surpassing this physical, vital, or mental Nature. This fixes the limits of our evolution here.

It might be suggested also that until something clearly recognizable like Supermind manifests itself with some definiteness and fullness or until it descends and takes possession of our earth-consciousness, we cannot be certain that it exists; till then mind holds the place as a general arbiter or field of reference for all knowledge and mind is incapable of any certain or absolute knowledge; it has to doubt all, to test all, and yet to achieve all, but cannot be secure in its knowledge or its achievement. That, incidentally, establishes the necessity of such a principle as the Supermind or Truth-Consciousness in any intelligible universe, for without it there is no issue, no goal for either life or knowledge. Consciousness cannot achieve its own entire meaning, its own supreme result without it; it will end in an inconsequence or a fiasco. To become aware of its own truth and all truth is the very aim of its existence and it cannot do so, so long as it has to tend toward truth, toward knowledge in ignorance and through the ignorance; it must develop or it must reach a power of itself whose very nature is to know, to see, to possess in its own power. This is what we call Supermind, and once it is admitted all the rest becomes intelligible. But, till then we are in doubt and it may be contended that even if Supermind is admitted as a reality, there can be no certainty of its advent and reign: till then all effort toward it may end in failure. It is not enough that the Supermind should be actually there above us, its descent a possibility or a future intention in Nature. We have no certainty of the reality of this descent until it becomes an objectivized fact in our earthly being. Light has often tried to descend upon the earth, but the Light remains unfulfilled and incomplete; man may reject the Light, the world is still full of darkness and the advent seems to be little more than a chance; this doubt is to some extent justified by the actualities of the past and still existing possibilities of the future. Its power to stand would disappear only if Supermind is once admitted as a consequent part of the order of the universe. If the evolution tends from Matter to Supermind, it must also tend to bring down Supermind into Matter and the consequences are inevitable.

The whole trouble of this incertitude arises from the fact that we do not look straight at the whole truth of the world as it is and draw from it the right conclusion as to what the world must be and cannot fail to be. This world is, no doubt, based ostensibly upon Matter, but its summit is Spirit and the ascent toward Spirit must be the aim and justification of its existence and the pointer to its meaning and purpose. But the natural conclusion to be drawn from the supremacy and summit existence of Spirit is clouded by a false or imperfect idea of spirituality that has been constructed by intellect in its ignorance and even by its too hasty and one-sided grasp at knowledge. The Spirit has been thought of not as something all-pervading and the secret essence of our being, but as something only looking down on us from the heights and drawing us only toward the heights and away from the rest of existence. So we get the idea of our cosmic and individual being as a great illusion, and departure from it and extinction in our consciousness of both individual and cosmos as the only hope, the sole release. Or we build up the idea of the earth as a world of ignorance, suffering, and trial and our only future an escape into heavens beyond; there is no divine prospect for us here, no fulfillment possible even with the utmost evolution on earth in the body, no victorious transformation, no supreme object to be worked out in terrestrial existence. But if Supermind exists, if it descends, if it becomes the ruling principle, all that seems impossible to mind becomes not only possible but inevitable. If we look closely, we shall see that there is a straining of mind and life on their heights toward their own perfection, toward some divine fulfillment, toward their own absolute. That and not only something beyond and elsewhere is the true sign, the meaning of this constant evolution, and the labor of continual birth and rebirth and the spiral ascent of Nature. But it is only by the descent of Supermind and the fulfillment of mind and life by their self-exceeding that this secret intention in things, this hidden meaning of Spirit and Nature can become utterly overt and in its totality realizable. This is the evolutionary aspect and significance of Supermind, but in truth it is an eternal principle existing covertly even in the material universe, the secret supporter of all creation, it is what makes the emergence of consciousness possible and certain in an apparently inconscient world and compels a climb in Nature toward a supreme spiritual Reality. It is, in fact, an already—and always—existent plane of being, the nexus of Spirit and Matter, holding in its truth and reality and making certain the whole meaning and aim of the universe.

If we disregard our present ideas of evolution, all changes—if we can regard consciousness and not life and form as the fundamental and essential evolutionary principle and its emergence and full development of its possibilities as the object of the evolutionary urge. The inconscience of Matter cannot be an insuperable obstacle; for in this inconscience can be detected an involved consciousness that has to evolve; life and mind are steps and instruments of that evolution, the purposeful drive and workings of the inconscient material Energy and precisely such as we can attribute to the presence of an involved consciousness, automatic, not using thoughts like the mind but guided by something like an inherent material instinct practically infallible in all its steps, not yet cognitive but miraculously creative. The entirely and inherently enlightened Truth-Consciousness we attribute to Supermind would be the same reality appearing at an ultimate stage of the evolution, finally evolved and no longer wholly involved as in Matter, or partly and imperfectly evolved, and therefore capable of imperfection and error as in life and mind, now possessed of its own natural fullness and perfection, luminously automatic, infallible. All the objections to a complete evolutionary possibility then fall away; it would, on the contrary, be the inevitable consequence contained not only in Nature as a whole but even in material Nature.

In this vision of things the universe will reveal itself in its unity and totality as a manifestation of a single Being, Nature as its power of manifestation, evolution as its process of gradual self-revelation here in Matter. We would see the divine series of the worlds as a ladder of ascent from Matter to supreme Spirit; there would reveal itself the possibility, the prospect of a supreme manifestation by the conscious and no longer a veiled and enigmatic descent of the Spirit and its powers in their fullness even into this lowest world of Matter. The riddle of the universe need be no longer a riddle; the dubious mystery of things would put off its enigma, its constant ambiguity; the tangled writings would become legible and intelligible. In this revelation, Supermind would take its natural place and no longer be a matter of doubt or questioning to an intelligence bewildered by the complexity of the world; it would appear as the inevitable consequence of the nature of mind, life, and Matter, the fulfillment of their meaning, their inherent principle and tendencies, the necessary perfection of their imperfection, the summit to which all are climbing, the consummation of divine existence, consciousness, and bliss to which it is leading, the last result of the birth of things and supreme goal of this progressive manifestation that we see here in life.

The full emergence of Supermind may be accomplished by a sovereign manifestation, a descent into earth-consciousness and a rapid assumption of its powers and disclosing of its forms and the creation of a supramental race and a supramental life: this must indeed be the full result of its action in Nature. But this has not been the habit of evolutionary Nature in the past upon earth and it may well be that this supramental evolution also will fix its own periods, though it cannot be at all a similar development to that of which earth has hitherto been the witness. But once it has begun, all must unavoidably and perfectly manifest and all parts of Nature must tend toward the greatest possible luminousness and perfection. It is this certainty that authorizes us to believe that mind and humanity also will tend toward the realization that will be far beyond our present dreams of perfection. A Mind of Light will replace the present confusion and trouble of this earthly ignorance; it is likely that even those parts of humanity that cannot reach it will yet be aware of its possibility and consciously tend toward it; furthermore, the life of humanity will be enlightened, uplifted, governed, harmonized by this luminous principle and even the body become something much less powerless, obscure, and animal in its propensities and capable instead of a new and harmonized perfection. It is this possibility that we have to look at and that would mean a new humanity uplifted into Light, capable of a spiritualized being and action, open to governance by some light of the Truth-Consciousness, capable even on the mental level and in its own order of something that might be called the beginning of a divinized life.

MIND OF LIGHT

A new humanity means for us the appearance, the development, of a type or race of mental beings whose principle of mentality would be no longer a mind in the Ignorance seeking for knowledge but even in its knowledge bound to the Ignorance, a seeker after Light but not its natural possessor, open to the Light but not an inhabitant of the Light, not yet a perfected instrument, Truth-Conscious and delivered out of the Ignorance. Instead, it would be possessed already of what could be called a Mind of Light, a mind capable of living in the truth, capable of being Truth-Conscious and manifesting in its life a direct in place of an indirect knowledge. Its mentality would be an instrument of the Light and no longer of the Ignorance. At its highest it would be capable of passing into the Supermind and from the new race would be recruited the race of supramental beings who would appear as the leaders of the evolution in earth-nature. Even, the highest manifestations of a Mind of Light would be an instrumentality of the Supermind, a part of it or a projection from it, a stepping beyond humanity into the superhumanity of the supramental principle. Above all, its possession would enable the human being to rise beyond the normalities of his present thinking, feeling, and being into those highest powers of the mind in its self-exceedings that intervene between its mentality and Supermind and can be regarded as steps leading toward the greater and more luminous principle. This advance like others in the evolution might not be reached and would naturally not be reached at one bound, but from the very beginning it would be inevitable: the pressure of the Supermind creating from above out of itself the Mind of Light would compel this certainty of the eventual outcome. The first gleamings of the new Light would carry in themselves the seed of its highest flamings; even in the first beginnings, the certainty of their topmost powers would be there, for this is the constant story of each evolutionary emergence: the principle of its highest perfection lies concealed in the involution that precedes and necessitates the evolution of the secret principle.

For throughout the story of evolution there are two complementary aspects that constitute its action and are necessary to its totality; there is hidden in the involution of Nature the secret power and principle of being that lies concealed under the veil cast on it by material Nature, and there is carried in that Nature itself the inevitable force of the principle compelling the process of emergence of its inherent powers and characters, the essential features that constitute its reality. As the evolutionary principle emerges, there are also two constant features of the process of the emergence: there are the gradations by which it climbs out of the involution and manifests more and more of its power, its possibilities, the force of the Godhead within it, and there is a constant manifestation of all types and forms of its being that are the visible, indicative, and efficient embodiments of its essential nature. There appear in the evolutionary process organized forms and activities of Matter, the types of life and the living beings, the types of mind and the thinking beings, the luminosities and greatnesses of the spiritual principle, and the spiritual beings whose nature, character, personality, mark the stages of the ascent toward the highest heights of the evolution and the ultimate largest manifestation of what it is in itself and must become by the force of time and the all-revealing Spirit. This is the real sense and drive of what we see as evolution: the multiplication and variation of forms is only the means of its process. Each gradation contains the possibility and the certainty of the grades beyond it: the emergence of more and more developed forms and powers points to more perfected forms and greater powers beyond them and each emergence of consciousness and the conscious beings proper to it enables the rise to a greater consciousness beyond and the greater order of beings up to the ultimate godheads of which Nature is striving and is destined to show herself capable. Matter developed its organized forms until it became capable of embodying living organisms; then life rose from the subconscience of the plant into conscious animal formations and through them to the thinking life of man. Mind founded in life developed intellect, developed its types of knowledge and ignorance, truth and error, till it reached the spiritual perception and illumination and now can see as in a glass dimly the possibility of Supermind and a Truth-Conscious existence. In this inevitable ascent the Mind of Light is a gradation, an inevitable stage. As an evolving principle it will mark a stage in the human ascent and evolve a new type of human being; this development must carry in it an ascending gradation of its own powers and types of an ascending humanity that will embody more and more the turn toward spirituality, capacity for Light, a climb toward a divinized manhood and the divine life.

In the birth of the Mind of Light and its ascension into its own recognizable self and its true status and right province there must be, in the very nature of things as they are and the very nature of the evolutionary process as it is at present, two stages. In the first, we can see the Mind of Light gathering itself out of the Ignorance, assembling its constituent elements, building up its shapes and types however imperfect at first, and pushing them toward perfection till it can cross the border of the Ignorance and appear in the Light, in its own Light. In the second stage we can see it developing itself in that greater natural light taking its higher shapes and forms till it joins the Supermind and lives as its subordinate portion or its delegate. In each of these stages it will define its own grades and manifest the order of its beings who will embody it and give to it a realized life. Thus there will be built up, first, even in the Ignorance itself, the possibility of a human ascent toward a divine living; then there will be, by the illumination of this Mind of Light in the greater realization of what may be called a gnostic mentality, in a transformation of the human being, even before the Supermind is reached, even in the earth-consciousness and in a humanity transformed, an illumined divine life.

SUPERMIND AND MIND OF LIGHT

The essential character of Supermind is a Truth-Consciousness that knows by its own inherent right of nature, by its own light: it has not to arrive at knowledge but possesses it. It may, indeed, especially in its evolutionary action, keep knowledge behind its apparent consciousness and bring it forward as if from behind the veil; but even then this veil is only an appearance and does not really exist: the knowledge was always there, the consciousness its possessor and present revealer. This too is only in the evolutionary play and on the supramental plane itself the consciousness lives always in an immediacy of knowledge and acts by a direct immediacy of knowledge. In Mind as we see it here the action is very different; it starts from an apparent absence of knowledge, a seeming ignorance or nescience, even, in material Nature, from an inconscience in which any kind of knowing does not seem to exist at all. It reaches knowledge or the action of knowledge by steps that are not at all immediate but rather knowledge at first seems utterly impossible and foreign to the very substance of this Matter. Yet, in the blindness of Matter itself there are signs of a concealed consciousness, which in its hidden fundamental being sees and has the power to act according to its vision and even by an infallible immediacy that is inherent in its nature. This is the same Truth that is apparent in Supermind but is here involved and seems not to be. The Mind of Light is a subordinate action of Supermind, dependent upon it even when not apparently springing direct from it, in which the secret of this connection becomes evident and palpable.

The Truth-Consciousness is not only a power of knowledge, it is a being of consciousness and knowledge, a luminous many-sided dynamis and play of the omniscient Spirit; in it there can be a spiritual feeling, a spiritual sensation, a spiritual essentiality of substance that knows and reveals, that acts and manifests in an omniscience that is one with omnipotence. In Mind this Truth-Consciousness and these workings of the Truth-Consciousness can be there and even though it limits itself in Mind and has a subordinate or an indirect working, its action can be essentially the same. There can even be a hidden immediacy that hints at the presence of something absolute and is evidence of the same omnipotence and omniscience. In the Mind of Light, when it becomes full-orbed, this character of the Truth reveals itself though in a garb that is transparent even when it seems to cover; for this, too, is a Truth-Consciousness and a self-power of knowledge. This, too, proceeds from the Supermind and depends upon it even though it is limited and subordinate. What we have called specifically the Mind of Light is indeed the last of a series of descending planes of consciousness in which the Supermind veils itself by a self-chosen limitation or modification of its self-manifesting activities, but its essential character remains the same: there is in it an action of light, of truth, of knowledge in which inconscience, ignorance, and error claim no place. It proceeds from knowledge to knowledge; we have not yet crossed over the borders of the Truth-Conscious into ignorance. The methods also are those of a self-luminous knowing and seeing and feeling and a self-fulfilling action within its own borders; there is no need to seek for something missing, no fumbling, no hesitation; all is still a gnostic action of a gnostic power and principle. There has been a descent from full Supermind into Mind, but this Mind though self-limited is not yet an agnostic consciousness unsure of itself or unsure of its workings; there is still a comprehending or an apprehending consciousness that goes straight to its object and does not miss its mark or have to hunt for it in the dark or in insufficient light: it sees, knows, puts its hand immediately on things of self and things of Nature. We have passed into Mind but Mind has still not broken its inherent connection with the supramental principle.

Still there is an increasing self-limitation that begins even with Overmind: Overmind is separated only by a luminous border on the full light and power of the supramental Truth and it still commands direct access to all that Supermind can give it. There is a further limitation or change of characteristic action at each step downward from Overmind to Intuition, from Intuition to Illumined Mind, from Illumined Mind to what I have called the Higher Mind: the Mind of Light is a transitional passage by which we can pass from Supermind and superhumanity to an illumined humanity. For the new humanity will be capable of at least a partly divinized way of seeing and living because it will live in the light and in knowledge and not in the obscuration of the Ignorance.

Still, again there will be a difference between the superhuman and the human, a difference in nature and power but a difference especially in the access and way of admission to the Truth-Consciousness and its activities; there may, indeed, be two orders of its truth, direct and half-direct, immediate and near or even only a reception at a distance. But this we must consider afterward; at present it is sufficient to mark certain differences in the descending order of gnostic mind that culminates here. We may say that there is a higher hemisphere of our being in which Mind luminous and aware of its workings still lives in the Light and can be seen as a subordinate power of the Supermind; it is still an agent of the Truth-Consciousness, a gnostic power that has not descended into the mental ignorance; it is capable of a mental gnosis that preserves its connection with the superior light and acts by its power. This is the character of Overmind in its own plane and of all the powers that are dependent on the Overmind. The Supermind works there but at one remove as if in something that it has put forth from itself but that is no longer entirely itself but is still a delegate of the Truth and invested with its authority.

We are moving toward a transitional border beyond which lies the possibility of the Ignorance, but the Ignorance is not yet here. In the order of the evolutionary descent we stand in the Mind of Light on that border, and a step downward can carry us beyond it into the beginnings of an ignorance that still bears on its face something of the luminosity that it is leaving behind it. On the other hand, in the ascending order of the evolution we reach a transition in which we see the light, are turned toward it, reflected in our consciousness and one further step carries us into the domain of the Light. The Truth becomes visible and audible to us and we are in immediate communication with its messages and illuminations and can grow into it and be made one with its substance. Thus there is a succession of ranges of consciousness that we can speak of as Mind but that belong practically to the higher hemisphere although in their ontological station they are within the domain of the lower hemisphere. For the whole of being is a connected totality and there is in it no abrupt passage from the principle of Truth and Light into its opposite. The creative truth of things works and can work infallibly even in the Inconscient: the Spirit is there in Matter and it has made a series of steps by which it can travel from it to its own heights in an uninterrupted line of gradations; the depths are linked to the heights and the Law of the one Truth creates and works everywhere.

Even in the material world, which seems to us a world of ignorance, a world of the workings of a blind and inconscient Force starting from inconscience and proceeding through Ignorance and reaching with difficulty toward an imperfect Light and Knowledge, there is still a secret Truth in things that arranges all, guides toward the Self many contrary powers of being, and rises toward its own heights where it can manifest its own highest truth and fulfill the secret purpose of the universe. Even this material world of existence is built upon a pattern of the truth in things that we call the Law of Nature, a truth from which we climb to a greater truth until we emerge in the Light of the Supreme. This world is not really created by a blind force of Nature: even in the Inconscient the presence of the supreme Truth is at work; there is a seeing Power behind it that acts infallibly, and the steps of the Ignorance itself are guided even when they seem to stumble; for, what we call the Ignorance is a cloaked Knowledge, a Knowledge at work in a body not its own but moving toward its own supreme self-discovery. This Knowledge is the covert Supermind, which is the support of the creation, and is leading all toward itself and guides behind this multitude of minds and creatures and objects that seems each to be following its own law of nature; in this vast and apparently confused mass of existence there is a law, a one truth of being, a guiding and fulfilling purpose of the world-existence. The Supermind is veiled here and does not work according to its characteristic law of being and self-knowledge, but without it nothing could reach its aim. A world governed by an ignorant mind would soon drift into a chaos; it could not in fact come into existence or remain in existence unless supported by the secret Omniscience of which it is the cover; a world governed by a blind inconscient force might repeat constantly the same mechanical workings but it would mean nothing and arrive nowhere. This could not be the cause of an evolution that creates life out of Matter, out of life mind, and a gradation of planes of Matter, Life, and Mind culminating in the emergence of Supermind. The secret truth that emerges in Supermind has been there all the time, but now it manifests itself and the truth in things and the meaning of our existence.

It is in this series of the order of existence and as the last word of the lower hemisphere of being, the first word of the higher hemisphere that we have to look at the Mind of Light and see what is its nature and the powers that characterize it and which it uses for its self-manifestation and workings, its connection with Supermind and its consequences and possibilities for the life of a new humanity.

GANDHI: SELECTIONS*

A: On God

My own experience has led me to the knowledge that the fullest life is impossible without an immovable belief in a Living Law in obedience to which the whole universe moves. A man without that faith is like a drop thrown out of the ocean bound to perish. Every drop in the ocean shares its majesty and has the honour of giving us the ozone of life.—*H*, 25-4-36, 84.

God as Truth and Love

There is an indefinable mysterious power that pervades everything. I feel it, though I do not see it. It is this unseen power that makes itself felt and yet defies proof, because it is so unlike all that I perceive through my senses. It transcends reason. But it is possible to reason out the existence of God to a limited extent.—*YI*, 11-10-28, 340.

I have made the world's faith in God my own, and as my faith is ineffaceable, I regard that faith as amounting to experience. However, as it may be said that to describe faith as experience is to tamper with Truth, it may perhaps be more correct to say that I have no word for characterizing my belief in God.—*Auto*, 341.

God is that indefinable something which we all feel but which we do not know. To me God is Truth and Love, God is ethics and morality. God is fearlessness, God is the source of light and life and yet He is above and beyond all these. God is conscience. He is even the atheism of the atheist. He transcends speech and reason. He is a personal God to those who need His touch. He is the purest essence. He simply Is to those who have faith. He is long suffering. He is patient but He is also terrible. He is the greatest democrat the world knows. He is the greatest tyrant ever known. *We are not, He alone is.*—*YI*, 5-3-28, 81.

You have asked me why I consider that God is Truth. In my early youth I was taught to repeat what in Hindu scriptures are known as one thousand names of God. But these one thousand names of God were by no means exhaustive. We believe—and I think it is the truth—that God has as many names as there are creatures and, therefore, we also say that God is nameless and since God has many forms we also consider Him formless, and since He speaks to us through many tongues we consider Him to be speechless and so on. And when I came to study Islam I found that Islam too had many names for God. I would say with those who say God is Love, God is Love. But deep down in me I used to say that though God may be God, God is Truth, above all. If it is possible for the human tongue to give the fullest description, I have come to the conclusion that for myself God is Truth. But two years ago, I went a step further and said Truth is God. You

Reprinted with permission from Nirmal Kumar Bose, *Selections from Gandhi* (Ahmedabad, India: Navajivan Publishing House, 1957). This selection follows the editing of John M. Koller and Patricia Koller, *A Sourcebook in Asian Philosophy* (New York: Macmillan, 1991), pp. 156–65.

*The following abbreviations are used for the sources in these selections: *Auto: An Autobiography or The Story of My Experiments with Truth; ABP: Amrit Bazar Patrika; H: The Harijan; IHR: Hind Swaraj or Indian Home Rule; IV: Gandhiji in Indian Villages; MR: The Modern Review; NAT: Speeches and Writings of Mahatma Gandhi; SA: Satyagraha in South Africa; Tagore: Young India, 1919–1922; and YI: Young India, 1919–1932.*

will see the fine distinction between the two statements, *viz.* that God is Truth and Truth is God. And I came to that conclusion after a continuous and relentless search after Truth which began nearly fifty years ago. I then found that the nearest approach to Truth was through love. But I also found that love has many meanings in the English language at least and that human love in the sense of passion could become a degrading thing also. I found, too, that love in the sense of *ahimsa* had only a limited number of votaries in the world. But I never found a double meaning in connection with truth and not even the atheists had demurred to the necessity or power of truth. But in their passion for discovering truth the atheists have not hesitated to deny the very existence of God—from their own point of view rightly. And it was because of this reasoning that I saw that rather than say God is Truth I should say Truth is God. I recall the name of Charles Bradlaugh who delighted to call himself an atheist, but knowing as I do something of him, I would never regard him as an atheist. I would call him a God-fearing man, though, I know, he would reject the claim. His face would redden if I would say, "Mr. Bradlaugh, you are a truth-fearing man and not a God-fearing man." I would automatically disarm his criticism by saying that Truth is God, as I have disarmed the criticism of many a young man. Add to this the difficulty that millions have taken the name of God and in His name committed nameless atrocities. Not that scientists very often do not commit cruelties in the name of truth. I know how in the name of truth and science inhuman cruelties are perpetrated on animals when men perform vivisection. There are thus a number of difficulties in the way, no matter how you describe God. But the human mind is a limited thing, and you have to labour under limitations when you think of a being or entity who is beyond the power of man to grasp. And then we have another thing in Hindu philosophy, *viz.* God alone is and nothing else exists, and the same truth you find emphasized and exemplified in the *Kalema* of Islam. There you find it clearly stated—that God alone is and nothing else exists. In fact the Sanskrit word for Truth is a word which literally means that which exists—*Sat.* For these and several other reasons that I can give you I have come to the conclusion that the definition—Truth is God—gives me the greatest satisfaction. And when you want to find Truth as God the only inevitable means is Love, *i.e.* non-violence, and since I believe that ultimately means and end are convertible terms, I should not hesitate to say that God is Love.

"What then is Truth?"

A difficult question, but I have solved it for myself by saying that it is what the voice within tells you. How, then, you ask, different people think of different and contrary truths? Well, seeing that the human mind works through innumerable media and that the evolution of the human mind is not the same for all, it follows that what may be truth for one may be untruth for another, and hence those who have made experiments have come to the conclusion that there are certain conditions to be observed in making those experiments. Just as for conducting scientific experiments there is an indispensable scientific course of instruction, in the same way strict preliminary discipline is necessary to qualify a person to make experiments in the spiritual realm. Everyone should, therefore, realize his limitations before he speaks of his inner voice. Therefore, we have the belief based upon experience, that those who would make individual search after truth as God, must go through several vows, as for instance, the vow of truth, the vow of *brahmacharya* (purity)—for you can not possibly divide your love for Truth and God with anything else—the vow of non-violence, of poverty and non-possession. Unless you impose on yourselves the five vows, you may not embark on the experiment at all. There are several other conditions prescribed, but I must not take you through all of them. Suffice it to say that those who have made these experiments know that it is not proper for everyone to claim to hear the voice of conscience and it is be-

This statue of Mahatma Gandhi stands atop a square plinth in Pietermaritzburg, South Africa (*Roger de la Harpe © Dorling Kindersley*)

cause we have at the present moment everyone claiming the right of conscience without going through any discipline whatsoever that there is so much untruth being delivered to a bewildered world. All that I can in true humility present to you is that truth is not to be found by anybody who has not got an abundant sense of humility. If you would swim on the bosom of the ocean of Truth you must reduce yourselves to a zero. Further than this I cannot go along this fascinating path.—*YI*, 31-12-31, 427.

GOD AS TRUTH AND THE LAW

I do not regard God as a person. Truth for me is God, and God's Law and God are not different things or facts, in the sense that an earthly king and his law are different. Because God is an Idea, Law Himself. Therefore, it is impossible to conceive God as breaking the Law. He, therefore, does not rule our actions and withdraw Himself. When we say He rules our actions, we are simply using human language and we try to limit Him. Otherwise, He and His Law abide everywhere and govern everything. Therefore, I do not think that He answers in every detail every request of ours, but there is no doubt that He rules our action, and I literally believe that not a blade of grass grows or moves without His will. The free will we enjoy is less than that of a passenger on a crowded deck.

"Do you feel a sense of freedom in your communion with God?"

I do. I do not feel cramped as I would on a boat full of passengers. Although I know that my freedom is less than that of a passenger, I appreciate that freedom as I have imbibed through and through the central teaching of the *Gita* that man is the maker of his own destiny in the sense that he has freedom of choice as to the manner in which he uses that freedom. But he is no controller of results. The moment he thinks he is, he comes to grief.—*H*, 23-3-40, 55.

Man was supposed to be the maker of his own destiny. It is partly true. He can make his destiny only in so far as he is allowed by the Great Power which overrides all our intentions, all our plans and carries out His own plans.

I call that Great Power not by the name of *Allah*, not by the name of *Khuda* or God but by the name of Truth. For me, Truth is God and Truth overrides all our plans. The whole truth is only embodied within the heart of that Great Power—Truth. I was taught from my early days to regard Truth as unapproachable—something that you cannot reach. A great Englishman taught me to believe that God is unknowable. He is knowable to the extent that our limited intellect allows.—*H*, 20-4-47, 113.

B: ON ACTION

HATRED CAN NEVER YIELD GOOD

Brute force has been the ruling factor in the world for thousands of years, and mankind has been reaping its bitter harvest all along, as he who runs may read. There is little hope of anything good coming out of it in the future. If light can come out of darkness, then alone can love emerge from hatred.—*SA*, 289.

It is my firm conviction that nothing enduring can be built upon violence.—*YI*, 15-11-28, 381.

NON-VIOLENCE

Non-violence implies as complete self-purification as is humanly possible.

Man for man the strength of non-violence is in exact proportion to the ability, not the will, of the non-violent person to inflict violence.

Non-violence is without exception superior to violence, i.e., the power at the disposal of a non-violent person is always greater than he would have if he was violent.

There is no such thing as defeat in non-violence. The end of violence is surest defeat.

The ultimate end of non-violence is surest victory if such a term may be used of non-violence. In reality where there is no sense of defeat, there is no sense of victory.—*H*, 12-10-35, 276.

The only condition of a successful use of this force is a recognition of the existence of the soul as apart from the body and its permanent nature. And this recognition must amount to a living faith and not mere intellectual grasp.—*Nat*, 166.

CONSEQUENCES OF NON-VIOLENCE

Q. Is love or non-violence compatible with possession or exploitation in any shape or form?

A. Love and exclusive possession can never go together.—*MR*, 1935, 412.

Military force is inconsistent with soul-force. Frightfulness, exploitation of the weak, immoral gains, insatiable pursuit after enjoyments of the flesh are utterly inconsistent with soul-force.—*YI*, 6-5-26, 164.

The principle of non-violence necessitates complete abstention from exploitation in any form.

Rural economy as I have conceived it eschews exploitation altogether, and exploitation is the essence of violence.—*H*, 4-11-39, 331.

No man could be actively non-violent and not rise against social injustice no matter where it occurred.—*H*, 20-4-40, 97.

NON-VIOLENCE ALWAYS APPLICABLE AND IN ALL SPHERES OF LIFE

Non-violence is a universal principle and its operation is not limited by a hostile environment. Indeed, its efficacy can be tested only when it acts in the midst of and in spite of opposition. Our non-violence would be a hollow thing and nothing worth, if it depended for its success on the goodwill of the authorities. (Here, reference is made to the British Government in India.)—*H*, 12-11-38, 326.

Truth and non-violence are no cloistered virtues but applicable as much in the forum and the legislatures as in the market place.—*H*, 8-5-37, 98.

Some friends have told me that truth and non-violence have no place in politics and worldly affairs. I do not agree. I have no use for them as a means of individual salvation. Their introduction and application in everyday life has been my experiment all along.—*ABP*, 30-6-44.

We have to make truth and non-violence, not matters for mere individual practice but for practice by groups and communities and nations. That at any rate is my dream. I shall live and die in trying to realize it. My faith helps me to discover new truths every day. *Ahimsa is* the attribute of the soul, and therefore, to be practised by everybody in all the affairs of life. If it cannot be practised in all departments, it has no practical value.—*H*, 2-3-40, 23.

THE MEANING OF NON-RESISTANCE

Hitherto the word "revolution" has been connected with violence and has as such been condemned by established authority. But the movement of Non-co-operation, if it may be considered a revolution, is not an armed revolt; it is an evolutionary revolution, it is a bloodless revolution. The movement is a revolution of thought, of spirit. Non-co-operation is a process of purification, and, as such, it constitutes a revolution in one's ideas. Its suppression, therefore, would amount to co-operation by coercion. Orders to kill the movement will be orders to destroy, or interfere with, the introduction of the spinning wheel, to prohibit the campaign of temperance, and an incitement, therefore, to violence. For any attempt to compel people by indirect methods to wear foreign clothes, to patronize drink-shops would certainly exasperate them. But our success will be assured when we stand even this exasperation and incitement. We must not retort. Inaction on our part will kill Government madness. For violence flourishes on response, either by submission to the will of the violator, or by counter-violence. My strong advice to every worker is to segregate this evil Government by strict non-co-operation, not even to talk or speak about it, but having recognized the evil, to cease to pay homage to it by co-operation.—*YI*, 30-3-21, 97.

Passive resistance is a method of securing rights by personal suffering; it is the reverse of resistance by arms. When I refuse to do a thing that is repugnant to my conscience, I use soul-force. For instance, the Government of the day has passed a law which is applicable to me. I do not like it. If by using violence I force the Government to repeal the law, I am employing what may be termed body-force. If I do not obey the law and accept the penalty for its breach, I use soul-force. It involves sacrifice of self.

Everybody admits that sacrifice of self is infinitely superior to sacrifice of others. Moreover, if this kind of force is used in a cause that is unjust, only the person using it suffers. He does not make others suffer for his mistakes. Men have before now done many things which were subsequently found to have been wrong. No man can claim that he is absolutely in the right or that a particular thing is wrong because he thinks so, but it is wrong for him so long as that is his deliberate judgment. It is therefore meet that he should not do that which he knows to be wrong, and suffer the consequence whatever it may be. This is the key to the use of soul-force.—*IHR*, 45.

The method of passive resistance adopted to combat the mischief is the clearest and safest, because, if the cause is not true, it is the resisters, and they alone, who suffer.—*NAT*, 305.

That is the way of *satyagraha* or the way of non-resistance to evil. It is the aseptic method in which the physician allows the poison to work itself out by setting in motion all the natural forces and letting them have full play.—*H*, 9-7-38, 173.

I accept the interpretation of *ahimsa*, namely, that it is not merely a negative state of harmlessness but it is a positive state of love, of doing good even to the evil-doer. But it does not mean helping the evil-doer to continue the wrong or tolerating it by passive acquiescence. On the contrary, love, the active state of *ahimsa*, requires you to resist the wrongdoer by dissociating yourself from him even though it may offend him or injure him physically.—*YI*, 25-8-20.

In its negative form, it *(ahimsa)* means not injuring any living being whether by body or mind. It may not, therefore, hurt the person of any wrongdoer or bear any ill-will to him and so cause him mental suffering. The statement does not cover suffering caused to the wrongdoer by natural acts of mine which do not proceed from ill-will. It, therefore, does not prevent me from withdrawing from his presence a child whom he, we shall imagine, is about to strike. Indeed, the proper practice of *ahimsa* requires me to withdraw the intended victim from the wrongdoer, if I am in any way the guardian of such a child. It was therefore most proper for the passive resisters of South Africa to have resisted the evil that the Union Government sought to do to them. They bore no ill-will to it. They showed this by helping the Government whenever it needed their help. "Their resistance consisted of disobedience of the orders of the Government even to the extent of suffering death at their hands." *Ahisma* requires deliberate self-suffering, not a deliberate injury of the supposed wrongdoer.—*NAT*, 346 (from *MR*, Oct. 1916).

If a man abused him, it would never do for him to return the abuse. An evil returned by another evil only succeeded in multiplying it, instead of leading to its reduction. It was a universal law that violence would never be quenched by superior violence but could only be quenched by non-violence or non-resistance. But the true meaning of non-resistance had often been misunderstood or even distorted. It never implied that a non-violent man should bend before the violence of an aggressor. While not returning the latter's violence by violence, he should refuse to submit to the latter's illegitimate demand even to the point of death. That was the true meaning of non-resistance.—*H*, 30-3-47, 85.

NON-VIOLENCE, MILITANT IN CHARACTER

Non-violence in its dynamic condition means conscious suffering. It does not mean meek submission to the will of the evil-doer, but it means the putting of one's whole soul against the will of the tyrant. Working under this law of our being, it is possible for a single individual to defy the whole might of an unjust empire to save his honour, his religion, his soul and lay the foundation for that empire's fall or its regeneration.— *YI*, 11-8-20.

Yours should not merely be a passive spirituality that spends itself in idle meditation, but it should be an active thing which will carry war into the enemy's camp.

Never has anything been done on this earth without direct action. I reject the word "passive resistance," because of its insufficiency and its being interpreted as a weapon of the weak.

What was the larger "symbiosis" that Buddha and Christ preached? Gentleness and love. Buddha fearlessly carried the war into the enemy's camp and brought down on its knees an arrogant priesthood. Christ drove out the money-changers from the temple of Jerusalem and drew down curses from heaven upon the hypocrites and the Pharisees. Both were for intensely direct action. But even as Buddha and Christ chastized, they showed unmistakable love and gentleness behind every act of theirs.—*YI*, 12-5-20.

Our aim is not merely to arouse the best in the Englishman but to do so whilst we are prosecuting our cause. If we cease to pursue our course, we do not evoke the best in him. The best must not be confounded with good temper. When we are dealing with any evil, we may have to ruffle the evil-doer. We have to run the risk, if we are to bring the best out of him. I have likened non-violence to aseptic and violence to antiseptic treatment. Both are intended to ward off the evil, and therefore cause a kind of disturbance which is often inevitable. The first never harms the evil-doer.—*H*, 30-3-40, 72.

NON-VIOLENCE, THE VIRTUE OF THE STRONG

Non-violence presupposes ability to strike. It is a conscious, deliberate restraint put upon one's desire for vengeance. But vengeance is any day superior to passive, effeminate and helpless submission. Forgiveness is higher still. Vengeance too is weakness. The desire for vengeance comes out of fear of harm, imaginary or real. A man who fears no one on earth would consider it troublesome even to summon up anger against one who is vainly trying to injure him.—*YI*, 12-8-26, 285.

Ahimsa is the extreme limit of forgiveness. But forgiveness is the quality of the brave. *Ahimsa* is impossible without fearlessness.—*YI*, 4-11-26, 384.

My creed of non-violence is an extremely active force. It has no room for cowardice or even weakness. There is hope for a violent man to be some day non-violent, but there is none for a coward. I have therefore said more than once in these pages that if we do not know how to defend ourselves, our women and our places of worship by the force of suffering, i.e., non-violence, we must, if we are men, be at least able to defend all these by fighting.—*YI*, 16-6-27, 196.

There are two ways of defence. The best and the most effective is not to defend at all, but to remain at one's post risking every danger. The next best but equally honourable method is to strike bravely in self-defence and put one's life in the most dangerous positions.—*YI*, 18-12-24, 414.

The strength to kill is not essential for self-defence; one ought to have the strength to die. When a man is fully ready to die, he will not even desire to offer violence. Indeed

I may put it down as a self-evident proposition that the desire to kill is in inverse proportion to the desire to die. And history is replete with instances of men who by dying with courage and compassion on their lips converted the hearts of their violent opponents.—*YI*, 23-1-30-27.

Non-violence and cowardice go ill together. I can imagine a fully armed man to be at heart a coward. Possession of arms implies an element of fear, if not cowardice. But true non-violence is an impossibility without the possession of unadulterated fearlessness.—*H*, 15-7-39, 201.

TRUE AND FALSE NON-VIOLENCE

Non-violence to be a potent force must begin with the mind. Non-violence of the mere body without the co-operation of the mind is non-violence of the weak or the cowardly, and has therefore no potency. If we bear malice and hatred in our bosoms and pretend not to retaliate, it must recoil upon us and lead to our destruction. For abstention from mere bodily violence not to be injurious, it is at least necessary not to entertain hatred if we cannot generate active love.

All the songs and speeches betokening hatred must be taboo.—*YI*, 2-4-31, 58.

The mysterious effect of non-violence is not to be measured by its visible effect. But we dare not rest content so long as the poison of hatred is allowed to permeate society. This struggle is a stupendous effort at conversion. We aim at nothing less than the conversion of the English. It can never be done by harbouring ill-will and still pretending to follow non-violence. Let those therefore who want to follow the path of non-violence and yet harbour ill-will retrace their steps and repent of the wrong they have done to themselves and the country.—*YI*, 2-4-31, 58.

If we are unmanly today, we are so, not because we do not know how to strike, but because we fear to die. He is no follower of Mahavira, the apostle of Jainism, or of Buddha or of the *Vedas* who, being afraid to die, takes flight before any danger, real or imaginary, all the while wishing that somebody else would remove the danger by destroying the person causing it. He is no follower of *ahimsa* who does not care a straw if he kills a man by inches by deceiving him in trade, or who would protect by force of arms a few cows and make away with the butcher or who, in order to do a supposed good to his country, does not mind killing off a few officials. All these are actuated by hatred, cowardice and fear. Here the love of the cow or the country is a vague thing intended to satisfy one's vanity or soothe a stinging conscience.

Ahimsa, truly understood, is in my humble opinion a panacea for all evils mundane and extra-mundane. We can never overdo it. Just at present we are not doing it at all. *Ahimsa* does not displace the practice of other virtues, but renders their practice imperatively necessary before it can be practised even in its rudiments. Mahavira and Buddha were soldiers, and so was Tolstoy. Only, they saw deeper and truer into their profession and found the secret of a true, happy, honourable and godly life. Let us be joint-sharers with these teachers, and this land of ours will once more be the abode of gods.—*NAT*, 348.

VIOLENCE, RATHER THAN COWARDICE

I do believe that, where there is only a choice between cowardice and violence, I would advise violence. I would rather have India resort to arms in order to defend her honour than that she should, in a cowardly manner, become or remain a helpless witness to her own dishonour.

But I believe that non-violence is infinitely superior to violence, forgiveness is more manly than punishment. Forgiveness adorns the soldier. But abstinence is forgiveness only when there is the power to punish; it is meaningless when it pretends to proceed from a helpless creature. But I do not believe India to be helpless. I do not believe myself to be a helpless creature. Strength does not come from physical capacity. It comes from an indomitable will.—*YI*, 11-8-20.

The people of a village near Bettiah told me that they had run away whilst the police were looting their houses and molesting their womenfolk. When they said that they had run away because I had told them to be non-violent, I hung my head in shame. I assured them that such was not the meaning of my non-violence. I expected them to intercept the mightiest power that might be in the act of harming those who were under their protection, and draw without retaliation all harm upon their own heads even to the point of death, but never to run away from the storm centre. It was manly enough to defend one's property, honour or religion at the point of the sword. It was manlier and nobler to defend them without seeking to injure the wrongdoer. But it was unmanly, unnatural and dishonourable to forsake the post of duty and, in order to save one's skin, to leave property, honour or religion to the mercy of the wrongdoer. I could see my way of delivering the message of *ahimsa* to those who knew how to die, not to those who were afraid of death.—*IV,* 254.

The weakest of us physically must be taught the art of facing dangers and giving a good account of ourselves. I want both the Hindus and the Mussalmans to cultivate the cool courage, to die without killing. But if one has not that courage, I want him to cultivate the art of killing and being killed, rather than in a cowardly manner flee from danger. For the latter in spite of his flight does commit mental *himsa*. He flees because he has not the courage to be killed in the act of killing.—*YI*, 20-10-21, 335.

CHINESE THOUGHT

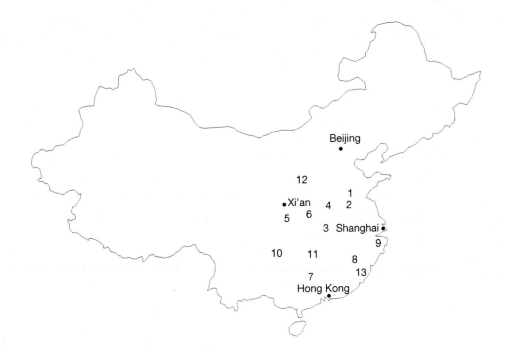

- Major cities today

1   Ch'u-fu (Confucius's birthplace, school, tomb, temple)

2   Tsou (Mencius's birthplace)

3   Lu-yi (traditional birthplace of Lao-tzu)

4   Meng (Chuang-tzu's birthplace)

5   Ch'ang-an (Fa-tsang's monastery)

6   Sung-shan (Bodhidharma's wall-gazing at Shaolin Monastery)

7   Canton (Hui-neng's birthplace and temple)

8   Yu-hsi (Chu Hsi's birthplace)

9   Yu-yao (Wang Yang-ming's birthplace)

10   Lung-ch'ang (Wang Yang-ming's exile and enlightenment)

11   Shao-shan (Mao Tse-tung's birthplace)

12   Yen'an (Mao's revolutionary headquarters during War of Liberation)

13   Changchou (Lin Yutang's birthplace)

CONFUCIAN ORIGINS

Twenty-five centuries of Chinese philosophy fall into three periods—classical, middle, and modern—each with its own distinctive flavor. Disputation marked the philosophical activity of the classical period, roughly 525–206 B.C.E. (late Chou (Zhou)* and Ch'in (Qin) dynasties). Some of the most famous debates in the history of Chinese thought occurred then. Confucianism (present section) and Taoism (Daoism) (next section) are the legacies most valued from that era. Synthesis characterized the middle period, 206 B.C.E.–1644 C.E. (Han through Ming dynasties). Controversy persisted but was overshadowed by the emergence of systems combining and reconciling diverse viewpoints. Chinese Buddhism and Neo-Confucianism are outstanding examples of the synthetic tendency. The impact of Western thought stamps the modern period, 1644 to the present (Ch'ing (Qing) Dynasty, Republic of China, and People's Republic of China). Chinese Marxism in Mainland China and the adaptation of Chinese philosophy to the contemporary Western philosophical scene overseas best illustrate the modern phase. Since the subjects of this section and the next—Confucianism and Taoism—are rooted in the classical period, additional background on that era will prove helpful.

The classical period is often described as the time when "the Hundred Schools contended," suggesting intense philosophical rivalry from the start. "The Hundred Schools" should be taken as a metaphor meaning "many" rather than as a precise figure. Six schools are commonly singled out as the major players of that era: Confucianism, Taoism, Mohism (utilitarians), School of Names (logicians), Yin

---

*The Pinyin version of Chinese names and words is given in parentheses after first being given in the Wade-Giles version. See the Preface for further information.

Yang School (cosmologists), and Legalism (totalitarians). Only two of them, the Confucian and the Mohist, were schools in the usual sense of ongoing teacher-student communities identified with specific viewpoints. The other four "schools" were the fabrication of a Han Dynasty historian; in retrospect, he grouped together unaffiliated individuals of an earlier period who happened to hold similar ideas. Various schools proposed conflicting solutions to the pressing moral, social, and political problems of the chaotic later Chou Dynasty (722–249 B.C.E.). The Confucians and Taoists (Daoists) disagreed on whether genuine virtue is cultivated (Confucians) or natural (Taoists). The Confucians and Mohists (followers of Mo-tzu (Mozi), fl. 479–438 B.C.E.) argued about applying the love ethic equally to everyone (Mohists) or selectively (Confucians). The Legalists, headed by Han Fei-tzu (Han Feizi, d. 233 B.C.E.), opposed the politically liberal Taoists and Confucians by advocating a program of strict government regimentation. On the sidelines of these mainstream disputes were the logicians and cosmologists. Hui Shih (Hui Shi, c. 380–c. 305 B.C.E.) and Kung-sun Lung (Gongsun Long, b. 380 B.C.E.) of the School of Names used paradoxes to convey subtle conceptual distinctions. The Yin Yang philosopher, Tsou Yen (Zou Yan, 305–240 B.C.E.), explained the alternating seasons as well as the succession of dynasties by means of the interactions of cosmic forces, such as Yin-Yang and the Five Agents (*wu-hsing (wuxing)*—metal, wood, water, fire, and earth).

Confucianism has taken the commanding role throughout the history of Chinese philosophy. During classical times, this school was led by five generations of brilliant thinkers and teachers. Confucius (Kongzi, 551–479 B.C.E.) in the first generation was succeeded by his most able student Tseng-tzu (Cengzi, 505–c. 436 B.C.E.) in the second, his grandson Tzu-ssu (Zisi, 492–431 B.C.E.) in the third, Mencius (Mengzi, 391–308 B.C.E.) in the fourth, and Hsun-tzu (Xunzi, fl. 298–238 B.C.E.) in the fifth. The latter two opened up the first significant split in the school, between the idealistic and realistic wings, over the issue of whether human nature is inherently good (Mencius) or evil (Hsun-tzu). Intense persecution of the Confucians under the Ch'in Dynasty (221–206 B.C.E.) brought the classical era to a close.

In the middle period, Confucianism swiftly rebounded. Tung Chung-shu (Dong Zhongshu, 176–104 B.C.E.) persuaded the Emperor Han Wu-ti (Han Wudi, r. 140–87 B.C.E.) to make Confucianism his official ideology and to fund a university for teaching the Confucian classics. Thus began Confucianism's privileged position at court, which, though broken at times, extended into the early twentieth century. Tung's own philosophy placed Confucian ethics on a metaphysical foundation drawn from Yin-Yang and Five Agents theory. His Yin-Yang Confucianism prevailed during the Han Dynasty (206 B.C.E.–220 C.E.) but was supplanted, first by Neo-Taoism and later by the Buddhist schools, in the centuries following the Han and through the T'ang (Tang) Dynasty (220–907). Then, in the Sung (Song, 960–1279) and Ming (1368–1644) dynasties, two varieties of Neo-Confucianism, synthesizing classical Confucianism with Neo-Taoism and Buddhism, captured and held the field until after the Ch'ing (Qing) Dynasty (1644–1911). They were Chu Hsi's (Zhu Xi's, 1130–1200) School of Principle and Wang Yangming's (Wang Yangming's, 1472–1529) School of Mind (see the introduction to the section on Neo-Confucianism).

In the modern period, Neo-Confucianism, still supreme, was attacked by those who advocated purging its Taoist and Buddhist elements and returning to earlier,

Statue of Confucius from the Confucius Temple in
Beijing. (*Forrest E. Baird*)

purer forms of Confucianism from Chou or Han times. Tai Chen (Dai Zhen,
1723–1777) was representative of that movement. Under Western influence in the
early twentieth century, K'ang Yu-wei (Kang Youwei, 1858–1927) attempted to
convert Confucianism into an established state religion, on the model of
Christianity in European countries; Fung Yu-lan (Feng Youlan, 1895–1990) reconstructed Sung Neo-Confucianism into a logical deductive system; and Hsiung
Shih-li (Xiong Shili, 1885–1968) refurbished Ming Neo-Confucianism. After
1949, all forms of Confucianism were criticized as idealistic and were repressed
by the militantly materialistic Chinese Marxism of Mao Tse-tung (Mao Zedong,
1893–1976). Finally, during the closing decades of the twentieth century,
Confucianism reinvented itself through interaction with Western philosophy outside Mainland China, in Taiwan and the United States.

*   *   *

The paramount figure in the Confucian lineage is also the most famous single individual in Chinese civilization. Confucius (551–479 B.C.E.) made his mark as a
scholar, teacher, and thinker. He is remembered as a man of impeccable manners,
sterling moral character, and a personal presence both dignified and magnetic.

During certain limited stretches of Chinese history, he was regarded even more highly—as the legitimate though uncrowned king of his time, or as a god. It is universally acknowledged that his contribution stands above all others in shaping the ideals and institutions of his culture. His Chinese name was K'ung Ch'iu (Kong Qiu). The West knows him as Confucius, because early missionaries latinized his Chinese title, K'ung Fu-tzu (Kong Fuzi, "Master K'ung"), and referred to him by that designation. His birthplace was the town of Ch'u-fu (Qufu) in present-day Shantung (Shandong) Province. In Confucius's time, it was the state of Lu, renown for its careful preservation of the ancient rites upon which the social stability of the early Chou Dynasty had been grounded. The sources of biographical information on this remarkable person contain some questionable and conflicting elements. The following facts, however, can be affirmed with confidence.

The K'ung family was of noble descent but poor by the time of the great man's birth. At age three, he lost his father; his mother also died before he reached maturity. He married at nineteen, and fathered at least one son and one daughter. His threefold professional goal crystallized early—to serve in government, to teach others, and to transmit to posterity the splendid culture of the early Chou Dynasty (1111–722 B.C.E.). Possessed of a deep love of learning by age fifteen, Confucius became one of the best-educated men of the day by his mid-twenties. He had a special fondness for poetry and music and was skilled in the performance of the latter. His reputation for excellent teaching was established by the age of thirty. As a teacher, Confucius rejected vocationalism while pioneering a liberal education that was strong in ethics, history, literature, and the fine arts. He admitted any student who could afford the token tuition—a bundle of dried meat. He is reputed to have instructed 3,000 students, seventy of whom became close disciples. Confucius entered government service under the Duke of Lu at the age of fifty-one, holding the offices of magistrate, minister of public works, and finally minister of justice. He is credited with some modest successes as an administrator. At the age of fifty-five (497 B.C.E.), he resigned from public office in Lu, under ambiguous circumstances. For the next thirteen years, Confucius wandered through neighboring states in the company of a small band of students, whom he continued to teach. He offered advice on government matters to local rulers and sometimes accepted temporary posts in their service. There were hardships to be endured—rejection, persecution, even attempted assassination. Confucius returned to teaching, perhaps also to a minor government post, in his hometown at the age of sixty-eight (484 B.C.E.). There he died five years later at age seventy-three.

History recognizes as the Confucian Canon a list of thirteen texts. Among these and of special importance are the Six Classics and the Four Books. The Six Classics are the works Confucius himself studied and taught. An older generation of scholarship credited him with the authorship of all six. Contemporary scholarship seems disinclined to acknowledge any involvement by Confucius in the literary production of these texts. The *Book of Odes* (*Shih ching (Shijing)*) is the first anthology of Chinese poetry. It contains 305 songs (poems were originally sung) on a wide variety of subjects, including courtship and marriage, hunting and war, agriculture, feasting, sacrifice, friendship, and morals. Confucius valued this collection for what it had to reveal about the mores and folkways of the early Chou culture he wished to revive for the improvement of his own age. The *Book of*

History (*Shu ching* (*Shujing*)) contains fifty-eight documents chronicling the lives of the great moral exemplars of the past. These include Yao and Shun from the Period of the Legendary Kings (third millennium B.C.E.); the great Yu, supposed founder of the Hsia (Xia) Dynasty (2183–1752 B.C.E.); and King Wen and Duke Chou, patriarchs of the Chou Dynasty (1111–249 B.C.E.). The *Book of Changes* (*I ching* (*Yijing*)) is an ancient book of Chinese divination based on diagrams of six either solid or broken lines, called hexagrams. Confucius had no use for divination, but he did find in this highly symbolic book a rich source of intuitive insight into how the world works relative to the moral situation of people's lives. The original *Book of Rites* (*Li ching* (*Lijing*)), written before Confucius, was badly damaged in the Burning of the Books (213 B.C.E.) under the First Emperor, Ch'in Shih Huang Ti (Qin Shi Huang Di). It was, for that reason, replaced in the Confucian Canon by three books on the same subject that postdated Confucius. What is now called the *Book of Rites* and is included among the Six Classics is the best of those three, the *Li chi* (*Liji*). It contains short pieces, written from the fourth to first centuries B.C.E. and compiled in the first century B.C.E., about religious ceremonies, social etiquette, customs, and social institutions. It also includes two chapters containing famous philosophical ideas. These two chapters were extracted by Chu Hsi in the twelfth century C.E. and presented separately as two of the Four Books. The *Spring and Autumn Annals* (*Ch'un-ch'iu* (*Chunqiu*)) records the history of twelve degenerate dukes who ruled during the later Chou Dynasty or Spring and Autumn Period (722–481 B.C.E.), when Confucius himself lived. Apparently, the merit Confucius found in this chronicle of decadence concerned the power of negative example in the formation of virtuous character. Last, the *Book of Music* (*Yueh ching* (*Yuejing*)) was probably a collection of early Chou ritual scores, since the prominent rites were always performed to musical accompaniment. Its inclusion testifies to the attention Confucius paid to the role of music in the harmonization of the soul. It was lost long ago, explaining why we more often hear of Five Classics than of Six.

The Four Books are believed to preserve the teaching original to Confucius. Like the Buddha, Socrates, and Jesus, Confucius himself wrote nothing. Disciples whom he inspired, however, produced masterpieces immortalizing his words. The Four Books grouping was the invention of the great Sung Dynasty Neo-Confucian, Chu Hsi (1130–1200), centuries after the books themselves were penned. He proclaimed that the *Analects* (*Lun-yu* (*Lunyu*)), the *Great Learning* (*Ta-hsueh* (*Daxue*)), the *Doctrine of the Mean* (*Chung-yung* (*Zhongyong*)), and the *Mencius* (*Meng-tzu* (*Mengzi*)) exclusively convey the pure teaching of Master K'ung. That teaching supposedly was handed down from Confucius to Tseng-tzu to Tzu-ssu to Mencius. Chu Hsi mistakenly thought Mencius had been the student of Tzu-ssu. It is more likely that Mencius received his instruction from disciples of Tzu-ssu. According to Chu Hsi, Tseng-tzu authored the *Great Learning* and Tzu-ssu the *Doctrine of the Mean*. Both these texts as well as the *Mencius*, he claimed, transmitted the views of Confucius, not those of their authors. Chu Hsi also wrote commentaries on the Four Books, interpreting them from the perspective of his own philosophy. From 1313 to 1905, the Four Books plus Chu Hsi's commentaries on them dominated the official syllabus for the imperial civil service examinations, giving them a role of unparalleled importance in the intellectual life of China during that era.

*   *   *

The *Analects* ("Assorted Sayings") of Confucius, all authorities agree, is the primary vehicle for the original thought of China's premier philosopher. It is the first reading offered in this section (translated by William Cheung). Written down by his followers from their recollections some decades after his death, it records conversations with his students and advice to rulers. There may well have been other early collections of the great man's sayings. This can reasonably be inferred because very few of the sayings attributed to Confucius in the books authored by Mencius and Hsun-tzu can be found in the *Analects*. The book is divided into 499 verses and twenty chapters. Thematic continuity rarely extends beyond a few verses, making the work appear fragmentary. Since the same set of themes is repeated throughout, it is possible, by means of careful content analysis, to distill the essence of the message and to present it in an organized fashion lacking in the original. Toward this end, the ethical, political, and religious philosophy of Confucius in the *Analects* will be reassembled as a coherent whole in this introduction.

The ethical ideal of Confucius in the *Analects,* his foremost concern, can be condensed into a single complex proposition: "The Gentleman follows the Way of self-cultivation of Virtue, observance of the Rites, devotion to Learning, and Public Service." Each part of this proposition needs to be explained. To begin with, the Gentleman (*chun-tzu (junzi)*) is the pivotal concept of the *Analects*. The word can be rendered also as "superior person," in contrast to "petty person" or one who is not noteworthy in any respect. The Chinese word originally referred to the hereditary heir of a nobleman ("lord's son"). Confucius redefined it to mean "a morally distinguished person." The Gentleman is noble in refinement, integrity, and lofty ethical character, regardless of inherited social standing. Discounting the gender bias of the patriarchal society in which Confucius lived, the ideal is as applicable to women as to men. Confucius surely believed his ideal could be realized. Yao, Shun, Yu, King Wen, and Duke Chou—those worthies of whom he read in the *Book of History*—were true gentlemen in his sense of the term. So was one of his disciples, Yen Yuan (Yan Yuan), the only one the Master recognized for that honor. Confucius never laid claim to such eminence for himself. What sets the Gentleman above the petty fellow is pursuit of the Way.

The Way (*tao (dao)*) in the *Analects* is the right course of conduct for individuals and governments, not a mysterious metaphysical ground of the universe as in the *Tao Te Ching* (*Daodejing,* see next section). Only metaphorically a pathway, in reality it is a set of moral principles. These principles are indeed sanctioned by Heaven, the ultimate religious authority for Confucius. But they are not right for that reason. Nor are they right because they bring beneficial results. These principles are right in and of themselves. One should follow the Way because it is right and for no other reason. Confucius believed that Heaven had created the universe with moral as well as physical laws. In Heaven's world, the rules are already set for us. The Gentleman follows the Way ordained by Heaven rather than aspiring to create his own. That Way is in fact the way of self-cultivation of Virtue, observance of the Rites, devotion to Learning, and Public Service.

Self-cultivation of Virtue is the very backbone of the Way. To cultivate means to enhance, refine, or perfect some latent quality. Confucius likened the process to an artisan polishing horn or carving jade. The latent quality the Gentleman is to polish and carve is Virtue. Virtue here refers both to moral excellence and to the charisma of the morally excellent person. To cultivate Virtue, therefore, is to develop one's moral character by acquiring the specific moral excellences Heaven has prescribed in the Way; it is also to enlarge the impact one has on others through the sheer force of moral integrity. A number of moral excellences are advocated in the *Analects*. Prominent among them are those that pertain directly to the social roles that constitute the Five Essential Human Relationships—husband and wife, father and son, elder and younger brother, ruler and minister, friend and friend. Filial piety, brotherly love, trustworthiness, and loyalty are some of these moral qualities. But for Confucius, three virtues were of supreme importance—Benevolence (*jen (ren)*), Righteousness (*i (yi)*), and Propriety (*li*).

Propriety is the virtue of treating others with courtesy, consideration, and respect. Righteousness is the virtue of fulfilling one's duties and responsibilities to family, community, nation, and world. Benevolence is the most emphasized and esteemed of the three. In its broad sense, it is equivalent to moral excellence in general. In its narrow sense, it means kindness, human-heartedness, love, or caring—no one English word covers all of its nuances. It is fundamentally a quality of the heart, a selfless concern for the well-being of other people. Behaviorally, it shows itself in supporting others in what one seeks for oneself (*chung (zhong)*) and in sparing others what one avoids for oneself (*shu*). Here we have the Golden Rule in Chinese dress, stated both positively and negatively. Here we have the perennial wisdom that to measure our treatment of others by our own likes and dislikes is morality in action. To these three virtues, Mencius added Wisdom (*chih (zhi)*) to make Four Constant Virtues. The later Confucian tradition added yet another, Sincerity (*hsin (xin)*). The Five Constant Virtues were likened unto a tree, Benevolence being the root, Righteousness the trunk, Propriety the branches, Wisdom the flower, and Sincerity the fruit.

Observance of the Rites points to formalities essential to keeping the Way. For the Rites are related to Virtue as outer form to inner spirit. The Rites without Virtue are empty and Virtue without the Rites ineffectual, lacking a suitable medium of expression. The Rites provide stylized patterns of conduct by means of which the common life of people in interaction with one another can be humanized and morally upgraded. The Rites provide the sole vehicle for the virtue of Propriety. They serve as conduits of Benevolence and Righteousness as well. The Rites include ceremonies that accompany affairs of state, traditional family rituals used in the burial of and bereavement for dead ancestors, and forms followed in offering sacrifices to sacred powers. They include also rules of appropriate conduct in all phases of human life, otherwise known as etiquette or manners. Social customs, mores and folkways, and institutionalized behavior of any description are all part of the Rites. As citizen of a state (Lu) keen on preserving the Rites of the early Chou Dynasty, Confucius avidly researched the Rites not only of early Chou but of the preceding Shang and Hsia dynasties too. He was apparently not interested in simply conserving relics of the dead past. Aware of the fact that history demands revision, he was concerned to remodel the old. Confucius witnessed a general deterioration in the practice of manners, customs, and traditions in his own day. He must have drawn a causal connection in his mind between the declining civility of his society and its widespread misery. For him, the Rites were not monotonous routines but living vessels of moral intercourse among people. As patterned behavior, they had a harmonizing effect upon participants. As channels for Benevolence, Righteousness, and Propriety, they brought a morally ennobling influence to society. Humanizing of the Rites is thought of as one of Confucius's finest contributions.

Devotion to Learning was a fixture in the life of Confucius from youth on. It was also a staple of the Way he preached. Confucius viewed education as the major moral regenerative force in society, its best hope. Learning, of course, needs to be coupled with reflection, because learning without thinking is undigested, while thinking without learning is unfounded. Confucius was a lifelong learner and a deep thinker. For him, the excellent teacher was one who can discover fresh meaning in old materials. His syllabus was the Six Classics, introduced earlier. His curriculum, accordingly, featured history, literature, the fine arts (music and dance at least), rites, and certain aspects of physical culture such as archery and carriage racing. Music, he thought, must be more than beautiful; it must also be uplifting. Good music, by definition, purifies the emotions the way lovely rituals purify the desires. Confucius believed profoundly in the liberating effect of education on the individual student and its civilizing effect on relationships. Education as he practiced it was not preparation for the job market but refinement of moral character and hence training in the Way.

Public Service is the ultimate purpose of the Gentleman. Virtue, the Rites, and Learning are not only legitimate ends unto themselves but also means to the further end of Public Service. They are mandated for the betterment of one's family, the nation, and humankind, not just for private enhancement. A strong sense of solidarity with others comes across in the *Analects,* where individual fulfillment is incorporated within the well-being of society as an organic whole. Though Confucius himself had only limited success in public office, to serve his society had been one of his three goals in life from early manhood. As a teacher, he inculcated his students with the aspiration to seek public office for the improvement of society. Many did, some making a better showing than their master had.

The political philosophy of Confucius in the *Analects* is secondary to the ethical. His politically oriented sayings suggest answers to three questions. First, when is the nation healthy? Answer: When there is harmony throughout the Five Essential Human Relationships. Confucianism is renown for its belief that the well-being of society at large depends on harmony in the relationships between husbands and wives, fathers and sons, elder and younger brothers, ruler and ministers, and friends. Other domestic and social relationships will follow suit. Only two of the five are cited in the *Analects*—father and son and ruler and minister. All five, however, are taught in the *Book of History* and in the *Doctrine of the Mean.* The full teaching also specifies the humane duties incumbent on both parties to each relationship, duties said to be implicit in the very meaning of each role name. Harmony will exist in society when all members honor the humane and virtuous duties that bind them together into a community. Morality, therefore, is the key to harmony, harmony a function of morality, and community the result of both. Ethics and politics overlap at this point.

Next question, when is the nation well governed? Answer: When rulers are Gentlemen. Confucius held that the ship of state is well piloted only when a gentleman-king and moral ministers are at the helm. Confucius often spoke with rulers about their office. He discoursed with them about the king's source of authority, qualifications, purpose, responsibility for establishing harmony, and strategy for achieving that harmony. In order to rule effectively, the ruler must above all be a Gentleman. The king gets his authority to rule from Heaven—the divine right of kings. The Son of Heaven (the king) rules by the Mandate of Heaven (Heaven's will). If the king fails to maintain harmony throughout his realm, social discord will disturb the balance of Nature. Natural catastrophes will then occur, indicating that the Mandate to rule has been withdrawn by Heaven. In that event, the king must be removed, by force if necessary. The qualifications for ruling are high moral character, leadership ability, intelligence, and a fine education (all marks of a Gentleman), not birth. The rightful purpose of his rule is not his own aggrandizement but the welfare of the people, measured by harmony throughout the kingdom. Everyone must cooperate if harmony is to prevail. The king, however, bears ultimate responsibility for it.

Sound strategy for achieving social harmony includes the rectification of names, rule by moral example, and rule by ceremony. The king's primary objective in ruling should be the rectification of names. The king must lead his people to behave according to the humane duties implicit in the meanings of their role names under the Five Essential Human Relationships. When fathers act like fathers and ministers act like ministers, and so on, their behavior coincides with that of their role names. By bringing behaviors into line with roles, the ruler rectifies names. How is he to do this? Not through law enforcement, for morality cannot be legislated. He works through the power of his own virtuous example. People learn morality best by example. As the grass bends with the wind, so the people's virtue will follow the ruler's lead. This is rule by moral example. The king's moral magnetism impacts the people directly in his skillful performance of public ceremonies. Such occasions are opportunities for the ruler to unify the people under his authority. This is ruling by ceremony.

Last question, what is the best system of government? Confucius never squarely addressed this question. It seems safe to assume, however, that he preferred feudal monarchy, patterned after the regime of the founders of the Chou Dynasty. For him, arguably, the system of government (monarchy, oligarchy, democracy, tyranny, etc.) was not of first importance; the moral integrity and example of its leaders were. Gentlemen rulers would bring harmony to any one of several acceptable systems of government. The moral tone of the society is more important than its form of government. There are several features of the political philosophy of Confucius, however, that resonate well with liberal democracy. Education should be accessible to all. The king should be chosen (elected?) for moral character and ability, not birth, and he should install ministers who exhibit those same qualities regardless of their parentage or connections. The welfare of the people should be the first concern of the state, not increasing the power and wealth of its leaders or their perpetuation in office. True, the people's welfare is seen largely in terms of social harmony. Enhancement of individual liberty, higher living standard, and technological progress are not mentioned. Order is nevertheless the basis for true liberty and economic sufficiency a condition of harmony. If monarchy is by implication the best form of government in the *Analects,* it is liberal, benevolent monarchy surely.

The religious philosophy of the *Analects* is hard to deduce, for the passages bearing on it are few, brief, and vague. Of particular difficulty is the question of Confucius's position vis-à-vis the colorful folk religion of his time, with its nature spirits in mountains and rivers, ancestral ghosts, demon possession, magic, divination techniques, astrology, and the pantheon of anthropomorphic protective deities of home and village. When asked about it by his disciples, Confucius redirected their attention to human problems. What might his reticence to give straight answers indicate? Tacit acceptance of belief? Polite rejection of it? Agnosticism? Indifference? All these possibilities have been defended by this commentator or that. What is beyond dispute, however, is Confucius's firm endorsement of the rituals employed in the worship of such sacred powers. As with all other Rites, these sacred ceremonies harmonize the personalities of the participants, provide vehicles of moral behavior, and occasion the manifestation of the Gentleman's charisma and the king's (when he is the celebrant) government.

Beyond the unanswerable question of Confucius's private views on Chinese folk religion as a system of belief lies his profound faith in Heaven. Heaven was for Confucius the ultimate reality and the ruler of the universe. Whatever exact theological idea he might have held in mind, if any, Confucius's references to Heaven suggest a single, spiritual, transcendent, personal, intelligent, purposive, holy Deity who rules by remote control through natural laws built into creation rather than by supernatural intervention. Revelation and miracle are never mentioned, nor are the issues of immortality and eschatology. If a label had to be put on Confucius's concept of Heaven, "deism" would perhaps be the best choice. Confucius's references to Heaven were often in the context of its Mandate, submission to which seems to have been the crux of his personal religious faith. The Mandate of Heaven applies to the divine right of kings to rule as sons of Heaven. It applies also to the moral and physical laws Confucius believed were part of the created universe. But it applies as well to the sphere of personal choice and action. Heaven's Mandate or will for each person's life is pursuit of the Way, regardless of consequences. All will turn out for the best when a person does what is right simply because it is right.

*   *   *

The *Great Learning* and the *Doctrine of the Mean* come after the *Analects* in the order of the Four Books established by Chu Hsi. On his authority, for centuries the accepted view of authorship and date attributed the *Great Learning* to Tseng-tzu and the *Doctrine of the Mean* to Tzu-ssu. Tseng-tzu had been the most able student and Tzu-ssu the brilliant grandson of the Master. As Confucius handed his teaching down to them, they recorded it in book form, according to Chu Hsi. Both texts were originally chapters Chu Hsi had extracted from the *Li chi*. Current scholarship regards the *Li chi* as a post-Confucian replacement for the pre-Confucian *Li ching* among the Six Classics. It is now seen as an anthology of Confucian writings from the fourth to the first centuries B.C.E., compiled in the first century B.C.E. For that reason, many contemporary scholars place the writing of the second and third of the Four Books at about 200 B.C.E. If accurate, this would nullify authorship by Tseng-tzu and Tzu-ssu and put these texts after rather than before the *Mencius*. Both texts reinforce the crucial Confucian idea that Heaven, Earth, and Mankind constitute a Cosmic Community based on Harmony. Harmony and Community are among the most vibrant themes in Confucian philosophy.

The great learning in the text by that name maintains that harmony radiates from the center through the concentric spheres of human life to the circumference. One could visualize this action on analogy with the ripple effect of a stone thrown into a pool of still water. The harmony within the personality of the self-cultivated individual Gentleman (who has first investigated things, extended his knowledge, made sincere his will, and rectified his mind) spills over into his family life, making the family functional. The harmony of well-regulated families spills over into the state, spreading order into the next larger concentric sphere of human life. Finally, the harmony of well-ordered states then spills over into the world, bringing the blessing of universal peace to all humankind. The centrifugal force of harmony within the communities of humankind is essentially what the *Great Learning* is about.

The doctrine of the mean in the text so named refers to a force much grander than the human force of harmony just described. The mean refers to a metaphysical force that suffuses not only humankind but also the whole universe. That force is the force of balance, equilibrium, or attunement. It is the cosmic force comparable to being on pitch or on key in music. The universe, informed by the mean, is naturally centered, in balance, attuned. Human nature, likewise informed by the mean, is intrinsically centered, balanced, attuned. The balance of Nature can be upset and the attunement of human nature lost. But in both cases that is a defect that enters after the fact of original centeredness. Since Heaven imparts human nature to people, the mean of the universe becomes the mean in people, making of Heaven, Earth, and Mankind a harmonic tri-unity based on the mean. In the *Doctrine of the Mean,* the Way (*tao*) becomes the pursuit of the centeredness, balance, or attunement inherent in human nature. The Gentleman is the person who has discovered and reunited with the mean in human nature. The sage-king in this text becomes correspondingly the ruler who applies the mean to government by keeping the affairs of state in tune with it. In the *Analects,* as in Aristotle, the mean refers simply to the principle of moderation in human choosing, finding the middle course between extremes. In the *Doctrine of the Mean,* the mean doctrine has undergone considerable amplification.

*   *   *

The last of the Four Books, in the order in which Chu Hsi raised them to prominence, is the *Mencius.* Selections from it constitute the second reading presented in this section (translated by D.C. Lau). This classic was written either by Mencius himself or by his immediate disciples, perhaps from his notes, maybe even with his help. Meng K'o (Meng Kou) was his Chinese name, Mencius a latinization of his title of respect, Meng-tzu ("Master Meng"). His birthplace was about fifty miles south of Ch'u-fu, where Confucius had been born. Though the two men were separated by a century, Mencius's life paralleled that of Confucius in some respects. He was an orphan at three, a failure at politics, a success at teaching, and an itinerant scholar-teacher-political advisor in his later years. He studied with disciples of Tzu-ssu, Confucius's grandson, not with Tzu-ssu himself as Chu Hsi held. The book named after him is divided into seven "books" of two parts each (A and B), broken down further into 261 chapters. The discussion of topics is much more sustained and systematic than that in the *Analects.* The first three books record Mencius's conversations with rulers of neighboring states during his wandering years. The fourth and seventh books contain paragraph-length sayings, without naming to whom he addressed them. The fifth book gives his answers to questions brought by one very inquisitive disciple, Wan Chang (Wan Zhang). The sixth and meatiest book recounts his famous debate with Kao-tzu (Gaozi) on the question of the moral condition of human nature. Mencius became the acknowledged leader of "right wing" or idealistic Confucianism, opposed to the "left wing" or realistic Confucianism of Hsun-tzu. Since the time of Chu Hsi, Mencius has been regarded as the most authoritative voice in the orthodox Confucian lineage after Confucius himself.

Generally recognized as Mencius's key contributions are the ideas of the original goodness of human nature, the universal moral law implanted in the human mind, and benevolent government. These ideas take on enhanced significance when viewed against the background of the debates from which they sprang. Mencius attacked positions espoused by Mo-tzu and Yang Chu (Yang Zhu), 440?–360? B.C.E.). Mo-tzu preached loving everyone equally, other families as much as one's own and enemies as much as friends. He grounded his love ethic in its social utility (consequences) and in the revealed will of God (authority). Yang Chu advocated a kind of laissez-faire individualism (everyone for himself or herself) that denied responsibilities of any kind to family, friend, or king. He favored as well the pursuit of personal pleasure, repugnant to the Confucian conscience. Mencius, for his part, was persuaded of the moral philosophy taught by Confucius. The Gentleman should follow the Way decreed by Heaven, the Way that featured self-cultivation of Virtue (Benevolence and Righteousness particularly, in Mencius's case), observance of the Rites, devotion to Learning, and Public Service. Mencius believed Mo-tzu was wrong about loving everyone equally. One should indeed love other families but not as devotedly as one's own, and enemies too but not to the same extent as friends. He disagreed further with Mo-tzu about love being right because backed by consequences and authority. This for him cheapened morality; the Gentleman acts on principle, not profit or threat of divine sanctions. He believed also that Yang Chu was mistaken in prioritizing self and pleasure above responsibility to serve society and loyalty to the ruler.

Why was the Confucian ethic right and the ethical policies of Mo-tzu and Yang Chu wrong? To debate an adversary involves attacking his position with reasons and defending one's own position with reasons. Confucius, because he preceded these adversaries, had not been confronted with the need for rational defense. Mencius, coming after them, found himself on the spot. Confucius had supplied him with an ethical ideal but not armed him with reasons for its defense. Mencius's primary contribution was inventing a defensible rationale for the Confucian ethic. Mencius discovered that rationale in the very nature of things—in the nature of the universe reflected in the nature of man.

Mencius based his naturalistic ethic on the universal moral law implanted in human nature. Confucius was right, and his opponents wrong, because the Confucian ethic alone is grounded in the very nature of humankind. Mo-tzu was wrong to teach that impartial love is obligatory. Loving other fathers and families as much as one's own is unnatural, a violation of the universal moral law implanted in human nature. Yang Chu was foolish to discount feelings of responsibility to family, friends, and ruler. Those feelings are natural, supported by the universal moral law inscribed on human nature. Confucius had kept private his views on human nature. Mencius, however, did not hesitate to articulate a feasible theory of human nature and deploy it in his naturalistic ethic. According to Mencius, the core of human nature (in contrast to the animal nature people share with bird and beast) is evaluating mind (*hsin (xin)*). Evaluating mind is the innate capacity to discern the difference between noble and base, right and wrong, proper and improper. This it can do, because the universal moral law is imprinted upon it. Heaven does not hand down the universal moral law the way Yahweh gave Moses the Ten Commandments on Mt. Sinai. The universal moral law *is* Heaven! There is no lawgiver; Heaven and Law are one and the same. The more that evaluating mind is cultivated, the clearer become the universal moral law and the rightness of the Way Confucius taught. The morally superior person, with evaluating mind fine-tuned, is able to attune character and conduct to the universal moral law that is Heaven.

Because it is equipped with evaluating mind informed by the universal moral law, human nature is inherently good. The idea of the original goodness of human nature is the hallmark of Mencius's teaching. A controversy raged in his day over the question of the moral condition of human nature. There were four competing positions. Mencius's position has just been indicated. Kao-tzu held that human nature is neutral; behavior is good or bad, but human nature itself is not. A third position maintained that human nature has a dual potential to become either good or bad developmentally, though it is originally blank. A fourth view contended that human nature is mixed, being inherently good in some people but inherently bad in others. No one in Mencius's own time proposed that human nature is inherently evil. That view found its champion in Hsun-tzu of the next generation. Mencius argued his position on the grounds that the "seeds" or "beginnings" of the Four Constant Virtues are innate in human nature. Though the seeds must be nurtured in order to mature, their very presence ensures the original goodness of human nature. The Four Constant Virtues are Benevolence, Righteousness, Propriety, and Wisdom. The feeling of commiseration with the suffering of others, he claimed, is the seed of Benevolence, the feeling of shame when elders scold the seed of Righteousness, the feeling of deference or compliance to parental wishes the seed of Propriety, and spontaneous approval or disapproval of the behavior of young siblings the seed of Wisdom. Every child, Mencius observed, is born with these four seeds as surely as with four limbs. And just as surely those seeds, unless hindered, will with nurture blossom into the Four Constant Virtues. Hindering factors explained moral decadence for Mencius. If one fails to nurture the seeds, or yields to adversity, or responds to drives rooted in the animal nature that exists alongside human nature in people, then the four seeds will not flower into the Four Constant Virtues.

The mainstay of Mencius's political philosophy was his insistence that the state function as a moral institution. The ruler must be a moral leader, a Gentleman, a sage-king, as were the great leaders of the past—Yao, Shun, and especially (for Mencius) Yu. The ruler must win the support of the people through benevolent ruling, because his right to rule stems not from the Mandate of Heaven alone; it stems equally from the consent of the governed. If the ruler fails to provide the people benevolent rule, he forfeits the Mandate of Heaven and his right to be called "king." He becomes "a mere fellow," no longer the monarch. Revolution and even regicide are moral rights of the people in extreme cases of misrule. A moral king's sole objective must be the welfare of the people. Measures that will enhance the quality of life for the people, Mencius taught, include equal distribution of land, reduction of taxes, pensions for the aged, minimal interference in the affairs of the people, and, perhaps above all, the provision at state expense of excellent moral education, enabling people to reach their full moral (hence human) potential. The Golden Rule must be extended to the administration of government. Benevolence and Righteousness must be its guiding principles. And the universal moral law must be the tribunal before which civil laws (as few as possible) answer. No matter that the form of such government is feudal monarchy; its spirit resonates with that of liberal democracy. Government can afford to be liberal, because human nature is certifiably good. Mencius's politics flow directly from his confidence in the moral goodness of human nature.

*   *   *

The last of the five great classical Confucians was Hsun-tzu, born a decade after Mencius died. The first breech in the Confucian school opened up between the right-wing idealistic school of Mencius and Hsun-tzu's left-wing realistic school. As fellow Confucians, they shared much in common, including the Gentleman ideal, emphasis on Benevolence and Righteousness, reliance on education as the main transformative force in people's lives, esteem for the ancient Rites, the principle of the rectification of names, and belief in humane government. The points on which they differed were the moral condition of human nature, the role of civil law enforcement, and the interpretation of Heaven.

Hsun-tzu rejected Mencius's theory that the four seeds are innate in human nature. Instead, he found human nature to be inherently evil, spoiled by greed and envy. Because human nature is originally corrupt, government cannot afford to be permissive, though it exists solely for the benefit of the people. Regulation of deviant behavior through tough laws strictly enforced is absolutely necessary. No universal moral law is written in human nature, accessed through evaluative mind. Civil law is the invention of human intelligence, not the reflection of a higher legal order. Heaven is merely the physical law by which Nature operates, not the universal moral law of Mencius or the eternal lawgiver of Confucius.

Hsun-tzu was more influential than Mencius in the late classical period and immediately thereafter. The Legalism of Han Fei-tzu, a student of Hsun-tzu's, came into vogue during the Ch'in Dynasty that followed the Chou. Once Chu Hsi incorporated Mencius into the orthodox succession from which Hsun-tzu was excluded, however, Mencius has far outshone his rival. The coupling of an optimistic view of human nature with liberal politics and of a pessimistic view with repressive politics surfaces in Western political philosophy as well as in the debate between Mencius and Hsun-tzu.

*   *   *

Supplementary reading on Confucius and Mencius falls into several categories. The first is standard works on the full history of Chinese philosophy: H.G. Creel, *Chinese Thought: From Confucius to Mao Tse-tung* (New York: Mentor Books, 1953); Fung Yu-lan, *A History of Chinese Philosophy,* 2nd ed., tr. Derk Bodde (Princeton, NJ: Princeton University Press, 1952); Fung Yu-lan, *A Short History of Chinese Philosophy,* ed. Derk Bodde (New York: The Free Press, 1948); Robert E. Allinson, *Understanding the Chinese Mind: The Philosophical Roots* (New

York: Oxford University Press, 1992); and Antonio S. Cua, ed., *Encyclopedia of Chinese Philosophy* (New York and London: Routledge, 2003).

Second, studies of the classical period of Chinese philosophy: E.R. Hughes, *Chinese Philosophy in Classical Times,* rev. ed. (London: Dent, 1954); A.C. Graham, *Disputers of the Tao: Philosophical Argument in Ancient China* (La Salle, IL: Open Court, 1989); Benjamin I. Schwartz, *The World of Thought in Ancient China* (Cambridge, MA: Harvard University Press, 1985); and Donald J. Munro, *The Concept of Man in Early China* (Stanford, CA: Stanford University Press, 1969).

Third, introductory level studies of Confucianism: Herrlee G. Creel, *Confucius and the Chinese Way* (New York: Harper Torchbooks, 1949); Wu-chi Liu, *A Short History of Confucian Philosophy* (Harmondsworth, Eng.: Penguin Books, 1955); Wu-chi Liu, *Confucius: His Life and Times* (Westport, CT: Greenwood Press, 1972); and Richard Wilhelm, *Confucius and Confucianism,* trs. George H. Danton and Annina Periam Danton (New York: Harcourt Brace Jovanovich, 1931).

Fourth, advanced studies of Confucianism: David L. Hall and Roger T. Ames, *Thinking Through Confucius* (Albany: SUNY Press, 1987); David S. Nivison, *The Ways of Confucianism* (La Salle, IL: Open Court, 1997); and Bryan W. Van Norden, ed., *Confucius and the Analects: New Essays* (Oxford, Eng.: Oxford University Press, 2001).

Fifth, studies in Confucian ethics: Philip J. Ivanhoe, *Confucian Moral Self Cultivation,* 2nd ed. (Indianapolis/Cambridge: Hackett, 2000); T.C. Kline III and Philip J. Ivanhoe, eds., *Virtue, Nature, and Moral Agency in the* Xunzi (Indianapolis/Cambridge: Hackett, 2000); Xiusheng Liu and Philip J. Ivanhoe, eds., *Essays on the Moral Philosophy of Mengzi* (Indianapolis/Cambridge: Hackett, 2002); and Philip J. Ivanhoe, *Ethics in the Confucian Tradition: The Thought of Mengzi and Wang Yangming,* 2nd ed. (Indianapolis/Cambridge: Hackett, 2002).

Last, studies relating Confucianism to various aspects of contemporary thought: Herbert Fingarette, *Confucius: The Secular as Sacred* (New York: Harper & Row, 1972); Tu Wei-ming, *Confucian Thought: Selfhood as Creative Transformation* (Albany: SUNY Press, 1985); Wm. Theodore de Bary and Tu Weiming, eds., *Confucianism and Human Rights* (New York: Columbia University Press, 1998); John H. Berthrong, *All Under Heaven: Transforming Paradigms in Confucian–Christian Dialogue* (Albany: SUNY Press, 1994); and Chenyang Li, ed., *The Sage and the Second Sex: Confucianism, Ethics, and Gender* (Chicago and La Salle, IL: Open Court, 2000).

CONFUCIUS, THE ANALECTS

BOOK I

1. Confucius said, "To learn and to practise what is learned time and again is pleasure, is it not? To have friends come from afar is happiness, is it not? To be unperturbed when not appreciated by others is gentlemanly, is it not?"

2. Yu Tzu said, "It is seldom that a man of filial piety* and brotherly love would be inclined to offend those above. There has not been a man inclined to cause disorder without the inclination to offend those above. The gentleman nourishes the roots. With the roots established, the Way grows. Are filial piety and brotherly love not the roots of benevolence?"

3. Confucius said, "Clever talk and a pretentious manner are seldom compatible with the benevolent."

4. Tseng Tzu said, "Each day I examine myself on three counts: whether or not I am loyal to those in whose behalf I act; whether or not I am trustworthy in my dealings with friends; whether or not I practise what is imparted."

5. Confucius said, "In leading a state of a thousand chariots, respect the office and be trustworthy; economise in the use of resources and love the people, and employ the people when it is timely."

6. Confucius said, "In the home, the young should behave with filial piety, and out in the world, with brotherly love. They should be prudent and trustworthy. They should love all people and be close to the benevolent. Having so done, their remaining strength should be used to learn literature."

7. Tzu Hsia said, "To revere virtue instead of beauty, to devote all strength to serving parents, to be willing to die in serving the lord, to speak with trustworthiness in dealings with friends: even though it is said this is not to have learned, I say this is."

8. Confucius said, "Without steadfastness, the gentleman would not command respect, and his learning would not be sound. Advocating loyalty and trustworthiness, he has no friend who is not his equal. He would not hesitate to correct his faults."

9. Tseng Tzu said, "To be prudent in mourning, and to remember those who have passed away before, is to enhance the virtue of the people."

Confucius, *Analects* (Lun Yu), Complete. Reprinted with permission from *The* Lun Yu *in English,* translated by William Cheung (Hong Kong and Richmond, BC: Confucian Publishing Company, 1999). (The numbering has been modified to match standard book and chapter.)
*Chinese traditional family concept of devotion, duty and respect which, according to the *Analects,* is extended to include all elders, living or dead.

Drawing of Confucius (551–479 B.C.E.). (EMG
Education Management Group)

10. Tzu Ch'in asked Tzu Kung, "To whichever state the Master travels, he always hears of its policies. Does he enquire or is he informed?"

Tzu Kung said, "The Master learns by being gentle, kind, courteous, modest and deferential. The Master's enquiry is different from that of others."

11. Confucius said, "Note the aspirations of the man during his father's lifetime,* and the conduct of the man after his father's death. If after three years he has not changed his father's way, this could be considered filial piety."

12. Yu Tzu said, "Harmony is the value of performing the rites.** Such was the beauty of the way of emperors past in matters great and small. Yet there are times when this is not acceptable. When there is harmony for harmony's sake, undisciplined by the rites, it is not acceptable."

---

*The code of conduct based on filial piety was that a man should act according to the wishes of his father. Therefore while his father was alive, a man's true character could not be judged by his conduct, only by his aspirations.

**Set rules of etiquette, codes of conduct and moral obligations which were formalised during the Chou Dynasty and advocated by Confucius.

13. Yu Tzu said, "When trustworthiness complements righteousness, words can be fulfilled. When courtesy complements the rites, shame and disgrace are kept afar. Thereby those closest are not lost and the honour of the ancestors is preserved."

14. Confucius said, "The gentleman does not seek to satiate himself in eating, does not seek ease in living, is quick in his dealings and prudent in speech, and keeps to the correctness of those with the Way. He can be considered as devoted to learning."

15. Tzu Kung said, "'Poor yet not a debased flatterer, rich yet not arrogant': what do you say?"
Confucius said, "It will suffice, but it is not equal to 'Poor yet happy, rich yet devoted to the rites.'"
Tzu Kung said, the *Odes** say,

> Like bone cut, like horn polished,
> Like jade carved, like stone ground

Is this what you mean?"
Confucius said, "T'su,** now I can begin to discuss the *Odes* with you. From what I have told you, you can deduce what is to come."

16. Confucius said, "Do not be concerned about others not appreciating you. Be concerned about your not appreciating others."

BOOK II

1. Confucius said, "To rule with virtue is like the North Star in its place, around which all other stars revolve, in homage."

2. Confucius said, "The three hundred verses of the *Odes* may be summed up in a single sentence which is, 'Think no evil.'"

3. Confucius said, "Lead through policies, discipline through punishments, and the people may be restrained but without a sense of shame. Lead through virtue, discipline through the rites, and there will be a sense of shame and conscientious improvements."

4. Confucius said: "At fifteen, I aspired to learning. At thirty, I established my stand. At forty, I had no delusions. At fifty, I knew my destiny. At sixty, I knew truth in all I heard. At seventy, I could follow the wishes of my heart without doing wrong."

5. Meng Yi Tzu asked about filial piety. Confucius said, "Without deviation."
As Fan Ch'ih drove the Master's carriage, Confucius recounted to this disciple, "Meng-Sun asked me about filial piety and I told him, 'Without deviation.'"
Fan Ch'ih said, "What did you mean?"

---

*One of the six classics compiled and edited by Confucius.
**Another name for Tzu Kung.

Confucius said, "Serve your parents during their lifetime according to the rites. When they die, bury them according to the rites and make sacrificial offerings to them according to the rites."

6. Meng Wu Po asked about filial piety. Confucius said, "Your parents' greatest worry should be your health."

7. Tzu Yu asked about filial piety. Confucius said, "Nowadays, to provide for parents is considered filial piety. But dogs and horses are so provided. Without respect, what is the difference?"

8. Tzu Hsia asked about filial piety. Confucius said, "Subtle is the countenance. The young bear the burden in work, and the elders enjoy the first choice in food and wine. But can this be considered filial piety?"

9. Confucius said, "For a whole day, I conversed with Hui who, as though dull-witted, did not contradict me. I reflected on his personal conduct after we had parted company, and found it sufficiently expressive. Hui is not dull-witted after all."

10. Confucius said, "Look into a man's motives, note his course, take heed of whether he is at ease, and how can a man hide, how can a man hide!"

11. Confucius said, "Exploring the old and deducing the new makes a teacher."

12. Confucius said, "The gentleman is unlike an implement."*

13. Tzu Kung asked about the gentleman. Confucius said, "Action takes precedence over words."

14. Confucius said, "The gentleman encompasses all and is not partial. The petty man is partial and does not encompass all."

15. Confucius said, "To learn without thinking is labour in vain. To think without learning is desolation."

16. Confucius said, "To attack extremes is harmful indeed."

17. Confucius said, "Yu, I shall instruct you about knowledge. To acknowledge what is known as known, and what is not known as not known is knowledge."

18. Tzu Chang wished to learn how to acquire the career of an official.
Confucius said, "Listen extensively and cast aside doubt. As for the rest, speak prudently, and there will be little accusation. Observe extensively and cast aside desolation. As for the rest, act prudently, and there will be little remorse. With little accusation about what is spoken and little remorse about what is done, there is the career of an official."

19. Duke Ai asked, "What must be done for the support of the people?"

*I.e., the gentleman has a limitless capacity to achieve good, not the limited value of a tool.

Confucius replied, "Elevate the honest above the wrong doers, and there will be support from the people. Elevate the wrong doers above the honest and there will not be support from the people."

20. Chi K'ang Tzu asked, "How may the people be instilled with respect, loyalty and encouragement?"

Confucius said, "Preside with dignity and there is respect, with filial piety and compassion and there is loyalty. Elevate the good and teach the incapable and there is encouragement."

21. Someone asked Confucius, "Why are you not in public office?"

Confucius said, "The *Book of History* says, 'great is filial piety' and 'all brothers are friends,' the realization of which is as to be in public office. What need is there to be in public office?"

22. Confucius said, "I know not what a man without trustworthiness may accomplish. Be it large or small, how could a carriage move without its yoke-bar?"

23. Tzu Chang asked about the future of the ten generations to come.

Confucius said, "The Yin inherited the rites of the Hsia. Their gain or loss can be deduced. The Chou inherited the rites of the Yin. Their gain or loss can be deduced. The future of whoever succeeds the Chou can be deduced for a hundred generations to come."

24. Confucius said, "To make sacrificial offerings other than to the family dead is to be a debased flatterer. To know what is right and not to do it is to be without courage."

BOOK III

1. Confucius said of Chi who has eight rows of eight dancers* each to perform in his courtyard, "If such is accepted, what might not be accepted!"

2. The three families** concluded with the "Yung."†

Confucius said, "'Attended by the lords and the dukes, the son of heaven‡ makes sacrificial offerings in solemn dignity': what can be derived from it in the hall of the three families?"

3. Confucius said, "If a man is without benevolence, then of what use are the rites? If a man is without benevolence, then of what use is music?"

4. Lin Fang asked about the roots of the rites.

"An excellent question indeed," said Confucius. "As to the rites, rather be modest than lavish. As to mourning, rather be grieving than meticulous."

---

*The prerogative of the emperor.
**The three leading families of the state of Lu, surnamed Meng-Sun, Shu-Sun and Chi-Sun, of noble descent, but not entitled to the prerogatives of the emperor.
†A passage from the *Odes*, the recitation of which was the emperor's prerogative.
‡The emperor.

5. Confucius said, "Even with lords, the Yi and the Ti* cannot be compared to the Hsia** without lords."

6. Chi was making a pilgrimage to T'ai Shan.†
Confucius said to Jan Yu,‡ "Can you not save this situation?"
The reply was, "I cannot."
Confucius said, "Alas, can T'ai Shan be considered not equal to Lin Fang?"§

7. Confucius said, "Gentlemen do not compete, except in archery. With both hands clasped, each greets the other in ascent. Having descended, they drink to each other. Their competition is gentlemanly."

8. Tzu Hsia asked, "What is meant by

> The pretty smile entices,
> The beautiful eyes enchant,
> Whiting before colour.

Confucius said, "Colour rendering comes after sketching."
Tzu Hsia said, "As the rites come after . . ."§§
Confucius said, "Shang, I am stimulated, and can begin to discuss the *Odes* with you."

9. Confucius said, "I can discuss the rites of the Hsia, but the Ch'i§§§ is not worthy to be cited. I can discuss the rites of the Yin, but Sung# is not worthy to be cited. The learned and the literature of Ch'i and Sung are not worthy of mention. If they were, I could cite them."

10. Confucius said, "At the *ti* offering, I wish not to see what comes after the *kuan*."***

11. Someone asked about the remark Confucius made on the ti offering.
Confucius said, "I do not know. But many under heaven know my remark. It is as what I show you here." And he referred to the palm of his hand.

12. In ancestral offerings, the ancestors' presence should be felt. In sacrificial offerings to the gods, the gods' presence should be felt.
Confucius said, "It is as if I had not made the offerings if I do not feel their presence."

13. Wang-Sun Chia asked Confucius, "What is meant by

*Uncivilized tribes to the East and the North respectively of China.
**The civilized peoples of China proper.
†Mountain, the worship of which was the emperor's prerogative.
‡Disciple, and official to the Chi Family.
§Confucius muses that the mountain god, T'ai Shan, would surely be more conscious than Lin Fang of the emperor's prerogative.
§§I.e., inner qualities should take precedence over the rites.
§§§A feudal state during the Chou Dynasty established for the descendants of the Hsia Dynasty.
#A feudal state during the Chou Dynasty established for the descendants of the Yin-Shang Dynasty.
***The *ti* offering was an ancestral offering made by lords every five years. The *kuan* was a wine pouring ritual which was performed at the start and the conclusion of the ti offering, to honour the ancestors whose tablets were placed in a formalised descending order. In Confucius' time, the lord of the state of Lu did not observe the prescribed ancestral order and traditions of the ti offering, which prompted Confucius' dismay.

Rather flatter the god of the kitchen
Than the god of the main chamber?"

Confucius said, "It should not be so. Having offended heaven, there would be nowhere to pray."

14. Confucius said, "The heritage of the Chou [Dynasty] is of the two dynasties.* How literature flourishes! I advocate the Chou.

15. On entering the grand temple,** Confucius asked about every detail. Someone said, "Who said that this young man of Tsou knows the rites? On entering the grand temple he asked about every detail."
Hearing this, Confucius said, "[Asking questions] is in accordance with the rites."

16. Confucius said, "In archery, to pierce the hide† is not the measure, as the archers' strength varies. It has been the way from ancient times."

17. Tzu Kung wished to dispense with the sacrifice of a live goat for the lunar offering.
Confucius said, "T'su,‡ you value the goat, I value the rites."

18. Confucius said, "In serving the lord, adhere completely to the rites, letting others take it to be debased flattery."

19. Duke Ting asked, "What do you say about how the lord should employ his subjects and how the subjects should serve their lord?"
Confucius replied, "The lord should employ his subjects in accordance with the rites. The subjects should serve their lord with loyalty."

20. Confucius said, "The *Kuan sui*§ expresses joy but not debauchery, sorrow but not morbidity."

21. Duke Ai asked Tsai Wo about the *she*.§§
Tsai Wo replied, "The Hsia Hou used the pine, the Yin used the cypress, and the Chou used the chestnut tree, said to have been selected to instil fear."
On hearing this, Confucius said, "What has been accomplished do not discuss; what is in progress, do not recommend to improve; what is past, do not censure."
Confucius said, "Kuan Chung was small-minded."
Someone said, "Was Kuan Chung not being frugal?"

22. Confucius said, "Kuan had three households, with attendants assigned different tasks. How could that be frugality?"

---

*The Hsia and the Yin-Shang.
**Established in the state of Lu at the command of the emperor to honour the memory of the Duke of Chou.
†I.e., the target.
‡Another name for Tzu Kung.
§A verse from the *Odes*.
§§When a state was established, it was customary to build a *she* or "shrine to the god of earth" in thanksgiving and commemoration. The founders of the Hsia, the Yin-Shang, and the Chou Dynasties respectively used pine, cypress and chestnut trees in the construction of their shrines because these were the types of trees growing in their three localities. The Chinese character for "chestnut tree" happens also to mean "fear." Confucius considers Tsai Wo's reply unreasonable.

"But did Kuan Chung not know the rites?"

Confucius said, "Lords have wooden screens at their doors. Kuan too had wooden screens at his doors. When lords toast one another, they use cup stands. Kuan too used cup stands. If Kuan Chung knew the rites, who does not?"*

23. Talking of music with the grand music master of Lu, Confucius said, "Music can be appreciated . . . stirringly in unison it begins. As it continues, how harmonious, how clear, how it grows unto its finale!"

24. An official of Yi asked to see Confucius, saying, "I have not missed meeting any gentleman who travels this way." The followers of Confucius presented the official to the Master. Emerging, he said, "Why should you, the pupils, be concerned with the loss? All under heaven have long been without the Way! Heaven will soon use your Master as a wooden *to*."**

25. Confucius considered *Shao*† as perfectly beautiful and perfectly good and considered *Wu*‡ as perfectly beautiful yet not perfectly good.

26. Confucius said, "When positioned above, without tolerance; when practising the rites, without respect; when mourning, without sorrow. Indeed, what am I to make of it!"

BOOK IV

1. Confucius said, "To live among the benevolent is good. To choose not to be with the benevolent . . . of this I know not!"

2. Confucius said, "Those not benevolent cannot long endure adversity, cannot long be happy. The benevolent are at ease with benevolence. The wise profit from benevolence."

3. Confucius said, "Only the benevolent can love or hate men."

4. Confucius said, "To aspire earnestly to benevolence is to be without vices."

5. Confucius said, "Riches and position are what men desire. If their attainment is to be by departing from the Way, do not have them. Poverty and lowliness are what men hate. If their abandonment is to be by departing from the Way, do not abandon them. If the gentleman abandons benevolence, how is he to live up to his reputation!

---

*Kuan Chung was not entitled to the privileges of lords as set out by the rites.

**The subsequent comments of the official following his audience with Confucius refer to the Master's lack of public office, and to the prevailing social disorder. The *to* was a bell used in ancient times to herald an official proclamation.

†Music adopted by the Emperor Shun when he gained rulership.

‡Music adopted by the Emperor Wu when he gained rulership. Confucius thought highly of the Emperor Shun whose predecessor abdicated in his favour because of his virtue. He thought less of Emperor Wu who, as good an emperor as he was, gained rulership by killing his predecessor.

The gentleman does not deviate from benevolence, not even during meals, during hectic times, nor in destitution."

6. Confucius said, "I have yet to meet the man who loves benevolence, or the man who hates what is not benevolent. Nothing surpasses the man who loves benevolence. The man who hates what is not benevolent is himself benevolent, for he prevents what is not benevolent being attached to him. There is indeed strength to be benevolent for a day! I have yet to meet the man whose strength is insufficient. If there be such a man, I have yet to meet him."

7. Confucius said, "Note the many kinds of faults in men to know benevolence."

8. Confucius said, "To hear in the morning that the Way prevails is to be able to die without regret in the night."

9. Confucius said, "A scholar who aspires to the Way but who is ashamed of wretched clothing and wretched food is not worthy of discussion."

10. Confucius said, "Anywhere under heaven for the gentleman there is nothing absolutely positive, there is nothing absolutely negative. Righteousness is his measure."

11. Confucius said, "The gentleman sets his heart on virtue, the petty man sets his heart on land.* The gentleman sets his heart on law, the petty man sets his heart on privilege."

12. Confucius said, "Conduct guided by profit is cause for much complaint."

13. Confucius said, "If a state is ruled with the rites and deference, what difficulties could there be? If a state is not ruled with the rites and deference, then of what use are the rites?"

14. Confucius said, "Do not be concerned when without official position, be concerned with where a stand is established. Do not be concerned when not appreciated, seek what can be appreciated."

15. Confucius said, "Ts'an,** the way I follow has one unifying principle."
Tseng Tzu said, "Yes."
After Confucius departed, his disciples asked, "What did he mean?"
Tseng Tzu said, "The way of the Master is simply loyalty and forgiveness."

16. Confucius said, "The gentleman understands righteousness, the petty man understands profit."

17. Confucius said, "Meet the virtuous and think how to be their match. Meet those not virtuous and examine yourself."

---

*I.e., on physical gain.
**Another name for Tseng Tzu.

18. Confucius said, "In serving parents, make suggestions tactfully, and if your aspirations are not pursued, still respect and do not disobey, bear burdens and do not complain."

19. Confucius said, "During your parents' lifetime, do not journey afar. If a journey has to be made, your direction must be told."

20. Confucius said, "If after three years* the father's way has not changed, this could be considered filial piety."

21. Confucius said, "Parents' ages should be known, for joy on one hand, for fear on the other."

22. Confucius said, "In ancient times, men hesitated to speak out, for their conduct, if falling short, would be shameful."

23. Confucius said, "It is seldom indeed that a man with temperance is lost."

24. Confucius said, "The gentleman wishes to be slow to speak but quick to act."

25. Confucius said, "With virtue there is no solitude, there is always company."

26. Tzu Yu said, "To be repetitive in serving the lord is to cause disgrace. To be repetitive with friends is to cause dispersion."

BOOK V

1. Confucius said of Kung-Yeh Ch'ang, "Marriageable indeed! Although he was tied with the black rope,** it was not his crime." He married his daughter to Kung-Yeh Ch'ang.

2. Confucius said of Nan Jung, "When the state is with the Way, he is not abandoned. When it is without the Way, he is free of punishment and persecution." He married his elder brother's daughter to Nan Jung.

3. Confucius said of Tzu Chien, "This man is indeed a gentleman! If the state of Lu had no gentlemen, how was he able to so attain?"

4. Tzu Kung asked, "What do you say about T'su?"
Confucius said, "You are an implement."
Tzu Kung said, "What sort of implement?"
Confucius said, "A *hu lien.*†"

---

*Three years after the father's death.
**In prison.
†A jade-encrusted bamboo implement used in sacrificial offerings as a container for grain.

5. Someone said, "Yung is benevolent and not an artful speaker."
Confucius said, "Of what use is artful speech? In self-defence such speech may often cause others' abhorrence. I do not know if he is benevolent, but of what use is artful speech?"

6. Confucius asked Ch'i-Tiao K'ai to assume public office. The reply was, "I am not yet to be so entrusted." Confucius was pleased.

7. Confucius said, "If the Way did not prevail, and I were on a raft drifting out at sea, Yu would be the one accompanying me." On hearing this, Tzu Lu was delighted. Confucius said, "Yu is more courageous than I. But from where would the materials be obtained?"*

8. Meng Wu Po asked if Tzu Lu was benevolent. Confucius said, "I do not know." When the question was repeated, Confucius said, "Yu** could be employed to manage the military responsibilities in a state of a thousand chariots, but I do not know if he is benevolent."
"And what about Ch'iu?"
Confucius said, "Ch'iu could be employed to head a community of a thousand households or a [ruling] family of a hundred chariots, but I do not know if he is benevolent."
"And what about Ch'ih?"
Confucius said, "His sash tied and standing at court, Ch'ih could be employed to converse with important guests, but I do not know if he is benevolent."

9. Confucius said to Tzu Kung, "Who is the better, you or Hui?"
The reply was, "How can I venture to compare myself with Hui? When Hui hears one thing, he is able to deduce ten. When I hear one thing, I may deduce two."
Confucius said, "You are not his equal. Neither of us is his equal."

10. Tsai Yu napped during the day. Confucius said, "Rotten wood cannot be carved nor a wall of dried dung trowelled. How would I rebuke Yu?" Confucius said, "I used to take a man at his word and trusted he would act accordingly. But now I listen to his words and note his actions. The change is due to Yu."

11. Confucius said, "I have yet to meet a man who is resolute."
Someone replied, "Shen Ch'eng?"
Confucius said, "Ch'eng is passionate. How could he be resolute?"

12. Tzu Kung said, "I do not wish to be imposed upon by others, nor do I wish to impose upon others."
Confucius said, "T'su,† that you have not attained."

13. Tzu Kung said, "The Master's literary pursuits are heard of but his words about nature and the Way of Heaven are not."

---

*The materials for construction of a raft. The allusion is that courage, while commendable, is insufficient by itself.
**Another name for Tzu Lu.
†Another name for Tzu Kung.

14. Tzu Lu was afraid that before he could act upon what he had heard there would be more.*

15. Tzu Kung asked, "Why was K'ung Wen Tzu called 'Wen'?"**
Confucius said, "He was quick and devoted to learning, and unashamed to ask of those below him. That is why he was called 'Wen.'"

16. Confucius said of Tzu Ch'an, "He has the way of the gentleman in four areas. He is courteous in his personal conduct. He is respectful in serving those above him. He is generous towards his people and righteous in employing the people."

17. Confucius said, "Yen P'ing Chung is good at dealing with people, and so there is respect, even after a long time."

18. Confucius said, "Tsang Wen Chung kept a *ts'ai*† in a house whose arches had landscape scenes and whose beams had seaweed patterns. What can be said of his wisdom!"

19. Tzu Chang asked, "On the three occasions when Tzu Wen assumed the public office of ling yin, he showed no signs of joy. On the three occasions when he was dismissed, he showed no signs of perturbation. He always briefed the new ling yin on policy matters. What do you say?"
Confucius said, "Loyalty indeed!"
Tzu Chang said, "Was that benevolence?"
Confucius said, "I do not know if that was benevolence."
"When Ts'ui Tzu assassinated the lord of Ch'i, Ch'en Wen Tzu who had ten teams of horses, abandoned his office and departed. Arriving in another state, he then said, 'The officials here are just the same as our Ts'ui Tzu.' He departed. Arriving in another state, he said again, 'The officials here are just the same as our Ts'ui Tzu,' and he departed. What do you say?"
Confucius said, "Pure indeed!"
Tzu Chang said, "Was that benevolence?"
Confucius said, "I do not know if that was benevolence."

20. Chi Wen Tzu thought three times before he acted. Hearing of this, Confucius said, "Twice is enough."

21. Confucius said, "Ning Wu Tzu was wise when the Way prevailed in the state, but dull-witted when the Way did not prevail in the state. His wisdom could be equalled, but his dull-wittedness could not be equalled."

---

*Meaning before he could fully absorb and implement Confucius' teachings, there would be more forthcoming.
**Posthumous recognition in the form of the addition of the character "Wen" to his name. "Wen" means "finesse."
†The *ts'ai* was a tortoise named for its place of origin, Ts'ai. The tortoise was used in divination and was held in such high esteem by Tsang Wen Chung that he fitted out a house in a manner he deemed pleasing to the tortoise. The landscape and seaweed decorative motifs were normally the prerogative of the emperor for his temples.

22. When he was in Ch'en, Confucius said, "Let us return. Let us return. The young people in our tang* are unrestrained and unpolished. Indeed they have accomplishments but they do not know how to tailor them to perfection."**

23. Confucius said, "Po Yi and Shu Ch'ih† bore no grudges, so there were few complaints."

24. Confucius said, "Who said that Wei-Sheng Kao is honest? When someone asked him for vinegar, he in turn asked for it from his neighbour, and then gave it as if it were his own."

25. Confucius said, "Clever talk, a pretentious manner and excessive courtesy were shameful to Tso Ch'iu Ming. [I] too consider them shameful. To harbour complaints against someone and yet befriend him was shameful to Tso Ch'iu Ming. [I] too consider it shameful."

26. When Yen Yuen and Chi Lu‡ were in attendance, Confucius said, "Why not tell me your aspirations."
Tzu Lu said, "I would like to share my horses and carriage, my clothes and furs with my friends, and not to regret it when they become worn."
Yen Yuen said, "I would like not to boast about my goodness and not to demand that services be extended to me."
Tzu Lu said, "I would like to hear to what my Master aspires."
Confucius said, "Comforting the aged, being trustworthy to friends, and caring for the young."

27. Confucius said, "All is lost! I have yet to meet the man who can see his own faults and censure himself!"

28. Confucius said, "In a [hamlet] of ten households, there must be men as loyal and trustworthy as [me] but they may be unequal in devotion to learning."

BOOK VI

1. Confucius said, "Yung can be employed in the seat that faces south."§

2. Chung Kung asked about Tzu-Sang Po Tzu. Confucius said, "He too can, for his directness."

---

*Feudal settlement of 500 families, used here to mean "community."
**Confucius was in the state of Ch'en to promote the Way. His efforts were not appreciated, and at this time, one of his disciples, Jan Ch'iu, was recalled to the state of Lu to take up public office. Predominantly for these reasons, Confucius pines for Lu and is concerned about the inexperience of the young, including Jan Ch'iu. Consequently, Confucius wishes also to return to Lu to make a positive contribution, to advocate the Way.
†Two sons of the lord of the state of Ku Chu in the Yin-Shang Dynasty who abdicated and became hermits.
‡Another name for Tzu Lu.
§The seat of a lord, south being the direction which the lord traditionally faced when seated at court.

Chung Kung said, "Is it not then acceptable for him to preside over the people with directness in implementing policies if he is respectful in living? Would there not be too much directness if there is directness in living and directness in implementing policies?"

Confucius said, "Yung, what you say is right."

3. Duke Ai asked, "Which disciple is devoted to learning?" Confucius replied, "There was Yen Hui, who was devoted to learning. He did not vent his anger on others nor make the same mistake twice. He lived a short life and died, unfortunately. Now there is none as devoted to learning, at least none of whom I have heard."

4. Tzu Hua went on a mission to Ch'i. When Jan Tzu requested grain for the mother of Ch'ih, Confucius said, "Give her one *fu.*" When Jan Tzu asked for more, Confucius said, "Give her one *yu.*"

Jan Tzu gave her five *ping** of grain.

Confucius said, "Ch'ih went to Ch'i clothed in furs and in a carriage drawn by well-fed horses. I have heard that a gentleman should help the needy, not the rich."

5. When Yuen Szu was head official to the family** and was given nine hundred measures of grain, he declined it. Confucius said, "Do not decline. Distribute it among your *lin, li, hsiang* and *tang.*"†

6. Confucius said of Chung Kung, "If the calf of a brindled cow has a coat of one colour and grown horns, would the gods of the mountains and rivers deny it even if men have reservations about its suitability?"

7. Confucius said, "Hui in his heart does not deviate from benevolence for three [months], while the others cease within a day or a moon."

8. Chi K'ang Tzu asked, "Is Chung Yu suited to public office?"

Confucius said, "Yu is decisive. What difficulties could there be in public office?"

Chi K'ang Tzu asked, "Is T'su suited to public office?"

Confucius said, "T'su is comprehending. What difficulties could there be in public office?"

Chi K'ang Tzu asked, "Is Ch'iu suited to public office?"

Confucius said, "Ch'iu is skillful. What difficulties could there be in public office?"

9. Chi sent an offer to Min Tzu Ch'ien to become head official of Fei. Min Tzu Ch'ien said, "Decline politely in my behalf. If the offer is made to me again, I will be at the River Wen."‡

10. Po Niu was seriously ill. Confucius visited him and held his hand through a window and said, "His death will be due to destiny. Such a man, such a serious illness! Such a man, such a serious illness!"

---

*One *fu* = 20.46 liters; one *yu* = 51.15 liters; one *ping* = 511.5 liters.

**Family of Confucius.

†Feudal settlements of 5 families, 25 families, 12,500 families and 500 families respectively.

‡Min Tzu Ch'ien discreetly declines the offer and makes it clear that he will leave the state of Lu rather than accept the offer.

11. Confucius said, "Virtuous indeed is Hui! One basket of food, one gourd of water, in a sparse alley. Hardship others cannot bear. Yet it does not change Hui's happiness. Virtuous indeed is Hui!"

12. Jan Ch'iu said, "It is not that I am not pleased with the Master's way, but that my strength is insufficient." Confucius said, "Where there is abandonment midway, strength is insufficient. Today you are drawing the line."*

13. Confucius said to Tzu Hsia, "You should be a gentleman scholar, not a petty scholar."

14. When Tzu Yu became head official of Wu Ch'eng, Confucius said, "Have you not found able men?"
Tzu Yu said, "There is Tan-T'ai Mieh Ming who does not take side paths. He has not come to Yen's house on unofficial matters."

15. Confucius said, "Meng Chih Fan does not boast. He was behind in the retreat, and last to enter through the gates, spurring his horse. He said, 'It was not bravery to be the last. My horse did not advance.'"

16. Confucius said, "Either the artfulness in speech of Chu T'o or the beauty of Sung Ch'ao . . . in this day and age, it is difficult to be spared!"

17. Confucius said, "Who can exit if not through the door? Through the Way, why none?"

18. Confucius said, "When substance overshadows refinement, there is the coarse man. When refinement overshadows substance, there is the court historian. When substance equates with refinement, there is the gentleman."

19. Confucius said, "Men live with honesty. The dishonest live, spared by fortune."

20. Confucius said, "Knowledge is not equal to devotion. Devotion is not equal to joy."

21. Confucius said, "It is possible to speak of lofty subjects with men who are above the average. It is not possible to speak of lofty subjects with men who are below the average."

22. Fan Ch'ih asked about wisdom. Confucius said, "To work for what is right for the people, and to respect the spirits and gods from afar, can be considered wisdom."
Fan Ch'ih asked about benevolence. Confucius said, "To be the first to face difficulties and the last to reap benefits can be considered benevolence."

23. Confucius said, "The wise enjoy the waters, the benevolent enjoy the mountains, the wise are active, the benevolent are placid, the wise are happy, the benevolent live long."

*Confucius tells Jan Ch'iu that it is only because he gives up or "draws the line" that he deems his own strength to be insufficient.

24. Confucius said, "With a single change, Ch'i could be Lu; with a single change Lu could be with the Way."*

25. Confucius said, "A *ku*** that is no longer a *ku! What a ku! What a ku!"*

26. Tsai Wo asked, "If a benevolent man were told that there was a man in a well, would he follow him?"

Confucius said, "Why should he? You might make a gentleman go there, but he cannot be trapped. You might try to deceive him, but he cannot be deluded."

27. Confucius said, "The gentleman studies literature extensively, is tempered by the rites, and is unlikely to go astray."

28. Confucius met with Nan Tzu.† Tzu Lu was not pleased. Confucius swore, "If I have done anything improper, may heaven forsake me, may heaven forsake me."

29. Confucius said, "The mean as a virtue is supreme indeed! For long it has been seldom among the people."

30. Tzu Kung said, "If the people are provided for extensively, and helped, what would you say? Can it be considered benevolence?"

Confucius said, "What has it to do with benevolence? Surely it is sagacious! Even Yao and Shun‡ found it difficult. As to the benevolent man, he establishes for others stands he wishes for himself. He brings others to reach where he wishes to reach himself. The ability to extend from self to others can be considered the direction towards benevolence."

BOOK VII

1. Confucius said, "To relate and not to invent, to believe in and to be devoted to antiquity. Permit me to compare myself to Lao P'eng."§

2. Confucius said, "To gain knowledge quietly, to learn without losing interest, to instruct others relentlessly, indeed, what difficulty for me?"

3. Confucius said, "Virtue not cultivated, learning not expounded, not able to accommodate righteousness having heard of it, not able to correct what is not good . . . they trouble me."

---

*In Confucius' view, the worldly pursuits of the wealthy state of Ch'i place it below the more spiritually oriented state of Lu. By the "single change," Confucius is thought to have meant an improvement in politics and education.

**The *ku* was a small drinking cup originally used in rituals. Its accepted size and shape had been altered to facilitate drinking and Confucius laments the predominance of drinking over rituals.

†A notorius wife of Duke Ling of Wei.

‡Ancient emperors much revered by Confucius.

§Virtuous official of the Yin-Shang Dynasty who had great respect for antiquity.

4. At leisure Confucius was sedate and tranquil.

5. Confucius said, "How weak I have become! For a long time I have not dreamed about the Duke of Chou."

6. Confucius said, "Aspire to the Way, align with virtue, abide by benevolence, and immerse yourself in the arts."

7. Confucius said, "I have yet to not instruct even someone who comes with a small bundle of dried meat."

8. Confucius said, "Without determination, there can be no revelation [of knowledge], without anxiety to express convictions, there can be no illumination. To have one corner [of a square] identified and not be able to revert by identifying the other three: there can be nothing further."

9. When Confucius was eating with a mourner, he never satiated himself.

10. On that day, the Master wept, and did not sing.

11. Confucius said to Yen Yuen, "Implementing it [the Way] when employed and keeping it safe when not, only you and I do so!"
Tzu Lu said, "If my Master led the three armies who would be with you?"
Confucius said, "Not the man who would die without remorse fighting a tiger or braving a river, but the man who would be devoted to planning and accomplishing tasks which he approaches with fear."

12. Confucius said, "If riches could be acquired, I would be willing to become even a whip holder. Since they cannot be acquired, I follow that to which I am devoted."

13. Confucius was prudent about abstinence, war and illness.

14. While in Ch'i, Confucius heard *Shao*.* For three [months] he did not know the taste of meat. He said, "I never imagined that music could attain such."

15. Jan Yu said, "Is the Master for the lord of Wei?"** Tzu Kung said, "I will ask him."
He then entered and said,
"What sort of men were Po Yi and Shu Ch'i?"
Confucius said, "Virtuous men of ancient times."
Tzu Kung asked, "Did they complain?"
Confucius said, "They sought and attained benevolence. What complaint could they have?"
Tzu Kung departed and said, "The Master is not for him."

---

*Music adopted by the Emperor Shun when he gained rulership.
**Duke Ch'u, who was established as lord of the state of Wei by the people while his father, K'uai K'ui, was still alive and residing in Chin, where he had been forced to flee by his father, Duke Ling of Wei. In the state of Chin, K'uai K'ui was recognised as the rightful lord of Wei.

16. Confucius said, "Simple meals, water to drink, bent elbow for pillow: therein is happiness. Riches and position without righteousness are to me as the floating clouds."

17. Confucius said, "Give me a few more years to learn at the age of fifty, and I will be unlikely to have major faults."

18. Confucius spoke *ya:** for poetry, books, and performing the rites, he always spoke *ya.*

19. The Duke of Yeh asked Tzu Lu about Confucius. Tzu Lu did not reply. Confucius said, "Why did you not say: 'He is a man whose determination makes him forget to eat, whose happiness makes him forget his troubles and who knows not that old age is stealing upon him'?"

20. Confucius said, "I was not born knowledgeable, I am devoted to antiquity and am quick to seek knowledge."

21. Confucius did not talk about prodigies, force, disorders and gods.

22. Confucius said, "When three men walk together, there is always something I can learn. Choose to follow what is good in them and correct what is not good."

23. Confucius said, "My virtue is from heaven. What can Huan T'ui** do to me?"

24. Confucius said, "My pupils, do you think that I conceal anything? I conceal nothing from you. I do not act without my pupils. This is Ch'iu."

25. The four teachings of Confucius: literature, conduct, loyalty and trustworthiness.

26. Confucius said, "I have not yet met a sage. I would accept meeting a gentleman."
Confucius said, "I have not yet met an altruistic man. I would accept meeting a man of principles. To have not taken as to have, to be vacant taken as to be filled, to be in adversity taken as to be at peace, it is difficult indeed to be principled."

27. In fishing, Confucius did not use a net. In fowling, Confucius did not shoot at a roosting bird.

28. Confucius said, "There are men who invent what they do not know. I do not. To listen extensively, to choose to follow what is good, to observe extensively to gain knowledge, are next to knowledge."

29. It was difficult to talk with the people of Hu Hsiang. The disciples were perplexed when a boy was received. Confucius said, "I am for his advancement, not for his regression. Is that too much? When a person cleanses himself in order to advance, be for his cleansing without vouching for his past."

---

*The dialect of Hao, the capital of the Western Chou Dynasty. Confucius demonstrated his profound respect for the past by using this older dialect for important matters.
**Official of the state of Sung who threatened to have Confucius killed.

30. Confucius said, "Is benevolence so far away? I wish for benevolence, and benevolence is attained."

31. A *szu pai** of Ch'en asked, "Does Duke Chao know the rites?" Confucius said, "He knows the rites."
Confucius retired. The *szu pai* greeted Wu-Ma Ch'i, showed him in, and said, "I have heard that the gentleman does not take sides. Does the gentleman take sides? The lord married someone from Wu who shares his surname, and referred to her as Wu Meng Tzu.** If the lord knows the rites, who does not know the rites?"
Wu-Ma Ch'i reported this to Confucius who said, "I am fortunate. When I make a mistake people know about it."

32. In singing, when the song was good, Confucius would have it repeated, then joined in the singing.

33. Confucius said, "In literature, I am barely comparable with others. But as to being a dedicated gentleman, this I have yet to attain."

34. Confucius said, "Would I venture to call myself a sage or a benevolent man? At most, it might be said that I so pursue without losing interest and instruct others relentlessly." Kung-Hsi Hua said, "This is what your disciples have not been able to learn."

35. Confucius was seriously ill. Tzu Lu asked to pray in his behalf. Confucius said, "Is it done?" Tzu Lu replied, "Yes. The ancient prayer was, 'Pray thee to the gods and deities above and below,'" Confucius said, "[I] have prayed so for a long time."

36. Confucius said, "With extravagance there is no humility, with frugality there is miserliness. Rather be miserly than without humility."

37. Confucius said, "The gentleman is free and bountiful. The petty man is bound and grieving."

38. Confucius was gentle yet strict, awe-inspiring yet not fearful, and courteous yet at ease.

BOOK VIII

1. Confucius said, "T'ai Po could indeed be called supreme in virtue! Three times he renounced his right to rule all under heaven, and the people had no opportunity to praise him."

2. Confucius said, "Courtesy without the rites is labour lost. Prudence without the rites is timidity. Courage without the rites is disorder. Honesty without the rites is impatience. When the gentleman cherishes his family, the people are inspired towards benevolence. When he does not desert that of long standing, the people are not stealthy."

---

*An official of the state of Ch'en in charge of judicial matters.
**She should be called Wu Chi. He is trying to hide that she is from the same clan.

3. Tseng Tzu was seriously ill. He summoned his disciples and said, "Uncover my feet, uncover my hands. The *Odes* say

> Shaking and tremulous
> As if faced with a deep pit,
> As if treading on thin ice,

and from now on I know I can be exempted from it, my young ones!"*

4. Tseng Tzu was seriously ill. When Meng Ching Tzu asked after him, Tseng Tzu said,

> "Sorrowful are the cries of a dying bird,
> Good are the words of a dying man.

The Way of the gentleman has three aspects which he values: in forming facial expressions, to avoid displays of bad temper and impropriety, in moderating countenance, to approach trustworthiness, in speaking, to avoid crudeness and the unreasonable. Matters of the *pien* and the *tou*** are in the care of officials with delegated duties."

5. Tseng Tzu said, "To be capable, yet to consult those not capable, to have plenty yet to consult those with little, to have and appearing to have not, to be of substance and appearing to be vacant, to be transgressed against, yet not to mind. I once had a friend who was so."

6. Tseng Tzu said, "The man who may be charged with the care of an orphan of six *ch'ih*† [tall], assigned powers over a hundred *li*‡ [square], and is not robbed of his principles when faced with crises, is a gentleman. He is a gentleman."

7. Tseng Tzu said, "A scholar must not be without scope and persistence, for his responsibility is weighty and his way is long. Benevolence is the responsibility he has taken upon himself: is it not weighty? Only after his death does it end: is it not long?"

8. Confucius said, "Thrive with the *Odes*, establish stands with the rites, and accomplish with music."

9. Confucius said, "The people may be made to follow, but may not be made to know."

10. Confucius said, "Inclining to courage and deploring poverty would cause disorder. Excessive deploring of men who are not benevolent would cause disorder."

---

*The imminent death of Tseng Tzu will release him from the concept of honouring parents by caring for one's own health.

**Pien* and *tou* are containers for food used in sacrifical offerings, and here represent details of the rites.

†The exact length of the ancient *ch'ih* is not clear. Here "six *ch'ih*" refers to the height of a person of fifteen years and under.

‡"A hundred *li*" can be interpreted as a "feudal settlement of 2,500 families" or "a hundred Chinese miles." "A hundred *li*" is used here to mean "a large state."

11. Confucius said, "Even with the fine talents of the Duke of Chou, the other qualities of a man who is arrogant and stinting would not be noteworthy."

12. Confucius said, "It is not easy to study for three years and not resort to gain."*

13. Confucius said, "Adhere to your beliefs and be devoted to learning. Secure to the death the good of the Way. Enter not a state in danger. Live not in a state in disorder. When all under heaven are with the Way, be visible. When without the Way, be secluded. When the state is with the Way, to be poor and lowly is shameful. When the state is without the Way, to have riches and position is shameful."

14. Confucius said, "When not in the official position, do not be involved with its policies."

15. Confucius said, "From when the music master Chih begins, till the conclusion of the *Kuan sui*,** how exhilarating to the ear."

16. Confucius said, "Unrestrained and not honest, ignorant and not conscientious, deficient and not trustworthy: I do not know about this!"

17. Confucius said, "Learn as if behind, and still be afraid of losing what has been learned."

18. Confucius said, "How magnificent: Shun and Yu† had all under heaven, yet they remained unaffected."

19. Confucius said, "Great indeed was Yao‡ as lord! How magnificent that great is heaven, that Yao was comparable! How bountiful that people had no words for it! How magnificent were his accomplishments! How glorious were his literary pursuits!"

20. Shun had five officials and all under heaven were governed. Emperor Wu had said he had ten able officials.
Confucius said, "It is true that talent is difficult to find. Following the T'ang and the Yu, talent should have been plentiful. Yet one was a woman, so there were nine. With two-thirds of all under heaven, yet still serving the Yin, the virtue of the Chou could indeed be called supreme."

21. Confucius said, "I can find no fault with Yu. He ate and drank sparingly yet did his best in the filial duties to the spirits [of ancestors] and gods. He wore wretched clothing yet donned the best ceremonial attire. He lived in bare dwellings yet he spent all his strength in irrigation projects. I can find no fault with Yu."

---

*Confucius deems it more admirable not to study with the aim of becoming an official, as many scholars of his day did.

**The first of the *Odes*.

†Ancient emperors revered by Confucius.

‡Ancient emperor revered by Confucius.

BOOK IX

1. Confucius seldom spoke of profit. He ascribed to destiny, he ascribed to benevolence.

2. The people of Ta Hang Tang said, "Confucius is great indeed! He has extensive learning, without having accomplished his name in any area."

Hearing of this, Confucius said to his disciples, "To what should I hold? To horsemanship? To archery? I shall hold to horsemanship."

3. Confucius said, "A ceremonial headdress of flax is prescribed by the rites. Today, silk is used for economy, and I follow the majority. To bow below* is prescribed by the rites. Today, bowing is done above, casually. Though contrary to the majority, bowing below is what I follow."

4. Confucius never allowed four things: he allowed no speculation, no absolute definitude, no inflexibility and no selfishness.

5. When threatened in K'uang, Confucius said, "With the death of Emperor Wen, has *wen* [culture] ceased to exist? If heaven had allowed *wen* to perish, then those who came after would not have had *wen*. Since heaven has not yet allowed *wen* to perish, what can the people of K'uang do to me?"

6. A senior head official asked Tzu Kung, "Is your Master a sage? How is it that he has so many abilities?" Tzu Kung said, "Because heaven allows him to be a sage and to have many abilities."

On hearing of this, Confucius said, "Does the senior head official know me? I was of lowly station when young. So I am able in many menial matters. Should a gentleman have many abilities? Not many."

7. Lao said, "The Master has said, 'I am not put to the test [in public office]. So I have many skills.'"

8. Confucius said, "Do I have wisdom? I have no wisdom. If a crude man asked me a question in all candour, I would tap its two extremes, doing my best."

9. Confucius said, "The Phoenix has not come. The River has no patterns.** This is the end for me!"

10. When Confucius saw men in mourning attire or in ceremonial headdress and garments, or who were blind, he would rise even if they were younger than he, and when passing by them, he would quicken his pace!†

---

*Chou Dynasty etiquette prescribed that exchange of courtesies should begin at the foot of the steps (to a hall, for example). In Confucius' day, most people dispensed with this formality, and exchange of courtesies commenced only when the guest reached the upper part of the hall.

**The Phoenix and river patterns Chart were good omens.

†To show respect by leaving whatever he was attending to at the time, and to make way for those in mourning and for the blind.

11. Yen Yuen sighed, lamented and said, "Look up to it [i.e., the Way], and it is ever higher. Penetrate it, and it is ever harder. See it ahead, and suddenly it is behind. The Master guides and steers men to goodness: I am extended through literature, I am tempered through the rites. Wishing to stop yet unable, having done my best with my talents, it seems to stand at such an awesome height, that even though I wish to follow, there is no course to it."

12. Confucius was seriously ill. Tzu Lu sent the disciples to be family officials.* When Confucius was better, he said, "Yu's** conduct is deceptive indeed. To have no family officials yet as if to have: who would I be deceiving? Deceiving heaven? I would rather die at the hands of my pupils, than at the hands of family officials. Even if I were not allowed a grand burial, would I die by the roadside?"

13. Tzu Kung said, "If there was a beautiful piece of jade, should it be kept safely in a box? Or should a good offer be sought for the sale of it?" Confucius said, "Sell it, indeed. Sell it, indeed. I for one await the offer."

14. Confucius wished to live among the nine tribes of Yi.† Someone said, "It is so sparse. How could you?" Confucius said, "With a gentleman living there, how could it be sparse?"

15. Confucius said, "I returned to Lu from Wei and then righted music, with the *ya* and the *sung*‡ in their places."

16. Confucius said, "Out in the world, of service to high-ranking officials, in the home, of service to father and elder brothers. Venture not to be lax in matters of mourning, not to be ensnared by drinking wine. Indeed, what difficulty for me?"

17. By a river, Confucius said, "What has passed has passed, like this . . . day and night, not pausing."

18. Confucius said, "I have yet to meet the man who is as devoted to virtue as to beauty."

19. Confucius said, "If work halts, as when it does only one basketful of earth short of completing a mound, it would be I who halt it. If work advances, as when it does with only one basketful of earth poured in levelling the ground, it would be I who make it proceed."

20. Confucius said, "One I could talk to, who would not slacken, would be Hui!"

21. Confucius said of Yen Yuen, "How piteous! I saw him advance. I had yet to see him halt."

22. Confucius said, "There are seedlings that do not bear flowers. There are flowers that do not bear fruits."

---

*At this time Confucius was not in public office and therefore it was improper for him to have family officials.

**Another name for Tzu Lu.

†Uncivilized tribes to the East of China.

‡The *ya* and the *sung* are sections in the *Odes.*

23. Confucius said, "Regard the young with apprehension, for who knows if the future will not be comparable to the present? At forty to fifty and still unheard of is to be not worthy of apprehension."

24. Confucius said, "Can severe words of advice not be followed? Their value is in the reforming. Can soothing words of endorsement not be pleasing? Their value is in the assessment. To be pleased, but not to assess. To follow, but not to reform. I know not what is to be done."

25. Confucius said, "Advocate loyalty and trustworthiness. Have no friends who are not your equals. Do not hesitate to correct faults."

26. Confucius said, "The three armies can be deprived of their commanding officer, but a common man cannot be deprived of his aspirations."

27. Confucius said, "Clothed in a shabby coat, yet unashamed to stand with men in furs of fox and raccoon-dog, is Yu.

> Not invidious, not avaricious.
> Naught but superb."

Tzu Lu recited [these lines] all his life.
Confucius said, "It is with the Way, but not quite superlative."

28. Confucius said, "Comes the cold of winter, then it is known that the pine and the cypress are the last to wither."

29. Confucius said, "With wisdom, there is no delusion, with benevolence, there is no worry, with courage, there is no fear."

30. Confucius said, "To learn together does not mean concurring in the pursuit of the Way. To concur in the pursuit of the Way does not mean establishing the same stand. To establish the same stand does not mean making the same value judgements."

31.   How the aspen plums blossom and dance!
      How can I not think of thee?
      Thine home is far.

Confucius said, "Perhaps there is no thinking, else how could it be far?"

BOOK X

1. Within his *hsiang* and *tang,** Confucius was unassuming and seemed inarticulate. At the ancestral shrine and at court, he spoke fluently, though with prudence.

---

*Feudal settlements of 12,500 families and 500 families respectively, used here to mean "native communities."

2. At court, [Confucius] conversed cordially with junior officials; with senior officials, he conversed formally. In the presence of his lord, he was politely constrained, and he was composed.

3. When summoned by his lord to receive guests, [Confucius] wore a serious expression and walked cautiously. He greeted those standing to his left and to his right and his robes flowed about him without disarray. He proceeded, quickening his pace, as if on wings. After the important guests had retired, he always reported on his duties, and said, "The guests have gone their way."

4. On entering the lord's gates, [Confucius] bowed respectfully as though unworthy, not pausing midway nor stepping on the threshold.

On passing by a designated seat, he wore a serious expression. He walked cautiously and spoke as though inadequate. He lifted the hem of his robes to ascend to the hall, and bowed respectfully, holding his breath.

On departing, he descended the first step, regaining his colour, and he was amicable. Having descended, he quickened his pace as if on wings.

On passing again a designated seat, he was politely constrained.

5. Holding the *kui*,* [Confucius] was bowed respectfully as though not qualified, holding it not above where hands are clasped in greeting, nor below where gifts are proffered. Serious, and appearing to shake, he walked gingerly, as though along a track. When the gifts were presented, he appeared relieved and he was relaxed when received informally.

6. The gentleman does not have robes trimmed in dark purple and red, and casual clothing in red and purple. In hot weather, he wears an unlined flaxen robe, donning another robe when he goes out.

Under a black robe, he wears black lambskin; under an undyed robe, fawnskin; under a yellow robe, fox fur.

His casual furs are long, but with short right sleeves.

The covers in his bedchamber are half as long again as the body.

Thick furs of fox and raccoon-dog are for seating. Except when in mourning, he wears jade ornaments. But for ceremonial garments, his skirts are cut on the bias.

He does not wear black lambskin or a dark headdress when paying a condolence call.

On the first day of each new moon, he always wears court attire and attends at court.

7. In abstinence, always wear the white garment which is of plain cloth. In abstinence, always change to the diet, always move to the chamber.**

8. Do not eat to the fill of the finest.

Do not eat to the fill of the best cuts.

---

*Jade tablet carried by an official on official business to display authority assigned to him by his lord. Protocol required a three-step process: formal presentation of the *kui*, formal presentation of the gifts, and the less formal reception that followed.

**Abstinence began with bathing, after which a simple garment was donned, a vegetarian diet adopted, and one retreated to a special chamber within the household set aside for abstinence, and convalescing during illness. Abstinence usually preceded sacrificial offerings.

Do not eat food that has turned and smells, or fish that has spoiled and meat that has gone bad.

Do not eat what looks bad.

Do not eat what smells bad.

Do not eat what is poorly cooked.

Do not eat at inappropriate times.

Do not eat what is not correctly cut.

Do not eat without the appropriate sauces.

Even when meat is plentiful, it should not overshadow the staples.

When the supply of wine is unlimited, do not become disorderly.

Do not have wine and dried meat purchased from the marketplace.

Do not eat too much from the side dish of ginger not cleared away.

9. Do not keep the meat overnight after a public sacrificial offering. Sacrificial meat does not last for more than three days.

Do not eat it after more than three days.

10. Do not converse while eating.

Do not talk once abed.

11. Even from a simple meal of soup and vegetables, always make a solemn offering.

12. When the mat is not straight, do not sit.

13. When drinking with people of the *hsiang*,* depart only after the elders.

14. When people of the *hsiang* perform exorcisms, wear court attire and stand on the eastern steps.**

15. When despatching his greetings to someone in another state prior to seeing him off, [Confucius] bowed repeatedly before the bearer.

16. When K'ang Tzu sent him medicine, he bowed, accepted it, and said, "Since [I] am not yet familiar with its properties, I shall not venture to try it."

17. When the stable caught fire, Confucius retired from court and said, "Is anyone hurt?" He did not ask about the horses.

18. When given food by the lord, always straighten the mat and try it immediately. When given uncooked meat by the lord, always cook it and make an offering from it. When given livestock by the lord, always rear it. In attendance to the lord at meals, when the lord is making the offering, try the food first.

19. In illness when visited by the lord, lie with head to the East, covered in court attire and draped with sash.

*Feudal settlement of 12,500 families, used here to mean "native land."

**Of the ancestral shrine, in the designated spot of the presiding person responsible to comfort and protect his ancestors.

20. When summoned by the lord, make ready to depart before the carriage is harnessed.

21. On entering the grand temple, ask about every detail.

22. At the death of a friend without family, [Confucius] said, "Let me be responsible for the funeral."

23. For gifts from a friend, even carriages and horses, if not sacrificial meat, he did not bow.

24. In bed, do not stretch out in repose. At leisure, do not assume the manner of a guest.

25. On seeing a man in mourning attire, even though familiar, always assume a different expression. On seeing a man in ceremonial headdress or a man who is blind, even though well known, assume the proper expression.
Towards a man with mourning attire, even a common tradesman, lean forward, placing the hands on the carriage cross-bar.*
When having a grand meal, always assume a different expression and rise in acknowledgement. And at sudden thunder or strong wind, always assume a different expression.

26. When ascending into the carriage, always stand correctly and hold on to the mounting cord. Within the carriage, do not look back, do not speak loudly, and do not point.

27. Startled, the birds took flight, and circled about before alighting together. [Confucius] said, "The hen-pheasants on the mountain bridge . . . Timely indeed! Timely indeed!" Tzu Lu made a meal of pheasant. Confucius savoured the aroma three times, but rose and departed.

BOOK XI

1. Confucius said, "Those of preceding eras who were with the rites and music are considered coarse men. Those of succeeding eras who are with the rites and music are considered gentlemen. In practice, I would rather follow those of preceding eras."

2. Confucius said, "Those who followed me to Ch'en and Ts'ai are all with me no longer."

3. "In virtuous conduct: Yen Yuen, Min Tzu Ch'ien, Jan Po Niu and Chung Kung; in speech: Tsai Wo and Tzu Kung; in policy matters: Jan Yu and Chi Lu; in literature: Tzu Yu and Tzu Hsia."

4. Confucius said, "Hui is not helping me! He is never displeased with what I say."

*As a mark of respect.

5. Confucius said, "What filial piety has Min Tzu Ch'ien! No one can dispute what even his parents and brothers say about him."

6. Nan Jung repeated "The white jade"* three times. Confucius married his elder brother's daughter to Nan Jung.

7. Chi K'ang Tzu asked, "Which disciple is devoted to learning?" Confucius replied, "There was Yen Hui, who was devoted to learning. He lived a short life and died, unfortunately. Now there is none."

8. When Yen Yuen died, Yen Lu** requested the carriage of Confucius for an outer coffin. Confucius said, "Whether they are talented or not talented, they are but our sons of whom we talk. Li† who is also dead, had an inner coffin but not an outer coffin. I would not walk for an outer coffin, for to follow in the footsteps of officials, walking would not do."‡

9. When Yen Yuen died, Confucius said, "Alas! Heaven is my bereavement! Heaven is my bereavement!"

10. When Yen Yuen died, Confucius wept excessively. His followers said, "Master, you are being excessive!" He said, "Excessive? But if not for him, then excessive for whom?"

11. When Yen Yuen died, the disciples wished to give him an elaborate burial. Confucius said, "Do it not." They gave him an elaborate burial anyway. Confucius said, "Hui looked upon me as a father, but I was not able to look upon him as a son. It was not my doing, it was my pupils."

12. Chi Lu asked about serving the spirits and gods. Confucius said, "Not able to serve the living, how is it possible to serve the spirits?" Chi Lu ventured to ask about death. Confucius said, "Not knowing about life, how is it possible to know about death?"

13. In attendance to Confucius, Min Tzu was formal, Tzu Lu was firm, Jan Yu and Tzu Kung were cordial. Confucius was happy. He lamented, "As for Yu, he is unlikely to die a natural death."

14. The people of Lu were about to reconstruct the treasury. Min Tzu Ch'ien said, "What do you say to keeping things as they are? Why must changes be made?"
Confucius said, "This man speaks seldom, but what he says is always valid."

15. Confucius said, "The *se*§ of Yu played within [my] door?" The disciples no longer respected Tzu Lu. Confucius said, "Yu has yet to enter the inner chamber, but he has ascended to the hall."

*Lines from the *Odes,* about prudence in speech.
**Yen Yuen's father.
†Confucius' son.
‡Confucius, himself previously an official, wished to preserve the dignity of officials. They were expected to travel by carriage.
§The *se* was an ancient, 25-string musical instrument, said to be played to best advantage by refined persons. As good a disciple and person as Yu was, Confucius, his teacher, considered there was room for improvement.

Confucian Temple
Apricot Rostrum Pavilion in the Confucius Temple,
Ch'u-fu (Qufu), Shantung (Shandong) Province.
According to tradition, Confucius gave lectures on this
site in his hometown. *(Forrest E. Baird)*

16. Tzu Kung asked, "Who is more virtuous, Shih or Shang?" Confucius said,
"Shih goes beyond, Shang falls short."
   Tzu Kung said, "Then is Shih better?"
   Confucius said, "To go beyond is the same as to fall short."

17. Chi was richer than the Duke of Chou, yet Ch'iu gathered more for him,
adding to his gains. Confucius said, "He is not my pupil. My young ones, you may beat
the drums and assail him."

18. [Confucius said,] "Ch'ai is dull-witted, Ts'an is simple-minded, Shih is remote, Yu is headstrong."

19. Confucius said, "Hui, who is almost perfect, is often without. T'su, who has
not accepted his destiny and has taken to trading, is often accurate in estimating."

20. Tzu Chang asked about the way of the altruistic man. Confucius said, "Not
traversing the worn way and not entering the inner chamber."

21. Confucius said, "His opinions are expressed with sincerity. Is he a gentleman? Or is he merely dignified by appearance?"

22. Tzu Lu asked, "Should actions be based on what is heard?" Confucius said, "With father and elder brothers still living, how can actions be based on what is heard?"*

Jan Yu asked, "Should actions be based on what is heard?" Confucius said, "Act on what is heard."

Kung-Hsi Hua said, "When Yu asked if actions should be based on what is heard, my Master said that his father and elder brothers are still living. When Ch'iu asked if actions should be based on what is heard, my Master said that he should act on what is heard. [I am] perplexed . . . may I enquire?"

Confucius said, "Ch'iu is deterred. Therefore I impel him. Yu is boundless. Therefore I deter him."

23. When Confucius was threatened in K'uang, Yen Yuen fell behind. Confucius said, "I thought you were dead." Yen Yuen said, "While my Master lives, how could [I] venture to die?"

24. Chi Tzu Jan** asked whether Chung Yu and Jan Ch'iu could be considered great officials.

Confucius said, "I thought you would ask about other than Yu and Ch'iu. Those considered great officials serve their lords with the Way until such is of no avail, then halt. Now, Yu and Ch'iu may be considered officials of convenience."

Chi Tzu Jan said, "In that case, would they just follow?"

Confucius said, "In patricide and regicide, they would not follow."

25. Tzu Lu sent Tzu Kao to be head official of Fei. Confucius said, "This destroys the son of another man."

Tzu Lu said, "There are the people, there are shrines to the *she chi.*† Why must book learning alone constitute learning?"

Confucius said, "This is why I hate artful speakers!"

26. Tzu Lu, Tseng Hsi, Jan Yu and Kung-Hsi Hua were seated in attendance to Confucius. Confucius said, "Do not be constrained with me because I am one day older than you, while ordinarily you would say, 'I am not appreciated.' What if you were appreciated?"

Tzu Lu replied promptly, "In a state of a thousand chariots caught between large states, with the addition of military operations and famine, if [I] were to rule, within three years the people would be made courageous, and their direction known."

Confucius smiled.

"Ch'iu, what about you?"

The reply was, "In a settlement of sixty to seventy, or even fifty to sixty measures if [I] were to rule, within three years the people would be made plentiful. As for the rites and music, I would rely on other gentlemen."

---

*According to the dictates of filial piety, parents and elder brothers had to be consulted first and respected.

**Member of the Chi Family, which employed Chung Yu and Jan Ch'iu.

†Shrines to the gods of earth and grain which received homage wherever they were erected, in states and their subordinate settlements.

"Ch'ih, what about you?"

The reply was, "I would not call myself capable, only willing to learn. In matters of the ancestral shrine and official gatherings, I would don the ceremonial attire and be willing to be a minor assistant."

"Tien, what about you?"

Strumming the *se,* striking a final note, putting the *se* aside, Tien rose and replied, "Mine is different and cannot compare with the other three."

Confucius said, "What does it matter? Each just speaks of his own aspirations."

Tseng Hsi said, "During late spring, with spring clothes, with five to six [adults] and six to seven boys, I would like to bathe in the River Yi, enjoy the breezes at the rain altar, and chant, before returning."

The Master sighed, lamented and said, "I am with Tien."

The three disciples departed. Tseng Hsi stayed behind. He said, "What do you say to that which the other three said?"

Confucius said, "Each just speaks of his own aspirations."

Tseng Hsi asked, "Then Master, why did you smile at Yu?"

Confucius said, "A state should be ruled with the rites. He spoke without deference. Therefore I smiled. Did Ch'iu not have a state in mind? A mere settlement of sixty to seventy or fifty to sixty measures is still a state, is it not? Did Ch'ih not have a state in mind? Ancestral shrines and official gatherings are matters for the lords, are they not? If Ch'ih were to have a minor role, who could have a major part?"

BOOK XII

1. Yen Yuen asked about benevolence. Confucius said, "To discipline self to fulfill the rites is benevolence. The day when self-discipline fulfills the rites, all under heaven would be with benevolence. Indeed, the practices of benevolence originate from self and not from others!"

Yen Yuen said, "May I ask for more details?" Confucius said, "Do not look at what is not in accordance with the rites; do not listen to what is not in accordance with the rites; do not speak when it is not in accordance with the rites; do not act when it is not in accordance with the rites."

Yen Yuen said, "[I], though not quick, will attempt to do things in accordance with these words."

2. Chung Kung asked about benevolence. Confucius said, "Beyond your door, conduct yourself as if meeting important guests. In employing the people, conduct yourself as if making important offerings. What you do not wish upon yourself, extend not to others. In the state there will be no complaints, in the family there will be no complaints."

Chung Kung said, "[I], though not quick, will attempt to do things in accordance with these words."

3. Szu-Ma Niu asked about benevolence. Confucius said, "The benevolent speak with effort."

Szu-Ma Niu asked, "Can a man be considered benevolent because he speaks with effort?"

Confucius said, "When doing is difficult, would speaking not be with effort?"*

4. Szu-Ma Niu asked about the gentleman. Confucius said, "The gentleman is without worry, without fear."

Szu-Ma Niu asked, "Can a man be considered a gentleman because he is without worry, without fear?"

Confucius said, "When upon self-examination there is no self-recrimination, why would there be worry, why would there be fear?"

5. Szu-Ma Niu was worried and said, "All men have brothers but I, who have none." Tzu-Hsia said, "Shang has heard that life and death are predestined, riches and position are up to heaven. The gentleman is respectful and does no wrong, courteous towards others, and is with the rites. All within the four seas are his brothers. Why should the gentleman be concerned about not having brothers?"

6. Tzu Chang asked about enlightenment. Confucius said, "To be unaffected by accumulative slander and nagging grievances can be considered as enlightened. To be unaffected by accumulative slander and nagging grievances can be considered as far-sighted."

7. Tzu Kung asked about ruling. Confucius said, "Sufficient food, sufficient arms, and the trust of the people."

Tzu Kung said, "If one had to be dispensed with, which of the three should be first?"

Confucius said, "Dispense with arms."

Tzu Kung said, "If one had to be dispensed with, which of the remaining two should be first?"

Confucius said, "Dispense with food. Death has always been since the beginning of time, but without trust, the people could not establish their stand."

8. Chi Tzu Ch'eng said, "For the gentleman substance is everything. What need is there for refinement?" Tzu Kung said, "A pity! Sir, as to what you have said about the gentleman, 'Four horses cannot overtake a man's tongue.' Refinement is as substance, substance is as refinement. The pelt of a tiger or leopard is as the pelt of a dog or goat."

9. Duke Ai asked Yu Jo, "In this time of famine, resources are insufficient. What is to be done?"

Yu Jo replied, "Why not tax the people one part in ten?"

Duke Ai said, "It is two parts in ten, and I deem it insufficient. What is to be done if the people are taxed one part in ten?"

The reply was, "If it is sufficient for the people, how could it be insufficient for the lord? If it is insufficient for the people, how could it be sufficient for the lord?"

10. Tzu Chang asked about exaltation of virtue and recognition of delusion. Confucius said, "Advocating loyalty and trustworthiness, and accommodating righteousness are to exalt virtue. Wishing a man would live forever when you love him and wishing a man would die when you hate him . . . having wished he would live forever, to wish he would die, is delusion.

---

*I.e., it would be difficult to live up to one's words.

It is without enrichment,
It only detracts."

11. Duke Ching of Ch'i asked Confucius about ruling. Confucius replied, "Let the lords be lords, the subjects be subjects, the fathers be fathers, the sons be sons."

Duke Ching said, "How well said! If the lords were unlike lords, the subjects unlike subjects, the fathers unlike fathers, the sons unlike sons, then even if there were grain, would I be able to eat it?"

12. Confucius said, "If anyone can resolve a legal dispute based on the evidence of only one side, it is Yu. Tzu Lu never delayed for a night keeping his promise."

13. Confucius said, "In hearing litigation, I am just like other men, but I try always to eliminate the need for litigation too."

14. Tzu Chang asked about ruling. Confucius said, "Be relentless, act loyally."

15. Confucius said, "Study literature extensively, temper it with the rites, and be unlikely to go astray."

16. Confucius said, "The gentleman helps others to accomplish good. He does not help others to accomplish vice. The petty man does the reverse."

17. Chi K'ang Tzu asked Confucius about ruling. Confucius replied, "Ruling is as right.* Sir, when you command with right, who would venture not to be with right?"

18. Chi K'ang Tzu, concerned about stealing, consulted Confucius. Confucius replied, "If you, sir, were not covetous, no one would steal, even if there were a reward for it."

19. Chi K'ang Tzu asked Confucius about ruling, "What would you say if those without the Way were to be killed for the sake of those with the Way?"

Confucius replied, "Sir, when you rule, why resort to killing? When you wish for good, the people will be good. The virtues of the lord are as the wind, the virtues of the people are as the grass. The grass bends with the wind."

20. Tzu Chang asked what a scholar must do to be considered successful. Confucius said, "What do you mean by 'successful'?"

Tzu Chang replied, "He must be famous in the state, he must be famous in the family."

Confucius said, "That is fame, not success. For to be successful, a man would be by nature honest and devoted to righteousness. He would take heed of what is spoken, and would note the countenance. He would care about remaining lowly. Such a man would be assured of success in the state, such a man would be assured of success in the family. To be famous, a man might appear benevolent but deviate in action, and live thus without doubting. Such a man would be assured of being famous in the state, such a man would be assured of being famous in the family."

*"Ruling" (cheng) and "right" (cheng) are cognate, showing that to rule is related to making right.

21. Accompanying Confucius to the grounds of the rain altar, Fan Ch'ih said, "I venture to ask about exaltation of virtue, dispelling of malevolence from within, and recognition of delusion." Confucius said, "What a good question! To put work before reward: is that not exaltation of virtue? To attack the vices of oneself and not the vices of others: is that not dispelling of malevolence from within? A sudden burst of anger forgetting self and kin: is that not delusion?"

22. Fan Ch'ih asked about benevolence. Confucius said, "Love your fellow men."
Fan Ch'ih asked about knowledge. Confucius said, "Know your fellow men." Fan Ch'ih did not comprehend. Confucius said, "Elevate the honest above the wrong doers, and the wrong doers can be made honest."
Fan Ch'ih retired. He went to see Tzu Hsia and said, "A while ago, I asked the Master about knowledge and he said, 'Elevate the honest above the wrong doers, and the wrong doers can be made honest.' What did he mean?"
Tzu Hsia said, "His words are rich with meaning. When Shun had all under heaven, from many he elected to elevate Kao T'ao and so those who were not benevolent were kept afar. When T'ang had all under heaven, from many he elected to elevate Yi Yin and so those who were not benevolent were kept afar."

23. Tzu Kung asked about friendship. Confucius said, "Give loyal advice and good guidance, until such is of no avail, then halt. Do not disgrace yourself."

24. Tseng Tzu said, "A gentleman makes friends through literature and that friendship ennobles benevolence."

Book XIII

1. Tzu Lu asked about ruling. Confucius said, "Work yourself before you work others." Tzu Lu enquired further. Confucius said, "Be relentless."

2. When he became head official to the family of Chi, Chung Kung asked about ruling. Confucius said, "Start with the officials and their delegated duties, pardon minor faults, elevate the virtuous and the talented."
Chung Kung said, "How am I to know the virtuous and the talented to elevate them?"
Confucius said, "Elevate those you know. As to those you do not know, would others deny them?"

3. Tzu Lu said, "If the lord of Wei offered my Master public office, with what would my Master start?"
Confucius said, "It would be protocol."
Tzu Lu said, "If that is so, the Master is taking a roundabout route! Why protocol?"
Confucius said, "Yu, how coarse you are. A gentleman evades what he does not know. When protocol is not instituted correctly, what is said is not accepted; when what is said is not accepted, matters are not accomplished; when matters are not accomplished, the rites and music do not thrive; when the rites and music do not thrive, punishments and penalties are not kept; when punishments and penalties are not kept, the

people are bewildered. Thus with protocol instituted, a gentleman may begin to speak and what is said may be enacted. What a gentleman says is but earnest."

4. Fan Ch'ih asked to learn agriculture. Confucius said, "I cannot compare with an old farmer." Fan Ch'ih asked to learn how to cultivate vegetables. Confucius said, "I cannot compare with an old vegetable farmer."

Fan Ch'ih departed. Confucius said, "Fan Hsu is a petty man indeed! When those above are devoted to the rites, the people will not venture to be disrespectful. When those above are devoted to righteousness, the people will not venture to be unsupporting. When those above are devoted to trustworthiness, the people will not venture to be untruthful. Thus people from everywhere will come, carrying their children. What need is there to learn agriculture?"

5. Confucius said, "To recite the three hundred verses of the *Odes,* yet not to succeed when given public office and not to be able to face it independently when sent anywhere on a mission: of what use are the many verses?"

6. Confucius said, "When he himself is right, there is action without his orders. When he himself is not right, he is not obeyed despite his orders."

7. Confucius said, "In their policies, [the states of] Lu and Wei are brothers."

8. Confucius said of the good attitude towards living of the young lord Ching of Wei, "At first when he had a little, he said, 'It is reasonable enough.' When he had a little more, he said, 'It is complete enough.' When he had riches, he said, 'It is fine enough.' "

9. When Confucius went to Wei, Jan Yu drove his carriage. Confucius said, "How populous indeed!"

Jan Yu said, "Being populous, what then?"

Confucius said, "Make them rich."

Jan Yu said, "Being rich, what then?"

Confucius said, "Teach them."

10. Confucius said, "If I were employed, something would be done within twelve [months], and there would be accomplishment within three years."

11. Confucius said, " 'If an altruistic man were to run a state for a hundred years, brutality could be overcome and killing could be eliminated.' How real these words!"

12. Confucius said, "Even if there is a divine emperor, benevolence will still take a generation."

13. Confucius said, "If he rights himself, what difficulty will he have in public office? If he is not able to right himself, how can he right others?"

14. When Jan Tzu retired from court, Confucius said, "Why are you so late?" The reply was, "There were policy matters." Confucius said, "Were they not family matters? If they were policy matters I would have heard of them even though I am not in office."

15. Duke Ting asked, "Is there such a thing as a single sentence bringing about the prosperity of a state?"

Confucius replied, "The sentence itself may not have such an effect. People have said that it is difficult to be the lord and not easy to be the subject . . . and if the difficulty of being the lord is acknowledged, is what is said not tantamount to a single sentence bringing about the prosperity of a state?"

Duke Ting said, "Is there such a thing as a single sentence bringing about the loss of a state?"

Confucius replied, "The sentence itself may not have such an effect. People have said that there is no happiness for he who is the lord, that there are only his words, not resisted . . . and if what he says is good, and not resisted, is it not so? But if what he says is not good, and not resisted, then is it not tantamount to a single sentence bringing about the loss of a state?"

16. The Duke of Yeh asked about ruling. Confucius said, "Those who are near are pleased, those who are far away long to come."

17. When he was head official of Chu Fu, Tzu Hsia asked about ruling. Confucius said, "Wish not for haste, look not to small profits. Wish for haste and there is no success. Look to small profits and important tasks are not accomplished."

18. The Duke of Yeh said to Confucius, "In our [community], a man who behaves with honesty would testify against his own father for stealing a goat." Confucius said, "In our [community], an honest man is different. A father would shield his son and a son would shield his father. And there is honesty."

19. Fan Ch'ih asked about benevolence. Confucius said, "At home, be courteous. At work, respectful. In dealing with people, be loyal. Such must not be abandoned, even when among the Yi and the Ti."*

20. Tzu Kung asked, "What can be considered as scholarly?" Confucius said, "Act with the sense of shame when sent anywhere on a mission, do not disgrace the commission of the lord, and such can be considered as scholarly."

Tzu Kung said, "I venture to ask what ranks next."

Confucius said, "Being praised for filial piety by family, and being praised for brotherly love by [the community]."

Tzu Kung said, "I venture to ask what ranks next."

Confucius said, "Being trustworthy in speech and being decisive in action, though in a strong and petty-minded manner: this can be considered to rank next."

Tzu Kung said, "And what of men in public office today?"

Confucius said, "Alas! Men of the *tou* and the *shao*** are not worth counting."

21. Confucius said, "If unable to be with those of the middle course, then be with the unrestrained and the prudish. The unrestrained advance and take. The prudish refrain from certain deeds."

---

*Uncivilized tribes to the East and the North respectively of China.

***Tou* and *shao* were small units of measurement. Confucius alludes to the insignificance of the men who "are not worth counting."

22. Confucius said, "People from the South have a saying, 'Men without principles should not practise divination and medicine.' How well said! 'Embarrassment shall be with those who lack the virtue of being principled.'" Confucius said, "It would be pointless to divine."*

23. Confucius said, "Gentlemen are harmonious and not clannish. Petty men are clannish and not harmonious."

24. Tzu Kung asked, "As to being loved by all in the [village], what do you say?" Confucius said, "It is not enough."
"As to being hated by all in the [village], what do you say?"
Confucius said, "It is not enough. It is not equal to being loved by the good men of the [village], and hated by those not good."

25. Confucius said, "The gentleman is easy to serve but difficult to please. Please him not with the Way and he is not pleased. And when he employs others, he evaluates abilities. The petty man is difficult to serve but easy to please. Please him not with the Way and he is still pleased. And when he employs others, he looks to blame."

26. Confucius said, "The gentleman is at peace without being arrogant. The petty man is arrogant without being at peace."

27. Confucius said, "Resoluteness, persistence, simplicity and slowness to speak are close to benevolence."

28. Tzu Lu asked, "What can be considered as scholarly?" Confucius said, "Enthusiasm, exhortation, amicability can be considered as scholarly, enthusiasm and exhortation among friends, and amicability among brothers."

29. Confucius said, "If altruistic men were to teach the people for seven years, they could be recruited."

30. Confucius said, "To send the people to battle without teaching them is to abandon them."

BOOK XIV

1. Hsien asked about shame. Confucius said, "When the state is with the Way, accept grain. When the state is without the Way, accept grain and be shamed."
"Can acting without the compulsion to win, boastfulness, complaint and covetousness, be called benevolent?"
Confucius said, "It can be called difficult, but I do not know whether it is benevolent."

---

*The unprincipled person's fate is clearly defined in *The Book of Change* and therefore divination is futile.

2. Confucius said, "A scholar with his heart set on property is not worthy to be called a scholar."

3. Confucius said, "When the state is with the Way, be bold in speech and be bold in action. When the state is without the Way, be bold in action and be humble in speech."

4. Confucius said, "A man who has virtue is sure to have something to say. A man who has something to say is not sure to have virtue. A man who has benevolence is sure to have courage. A man who has courage is not sure to have benevolence."

5. Nan-Kung K'uo consulted Confucius, saying, "Yi was good in archery. Ao was capable of capsizing enemy craft. Both died untimely deaths. Yu and Chi involved themselves in agriculture and had all under heaven." The Master did not respond.
Nan-Kung K'uo departed. Confucius said, "This man is a gentleman indeed. This man has high regard for virtue indeed."

6. Confucius said, "There are times when a gentleman is not benevolent, but at no time is a petty man benevolent."

7. Confucius said, "Can you not make someone you love work hard? Can you not instruct someone who is loyal?"

8. Confucius said, "In the making of state documents, P'i Ch'en did the draft, Shih Shu commented upon it, Tzu Yu, an official of protocol, improved upon it, and Tzu Ch'an of Tung Li added colour to it."

9. Someone asked about Tzu Ch'an. Confucius said, "He is generous towards people." When asked about Tzu Hsi, Confucius said, "What a man! What a man!" When asked about Kuan Chung, Confucius said, "As for this man, he took over three-hundred [households from the fief of the family Po in the city of P'ien]. Despite being reduced to simple meals, Po had no words of complaint for the rest of his years."

10. Confucius said, "To be poor and without complaint is difficult. To be rich and without arrogance is easy."

11. Confucius said, "Meng Kung Ch'o would excel as an official to the family of Chao or Wei,* but he could not be an official of T'eng or Hsueh."**

12. Tzu Lu asked about the accomplished man.
Confucius said, "If a man has the wisdom of Tsang Wu Chung, the uncovetousness of Kung Ch'o, the courage of Pien Chuang Tzu, the skills of Jan Ch'iu, and refines them with the rites and music, he could be called an accomplished man." Confucius added, "Nowadays the accomplished man is not necessarily as such. If a man thinks of righteousness where he sees profit, risks his life where he sees others endangered, and does not forget words he has spoken at any time of his life, he could be called an accomplished man too."

---

*Powerful families poised to take over the state of Chin.
**Minor states which Confucius deemed difficult to administer.

13. Confucius asked Kung-Ming Chia about Kung-Shu Wen Tzu, "Is it true that the gentleman does not speak, does not smile and does not take?"

Kung-Ming Chia replied, "Those who say so exaggerate. The gentleman speaks only when it is timely, and people do not resent his speaking. He smiles only when he is happy, and people do not resent his smiling. He takes only when it is right, and people do not resent his taking."

Confucius said, "Is that indeed how he was?"

14. Confucius said, "Still occupying Fang, Tsang Wu Chung sought to establish his line of succession in Lu. Although it is said that he was not blackmailing his lord, I do not believe so."

15. Confucius said, "Duke Wen of Chin was crafty and not upright, Duke Huan of Ch'i was upright and not crafty."

16. Tzu Lu said, "When Duke Huan had the young lord Chiu killed, Chao Hu died with his lord, but Kuan Chung did not." Tzu Lu added, "Did Kuan Chung lack benevolence?" Confucius said, "It was through the strength of Kuan Chung that Duke Huan was able to unite the lords nine times without using military force. Such was his benevolence. Such was his benevolence."

17. Tzu Kung said, "Did Kuan Chung lack benevolence when not only did he not die with the young lord Chiu, but went on to assist Duke Huan, who had the young lord killed?"

Confucius said, "When Kuan Chung was assisting Duke Huan, the lords were made conciliatory and all under heaven were united. To this day, the people benefit from it. If not for Kuan Chung, we could be wearing our hair down and our robes folded to the left.* Surely Kuan Chung was unlike the average man or woman who would commit suicide and die unknown in a ditch, to remain faithful."

18. Chuan, official to the family of Kung-Shu Wen Tzu, was promoted along with Wen Tzu to rank with the lords. Hearing of it, Confucius said, "Indeed he can be called *wen*."**

19. When Confucius spoke about lack of the Way in Duke Ling of Wei, K'ang Tzu said, "How then does he not lose his state?"

Confucius said, "Chung-Shu Yu takes charge of important guests, Chu T'o takes charge of the ancestral shrine and Wang-Sun Chia takes charge of the military. How then could he lose it?"

20. Confucius said, "When what a man speaks is guiltless, what he does is difficult."

21. Ch'en Ch'eng Tzu had Duke Chien assassinated. Confucius cleansed himself ceremonially before attending court. Reporting to Duke Ai, he said, "Ch'en Heng† has had his lord assassinated. I ask that he be suppressed." The duke said, "Report it to the

---

*Like the uncivilized tribes.
**Posthumous recognition, in the form of the addition of the character "*Wen*" to his name. "*Wen*" means "finesse."
†Another name for Ch'en Ch'eng Tzu

three leaders."* Confucius said, "Following as I do in the footsteps of officials, I dared not withhold my report. Yet my lord said, 'Report it to the three leaders.'"

The report made to the three leaders was of no avail. Confucius said, "Following as I do in the footsteps of officials, I dared not withhold my report."

22. Tzu Lu asked about serving the lord. Confucius said, "Do not deceive him, rather offend him."

23. Confucius said, "The gentleman comprehends what is above. The petty man comprehends what is below."

24. Confucius said, "In ancient times, learning was for self [improvement]. Nowadays learning is for [impressing] others."

25. Ch'u Po Yu sent a messenger to Confucius. Confucius asked him to be seated and said, "How does your lord fare?" The reply was, "My lord wishes to minimize his mistakes, but without success."

The messenger departed, and Confucius said, "What a messenger indeed! What a messenger indeed!"

26. Confucius said, "When not in the official position, do not be involved with its policies."

Tseng Tzu said, "A gentleman does not think about what is outside his official position."

27. Confucius said, "A gentleman is ashamed if his words outshine his actions."

28. Confucius said, "The way of the gentleman has three aspects of which I am incapable: with benevolence, there is no worry, with wisdom, there is no delusion, with courage, there is no fear." Tzu Kung said, "The Master describes himself!"

29. Tzu Kung was grading people. Confucius said, "How virtuous is T'su! As for me, there is not the time."

30. Confucius said, "Do not be concerned about others not appreciating you. Be concerned about your own inabilities."

31. Confucius said, "Without unduly anticipating deceit, without suspecting distrust, yet still able to sense them, is a man not virtuous?"

32. Wei-Sheng Mu said to Confucius, "Ch'iu, besides artfulness in speech, what do you achieve by busying yourself like this?"

Confucius said, "I dare not presume myself an artful speaker. I merely deplore inflexibility."

33. Confucius said, "A superior horse is praised not for its strength but rather for its finer qualities."

---

*Heads of the three leading families of the state of Lu.

34. Someone said, " 'Repay complaint with virtue.' What do you say?"
Confucius said, "And how should virtue be repaid? Repay complaint with honesty, and virtue with virtue."

35. Confucius said, "There may well be none who appreciates me!" Tzu Kung said, "Why is there none who appreciates my Master?" Confucius said, "I complain not against heaven nor accuse men. I learn what is below to comprehend what is above. It is heaven that appreciates me!"

36. Kung-Po Liao criticised Tzu Lu in front of Chi-Sun. Tzu-Fu Ching Po reported this and said, "The gentleman is deluded by what Kung-Po Liao says, but I can still have him put to death."
Confucius said, "When the Way prevails, it is destiny. When the Way is abandoned, it is destiny. What is Kung-Po Liao in the face of destiny?"

37. Confucius said, "There are the virtuous who shun the world. Then there are those who shun the place. Then there are those who shun the countenance. Then there are those who shun the word."
Confucius said, "There are seven men who have done so."

38. Tzu Lu stayed for the night at the Stone Gate. The [next] morning the gatekeeper said, "From where do you come?" Tzu Lu said, "From the K'ung."* The gatekeeper said, "He who knows what is impossible yet attempts to do it."

39. As Confucius was playing the [stone chimes] in Wei, a man carrying a basket passed the K'ung door, saying, "The player has heart indeed." Presently, he said, "How crude for the [stone chimes] to continue. If he knew better, he would cease.

> When the waters are deep, swim.
> When the waters are shallow, lift your hem in crossing."

Confucius said, "With such decisiveness, nothing would be difficult!"

40. Tzu Chang said, "The *Book* [*of History*] says, 'Kao Tsung was in the [place of mourning] for three years without speaking.' Why was this?"
Confucius said, "Why is Kao Tsung singled out, when men of ancient times were all so? When a lord died, a hundred officials submitted themselves and listened to the [prime minister] for three years."

41. Confucius said, "When those above are devoted to the rites, the people will serve obediently."

42. Tzu Lu asked about the gentleman. Confucius said, "Cultivate yourself to be respectful."
Tzu Lu said, "Is that all?"
Confucius said, "Cultivate yourself to put others at ease."
Tzu Lu said, "Is that all?"

*Household of Confucius or K'ung.

Confucius said, "Cultivate yourself to put the people at ease. Even Yao and Shun found it difficult to cultivate themselves to put the people at ease."

43. Yuen Jang waited, squatting. Confucius said,

> "Young, but without humility and brotherly love,
> Grown, but without anything commendable,
> Old but cheating death, What thievery!"
> Confucius tapped him on the leg with his stick.

44. Someone asked about the errand boy of Ch'ueh Tang and said, "Is he gaining?" Confucius said, "I have seen him [presume to take] a designated seat. I have seen him walk alongside his seniors. He does not look for [progress]. He desires hasty accomplishments."

BOOK XV

1. Duke Ling of Wei asked Confucius about military manoeuvers. Confucius replied, "As to matters of the *tsu* and the *tou*,* I have been fortunate to hear about them, but I have yet to learn about military matters." The following day, Confucius departed.

2. At Ch'en, when food was scarce and the followers fell ill, perturbed, Tzu Lu said, "How could a gentleman be so poor?" Confucius said, "There are times when even a gentleman is poor, but when a petty man is poor, disaster befalls the world!"

3. Confucius said, "T'su, do you think that I learn extensively to gain knowledge?" The reply was, "Yes. Is it not so?" Confucius said, "No. I have one unifying principle."

4. Confucius said, "Yu, rare indeed are those who know virtue."

5. Confucius said, "There was one who did not have to do much when ruling and he was Shun! All he did was to sit courteously facing south!"**

6. Tzu Chang asked about conduct. Confucius said, "Be loyal and trustworthy in speech and be sincere and respectful in conduct. Conduct should be so even when you are in the [uncivilized] states of Man and Mo. Even when you are in your [neighboring communities], should your speech not be loyal and trustworthy, and your conduct not sincere and respectful? Be standing and see it planted before you. Be seated in the carriage and see it on the wooden bar in front. Such is conduct."

7. Confucius said, "How honest is Shih Yu! When the state is with the Way, he is like the arrow. When the state is without the Way, he is like the arrow."

*Vessels for sacrificial offerings, here representing details of the rites.
**The emperor's chair traditionally faces south.

"How gentlemanly is Ch'u Po Yu! When the state is with the Way, he assumes public office. When the state is without the Way, he enfolds his principles."

8. Confucius said, "Not to converse with a man worthy of conversation is to waste the man. To converse with a man not worthy of conversation is to waste words. The wise waste neither men nor words."

9. Confucius said, "Men with aspiration and men with benevolence do not sacrifice benevolence to remain alive, but would sacrifice themselves for benevolence."

10. Tzu Kung asked how to be benevolent. Confucius said, "The craftsman who wishes to work well has first to sharpen his implements. To live in a state, serve the virtuous among its officials and befriend the benevolent among its scholars."

11. Yen Yuen asked how to run a state. Confucius said, "Implement the Hsia calendar, ride the Yin carriages, wear the Chou ceremonial headdress, and let the music be that of the Shao dance. Banish the sounds of Cheng and keep artful speakers afar. The sounds of Cheng are debauched and artful speakers are desolating."

12. Confucius said, "Men who do not care about the future, will soon have trouble."

13. Confucius said, "All is lost! I have yet to meet the man who is as devoted to virtue as to beauty."

14. Confucius said, "Was Tsang Wen Chung a thief of his position? He knew that Liu Hsia Hui was virtuous, yet he did not establish Liu Hsia Hui as his equal."

15. Confucius said, "Be strict with yourself but least reproachful of others and complaint is kept afar."

16. Confucius said, "I know not what is to be done about those who do not say, 'What is to be done? What is to be done?'"

17. Confucius said, "Gathered together all day long, what is spoken does not touch upon righteousness, and the inclination is to act with inane cleverness . . . difficult indeed!"

18. Confucius said, "With righteousness as his substance, the gentleman acts in accordance with the rites, expresses himself with humility and is complete with trustworthiness. He is a gentleman indeed!"

19. Confucius said, "The gentleman is distressed about his own inabilities and does not distress himself about others not appreciating him."

20. Confucius said, "The gentleman deplores dying without having lived up to his reputation."

21. Confucius said, "The gentleman demands of himself. The petty man demands of others."

22. Confucius said, "The gentleman is conceited but not competitive, socializes but does not take sides."

23. Confucius said, "The gentleman does not elevate a man because of what he speaks, nor abandon what is spoken because of the speaker."

24. Tzu Kung asked, "Is there a word with which to act in accordance throughout a lifetime?" Confucius said, "It is 'forgiveness.' What you do not wish upon yourself, extend not to others."

25. Confucius said, "Whom among men can I chastise or celebrate? Those whom I celebrate have been put to the test. So were the people of the three dynasties* who were able to be honest in keeping with the Way."

26. Confucius said, "I can recall when court historians would leave some things unrecorded, and horse owners would loan others their horses to ride. But not nowadays!"

27. Confucius said, "Clever talk disorders virtue. Intolerance in small matters disorders big plans."

28. Confucius said, "When people hate, take heed. When people love, take heed."

29. Confucius said, "Men can expand the Way. The Way cannot expand men."

30. Confucius said, "Having made a mistake, not to correct it is a mistake indeed."

31. Confucius said, "I tried thinking all day not eating, and all night not sleeping. It was without gain, and not equal to learning."

32. Confucius said, "The gentleman works towards the Way and does not work towards sustenance. Plough and there is hunger. Learn and there is the salary of an official. The gentleman worries about the Way and does not worry about poverty."

33. Confucius said, "What is attained with wisdom but not secured with benevolence will be lost despite its acquisition. What is attained with wisdom, secured with benevolence but not presided over with dignity will not be respected by the people. What is attained with wisdom, secured with benevolence, presided over with dignity but not enacted in accordance with the rites will not yet be goodness."

34. Confucius said, "Petty cleverness is not for the gentleman as are great tasks. Great tasks are not for the petty man as is petty cleverness."

35. Confucius said, "For the people, benevolence is more important than fire and water. I have seen men die attempting to master fire and water, but have yet to see men die attempting to master benevolence."

*The Hsia (circa 2100–1600 B.C.E.), the Yin-Shang (circa 1600–1111 B.C.E.) and the Chou (circa 1111–249 B.C.E.).

36. Confucius said, "Where benevolence is concerned, do not defer to the teacher."

37. Confucius said, "The gentleman is faithful to what is right, irrespective of others' faith in him."

38. Confucius said, "In serving a lord, respect for the office takes precedence over sustenance."

39. Confucius said, "Teach without discrimination."

40. Confucius said, "When the ways are not the same, work not in association."

41. Confucius said, "The official word is simply for comprehension."*

42. Mien, the music master** went to see Confucius. On reaching the steps, Confucius said, "You are at the steps." On reaching the mat, Confucius said, "You are at the mat." When all were seated, Confucius told him where everyone was.

After music master Mien had departed, Tzu Chang asked, "Was how you spoke to the music master the way?" Confucius said, "Yes. This is certainly the way to assist a music master."

BOOK XVI

1. When Chi was about to attack Chuan Yu, Jan Yu and Chi Lu went to see Confucius and said, "Chi will soon take action against Chuan Yu."

Confucius said, "Ch'iu, is it not obvious that it is your fault? Chuan Yu was designated long ago by a former emperor to be responsible for Meng to the East. Furthermore it lies within the state boundaries and is serving the same *she chi*.† Why resort to attack?"

Jan Yu said, "My lord wishes it. We the two officials do not."

Confucius said, "Ch'iu, Chou Jen has said, 'Take the position appropriate to the abilities displayed, and when falling short, relinquish it.' Of what use to the blind are assistants who do not hold them when they are in danger, nor steady them when they lose their balance? Besides your words are wrong. Whose fault is it if the tiger and the one-horned beast escape from the cages, or if the tortoise shell and the jade are damaged in their cages?"

Jan Yu said, "But now Chuan Yu is well fortified and close by Fei. If we do not take it now, our descendants will be troubled for generations to come."

---

*Confucius appears to be reproaching the use of elaborate language by some officials.
**In Confucius' time, music masters were blind.
†*She chi*, being shrines to the gods of earth and grain, received homage wherever they were erected, in states and their subordinate settlements, such as Lu and Chuan Yu respectively.

Confucius said, "Ch'iu, the gentleman deplores those who do not say what they covet and use disguised words. I have heard that the lord of a state or a family concerns himself not with scarcity, but rather with uneven distribution, not with poverty but with discontent. For where there is even distribution, there is no poverty, where there is harmony there is no scarcity, and where there is contentment, there is no overthrowing. Thus when the people afar are unsupporting, bring them round by cultivating literature and virtue. Having brought the people round, make them content. Now in assisting your lord, you are unable to bring round the unsupporting people afar, leaving the state divided, in discord and not secure, and you are planning to battle within the state. I fear the trouble with Chi-Sun lies not in Chuan Yu, but rather within his own walls."

2. Confucius said, "When all under heaven are with the Way, the rites, music and military conquests are initiated by the son of heaven.* When all under heaven are not with the Way, the rites, music and military conquests are initiated by the [feudal] lords. When initiated by the lords, they rarely last beyond ten generations. When initiated by the officials, they rarely last beyond five generations. When the destiny of the state is in the hands of the officials to the family, they rarely last beyond three generations. When all under heaven are with the Way, rulership is not for the officials. When all under heaven are with the Way, there is no discussion among the people."

3. Confucius said, "It has been five generations since responsibility for the [payment] of officials was taken away from the chambers of the dukes. It has been four generations since rulership was seized by the officials. Thus the descendants of the three families of Huan are weak indeed."

4. Confucius said, "There are the three friends with whom there is gain and the three friends with whom there is loss. Befriend the honest, befriend the faithful and befriend those who listen extensively, and there is gain indeed. Befriend those who appear honourable, befriend those who are good at pleasing, and befriend those who appear to be artful in speech, and there is loss indeed."

5. Confucius said, "There are the three enjoyments through which there is gain and the three enjoyments through which there is loss. Enjoy regulating with the rites and music, enjoy speaking of the good in others, and enjoy having many virtuous friends and there is gain indeed. Enjoy indulging in arrogance, enjoy wandering in idleness, and enjoy indulging in feasts and there is loss indeed."

6. Confucius said, "In attendance to the gentleman, there are the three pitfalls: in speech, if what is spoken is not realized, that can be called rashness. In speech, if what is realized is unspoken, that can be called concealment. If what is spoken is spoken before observing the countenance, that can be called blindness."

7. Confucius said, "For the gentleman there are the three abstentions: in his youth, when his blood** runs unsettled, he should abstain from physical beauty. In his

---

*The emperor.
**In the original text, the reference is to "blood and ch'i," ch'i being the vital energy of the universe. Blood and ch'i are said to be the basic constituents of human life.

prime when his blood runs full, he should abstain from provocation. In his old age, when his blood runs weak, he should abstain from acquisitiveness."

8. Confucius said, "For the gentleman there are the three apprehensions: he is apprehensive of destiny, he is apprehensive of the great men, he is apprehensive of the sages' words. The petty man, without knowledge of destiny and without apprehension, slights the great men and makes a mockery of the sages' words."

9. Confucius said, "Those born with knowledge rank high. Those who acquire knowledge through learning rank next. Those who learn when in difficulty rank next. Those who do not learn even when in difficulty rank lowest among the people."

10. Confucius said, "For the gentleman there are the nine things of which he thinks:

> In seeing, he thinks of enlightenment,
> In listening he thinks of clarity,
> In countenance, he thinks of gentleness,
> In facial expression, he thinks of courtesy,
> In speech, he thinks of loyalty,
> In serving, he thinks of respect,
> In doubt, he thinks of questioning,
> In anger, he thinks of difficulties,
> In considering acquisition, he thinks of righteousness."

11. Confucius said, " 'To feel left behind on meeting with what is good, to feel the hand scalded by boiling water on meeting with what is not good.' Indeed I have met such a man. Indeed I have heard the saying.

" 'To live in seclusion in keeping with aspirations, to act with righteousness in reaching the Way.' Indeed I have heard the saying. I have yet to meet such a man."

12. Duke Ching of Ch'i had a thousand teams of horses. On the day he died, the people found nothing virtuous about him to praise. Po Yi and Shu Ch'i starved at the foot of [Mount] Shou Yang. The people still praise them today. Is this what it means?

13. Ch'en K'ang asked Po Yu, "Have you heard anything different?"

The reply was, "No. Once [my father] was standing alone as I hurried through the courtyard, and he said, 'Have you studied the *Odes?*' I replied, 'Not yet.' 'Without having studied the *Odes,* you could not converse.' I retired to study the *Odes.*

"Another day [my father] was standing alone once again as I hurried through the courtyard, and he said, 'Have you studied the rites?' I replied, 'Not yet.' 'Without having studied the rites, you could not establish a stand.' I retired to study the rites. These are the two things I have heard."

Ch'en K'ang retired and said in delight, "I asked one [question] and received three [answers]: I heard about the *Odes,* I heard about the rites, and I heard that the gentleman keeps his son at arm's length."

14. The lord of a state calls his wife "my lady." The lady calls herself "your humble servant." Within the state people call her "the lord's lady" and when they are in a foreign state, they call her "the lord's modest lady." People of foreign states call her "the lord's lady."

BOOK XVII

1. Yang Huo wished to see Confucius, but when Confucius declined, Yang Huo sent him the gift of a piglet.

Confucius picked a time when Yang Huo was not home to pay him a return courtesy visit. Enroute, he chanced to meet Yang Huo, who said to Confucius, "Come, I would speak with you." Yang Huo continued, "Can a man be called benevolent who, possessed of treasure, allows the state to be in confusion? I would say not. Can a man be called wise who, devoted to public service, misses many chances? I would say not. The days and moons pass. Time is not on our side." Confucius said, "Yes, I shall assume public office."

2. Confucius said, "So close to each other in nature, yet so far from each other through experience."

3. Confucius said, "Only the wisest and the most dull-witted are unchangeable."

4. Confucius went to Wu Ch'eng. There he heard sounds of stringed instruments and singing. The Master smiled and said, "Would a butcher's knife be used for the killing of a chicken!"

Tzu Yu replied, "But I have previously heard my Master say, 'The gentleman learns the Way and loves the people, the people learn the Way and serve obediently.'"

Confucius said, "My pupils, Yen's words are true. I spoke before in jest."

5. Kung-Shan Fu Jao revolted at Fei and summoned Confucius. Confucius wished to go.

Displeased, Tzu Lu said, "Do not go. Why should you go to Kung-Shan?"

Confucius said, "Would I be summoned without reason? If I am to be employed, it will be for the making of the Chou in the East."*

6. Tzu Chang asked Confucius about benevolence. Confucius said, "The ability to enact the five everywhere under heaven is benevolence."

Asked to elaborate, Confucius said, "Courtesy, tolerance, trustworthiness, quickness and generosity. With courtesy there is no mockery. With tolerance there is support from people. With trustworthiness there are entrusted responsibilities from people. With quickness there is merit. With generosity people can be employed willingly."

7. Fo Pi summoned Confucius. Confucius wished to go.

Tzu Lu said, "I have previously heard my Master say that the gentleman does not join those who themselves are not good. What are you about now going to Fo Pi who revolted at Chung Mou?"

Confucius said, "Yes, it is true I said that. But would you not say that it is hardness indeed that could not be ground thin? Would you not say that it is whiteness indeed that could not be dyed black? Would I not be like a gourd that is only hung, not eaten?"

---

*The implication is that if Confucius were to accept employment from the rebel, he would utilise it for the noble objective of rekindling the past glory of the Chou Dynasty by its establishment in a geographical location to the East, namely Fei.

8. Confucius said, "Yu, have you heard of the six qualities and the six failures?" The reply was, "Not yet."

Confucius said, "Sit down and I shall tell you about them. Be inclined to benevolence but not to learning, and dull-wittedness is the failure. Be inclined to wisdom, but not to learning, and aimlessness is the failure. Be inclined to trustworthiness, but not to learning, and thievery is the failure. Be inclined to honesty, but not to learning, and impatience is the failure. Be inclined to courage, but not to learning, and disorder is the failure. Be inclined to resoluteness, but not to learning, and lack of restraint is the failure."

9. Confucius said, "Why is it that my young ones do not study the *Odes?* The *Odes* can enhance inspiration, can enhance observation, can enhance socializing, can enhance the process for complaint . . . be it to serve your fathers on one hand, be it to serve your lords on the other hand, or to gain knowledge of names of birds and animals, plants and trees."

10. Confucius said to Po Yu, "Have you studied 'the *Chou Nan*' and 'the *Chao Nan*'?* A man who has not studied 'the *Chou Nan*' and 'the *Chao Nan*' is like a man who stands with his face towards a wall."

11. Confucius said, "Indeed 'rites' means more than 'jade and silk'! Indeed 'music' means more than 'bells and drums'!"

12. Confucius said, "A man of stern countenance who quivers within is like a petty man who steals through holes he bores and over walls."

13. Confucius said, "A pleaser of the whole [native land] is a thief of virtue."

14. Confucius said, "To spread hearsay mindlessly is to abandon virtue."

15. Confucius said, "Is it possible to work with crude men in serving the lord? Before they acquire what they want, they are concerned that they cannot acquire it. After they acquire it, they are concerned that they will lose it. And when they are concerned about losing it, there is nothing to which they will not resort."

16. Confucius said, "In ancient times, the people had three failings which perhaps no longer exist today. In ancient times, the unrestrained were unruly but today the unrestrained are aimless. In ancient times, the conceited were aloof, but today the conceited are angry and aggressive. In ancient times, the dull-witted were honest, but today the dull-witted are deceitful."

17. Confucius said, "Clever talk and a pretentious manner are seldom compatible with the benevolent."

18. Confucius said, "It is hateful for purple to displace red. It is hateful for the sounds of Cheng to be confused with the music of *ya.*** It is hateful for sharpened tongues to overthrow states."

---

*The opening sections of the *Odes*
**Court music of the Chou Dynasty.

19. Confucius said, "I wish not to speak." Tzu Kung said, "If my Master does not speak, then what would we young ones relate?" Confucius said, "Does heaven speak? The four seasons prevail, a hundred things grow, and does heaven speak?"

20. Ju Pei wished to see Confucius. Confucius declined to see him, begging illness. And as soon as the messenger stepped out of the door, Confucius fetched his *se** and sang so that the messenger could hear him.

21. Tsai Wo asked, "As to the three-year mourning period, one year is long enough. If for three years the gentleman does not practise the rites, his rites will deteriorate. If for three years, he does not practise music, his music will decline. The old grain exhausted, the new grain ripened, the flame of the firewood rekindled** . . . indeed one year is enough."
Confucius said, "Would you be at ease eating rice† and wearing finery?"
Tsai Wo said, "Yes."
Confucius said, "If you would be at ease then do so. As for the gentleman in mourning, delicious food he eats is not tasty, music he hears does not make him happy, and he cannot live at ease. Therefore he does not do so. Now if you would be at ease then do so."
Tsai Wo departed. Confucius said, "Yu is not benevolent! A child does not leave his parents' bosom until three years after his birth. Moreover the three-year mourning period is the popular practice among all under heaven. Was Yu not loved by his parents for three years?"

22. Confucius said, "People who satiate themselves, without putting their hearts into anything all day, are difficulties indeed. Are there not chess players who are more virtuous than they?"

23. Tzu Lu said, "Does the gentleman have high regard for courage?" Confucius said, "The gentleman has higher regard for righteousness. The gentleman who has courage but not righteousness will cause disorder. The petty man who has courage but not righteousness will cause thievery."

24. Tzu Kung said, "Does the gentleman have hatred too?" Confucius said, "Yes, he has hatred. He hates people who talk about others' vices. He hates people who malign those above. He hates people who have courage but not the rites. He hates people who are stubbornly brave and close-minded."
He added, "T'su, do you have hatred too?"
"I hate people who plagiarize in the name of wisdom. I hate people who abandon humility in the name of courage. I hate people who slander in the name of honesty."

25. Confucius said, "Only women and petty men are difficult to handle. Be close to them and they are not humble, keep them at arm's length and they complain."

26. Confucius said, "It is fatal to be hated still at the age of forty."

---

*Ancient 25-string musical instrument said to be played to best advantage by refined persons.
**An annual process.
†A luxury.

BOOK XVIII

1. Wei Tzu left [the tyrant Emperor Chou], Chi Tzu was enslaved because of him, and Pi Kan died for recommending improvements to him. Confucius said, "The Yin [Dynasty] had three benevolent men."

2. The magistrate Liu Hsia Hui was dismissed three times from public office. Someone said, "Should you not leave?" Liu Hsia Hui said, "Serving people with honesty according to the Way, where could I go without being dismissed three times from public office? If I could serve people wrongly against the Way, would there be a need for me to leave my home state?"

3. Duke Ching of Ch'i considered how he should treat Confucius, and said, "I shall not treat him like Chi. I shall treat him like someone between Chi and Meng." Duke Ching of Ch'i said, "I am old and incapable of using him." Confucius departed.*

4. Someone from Ch'i sent a gift of female musicians. Chi Huan Tzu accepted it, and court was not convened for three days. Confucius departed.

5. As Confucius was passing by, the wild man of Ch'u met his carriage, singing,

> Phoenix, oh phoenix,
> Thine virtue declined,
> What is past unalterable,
> What will come undefined.
> Refrain! Refrain!
> Desolate the public office of the day!

Confucius descended to speak with him, but the wild man quickened his pace to shun him. Confucius was unable to speak with him.

6. The tall hermit and the stout hermit** were ploughing together. Confucius was passing by and sent Tzu Lu to ask for directions for crossing the waters. The tall hermit said, "Who is the one holding the reins?" Tzu Lu said, "It is K'ung Ch'iu." "Is he the K'ung Ch'iu of Lu?" "Yes." "He knows the direction."

Tzu Lu asked the stout hermit. The stout hermit said, "Who are you?" "I am Chung Yu." "The pupil of K'ung Ch'iu of Lu?" The reply was, "Yes." "Continuously the waters flow in the same manner everywhere under heaven and who can change that? As for you, would it not be better to follow the man who shuns the world than to follow he who shuns people?" He continued to work on the soil.

---

*Duke Ching was the ruling lord of the state of Ch'i, to which Confucius travels after leaving his home state of Lu. Hence in weighing how Confucius should be ranked, were he to be employed in Ch'i, the duke refers to two officials serving in Lu: Chi was a high-ranking official whom historians consider to have usurped power and authority at a time when the ruling lord of Lu was said to be internally weak. Meng was an official of lesser rank. Duke Ching was apparently unwilling to employ Confucius in a post deemed to be less than he deserved.

**Some sources adopted Ch'ang Chu and Chieh Ni as proper names which mean respectively, "the tall one of the waters" and "the stout one of the waters." The original names of the hermits were not known at the time the *Lun Yu* was compiled.

Tzu Lu departed to report to Confucius.

The Master sighed and said, "Birds and animals are not for company. If I were not with people, with whom would I be? If all under heaven were with the Way, Ch'iu would not have to make changes!"

7. Tzu Lu fell behind. He chanced to meet an old man carrying a basket on a stick. Tzu Lu asked, "Have you seen my Master?"

The old man said, "You do not use your four limbs well, you cannot distinguish the five types of grain—who be your Master?" He drove his stick into the ground and began to weed.

Tzu Lu stood with his hands clasped respectfully.

Tzu Lu was asked to stay for the night. Chicken killed, and millet prepared for the meal, the old man presented his two sons to Tzu Lu.

The next day, Tzu Lu departed and reported to Confucius. Confucius said, "He must be a hermit," and sent Tzu Lu back to see him. But when he arrived, the old man had departed.

Tzu Lu said, "It is not righteous for him not to assume public office. If the duties between old and young are not abandoned, how is it that righteousness between lords and subjects is abandoned? It is to cause disorder to the most important part of the social system for the sake of remaining untainted. For the gentleman, to assume public office is to act righteously irrespective of the knowledge that the Way does not prevail."

8. Of those who kept away from public office, namely Po Yi, Shu Ch'i, Yu Chung, Yi Yi, Chu Chang, Liu Hsia Hui and Shao Lien, Confucius said, "Po Yi and Shu Ch'i did not compromise their aspirations and did not disgrace themselves." Of Liu Hsia Hui and Shao Lien, he said, "They compromised their aspirations and disgraced themselves. They spoke in keeping with the social system. They acted in keeping with careful consideration. But that was about all they did." Of Yu Chung and Yi Yi, he said, "They spoke freely as hermits. They kept themselves pure. They kept to their right when they abandoned public office. I am different from them, for to me nothing is absolute."*

9. The grand music master, Chih, departed for Ch'i. The musician of the second rank, Kan, departed for Ch'u. The musician of the third rank, Liao, departed for Ts'ai. The musician of the fourth rank, Ch'ueh, departed for Ch'in. The [drum] player, Fang Shu, departed for the river. The [hand-drum] player, Wu, departed for the River Han. An assistant to the music master, Yang, and the [stone chimes] player, Hsiang, departed for the sea.**

10. The Duke of Chou said to the Duke of Lu,† "The gentleman does not neglect his relatives, nor give his officials cause to complain about not being utilised. He does not abandon officials of long standing if they have not made serious mistakes. He does not look for one man to bear all the blame."

---

*Confucius names men who were considered to be able, learned and fit for public office, but who lived the lives of recluses because of the corrupting influences of their social circumstances.

**An apparent reference to the flight of musicians due to the decline of the rites and music in the state of Lu.

†His son.

11. The Chou had eight scholars: Po Ta, Po K'uo, Chung T'u, Chung Hu, Shu Yeh, Shu Hsia, Chi Sui and Chi Kua.

BOOK XIX

1. Tzu Chang said, "The scholar, when he sees danger, is willing to give his life. When he sees acquisition, he thinks of righteousness. In offerings, he thinks of respectfulness. In mourning, he thinks of sorrow. That is all."

2. Tzu Chang said, "Holding to virtue without expansion, believing in the Way without adherance: is this to have or to have not?"

3. Tzu Hsia's disciples asked Tzu Chang about friendship. Tzu Chang said, "What does Tzu Hsia say?" The reply was, "Tzu Hsia says 'Befriend those whom you should, and spurn those whom you should not.'"

Tzu Chang said, "What I have heard is different, that 'The gentleman reveres the virtuous and is accommodating towards others, compliments the good and is sympathetic towards the incapable.' If I were very virtuous, could I be unaccommodating towards others? If I were not virtuous, I would be spurned by others. How could I spurn others?"

4. Tzu Hsia said, "Although they are the lesser ways,* they are noteworthy. However the gentleman does not take them because he fears that they would muddy his future pursuits."

5. Tzu Hsia said, "With every day, to acknowledge what is lacking. With every [month], not to forget what has been acquired. This can be called devotion to learning."

6. Tzu Hsia said, "To learn extensively and adhere to aspirations, to question enthusiastically and reflect upon yourself: there is benevolence."

7. Tzu Hsia said, "As the craftsman of a hundred trades in a workshop accomplishes the task, so the gentleman learns to attain the way."

8. Tzu Hsia said, "The petty man is sure to gloss over his faults."

9. Tzu Hsia said, "The gentleman gives three different impressions. Seen from afar, he is awe-inspiring. On approaching closer, he is gentle. On listening, his words are stern."

10. Tzu Hsia said, "The gentleman should gain the trust of the people before he employs their services. Without trust the people would consider their employment as exploitation. The gentleman should gain the trust of his lord before he recommends improvements. Without trust, the lord would consider his recommendations as contemptuous."

---

*As Confucius' disciple, Tzu Hsia perhaps refers here to lesser schools of thought, and the principles and practices of artisans and men of science, which were as tributaries flowing into the mainstream of civilization.

11. Tzu Hsia said, "Step not away from great virtues. Accept ins and outs with small virtues."

12. Tzu Yu said, "Tsu Hsia accepts his young disciples as long as they can sweep the floors, converse fluently with and attend correctly to his guests. But these are mere branches of learning and not the roots. What is to be done?"

On hearing this, Tzu Hsia said, "Ah, but Yen Yu exaggerates! Is the gentleman's way to distinguish what is to be imparted first and what is to be taught later, like categorizing plants and trees? How is the gentleman's way false? It is only the sage who can unite the first and the last."

13. Tzu Hsia said, "Excel in public office and learn. Excel in learning and assume public office."

14. Tzu Yu said, "In mourning, halt with sorrow."

15. Tzu Yu said, "My friend Chang is difficult to equal, but not yet benevolent."

16. Tseng Tzu said, "Tall as Chang stands, it is difficult to be with him in the pursuit of benevolence."

17. Tseng Tzu said, "I have heard from the Master that people who have not done their utmost, would do so when mourning their parents."

18. Tseng Tzu said, "I have heard from the Master that the filial piety of Meng Chuang Tzu can be equalled, except where he keeps his father's officials and his father's policies unchanged, which is difficult to equal."

19. When Yang Fu was employed as magistrate by Meng, he consulted Tseng Tzu. Tseng Tzu said, "Those above have lost the Way and the people have long been disoriented. Be sorrowful and sympathetic, and do not rejoice to uncover truth."

20. Tzu Kung said, "The badness of Chou might not have been so bad, which is why the gentleman hates to be with the notorious, through whom all the badness under heaven is attributed to him."

21. Tzu Kung said, "When the gentleman errs, it is like an eclipse of the sun or the moon. He errs and all men see it. He corrects and all men look up to him."

22. Kung-Sun Ch'ao of Wei asked Tzu Kung, "How did Chung Ni [i.e., Confucius] learn?" Tzu Kung said, "The way of King Wen and King Wu has not fallen completely and is still with men. The virtuous gain knowledge of its greater principles and those who are not virtuous gain knowledge of its lesser principles. Nowhere does the way of Wen and Wu not exist. How could the Master not learn and why would there be a teacher?"

23. Shu-Sun Wu Shu said to the officials at court, "Tzu Kung is more virtuous than Chung Ni [i.e., Confucius]." Tzu-Fu Ching Po reported this to Tzu Kung.

Tzu Kung said, "Let us use surrounding walls in an analogy. T'su's walls are shoulder-high, so you may look over them and see the loveliness of the house within.

The Master's walls are [twenty or thirty feet] high and so, if you are denied entry, you will not be able to see the beauty of the ancestral shrine nor the riches of a hundred officials. Those who succeed in gaining entry are perhaps few, and so would what was said not be fitting?"

24. Shu-Sun Wu Shu chastised Chung Ni [i.e., Confucius]. Tzu Kung said, "It is of no avail. Chung Ni cannot be chastised. Others who are virtuous are as knolls and hills which can be climbed. Chung Ni is as the sun and moon which cannot be climbed. Would it matter to the sun and moon if a man wished to shun them? Or would it be apparent that he does not know his own measure?"

25. Ch'en Tzu Ch'in said to Tzu Kung, "Sir, are you not just being courteous? How could Chung Ni [i.e., Confucius] be more virtuous than you?"

Tzu Kung said, "From a single sentence, the gentleman can be considered wise. From a single sentence, he can be considered unwise. His words cannot be without prudence. The Master cannot be equalled just as heaven cannot be reached by ascending any steps. If the Master were to rule a state, as it is said, he would establish his stand and others would be able to establish theirs. He would advocate the Way and it would prevail. He would settle his people and others would come. He would motivate his people and they would be in harmony. In life he is honoured and in death there will be sorrow. How could he be equalled?"

BOOK XX

1. Yao said,

> Ah, Shun.
> The destiny of heaven has been bestowed upon you,
> Hold genuinely to the mean.
> With all within the four seas in dire poverty,
> The endowment of heaven would cease for all eternity.

Yu was also thus bequeathed by Shun.

T'ang said, "I your humble Lu venture to offer this black heifer, and to declare and report to my majestic emperors: I venture not to pardon those who have sinned. I do not shelter the subjects of my emperors, for the choice is my emperors. If I sin, spare the tens of thousands everywhere. If the tens of thousands everywhere sin, the sin is mine."

The Chou was blessed with many altruistic men.

> Even close relatives
> Are not equal to benevolent men.
> If the people have faults
> It is solely because of me.

Be prudent about weights and measures, scrutinize laws and practices, reinstate abandoned official posts, and everywhere your policies will prevail. Restore states that had been ruined, revive lines that had died away, elevate those who had kept away from public office, and the hearts of all the people under heaven will be yours.

Confucius's Tomb in the Confucius Forest, Ch'u-fu (Qufu), Shantung (Shandong) Province. Confucius and his descendants since 478 B.C.E. are buried in this, the largest and oldest family cemetery in the world. (*Forrest E. Baird*)

Food for the people, mourning and sacrificial offerings are important.

With tolerance there is support from people. With trustworthiness there are entrusted responsibilities from the people. With quickness there is merit. With justice there is pleasure.

2. Tzu Chang asked Confucius, "What are the qualifications of public office?"

Confucius said, "Revere the five forms of goodness and abandon the four vices and you can qualify for public office."

Tzu Chang said, "What can be called 'the five forms of goodness'?"

Confucius said, "The gentleman is generous but not extravagant, works without complaint, has desires without being greedy, is at peace but not arrogant, and commands respect but not fear."

Tzu Chang said, "What can be called 'generous but not extravagant'?"

Confucius said, "Give the people what is profitable for them, and is this not generous but not extravagant? Choose to work the people only when it is timely, and who would complain? Wish for what is benevolent, and could that be greedy? Be the gentleman dealing with the many or the few, the great or the small, he ventures not to be improper, and thus would he not be at peace but not arrogant? The gentleman rights his clothes and headdress and gazes ahead with reverence, inspiring awe and causing people to be apprehensive. Is this not commanding respect but not fear?"

Tzu Chang said, "What can be called 'the four vices'?"

Confucius said, "To put to death without teaching can be called cruelty. To judge results without prerequisites can be called tyranny. To impose deadlines on improper orders, can be called thievery. As when giving in the procedure of receipt and disbursement, to stint can be called officious."

3. Confucius said, "Without knowing destiny, it is not possible to be a gentleman. Without knowing the rites, it is not possible to establish a stand. Without knowing words, it is not possible to know people."

MENCIUS

BOOK VI, PART A

1. Kao Tzu said, "Human nature is like the *ch'i* willow. Dutifulness is like cups and bowls. To make morality out of human nature is like making cups and bowls out of the willow."

"Can you," said Mencius, "make cups and bowls by following the nature of the willow? Or must you mutilate the willow before you can make it into cups and bowls? If you have to mutilate the willow to make it into cups and bowls, must you, then, also mutilate a man to make him moral? Surely it will be these words of yours men in the world will follow in bringing disaster upon morality."

2. Kao Tzu said, "Human nature is like whirling water. Give it an outlet in the east and it will flow east; give it an outlet in the west and it will flow west. Human nature does not show any preference for either good or bad just as water does not show any preference for either east or west."

"It certainly is the case," said Mencius, "that water does not show any preference for either east or west, but does it show the same indifference to high and low? Human nature is good just as water seeks low ground. There is no man who is not good; there is no water that does not flow downwards.

"Now in the case of water, by splashing it one can make it shoot up higher than one's forehead, and by forcing it one can make it stay on a hill. How can that be the nature of water? It is the circumstances being what they are. That man can be made bad shows that his nature is no different from that of water in this respect."

3. Kao Tzu said, "The inborn is what is meant by 'nature.'"

"Is that," said Mencius, "the same as 'white is what is meant by "white"'?"

"Yes."

"Is the whiteness of white feathers the same as the whiteness of white snow and the whiteness of white snow the same as the whiteness of white jade?"

"Yes."

"In that case, is the nature of a hound the same as the nature of an ox and the nature of an ox the same as the nature of a man?"

4. Kao Tzu said, "Appetite for food and sex is nature. Benevolence is internal, not external; rightness is external, not internal."

Reprinted with permission from D.C. Lau, tr., *Mencius* (Harmondsworth, UK: Penguin, 1970).

"Why do you say," said Mencius, "that benevolence is internal and rightness is external?"

"That man there is old and I treat him as elder. He owes nothing of his elderliness to me, just as in treating him as white because he is white I only do so because of his whiteness which is external to me. That is why I call it external."

"The case of rightness is different from that of whiteness. 'Treating as white' is the same whether one is treating a horse as white or a man as white. But I wonder if you would think that 'treating as old' is the same whether one is treating a horse as old or a man as elder? Furthermore, is it the one who is old that is dutiful, or is it the one who treats him as elder that is dutiful?"

"My brother I love, but the brother of a man from Ch'in I do not love. This means that the explanation lies in me. Hence I call it internal. Treating an elder of a man from Ch'u as elder is no different from treating an elder of my own family as elder. This means that the explanation lies in their elderliness. Hence I call it external."

"My enjoyment of the roast provided by a man from Ch'in is no different from my enjoyment of my own roast. Even with inanimate things we can find cases similar to the one under discussion. Are we, then, to say that there is something external even in the enjoyment of roast?"

5. Meng Chi-tzu asked Kung-tu Tzu, "Why do you say that rightness is internal?"

"It is the respect in me that is being put into effect. That is why I say it is internal."

"If a man from your village is a year older than your eldest brother, which do you respect?"

"My brother."

"In filling their cups with wine, which do you give precedence to?"

"The man from my village."

"The one you respect is the former; the one you treat as elder is the latter. This shows that it is in fact external, not internal."

Kung-tu Tzu was unable to find an answer and gave an account of the discussion to Mencius.

Mencius said, "[Ask him,] 'Which do you respect, your uncle or your younger brother?' He will say, 'My uncle.' 'When your younger brother is impersonating an ancestor at a sacrifice, then which do you respect?' He will say, 'My younger brother.' You ask him, 'What has happened to your respect for your uncle?' He will say, 'It is because of the position my younger brother occupies.' You can then say, '[In the case of the man from my village] it is also because of the position he occupies. Normal respect is due to my elder brother; temporary respect is due to the man from my village.' "

When Meng Chi-tzu heard this, he said, "It is the same respect whether I am respecting my uncle or my younger brother. It is, as I have said, external and does not come from within."

"In winter," said Kung-tu Tzu, "one drinks hot water, in summer cold. Does that mean that even food and drink can be a matter of what is external?"

6. Kung-tu Tzu said, "Kao Tzu said, 'There is neither good nor bad in human nature,' but others say, 'Human nature can become good or it can become bad, and that is why with the rise of King Wen and King Wu, the people were given to goodness, while with the rise of King Yu and King Li, they were given to cruelty.' Then there are others who say, 'There are those who are good by nature, and there are those who are bad by nature. For this reason, Hsiang could have Yao as prince, and Shun could have the Blind Man as father, and Ch'i, Viscount of Wei and Prince Pi Kan could have Tchou as nephew as well as sovereign.' Now you say human nature is good. Does this mean that all the others are mistaken?"

"As far as what is genuinely in him is concerned, a man is capable of becoming good," said Mencius. "That is what I mean by good. As for his becoming bad, that is not the fault of his native endowment. The heart of compassion is possessed by all men alike; likewise the heart of shame, the heart of respect, and the heart of right and wrong. The heart of compassion pertains to benevolence, the heart of shame to dutifulness, the heart of respect to the observance of the rites, and the heart of right and wrong to wisdom. Benevolence, dutifulness, observance of the rites, and wisdom do not give me a lustre from the outside, they are in me originally. Only this has never dawned on me. That is why it is said, 'Seek and you will find it; let go and you will lose it.' There are cases where one man is twice, five times or countless times better than another man, but this is only because there are people who fail to make the best of their native endowment. The *Odes* say,

> Heaven produces the teeming masses,
> And where there is a thing there is a norm.
> If the people held on to their constant nature,
> They would be drawn to superior virtue. [*Ode* #260.]

Confucius commented, 'The author of this poem must have had knowledge of the Way.' Thus where there is a thing there is a norm, and because the people hold on to their constant nature they are drawn to superior virtue."

7. Mencius said, "In good years the young men are mostly lazy, while in bad years they are mostly violent. Heaven has not sent down men whose endowment differs so greatly. The difference is due to what ensnares their hearts. Take the barley for example. Sow the seeds and cover them with soil. The place is the same and the time of sowing is also the same. The plants shoot up and by the summer solstice they all ripen. If there is any unevenness, it is because the soil varies in richness and there is no uniformity in the benefit of rain and dew and the amount of human effort devoted to tending it. Now things of the same kind are all alike. Why should we have doubts when it comes to man? The sage and I are of the same kind. Thus Lung Tzu said, 'When someone makes a shoe for a foot he has not seen, I am sure he will not produce a basket.' All shoes are alike because all feet are alike. All palates show the same preferences in taste. Yi Ya was simply the man first to discover what would be pleasing to my palate. Were

the nature of taste to vary from man to man in the same way as horses and hounds differ from me in kind, then how does it come about that all palates in the world follow the preferences of Yi Ya? The fact that in taste the whole world looks to Yi Ya shows that all palates are alike. It is the same also with the ear. The fact that in sound the whole world looks to Shih K'uang shows that all ears are alike. It is the same also with the eye. The whole world appreciates the good looks of Tzu-tu; whoever does not is blind. Hence it is said: all palates have the same preference in taste; all ears in sound; all eyes in beauty. Should hearts prove to be an exception by possessing nothing in common? What is it, then, that is common to all hearts? Reason and rightness. The sage is simply the man first to discover this common element in my heart. Thus reason and rightness please my heart in the same way as meat pleases my palate."

8. Mencius said, "There was a time when the trees were luxuriant on the Ox Mountain, but as it is on the outskirts of a great metropolis, the trees are constantly lopped by axes. Is it any wonder that they are no longer fine? With the respite they get in the day and in the night, and the moistening by the rain and dew, there is certainly no lack of new shoots coming out, but then the cattle and sheep come to graze upon the mountain. That is why it is as bald as it is. People, seeing only its baldness, tend to think that it never had any trees. But can this possibly be the nature of a mountain? Can what is in man be completely lacking in moral inclinations? A man's letting go of his true heart is like the case of the trees and the axes. When the trees are lopped day after day, is it any wonder that they are no longer fine? If, in spite of the respite a man gets in the day and in the night and of the effect of the morning air on him, scarcely any of his likes and dislikes resembles those of other men, it is because what he does in the course of the day once again dissipates what he has gained. If this dissipation happens repeatedly, then the influence of the air in the night will no longer be able to preserve what was originally in him, and when that happens, the man is not far removed from an animal. Others, seeing his resemblance to an animal, will be led to think that he never had any native endowment. But can that be what a man is genuinely like? Hence, given the right nourishment there is nothing that will not grow, while deprived of it there is nothing that will not wither away. Confucius said, 'Hold on to it and it will remain; let go of it and it will disappear. One never knows the time it comes or goes, neither does one know the direction.' It is perhaps to the heart this refers."

9. Mencius said, "Do not be puzzled by the King's lack of wisdom. Even a plant that grows most readily will not survive if it is placed in the sun for one day and exposed to the cold for ten. It is very rarely that I have an opportunity of seeing the King, and as soon as I leave, those who expose him to the cold arrive on the scene. What can I do with the few new shoots that come out? Now take yi,* which is only an art of little consequence. Yet if one does not give one's whole mind to it, one will never master it. Yi Ch'iu is the best player in the whole country. Get him to teach two people to play, one of whom concentrates his mind on the game and listens only to what Yi Ch'iu has to say, while the other, though he listens, dreams of an approaching swan and wants to take up his bow and corded arrow to shoot at it. Now even though this man shares the lessons with the first, he will never be as good. Is this because he is less clever? The answer is, 'No.'"

*[The ancient name for the game of wei ch'i, better known in the West by the name go.]

10. Mencius said, "Fish is what I want; bear's palm is also what I want. If I cannot have both, I would rather take bear's palm than fish. Life is what I want; dutifulness is also what I want. If I cannot have both, I would rather take dutifulness than life. On the one hand, though life is what I want, there is something I want more than life. That is why I do not cling to life at all costs. On the other hand, though death is what I loathe, there is something I loathe more than death. That is why there are troubles I do not avoid. If there is nothing a man wants more than life, then why should he have scruples about any means, so long as it will serve to keep him alive? If there is nothing a man loathes more than death, then why should he have scruples about any means, so long as it helps him to avoid trouble? Yet there are ways of remaining alive and ways of avoiding death to which a man will not resort. In other words, there are things a man wants more than life and there are also things he loathes more than death. This is an attitude not confined to the moral man but common to all men. The moral man simply never loses it.

"Here is a basketful of rice and a bowlful of soup. Getting them will mean life; not getting them will mean death. When these are given with abuse, even a wayfarer would not accept them; when these are given after being trampled upon, even a beggar would not accept them. Yet when it comes to ten thousand bushels of grain one is supposed to accept without asking if it is in accordance with the rites or if it is right to do so. What benefit are ten thousand bushels of grain to me? [Do I accept them] for the sake of beautiful houses, the enjoyment of wives and concubines, or for the sake of the gratitude my needy acquaintances will show me? What I would not accept in the first instance when it was a matter of life and death I now accept for the sake of beautiful houses; what I would not accept when it was a matter of life and death I now accept for the enjoyment of wives and concubines; what I would not accept when it was a matter of life and death I now accept for the sake of the gratitude my needy acquaintances will show me. Is there no way of putting a stop to this? This way of thinking is known as losing one's original heart."

11. Mencius said, "Benevolence is the heart of man, and rightness his road. Sad it is indeed when a man gives up the right road instead of following it and allows his heart to stray without enough sense to go after it. When his chickens and dogs stray, he has sense enough to go after them, but not when his heart strays. The sole concern of learning is to go after this strayed heart. That is all."

12. Mencius said, "Now if one's third finger is bent and cannot stretch straight, though this neither causes any pain nor impairs the use of the hand, one would think nothing of the distance between Ch'in and Ch'u if someone able to straighten it could be found. This is because one's finger is inferior to other people's. When one's finger is inferior to other people's, one has sense enough to resent it, but not when one's heart is inferior. This is what is called a lack of knowledge of priorities."

13. Mencius said, "Even with a *t'ung* or a *tzu* tree one or two spans thick, anyone wishing to keep it alive will know how it should be tended, yet when it comes to one's own person, one does not know how to tend it. Surely one does not love one's person any less than the *t'ung* or the *tzu?* This is unthinking to the highest degree."

14. Mencius said, "A man loves all parts of his person without discrimination. As he loves them all without discrimination, he nurtures them all without discrimination.

If there is not one foot or one inch of his skin that he does not love, then there is not one foot or one inch that he does not nurture. Is there any other way of telling whether what a man does is good or bad than by the choice he makes? The parts of the person differ in value and importance. Never harm the parts of greater importance for the sake of those of smaller importance, or the more valuable for the sake of the less valuable. He who nurtures the parts of smaller importance is a small man; he who nurtures the parts of greater importance is a great man. Now consider a gardener. If he tends the common trees, while neglecting the valuable ones, then he is a bad gardener. A man who takes care of one finger to the detriment of his shoulder and back without realizing his mistake is a muddled man. A man who cares only about food and drink is despised by others because he takes care of the parts of smaller importance to the detriment of the parts of greater importance. If a man who cares about food and drink can do so without neglecting any other part of his person, then his mouth and belly are much more than just a foot or an inch of his skin."

15. Kung-tu Tzu asked, "Though equally human, why are some men greater than others?"

"He who is guided by the interests of the parts of his person that are of greater importance is a great man; he who is guided by the interests of the parts of his person that are of smaller importance is a small man."

"Though equally human, why are some men guided one way and others guided another way?"

"The organs of hearing and sight are unable to think and can be misled by external things. When one thing acts on another, all it does is attract it. The organ of the heart can think. But it will find the answer only if it does think; otherwise, it will not find the answer. This is what Heaven has given me. If one makes one's stand on what is of greater importance in the first instance, what is of smaller importance cannot displace it. In this way, one cannot but be a great man."

16. Mencius said, "There are honours bestowed by Heaven, and there are honours bestowed by man. Benevolence, dutifulness, conscientiousness, truthfulness to one's word, unflagging delight in what is good,—these are honours bestowed by Heaven. The position of a Ducal Minister, a Minister, or a Counsellor is an honour bestowed by man. Men of antiquity bent their efforts towards acquiring honours bestowed by Heaven, and honours bestowed by man followed as a matter of course. Men of today bend their efforts towards acquiring honours bestowed by Heaven in order to win honours bestowed by man, and once the latter is won they discard the former. Such men are deluded to the extreme, and in the end are sure only to perish."

17. Mencius said, "All men share the same desire to be exalted. But as a matter of fact, every man has in him that which is exalted. The fact simply never dawned on him. What man exalts is not truly exalted. Those Chao Meng exalts, Chao Meng can also humble. The *Ode* says,

> Having filled us with drink,
> Having filled us with virtue,... [*Ode* #247.]

The point is that, being filled with moral virtue, one does not envy other people's enjoyment of fine food and, enjoying a fine and extensive reputation, one does not envy other people's fineries."

18. Mencius said, "Benevolence overcomes cruelty just as water overcomes fire. Those who practise benevolence today are comparable to someone trying to put out a cartload of burning firewood with a cupful of water. When they fail to succeed, they say water cannot overcome fire. For a man to do this is for him to place himself on the side of those who are cruel to the extreme, and in the end he is sure only to perish."

19. Mencius said, "The five types of grain are the best of plants, yet if they are not ripe they are worse than the wild varieties. With benevolence the point, too, lies in seeing to its being ripe."

20. Mencius said, "In teaching others archery, Yi naturally aims at drawing the bow to the full, and the student naturally also aims at drawing the bow to the full. In teaching others, the master carpenter naturally does so by means of compasses and square, and the student naturally also learns by means of compasses and square."

TAOIST ALTERNATIVES

Of the six schools of Chinese philosophy attributed to the classical period, only Confucianism and Taoism (Daoism) survived the collapse of the Ch'in Dynasty in 206 B.C.E. Mohism, the School of Names, the Yin Yang School, and Legalism vanished. Yin-Yang theory lived on in the Confucian and Taoist systems, and Legalist principles continued to influence the way emperors ruled. But as separate forces, these four waned. Confucianism and Taoism, in contrast, entered the middle period of Chinese philosophy as major players. Once joined by Buddhism, those three wrote the script for the main act. In retrospect, then, Confucianism and Taoism may be considered the mainstays of the classical period, the protagonist and antagonist respectively. Mohism was in point of fact the first serious threat to the primacy of Confucianism. Taoism, however, posed the lasting challenge.

From its inception during the later Chou Dynasty, Taoism was an odd mix. That label was applied to diverse figures and activities. The Chinese themselves recognize the patchwork nature of Taoism by distinguishing between Taoist Philosophy (*tao-chia (daojia)*) and Taoist Religion (*tao-chiao (daojiao)*). Even that distinction does not include all the unconnected elements associated with Taoism during classical times. Lao-tzu (Laozi) and Chuang-tzu (Zhuangzi) were not connected as a "school" of Taoist Philosophy until the early Han Dynasty (second century B.C.E.), and the components of the Taoist Religion did not mesh until late in that dynasty (second century C.E.). The thread common to all these disparate elements was the aspiration for immortality. Immortality, however, meant something different for the philosophy than for the religion. Taoist Philosophy took it to be a state of mystical union with Tao (Dao), the Absolute, reached through meditation. Taoist Religion understood it as the transmutation of the physical body from the conditions of mortality (disease, old age, death) to great longevity if not deathlessness, rejuvenation, invulnerability to disease and harm, and occult powers of body and psyche. This physical immortality was obtained through unusual dietary and gymnastic practices, alchemy, and the ingestion of magical plants sought in remote places. This section touches on Taoist Religion but concentrates on Taoist Philosophy.

The history of Taoist Philosophy reached its highpoint during the first period of Chinese philosophy (525–206 B.C.E.). The two classic works appearing then, the *Lao-tzu* and *Chuang-tzu*, remain that school's unexcelled literary treasures. Brief, enigmatic, and tantalizing, they have provided generations of Taoist thinkers ample food for thought. For that reason, the history of this school has been virtually the history of the interpretation of its two seminal texts. Also worthy of note from the initial period is Yang Chu, classified by some later scholars as another early Taoist, though of a stripe very different from Lao-tzu and Chuang-tzu. Mencius criticized him for his radical individualism, disregard for social obligations, and hedonistic tendency.

During the middle period of Chinese philosophy (206 B.C.E.–1644 C.E.), philosophical Taoism launched the lone postclassical innovation of significance in its tradition—Neo-Taoism. A short-lived movement following the fall of the Han Dynasty, it took two directions, one 361 and the other ethical. Wang Pi (Wang Bi, 226–249 C.E.), and Kuo Hsiang (Guo Xiang, 252–312 C.E.) probed the all-important metaphysical concept of Tao. Wang Pi is credited with inventing, in his commentary on the *Lao-tzu*, the idea of principle (*li*) to explain Tao. Principle is the abstract universal or Absolute that generates, regulates, and defines everything in the world. Kuo Hsiang advanced the radical belief that Tao as principle is literally nonexistent. In his commentary on the *Chuang-tzu*, he maintained that concrete particulars are self-sufficient, each containing its own built-in principle, voiding the need Wang Pi saw for one overarching Tao as ground of all.

The other thrust of the Neo-Taoist movement was the School of Pure Conversation. Its members held the ethical theory that the good life consists in cultivating one's capacity to appreciate the higher pleasures—music, art, literature, philosophy—and in engaging in brilliant discourse about them. Nor would they exclude from such a life the tempered enjoyment of eating, drinking, recreation, travel, friendship, and family life. This is hedonism, of course, but of the refined not the vulgar sort. Vulgar hedonism, however, also claimed a place in Neo-Taoism with the so-called Seven Sages of the Bamboo Grove, who are said to have carried Taoist completely spontaneous behavior to excess. Neo-Taoism inherited its hedonism from Yang Chu, accounting for the fact that a crucial chapter in the *Lieh-tzu (Liezi)* is entitled "Yang Chu's Garden of Pleasure." The *Lieh-tzu*, sometimes called the third classic of Taoist Philosophy, is in the opinion of contemporary scholarship a work of the Neo-Taoist period (ca. 300 C.E.) incorrectly assigned by tradition to the earlier era of the other two classics.

Unlike Confucianism, which continues to evolve, Taoist Philosophy advanced no further than Neo-Taoism. Taoist Religion, however, experienced vigorous development over ensuing centuries. But Taoist Philosophy became primarily a rallying point for numerous intellectuals who personally identified with the mysticism of the two Taoist classics, the *Lao-tzu* and the *Chuang-tzu*, or with the refined hedonism of the *Lieh-tzu*. The best commentaries on the classics continued to stimulate interest, and new commentaries were written, but none commanded attention sufficient to spark a new departure in Taoist thought. Taoist

Philosophy did, however, play an important role in two other movements during the remainder of the middle period. It loaned Buddhism a basic Chinese philosophical vocabulary for the translation of Indian texts when Buddhism was taking root in China during the first five centuries C.E. It also contributed the central concept of principle (*li*) to the synthesis of Confucianism and Taoism culminating in Chu Hsi's work in the Sung Dynasty. The shape of Taoist Philosophy during the modern period (1644–present) remains unchanged. Study and personal appropriation of the *Lao-tzu* and *Chuang-tzu* classics continues as before. It is to the examination of these two texts, paramount throughout the history of Taoist Philosophy, that we now turn, honoring precedent by taking the *Lao-tzu* first.

*   *   *

Who was Lao-tzu, and what might his connection have been with the book bearing that name? A quest for the identity of Lao-tzu uncovers a trail of three stages marked by clues that start in obscure history and end in flamboyant mythology. The pre-Han sources (fourth and third centuries B.C.E.) focus on a figure indicated only as Lao Tan (Lao Dan, "Old Tan"), an affectionate nickname lacking historical precision. This Lao Tan was supposedly visited by Confucius, to whom he was senior and superior in knowledge of the Rites or of the Tao. Association with the historically confirmed Confucius would place Lao Tan squarely in the sixth century B.C.E. One fourth-century B.C.E. source equates Lao Tan with Lao-tzu ("Old Master"), a nickname of endearment and respect with even less historical value, appearing here for the first time in the literature. Materials from the third-century B.C.E. describe Lao Tan as a retired imperial archivist and author of a text entitled the *Lao-tzu*. Identification of Lao Tan with Lao-tzu is the pre-Han basis for assigning to Lao-tzu the sixth-century authorship of a book using his name as its title. The book has come down through Chinese history with that pedigree, seriously doubted by many scholars today.

The second stage in the quest features a source that invests Lao-tzu with a precise identity, factual or fictitious. In Ssu-ma Ch'ien's (Sima Qian's) biography of Lao-tzu, one of many biographies of ancient worthies in his *Records of the Historian* (ca. 90 B.C.E.), the Lao Tan nickname recedes; Lao-tzu receives instead a real name, Li Erh (Li Er), and a specific birthplace, in what is now Honan (Henan) Province. Two stories are told of him that help flesh out the impression of his personality. In the first, Lao-tzu is an imperial archivist whom Confucius seeks out at the Chou court for instruction in the Rites; the interview goes badly, for Confucius withdraws bewildered. The second story elaborates on Lao-tzu's authorship of the classic named after him. Believing the Chou Dynasty about to collapse, Lao-tzu flees to the west. At the frontier, the gatekeeper implores him to record his wisdom on *tao (dao,* "way") and *te (de,* "power") before leaving China. He complies by scribbling a manuscript of 5,000 characters in two parts, then exits. Ssu-ma Ch'ien imputes one more thing of significance to Lao-tzu—great longevity of about 200 years, acquired through union with the Tao. This portrait of Lao-tzu, minus the longevity claim, has been accepted by Taoist Philosophy ever since Ssu-ma Ch'ien's day, until recent scholarship challenged it.

The late Han sources of the third stage take the quest beyond the human though historically uncertain Lao-tzu of Taoist Philosophy to the deified, mythological Lao-tzu of Taoist Religion. Sacrifices to Lao-tzu as a god are known to have commenced in the middle of the second century C.E. At that time, beliefs were circulating that Lao-tzu was really a divine being coeternal with the primeval chaos. He had undergone many marvelous transformations before the creation of the universe and numerous earthly incarnations after it, usually through miraculous birth and always in the role of savior. Sometimes he had come to offer counsel to the sage-kings of China's ancient past. Once he had come to journey beyond China's western border and on to India, where he changed into the Buddha for the conversion of barbarians to faith in Tao. Further, he is coming again to establish a kingdom on earth where physical immortality will abound. Another tradition denies to the heavenly Lao-tzu earthly incarnations but has him commission human emissaries to do his work on earth, equipping them with a divinely revealed scripture (the *Lao-tzu*) and the power of faith healing, charging them also to found through rebellion a separate church-state. Such beliefs in Lao-tzu's divinity continued to mount through the T'ang and Sung dynasties, inspiring faith and hope in the hearts of multitudes and spurring not a few uprisings. Even today, in Taoist temples throughout the Chinese world, Lao-tzu as T'ai-shang Lao-chun (Taishang Laojun, "Lord Lao the Most High") appears among the trinity of deities on the high altar.

After Lao-tzu the person comes discussion of *Lao-tzu* the book. Scholars are divided on authorship and date. Some authorities today, believing the traditional account conveyed by the pre-Han and early Han sources just mentioned, opt for single authorship by Lao Tan/Li Erh (alias Lao-tzu), a senior contemporary of Confucius, in the sixth century B.C.E. Other experts date the book at about 250 B.C.E., when its existence was first documented in pre-Han sources. These experts tend to think the book is the work of many hands, since it appears piecemeal rather than unified. Both these popular views were put on hold by a major 1993 archaeological discovery at Kuotien (Guodian) in central east China. There, three untitled bundles of bamboo strips were recovered from a tomb, strips on which two-fifths of the material in the *Lao-tzu* is inscribed. The implications of this find are still being studied. What seems likely at this point is that many hands were involved in the production of what eventually became the *Lao-tzu* we have today, that the production went through many revisions over time, and that composition began sometime prior to 350 B.C.E. The Kuotien *Lao-tzu* shows signs of being a work in progress.

Analysis of the structure of the completed book is complicated by manuscript differences. The text accepted for centuries as the standard is the text Wang Pi included in his eminent commentary on the *Lao-tzu* (third century C.E.). That text, following an order established at least as early as the first century B.C.E., divides the work into eighty-one chapters in two parts, Chapters 1–37 comprising Book One and Chapters 38–81 Book Two. In 1973, two silk manuscripts of the text, dating about 200 B.C.E. or 450 years earlier than Wang Pi's, were unearthed from a Han tomb at Ma-wang-tui (Mawangdui), also in central east China. These much older manuscripts reverse the two parts and contain practically no chapter division markers. Some experts claim the Wang Pi text belongs to a manuscript tradition just as old. Further, the Ma-wang-tui manuscripts were the property of the Huang-Lao sect, who blended Taoism with Legalism; that sect may have had special reasons for reordering the two parts. On the other hand, the arrangement of materials in the Wang Pi text makes better sense and its division into chapters seems more advanced, arguing for the likelihood that of the two it is the altered version. Also contested is the suggestion that each chapter is reducible to a mosaic of very short fragments from different sources. What, therefore, was the structure of the first complete text? The evidence to date is inconclusive.

The book bears three names. At first, it was called the *Lao-tzu* after its supposed author. Once it had achieved status as a classic, it acquired its other familiar title, the *Tao-te ching (Daodejing,* "The Classic of the Way and the Power"). *Tao* and *te* are not only its key words but also the first words of Book One and Book Two, respectively, in the Wang Pi text (the opposite in the Ma-wang-tui). According to a convention applied to many ancient untitled writings, the first word of the text eventually became its name. In the present case, the first word of each of its two parts jointly provided a second title. In addition, since the early Han, the book has been referred to, less commonly, as *The Book of the Five Thousand Characters,* because of its approximate length and Ssu-ma Ch'ien's narrative of Lao-tzu's writing a book of that word count on his departure from China. By whatever name, this classic ranks among the most esteemed in world literature. English translations alone, beginning with James Legge's in 1861, number about 100, with fresh efforts appearing almost yearly. There are scores of translations in German and French as well, not to mention those in numerous other European and Asian languages.

The meaning of this most cryptic of ancient Chinese classics, the first selection offered in this section (Wing-tsit Chan translation), is far from self-evident. The reader must create a coherent interpretation around its recurring themes, foremost of which is Tao ("way," "road," or "path"). In the early period, this celebrated Chinese word usually indicated an ethical path of right living. Here it is elevated to a metaphysical principle, the Absolute, in the same league with Brahman (Upanishads) and the Truth Body of Buddha (Mahayana Buddhism). As viewed by humans, Tao has two aspects—the secret and the manifest (*Lao-tzu,* Chapter 1), like the two sides of the moon. Secret Tao is beyond the range of ordinary knowing (14, 21) but accessible to extraordinary cognition through mind-emptying meditation (10, 12, 28). The mystical knowledge of secret Tao is incommunicable. We cannot say what its essential nature is. Secret Tao cannot be articulated (1); it is nameless (14, 32, 41); he who knows it is speechless (56). But we can say what secret Tao is not. It is nonbeing (40), empty (4), formless (25), not a discrete object with shape and features or a recognizable force like heat or sound. And we can say what secret Tao is like. It is like water, because it benefits all creatures gently and humbly (8), and because it is where the many reunite into one (32). Feminine analogues (mother, mysterious female) associate it with procreation (1, 25, 52), while other analogues (valley spirit, gate, bellows, jar) connote the hollow from which something emerges. Much of this combines, finally, to allow us to say what secret Tao does. It generates the creatures of heaven and earth (1, 2, 42, 52). It also ennatures (39) and sustains (7, 34, 51) them. All this can be communicated about secret Tao without encroaching on the mystery of its inner essence.

Tao's outer form, on the other hand, is open to all and communicable. The manifest Tao discloses itself in the way Nature works, and Nature is forever underway, always on the go. Within the flux a constant can be observed, a master plan, pattern, or principle—return through the opposite. *Return* denotes a curved course that reverts to its departure point (16, 40). Opposites, in this view, cooperate in a joint venture or common cause (2, 26, 39, 42). Nature comes full circle propelled by the alternation of opposites, seen in the endless cycles of day and night, summer and winter, high and low tide, full and new moon. Returning through the opposite is Tao manifest in the way Nature works. Humans are advised to copy Nature and conform to the Way (23) by turning back when a limit or extreme is reached. There comes a point when learning should give way to simple-mindedness (20, 81); the male to the female, the white to the black, honor to disgrace (28); attack to retreat, strength to weakness, fullness to emptiness, the big to the small. In this spirit, the text advocates reducing the population, decentralizing the state, disarming, retarding technology, and recalling diplomats (80). The ideal of unlimited progress is a snare and a delusion if it is natural for everything in the world to return.

The theme of return leads to consideration of Te ("virtue," "power"), a concept as important as Tao in the *Tao-te ching*. The word *te* in its earliest traceable usage (twelfth century B.C.E.) refers to the king's outward forcefulness, which earns him Heaven's mandate to rule. By the time of Confucius (sixth century B.C.E.), it means the moral virtue of the Gentleman, the inner force behind his charisma. In the Taoist classics, it designates the power in anything to actualize its full potential. In humans, Te is the innate power to become fully and authentically human. It is the Tao within, comparable to Atman, the Brahman within (Upanishads). To this natural potency the text urges a return. Return implies departure; people have lost touch with their inborn energy and are surviving on a substitute. Operating by means of the substitute is a departure from Te, reconnecting with the original a return to it. Discredited with the substitute as its unnatural byproducts are affluence (prompted by greed), education (pseudo wisdom), reason (mere cleverness), refinement (a facade), and self-cultivated benevolence and righteousness (contrived, ineffectual), the last a veiled attack on Mencius (18, 19, 38). Genuine benevolence and righteousness spring spontaneously from the natural power, without need of cultivation. A person is to hold the substitute energy in reserve while drawing on the original, thus returning to the pristine state of a newborn babe or uncarved block (28).

Inaction (*wu wei (wuwei)*) is another theme fundamental to the *Lao-tzu* and one easily misunderstood. "Taking no action" has nothing to do with inactivity prompted by laziness, apathy, timidity, or neglect. The term has several nuances, all of them positive. First, taking no action means refraining from action likely to prove counterproductive. The text counsels not meddling in the affairs of others or interfering with a process that is moving ahead well enough on its own (3, 29, 44, 48, 57, 63, 64). Second, taking no action in some passages concerns the energy source behind action. It means allowing Te to empower action, rather than drawing on the substitute. Te alone can supply the dynamic for humane action. Harnessed to Te, action flows effortlessly, spontaneously. One feels one does nothing, yet everything needful gets done (38, 47, 48). Third, taking no action sometimes concerns the guidance of action. It is being guided by wisdom one cannot readily identify as one's own. So guided, again one feels inactive in the midst of action, like a bystander. This higher wisdom usually takes one successfully along the course of least resistance; any other course provokes its own obstruction (22, 43). Or the higher wisdom may take one in an unexpected direction, even away from one's goal rather than toward it. The Way always returns through the opposite, reaching the goal after coming full circle (2, 7, 15, 22, 36, 43). The mystical flavor of philosophical Taoism comes across in the inaction doctrine.

The last of the main themes of the *Lao-tzu* is the Taoist Sage, the ideal human according to this text. The life of the Taoist Sage is completely natural and spontaneous, not a matter of deliberate self-cultivation like the life of the Confucian Gentleman. The Sage knows Tao, secret Tao mystically through mind-emptying meditation (1, 10, 56, 81) and manifest Tao by observing the way Nature works (16, 40). Knowing the Tao, the Sage reflexively conforms to it (15, 21, 22, 23,

54). Conforming to the Tao whose Way is return, the Sage reconnects with Te, the Tao within (18, 19, 20, 28, 38). Having recentered on Te, the Sage practices inaction, refraining from counterproductive action and trusting Te to empower and guide humane action (2, 36, 48, 57). The *Lao-tzu,* further, contains advice for rulers. Like the *Republic* of Plato, this Taoist classic would have sages be kings. The Sage-King rules by setting the example of conforming to Tao, returning to Te, and practicing inaction, an example from which the empire prospers (3, 10, 17, 32, 37, 57, 59, 66, 78). He interferes as little as possible in the lives of his subjects. Insofar as he has any formulated policy, it seems to follow the lines of deregulation, decentralization, disarmament, diplomatic isolationism, and technological restraint (30, 31, 57, 80). Whether such policy is to be taken as corrective of temporary excesses or normative for all times is not clear. The welfare of the state, however, is a concern this text shares with almost all the stellar works of early Chinese philosophy.

*   *   *

The *Chuang-tzu* is the other masterwork of Taoist Philosophy from the classical era. The man credited with its authorship bore the name Chuang Chou (Zhuang Zhou). Chuang-tzu is the title of respect conferred on him posthumously, after the fame of his book was established. His probable dates are 369–286 B.C.E. Virtually all that is known about him comes from the biographical sketch in Ssu-ma Ch'ien's *Records of the Historian.* Complications such as those surrounding the question of Lao-tzu's historicity are absent in the case of Chuang-tzu, and scholars are willing to take the ancient historian's account at face value. In that source, we learn that Chuang-tzu came from the state of Sung in Honan Province, resigned a minor post and refused a prime ministership in order to adopt a hermit's existence, and wrote a book of 100,000 words. He was a contemporary of Mencius but unacquainted with him. Hui Shih of the School of Names, however, is known to have been his friend and in the *Chuang-tzu* his frequent dialogue partner. Since so much of the book appears fanciful, stories found there about its author are subject to suspicion. So are the conversations put into the mouths of Confucius, Lao Tan, Yang Chu, Lieh-tzu, and other famous personages of the early period.

Chuang-tzu the book, authorities now believe, is a condensation by the Neo-Taoist philosopher, Kuo Hsiang, of a once larger compendium of pieces written over a two-century period by many hands. Kuo Hsiang arranged in three parts the thirty-three chapters he kept, to which he added the definitive commentary, the oldest extant on that work. Those three parts he called the Inner Chapters (1–7), the Outer Chapters (8–22), and the Miscellaneous Chapters (23–33). The Inner Chapters he regarded as genuine (written by Chuang-tzu) and named each according to its central theme. The Outer Chapters he judged doubtful and the Miscellaneous Chapters inauthentic as far as Chuang-tzu authorship is concerned; these chapters for the most part he gave titles taken from important words in their first lines. Contemporary scholarship agrees on the genuineness of the Inner Chapters but thinks they were crafted together by later editors out of fragments jotted down by the master about 320 B.C.E. As for the remaining twenty-six chapters, one highly reputed expert today offers a feasible analysis. He considers Chapters 12 to 22 to have been written by Chuang-tzu's immediate disciples just after his death and to be consistent with his position. Chapters 8 to 11 and 28 to 31 he believes come from sources more distant from Chuang-tzu's thought and time period; he dates them late in the third century B.C.E. And Chapters 23 to 27 and 32 to 33 he sees as a potpourri of elements with little connection to Chuang-tzu's thinking, composed in the second century B.C.E. The comments that follow on the *Chuang-tzu* pertain only to the surely authentic part of the work—the Inner Chapters.

What is the relationship between the two texts named after Lao-tzu and Chuang-tzu? For centuries, the *Chuang-tzu* was looked upon as a sequel to the *Lao-tzu*. Most scholars today, however, regard them as isolated productions, and some would reverse their order of appearance. Ssu-ma T'an (Sima Tan, d. 110 B.C.E.) retrospectively grouped the classical Chinese philosophers into the "Six Schools" in his *Han History*. He first coupled these two works under the heading of the School of Taoist Philosophy. Because his system of classification caught on, the two essential Taoist classics, like twins, have led parallel lives. Consequently, we now take their linkage under one school for granted. Their popularity relative to each other has fluctuated over the centuries. The *Lao-tzu* was preferred during the Han Dynasty, the *Chuang-tzu* for some time following it. Since they came to light in the West 150 years ago, the *Lao-tzu* has overshadowed its companion in terms of translations, scholarship, and readership. But with a recent surge of interest in the *Chuang-tzu,* attention to each one is today more equally balanced. When the two books are studied side by side, similarities and differences can be noted. We today, accustomed to regarding both books as Taoist, tend to weight the similarities more heavily. Apparently, in Ssu-ma T'an's time, the opposite occurred, and many viewed his joining of the two works under one caption as unjustified. If the two are twins, their bond is fraternal not identical.

The Inner Chapters of the *Chuang-tzu* share with the *Lao-tzu* a set of key concepts. No significant differences divide these texts in their understanding of Tao (the Way), Te (virtue or power), Inaction, Opposites, Return, or the Sage. Beyond general ideological agreement, however, lie differences in intended readership and in rhetorical style. The *Lao-tzu* offers advice to rulers on statecraft and governance, whereas the *Chuang-tzu* in its Inner Chapters mounts but a single passage on that subject (Chap. 7). Some commentators conclude that the former originally addressed persons engaged in public affairs, while the latter made its appeal to nonpolitical types, like Chuang-tzu himself, attracted to a quieter life. The claim that the *Chuang-tzu* is the only classic of any ancient school preferring seclusion to public office is cited as the main obstacle in Ssu-ma T'an's day to pairing the two books as Taoist. As for rhetorical style, what we find in the *Lao-tzu* is straight discursive discourse. The *Chuang-tzu*, on the other hand, is variety epitomized: There are fantastic anecdotes, thought-provoking conversations, stunning images, humorous nicknames, grotesque evocations, touches of sensitivity to Nature and craftsmanship, all enlisted into the service of philosophy. Both works are baffling in a way that tends to hold the reader enthralled. But the *Chuang-tzu* especially exudes a charm hard to match.

The consciousness of the Sage in contrast to that of the nonsage is the unifying theme and unique contribution of the Inner Chapters (second selection in this section, A.C. Graham translation). The Sage's awareness is far superior in range, power, freedom, and clarity to what most people experience. The Sage is attuned to the mystical presence of Tao everywhere, whereas the nonsage finds the world Tao-less (Chaps. 2, 4, 5). The Sage, surveying earth from the vantage point of Heaven, is surrounded by beauty and wonder (Chaps. 2, 6). The nonsage finds it difficult to even imagine such heights (Chaps. 1, 4). The Sage beholds an integrated scene, the nonsage a fragmented one (Chaps. 1, 2, 5). The Sage, accepting uncontrollable circumstances, enjoys tranquillity and contentment, while his unfortunate counterpart struggles with cares and worries (Chaps. 3, 4, 5, 6). The Sage uses the mind like a mirror, responding appropriately without pondering or weighing. The nonsage, poor chap, using the mind like a computer, tries to figure things out but is left with uncertainty and confusion (Chaps. 6, 7). Chuang-tzu captures his point vividly in an image and a fantasy. The image is of the immortals of Taoist religion with their limitless powers; they sky-surf the wind and clouds and frolic among the planets. In the fantasy, which launches the book, a fish grows from a tiny egg to a size so big the sea itself can no longer contain it, then metamorphoses into a gigantic bird streaking through infinite space like a comet. Meanwhile, a cicada, a dove, and a quail, low fliers all, scoff at reports of the space bird's miraculous voyage. The application to the consciousness of Sage and nonsage is fairly transparent.

How might sage consciousness be realized? The impediment to be removed is reason with its need to decide truth or falsity. Of two strategies for coping with the problem, one is mystical and the other philosophical. The mystical approach circumvents reason through mind-emptying meditation (Chaps. 2, 4, 6, 7). The philosophical approach (Chap. 2) proposes to undo reason with reasoning. Test cases are presented in which reason cannot reasonably decide truth or falsity. For example, since words receive their meanings arbitrarily, and any word could just as well carry a meaning opposite to what convention assigns it, how can one tell if anything one says is true or false? If "rock" could just as well refer to water and "hard" to what is soft, how can one tell if "rock is hard" is true or false? If words are not true or false, how can statements formed out of words be true or false? Again, two individuals finish a debate, and the judges declare one of them the winner. His argument was stronger, but his proposition may in fact have been false. The loser's argument was weaker, but his proposition may have been true. We can decide the strength or weakness of arguments, but how can we decide the truth or falsity of the propositions argued? How can we ever be sure that what we take for truth is not just clever argumentation, or falsity clumsy argumentation? Further, Chuang-tzu asks if at any given moment one can decide whether one is dreaming or awake, for dreaming seems to be waking until one awakens to discover it was a dream after all. Chuang-tzu climaxes his exposé of reason with his famous butterfly paradox. He is dreaming of being a butterfly, when the thought strikes him that maybe he is really the dream of the butterfly he is dreaming about. Who is the dreamer and who the dream? The inability of reason to decide such cases is reason's undoing. The force of Chuang-tzu's reasoning is to free consciousness from reason, with its impossible demand to decide truth or falsity, and to usher in the suprarational consciousness of the Sage.

*   *   *

Competent discussions of both philosophical and religious Taoism include Holmes Welch, *Taoism: The Parting of the Way,* rev. ed. (Boston: Beacon Press, 1965); Herrlee G. Creel, *What Is Taoism?* (Chicago: University of Chicago Press, 1970); John Blofeld, *Taoism: The Road to Immortality* (Boulder, CO: Shambhala, 1978); and Livia Kohn, ed., *Daoism Handbook* (Leiden: E.J. Brill, 2000). For more advanced studies of the *Lao-tzu,* consult Max Kaltenmark, *Lao Tzu and*

Taoism, tr. Roger Graves (Stanford: Stanford University Press, 1969); Michael LaFargue, *Tao and Method: A Reasoned Approach to the Tao-te-ching* (Albany: SUNY Press, 1994); Livia Kohn and Michael LaFargue, eds., *Lao-tzu and the Tao-te-ching* (Albany: SUNY Press, 1998); and Mark Csikszentmihalyi and Philip J. Ivanhoe, eds., *Religious and Philosophical Aspects of the Laozi* (Albany: SUNY Press, 1999). For more advanced studies of the *Chuang-tzu*, see Herbert A. Giles, *Zhuangzi: Mystic, Moralist, and Social Reformer* (London: George Allen & Unwin, 1981); Kuang-ming Wu, *Chuang-tzu: World Philosopher at Play* (New York: Crossroad, 1982); Victor H. Mair, ed., *Experimental Essays on Chuang-tzu* (Honolulu: University of Hawaii Press, 1983); Robert E. Allinson, *Chuang-tzu for Spiritual Transformation: An Analysis of the Inner Chapters* (Albany: SUNY Press, 1989); Kuang-ming Wu, *The Butterfly as Companion: Meditations on the First Three Chapters of the Chuang Tzu* (Albany: SUNY Press, 1990); Paul Kjellberg and Philip J. Ivanhoe, eds., *Essays on Skepticism, Relativism, and Ethics in the Zhuangzi* (Albany: SUNY Press, 1996); and Roger T. Ames, ed., *Wandering at Ease in the Zhuangzi* (Albany: SUNY Press, 1998).

LAO TZU, TAO-*TE* CHING

The Tao that can be told of is not the eternal Tao;   1
The name that can be named is not the eternal name.
The Nameless is the origin of Heaven and Earth;
The Named is the mother of all things.
Therefore let there always be non-being, so we may see their subtlety,
And let there always be being, so we may see their outcome.
The two are the same,
But after they are produced, they have different names.
They both may be called deep and profound.
Deeper and more profound, The door of all subtleties!

When the people of the world all know beauty as beauty,   2
There arises the recognition of ugliness.
When they all know the good as good,
There arises the recognition of evil.
Therefore:
Being and non-being produce each other;
Difficult and easy complete each other;
Long and short contrast each other;
High and low distinguish each other;
Sound and voice harmonize each other;
Front and behind accompany each other.
Therefore the sage manages affairs without action
And spreads doctrines without words.
All things arise, and he does not turn away from them.
He produces them but does not take possession of them.
He acts but does not rely on his own ability.
He accomplishes his task but does not claim credit for it.
It is precisely because he does not claim credit that his accomplishment remains with him.

Do not exalt the worthy, so that the people shall not compete.   3
Do not value rare treasures, so that the people shall not steal.
Do not display objects of desire, so that the people's hearts shall not be disturbed.
Therefore in the government of the sage,
He keeps their hearts vacuous,
Fills their bellies,
Weakens their ambitions,
And strengthens their bones,
He always causes his people to be without knowledge (cunning) or desire,
And the crafty to be afraid to act.
By acting without action, all things will be in order.

Tao is empty (like a bowl).   4
(It may be used) but its capacity is never exhausted.
It is bottomless, perhaps the ancestor of all things.
It blunts its sharpness,
It unties its tangles.
It softens its light.

The Way of Lao Tzu, tr. by Wing-tsit Chan (New York: Macmillan/Library of Liberal Arts, 1963).

Lao Tzu on a Water Buffalo. According to legend, in his old age Lao Tzu (Laozi) became disillusioned by the decline of the state of Chou (Zhou) and decided to leave civilization for the Western wilderness. The gatekeeper recognized him as a great teacher and convinced him to record his teachings before he left. Lao-tzu obliged and in three days wrote the Tao Te Ching before riding his water buffalo into the sunset. (*Burstein Collection, Corbis, NY*)

It becomes one with the dusty world.
Deep and still, it appears to exist forever.
I do not know whose son it is.
It seems to have existed before the Lord.

5   Heaven and Earth are not humane.
They regard all things as straw dogs.
The sage is not humane.
He regards all people as straw dogs.
How Heaven and Earth are like a bellows!
While vacuous, it is never exhausted. When active, it produces even more.
Much talk will of course come to a dead end.
It is better to keep to the center.

6   The spirit of the valley never dies.
It is called the subtle and profound female.
The gate of the subtle and profound female
Is the root of Heaven and Earth.
It is continuous, and seems to be always existing.
Use it and you will never wear it out.

7   Heaven is eternal and Earth everlasting.
They can be eternal and everlasting because they do not exist for themselves,

And for this reason can exist forever.
Therefore the sage places himself in the background but finds himself in the foreground.
He puts himself away, and yet he always remains.
Is it not because he has no personal interests?
This is the reason why his personal interests are fulfilled.

The best (man) is like water.   8
Water is good; it benefits all things and does not compete with them.
It dwells in (lowly) places that all disdain.
This is why it is so near to Tao.
(The best man) in his dwelling loves the earth.
In his heart, he loves what is profound.
In his associations, he loves humanity.
In his words, he loves faithfulness.
In government, he loves order.
In handling affairs, he loves competence.
In his activities, he loves timeliness.
It is because he does not compete that he is without reproach.

To Hold and fill a cup to overflowing   9
Is not as good as to stop in time.
Sharpen a sword-edge to its very sharpest,
And the (edge) will not last long.
When gold and jade fill your hall,
You will not be able to keep them.
To be proud with honor and wealth
Is to cause one's own downfall.
Withdraw as soon as your work is done.
Such is Heaven's Way.

Can you keep the spirit and embrace the One without departing from them?   10
Can you concentrate your vital force and achieve the highest degree of weakness like an infant?
Can you clean and purify your profound insight so it will be spotless?
Can you love the people and govern the state without knowledge (cunning)?
Can you play the role of the female in the opening and closing of the gates of Heaven?
Can you understand all and penetrate all without taking any action?
To produce things and to rear them,
To produce, but not to take possession of them,
To act, but not to rely on one's own ability,
To lead them, but not to master them—
This is called profound and secret virtue.

Thirty spokes are united around the hub to make a wheel,   11
But it is on its non-being that the utility of the carriage depends.
Clay is molded to form a utensil,
But it is on its non-being that the utility of the utensil depends.
Doors and windows are cut out to make a room,
But it is on its non-being that the utility of the room depends.
Therefore turn being into advantage, and turn non-being into utility.

The five colors cause one's eyes to be blind.   12
The five tones cause one's ears to be deaf.
The five flavors cause one's palate to be spoiled.
Racing and hunting cause one's mind to be mad.
Goods that are hard to get injure one's activities.

For this reason the sage is concerned with the belly and not the eyes.
Therefore he rejects the one but accepts the other.

13   Be apprehensive when receiving favor or disgrace.
Regard great trouble as seriously as you regard your body.
What is meant by being apprehensive when receiving favor or disgrace?
Favor is considered inferior.
Be apprehensive when you receive them and also be apprehensive when you lose them.
This is what is meant by being apprehensive when receiving favor or disgrace.
What does it mean to regard great trouble as seriously as you regard the body?
The reason why I have great trouble is that I have a body.
If I have no body,
What trouble could I have?
Therefore he who values the world as his body may be entrusted with the empire.
He who loves the world as his body may be entrusted with the empire.

14   We look at it and do not see it;
Its name is The Invisible.
We listen to it and do not hear it;
Its name is The Inaudible.
We touch it and do not find it;
Its name is The Subtle (formless).
These three cannot be further inquired into,
And hence merge into one.
Going up high, it is not bright, and coming down low, it is not dark.
Infinite and boundless, it cannot be given any name;
It reverts to nothingness.
This is called shape without shape,
Form without objects.
It is The Vague and Elusive.
Meet it and you will not see its head.
Follow it and you will not see its back.
Hold on to the Tao of old in order to master the things of the present.
From this one may know the primeval beginning (of the universe).
This is called the bond of Tao.

15   Of old those who were the best rulers were subtly mysterious and profoundly penetrating;
Too deep to comprehend.
And because they cannot be comprehended,
I can only describe them arbitrarily:
Cautious, like crossing a frozen stream in the winter,
Being at a loss, like one fearing danger on all sides,
Reserved, like one visiting,
Supple and pliant, like ice about to melt.
Genuine, like a piece of uncarved wood,
Open and broad, like a valley,
Merged and undifferentiated, like muddy water.
Who can make muddy water gradually clear through tranquility?
Who can make the still gradually come to life through activity?
He who embraces this Tao does not want to fill himself to overflowing.
It is precisely because there is no overflowing that he is beyond wearing out and renewal.

16   Attain complete vacuity.
Maintain steadfast quietude.
All things come into being,

And I see thereby their return.
All things flourish,
But each one returns to its root.
This return to its root means tranquility.
It is called returning to its destiny.
To return to destiny is called the eternal (Tao).
To know the eternal is called enlightenment.
Not to know the eternal is to act blindly to result in disaster.
He who knows the eternal is all-embracing.
Being all-embracing, he is impartial.
Being impartial, he is kingly (universal).
Being kingly, he is one with Nature.
Being one with Nature, he is in accord with Tao.
Being in accord with Tao, he is everlasting
And is free from danger throughout his lifetime.

The best (rulers) are those whose existence is (merely) known by the people.   17
The next best are those who are loved and praised.
The next are those who are feared.
And the next are those who are despised.
It is only when one does not have enough faith in others that others will have no faith in him.
(The great rulers) value their words highly.
They accomplish their task; they complete their work.
Nevertheless their people say that they simply follow Nature.

When the great Tao declined,   18
The doctrine of humanity and righteousness arose.
When knowledge and wisdom appeared,
There emerged great hypocrisy.
When the six family relationships are not in harmony,
There will be the advocacy of filial piety and deep love to children.
When a country is in disorder,
There will be the praise of loyal ministers.

Abandon sageliness and discard wisdom;   19
Then the people will benefit a hundredfold.
Abandon humanity and discard righteousness;
Then the people will return to filial piety and deep love.
Abandon skill and discard profit;
Then there will be no thieves or robbers.
However, these three things are ornaments (wen) and are not adequate.
Therefore let people hold on to these:
Manifest plainness,
Embrace simplicity,
Reduce selfishness,
Have few desires.

Abandon learning and there will be no sorrow.   20
How much difference is there between "Yes, sir," and "Of course not"?
How much difference is there between "good" and "evil"?
What people dread, do not fail to dread.
But, alas, how confused, and the end is not yet.
The multitude are merry, as though feasting on a day of sacrifice.
Or like ascending a tower in the springtime.
I alone am inert, showing no sign (of desires),

Like an infant that has not yet smiled.
Wearied, indeed, I seem to be without a home.
The multitude all possess more than enough.
I alone seem to have lost all.
Mine is indeed the mind of an ignorant man,
Indiscriminate and dull!
Common folks are indeed brilliant;
I alone seem to be in the dark.
Common folks see differences and are clear-cut;
I alone make no distinctions.
I seem drifting as the sea;
Like the wind blowing about, seemingly without destination.
The multitude all have a purpose;
I alone seem to be stubborn and rustic.
I alone differ from others,
And value drawing sustenance from Mother (Tao).

21   The all-embracing quality of the great virtue follows alone from the Tao.
The thing that is called Tao is eluding and vague.
Vague and eluding, there is in it the form.
Eluding and vague, in it are things.
Deep and obscure, in it is the essence.
The essence is very real; in it are evidences.
From the time of old until now, its name (manifestations) ever remains.
By which we may see the beginning of all things.
How do I know that the beginnings of all things are so?
Through this (Tao).

22   To yield is to be preserved whole.
To be bent is to become straight.
To be empty is to be full.
To be worn out is to be renewed.
To have little is to possess.
To have plenty is to be perplexed.
Therefore the sage embraces the One
And becomes the model of the world.
He does not show himself; therefore he is luminous.
He does not justify himself; therefore he becomes prominent.
He does not boast of himself; therefore he is given credit.
He does not brag; therefore he can endure for long.
It is precisely because he does not compete that the world cannot compete with him.
Is the ancient saying, "To yield is to be preserved whole," empty words?
Truly he will be preserved and (prominence and credit) will come to him.

23   Nature says few words.
For the same reason a whirlwind does not last a whole morning.
Nor does a rainstorm last a whole day.
What causes them?
It is Heaven and Earth (Nature).
If even Heaven and Earth cannot make them last long,
How much less can man?
Therefore he who follows Tao is identified with Tao.
He who follows virtue is identified with virtue.
He who abandons (Tao) is identified with the abandonment (of Tao).
He who is identified with Tao—Tao is also happy to have him.

He who is identified with virtue—virtue is also happy to have him.
And he who is identified with the abandonment (of Tao)—the abandonment (of Tao) is also happy to abandon him.
It is only when one does not have enough faith in others that others will have no faith in him.

He who stands on tiptoe is not steady.   24
He who strides forward does not go.
He who shows himself is not luminous.
He who justifies himself is not prominent.
He who boasts of himself is not given credit.
He who brags does not endure for long.
From the point of view of Tao, these are like remnants of food and tumors of action,
Which all creatures detest.
Therefore those who possess Tao turn away from them.

There was something undifferentiated and yet complete,   25
Which existed before heaven and earth.
Soundless and formless, it depends on nothing and does not change.
It operates everywhere and is free from danger.
It may be considered the mother of the universe.
I do not know its name; I call it Tao.
If forced to give it a name, I shall call it Great.
Now being great means functioning everywhere.
Functioning everywhere means far-reaching.
Being far-reaching means returning to the original point.
Therefore Tao is great.
Heaven is great.
Earth is great.
And the king is also great.
There are four great things in the universe, and the king is one of them.
Man models himself after Earth.
Earth models itself after Heaven.
Heaven models itself after Tao.
And Tao models itself after Nature.

The heavy is the root of the light.   26
The tranquil is the ruler of the hasty.
Therefore the sage travels all day
Without leaving his baggage.
Even at the sight of magnificent scenes,
He remains leisurely and indifferent.
How is it that a lord with ten thousand chariots
Should behave lightheartedly in his empire?
If he is lighthearted, the minister will be destroyed.
If he is hasty, the ruler is lost.

A good traveler leaves no track or trace.   27
A good speech leaves no flaws.
A good reckoner uses no counters.
A well-shut door needs no bolts, and yet it cannot be opened.
A well-tied knot needs no rope and yet none can untie it.
Therefore the sage is always good in saving men and consequently no man is rejected.
He is always good in saving things and consequently nothing is rejected.
This is called following the light (of Nature).
Therefore the good man is the teacher of the bad,

And the bad is the material from which the good may learn.
He who does not value the teacher,
Or greatly care for the material,
Is greatly deluded although he may be learned.
Such is the essential mystery.

28   He who knows the male and keeps to the female
Becomes the ravine of the world.
Being the ravine of the world,
He will never depart from eternal virtue,
But returns to the state of infancy.
He who knows the white and yet keeps to the black
Becomes the model for the world.
Being the model for the world,
He will never deviate from eternal virtue,
But returns to the state of the non-ultimate.
He who knows glory but keeps to humility
Becomes the valley of the world.
Being the valley of the world,
He will be proficient in eternal virtue,
And returns to the state of simplicity (uncarved wood).
When the uncarved wood is broken up, it is turned into concrete things.
But when the sage uses it, he becomes the leading official.
Therefore the great ruler does not cut up.

29   When one desires to take over the empire and act on it (interfere with it),
I see that he will not succeed.
The empire is a spiritual thing, and should not be acted on.
He who acts on it harms it.
He who holds on to it loses it.
Among creatures some lead and some follow.
Some blow hot and some blow cold.
Some are strong and some are weak.
Some may break and some may fall.
Therefore the sage discards the extremes, the extravagant, and the excessive.

30   He who assists the ruler with Tao does not dominate the world with force.
The use of force usually brings requital.
Wherever armies are stationed, briers and thorns grow.
Great wars are always followed by famines.
A good (general) achieves his purpose and stops,
But dares not seek to dominate the world.
He achieves his purpose but does not brag about it.
He achieves his purpose but does not boast about it.
He achieves his purpose but is not proud of it.
He achieves his purpose but only as an unavoidable step.
He achieves his purpose but does not aim to dominate.
(For) after things reach their prime, they begin to grow old,
Which means being contrary to Tao.
Whatever is contrary to Tao will soon perish.

31   Fine weapons are instruments of evil.
They are hated by men.
Therefore those who possess Tao turn away from them.
The good ruler when at home honors the left.

When at war he honors the right.
Weapons are instruments of evil, not the instruments of a good ruler.
When he uses them unavoidably, he regards calm restraint as the best principle.
Even when he is victorious, he does not regard it as praiseworthy,
For to praise victory is to delight in the slaughter of men.
He who delights in the slaughter of men will not succeed in the empire.
In auspicious affairs, the left is honored.
In inauspicious affairs, the right is honored.
The lieutenant general stands on the left.
The senior general stands on the right.
This is to say that the arrangement follows that of funeral ceremonies.
For the slaughter of the multitude, let us weep with sorrow and grief.
For a victory, let us observe the occasion with funeral ceremonies.

Tao is eternal and has no name.   32
Though its simplicity seems insignificant, none in the world can master it.
If kings and barons would hold on to it, all things would submit to them spontaneously.
Heaven and earth unite to drip sweet dew.
Without the command of men, it drips evenly over all.
As soon as there were regulations and institutions, there were names.
As soon as there are names, know that it is time to stop.
It is by knowing when to stop that one can be free from danger.
Analogically, Tao in the world may be compared to rivers and streams running into the
    sea.

He who knows others is wise;   33
He who knows himself is enlightened.
He who conquers others has physical strength.
He who conquers himself is strong.
He who is contented is rich.
He who acts with vigor has will.
He who does not lose his place (with Tao) will endure.
He who dies but does not really perish enjoys long life.

The Great Tao flows everywhere.   34
It may go left or right.
All things depend on it for life, and it does not turn away from them.
It accomplishes its task, but does not claim credit for it.
It clothes and feeds all things but does not claim to be master over them.
Always without desires, it may be called The Small.
All things come to it and it does not master them; it may be called The Great.
Therefore (the sage) never strives himself for the great, and thereby the great is
    achieved.

Hold fast to the great form (Tao),   35
And all the world will come.
They come and will encounter no harm;
But enjoy comfort, peace, and health.
When there are music and dainties,
Passing strangers will stay.
But the words uttered by Tao,
How insipid and tasteless!
We look at it; it is imperceptible.
We listen to it; it is inaudible.
We use it; it is inexhaustible.

36
In order to contract,
It is necessary first to expand.
In order to weaken,
It is necessary first to strengthen.
In order to destroy,
It is necessary first to promote.
In order to grasp,
It is necessary first to give.
This is called subtle light.
The weak and the tender overcome the hard and the strong.
Fish should not be taken away from water.
And sharp weapons of the state should not be displayed to the people.

37
Tao invariably takes no action, and yet there is nothing left undone.
If kings and barons can keep it, all things will transform spontaneously.
If, after transformation, they should desire to be active,
I would restrain them with simplicity, which has no name.
Simplicity, which has no name, is free of desires.
Being free of desires, it is tranquil.
And the world will be at peace of its own accord.

38
The man of superior virtue is not (conscious of) his virtue,
And in this way he really possesses virtue.
The man of inferior virtue never loses (sight of) his virtue,
And in this way he loses his virtue.
The man of superior virtue takes no action, but has no ulterior motive to do so.
The man of inferior virtue takes action, and has an ulterior motive to do so.
The man of superior humanity takes action, but has no ulterior motive to do so.
The man of superior righteousness takes action, and has an ulterior motive to do so.
The man of superior propriety takes action,
And when people do not respond to it, he will stretch his arms and force it on them.
Therefore when Tao is lost, only then does the doctrine of virtue arise.
When virtue is lost, only then does the doctrine of humanity arise.
When humanity is lost, only then does the doctrine of righteousness arise.
When righteousness is lost, only then does the doctrine of propriety arise.
Now, propriety is a superficial expression of loyalty and faithfulness, and the beginning
    of disorder.
Those who are the first to know have the flowers of Tao but are the beginning of ignorance.
For this reason the great man dwells in the thick, and does not rest with the thin.
He dwells in the fruit, and does not rest with the flower.
Therefore he rejects the one, and accepts the other.

39
Of old those that obtained the One:
Heaven obtained the One and became clear.
Earth obtained the One and became tranquil.
The spiritual beings obtained the One and became divine.
The valley obtained the One and became full.
The myriad things obtained the One and lived and grew.
Kings and barons obtained the One and became rulers of the empire.
What made them so is the One.
If heaven had not thus become clear,
It would soon crack.
If the earth had not thus become tranquil,
It would soon be shaken.
If the spiritual beings had not thus become divine,

They would soon wither away.
If the valley had not thus become full,
It would soon become exhausted.
If the myriad things had not thus lived and grown,
They would soon become extinct.
If kings and barons had not thus become honorable and high in position,
They would soon fall.
Therefore humble station is the basis of honor.
The low is the foundation of the high.
For this reason kings and barons call themselves children without parents, lonely people
    without spouses, and men without food to eat.
Is this not regarding humble station as the basis of honor?
Is it not?
Therefore enumerate all the parts of a chariot as you may, and you still have no chariot.
Rather than jingle like the jade,
Rumble like the rocks.

Reversion is the action of Tao.   40
Weakness is the function of Tao.
All things in the world come from being.
And being comes from non-being.

When the highest type of men hear Tao,   41
They diligently practice it.
When the average type of men hear Tao,
They half believe in it.
When the lowest type of men hear Tao,
They laugh heartily at it.
If they did not laugh at it, it would not be Tao.
Therefore there is the established saying:
The Tao which is bright appears to be dark.
The Tao which goes forward appears to fall backward.
The Tao which is level appears uneven.
Great virtue appears like a valley (hollow).
Great purity appears like disgrace.
Far-reaching virtue appears as if insufficient.
Solid virtue appears as if unsteady.
True substance appears to be changeable.
The great square has no corners.
The great implement (or talent) is slow to finish (or mature).
Great music sounds faint.
Great form has no shape.
Tao is hidden and nameless.
Yet it is Tao alone that skillfully provides for all and brings them to perfection.

Tao produced the One.   42
The One produced the two.
The two produced the three.
And the three produced the ten thousand things.
The ten thousand things carry the yin and embrace the yang, and through the blending of
    the material force they achieve harmony.
People hate to be children without parents, lonely people without spouses, or men without
    food to eat,
And yet kings and lords call themselves by these names.
Therefore it is often the case that things gain by losing and lose by gaining.

What others have taught, I teach also:
"Violent and fierce people do not die a natural death."
I shall make this the father of my teaching.

43   The softest things in the world overcome the hardest things in the world.
Non-being penetrates that in which there is no space.
Through this I know the advantage of taking no action.
Few in the world can understand the teaching without words and the advantage of tak-
   ing no action.

44   Which does one love more, fame or one's own life?
Which is more valuable, one's own life or wealth?
Which is worse, gain or loss?
Therefore he who has lavish desires will spend extravagantly.
He who hoards most will lose heavily.
He who is contented suffers no disgrace.
He who knows when to stop is free from danger.
Therefore he can long endure.

45   What is most perfect seems to be incomplete;
But its utility is unimpaired.
What is most full seems to be empty;
But its usefulness is inexhaustible.
What is most straight seems to be crooked.
The greatest skill seems to be clumsy.
The greatest eloquence seems to stutter.
Hasty movement overcomes cold,
(But) tranquility overcomes heat.
By being greatly tranquil,
One is qualified to be the ruler of the world.

46   When tao prevails in the world, galloping horses are turned back to fertilize (the fields with
   their dung).
When Tao does not prevail in the world, war horses thrive in the suburbs.
There is no calamity greater than lavish desires.
There is no greater guilt than discontentment.
And there is no greater disaster than greed.
He who is contented with contentment is always contented.

47   One may know the world without going out of doors.
One may see the Way of Heaven without looking through the windows.
The further one goes, the less one knows.
Therefore the sage knows without going about,
Understands without seeing,
And accomplishes without any action.

48   The pursuit of learning is to increase day after day.
The pursuit of Tao is to decrease day after day.
It is to decrease and further decrease until one reaches the point of taking no action.
No action is undertaken, and yet nothing is left undone.
An empire is often brought to order by having no activity.
If one (likes to) undertake activity, he is not qualified to govern the empire.

49   The sage has no fixed (personal) ideas.
He regards the people's ideas as his own.

I treat those who are good with goodness,
And I also treat those who are not good with goodness.
Thus goodness is attained.
I am honest to those who are honest,
And I am also honest to those who are not honest.
Thus honesty is attained.
The sage, in the government of his empire, has no subjective viewpoint.
His mind forms a harmonious whole with that of his people.
They all lend their eyes and ears, and he treats them all as infants.

Man comes in to life and goes out to death.   50
Three out of ten are companions of life.
Three out of ten are companions of death.
And three out of ten in their lives lead from activity to death.
And for what reason?
Because of man's intensive striving after life.
I have heard that one who is a good preserver of his life will not meet tigers or wild buffaloes,
And in fighting will not try to escape from weapons of war.
The wild buffalo cannot butt its horns against him,
The tiger cannot fasten its claws in him,
And weapons of war cannot thrust their blades into him.
And for what reason?
Because in him there is no room for death.

Tao produces them.   51
Virtue fosters them.
Matter gives them physical form.
The circumstances and tendencies complete them.
Therefore the ten thousand things esteem Tao and honor virtue.
Tao is esteemed and virtue is honored without anyone's order!
They always come spontaneously.
Therefore Tao produces them and virtue fosters them.
They rear them and develop them.
They give them security and give them peace.
They nurture them and protect them.
(Tao) produces them but does not take possession of them.
It acts, but does not rely on its own ability.
It leads them but does not master them.
This is called profound and secret virtue.

There was a beginning of the universe   52
Which may be called the Mother of the universe.
He who has found the mother (Tao)
And thereby understands her sons (things),
And having understood the sons,
Still keeps to its mother,
Will be free from danger throughout his lifetime.
Close the mouth.
Shut the doors (of cunning and desires).
And to the end of life there will be (peace) without toil.
Open the mouth.
Meddle with affairs.
And to the end of life there will be no salvation.
Seeing what is small is called enlightenment.
Keeping to weakness is called strength.

Use the light.
Revert to enlightenment.
And thereby avoid danger to one's life—
This is called practicing the eternal.

53   If I had but little knowledge
I should, in walking on a broad way,
Fear getting off the road.
Broad ways are extremely even,
But people are fond of bypaths.
The courts are exceedingly splendid,
While the fields are exceedingly weedy,
And the granaries are exceedingly empty.
Elegant clothes are worn,
Sharp weapons are carried,
Foods and drinks are enjoyed beyond limit,
And wealth and treasures are accumulated in excess.
This is robbery and extravangance.
This is indeed not Tao (the Way).

54   He who is well established (in Tao) cannot be pulled away.
He who has a firm grasp (of Tao) cannot be separated from it.
Thus from generation to generation his ancestral sacrifice will never be suspended.
When one cultivates virtue in his person, it becomes genuine virtue.
When one cultivates virtue in his family, it becomes overflowing virtue.
When one cultivates virtue in his community, it becomes lasting virtue.
When one cultivates virtue in his country, it becomes abundant virtue.
When one cultivates virtue in the world, it becomes universal.
Therefore the person should be viewed as a person.
The family should be viewed as a family.
The community should be viewed as a community.
The country should be viewed as a country.
And the world should be viewed as the world.
How do I know this to be the case in the world?
Through this.

55   He who possesses virtue in abundance
May be compared to an infant.
Poisonous insects will not sting him.
Fierce beasts will not seize him.
Birds of prey will not strike him.
His bones are weak, his sinews tender, but his grasp is firm.
He does not yet know the union of male and female,
But his organ is aroused,
This means that his essence is at its height.
He may cry all day without becoming hoarse,
This means that his (natural) harmony is perfect.
To know harmony means to be in accord with the eternal.
To be in accord with the eternal means to be enlightened.
To force the growth of life means ill omen.
For the mind to employ the vital force without restraint means violence.
After things reach their prime, they begin to grow old,
Which means being contrary to Tao.
Whatever is contrary to Tao will soon perish.

He who knows does not speak.

56

He who speaks does not know.

Close the mouth.

Shut the doors.

Blunt the sharpness.

Untie the tangles.

Soften the light.

Become one with the dusty world.

This is called profound identification.

Therefore it is impossible either to be intimate and close to him or to be distant and indifferent to him.

It is impossible either to benefit him or to harm him.

It is impossible either to honor him or to disgrace him.

For this reason he is honored by the world.

Govern the state with correctness.

57

Operate the army with surprise tactics.

Administer the empire by engaging in no activity.

How do I know that this should be so?

Through this:

The more taboos and prohibitions there are in the world,

The poorer the people will be.

The more sharp weapons the people have,

The more troubled the state will be.

The more cunning and skill man possesses,

The more vicious things will appear.

The more laws and orders are made prominent,

The more thieves and robbers there will be.

Therefore the sage says:

I take no action and the people of themselves are transformed.

I love tranquility and the people of themselves become correct.

I engage in no activity and the people of themselves become prosperous.

I have no desires and the people of themselves become simple.

When the government is non-discriminative and dull,

58

The people are contented and generous.

When the government is searching and discriminative,

The people are disappointed and contentious.

Calamity is that upon which happiness depends;

Happiness is that in which calamity is latent.

Who knows when the limit will be reached?

Is there no correctness (used to govern the world)?

Then the correct again becomes the perverse.

And the good will again become evil.

The people have been deluded for a long time.

Therefore the sage is as pointed as a square but does not pierce.

He is as acute as a knife but does not cut.

He is as straight as an unbent line but does not extend.

He is as bright as light but does not dazzle.

To rule people and to serve Heaven there is nothing better than to be frugal.

59

Only by being frugal can one recover quickly.

To recover quickly means to accumulate virtue heavily.

By the heavy accumulation of virtue one can overcome everything.

If one can overcome everything, then he will acquire a capacity the limit of which is beyond anyone's knowledge.

When his capacity is beyond anyone's knowledge, he is fit to rule a state.

He who possesses the Mother (Tao) of the state will last long.

This means that the roots are deep and the stalks are firm, which is the way of long life and everlasting vision.

60   Ruling a big country is like cooking a small fish.
If Tao is employed to rule the empire,
Spiritual beings will lose their supernatural power.
Not that they lose their spiritual power,
But their spiritual power can no longer harm people.
Not only will their supernatural power not harm people,
But the sage also will not harm people.
When both do not harm each other,
Virtue will be accumulated in both for the benefit (of the people).

61   A big country may be compared to the lower part of a river.
It is the converging point of the world;
It is the female of the world.
The female always overcomes the male by tranquility,
And by tranquility she is underneath.
A big state can take over a small state if it places itself below the small state;
And the small state can take over a big state if it places itself below the big state.
Thus some, by placing themselves below, take over (others),
And some, by being (naturally) low, take over (other states).
After all, what a big state wants is but to annex and herd others,
And what a small state wants is merely to join and serve others.
Since both big and small states get what they want,
The big state should place itself low.

62   Tao is the storehouse of all things.
It is the good man's treasure and the bad man's refuge.
Fine words can buy honor,
And fine deeds can gain respect from others.
Even if a man is bad, when has (Tao) rejected him?
Therefore on the occasion of crowning an emperor or installing the three ministers,
Rather than present large pieces of jade preceded by teams of four horses,
It is better to kneel and offer this Tao.
Why did the ancients highly value this Tao?
Did they not say, "Those who seek shall have it and those who sin shall be freed"?
For this reason it is valued by the world.

63   Act without action.
Do without ado.
Taste without tasting.
Whether it is big or small, many or few, repay hatred with virtue.
Prepare for the difficult while it is still easy.
Deal with the big while it is still small.
Difficult undertakings have always started with what is easy.
And great undertakings have always started with what is small.
Therefore the sage never strives for the great,
And thereby the great is achieved.
He who makes rash promises surely lacks faith.
He who takes things too easily will surely encounter much difficulty.

For this reason even the sage regards things as difficult.
And therefore he encounters no difficulty.

What remains still is easy to hold.   64
What is not yet manifest is easy to plan for.
What is brittle is easy to crack.
What is minute is easy to scatter.
Deal with things before they appear.
Put things in order before disorder arises.
A tree as big as a man's embrace grows from a tiny shoot.
A tower of nine stories begins with a heap of earth.
The journey of a thousand li starts from where one stands.
He who takes action fails.
He who grasps things loses them.
For this reason the sage takes no action and therefore does not fail.
He grasps nothing and therefore he does not lose anything.
People in their handling of affairs often fail when they are about to succeed.
If one remains as careful at the end as he was at the beginning, there will be no failure.
Therefore the sage desires to have no desire,
He does not value rare treasures.
He learns to be unlearned, and returns to what the multitude has missed (Tao).
Thus he supports all things in their natural state but does not take any action.

In ancient times those who practiced Tao well   65
Did not seek to enlighten the people, but to make them ignorant.
People are difficult to govern because they have too much knowledge.
Therefore he who rules the state through knowledge is a robber of the state;
He who rules a state not through knowledge is a blessing to the state.
One who knows these two things also (knows) the standard.
Always to know the standard is called profound and secret virtue.
Virtue becomes deep and far-reaching,
And with it all things return to their original state.
Then complete harmony will be reached.

The great rivers and seas are kings of all mountain streams   66
Because they skillfully stay below them.
That is why they can be their kings.
Therefore, in order to be the superior of the people,
One must, in the use of words, place himself below them.
And in order to be ahead of the people,
One must, in one's own person, follow them.
Therefore the sage places himself above the people and they do not feel his weight.
He places himself in front of them and the people do not harm him.
Therefore the world rejoices in praising him without getting tired of it.
It is precisely because he does not compete that the world cannot compete with him.

All the world says that my Tao is great and does not seem to resemble (the ordinary).   67
It is precisely because it is great that it does not resemble (the ordinary).
If it did resemble, it would have been small for a long time.
I have three treasures. Guard and keep them:
The first is deep love,
The second is frugality,
And the third is not to dare to be ahead of the world.
Because of deep love, one is courageous.
Because of frugality, one is generous.

Because of not daring to be ahead of the world, one becomes the leader of the world.
Now, to be courageous by forsaking deep love,
To be generous by forsaking frugality,
And to be ahead of the world by forsaking following behind—This is fatal.
For deep love helps one to win in the case of attack,
And to be firm in the case of defense.
When Heaven is to save a person,
Heaven will protect him through deep love.

68   A skillful leader of troops is not oppressive with his military strength.
A skillful fighter does not become angry.
A skillful conqueror does not compete with people.
One who is skillful in using men puts himself below them.
This is called the virtue of non-competing.
This is called the strength to use men.
This is called matching Heaven, the highest principle of old.

69   The strategists say:
"I dare not take the offensive but I take the defensive;
I dare not advance an inch but I retreat a foot."
This means:
To march without formation,
To stretch one's arm without showing it,
To confront enemies without seeming to meet them,
To hold weapons without seeming to have them.
There is no greater disaster than to make light of the enemy.
Making light of the enemy will destroy my treasures.
Therefore when armies are mobilized and issues joined,
The man who is sorry over the fact will win.

70   My doctrines are very easy to understand and very easy to practice,
But none in the world can understand or practice them.
My doctrines have a source (Nature); my deeds have a master (Tao).
It is because people do not understand this that they do not understand me.
Few people know me, and therefore I am highly valued.
Therefore the sage wears a coarse cloth on top and carries jade within his bosom.

71   To know that you do not know is the best.
To pretend to know when you do not know is a disease.
Only when one recognizes this disease as a disease can one be free from the disease.
The sage is free from the disease.
Because he recognizes this disease to be disease, he is free from it.

72   When the people do not fear what is dreadful,
Then what is greatly dreadful will descend on them.
Do not reduce the living space of their dwellings.
Do not oppress their lives.
It is because you do not oppress them that they are not oppressed.
Therefore the sage knows himself but does not show himself.
He loves himself but does not exalt himself.
Therefore he rejects the one but accepts the other.

73   He who is brave in daring will be killed.
He who is brave in not daring will live.
Of these two, one is advantageous and one is harmful.

Who knows why Heaven dislikes what it dislikes?
Even the sage considers it a difficult question.
The Way of Heaven does not compete, and yet it skillfully achieves victory.
It does not speak, and yet it skillfully responds to things.
It comes to you without your invitation.
It is not anxious about things and yet it plans well.
Heaven's net is indeed vast.
Though its meshes are wide, it misses nothing.

The people are not afraid of death.   74
Why, then, threaten them with death?
Suppose the people are always afraid of death and we can seize those who are vicious
    and kill them,
Who would dare to do so?
There is always the master executioner (Heaven) who kills.
To undertake executions for the master executioner is like hewing wood for the mas-
    ter carpenter.
Whoever undertakes to hew wood for the master carpenter rarely escapes injuring his own
    hands.

The people starve because the ruler eats too much tax-grain.   75
Therefore they starve.
They are difficult to rule because their ruler does too many things.
Therefore they are difficult to rule.
The people take death lightly because their ruler strives for life too vigorously.
Therefore they take death lightly.
It is only those who do not seek after life that excel in making life valuable.

When man is born, he is tender and weak.   76
At death, he is stiff and hard.
All things, the grass as well as trees, are tender and supple while alive.
When dead, they are withered and dried.
Therefore the stiff and the hard are companions of death.
The tender and the weak are companions of life.
Therefore if the army is strong, it will not win.
If a tree is stiff, it will break.
The strong and the great are inferior, while the tender and the weak are superior.

Heaven's way is indeed like the bending of a bow.   77
When (the string) is high, bring it down.
When it is low, raise it up.
When it is excessive, reduce it.
When it is insufficient, supplement it.
The Way of Heaven reduces whatever is excessive and supplements whatever is insufficient.
The way of man is different.
It reduces the insufficient to offer to the excessive.
Who is able to have excess to offer to the world?
Only the man of Tao.
Therefore the sage acts, but does not rely on his own ability.
He accomplishes his task, but does not claim credit for it.
He has no desire to display his excellence.

There is nothing softer and weaker than water,   78
And yet there is nothing better for attacking hard and strong things.
For this reason there is no substitute for it.

All the world knows that the weak overcomes the strong and the soft overcomes the hard.
But none can practice it.
Therefore the sage says:
He who suffers disgrace for his country
Is called the lord of the land.
He who takes upon himself the country's misfortunes
Becomes the king of the empire.
Straight words seem to be their opposite.

79   To patch up great hatred is surely to leave some hatred behind.
How can this be regarded as good?
Therefore the sage keeps the left-hand portion (obligation) of a contract
And does not blame the other party.
Virtuous people attend to their left-hand portions,
While those without virtue attend to other people's mistakes.
"The Way of Heaven has no favorites.
It is always with the good man."

80   Let there be a small country with few people.
Let there be ten times and a hundred times as many utensils
But let them not be used.
Let the people value their lives highly and not migrate far.
Even if there are ships and carriages, none will ride in them.
Even if there are arrows and weapons, none will display them.
Let the people again knot cords and use them (in place of writing).
Let them relish their food, beautify their clothing, be content with their homes, and delight
    in their customs.
Though neighboring communities overlook one another and the crowing of cocks and
    barking of dogs can be heard,
Yet the people there may grow old and die without ever visiting one another.

81   True words are not beautiful;
Beautiful words are not true.
A good man does not argue;
He who argues is not a good man.
A wise man has no extensive knowledge;
He who has extensive knowledge is not a wise man.
The sage does not accumulate for himself.
The more he uses for others, the more he has himself.
The more he gives to others, the more he possesses of his own.
The Way of Heaven is to benefit others and not to injure.
The Way of the sage is to act but not to compete.

CHUANG TZU, THE BOOK OF CHUANG TZU: THE SEVEN INNER CHAPTERS

CHAPTER 1: GOING RAMBLING WITHOUT A DESTINATION*

In the North Ocean there is a fish, its name is the K'un; the K'un's girth measures who knows how many thousand miles. It changes into a bird, its name is the P'eng; the P'eng's back measures who knows how many thousand miles. When it puffs out its chest and flies off, its wings are like clouds hanging from the sky. This bird when the seas are heaving has a mind to travel to the South Ocean. (The South Ocean is the Lake of Heaven.) In the words of the *Tall Stories*, 'When the P'eng travels to the South Ocean, the wake it thrashes on the water is three thousand miles long, it mounts spiraling on the whirlwind ninety thousand miles high, and is gone six months before it is out of breath.' (The *Tall Stories of Ch'i* is a record of marvels.) Is the azure of the sky its true colour? Or is it that the distance into which we are looking is infinite? It never stops flying higher till everything below looks the same as above (heat-hazes, dust-storms, the breath which living things blow at each other).

If a mass of water is not bulky enough it lacks the strength to carry a big boat. When you upset a bowl of water over a dip in the floor, a seed will make a boat for it, but if you put the bowl there it jams, because your boat is too big for such shallow water. If the mass of the wind is not bulky enough it lacks the strength to carry the great wings. So it is only when the bird is ninety thousand miles high, with the wind underneath it, that it rests its weight on the wind; and it must have the blue sky on its back and a clear view ahead before it will set its course for the South.

A cicada and a turtle-dove laughed at it, saying, "We keep flying till we're bursting, stop when we get to an elm or sandalwood, and sometimes are dragged back to the ground before we're there. What's all this about being ninety thousand miles up when he travels south?"

Someone off to the green of the woods, with enough for three meals will be home with his belly still full; someone going thirty miles pounds grain for the days he will be away; someone going three hundred miles lays in grain to last three months. What do these two creatures know? Little wits cannot keep up with great, or few years with many. How would we know that this is so? The mushroom of a morning does not know old and new moon, the cricket does not know spring and autumn; their time is too short. South of Ch'u there is the tree Ming-ling, which grows through a spring of five hundred years, declines through an autumn of five hundred years; in the remotest past there was

A.C. Graham, *The Seven Inner Chapters and Other Writings from the Book of Chuang-tzu* (London: George Allen & Unwin, 1981), pp. 43–99. Reprinted by permission.

*The pieces which the compilers of *Chuang-tzu* assembled in "Going rambling without a destination" are all on the theme of soaring above the restricted viewpoints of the worldly. Escape the fixed routes to worldly success and fame, defy all reproaches that you are useless, selfish, indifferent to the good of the Empire, and a perspective opens from which all ordinary ambitions are seen as negligible, the journey of life becomes an effortless ramble.

the great tree Ch'un, with eight thousand years for its spring and eight thousand for its autumn; it is only nowadays that P'eng-tsu is uniquely famous for living long, and is it not sad that common men should think him insurpassable?

(T'ang's questions to Chi were about this. "In the North where nothing grows there is a vast sea, which is the Lake of Heaven. There is a fish there, several thousand miles broad, no one knows how long; its name is the K'un. There is a bird there, its name is the P'eng, its back is as big as Mount T'ai, its wings are like clouds hanging from the sky. It mounts the whirlwind in a ram's horn spiral ninety thousand miles high, and only when it is clear of the clouds, with the blue sky on its back, does it set its course southward to journey to the South Ocean. A quail laughed at it, saying 'Where does he think he's going? I do a hop and a skip and up I go, and before I've gone more than a few dozen yards come fluttering down among the bushes. That is the highest one can fly, where does he think he's going?'" This was in disputation about the small and the great.)

Those, then, who are clever enough to do well in one office or efficient enough to protect one district, whose powers suit one prince and are put to the test in one state, are seeing themselves as the little birds did, and Sung Jung* smiled at them in disdain. Not only that, he refused to be encouraged though the whole world praised him, or deterred though the whole world blamed him, he was unwavering about the division between inward and outward, discriminating about the boundary between honour and disgrace—but then he soared no higher. (He was too concerned about the world to break clean away.) Or that Lieh-tzu** now, he journeyed with the winds for his chariot, a fine sight it must have been, and did not come back for fifteen days. (Even so, there was something he failed to plant in his own soil.) The former of them, in the hope of bringing blessings to the world, failed to break clean away; the latter, even if he did save himself the trouble of going on foot, still depended on something to carry his weight. As for the man who rides a true course between heaven and earth, with the changes of the Six Energies† for his chariot, to travel into the infinite, is there anything that he depends on? As the saying goes,

> The utmost man is selfless,
> The daemonic man takes no credit for his deeds,
> The sage is nameless.

*   *   *

---

    *Sung Jung is the philosopher Sung Hsing of "Below in the empire," one of whose doctrines was that "To be insulted is not disgraceful." Chuang-tzu sees his refusal to feel devalued by other men's judgements as a first step to escape from the world, but regrets that he still thought it his duty to get involved in politics for the good of the empire.

    **Lieh-tzu, later ranked among the greatest Taoist sages, is apparently seen by Chuang-tzu as a man who missed the final liberation by mistakenly seeking the Way through magic; in the single story about him in the *Inner Chapters* he is misled by a sorcerer before he attains the true Way. Neither of them quite achieves a selflessness indifferent to winning credit for deeds and having an honoured name.

    †The "Six Energies" which activate the cyclic motions of heaven and earth are traditionally enumerated as Yin and Yang, wind and rain, dark and light.

Yao resigned the Empire to Hsu Yu,* saying

"When the sun or the moon is up, if the torch fires are not put out, aren't we taking too much trouble to light the world? When the timely rains fall, if we go on flooding the channels, aren't we working too hard to water the fields? While you, sir, are in your place the Empire is in order, yet here I still am in the seat of honour. In my own eyes I do not deserve it; let me make you a present of the Empire."

"If you order things as Emperor, it's that already the Empire is in order; and if I were to see any point in taking your place, would it be for the sake of the name? The name is the guest of the substance. Would it be for the sake of the substance? The tit that nests in the deep forest wants no more than one branch, the mole that drinks in the Yellow River no more than a bellyful. Go back where you belong, my lord, the Empire is no use to me. Even when the chief cook does run a disorderly kitchen, the priest and the medium will not step over the jars and dishes to take his place."

*   *   *

Chien Wu put a question to Lien Shu,

"I heard Chieh Yu** say something, he talked big but there was no sense in it, he left the firm ground and never came back. I was amazed and frightened by his words, which streamed on into the infinite like the Milky Way, wild extravagances, nothing to do with man as he really is.

"What did he say?"

"In the mountains of far-off Ku-yi there lives a daemonic man, whose skin and flesh are like ice and snow, who is gentle as a virgin. He does not eat the five grains but sucks in the wind and drinks the dew; he rides the vapour of the clouds, yokes flying dragons to his chariot, and roams beyond the four seas. When the daemonic in him concentrates it keeps creatures free from plagues and makes the grain ripen every year.

"I thought him mad and wouldn't believe him."

"Yes, the blind can never share in the spectacle of emblems and ornaments, nor the deaf in the music of drums and bells. Is it only in flesh and bone that there is blindness and deafness? The wits have them too. When he spoke these words he was like a girl who waits for a suitor to come. This man, this Power that is in him, would merge the myriad things and make them one. The age has an incessant urge towards misrule, who are these people so eager to make the business of the empire theirs? This man no other thing will wound; though the great floods rise to the sky he will not drown, though metal and stone fuse in the great droughts and moors and mountains char he will not burn. From this man's very dust and siftings you could smelt and mould a Yao or Shun. Who are these people so determined to make other things their business?

*In Confucian legend the pre-dynastic emperor Yao is a sage who when his time is over abdicates to the man best fitted to rule in his place, Shun. Yangists and Taoists delighted in imagining a recluse Hsu Yu who disdained the offer of Yao's throne. In this and the next episode Chuang-tzu introduces a further refinement: Yao himself understood that the good order of his reign came not from his own policies but from individuals cultivating the Power in them in private, Hsu Yu and the nameless man on Mount Ku-yi. In ancient Chinese thought political order results directly from the mysterious influence of the Power in the ruler and his political acts are merely its by products. For a modern reader, this is a strange conceptualisation, but we may express Chuang-tzu's insight in more familiar terms—the social fabric coheres or dissolves by the action of influences which have little to do with the deliberate policies of rulers, and which may be emanating from humble publicly unnoticed individuals.

**Chieh Yu, the madman of Ch'u who mocked Confucius, is Chuang-tzu's favourite character in the Confucius story.

"A man of Sung who traded in ceremonial caps travelled to the Yueh tribes, but the men of Yueh who cut their hair short and tattoo their bodies had no use for them. Yao who reduced the people of the Empire to order, and imposed regular government on all within the seas, went off to see the Four in the mountains of far-off Ku-yi, on the north bank of Fen River, and in a daze forgot his empire there."

*   *   *

Said Hui Shih to Chuang-tzu

"The King of Wei gave me the seeds of a great calabash. I planted them, they grew up, with gourds of five bushels. When you filled them with water or soup they weren't solid enough to stay upright, if you split them to make ladles they sagged and spilled over. It's not that they weren't impressively big, but because they were useless I smashed them to bits."

"You really are clumsy, sir, in finding uses for something big. There was a man of Sung who was expert in making a salve to keep hands from chapping. For generations the clan had been silk-bleachers by trade. A stranger heard about it, and asked to buy the secret for a hundred pieces of gold. The man assembled his clan and talked it over. 'For generations,' he said, 'we have been silk-bleaching, for no more than a few pieces. Now in one morning we can sell the art for a hundred. I propose we give it to him.'

"The stranger when he got it recommended it to the King of Wu. There was trouble with Yueh, and the King of Wu made him a general. That winter he fought a battle by water with the men of Yueh. He utterly defeated the men of Yueh, and was enfiefed in a bit of the conquered territory.

"In their ability to keep hands from chapping, there was nothing to choose between them; if one of them got a fief for it while the other stayed a silk bleacher, it's that they put it to different uses. Now if you had five-bushel calabashes, why didn't it occur to you to make them into those big bottles swimmers tie to their waists, and go floating away over the Yangtse and the Lakes? If you worried because they sagged and wouldn't hold anything, isn't it that you still have a heart where the shoots grow up tangled?"

*   *   *

Said Hui Shih to Chuang-tzu

"I have a great tree, people call it the tree-of-heaven. Its trunk is too knobbly and bumpy to measure with the inked line, its branches are too curly and crooked to fit compasses or L-square. Stand it up in the road and a carpenter wouldn't give it a glance. Now this talk of yours is big but useless, dismissed by everyone alike."

"Haven't you ever seen a wild cat or a weasel? It lurks crouching low in wait for strays, makes a pounce east or west as nimble uphill or down, and drops plumb into the snare and dies in the net. But the yak now, which is as big as a cloud hanging from the sky, this by being able to be so big is unable to catch as much as a mouse. Now if you have a great tree and think it's a pity it's so useless, why not plant it in the realm of Nothingwhatever, in the wilds which spread out into nowhere, and go roaming away to do nothing at its side, ramble around and fall asleep in its shade?

> Spared by the axe
> No thing will harm it.
> If you're no use at all,
> Who'll come to bother you?"

CHAPTER 2: THE SORTING WHICH EVENS THINGS OUT*

Tzu-ch'i of Nan kuo reclined elbow on armrest, looked up at the sky and exhaled, in a trance as though he had lost the counterpart of himself. Yen-ch'eng Tzu-yu stood in waiting before him.

"What is this?" he said. "Can the frame really be made to be like withered wood, the heart like dead ashes? The reclining man here now is not the reclining man of yesterday."

"You do well to ask that, Tzu-yu! This time I had lost my own self, did you know it? You hear the pipes of men, don't you, but not yet the pipes of earth, the pipes of earth but not yet the pipes of Heaven?"**

"I venture to ask the secret of it."

"That hugest of clumps of soil† blows out breath, by name the 'wind.' Better if it were never to start up, for whenever it does ten thousand hollow places burst out howling, and don't tell me you have never heard how the hubbub swells! The recesses in mountain forests, the hollows that pit great trees a hundred spans round, are like nostrils, like mouths, like ears, like sockets, like bowls, like mortars, like pools, like puddles. Hooting, hissing, sniffing, sucking, mumbling, moaning, whistling, wailing, the winds ahead sing out AAAH!, the winds behind answer EEEH!, breezes strike up a tiny chorus, the whirlwind a mighty chorus. When the gale has passed, all the hollows empty, and don't tell me you have never seen how the quivering slows and settles!"

"The pipes of earth, these are the various hollows; the pipes of men, these are rows of tubes. Let me ask about the pipes of Heaven."

"Who is it that puffs out the myriads which are never the same, who in their self-ending is sealing them up, in their self-choosing is impelling the force into them?

"Heaven turns circles, yes!
Earth sits firm yes!
Sun and moon vie for a place, yes!
Whose is the bow that shoots them?
Whose is the net that holds them?

Who is it sits with nothing to do and gives them the push that sends them?

*The last word in the title *Ch'i wu lun* is sometimes understood as "discourse" ("The discourse on evening things out"), sometimes in its more basic sense of "sort out (in coherent discourse)." Comparison with the three-word titles of the other *Inner Chapters* favours the latter alternative. *Lun,* "sorting out," is the one kind of thinking always mentioned with approval in *Chuang-tzu.* Outside Taoism it suggests grading in superior and inferior categories, but Chuang-tzu detaches it from valuation, turns it into "the sorting which evens things out."

The theme of the chapter is the defence of a synthesising vision against Confucians, Mohists and Sophists, who analyse, distinguish alternatives and debate which is right or wrong. It contains the most philosophically acute passages in the *Inner Chapters*—obscure, fragmented, but pervaded by the sensation, rare in ancient literatures, of a man jotting the living thought at the moment of its inception. It is a pity that the Syncretist who assembled the chapter seems to have been out of sympathy with these intellectual subtleties designed to discredit the intellect, for he has relegated a number of closely related passages to the *Mixed Chapters* [not included here].

**Chuang-tzu's parable of the wind compares the conflicting utterances of philosophers to the different notes blown by the same breath in the long and short tubes of the pan-pipes, and the noises made by the wind in hollows of different shapes. It is natural for differently constituted persons to think differently; don't try to decide between their opinions, listen to Heaven who breathes through them.

†A phrase peculiar to the *Inner Chapters* that seems to conjure up an image of the universe so far in the distance that it is no bigger than a clod you could hold in your hand.

"Shall we suppose, yes, that something triggers them off then seals them away, and they have no choice?

Or suppose, yes, that wheeling in their circuits they cannot stop themselves?

Do the clouds make the rain?
Or the rain the clouds?
Whose bounty bestows them?

Who is it sits with nothing to do as in ecstasy he urges them?

The winds rise in the north
Blow west blow east,
And now again whirl high above.
Who breathes them out, who breathes them in?

Who is it sits with nothing to do and sweeps between and over them?"

*   *   *

"Great wit is effortless,
Petty wit picks holes.
Great speech is flavourless,
Petty speech strings words.

"While it sleeps, the paths of souls cross:
When it wakes, the body opens.
Whatever we sense entangles it:
Each day we use that heart of ours for strife.

The calm ones, the deep ones, the subtle ones.

"Petty fears intimidate,
The supreme fear calms.*
It shoots like the trigger releasing the string on the notch,"

Referring to its manipulation of "That's it, that's not."

It ties us down as though by oath, by treaty,"

referring to its commitment to the winning alternative.

"Its decline is like autumn and winter,"

speaking of its daily deterioration. As it sinks, that which is the source of its deeds cannot be made to renew them.

"It clogs as though it were being sealed up,"

*The "supreme fear" which calms would be the fear of death, reconciliation with which is Chuang-tzu's central concern.

speaking of its drying up in old age. As the heart nears death, nothing can make it revert to the Yang.

Pleasure in things and anger against them, sadness and joy, forethought and regret, change and immobility, idle influences that initiate our gestures—music coming out of emptiness, vapour condensing into mushrooms—alternate before it day and night and no one knows from what soil they spring. Enough! The source from which it has these morning and evening, is it not that from which it was born?

*   *   *

"Without an Other there is no Self, without Self no choosing one thing rather than another."

This is somewhere near it, but we do not know in whose service they are being employed. It seems that there is something genuinely in command, and that the only trouble is we cannot find a sign of it. That as 'Way' it can be walked is true enough, but we do not see its shape; it has identity but no shape. Of the hundred joints, nine openings, six viscera all present and complete, which should I recognise as more kin to me than another? Are you people pleased with them all? Rather, you have a favourite organ among them.* On your assumption, does it have the rest of them as its vassals and concubines? Are its vassals and concubines inadequate to rule each other? Isn't it rather that they take turns as each other's lord and vassals? Or rather than that, they have a genuine lord present in them. If we seek without success to grasp what its identity might be, that never either adds to nor detracts from its genuineness.

*   *   *

Once we have received the completed body we are aware of it all the time we await extinction. Is it not sad how we and other things go on stroking or jostling each other, in a race ahead like a gallop which nothing can stop? How can we fail to regret that we labour all our lives without seeing success, wear ourselves out with toil in ignorance of where we shall end? What use is it for man to say that he will not die, since when the body dissolves the heart dissolves with it? How can we not call this our supreme regret? Is man's life really as stupid as this? Or is it that I am the only stupid one, and there are others not so stupid? But if you go by the completed heart and take it as your authority, who is without such an authority? Why should it be only the man who knows how things alternate and whose heart approves its own judgements who has such an authority? The fool has one just as he has. For there to be "That's it, that's not" before they are formed in the heart would be to "go to Yueh today and have arrived yesterday."** This would be crediting with existence what has no existence; and if you do that even the daemonic Yu could not understand you, and how can you expect to be understood by me?

*   *   *

Saying is not blowing breath, saying says something; the only trouble is that what it says is never fixed. Do we really say something? Or have we never said anything? If

---

*[Chuang-tzu is referring to the heart, the organ of thought and asking,] "Should it be allowed to take charge of our lives? Isn't it merely one of many organs each with its own functions within an order which comes from beyond us, from the Way?"

**A paradox of the Sophist Hui Shih, here mentioned only for its absurdity.

you think it different from the twitter of fledgelings, is there proof of the distinction? Or isn't there any proof? By what is the Way hidden, that there should be a genuine or a false? By what is saying darkened, that sometimes "That's it" and sometimes "That's not"? Wherever we walk how can the Way be absent? Whatever the standpoint how can saying be unallowable? The Way is hidden by formation of the lesser, saying is darkened by its foliage and flowers. And so we have the "That's it, that's not" of Confucians and Mohists, by which what is *it* for one of them for the other is not, what is *not* for one of them for the other is. If you wish to affirm what they deny and deny what they affirm, the best means is Illumination.

No thing is not "other," no thing is not "it." If you treat yourself too as "other" they do not appear, if you know of yourself you know of them. Hence it is said:

" 'Other' comes out from 'it,' 'it' likewise goes by 'other,' "

the opinion that "it" and "other" are born simultaneously. However,

"Simultaneously with being alive one dies,"

and simultaneously with dying one is alive, simultaneously with being allowable something becomes unallowable and simultaneously with being unallowable it becomes allowable. If going by circumstance that's it then going by circumstance that's not, if going by circumstance that's not then going by circumstance that's it. This is why the sage does not take this course, but opens things up to the light of Heaven; his too is a "That's it" which goes by circumstance.*

*   *   *

What is It is also Other, what is Other is also It. There they say "That's it, that's not" from one point of view, here we say "That's it, that's not" from another point of view. Are there really It and Other? Or really no It and Other? Where neither It nor Other finds its opposite is called the axis of the Way. When once the axis is found at the centre of the circle there is no limit to responding with either, on the one hand no limit to what is *it*, on the other no limit to what is not. Therefore I say: "The best means is Illumination." Rather than use the meaning to show that

"The meaning is not the meaning,"

use what is *not* the meaning. Rather than use a horse to show that

"A horse is not a horse"

use what is *not* a horse. Heaven and earth are the one meaning, the myriad things are the one horse.**

---

*Chuang-tzu sees it as the lesson of disputation that one is entitled to affirm or deny anything of anything. He thinks of Confucians and Mohists who stick rigidly to their affirmations and denials as lighting up little areas of life and leaving the rest in darkness; the Illumination of the sage is a vision which brings everything to light.

**There are extant essays by the Sophist Kung-sun Lung arguing that "A white horse is not a horse" and "When no thing is not the meaning the meaning is not the meaning." Chuang-tzu thinks he was wasting his time; since all disputation starts from arbitrary acts of naming, he had only to pick something else as the meaning of the word, name something else "horse," and then for him what the rest of us call a horse would not be a horse.

*   *   *

Allowable?—allowable. Unallowable?—unallowable. The Way comes about as we walk it; as for a thing, call it something and that's so. Why so? By being so. Why not so? By not being so. It is inherent in a thing that from somewhere that's so of it, from somewhere that's allowable of it; of no thing is it not so, of no thing is it unallowable. Therefore when a "That's it" which deems* picks out a stalk from a pillar, a hag from beautiful Hsi Shih, things however peculiar or incongruous, the Way interchanges them and deems them one. Their dividing is formation, their formation is dissolution; all things whether forming or dissolving in reverting interchange and are deemed to be one. Only the man who sees right through knows how to interchange and deem them one; the "That's it" which deems he does not use, but finds for them lodging-places in the usual. The "usual" is the usable, the "usable" is the interchangeable, to see as "interchangeable" is to grasp; and once you grasp them you are almost there. The "That's it" which goes by circumstance comes to an end; and when it is at an end, that of which you do not know what is so of it you call the "Way."

To wear out the daemonic-and-illumined in you deeming them to be one without knowing that they are the same I call "Three every morning." What do I mean by "Three every morning?" A monkey keeper handing out nuts said, "Three every morning and four every evening." The monkeys were all in a rage. "All right then," he said, "four every morning and three every evening." The monkeys were all delighted. Without anything being missed out either in name or in substance, their pleasure and anger were put to use; his too was the "That's it" which goes by circumstance. This is why the sage smooths things out with his "That's it, that's not," and stays at the point of rest on the potter's wheel of Heaven. It is this that is called "Letting both alternatives proceed."**

*   *   *

The men of old, their knowledge had arrived at something: at what had it arrived? There were some who thought there had not yet begun to be things—the utmost, the exhaustive, there is no more to add. The next thought there were things but there had not yet begun to be borders. The next thought there were borders to them but there had not yet begun to be "That's it, that's not." The lighting up of "That's it, that's not" is the reason why the Way is flawed. The reason why the Way is flawed is the reason why love becomes complete. Is anything really complete or flawed? Or is nothing really complete or flawed? To recognise as complete or flawed is to have as model the Chao when they play the zither; to recognise as neither complete nor flawed is to have as model the Chao when they don't play the zither. Chao Wen strumming on the zither, Music-master K'uang propped on his stick, Hui Shih leaning on the sterculia, had the three men's knowledge much farther to go? They were all men in whom it reached a culmination, and therefore was carried on to too late a time. It was only in being preferred by them that what they knew about differed from an Other; because they preferred it they wished to illumine it, but they illumined it without the Other being illumined, and so the end of it all was the darkness of chop logic: and his own son too ended with only Chao Wen's

---

*"The 'That's it' which deems" (*wei shih*): in disputation over whether an object fits the name "ox" the object is "deemed" (*wei*) an ox by the judgement "That's it" (*shih*). Chuang-tzu allows the flexible " 'That's it' which goes by circumstance (yin shih), but rejects absolutely the rigid " 'That's it' which deems."

**"Letting both alternatives proceed": in disputation a decision to call an object "X" "proceeds" (*hsing*) to all objects of the same kind. But for Chuang-tzu one never loses the right to shift from one alternative to the other and allow either to "proceed" from the instance to the kind.

zither string, and to the end of his life his musicianship was never completed. May men like this be said to be complete? Then so am I. Or may they not be said to be complete? Then neither am I, nor is anything else.

Therefore the glitter of glib implausibilities is despised by the sage. The "That's it" which deems he does not use, but finds for things lodging-places in the usual. It is this that is meant by "using Illumination."

*   *   *

"Now suppose that I speak of something, and do not know whether it is of a kind with the 'it' in question or not of a kind. If what is of a kind and what is not are deemed of a kind with one another, there is no longer any difference from an 'other.' "

However, let's try to say it.

There is "beginning," there is "not yet having begun having a beginning."

—There is "there not yet having begun to be that 'not yet having begun having a beginning.' "

There is "something," there is "nothing."

—There is "not yet having begun being without something."

—There is "there not yet having begun to be that 'not yet having begun being without something.' "

All of a sudden "*there* is nothing", and we do not yet know of something and nothing really which there is and which there is not. Now for my part I have already referred to something, but do not yet know whether my reference really referred to something or really did not refer to anything.*

*In this and the next passage Chuang-tzu criticises two supposed examples of describing in words the whole out of which things divide. He thinks that analysis always leaves an overlooked remainder, and that the whole cannot be recovered by putting the parts together again. According to the current logic, an object either is an ox or is not, so that having distinguished the alternatives we ought to be able to recover the totality by adding non-oxen to oxen. Chuang-tzu's refutation of this assumption is highly elliptical, and it is possible that he intends his effect of making the mind fly off in a new direction at every re-reading. But in Chinese as in other philosophy a gap in the argument which hinders understanding (as distinct from a flaw in an argument which we do understand) can generally be filled by exploring implicit questions and presuppositions in the background. Here Chuang-tzu is picking out points in common between oxen and non-oxen which distinguish them both from a still remaining Other. In the first place both have a beginning, which excludes from them whatever preceded the beginning of things. Can we continue, by negating and adding, to incorporate this remainder into the totality? What preceded things is that in which they "had not yet begun to have a beginning." But in saying this retrospectively we speak as though things were somehow present before they began; we are driven to a further negation, "There had not yet begun to be that 'not yet having begun having a beginning.' "

It is also common to oxen and non-oxen that they are "something," what there is, in contrast with "nothing," what there is not. As empty space nothingness is a measurable part of the cosmos; but can we not arrive at the totality by adding Nothing to Something? Here Chuang-tzu assumes a position far from obvious to a modern reader but implicit throughout early Taoist literature. There can be Nothing only when there is Something, a void only when there are objects with intervals between them, and both divide out from a whole which is neither one nor the other. Each thing has limited properties, is "without something," but the whole out of which it differentiates is both "without anything," since things have not yet emerged, and "without nothing," since everything emerges from it. Then having added Nothing to Something, I have still to add a remainder which "has not yet begun to be without something." But again we are speaking retrospectively as though there were already things to be present or absent, and again we have to negate: "There had not yet begun to be that 'not yet having begun to be without something.' " Both Chuang-tzu's sequences are no doubt intended to lead to an infinite regress.

He concludes with the simpler point that as soon as we introduce Nothing as the remainder we contradict ourselves by saying "There is" even of what there is not, Nothing.

*   *   *

"Nothing in the world is bigger than the tip of an autumn hair, and Mount T'ai is small; no one lives longer than a doomed child, and P'eng-tsu died young; heaven and earth were born together with me, and the myriad things and I are one."

Now that we are one, can I still say something? Already having called us one, did I succeed in not saying something? One and the saying makes two, two and one make three. Proceeding from here even an expert calculator cannot get to the end of it, much less a plain man. Therefore if we take the step from nothing to something we arrive at three, and how much worse if we take the step from something to something! Take no step at all, and the "That's it" which goes by circumstance will come to an end.*

*   *   *

The Way has never had borders, saying has never had norms. It is by a "That's it" which deems that a boundary is marked. Let me say something about the marking of boundaries. You can locate as there and enclose by a line, sort out and assess, divide up and discriminate between alternatives, compete over and fight over: these I call our Eight Powers. What is outside the cosmos the sage locates as there but does not sort out. What is within the cosmos the sage sorts out but does not assess. The records of the former kings in the successive reigns in the Annals the sage assesses, but he does not argue over alternatives.

To "divide," then, is to leave something undivided: to "discriminate between alternatives" is to leave something which is neither alternative. "What?" you ask. The sage keeps it in his breast, common men argue over alternatives to show it to each other. Hence I say: "To 'discriminate between alternatives' is to fail to see something."

*   *   *

The greatest Way is not cited as an authority,
The greatest discrimination is unspoken,
The greatest goodwill is cruel,
The greatest honesty does not make itself awkward,
The greatest courage does not spoil for a fight.

When the Way is lit it does not guide,
When speech discriminates it fails to get there,
Goodwill too constant is at someone's expense,
Honesty too clean is not to be trusted,
Courage that spoils for a fight is immature.

These five in having their corners rounded off come close to pointing the direction. Hence to know how to stay within the sphere of our ignorance is to attain the highest.

---

*Hui Shih had said that "Heaven and earth are one unit." At first sight one might expect Chuang-tzu to agree with that at least. But to refuse to distinguish alternatives is to refuse to affirm even "Everything is one" against "Things are many." He observes that in saying it the statement itself is additional to the One which is about, so that already there are two (Plato makes a similar point about the One and its name in *The Sophist*). It may be noticed that Chuang-tzu never does say that everything is one (except as one side of a paradox), [but] always speaks subjectively of the sage treating as one.

Who knows an unspoken discrimination, an untold Way? It is this, if any is able to know it, which is called the Treasury of Heaven. Pour into it and it does not fill, bale out from it and it is not drained, and you do not know from what source it comes. It is this that is called our Benetnash Star.*

*   *   *

Therefore formerly Yao asked Shun

"I wish to smite Tsung, K'uai and Hsu-ao. Why is it that I am not at ease on the south-facing throne?"

"Why be uneasy," said Shun, "if these three still survive among the weeds? Formerly ten suns rose side by side and the myriad things were all illumined, and how much more by a man in whom the Power is brighter than the sun!"

*   *   *

Gaptooth put a question to Wang Ni.

"Would you *know* something of which all things agreed 'That's it'?"

"How would I know that?"

"Would you know what you did not know?"

"How would I know that?"

"Then does no thing know anything?"

"How would I know that? However, let me try to say it—'How do I know that what I call knowing is not ignorance? How do I know that what I call ignorance is not knowing?'**

"Moreover, let me try a question on you. When a human sleeps in the damp his waist hurts and he gets stiff in the joints; is that so of the loach? When he sits in a tree he shivers and shakes; is that so of the ape? Which of these three knows the right place to live? Humans eat the flesh of hay-fed and grain-fed beasts, deer eat the grass, centipedes relish snakes, owls and crows crave mice; which of the four has a proper sense of taste? Gibbons are sought by baboons as mates, elaphures like the company of deer, loaches play with fish. Mao-ch'iang and Lady Li were beautiful in the eyes of men; but when the fish saw them they plunged deep, when the birds saw them they flew high, when the deer saw them they broke into a run. Which of these four knows what is truly beautiful in the world? In my judgement the principles of Goodwill and Duty, the paths of 'That's it, that's not,' are inextricably confused; how could I know how to discriminate between them?"

"If you do not know benefit from harm, would you deny that the utmost man knows benefit from harm?

"The utmost man is daemonic. When the wide woodlands blaze they cannot sear him, when the Yellow River and the Han freeze they cannot chill him, when swift thunderbolts smash the mountains and whirlwinds shake the seas they cannot startle him.

---

*The star at the far end of the handle of the Dipper. The Dipper by turning its handle up, down, east and west, marks the progress of the four seasons. As a metaphor for the prime mover of things Chuang-tzu chooses not the stationary North Star but the circumpolar star which initiates the cyclic motions.

**Gaptooth is pressing for an admission that there must be something which is knowable: (1) Would you know something which everyone agrees on? Wang Ni denies it, perhaps because there could be no independent viewpoint from which to judge a universally shared opinion. (2) Then at least one knows what one does not know. But that is a contradiction, or so Chuang-tzu thinks (like Meno in Plato's dialogue); the Mohist *Canon* B 48 discusses this problem, and points out that one can know something by name without knowing what objects fit the name. (3) Then one knows that no one knows anything—another contradiction.

A man like that yokes the clouds to his chariot, rides the sun and moon and roams beyond the four seas; death and life alter nothing in himself, still less the principles of benefit and harm!"

* * *

Ch'u-ch'ueh-tzu asked Ch'ang-wu-tzu
"I heard this from the Master: 'The sage does not work for any goal, does not lean towards benefit or shun harm, does not delight in seeking, does not fix a route by a Way, in saying nothing says something and in saying something says nothing, and roams beyond the dust and grime.' The Master thought of the saying as a flight of fancy, but to me it seemed the walking of the most esoteric Way. How does it seem to you?"
"This is a saying which would have puzzled the Yellow Emperor, and what would old Confucius know about it? Moreover you for your part are counting your winnings much too soon; at the sight of the egg you expect the cock-crow, at the sight of the bow you expect a roasted owl. Suppose I put it to you in abandoned words, and you listen with the same abandon:

'Go side by side with the sun and moon,
Do the rounds of Space and Time.
Act out their neat conjunctions,
Stay aloof from their convulsions.
Dependents each on each, let us honour one another.
Common people fuss and fret,
The sage is a dullard and a sluggard.
Be aligned along a myriad years, in oneness, wholeness, simplicity.
All the myriad things are as they are,
And as what they are make up totality.'

How do I know that to take pleasure in life is not a delusion? How do I know that we who hate death are not exiles since childhood who have forgotten the way home? Lady Li was the daughter of a frontier guard at Ai. When the kingdom of Chin first took her the tears stained her dress; only when she came to the palace and shared the King's square couch and ate the flesh of hay-fed and grain-fed beasts did she begin to regret her tears. How do I know that the dead do not regret that ever they had an urge to life? Who banquets in a dream at dawn wails and weeps, who wails and weeps in a dream at dawn goes out to hunt. While we dream we do not know that we are dreaming, and in the middle of a dream interpret a dream within it; not until we wake do we know that we were dreaming. Only at the ultimate awakening shall we know that this is the ultimate dream. Yet fools think they are awake, so confident that they know what they are, princes, herdsmen, incorrigible! You and Confucius are both dreams, and I who call you a dream am also a dream. This saying of his, the name for it is 'a flight into the extraordinary'; if it happens once in ten thousand ages that a great sage knows its explanation it will have happened as though between morning and evening."

* * *

You and I having been made to argue over alternatives, if it is you not I that wins, is it really you who are on to it, I who am not? If it is I not you that wins, is it really I who am on to it, you who are not? Is one of us on to it and the other of us not? Or are both of us on to it and both of us not? If you and I are unable to know where we stand, others will surely be in the dark because of us. Whom shall I call in to decide it? If I get someone of your party to decide it, being already of your party how can he decide it? If I get someone of my party to decide it, being already of my party how can he decide it? If I get someone of a party different from either of us to decide it, being already of a party different from either of us how can he decide it? If I get someone of the same party as both of us to decide it, being already of the same party as both of us how can he decide it? Consequently you and I and he are all unable to know where we stand, and shall we find someone else to depend on?

It makes no difference whether the voices in their transformations have each other to depend on or not. Smooth them out on the whetstone of Heaven, use them to go by and let the stream find its own channels; this is the way to live out your years. Forget the years, forget duty, be shaken into motion by the limitless, and so find things their lodging-places in the limitless.

What is meant by "Smooth them out on the whetstone of Heaven"? Treat as "it" even what is not, treat as "so" even what is not. If the "it" is really it, there is no longer a difference for disputation from what is not it; if the "so" is really so, there is no longer a difference for disputation from what is not so.*

* * *

The penumbra asked the shadow:

"Just then you were walking, now you stop; just then you were sitting, now you stand. Why don't you make up your mind to do one thing or the other?"

"Is it that there is something on which I depend to be so? And does what I depend on too depend on something else to be so? Would it be that I depend on snake's scales, cicada's wings? How would I recognise why it is so, how would I recognise why it is not so?"

* * *

Last night Chuang Chou dreamed he was a butterfly, spirits soaring he was a butterfly (is it that in showing what he was he suited his own fancy?), and did not know about Chou. When all of a sudden he awoke, he was Chou with all his wits about him. He does not know whether he is Chou who dreams he is a butterfly or a butterfly who dreams he is Chou. Between Chou and the butterfly there was necessarily a dividing; just this is what is meant by the transformations of things.

CHAPTER 3: WHAT MATTERS IN THE NURTURE OF LIFE**

My life flows between confines, but knowledge has no confines. If we use the confined to follow after the unconfined, there is danger that the flow will cease; and when it ceases, to exercise knowledge is purest danger.

---

*Since anything may at one time or another be picked out as "it," if it were really the name of something (in Western grammatical terms, if it were not a pronoun but a noun) it would be the name of everything. Chuang-tzu likes the thought that instead of selecting and approving something as "it" one may use the word to embrace and approve everything, to say "Yes!" to the universe.

**The theme of this chapter is the recovery of the spontaneity of vital process when we abandon analytic knowledge and trust to the daemonic insight and aptitude which enters us from beyond, from Heaven. The chapter is short and scrappy, surely because of textual mutilation; it is unlikely that the compilers were short of material on so basic a theme.

Zhuangzi Dreaming of a Butterfly by LuZhi. In a famous section from his book, Chuang Tzu (Zhuangzi) tells how he once dreamed he was a butterfly who knew nothing of Chuang Tzu, the person. But when he awoke, he was left wondering: Was he really Chuang Tzu who dreamt he was a butterfly or a butterfly who was now dreaming he was Chuang Tzu?

> Doer of good, stay clear of reputation.
> Doer of ill, stay clear of punishment.
> Trace the vein which is central and make it your standard.
> You can protect the body,
> keep life whole,
> nurture your parents,
> last out your years.

Hence, as the ground which the foot treads is small, and yet, small as it is, it depends on the untrodden ground to have scope to range, so the knowledge a man needs is little, yet little as it is he depends on what he does not know to know what is meant by "Heaven." If you know the ultimate One, the ultimate Yin, the ultimate eye, the ultimate adjuster, the ultimate in scope, the ultimately truthful, the ultimately fixed, you have attained the utmost. The ultimate One makes things interchangeable, the ultimate Yin* unravels them, the ultimate eye looks out at them, the ultimate adjuster sets a route by them, the ultimate in scope identifies with them, the ultimately truthful verifies them, the ultimately fixed supports them.

*Instead of exerting his energies in the active or Yang phase to unravel a problem, the sage lets them withdraw in the passive or Yin phase to an absolute stillness in which he sees problems unravel of themselves.

If to embrace them all we have Heaven and to stay on course have its light, if in obscurity we have the axis* on which things turn, and to start from have that which is other than ourselves, then our unravelling will resemble failing to unravel, our knowing will resemble ignorance. The questions which we put to that which we know only by being ignorant cannot have confines yet cannot be without confines. If when we wrench everything apart there are objects, each in its own position past or present, and we cannot afford to leave any of them out of account, then can it be denied that there is a grand total of all? Why not after all put your questions to *it*?

Why be bothered by doubts? If you use the undoubted to unravel the doubted and transfer it to the undoubted, this is to have too much respect for the undoubted. Use the unlevel to level and your levelling will not level, use the untested to test and your testing will not test. The sight of the eye is only something which it employs, it is the daemonic in us which tests. It is no new thing that the sight of the eye does not prevail over the daemonic; and is it not sad that fools should depend on what they see and confine themselves to what is of man, so that their achievements are external?

Therefore the capacity of the eye to see presents dangers, the capacity of the ear to hear presents dangers, the capacity of the heart for perilous ambitions presents dangers. All ability in what concerns the organs presents dangers. When the dangers become actual it is too late to mend, as misfortune grows complications multiply, recovery depends on effective action, success depends on prolonged effort; and is it not sad that men should think of the organs as their greatest treasures? Therefore that there is no end to ruined states and massacred peoples is because we do not know how to put our questions to *it*.

*   *   *

Cook Ting was carving an ox for Lord Wen-hui. As his hand slapped, shoulder lunged, foot stamped, knee crooked, with a hiss! with a thud! the brandished blade as it sliced never missed the rhythm, now in time with the Mulberry Forest dance, now with an orchestra playing the Ching-shou.

"Oh, excellent!" said Lord Wen-hui. "That skill should attain such heights!"

"What your servant cares about is the Way, I have left skill behind me. When I first began to carve oxen, I saw nothing but oxen wherever I looked. Three years more and I never saw an ox as a whole. Nowadays, I am in touch through the daemonic in me, and do not look with the eye. With the senses I know where to stop, the daemonic I desire to run its course. I rely on Heaven's structuring, cleave along the main seams, let myself be guided by the main cavities, go by what is inherently so. A ligament or tendon I never touch, not to mention solid bone. A good cook changes his chopper once a year, because he hacks. A common cook changes it once a month, because he smashes. Now I have had this chopper for nineteen years, and have taken apart several thousand oxen, but the edge is as though it were fresh from the grindstone. At that joint there is an interval, and the chopper's edge has no thickness; if you insert what has no thickness where there is an interval, then, what more could you ask, of course there is ample room to move the edge about. That's why after nineteen years the edge of my chopper is as though it were fresh from the grindstone.

---

*The still point at the centre of us from which we can watch the cycles of events as though from the motionless centre of a rotating wheel.

"However, whenever I come to something intricate, I see where it will be hard to handle and cautiously prepare myself, my gaze settles on it, action slows down for it, you scarcely see the flick of the chopper—and at one stroke the tangle has been unravelled, as a clod crumbles to the ground. I stand chopper in hand, look proudly round at everyone, dawdle to enjoy the triumph until I'm quite satisfied, then clean the chopper and put it away."

"Excellent!" said Lord Wen-hui. "Listening to the words of Cook Ting, I have learned from them how to nurture life."

*   *   *

When Kung-wen Hsuan saw the Commander of the Right, he said in astonishment "What man is this? Why is he so singular? Is it from Heaven or from man?*

"It is from Heaven, not from man. When Heaven engenders something it causes it to be unique; the guise which is from man assimilates us to each other. By this I know it is from Heaven, not from man."

*   *   *

The pheasant of the woodlands walks ten paces for one peck, a hundred paces for one drink, but has no urge to be looked after in a cage. One's daemon does not find it good even to be a king.

When Old Tan died Ch'in Yi went in to mourn him, wailed three times and came out.

"Were you not the Master's friend?" said a disciple.

"I was."

"Then is it decent to mourn him like this?"

"It is. I used to think of him as the man, but now he is not. Just now as I came in to mourn him, there were old people bewailing him as they would wail for their sons, young people bewailing him as they would wail for their mothers. As to how he made them gather here—there were surely some who were saying what they had no urge to say, wailing when they had no urge to wail. This is to hide from Heaven and turn away from what we truly are, and forget the gift that we received; of old it was called 'the punishment for hiding from Heaven.' In coming when he did, the Master was on time; in departing when he did, the Master was on course. Be content with the time and settled on the course, and sadness and joy cannot find a way in. Of old this was called 'God's loosing of the bonds.'**

"If the meaning is confined to what is deemed the 'firewood.' as the fire passes on from one piece to the next we do not know it is the 'cinders.'"†

---

*The commentators suppose Kung-wen Hsuan to be singular in the number of his feet, having a chopped foot like the men condemned for crimes in *The Signs of Fullness of Power.* But the story makes more sense if he is singular in appearance or character, a freak or eccentric.

**If Old Tan had been the great teacher he seemed, his disciples would have learned to take his death with equanimity instead of making all this fuss.

†This final sentence is obscure. I take it to be using the terminology of disputation. We divide up the changing totality, use names such as "living" and "firewood" to detach the partial and temporary, and then suppose that death and burning bring them to an end, forgetting that they are the same thing as what in the next phase in the endless process of transformation will be named "dead" and "cinders."

CHAPTER 4: WORLDLY BUSINESS AMONG MEN*

1. FIRST SERIES

Yen Hui called on Confucius and asked leave to travel.

"Where are you off to?"

"I am going to Wey."

"What will you do there?"

"I hear that the lord of Wey is young in years and wilful in deeds. He is careless of the cost to his state and blind to his own faults; he is so careless of the cost in men's lives that the dead fill the state to its borders as though it had been ravaged with fire and slaughter. No, the people have nowhere to turn. I have heard you say, sir: 'Never mind the well ruled states, go to the misruled states; at a doctor's gate it is mostly the sick that call.' I wish to think out what to do in the light of what you taught me, in the hope that the state may be restored to health."

"Hmm. I am afraid that you are simply going to your execution. One doesn't want the Way to turn into a lot of odds and ends. If it does it becomes multiple, when it's multiple it gets you muddled, when you're muddled you worry, and once you worry there's no hope for you. The utmost man of old established in other people only what he had first established in himself. Until it is firmly established in yourself, what time have you to spare for the doings of tyrants?

"Besides, do you after all understand that the thing by which the Power in us is dissipated is the very thing by which knowledge is brought forth? The Power is dissipated by making a name, knowledge comes forth from competition. To 'make a name' is to clash with others, 'knowledge' is a tool in competition. Both of them are sinister tools, of no use in perfecting conduct.

"Then again, to be ample in Power and solid in sincerity but lack insight into others' temperaments, not enter into competition for reputation but lack insight into others' hearts, yet insist in the presence of the tyrant on preaching about Goodwill and Duty and the lines laid down for us, this amounts to taking advantage of someone's ugliness to make yourself look handsome. The name for it is 'making a pest of oneself.' Make a pest of oneself, and others will certainly make pests of themselves in return. I rather fancy that someone is going to be a pest to you.

"Another thing: if you do think he favours clever people and dislikes fools, will it do you any good to try to be especially clever? Better not get into an argument. A king or duke is sure to pit his wits against one's own with the whole weight of his authority behind him.

> Your eye he'll dazzle,
> Your look he'll cow,
> Your mouth he'll manage,
> Your gesture he'll shape,
> Your heart he'll form.

---

*This chapter has two sets of episodes. The first considers the devious and intractable problems of the Taoist in office: to what extent can he live the enlightened life and hope to bring his ruler nearer to the Way? The second proclaims the advantages of being useless, unemployable, so that the government leaves you alone.

"You will find yourself using fire to quell fire, water to quell water, the name for it is 'going from bad to worse.' Being submissive at the start that is how you will always be. I am afraid that he will lose faith in your fulsome words, and so you'll be sure to die at the tyrant's hands.

"One more point. Formerly Kuan Lung-feng was executed by Chieh and Prince Pi-kan by Chow. Both were men meticulous in their personal conduct who as ministers offended emperors by sympathising with their subjects. Consequently their lords found their meticulousness a reason to get rid of them. These were men who desired a good name. And formerly Yao attacked Tsung, Chih and Hsu-ao, Yu attacked Yu-hu, the countries were reduced to empty wastes and hungry ghosts, the rulers were executed. There was no end to their calls to arms, no respite in their aspiration to great deeds. All these men were seekers of the name or the deed, and don't tell me you haven't heard of them! A good name, a great deed, tempt even the sage, and do you think you're any better?

"However, I am sure you have something in mind. Let me hear about it."

"Would it do," said Hui, "to be punctilious and impartial, diligent and single-minded?"

"O no, that's no good at all! To sustain the Yang at its height without reverting to the Yin puts one under great stress, the tension shows in one's face. It is something which ordinary people prefer not to defy, so they suppress what the other man is stirring up in them in order to calm their own hearts. Even what are named 'powers which progress from day to day' will not grow to the full in him, let alone the supreme Power! He will stay obstinately as he is and refuse to reform, outwardly agreeing with you but inwardly insensible, and what's the good of that?"

"In that case," said Hui, "inwardly I shall be straight but outwardly I shall bend, I shall mature my own judgement yet conform to my betters. In being 'inwardly straight', I shall be of Heaven's party. One who is of Heaven's party knows that in the eyes of Heaven he is just as much a son as the Son of Heaven is, and is he the only one who, when speaking on his own account, has an urge which carries him away and other people applaud, or which carries him away and other people disapprove? Such a one is excused by others as childlike. It is this that I mean by 'being of Heaven's party.'

"In 'outwardly bending' I shall be of man's party. Lifting up the tablet in his hands and kneeling and bowing from the waist are the etiquette of a minister; everyone else does it, why should I presume to be an exception? If you do what others do, the others for their part will find no fault in you. It is this that I mean by 'being of man's party.'

"In 'maturing my own judgement yet conforming to my betters' I shall be of the party of the men of old. The words, although in substance instructions or criticisms, belong to the men of old, I can't be held responsible for them. Such a person can be as straight as he likes without getting into trouble. It is this that I mean by 'being of the party of the men of old.' How will that do?"

"Oh no, that's no good at all! Too much organising. If you stick to the forms and don't get too familiar, even if you're stupid you will escape blame. But that's all that can be said for it. How would you succeed in making a new man of him? It's still taking the heart as one's authority."

"I have nothing more to propose," said Hui. "I venture to ask the secret of it."

"Fast, and I will tell you," said Confucius. "Doing something thought out in the heart, isn't that too easy? Whoever does things too easily is unfit for the lucid light of Heaven."

"I am of a poor family, I have not drunk wine or eaten a seasoned dish for months. Would that count as fasting?"

"That kind of fasting one does before a sacrifice, it is not the fasting of the heart."

"I venture to inquire about the fasting of the heart."

"Unify your attention. Rather than listen with the ear, listen with the heart. Rather than listen with the heart, listen with the energies. Listening stops at the ear, the heart at what tallies with the thought. As for 'energy,' it is the tenuous which waits to be roused by other things. Only the Way accumulates the tenuous. The attenuating is the fasting of the heart."

"When Hui has never yet succeeded in being the agent, a deed derives from Hui. When he does succeed in being its agent, there has never begun to be a Hui.—Would that be what you call attenuating?"

"Perfect! I shall tell you. You are capable of entering and roaming free inside his cage, but do not be excited that you are making a name for your self. When the words penetrate, sing your native note; when they fail to penetrate, desist. When there are no doors for you, no outlets, and treating all abodes as one you find your lodgings in whichever is the inevitable, you will be nearly there.

"To leave off making footprints is easy,* never to walk on the ground is hard. What has man for agent is easily falsified, what has Heaven for agent is hard to falsify. You have heard of using wings to fly. You have not yet heard of flying by being wingless; you have heard of using the wits to know, you have not yet heard of using ignorance to know.

"This I call 'going at a gallop while you sit.' If the channels inward through eyes and ears are cleared, and you expel knowledge from the heart, the ghostly and daemonic will come to dwell in you, not to mention all that is human! This is to transform with the myriad things, here Shun and Yu found the knot where all threads join, here Fu-hsi and Chi Ch'u finished their journey, not to speak of lesser men!"**

*   *   *

Tzu-kao the Duke of She, about to go on a mission to Ch'i, consulted Confucius.

"The mission on which His Majesty has sent me is most weighty; and the way Ch'i treats emissaries, you know, is to be most respectful but put things off indefinitely. It is no use forcing the pace even with a commoner, not to speak of the lord of a state! I am very uneasy about it. You once said to me: 'There are few enterprises, great or small, in

---

*I.e., it is easy to withdraw from the world as a hermit, hard to remain above the world while living in it.

"Look up to the easer of our toils.
In the empty room the brightness grows.
The blessed, the auspicious, stills the stilled.
The about to be does not stay still.

**For Yen Hui (the favourite disciple of Confucius) to go to the King full of good intentions and well thought out plans will do harm in stead of good. He must first train the motions in himself which can spontaneously move another in the direction of the Way. He must trust to the ch'i (translated "energies"), the breath and other energising fluids which alternate between activity as the Yang and passivity as the Yin (as in breathing out and in), training them with the meditative technique including controlled breathing. When the purified fluid has become perfectly tenuous the heart will be emptied of conceptual knowledge, the channels of the senses will be cleared, and he will simply perceive and respond. Then the self dissolves, energies strange to him and higher than his own (the "daemonic") enter from outside, the agent of his actions is no longer the man but Heaven working through him, yet paradoxically (and it is in hitting on this paradox that Hui convinces Confucius that he understands) in discovering a deeper self he becomes for the first time truly the agent. He no longer has deliberate goals, the "about to be" at the centre of him belongs to the transforming processes of heaven and earth. Then he will have the instinct for when to speak and when to be silent, and will say the right thing as naturally as a bird sings.

which we are not under pressure to push for success. If the enterprise fails, we are sure to suffer the penalties of the Way of Man, and if it succeeds we are sure to suffer the maladies of the Yin and Yang. To escape ill consequences whether he succeeds or not—only the Man of Power is capable of that.' I am one who sticks to a diet of plain and simple foods, no one at my kitchen stove ever grumbles about the heat, but now I get orders in the morning and by evening am drinking iced water; surely I must be getting a fever? Before I even have access to the facts of the case I am already suffering those 'maladies of the Yin and Yang'; and if the enterprise fails I shall surely suffer your 'penalties of the Way of Man' as well. This is getting the worst of it both ways. I am inadequate to bear my responsibilities as a minister, and only hope you have some advice to give me."

"In the world there are two supreme commandments," said Confucius. "One of them is destiny, the other duty. A child's love of his parents is destined: it cannot be dispelled from the heart. A minister's service to his lord is duty;* wherever he may go his lord is his lord. The commandments from which there is no escape between heaven and earth, these are what I call the supreme ones. This is why in the service of parents there is no higher degree of filial conduct than to live contentedly wherever they may dwell, in the service of a lord no fuller measure of loyalty than to perform his tasks contentedly whatever they may be, and in the service of one's own heart no higher degree of Power than, without joy and sorrow ever alternating before it, to know that these things could not be otherwise, and be content with them as our destiny. It is inherent in serving either as a son or as a minister that there is something which is inevitable. If you act on the facts of the situation, forgetful of your own person, how can it ever occur to you that it would please you more to save your life than to die? Go, sir, it is well that you should.

"Allow me to repeat to you some things I have heard. Whenever we are dealing with neighbours we have to rub along with each other on a basis of trust; but with people more distant we have to show our good faith in words, and the words must have some messenger. To pass on the words of parties both of whom are pleased or both of whom are angry with each other is the most difficult thing in the world. In the one case there are sure to be a lot of exaggerated compliments, in the other a lot of exaggerated abuse. Every sort of exaggeration is irresponsible, and if language is irresponsible trust in it fails, and the consequence of that is that the messenger is a doomed man. Therefore the book of rules says: 'If you report the straightforward facts and omit the exaggerated language, you will be safe enough.'

"Another point: competitors in a game of skill begin in a bright Yang mood, but it is apt to end up by darkening to Yin; when they have gone too far they play more and more unfair tricks. Drinkers at a formal banquet are mannerly at first, but generally end up too boisterous; when they have gone too far the fun gets more and more reckless. This happens in all sorts of affairs. What begins as courtly is liable to end up vulgar; things which at the start were simple enough sooner or later are sure to get out of hand. Words are wind and waves, deeds fulfil or discredit them. It is easy for wind and waves to make a stir, and as easy for fulfilment or discrediting to endanger. Therefore the anger which is aroused has no other source than the cunning in wording and bias in phrasing.

---

*It is remarkable to find Chuang-tzu talking like a moralist about the "duty" to serve the ruler, especially since elsewhere he always uses the word unfavourably. However, this is the single episode in which an inquirer is under specific orders from his ruler. Chuang-tzu does not question the institutions of family and state, although he does not talk about them much. You do in the last resort acknowledge a duty to the state in which you live, and if by choice or necessity you come to be in office you accept its rules as belonging to the "inevitable." However narrow the limits, as long as you preserve the responsiveness of your energies you can still, like Hui in the last episode, "roam free inside the cage."

"When an animal faces death it does not choose its cry, the viciousness is in its very breath, and then it generates the blood lust in hunter and hunted alike. If you go too far in trying to force a conclusion, the other is sure to respond with poor judgement, and he will not even know what is happening to him. If he does not even know what is happening to him, who can guess where it will end? Therefore the book of rules says: 'Do not deviate from the orders, do not push for success. To exceed due measure is to go beyond your commission.' To deviate from the orders and push for success will endanger the enterprise. A fine success takes time, an ugly outcome is irreparable; can you afford not to be careful?

"Besides, to let the heart roam with other things as its chariot, and by trusting to the inevitable nurture the centre of you, is the farthest one can go. Why should there be anything you have initiated in the reply you bring back? The important thing is to fulfil what is ordained for you; and that is the most difficult thing of all."*

*   *   *

When Yen Ho was appointed tutor of the heir apparent of Duke Ling of Wey, he inquired of Ch'u Po-yu.

"Let us imagine the case of a man with a Power in him which Heaven has made murderous. If I behave recklessly in his company it will endanger our country; if I behave decently in his company it will endanger my life. He has just enough wit to know that a man has erred, but not to know why he erred. How would I deal with someone like that?"

"A good question indeed! Be alert, on guard! Get your own person rightly adjusted! In your demeanour what matters is to get close, in your heart what matters is to be at peace. However, there are difficulties on both points. In getting close you don't want to be drawn in, and you don't want the peace in your heart to escape outside. If by your demeanour getting too close you are drawn in, it will be downfall, ruin, collapse, trampling. If the peace in your heart escapes outside, it will become repute, fame, a disaster, a curse.

"When he wants to play the child, join him in playing the child. When he wants to jump the fences, join him in jumping the fences. When he wants to burst the shores, join him in bursting the shores. Fathom him right through, and be drawn into the unblemished in him.

"Don't you know about the praying mantis? It will wave its arms furiously and stand bang in the middle of a rut, it doesn't know that the weight of the wheel is too much for its strength. This is because the stuff it's made of is too noble. Be alert, on guard! If you confront him with something accumulating in you which takes pride in your own nobility, you won't last long. And don't you know what a keeper of tigers does? He daren't give them a live animal because they will get into a rage killing it, or a whole animal either, because they will get into a rage tearing it apart. He keeps track of the times when they will be hungry or full, and has the secret of their angry hearts. Tigers are a different breed from men, but when they fawn on the man who feeds them it is because he goes along with their dispositions; and so if they get murderous it is because he thwarts their dispositions.

---

*"What is ordained for you": the king's decree and/or what Heaven destines for you. Paradoxically, it is supremely difficult to act out your destiny, to surrender to the impulse from Heaven instead of thinking in terms of self interest and morality.

"The man who loves his horse will pamper it with a basket for its dung and a clam shell for its piss. But if a fly or mosquito should happen to hover near, and he slaps it unexpectedly, the horse will burst its bit and smash his head and kick in his chest. There was nothing wrong with the intention but the love did damage. You can't be too careful."

2. SECOND SERIES

When Carpenter Shih was travelling to Ch'i he came to a village at a bend in the road, and saw the chestnut-leaved-oak by the altar of the god of the soil. It was broad enough to give shade to several thousand oxen and measured by the tape a hundred spans round; it was so high that it overlooked the hills and the lowest branches were seventy feet up; boughs from which you might make a boat could be counted by the dozen. The crowd gazing at it was like the throng in a market, but Carpenter Shih did not give it a glance; he walked straight on without a pause.

When his apprentice had had his fill of gazing at it he ran to catch up with Carpenter Shih.

"Since I took up the axe to serve you, sir, I have never seen such noble timber. Why is it that you didn't deign to look at it, didn't even pause as you walked?"

"Enough, don't mention it again. That's good-for-nothing wood. Make a boat from it and it will sink, make a coffin and it will rot at once, make a bowl and it will break at once, make a gate or door and it will ooze sap, make a pillar and it will be worm-holed. This wood is wretched timber, useless for anything; that's why it's been able to grow so old."

When Carpenter Shih came home, the sacred oak appeared in a dream and said to him,

"With what do you propose to compare me? Would it be with the fine-grained woods? As for the sort that bear fruits or berries, the cherry-apple, pear, orange, pumelo, when the fruit ripens they are stripped, and in being stripped they are disgracefully abused, their branches broken, their twigs snapped off. These are trees which by their own abilities make life miserable for themselves; and so they die in mid-path without lasting out the years assigned to them by Heaven, trees which have let themselves be made victims of worldly vulgarity. Such are the consequences with all things. I would add that this quest of mine to become of no possible use to anyone has been going on for a long time: only now, on the verge of death, have I achieved it, and to me it is supremely useful. Supposing that I had been useful too, would I have had the opportunity to grow so big?

"Besides, you and I are both things, what nonsense! that one of us should think it is the other which is the thing: and the good-for-nothing man who is soon to die, what does he know of the good-for-nothing tree?"

When Carpenter Shih woke up he told his dream.

"If it prefers to be useless," said the apprentice, "why is it serving as the sacred tree?"

"Hush! Don't say it. It's simply using that as a pretext, thinks of itself as pestered by people who don't appreciate it. Aren't the ones which don't become sacred trees in some danger of being clipped? Besides, what that tree is protecting has nothing to do with the vulgar, and if we praise it for doing a duty won't we be missing the point?"

*   *   *

When Tzu-ch'i of Nan-po was rambling on the Hill of Shang, he saw a great tree which stood out from the rest. You could tether a thousand teams of horses to it, and they would all find shelter in its shade.

"What tree is this?" said Tzu-ch'i. "The timber must be quite out of the ordinary, I should think."

But when he looked up at the slimmer branches, they were too crooked to make beams and rafters. When he looked down at the trunk, the grain was too twisted and loose to make coffins. If you licked a leaf it stung the mouth and left a sore, if you took a sniff it made you delirious for a full three days.

"This indeed is wretched timber," said Tzu-ch'i, "which is why it has grown to be so big. Aha! That's why the most daemonic of men are made of such poor stuff!"

* * *

There is a place in Sung, Ching-shih, where catalpas, cypresses and mulberries thrive. But a tree an arm-length or two round will be chopped down by someone who wants a post to tether his monkey, a tree of three or four spans by someone seeking a ridge-pole for an imposing roof, a tree of seven or eight spans by the family of a noble or rich merchant looking for a sideplank for his coffin. So they do not last out the years Heaven assigned them, but die in mid-journey under the axe. That is the trouble with being stuff which is good for something. Similarly in the sacrifice to the god of the river it is forbidden to cast into the waters an ox with a white forehead, a pig with a turned-up snout or a man with piles. These are all known to be exempt by shamans and priests, being things they deem bearers of ill-luck. They are the very things which the daemonic man will deem supremely lucky.

* * *

Cripple Shu—his chin is buried down in his navel, his shoulders are higher than his crown, the knobbly bone at the base of his neck points at the sky, the five pipes to the spine are right up on top, his two thighbones make another pair of ribs. By plying the needle and doing laundry he makes enough to feed himself, and when he rattles the sticks telling fortunes for a handful of grain he is making enough to feed ten. If the authorities are press-ganging soldiers the cripple strolls in the middle of them flipping back his sleeves; if they are conscripting work parties he is excused as a chronic invalid: if they are doling out grain to the sick he gets three measures, and ten bundles of firewood besides. Even someone crippled in body manages to support himself and last out the years assigned him by Heaven. If you make a cripple of the Power in you, you can do better still!

When Confucius travelled to Ch'u, Chieh Yü the madman of Ch'u wandered at his gate crying

"Phoenix! Phoenix!
What's to be done about Power's decline?
Of the age to come we can't be sure,
To the age gone by there's no road back.

When the Empire has the Way
The sage succeeds in it.
When the Empire lacks the Way
The sage survives in it.
In this time of ours, enough
If he dodges execution in it.

Good luck is lighter than a feather,
None knows how to bear its weight.
Mishap is heavier than the earth,
None knows how to get out of the way.

Enough, enough!
Of using Power to reign over men.
Beware, beware!
Of marking ground and bustling us inside.

Thistle, thistle,
Don't wound me as I walk.
My walk goes backward and goes crooked,
Don't wound my feet.

The trees in the mountains plunder themselves,
The grease in the flame sizzles itself.
Cinnamon has a taste,
So they hack it down.
Lacquer has a use,
So they strip it off.

All men know the uses of the useful, but no one knows the uses of the useless."*

CHAPTER 5: THE SIGNS OF FULLNESS OF POWER**

There was a man with a chopped foot in Lu, Wang T'ai, who had as many disciples in his retinue as Confucius himself. Ch'ang Chi asked Confucius

"Wang T'ai had his foot chopped off, but the disciples in his train divide Lu down the middle with yours. When he stands up he doesn't teach, when he sits down he doesn't

---

*Cf. *Analects* of Confucius, Chapter 18 [page 346 in this volume]: "As Confucius was passing by, the wild man of Ch'u met his carriage singing,

Phoenix, oh phoenix,
Thine virtue declined,
What is past unalterable,
What will come undefined.
Refrain! Refrain!
Desolate the public office of the day!

Confucius descended to speak with him, but the wild man quickened his pace to shun him. Confucius was unable to speak with him."

This ballad ironically welcomes Confucius, preaching ideal government in a decadent age, as the phoenix which comes as an auspicious omen when there is a sage on the throne. Chuang-tzu has written a version of his own (it must be his, for the unqualified praise of uselessness is a theme which, even in *Chuang-tzu*, is peculiar to his own writings. The use of Chieh Yu as a spokesman of Taoism is also confined to him.

**The test that a man lives by the Power in himself, and is wholly independent of every thing outside him, is his indifference to the great irreparable disasters, death and bodily deformity, an indifference which makes others too ignore even such an obstructive sign of mutilation and social condemnation as a foot chopped off for a crime. The theme of death belongs to *The Teacher Who Is the Ultimate Ancestor;* stories about mutilated criminals, freaks and cripples are collected in this chapter. They are characteristic of Chuang-tzu's own writing, almost disappearing from the book after the end of the *Inner Chapters*.

talk things over, yet they go to him empty and come away full. Is there indeed a word-
less teaching, or a heart which is whole though the body is deformed? What man is this?"

"The Master is a sage," said Confucius. "I should already have gone to him myself if I hadn't been putting it off. And if *I* would want him as teacher, is it surprising
that lesser men do? Never mind our country Lu, I'll pull in the whole world to come
with me to follow him."

"If in spite of his chopped foot he is greater than you, sir, he must indeed be quite
out of the ordinary. Is there something special about the use to which such a man puts
the heart?"

"Death and life are mighty indeed, but he refuses to alter with them; though
heaven were to collapse and earth subside he would not be lost with them. He is aware
of the Flawless and is not displaced with other things; he does his own naming of the
transformations of things and holds fast to their Ancestor."

"What do you mean?"

"If you look at them from the viewpoint of their differences, from liver to gall is
as far as from Ch'u to Yueh; if you look at them from the viewpoint of their sameness,
the myriad things are all one. Such a man cannot even tell apart the functions of eyes
and ears, and lets the heart go roaming in the peace which is from the Power. As for
other things, he looks into that in which they are one, and does not see what each of
them has lost; he regards losing his own foot as he would shaking off mud."

"His concern is for himself, he uses his wits to discover his own heart, his heart
to discover the unchanging heart beyond it. Why should others congregate around him?"

"None of us finds his mirror in flowing water, we find it in still water. Only the
still can still whatever is stilled. Among all that owe their destiny to the earth, only the
pine and cypress are due on course; winter and summer they are the same green. Among
all that owe their destiny to Heaven, only Yao and Shun are due on course; they stand
at the head of the myriad things. One blessed with the ability to set life due on course
does it for every living thing.

"The test that one holds fast to the Beginning is the fact of not being afraid. A single brave knight will boldly enter a battle of great armies; if this can be done even by a
man capable of exerting himself out of ambition to make a name, how much more by
one who makes heaven and earth his palace and the myriad things his storehouse, his
trunk and limbs a place where he lodges and his eyes and ears images which he perceives, who treats as one all that wit knows and has a heart which never dies! He will
pick his own day to rise out of the world. As for other men, it is for them to follow in
his train; why should he want to make others his business?"

*   *   *

Shen-t'u Chia, a man with a chopped foot, was fellow student under Po-hun
Nobody with Tzu-ch'an the Prime Minister of Cheng.

"If I make the first move to leave, you stay," said Tzu-ch'an. "If you make the first
move to leave, I stay."

Next day he found himself sitting with him again for the same lesson on the same mat.

"If I leave you stay, if you leave I stay. I shall now leave. Would it bother you too
much to stay? Or would you rather not? And if you do not make way when you see the
Prime Minister, are you putting yourself on a level with the Prime Minister?"

"So there's really the Prime Minister, you say, here among our Master's pupils?
That's the one who being you is pleased it's you who's Prime Minister and turns his

back on everyone else. I have heard it said: 'If your mirror is bright* the dust will not settle, if the dust settles it's that your mirror isn't bright. Keep company long enough with a man of worth and there will be no crime in you.' The teacher you now acknowledge as the greatest is our Master, yet you can still talk to me like this. Don't you think that's a crime?"

"After *that* happened to you, you would still argue with Yao which of you is the better man. If you reckon it all up, isn't there even enough Power in you to take an honest look at yourself?"

"There are many of us who would freely tell you about their crimes, thinking that they did not deserve to suffer; there are a few of us who would refuse to tell you about their crimes, thinking that they did not deserve to he spared; but as for recognising the inescapable and being content with it as destined, only the man who does have Power in him is capable of that. To stray within the range of archer Yi's bow and not be hit is destiny. Plenty of people who have whole feet laugh at me because I haven't; I get into a furious temper, but if I go to the Master's place the mood has passed before I come home. I do not know whether it is the Master cleansing me by his goodness or my own self-awakening. I have been going around with the Master for nineteen years now, and was never aware that I'm a man with a chopped foot. You and I are roaming now on the inside of the flesh-and-bone, yet you haul me out to take a look from the outside of the flesh-and-bone. Don't you think that's a crime?"

Tzu-ch'an, taken aback, corrected his expression and bearing. "You don't have to say any more," he said.

*   *   *

There was a man with a chopped foot in Lu, Shu-shan Choptoes, who came walking on his heels to see Confucius.

"You were careless," said Confucius. "After getting into such trouble before, what is the point of coming to me now?"

"I simply did not have the sense to care, and took my own safety for granted, that is how I lost my foot. Coming to you now, what gave the foot its worth still survives in me, which is why I am concerned to keep it intact. There is nothing which heaven refuses to cover over or earth to support; I thought of you, sir, as my heaven and earth, how could I have known that you would turn out like this?"

"That was rude of me, why don't you come in, sir? Allow me to instruct you in what I have heard."

When Choptoes left, Confucius said,

"My disciples, be diligent! That Choptoes was condemned to have his foot chopped off, but he is still concerned to study in order to make amends for his former wicked conduct, and how much more the man in whom Power remains whole!"

Choptoes told Old Tan,

"As an aspirant to be the utmost man, Confucius has some way to go, wouldn't you say? Why did he bother to keep coming to learn from you? He still has an urge to have his name bandied about as someone unique and extraordinary. Doesn't he know that the utmost man would think of it as fettering and handcuffing himself?"

"Why not just get him to recognise death and life as a single strand," said Old Tan, "and the allowable and the unallowable as strung on a single thread? Surely it's possible to shake off his fetters and handcuffs?"

---

*If the disciple's mind, unclouded by egoism, lucidly reflects the master's teaching, he will be faultless.

"When Heaven does the punishing, how can they be shaken off?"

(He thought of the mutilation as a bodily feature, of the rites as his supports, of knowing what to do as a matter of timeliness, of Power as the capacity to stay on course.

"He thought of the mutilation as a bodily feature": he took the truncation for granted.

"Of the rites as his supports": as the means to conduct himself among the worldly.

"Of knowing what to do as a matter of timeliness": of doing whatever is inevitable in the circumstances.

"Of Power as the capacity to stay on course" means that he went to old Confucius with people who had their feet, and that the others genuinely regarded him as heedful in his conduct.)*

* * *

Duke Ai of Lu put a question to Confucius.

"In Wey there was a hideous man called Uglyface T'o. Young men who lived with him were so fascinated that they couldn't leave, the girls who when they saw him begged their parents 'I would rather be his concubine than anyone else's wife' could be counted in dozens. No one ever heard him say anything new, all he ever did was chime in with others. Without the throne of a lord of men from which to save a man from death, or mounting revenues with which to make waning bellies wax, and on top of that ugly enough to give the whole world a fright, chiming in without saying anything new, in knowledge content to stay within the bounds of the ordinary, none the less wild creatures would couple where he stood. This was obviously a man with something different about him. I summoned him to court to observe him, and he really was ugly enough to frighten the whole world. He stayed with me, and before it was time to start counting in months I was getting interested in the sort of man he was; before a year was up he had all my faith. The state lacked a chief minister, I put him in charge. He accepted only after a hesitation, in an apathetic voice as though he were declining. Embarrassing for me! But in the end I did get the state into his hands. Not long afterwards he left me and went away. I was as moved as if I had been bereaved, as if there were no one left with whom to share the joy of this state. What man was this?"

"To tell a story about myself," said Confucius, "I was once sent on a mission to Ch'u, and happened to see some little pigs sucking at their dead mother. Not long after, in the batting of an eye lid they all abandoned her and ran. It was just that they did not see themselves in her, did not recognise their own kind in her. What they loved in their mother was not her shape, but what made her shape move. Men who die in battle require no coffin plumes at their burial, a man with chopped feet will not grudge you the loan of his shoes; neither possesses what made them matter.

"Cripple Lipless with the crooked legs advised Duke Ling of Wey; the Duke was so pleased with him that when he looked at normal men their legs were too lanky. Pitcherneck with the big goitre advised Duke Huan of Ch'i; the Duke was so pleased with him that when he looked at normal men their necks were too scrawny. To the extent then that Power stands out, we lose sight of the bodily shape. When men do not lose sight of what is out of sight but do lose sight of what is in plain sight, we may speak of 'the oversight which is seeing things as they are.'

*Choptoes is learning the accepted code of manners as a practical convenience, without any inner allegiance. The real cripple is Confucius himself, who cannot live without the code to support him. Not that it is his fault; he was born a defective man, mutilated and imprisoned by Heaven, as he admits in a later episode.

"When a girl becomes a concubine of the Son of Heaven, they will not clip her nails or pierce her ears; a man with a new bride stays away from court and cannot be sent on any more missions. If we have such regard even for the whole in body, how much more for the man who keeps the Power in him whole! Now Uglyface T'o is trusted before he says a word, is accepted as an intimate without any deed to his credit, makes someone hand over his state and fear only that he will not accept it; he is evidently one in whom the stuff is whole but the Power has failed to shape the body."

"What do you mean by his stuff being whole?"

"Death and life, survival and ruin, success and failure, poverty and riches, competence and incompetence, slander and praise, hunger and thirst, these are the mutations of affairs, the course of destiny. They alternate before us day and night, and knowledge cannot measure back to where they began. Consequently there is no point in letting them disturb one's peace, they are not to be admitted into the Magic Storehouse. To maintain our store in peace and joy, and let none of it be lost through the senses though the channels to them are cleared, to ensure that day and night there are no fissures and it makes a springtime it shares with everything, this is to be a man who at every encounter generates the season in his own heart. This is what I mean by his stuff being whole."

"What do you mean by the Power failing to shape the body?"

"Being level is the culmination of water coming to rest. That the water-level can serve as standard is because it is protected from within and undisturbed from outside. As the saying goes, 'The wind passing over the river takes some of it away, the sun passing over the river takes some of it away'; but even if wind and sun were both to abide with the river, the river would suppose that they had never begun to infringe on it, for it is something which issues forth from springs of its own. The filling of a contour by whirling water, still water, flowing water, water bubbling up, water dripping down, water gushing from the side, water dammed and diverted, stagnant water, water with several sources, makes the same deep pool. Hence the water abiding with the earth fills its contours, the shadow abiding with the shape fills its contours, any thing abiding with another thing fills its contours. The Power is the wholly at peace with itself on the course which is in accord. That the Power fails to shape the body is because other things are unable to keep their distance from it."

On another day Duke Ai told Min-tzu:

"Not so long ago I thought I had nothing to learn about lording it over the empire from the south-facing throne, controlling the people from the centre and worrying how to keep them alive. Now that I have heard the words of the utmost man, I am afraid that I lack the substance of it, and that by neglecting the care of my own person I shall ruin the state. I and Confucius are not lord and vassal, he is simply a friend who has put me in his debt."*

*   *   *

*For ancient Chinese thought, which does not make a distinction in kind between the mental and the physical, it is the Power, the capacity to respond without reflection according to the Way, which enables the body to grow into its proper shape. How then can Power be at its height in cripples and freaks? In according with the Way, the sage is sensitive to and adapts to all pressures from outside. The Power in shaping the body is like the water which, irrespective of its source, has a shape imposed on it by the topography of the place. It seems indeed that it is we ourselves, we ordinary folk, who by crowding round T'o from the day of his birth because the charm of pure spontaneity so attracts us, have forced his superbly sensitive and malleable organism into a shape we judge to be ugly.

If you step on someone's foot in the market you make a formal apology for your carelessness; an elder brother says he hopes it didn't hurt; father and mother are too close kin to say anything at all. Hence it is said:

In utmost courtesy there is something not done as man.
Utmost duty isn't towards another.
Utmost knowledge doesn't plan.
Utmost goodwill is kin to no one.
Utmost honesty doesn't bother about money.

Hence, wherever the sage roams, for him knowledge is a curse, commitment is a glue, putting others in his debt is trafficking, getting credit for his deeds is peddling. Since the sage does not plan, what use has he for knowledge? Since he does not chop in pieces, what use has he for glue? Since he loses nothing, what use has he for repayments? Since he does not treat things as commodities, what use has he for peddling? For these four things, he buys at the market of Heaven. To 'buy at the market of Heaven' is to be fed by Heaven. Having received his food from Heaven, what use has he for man? He has the shape of a man, is without what is essentially man. He has the shape of a man, and therefore congregates with men; he is without what is essentially man, and therefore 'That's it, that's not' are not found in his person. Indiscernibly small, that which attaches him to man! Unutterably vast, the Heaven within him which he perfects in solitude!"

Said Hui Shih to Chuang-tzu
"Can a man really be without the essentials of man?"
"He can."
"If a man is without the essentials of man, how can we call him a man?"
"The Way gives him the guise, Heaven gives him the shape, how can we refuse to call him a man?"
"But since we do call him a man, how can he be without the essentials of man?"
"Judging 'That's it, that's not' is what I mean by 'the essentials of man.' What I mean by being without the essentials is that the man does not inwardly wound his person by likes and dislikes, that he constantly goes by the spontaneous and does not add anything to the process of life."
"If he does not add anything to the process of life, how can there be any such thing as his person?"
"The Way gives us the guise, Heaven gives us the shape: do not inwardly wound yourself by likes and dislikes. But now you

Go on pushing your daemon outside,
Wearing your quintessence away.
You loll on a treetrunk and mumble,
Drop off to sleep held up by withered sterculia.*
It was Heaven that chose you a shape,
But you sing chop logic as your native note."

*Hui Shih is mentioned elsewhere as leaning on wood of the wu-t'ung tree (sterculia platanifolia), presumably a desk or armrest made of it. One may guess that this is a concrete memory of the exhausted sophist drooping over desiccated wood which for Chuang-tzu sums up his impression of the unnatural and sterile effort of purely analytic thinking.

CHAPTER 6: THE TEACHER WHO IS THE ULTIMATE ANCESTOR*

"To know what is Heaven's doing and what is man's is the utmost in knowledge. Whoever knows what Heaven does lives the life generated by Heaven. Whoever knows what man does uses what his wits know about to nurture what they do not know about. To last out the years assigned you by Heaven and not be cut off in mid-course, this is perfection of knowledge."

However, there's a difficulty. Knowing depends on something with which it has to be plumb; the trouble is that what it depends on is never fixed. How do I know that the doer I call "Heaven" is not the man? How do I know that the doer I call the "man" is not Heaven? Besides, there can be true knowledge only when there is a true man. What do we mean by the "True Man"? The True Men of old did not mind belonging to the few, did not grow up with more cock than hen in them, did not plan out their actions. Such men as that did not regret it when they missed the mark, were not complacent when they hit plumb on. Such men as that climbed heights without trembling, entered water without a wetting, entered fire without burning. Such is the knowledge which is able to rise out of the world on the course of the Way. The True Men of old slept without dreaming and woke without cares, found one food as sweet as another, and breathed from their deepest depths. (The breathing of the True Man is from down in his heels, the breathing of plain men is from their throats; as for the cowed, the submissive, they talk in gulps as though retching. Wherever desires and cravings are deep, the impulse which is from Heaven is shallow.)

The True Men of old did not know how to be pleased that they were alive, did not know how to hate death, were neither glad to come forth nor reluctant to go in; they were content to leave as briskly as they came. They did not forget the source where they began, did not seek out the destination where they would end. They were pleased with the gift that they received, but forgot it as they gave it back. It is this that is called "not allowing the thinking of the heart to damage the Way, not using what is of man to do the work of Heaven." Such a one we call the True Man. Such men as that had unremembering hearts, calm faces, clear brows. They were cool like autumn, warm like spring; they were pleased or angry evenly through the four seasons, did what fitted in with other things, and no one knew their high point. The True Man of Old—

> His figure looms but suffers no landslides:
> He seems to lack but takes no gifts.
> Assured! his stability, but not rigid:
> Pervasive! his tenuous influence, but it is not on display.
> Lighthearted! Seems to be doing as he pleases:
> Under compulsion! Inevitable that he does it.
> Impetuously! asserts a manner of his own:
> Cautiously! holds in the Power which is his own.
> So tolerant! in his seeming worldliness:
> So arrogant! in his refusal to be ruled.
> Canny! Seems he likes to keep his mouth shut:
> Scatterbrained! Forgets every word that he says.

*The Taoist does not take the heart, the organ of thought, as his teacher or authority; the only instructor he recognises is the ultimate Ancestor who generates all things, whose guidance is discovered in reverting to pure spontaneity. Its profoundest lesson is reconciliation with death, by a surrender without protest to the process of living and dying as mere episodes in the endless transformations of heaven and earth.

The True Men of old used what is Heaven's to await what comes, did not let man intrude on Heaven. The True Men of old used the eye to look at the eye, the ear to look at the ear, the heart to recover the heart. Such men as that when they were level were true to the carpenter's line, when they were altering stayed on course. Hence they were one with what they liked and one with what they disliked, one when they were one and one when they were not one. When one they were of Heaven's party, when not one they were of man's party. Someone in whom neither Heaven nor man is victor over the other, this is what is meant by the True Man.*

*   *   *

Death and life are destined; that they have the constancy of morning and evening is of Heaven. Everything in which man cannot intervene belongs to the identities of things. Those have Heaven only as their father, yet still for our part we love them, and how much more that which is exalted above them! A man thinks of his lord merely as better than himself, yet still for his part will die for him, and how much more for the truest of lords!

That hugest of clumps of soil loads me with a body, has me toiling through a life, eases me with old age, rests me with death; therefore that I find it good to live is the very reason why I find it good to die. We store our boat in the ravine, our fishnet in the marsh, and say it's safe there; but at midnight someone stronger carries it away on his back, and the dull ones do not know it. The smaller stored in the bigger has its proper place, but still has room to escape; as for the whole world stored within the world, with nowhere else to escape, that is the ultimate identity of an unchanging thing. To have happened only on man's shape is enough to please us; if a shape such as man's through ten thousand transformations never gets nearer to a limit, can the joys we shall have of it ever be counted? Therefore the sage will roam where things cannot escape him and all are present. That he finds it good to die young and good to grow old, good to begin and good to end, is enough for men to take him as their model; and how much more that to which the myriad things are tied, on which we depend to be transformed just once!

*   *   *

As for the Way, it is something with identity, something to trust in, but does nothing, has no shape. It can be handed down but not taken as one's own, can be grasped but not seen. Itself the trunk, itself the root, since before there was a heaven and an earth inherently from of old it is what it was. It hallows ghosts and hallows God, engenders heaven, engenders earth; it is farther than the utmost pole but is not reckoned high, it is under the six-way oriented but is not reckoned deep, it was born before heaven and earth but is not reckoned long-lasting, it is elder to the most ancient but is not reckoned old. Hsi-wei found it, and with it dangled heaven and earth in his hand; Fu-hsi found it,

---

*At the end of Chapter 5, Chuang-tzu took the side of Heaven against man; here he tries to resolve the dichotomy. As in several examples in Chapter 2, he starts from a preliminary formulation, either his own or quoted from some unknown source, and then raises a doubt. The formulation takes the dichotomy for granted, and lays it down that the purpose of man's thought and action is to nourish the spontaneous process which is from Heaven, as in the support of the body, which is engendered by Heaven to last to a ripe old age provided that man looks after it properly. But can one make an ultimate distinction between the spontaneous motion and the deliberate action? The reformulation at the end attacks the dichotomy with the paradox that the sage remains fundamentally one with things whether he is being united with them by Heaven or is dividing himself off as a thinking man.

and with it ventured into the Mother of all breath. The Dipper which guides the stars found it, and through all the ages points unerringly; the sun and moon found it, and through all the ages never rest. K'an p'i found it and ventured into Mount K'un-lun, P'ing yi found it and swam the great river, Chien Wu found it and settled on Mount T'ai, the Yellow Emperor found it and rose up in the cloudy sky, Chuan Hsu found it and settled in the Black Palace. Yu Ch'iang who found it stands in the farthest North, the Western Queen Mother who found it sits in Shao-kuang; none knows their beginning, none knows their end. P'eng-tsu found it, who lived right back in the time of Shun, right down to the Five Tyrants. Fu Yueh found it, and used it to minister to Wu Ting, ere long possessor of the Empire; he rides the East Corner and straddles Sagittarius and Scorpio, a neighbour to all the constellated stars.

*   *   *

Tzu-k'uei of Nan-po asked the woman Chu,
"You are old in years, how is it that you look as fresh as a child?"
"I have heard the Way."
"Can the Way be learned?"
"Mercy me, it can't be done, you're not the man for it! That Pu-liang Yi had the stuff of a sage but not the Way of a sage, I have the Way of a sage but not the stuff of a sage. I wanted to teach it to him; could it be that he would really become a sage? In any case it's not so hard to tell the Way of a sage to someone with the stuff of a sage. I wouldn't leave him alone until I'd told him: three days in a row and he was able to put the world outside him. When he had got the world outside him I still wouldn't leave him alone, and by the seventh day he was able to put the things we live on outside him. When he got the things we live on outside him, again I wouldn't leave him alone, and by the ninth day he was able to put life itself outside him. Once he had got life itself outside him, he could break through to the daylight, and then he could see the Unique, and then he could be without past and present, and then he could enter into the undying, unliving. That which kills off the living does not die, that which gives birth to the living has never been born. As for the sort of thing it is, it is there to escort whatever departs, is here to welcome whatever comes, it ruins everything and brings everything about. Its name is 'At home where it intrudes'. What is 'at home where it intrudes' is that which comes about only where it intrudes into the place of something else."
"Where did you of all people come to hear of that?"
"I heard it from Inkstain's son, who heard it from Bookworm's grandson, who heard it from Wide-eye, who heard it from Eavesdrop, who heard it from Gossip, who heard it from Singsong, who heard it from Obscurity, who heard it from Mystery, who heard it from what might have been Beginning."

*   *   *

Four men, Masters Ssu, Yu, Li, and Lai, were talking together.
"Which of us is able to think of nothingness as the head, of life as the spine, of death as the rump? Which of us knows that the living and the dead, the surviving and the lost, are all one body? He shall be my friend."
The four men looked at each other and smiled, and none was reluctant in his heart. So they all became friends.
Soon Master Yu fell ill, and Master Ssu went to inquire.
"Wonderful! how the maker of things is turning me into this crumpled thing. He hunches me and stick out my back, the five pipes to the spine run up above my head,

my chin hides down in my navel, my shoulders are higher than my crown, the knobbly bone in my neck points up at the sky. The energies of Yin and Yang are all awry."

His heart was at ease and he had nothing to do. He tottered out to look at his reflection in the well.

"Ugh! The maker of things still goes on turning me into this crumpled thing."

"Do you hate it?"

"No, why should I hate it? Little by little he'll borrow my left arm to transform it into a cock, and it will be why I am listening to a cock-crow at dawn. Little by little he'll borrow my right arm to transform it into a crossbow, and it will be why I am waiting for a roasted owl for my dinner. Little by little he'll borrow and transform my buttocks into wheels, my daemon into a horse, and they'll be there for me to ride, I'll never have to harness a team again! Besides, to get life is to be on time and to lose it is to be on course; be content with the time and settled on the course, and sadness and joy cannot find a way in. This is what of old was called 'being loosed from the bonds'; and whoever cannot loose himself other things bind still tighter. And it is no new thing after all that creatures do not prevail against Heaven. What would be the point in hating it?"

Soon Master Lai fell ill, and lay panting on the verge of death. His wife and children stood in a circle bewailing him. Master Li went to ask after him.

"Shoo! Out of the way!" he said. "Don't startle him while he transforms."

He lolled against Lai's door and talked with him.

"Wonderful, the process which fashions and transforms us! What is it going to turn you into, in what direction will it use you to go? Will it make you into a rat's liver? Or a fly's leg?"

"A child that has father and mother, go east, west, north, south, has only their commands to obey; and for man the Yin and Yang are more than father and mother. Something other than me approaches, I die; and if I were to refuse to listen it would be defiance on my part, how can I blame him? That hugest of clumps of soil loaded me with a body, had me toiling through a life, eased me with old age, rests me with death; therefore that I found it good to live is the very reason why I find it good to die. If today a master swordsmith were smelting metal, and the metal should jump up and say 'I insist on being made into an Excalibur,' the swordsmith would surely think it metal with a curse on it. If now having once happened on the shape of a man, I were to say 'I'll be a man, nothing but a man,' he that fashions and transforms us would surely think me a baleful sort of man. Now if once and for all I think of heaven and earth as a vast foundry, and the fashioner and transformer as the master smith, wherever I am going why should I object? I'll fall into a sound sleep and wake up fresh."

*   *   *

The three men, Master Sang-hu, Meng Tzu-fan and Master Ch'in-chang, were talking together.

"Which of us can be *with* where there is no being with, be *for* where there is no being for? Which of us are able to climb the sky and roam the mists and go whirling into the infinite, living forgetful of each other for ever and ever?"

The three men looked at each other and smiled, and none was reluctant in his heart. So they became friends.

After they had been living quietly for a while Master Sang-hu died. Before he was buried, Confucius heard about it and sent Tzu-kung to assist at the funeral. One of the men was plaiting frames for silkworms, the other strumming a zither, and they sang in unison

"Hey-ho, Sang-hu!
Hey ho, Sang-hu!
You've gone back to being what one truly is,
But we go on being human, O!"

Tzu-kung hurried forward and asked.

"May I inquire whether it is in accordance with the rites to sing with the corpse right there at your feet?"

The two men exchanged glances and smiled.

"What does he know about the meaning of the rites?"

Tzu-kung returned and told Confucius

"What men are these? The decencies of conduct are nothing to them, they treat the very bones of their bodies as outside them. They sing with the corpse right there at their feet, and not a change in the look on their faces. I have no words to name them. What men are these?"

"They are the sort that roams beyond the guidelines," said Confucius. "I am the sort that roams within the guidelines. Beyond and within have nothing in common, and to send you to mourn was stupid on my part. They are at the stage of being fellow men with the maker of things, and go roaming in the single breath that breathes through heaven and earth. They think of life as an obstinate wart or a dangling wen, of death as bursting the boil or letting the pus. How should such men as that know death from life, before from after? They borrow right-of-way through the things which are different but put up for the night in that body which is the same. Self-forgetful right down to the liver and the gall, leaving behind their own ears and eyes, they turn start and end back to front, and know no beginning-point or standard. Heedlessly they go roving beyond the dust and grime, go rambling through the lore in which there's nothing to *do*. How could they be finicky about the rites of common custom, on watch for the inquisitive eyes and ears of the vulgar?"

"In that case, sir, why depend on guidelines yourself?"

"I am one of those condemned by the sentence of Heaven. However, let us see what we can do together."

"I venture to ask the secret of it."

"As fish go on setting directions for each other in the water, men go on setting directions for each other in the Way. For the fish which set directions for each other in the water, you dig a pool and their nurture is provided for. For us who set directions for each other in the Way, if we cease to be busy life fixes its own course. When the spring dries up and the fish are stranded together on land, they spit moisture at each other and soak each other in the foam, but they would be better off forgetting each other in the Yangtse or the Lakes. Rather than praise sage Yao and condemn tyrant Chieh, we should be better off if we could forget them both and let their Ways enter the transformations. As the saying goes, 'Fish forget all about each other in the Yangtse and the Lakes, men forget all about each other in the lore of the Way.'"

"Let me ask about extraordinary men."

"Extraordinary men are extraordinary in the eyes of men but ordinary in the eyes of Heaven. As the saying goes, 'Heaven's knave is man's gentle man, man's gentleman is Heaven's knave.'"

* * *

Yen Hui put a question to Confucius.

"Meng-sun Ts'ai wailed when his mother died but did not shed a tear, in his inward heart he did not suffer, conducting the funeral he did not grieve. In spite of these three failings, he is renowned as the best of mourners throughout the state of Lu. Are there really people who win a name for it without possessing the substance? I am utterly amazed at it."

"That Meng-sun has the whole secret, he has taken the step beyond knowledge. If you merely simplify it you don't succeed, finishing with it altogether does simplify something. Meng-sun does not know what he depended on to be born, does not know what he will depend on to die, does not know how to be nearer to the time before or the time after. If in transforming he has become one thing instead of another, is it required that what he does not know terminated in being transformed? Besides, at the stage of being transformed how would he know about the untransformed? At the stage of being untransformed, how would he know about the transformed? Is it just that you and I are the ones who have not yet begun to wake from our dream?

"Moreover he has convulsions of the body without damage to the heart, has abodes for no longer than a morning but no true death. It's just that Meng-sun has come awake. When another man wails he wails too; it is simply that, all the way up from that which they depend on to be-about-to be, he is with him in recognising him as 'I.' How would I know what it is I call recognising as 'I'?

"You dream that you are a bird and fly away in the sky, dream that you are a fish and plunge into the deep. There's no telling whether the man who speaks now is the waker or the dreamer. Rather than go towards what suits you, laugh: rather than acknowledge it with your laughter, shove it from you. Shove it from you and leave the transformations behind; then you will enter the oneness of the featureless sky."

Yi-erh-tzu visited Hsu Yu.

"What riches did you get from Yao?" said Hsu Yu.

"Yao told me: 'Be sure to devote yourself to Goodwill and Duty and say plainly "That's it, that's not."'"

"Then what do you think you're doing here? When that Yao has already branded your hide with Goodwill and Duty, and snipped off your nose with his 'That's it, that's not,' how are you going to roam that free and easy take-any-turn-you-please path?"

"At any rate I should like to roam by its hedges."

"No. Blind pupils can never share in the sight of beautiful eyebrows and face, nor pupilless eyes in the spectacle of green and yellow vestments."

"Wu-chuang losing his beauty, Chu-liang his strength, the Yellow Emperor his wisdom, were all simply in the course of being smelted and hammered. How do we know that the maker of things will not make my brand fade and my snipped nose grow, so that finding myself whole again I can be your disciple?"

"Hmm, we can't be sure. Let me put it for you in a few words. My Teacher, O my Teacher! He chops fine the myriad things but it is not cruelty, his bounty extends to a myriad ages but it is not goodwill, he is elder to the most ancient but it is not growing old, he overhangs heaven and bears up earth and cuts up and sculpts all shapes but it is not skill—

"It is over *this* that you have to roam."

(Therefore when the sage goes to war, though he ruins states he does not lose men's hearts; the benefits of his bounty extend to a myriad ages, but he is not deemed to love mankind. Hence to delight in being expert in things is not sagehood, to be more kin to some than to others is not goodwill, to pry into what is Heaven's is not cleverness. If your benefits and harms do not interchange you are not a gentleman, if in pursuit of a name you lose your own self you are not a knight, if by forgetting what you are you fail to be genuine you are not a master of men. As for such as Hu Pu-hsieh, Wu Kuang, Po Yi, Shu Ch'i, Chi-tzu, Hsu Yu, Chi T'o, Shen-t'u Ti, they were men who served what served others, were suited by what suited others, not by what suited themselves.)*

* * *

"I make progress," said Yen Hui.
"Where?" said Confucius.
"I have forgotten about rites and music."
"Satisfactory. But you still have far to go."
Another day he saw Confucius again.
"I make progress."
"Where?"
"I have forgotten about Goodwill and Duty."
"Satisfactory. But you still have far to go."
Another day he saw Confucius again.
"I make progress."
"Where?"
"I just sit and forget."
Confucius was taken aback.
"What do you mean, just sit and forget?"

"I let organs and members drop away, dismiss eyesight and hearing, part from the body and expel knowledge, and go along with the universal thoroughfare. This is what I mean by 'just sit and forget.'"

"If you go along with it, you have no preferences; if you let yourself transform, you have no norms. Has it really turned out that you are the better of us? Oblige me by accepting me as your disciple."

* * *

Master Yu was friendly with Master Sang, and it had been raining incessantly for ten days. "I am afraid Sang will be in trouble," said Yu, and wrapping up some rice took it him for his dinner. When he reached Sang's gate there was a sound as much like wailing as singing, to the strumming of a zither

"Was it father?—Was it mother?—Heaven?—Man?"

There was something in it of a voice too frail to hold out and in a hurry to finish the verse.

Entering, Master Yu asked

"The verse you were singing, what did you mean by it?"

"I was imagining who it might be that brought me so low, and can't find an answer. How could my father and mother have wanted me to be poor? Heaven is impartial to everything it covers, earth to everything it carries; why would heaven and earth discriminate to make me poor? I can't find out who it is that did it. That nonetheless I have sunk so low—shall we say it's destiny?"

---

*The list of names at the end is of men who pointlessly sacrificed themselves on trifling points of honour.

CHAPTER 7: RESPONDING TO THE EMPERORS AND KINGS*

1. FIRST SERIES

Gaptooth asked questions of Wang Ni, four times asked and four times he did not know. So Gaptooth hopped about in great delight, and went on a journey to tell Master Reedcoat.

"Didn't you know it until now?" said Master Reedcoat. "The House of Yu-yu is not equalling the House of T'ai. Our Emperor, yes, he still keeps a store of kindness to get a hold on men, and he does indeed win them, but he has never begun to draw from the source which is not man. He of the House of T'ai slept sound and woke up fresh; at one moment he deemed himself the logician's 'horse,' at the next his 'ox'; his knowledge was essential and trustworthy, the Power in him utterly genuine, and he had never begun to enter a realm which is not man."**

*   *   *

Chien Wu visited mad Chieh Yu.

"What did Noonbegin tell you?" asked mad Chieh Yu.

"He told me that a lord of men issues on his own authority rules, conventions, forms and regulations, and who dares refuse to obey and be reformed by them?"

"That's a bullying sort of a Power. As far as ordering the Empire is concerned, you might as well go wading through oceans, boring holes in rivers, or commanding mosquitos to carry mountains on their backs. When the sage sets in order, is he ordering the external? It is simply a matter of straightening oneself out before one acts, of being solidly capable of doing one's own work.

"The birds fly high to be out of danger from the stringed arrows, the field-mice go burrowing deep under the sacred hill, where no one can trouble them by digging down and smoking them out. Even those two creatures know better than that."

*   *   *

Heaven-based roamed on the south side of Mount Vast, and came to the bank of the River Limpid. Happening to meet a man without a name, he asked him.

"Permit me to inquire how one rules the Empire."

"Away! You're a bumpkin! What a dreary thing to talk about! I am just in the course of becoming fellow man with the maker of things; and when I get bored with

---

*This last of the *Inner Chapters* collects Chuang-tzu's few observations on ideal kingship. For the Syncretist editor this would be the greatest of themes, but it is plain that to find anything remotely relevant in Chuang-tzu's literary remains he had to scrape the bottom of the barrel. The first item is the conclusion of a dialogue already used in Chapter 2; he must have chopped it off and added the introduction which resumes the previous exchanges ("Gaptooth asked questions of Wang Ni, four times asked and four times he did not know").

The editor found only four items directly concerned with kingship, which we distinguish as the "First series." The "Second series" illustrates aspects of sagehood which he perhaps thought especially relevant to government. Thus his reason for including the penultimate episode might be that it introduces the metaphor of the sage's heart as a mirror, important in the Syncretist theory of kingship.

**Gaptooth and his friends live under the rule of the legendary Shun (whose family was the Yu-yu), one of the ideal sages of Confucians. But Shun preferred the morality which is from man to the spontaneity which is from Heaven. Chuang-tzu would rather imagine a sage in the remotest past (the meaning of *T'ai* is "ultimate") before there was even the dichotomy of Heaven and man, long before there were logicians distinguishing between "X" and "Y," "ox" and "horse."

that, I shall ride out on the bird which fades into the sky beyond where the six directions end, to travel the realm of Nothingwhatever and settle in the wilds of the Boundless. What do you mean by stirring up thoughts in my heart about such a trifle as ruling the Empire?"

He repeated the question. Said the man without a name

"Let your heart roam in the flavourless, blend your energies with the featureless, in the spontaneity of your accord with other things leave no room for selfishness, and the Empire will be order."*

What is significant about the nameless man's remarks about government is not the content but the perspective in which the government of the Empire is seen; it is of negligible importance, yet as important as anything else in the world.

*   *   *

Yang Tzu-chu visited Old Tan.

"Suppose we have a man," he said, "who is alert, energetic, well informed, clear headed and untiring in learning the Way: may someone like that be ranked with the enlightened Kings?"

"To the sage this is a slave's drudgery, an artisan's bondage, wearing out the body, fretting the heart. Besides, it's the elegant markings of tiger and leopard which attract the hunter, and it's the spryest of monkeys and the dog which catches the rat that get themselves on the leash. Can someone like that be ranked with the enlightened kings?"

Yang Tzu-chu was taken aback.

"May I ask how an enlightened king rules?"

"When the enlightened king rules
His deeds spread over the whole world
but seem not from himself:
His riches are loaned to the myriad things
but the people do not depend on him.
He is there, but no one mentions his name.
He lets things find their own delight.

He is one who keeps his foothold in the immeasurable and roams where nothing is."

2. SECOND SERIES

In Cheng there was a daemonic shaman called Chi Hsien, who knew whether a man would live or die, be ruined or saved, be lucky or unlucky, be cut off too soon or last out his term, and set the date within a year, a month, ten days, the day; it was daemonic, no less. When the people of Cheng saw him they all shunned him and fled. When Lieh-tzu saw him he was drunk at heart, and returned to tell Hu-tzu about him.

---

*This is the single passage which specifically distinguishes two stages of sagehood: (1) the ecstatic roaming as "fellow man with the maker of things," without yet ceasing to be human, like the two mourners singing to the zither who shocked Confucius; (2) the final withdrawal into the impassivity beyond life and death of the mourner Meng–sun, for whom past and present are the same, and everyone else is as much "I" as he is, and all the experience of the senses is revealed as a dream. It is a curious paradox of the Taoist mockery of deliberation that the final take-off seems to depend on a choice, perhaps on the verge of death. Confucius says of the cripple Wang T'ai that he "will pick his own day to rise out of the world."

Mount T'ai Shan (Taishan), the sacred "First Mountain of China." Taoist pilgrims (and sightseers) still climb the 6,660 steps to the top of the 1,545 meter peak. (*Forrest E. Baird*)

"Master, once I thought that your Way was the highest, but there is another which is higher still."

"With you I have exhausted its scriptures but not yet exhausted its substance: have you really grasped the Way? With so many hens but no cock, what eggs can you expect from them? In matching the Way to the world you have to exert yourself too actively, and that is how you give a man the opportunity to read your face. Try bringing him here, let him take a look at me."

Next day Lieh-tzu did bring him to see Hu-tzu. Coming out, the man said to Lieh-tzu,

"Hmm, your master is a dead man. He won't revive, his days are not to be counted in tens. I saw a strange thing in him, saw damp ash in him."

Lieh-tzu went in with tears soaking the lapels of his coat, and told Hu-tzu about it.

"Just now," said Hu-tzu, "I showed him the formation of the ground. The shoots as they went on sprouting were without vibration but without pause. I should think he saw me as I am when I hold down the impulses of the Power. Try bringing him here again."

Next day he brought him to see Hu-tzu again. Coming out, he told Lieh-tzu,

"A lucky thing your master happened to meet me! He's recovered, the ash is aflame, he's alive. I saw him holding down the arm of the scales."

Lieh-tzu went in and told Hu-tzu.

"Just now," said Hu-tzu, "I showed him Heaven and the fertilised ground. Names and substances had not found a way in, but the impulses were coming up from my heels. I should think he saw my impulses towards the good. Try bringing him here again."

Next day he brought him to see Hu-tzu again. Coming out, he told Lieh-tzu,

"Your master does not fast, I cannot read anything in his face. Let him try fasting, I'll read his face again."

Lieh-tzu went in and told Hu-tzu.

"Just now I showed him the absolute emptiness where there is no foreboding of anything. I should think he saw me as I am when I level out the impulses of the breath. Try bringing him here again."

Next day he brought him to see Hu-tzu again. Before the man had come to a standstill he lost his head and ran.

"Go after him," said Hu-tzu.

Lieh-tzu went after him but failed to catch up. He returned and reported to Hu-tzu, "He's vanished, he's lost, I couldn't catch up."

"Just now," said Hu-tzu, "I showed him how it is before ever we come out of our Ancestor.

> With him I attenuated, wormed in and out,
> Unknowing who or what we were.
> It made him think he was fading away,
> It made him think he was carried off on the waves.

"That's why he fled."

Only then did Lieh-tzu conclude that he had never begun to learn, and went off home. For three years he did not leave the house.

> He cooked the dinner for his wife,
> Fed the pigs as though feeding people,
> Remained aloof in all his works.
> From the carved gem he returned to the unhewn block:
> Unique, in his own shape, he took his stand.
> Didn't tidy up the raggle-taggle.
> That's how he was to the end of his days.*

*   *   *

> Don't be a medium possessed by your name,
> Don't be a stockroom for schemes.
> Don't take the weight of affairs on your shoulders,
> Don't be the man-in-charge of wisdom.

Become wholly identified with the limitless and roam where there is no foreboding of anything. Exhaust all that you draw from Heaven and never have gain in sight; simply keep yourself tenuous. The utmost man uses the heart like a mirror; he does not escort things as they go or welcome them as they come, he responds and does not store. Therefore he is able to conquer other things without suffering a wound.

*   *   *

---

*Here as in Chapter 1 Lieh-tzu is the Taoist led astray by the fascination of magical powers. His teacher Hu-tzu is not interested in fortune-telling, since he can withdraw beyond life and death to that serenity (with "a heart like dead ash" and "a frame like withered wood," which is outwardly indistinguishable from death. As elsewhere in the *Inner Chapters* the only technique assumed is the control of the *ch'i* (the breath and other energies of the body) by breathing which is very deep, "from the heels," and so even that the adept seems not to be breathing at all. For the uninitiated who cling to life, the merest glimpse of this state overwhelms with the horror of self-dissolution in ultimate solitude.

The Emperor of the South Sea was Fast, the Emperor of the North Sea was Furious, the Emperor of the centre was Hun-t'un.* Fast and Furious met from time to time in the land of Hun-t'un, who treated them very generously. Fast and Furious were discussing how to repay Hun-t'un's bounty.

"All men have seven holes through which they look, listen, eat, breathe; he alone doesn't have any. Let's try boring them."

Every day they bored one hole, and on the seventh day Hun-t'un died.

---

*Hun-t'un is the primal blob which first divided into heaven and earth and then differentiated as the myriad things. In Chinese cosmology the primordial is not a chaos reduced to order by imposed law, it is a blend of everything rolled up together; the word is a reduplicative of the type of English "hotchpotch" and "rolypoly," and diners in Chinese restaurants will have met it in the form "wuntun" as a kind of dumpling.

BUDDHIST INNOVATIONS

The two preceding sections, on Confucianism and Taoism, survey the highlights of Chinese philosophy in its classical period, when disputation among schools prevailed. This section and the next examine Buddhism and Neo-Confucianism, the most influential movements of the middle period, from Han through Ming dynasties (206 B.C.E.–1644 C.E.). The mood of philosophy shifted during these eighteen centuries. Debates and rivalries were overshadowed by alliances, appropriation of ideas, and reconciliation of differences among schools, as major developments throughout the period attest. Yin-Yang Confucianism (second century B.C.E.) fused two systems unrelated in classical times. Neo-Taoism (third century C.E.) esteemed Confucius along with Lao-tzu and Chuang-tzu. Chinese Buddhism (third-ninth centuries C.E.) borrowed from Neo-Taoism, and Buddhist schools learned from one another. Finally, Neo-Confucianism during the Sung (960–1279 C.E.) and Ming (1368–1644 C.E.) dynasties blended Taoism and Buddhism into Confucianism. Certain schools that had flourished in classical times perished, while new versions of Confucianism and Taoism joined by Buddhism led the way. The Buddhist legacy to Chinese philosophy is the theme of the present chapter.

A brief overview of Buddhism's career in China will help set the stage for the discussion to follow. Missionary monks introduced the Indian faith into China midway through the first century C.E. The Chinese initially rejected the unfamiliar religion from South Asia. They embraced it only after it adapted to the local culture by linking itself to Taoism. The six main schools of Chinese Buddhism matured during the T'ang Dynasty (618–907). Buddhism had by then become the dominant religious and philosophical force in China. Imperial persecution in the

middle of the ninth century, however, arrested its phenomenal expansion as a religion and terminated its philosophical evolution. The Buddhism of the past
millennium—emphasizing salvation by faith, ritual, and symbolism, not
philosophy—survived in the shadow of resurgent Confucianism. The communist
regime that took power in 1949 attacked Confucianism while curtailing
Buddhism and Taoism. Following the repressive Cultural Revolution
(1966–1976) that left China a spiritual wasteland, Buddhist religious practice
has enjoyed a revival. Unfortunately, no philosophical originality has surfaced
in Chinese Buddhism since its zenith in the T'ang. The spotlight here, consequently, is on the fifth through ninth centuries C.E., when Buddhism ruled the
field of Chinese philosophy.

The outstanding Chinese contribution to Buddhist thought is belief in the
Absolute—the ultimate reality that contains the world while being contained by
it. As primary reality, the Absolute is self-sufficient, eternal, and unchanging. As
container, it is comparable to a womb within which all things are conceived and
sustained. As content, it resembles an embryo gestating within all things, their
inner essence or secret substance. The function of the Absolute as source and
ground of the world is required by the dependent, temporal, changing character
of that world, which could not have caused itself and yet exists. The nature of the
Absolute, however, is unfathomable, totally beyond the capacity of human understanding. Belief in the Absolute is fundamental also to the Upanishadic-
Vedantic tradition of Hinduism in India (see introductions to the first and third
sections of this text, pages 3–8 and 135–149) and to Taoism in China (see introduction to the previous section, pages 361–370). Such a belief is nevertheless re-
pudiated by all the schools of Indian Buddhism (see introduction to the second
section, pages 83–94). Chinese Buddhism is indeed rooted in the Mahayana
branch of Buddhism, established in India between the first century B.C.E. and the
fourth century C.E.. But on this crucial point, Chinese Buddhism, with few ex-
ceptions, deviates radically from its Indian heritage and pioneers a new direction
in Buddhist thought. Arguably, Chinese Buddhism acquired its belief in the
Absolute as part of the accommodation to Taoism that won it acceptance in
Chinese culture. The unspeakable Tao of Taoism is a powerful expression of the
Absolute. The Absolute of Chinese Buddhism is no less powerful.

*   *   *

Credit for consolidating Chinese Buddhism's belief in the Absolute belongs to a
text known as *The Awakening of Faith in the Mahayana* (offered here in the Yoshito
S. Hakeda translation under the simplified title, *The Awakening of Faith*).
Contemporary scholarship inclines toward the view that this text was originally
penned in Chinese by an unknown Chinese author of the fifth or sixth century C.E.
The story accompanying this classic since it first appeared in China, however, is
quite different. According to that story, the text was composed in Sanskrit by an eminent Indian author of the first or second century C.E., then translated into Chinese
at the midpoint of the sixth. Recent scholarship has rejected this account for good
reason. There is no trace of the work in Sanskrit literature—no copy of the text, no
commentary on it, and no reference to it in other Indian sources. Presence of the
text in China, on the other hand, has been well documented since the sixth century
C.E.. The earliest extant copy (Chinese title: *Ta-ch'eng ch'i-hsin lun*
(Dachengqixinlun)), several commentaries, and important literary cross-references

date from that time. Undeniably, the text exhibits some of the trappings of an Indian Buddhist text, including many Sanskrit technical terms and doctrines of Indian origin. In an age when Chinese Buddhists were looking to India for the authentic Buddhism, giving a Chinese composition a Sanskrit veneer would make its presentation of a belief in the Absolute more credible.

The Awakening of Faith in the Mahayana is laced with perplexing jargon. Six Sanskrit terms drawn from the technical vocabulary of Indian Mahayana Buddhism confront the reader of this short work at every turn, all together more than 200 times. These expressions pose a serious obstacle to easy comprehension of the text and yet hold the key to its deeper meaning. Their crux is the Absolute, which Indian Buddhism denies but Chinese Buddhism in general affirms. *The Awakening of Faith in the Mahayana* co-opts Sanskrit terms that in India do not signify the Absolute and redeploys them to denote the Absolute while connoting different aspects of it. These terms function like a chorus sounding one grand chord that proclaims and extols the Absolute. The result is a new departure in Buddhist thought. The following list explains these terms, arranged according to frequency of usage.

Suchness (tathata) means literally "the state that is really so." It refers in Indian Buddhism to the actuality of things in contrast to their appearance. It indicates in this text that the Absolute is indefinable by pointing to it without characterizing it.

Mind (chitta, vijnana) is associated in Indian Buddhism with the mind-only doctrine of the Yogachara School, according to which perceptions alone are real; subjects behind and objects outside perceptions are illusory (Subjective Idealism). This text likens the Absolute to a cosmic Mind that creates subjects and objects by thinking them and thus enfolds the whole world as its idea (Absolute Idealism).

Dharmakaya means literally the "Essence-body" (of Buddha). It joins the Bliss-body (Sambhogakaya) and the Transformation-body (Nirmanakaya) in a famous Mahayana doctrine known as the "Three Bodies of Buddha" (Trikaya). In Indian Buddhism, it alludes to either the Buddha's teaching or his omniscient consciousness. In this text, it is another name for the Absolute, the essential reality that embodies the whole world.

Tathagata-garbha means literally "Buddha-womb" or "Buddha-embryo," "Tathagata" referring to Buddha. In Indian Buddhism, it indicates the seed of enlightenment natural to all sentient creatures. In this text, it characterizes the Absolute both as the cosmic womb wherein the world gestates and as the "Buddha-essence" gestating within all things.

Mahayana means literally "big vehicle." In Indian Buddhism, it refers to a branch of the religion. In this text, it is a metaphor for the Absolute, the all-inclusive receptacle, faith in which this work strives to awaken.

Storehouse Consciousness (alaya-vijnana) is connected in Indian Buddhism with the Yogachara school, where it denotes the subconscious mind of sentient beings. In this text, it points to the memory bank of the universal Mind (the Absolute).

Other technical Sanskrit terms of importance in this text are "One World of Reality" *(dharmadhatu)* and "Realm of the Tathagata" *(tathagatadhatu)*. They refer not to the Absolute but to the extraordinary character of the world grounded in the Absolute.

The heart of this groundbreaking work is the third and fourth of its five parts. Commentators turn the complexity of these two parts into a simple formula—One Mind, Two Aspects, Three Greatnesses, Four Faiths, and Five Practices. *One Mind:* The Absolute (Mahayana) is analogous to a single all-inclusive consciousness that creates the world by thinking it. *Two Aspects:* One Mind is both cosmic container (Absolute aspect) and its contents (aspect of phenomena). The container, the Absolute in itself (Suchness), is indefinable and yet worthy of the highest accolades. The contents, conceived and retained within One Mind (Tathagata-garbha, Storehouse Consciousness), are two mind-sets—enlightenment and nonenlightenment. They share the same database but configure it differently, imagining alternative realities. Nonenlightenment envisions the individual subject, without any Absolute, isolated at the center of a fragmented world of independently existing material objects. Craving, attachment, and suffering ensue (Samsara). Enlightenment, conversely, visualizes a unified world of interdependent subjects and objects issuing from the Absolute (One Mind, Suchness, Dharmakaya). Craving, attachment, and suffering vanish with such a vision (Nirvana). Both mind-sets also coexist in human consciousness, permeating each other, phasing in and out, switching back and forth. Enlightenment is the original mode, eclipsed by nonenlightenment when the mind becomes agitated, recovered by meditative calming of the mind. Samsara in human experience is nonenlightenment switched on and enlightenment switched off. Nirvana is enlightenment switched on and nonenlightenment switched off. Samsara and Nirvana thus also intermingle and alternate, neither identical nor different.

Three Greatnesses: The Absolute (Suchness, Dharmakaya, One Mind, Tathagata-garbha) is lauded for three properties—its eternal essence, its excellent attributes, and its compassionate influences. The influences actualize in the great host of heavenly and earthly Buddhas, who channel the creative work of the Absolute into the liberation of all sentient creatures. *Four Faiths:* Faith finds its true destiny in the Ultimate Source and the Three Treasures. Since this work's purpose is to awaken faith in the Absolute, what is here called the "Ultimate Source" takes priority. The Three Treasures embraced by all Buddhists are the Buddha, the Dharma (teaching), and the Sangha (Buddhist community). *Five Practices:* In the Mahayana branch of Buddhism, bodhisattvas achieve enlightenment by mastering the six perfections of charity, morality, patience, zeal, cessation (meditative calm), and clear observation (wisdom). These six are compressed into the Five Practices by joining the last two. Explaining how cessation and clear observation lead to awakened awareness of the Absolute (Suchness, Dharmakaya) is the thrust of the end of part four of *The Awakening of Faith.* By incorporating tenets crucial to Indian Buddhism in general (Three Treasures) and the Mahayana sect in particular (Three Bodies of Buddha, six perfections of the bodhisattva, Samsara = Nirvana), our text honors the Indian heritage even while superseding it.

This forceful proclamation of the Absolute impacted the four major Buddhist schools that originated in China, but not the two Indian imports. From India came the Madhyamika and Yogachara schools (discussed in the introduction to the second section of this text). The Chinese counterpart of Madhyamika was named the Three-Treatise School (San-lun (Sanlun)), because it rested on three Sanskrit texts translated by Kumarajiva (344–413), initiator of the school in China. Its greatest master was Chi-tsang (Jizang, 549–623). He claimed to hold no views of his own, proposing instead to refute all conceptualized positions through a sophisticated dialectical process designed to surpass conceptuality itself. It is therefore impossible to say whether or not he stood with those East Asian Buddhists who found in the Madhyamika teaching of Emptiness a sly pointer to the Absolute beyond the merely provisional existence of the world. What can be said, however, is that his writings quote extensively from *The Awakening of Faith.* The other Indian school, Yogachara, was called in China the Dharma-Character School (Fa-hsiang (Faxiang)) for its insistence that everything (all dharmas) is mental in character. Its founder was Hsuan-tsang (Xuanzang, 596–664), the most famous of the Chinese Buddhist pilgrims to visit India. There is no suggestion of the Absolute in his brand of Subjective Idealism.

Of the four schools invented by the Chinese that backed a belief in the Absolute, two were notable for theory, two for practice. The homegrown schools of Buddhist philosophy were the Heavenly Terrace School (T'ien-t'ai (Tiantai)), named after a sacred mountain where its founder Chih-i (Zhiyi, 538–597) taught, and the Flower Garland School (Hua-yen (Huayan)), based on a scripture with that title. Both espoused the doctrine of Totality, which posits the interconnection of all things within one cosmic web. Both also found Totality to be the creation of one universal Mind, deriving their Absolute Idealism from *The Awakening of Faith.* The two schools of practice born in China were the Meditation School (Ch'an (Chan)) and the Pure Land School (Ching-t'u (Jingtu)). They as well had ties to *The Awakening of Faith.* Though emphasizing meditation and ridiculing formal doctrine, the Ch'an School still managed to absorb the Emptiness, Mind-only, and Totality ideas propagated by Hua-yen. Awakening to the Absolute (Buddha-essence) is its aspiration. Ching-t'u embraced *The Awakening of Faith,* because a passage near the end of that work endorses this school's devotion to the heavenly Buddha Amitabha. The great persecution halfway through the ninth century led to the demise of the four philosophical schools as separate entities (San-lun, Fa-hsiang, T'ien-t'ai, and Hua-yen). The influence of Hua-yen endured, nonetheless, in Ch'an and Ching-t'u, a mixture of which has marked Chinese Buddhism ever since.

*   *   *

The Flower Garland or Hua-yen School, in the T'ang Dynasty (618–907), represented the culmination of the Chinese transformation of Buddhist philosophy. Hua-yen followed *The Awakening of Faith* in expanding the Emptiness, Mind-only, and Buddha-essence ideas of Indian Buddhism to make them indicate the Absolute. These it then combined with native Chinese beliefs about the goodness and harmony of Nature, beliefs reflected in Confucianism and Taoism as well as in T'ien-t'ai Buddhism. A synthesis highly unique and authentically Chinese resulted. This synthesis influenced the Meditation (Ch'an) and Pure Land (Ching-t'u) schools. Through them it provided the philosophical component of Buddhism in China since the end of the T'ang, when Hua-yen disappeared as an independent school. The school took its name and inspiration from the *Flower Garland Sutra,* an enormous Sanskrit scripture (*Avatamsaka Sutra*) of the third or fourth century, first translated into Chinese (*Hua-yen ching (Huayan jing)*) in the fifth century. Hua-yen had arranged all the Buddhist schools in five ranks, from elementary to advanced, and placed itself at the apex as their epitome. Experts today would agree: Hua-yen deserves the reputation of being the most inclusive, evolved, and original of the Buddhist philosophical schools of China.

Hua-yen fashioned its philosophy out of what is essentially a sublime experience. That experience explains the dazzling fantasy with which the *Flower Garland Sutra* climaxes. There the hero, after a long spiritual pilgrimage, reaches enlightenment when his normal perception of the everyday world is transfigured. He is privileged to behold the True World *(dharmadhatu),* this world as it really is, undiminished and undistorted, with its full glory revealed. The True World, he discovers, is supremely vibrant, radiant, beautiful, integrated, and harmonious. Above all, it is transparently the embodiment of the Buddha-essence *(tathagata-garbha),* hence a sacred place of awe and spiritual fulfillment (Nirvana). The veracity of the True World over the world of normal perception is vouchsafed by the fact that Buddhas and bodhisattvas perceive our world this way. They also intuit that the True World exists in and by the creative imagination of One Absolute Mind. Attuned to that Mind, they can in meditative visualization reshape the conditions of the world to advance sentient beings toward enlightenment. The *Flower Garland Sutra's* exalted world-vision influenced *The Awakening of Faith* in its terminology of "One World of Reality" *(dharmadhatu)* and "Realm of the Tathagata" *(tathagatadhatu).* Hua-yen drew its fascination with the True World from both these sources.

Fa-tsang (Fazang, 643–712) is honored as the brilliant systematizer of the Flower Garland School and as the third of its five great "patriarchs." These five, Hua-yen contended, cap an unbroken succession of supreme Buddhist leaders descending from Gautama Buddha himself, a claim geared to enhance its own tradition. In addition to his famous expositions of the *Flower Garland Sutra,* Fa-tsang wrote what is considered the definitive commentary (out of 170) on *The Awakening of Faith in the Mahayana.* In that commentary, he elevated the Buddha-essence concept *(tathagata-garbha),* making it the main name for the Absolute Reality that undergirds and suffuses our transitory world. Fa-tsang as a teenager devoted himself to the Buddhist life under the tutelage of the second patriarch, Chih-yen (Zhiyan). He delayed ordination until the age of twenty-eight, when the Empress Wu Tse-t'ien (Wu Zetian, 625–705), the only woman to officially rule China, made him abbot of a new monastery near the capital. For political as well as personal reasons, she gave state patronage to Buddhism. She recognized Fa-tsang's genius for making clear the subtleties of Hua-yen thought. Stories about Fa-tsang's ingenuity in instructing the Empress Wu enliven the history of this school at its peak.

Fa-tsang attempted the difficult task of transposing into philosophical theory the extraordinary experience of the True World unveiled. The wonder and divinity of the True World he meant to capture in his concept of the Unity of Principle and Facts. Facts are simply all the ordinary objects of the world from the standpoint of the external properties that make them recognizable as this animal or that plant. Principle is the inner substance of Facts that grounds their existence—the Absolute or, as Fa-tsang preferred, the Buddha-essence. Facts and Principle are inseparable, because Facts cannot exist without Principle, and Principle never exists independently of Facts. They are in the last analysis only the outside and inside of the same set of objects. Locating the Absolute inside objects as their Buddha-essence renders them wondrous and divine. Further, the cohesion and harmony of the True World Fa-tsang expressed philosophically in his version of the Totality doctrine, Hua-yen's most distinctive gift to Buddhist thought. Totality for Fa-tsang implied both the interconnection and the interaction of all Facts. Interconnection he explained in terms of "mutual interpenetration" and "mutual identity." All Facts are mutually identical, because, despite differences in external appearance, their inner substance (core reality) is the same Buddha-essence, Principle, Absolute. All Facts mutually interpenetrate, because each one is present in all and all in each one. This abstruse idea Fa-tsang sought to make intelligible through an image from Indian mythology and a visual aid he contrived for the edification of the Empress Wu. The image was of Indra's Jewel Net, at the intersections of which were fixed jewels reflecting all the net's other jewels. Each jewel thus "contained" all the others and was in turn "contained" by them. The visual aid invented for the benefit of the Empress Wu was a circle of mirrors surrounding a Buddha statue, so arranged that each mirror reflected not only the central Buddha but also every other mirror with its Buddha and its reflections of Buddha-laden mirrors in receding sets ad infinitum. This construction had the added pedagogical value of suggesting that since the content of each mirror was the Buddha, the Buddha-essence is the inner substance of all Facts, making them divine. The interaction aspect of Totality Fa-tsang explained as each Fact simultaneously sending and receiving ripple effects to and from every other Fact throughout the universe. In the True World, the existence and nature of each Fact conditions and is conditioned by the existence and nature of the Totality. This mutual interdependence or intercausality concept spoke to the amazing vibrancy and energy of the True World. Finally, the ability of Buddhas and bodhisattvas to alter the world by meditative visualization Fa-tsang construed in the context of the Absolute Idealism he derived from *The Awakening of Faith.* Since the world exists in the creative imagination of One Universal Mind, higher beings properly plugged into that Absolute Mind could work through it to modify the world.

Fa-tsang's *Treatise on the Golden Lion* (included here in the Wing-tsit Chan translation) is widely recognized as the most representative of his many writings. Fa-tsang is said to have based it on an actual lesson he taught the Empress Wu. When she could not grasp his exposition of the *Flower Garland Sutra,* he opened her understanding by using a golden lion statue that graced her palace courtyard. All but two of the ten sections comprising this work contain only a few lines. Yet the gist of Fa-tsang's elaborate system is compressed therein. Sections 1 to 5 allude to the Unity of Principle and Facts, with the lion symbolizing Facts and the precious gold standing for Principle or the Absolute or the divine Buddha-essence or Emptiness in its extended sense popular in East Asian Buddhism. Just as form and material are inseparable in the golden lion, so also are Facts and the Principle that gives substance to their existence. Section 6 lays out the assemblage of Buddhist schools in five ranks with Hua-yen crowned over the rest. Sections 7 and 8 are the most difficult to understand; they suggest the mutual identity, interpenetration, and intercausality of Facts within one grand Totality and belief in Absolute Idealism. Finally, sections 9 and 10 associate Hua-yen with a new and typically Chinese approach to meditation known as Sudden Enlightenment. This approach helped forge a partnership in which Hua-yen contributed the theory and Ch'an the practice that converts theory into experience.

* * *

The Meditation (Ch'an) School incorporates another Chinese Buddhist innovation—the method of sudden enlightenment. Introduced into Chinese Buddhism a century before Ch'an arose, the method owes its solid reputation to Ch'an. All the innovations of Buddhism in China both retain and, paradoxically, contradict articles of Indian Buddhist faith. Belief in the Absolute is a prime example. China acknowledges the Indian position on emptiness (absence of self-existence) but limits it to the material world while inserting as the necessary ground of that world an Absolute Reality, calling it, ironically, Emptiness as well as Suchness, Mind, Buddha-essence, and so on. Another example is Chinese Buddhism's vision of the True World. Without relinquishing suffering, karma, and rebirth, China inverts the negative Indian worldview into a magnificently positive one, integrating Nirvana and Samsara. The method of sudden enlightenment is a third example. Ch'an admits that gradual enlightenment, the Indian practice, works and even adopts some of its ways, but denounces it nonetheless in favor of the sudden approach. Ch'an is renown as a school of practice rather than philosophy. It espouses a philosophy, however, quietly not boisterously, borrowed not original. At first, Ch'an identified with the Emptiness philosophy of the *Perfection of Wisdom* literature, the *Diamond Sutra* (see section two) in particular. Later, in the ninth century, it embraced the Hua-yen philosophy. Ch'an has conveyed that system ever since the Hua-yen School declined at the end of the T'ang Dynasty. Ch'an's Four Precepts set forth its fundamental creed. They state that Ch'an (1) is transmitted privately from master to disciple rather than publicly through scripture, (2) speaks through nonverbal messages and riddles, (3) pierces to the innermost core of a person, and (4) reveals the divine Buddha-essence within, effecting reunion with it. Ch'an has stood firm in China for fifteen centuries and in its Japanese guise (Zen) has won a robust Western following.

The Meditation School assigns a special role in its teaching to its own history. That teaching is replete with stories (not theories) of colorful masters whose outrageous actions and baffling pronouncements have somehow triggered enlightenment Ch'an-style for earnest students over the centuries. The official tale told by Ch'an about its origins is clouded by legends concerning its first and second founders. Bodhidharma (460–534) is reputed to be the Indian monk who brought Ch'an to southern China in about 520, then moved north where, at the famous Shao-lin monastery, he sat transfixed in meditation before a wall for nine years. He claimed to be the twenty-eighth Indian and first Chinese patriarch of Buddhism, hence the sole heir in his age to the Buddha's supreme authority. Other schools of Chinese Buddhism, T'ien-t'ai and Hua-yen for example, made similar boasts about their founders. Since nothing in Indian Buddhism supports the idea of patriarchal succession, it seems to be a Chinese invention of the T'ang Dynasty to confer superiority upon a tradition. The Four Precepts, attributed to Bodhidharma, were probably formulated several centuries after his time.

Hui-neng (Huineng, 638–713) is considered the Sixth Patriarch and second founder of Ch'an. He is credited with turning the school away from ethereal Indian practices and toward Chinese pragmatism. Biographies of him are abundant but short on certified fact. His official story claims he was born in southern China, made his living selling firewood, and in early manhood had his mind dramatically opened upon hearing the *Diamond Sutra* recited. Sometime later he journeyed northward to study under Hung-jen, the Fifth Patriarch. As a lay disciple in Hung-jen's (Hongren's) monastery, he was put to work in the kitchen. Although at the bottom of the monastery echelon, he, an illiterate, managed to surpass the senior monk, Shen-hsiu (Shenxiu), in a poetry contest in which each set forth his comprehension of Ch'an. Discerning from the poems that this kitchen helper, rather than his most brilliant student, grasped the true spirit of Ch'an, Hung-jen conferred upon Hui-neng at approximately age thirty-six the office of Sixth Patriarch, then bade him flee to the South and not preach for three years. After that time elapsed, Hui-neng was finally ordained a Buddhist priest at age thirty-nine and began his long preaching ministry there. He died in 713.

The later history of Ch'an appears reliable. At the Great Dharma Assembly convened in 732 by Hui-neng's disciple and advocate, Shen-hui (Shenhui, 670–762), Ch'an split into Northern and Southern branches over the issues of gradual versus sudden enlightenment and entitlement to the patriarchy. The Northern School, defending the gradual method (Indian) and the patriarchal claim of Hui-neng's rival, Shen-hsiu, soon declined. The Southern School under Shen-hui triumphed in acclaiming Hui-neng the Sixth Patriarch and in advancing the sudden method (Chinese). Many skillful masters appeared in the Southern tradition during the remainder of the eighth century. Their radical methods for catalyzing self-discovery (shouting and beating) became staples of Ch'an training. After the great persecution of Buddhism that began in 845, family groups known as the Five Houses pursued distinctive approaches to Ch'an. Two of them, Lin-chi (Linji) and Ts'ao-tung (Caodong), absorbed the rest, then in the Sung Dynasty (960–1279) emerged as full-fledged schools. They disagreed primarily over the use of training problems in meditation. Training problems (*kung-an (gong'an)*) in Chinese, *koan* in Japanese) engage reason but are incapable of rational solution; struggling with one to the point of desperation finally rockets the mind beyond rationality to genuine insight. Lin-chi advocated their use; Ts'ao-tung preferred sitting quietly with an alert mind. In Japan, these two became the Rinzai and Soto schools of Zen (the Japanese equivalent of Ch'an, both words meaning "meditation"). Ch'an in China since Sung times has changed little.

The *Platform Scripture* (given here also in the Wing-tsit Chan translation) is the pivotal text for the Ch'an School. Four preliminary topics invite comment before discussing the work's meaning. First, the unabridged title amounts to an abstract of the whole. It describes the work as a sermon preached from a temple platform by Hui-neng, the Sixth Patriarch, recorded by his disciple Fa-hai (Fahai). It assigns the text prominence among the *Perfection of Wisdom* books, thus orienting it toward the philosophy of Emptiness. (For Ch'an, Emptiness indicates the absence of self-existence but presence of the divine Buddha-essence/Absolute in our world.) It also specifies the theme of the work as the method of sudden enlightenment taught by the Southern School of Ch'an (Zen). Second, the issues of authorship and date cannot be resolved with evidence presently available. Some authorities hold that the *Platform Scripture* was indeed the preaching of Hui-neng, recorded from memory by his disciple Fa-hai in 714, the year after Hui-neng's death. Others conjecture that the scripture was contrived by an unidentified student of Shen-hui's in about 780 to 800. They reason that certain features of the text presuppose Shen-hui's death (762) and echo his writings. Third, the original text is not in our possession. What we have is a handful of copies whose dates span six centuries. The oldest is the Tun-huang (Dunhuang) version (830–860), the latest the Ming Canon version (1440). Comparison of the two shows that the text changed dramatically during transmission. Additions almost doubled its size, wording was revised, segments rearranged, and a much larger dose of Hua-yen philosophy injected. The Ming Canon version is the one most modern Buddhists know and revere. But the Tun-huang, closest to the original, is the one presented here. Finally, analysis of the Tun-huang version reveals a simple structure. It consists of two main parts—Sermon (sections 1–37) and Miscellany (sections 38–57). Scholars contest the authenticity of the second part. The first part alone, they believe, reflects the original text. That part has three subparts: Hui-neng's autobiography (sections 2–12), the sermon itself (sections 13–33), and the preacher's response to questions (sections 34–37). The spotlight falls, logically, on the sermon. There we find elaboration of the primary theme—the method of sudden enlightenment.

The method of sudden enlightenment defines itself through contrast to the gradual method. First, what is the advantage of the sudden method over the gradual? Both methods result in enlightenment, but the sudden method provides a short cut, gaining the objective directly without an extra step needlessly required by the gradual. The greater practicality of the Southern School's method distinguished it above that of the Northern School, still wedded to the more complicated Indian approach, and earned Hui-neng recognition as the second founder of a truly Chinese Ch'an. Second, the gradual method, mainstream for both Indian and Chinese meditation before Hui-neng's time, prescribes seclusion from society with hours of quiet sitting until normal consciousness is suspended and the mind rendered profoundly blank. Let us call this "Mind Voiding" and take it as typical of the gradual method. With the sudden method, on the other hand, the practitioner continues fully engaged in life. Retreat from society is unnecessary (though permissible for monks). As for long periods of quiet sitting, the *Platform Scripture* dismisses them altogether; later Ch'an, however, found a place for them in its monastery training program. The point is to remain riveted on the present as it passes like a parade in review, engrossed in the "here-and-now," released from habituation (tuning out the familiar), unattached to any one moment (lest the rest slip by unnoticed), and not distracted by stray thoughts. This frame of mind can be called "Steady Alertness." Habituation, attachment, and distraction are common psychological processes among the unenlightened, but they warp comprehension of reality. Steady Alertness is their remedy, deliberate and unimpeded receptivity to the ever-changing present. Finally, both methods produce awareness of our everyday world as the True World, laden with, unified by, and immersed in the divine Buddha-essence (Suchness, Emptiness, Mind, Absolute). Steady Alertness takes the meditator directly there, while Mind Voiding arrives indirectly through the intermediate stop of suspended consciousness, achieved after years of effort. Realization of our everyday world as the True World binds Hua-yen theory and Ch'an practice together as partners in a joint venture.

Enigmas in the sermon central to the *Platform Scripture* (sections 13–33) dissolve in light of this analysis of the method of sudden enlightenment. The sermon may best be read as a series of comments on Steady Alertness.

The identity of calmness and wisdom (sections 13 and 15): Calmness and wisdom are two of the six perfections a bodhisattva vows to master. Calmness points to psychological and wisdom to cognitive aspects of Steady Alertness. They are two sides of the same coin. Calmness is simply sustained attention to the flow of life as it passes in review, undaunted by habituation, attachment, or distraction. Wisdom pertains to what is comprehended in that state of mind—the everyday world as the True World.

The identity of calmness and straightforward mind (section 14): Another coupling of the psychological and cognitive dimensions of Steady Alertness underscores the veracity rather than the content of the cognitive. Straightforward mind is the awareness that grasps the truth of the matter. The psychologically calmed mind is also cognitively set straight, corrected, relieved of all delusion.

Nonattachment as the foundation (section 17): Nonattachment is a psychological staple of Steady Alertness. Consciousness cannot sustain receptivity to the here-and-now unless it avoids fixation on single items in the flow as well as distraction by roving thoughts extrinsic to it. Both fixation and distraction break the continuity of the flow.

Sitting in meditation equated with calmness (sections 18–19): The *Platform Scripture* routinely disparages sitting quietly with a blank mind, associated with the gradual method. Here, however, the text redeems quiet sitting by declaring it a beneficial occasion to practice opening attention to the fullness of the present rather than closing it down into a mental vacuum.

Traditional Mahayana doctrines revised (sections 20–31): The sermon concludes with a sequence of obscure sections suggesting that some high Mahayana teachings have Steady Alertness as their deeper meaning. The Three Bodies of Buddha, the Four Great Vows of the Bodhisattva, Repentance, the Three Refuges, and the Great Wisdom Perfection are treated in this fashion. Steady Alertness, in sum, is the hub where the spokes of the sermon meet.

*   *   *

Readers wishing to consider the broader historical context of Chinese Buddhist philosophy are advised to consult Wing-tsit Chan, ed., *A Source Book in Chinese Philosophy* (Princeton, NJ: Princeton University Press, 1963); Kenneth K.S. Ch'en, *Buddhism in China: A Historical Survey* (Princeton, NJ: Princeton University Press, 1964) and *The Chinese Transformation of Buddhism* (Princeton, NJ: Princeton University Press, 1973); and Fung Yu-lan, *A History of Chinese Philosophy*, 2 vols., tr. Derk Bodde (Princeton, NJ: Princeton University Press, 1953).

Further explorations of the Hua-yen School include Garma C.C. Chang, *The Buddhist Teaching of Totality: The Philosophy of Hua-yen Buddhism* (University Park: Pennsylvania State University Press, 1971); Thomas Cleary, *Entry into the Inconceivable: An Introduction to Hua-yen Buddhism* (Honolulu: University of Hawaii Press, 1983); and Francis D. Cook, *Hua-yen Buddhism: The Jewel Net of Indra* (University Park: Pennsylvania State University Press, 1977). For a comparison of Hua-yen thought with A.N. Whitehead's process philosophy, see Steve Odin, *Process Metaphysics and Hua-yen Buddhism: A Critical Study of Cumulative Penetration Vs. Interpenetration* (Albany: SUNY Press, 1982).

Competent studies of Ch'an Buddhism are numerous. The standard work on the history of Ch'an is Heinrich Dumoulin, *Zen Buddhism: A History,* 2 vols., trs. James W. Heisig and Paul Knitter (New York: Macmillan, 1988). The outstanding scholar of Ch'an (Zen) is Daisetz Teitaro Suzuki. Of his many excellent books on the subject, the most profound is *Essays in Zen Buddhism,* 3 vols. (New York: Samuel Weiser, 1953). The classical study of the *Platform Scripture* is Suzuki's *The Zen Doctrine of No-Mind: The Significance of the Sutra of Hui-neng* (London: Rider, 1958).

THE AWAKENING OF FAITH

INVOCATION

I take refuge in [the *Buddha,*] the greatly Compassionate One, the Savior of the world, omnipotent, omnipresent, omniscient, of most excellent deeds in all the ten directions;

And in [the *Dharma,*] the manifestation of his Essence, the Reality, the sea of Suchness, the boundless storehouse of excellencies;

[And in the *Sangha,* whose members] truly devote themselves to the practice,

May all sentient beings be made to discard their doubts, to cast aside their evil attachments, and to give rise to the correct faith in the Mahayana, that the lineage of the Buddhas may not be broken off.

THE CONTENTS OF THE DISCOURSE

There is a teaching (dharma) which can awaken in us the root of faith in the Mahayana, and it should therefore be explained. The explanation is divided into five parts. They are (1) the Reasons for Writing; (2) the Outline; (3) the Interpretation; (4) on Faith and Practice; (5) the Encouragement of Practice and the Benefits Thereof.

PART I: THE REASONS FOR WRITING

Someone may ask the reasons why I was led to write this treatise. I reply: there are eight reasons.

The first and the main reason is to cause men to free themselves from all sufferings and to gain the final bliss; it is not that I desire worldly fame, material profit, or respect and honor.

The second reason is that I wish to interpret the fundamental meaning [of the teachings] of the Tathagata so that men may understand them correctly and not be mistaken about them.

The third reason is to enable those whose capacity for goodness has attained maturity to keep firm hold upon an unretrogressive faith in the teachings of Mahayana.

The fourth reason is to encourage those whose capacity for goodness is still slight to cultivate the faithful mind.

The fifth reason is to show them expedient means (*upaya*) by which they may wipe away the hindrance of evil karma, guard their minds well, free themselves from stupidity and arrogance, and escape from the net of heresy.

The Awakening of Faith: Attributed to Ashvaghosha, translated by Yoshito S. Hakeda (New York: Columbia University Press, 1967). Reprinted by permission.

The sixth reason is to reveal to them the practice [of two methods of meditation], cessation [of illusions] and clear observation (*shamatha* and *vipashyana;* Ch., *chih-kuan*), so that ordinary men and the followers of Hinayana may cure their minds of error.

The seventh reason is to explain to them the expedient means of single-minded meditation (*smriti*) so that they may be born in the presence of the Buddha and keep their minds fixed in an unretrogressive faith.

The eighth reason is to point out to them the advantages [of studying this treatise] and to encourage them to make an effort [to attain enlightenment]. These are the reasons for which I write this treatise.

Question: What need is there to repeat the explanation of the teaching when it is presented in detail in the sutras?

Answer: Though this teaching is presented in the sutras, the capacity and the deeds of men today are no longer the same, nor are the conditions of their acceptance and comprehension. That is to say, in the days when the Tathagata was in the world, people were of high aptitude and the Preacher excelled in his form, mind, and deeds, so that once he had preached with his perfect voice, different types of people all equally understood; hence, there was no need for this kind of discourse. But after the passing away of the Tathagata, there were some who were able by their own power to listen extensively to others and to reach understanding; there were some who by their own power could listen to very little and yet understand much; there were some who, without any mental power of their own, depended upon the extensive discourses of others to obtain understanding; and naturally there were some who looked upon the wordiness of extensive discourses as troublesome, and who sought after what was comprehensive, terse, and yet contained much meaning, and then were able to understand it. Thus, this

Wall relief of the Buddha carved on the outside of the Azure Clouds Temple in the Fragrant Hills, Beijing. (*Forrest E. Baird*)

discourse is designed to embrace, in a general way, the limitless meaning of the vast and profound teaching of the Tathagata. This discourse, therefore, should be presented.

PART 2: OUTLINE

The reasons for writing have been explained. Next the outline will be given. Generally speaking, Mahayana is to be expounded from two points of view. One is the principle and the other is the significance.

The principle is "the Mind of the sentient being." This Mind includes in itself all states of being of the phenomenal world and the transcendental world. On the basis of this Mind, the meanings of Mahayana may be unfolded. Why? Because the absolute aspect of this Mind represents the essence *(svabhava)* of Mahayana; and the phenomenal aspect of this Mind indicates the essence, attributes *(lakshana),* and influences *(kriya)* of Mahayana itself.

Of the significance [of the adjective *maha* (great) in the compound, *Mahayana*], there are three aspects: (1) the "greatness" of the essence, for all phenomena (dharma) are identical with Suchness and are neither increasing nor decreasing; (2) the "greatness" of the attributes, for the *Tathagata-garbha* is endowed with numberless excellent qualities; (3) the "greatness" of the influences, for the influences [of Suchness] give rise to the good causes and effects in this and in the other world alike.

[The significance of the term *yana* (vehicle) in the compound, *Mahayana.* The term *yana* is introduced] because all Enlightened Ones (Buddhas) have ridden [on this vehicle], and all Enlightened Ones-to-be (Bodhisattvas), being led by this principle, will reach the stage of Tathagata.

PART 3: INTERPRETATION

The part on outline has been given; next the part on interpretation [of the principle of Mahayana] will be given. It consists of three chapters: (1) Revelation of the True Meaning; (2) Correction of Evil Attachments; (3) Analysis of the Types of Aspiration for Enlightenment.

CHAPTER ONE: REVELATION OF TRUE MEANING

I. ONE MIND AND ITS TWO ASPECTS

The revelation of the true meaning [of the principle of Mahayana can be achieved] by [unfolding the doctrine] that the principle of One Mind has two aspects. One is the aspect of Mind in terms of the Absolute *(tathata;* Suchness), and the other is the aspect of

Mind in terms of phenomena (samsara; birth and death). Each of these two aspects embraces all states of existence. Why? Because these two aspects are mutually inclusive.

A. THE MIND IN TERMS OF THE ABSOLUTE

The Mind in terms of the Absolute is the one World of Reality (*dharmadhatu*) and the essence of all phases of existence in their totality.

That which is called "the essential nature of the Mind" is unborn and is imperishable. It is only through illusions that all things come to be differentiated. If one is freed from illusions, then to him there will be no appearances (*lakshana*) of objects [regarded as absolutely independent existences]; therefore all things from the beginning transcend all forms of verbalization, description, and conceptualization and are, in the final analysis, undifferentiated, free from alteration, and indestructible. They are only of the One Mind; hence the name Suchness. All explanations by words are provisional and without validity, for they are merely used in accordance with illusions and are incapable [of denoting Suchness]. The term Suchness likewise has no attributes [which can be verbally specified]. The term Suchness is, so to speak, the limit of verbalization wherein a word is used to put an end to words. But the essence of Suchness itself cannot be put an end to, for all things [in their Absolute aspect] are real; nor is there anything which needs to be pointed out as real, for all things are equally in the state of Suchness. It should be understood that all things are incapable of being verbally explained or thought of; hence, the name Suchness.

Question: If such is the meaning [of the principle of Mahayana], how is it possible for men to conform themselves to and enter into it?

Answer: If they understand that, concerning all things, though they are spoken of, there is neither that which speaks, nor that which can be spoken of, and though they are thought of, there is neither that which thinks, nor that which can be thought of, then they are said to have conformed to it. And when they are freed from their thoughts, they are said to have entered into it.

Next, Suchness has two aspects if predicated in words. One is that it is truly empty (*shunya*), for [this aspect] can, in the final sense, reveal what is real. The other is that it is truly nonempty (*a-shunya*), for its essence itself is endowed with undefiled and excellent qualities.

1. TRULY EMPTY

[Suchness is empty] because from the beginning it has never been related to any defiled states of existence, it is free from all marks of individual distinction of things, and it has nothing to do with thoughts conceived by a deluded mind.

It should be understood that the essential nature of Suchness is neither with marks nor without marks; neither not with marks nor not without marks; nor is it both with and without marks simultaneously; it is neither with a single mark nor with different marks; neither not with a single mark nor not with different marks; nor is it both with a single and with different marks simultaneously.

In short, since all unenlightened men discriminate with their deluded minds from moment to moment, they are alienated [from Suchness]; hence, the definition "empty"; but once they are free from their deluded minds, they will find that there is nothing to be negated.

2. TRULY NONEMPTY

Since it has been made clear that the essence of all things is empty, i.e., devoid of illusions, the true Mind is eternal, permanent, immutable, pure, and self-sufficient; therefore, it is called "nonempty." And also there is no trace of particular marks to be noted in it, as it is the sphere that transcends thoughts and is in harmony with enlightenment alone.

B. THE MIND IN TERMS OF PHENOMENA

1. THE STOREHOUSE CONSCIOUSNESS

The Mind as phenomena (samsara) is grounded on the *Tathagata-garbha*. What is called the Storehouse Consciousness is that in which "neither birth nor death (nirvana)" diffuses harmoniously with "birth and death (samsara)," and yet in which both are neither identical nor different. This Consciousness has two aspects which embrace all states of existence and create all states of existence. They are: (1) the aspect of enlightenment, and (2) the aspect of nonenlightenment.

a. THE ASPECT OF ENLIGHTENMENT

(1) Original Enlightenment: The essence of Mind is free from thoughts. The characteristic of that which is free from thoughts is analogous to that of the sphere of empty space that pervades everywhere. The one [without any second, i.e., the absolute] aspect of the World of Reality (*dharmadhatu*) is none other than the undifferentiated Dharmakaya, the "Essence-body" of the Tathagata. [Since the essence of Mind is] grounded on the Dharmakaya, it is to be called the original enlightenment. Why? Because "original enlightenment" indicates [the essence of Mind *(a priori)*] in contradistinction to [the essence of Mind in] the process of actualization of enlightenment; the process of actualization of enlightenment is none other than [the process of integrating] the identity with the original enlightenment.

(2) The Process of Actualization of Enlightenment: Grounded on the original enlightenment is nonenlightenment. And because of nonenlightenment, the process of actualization of enlightenment can be spoken of.

Now, to be [fully] enlightened to the fountainhead of Mind is called the final enlightenment; and not to be enlightened to the fountainhead of Mind, nonfinal enlightenment.

What is the meaning of this? An ordinary man becomes aware that his former thoughts were wrong; then he is able to stop *(nirodha)* such thoughts from arising again. Although this sometimes may also be called enlightenment, [properly it is not enlightenment at all] because it is not enlightenment [that reaches the fountainhead of Mind].

The followers of Hinayana, who have some insight, and those Bodhisattvas who have just been initiated become aware of the changing state *(anyathatva)* of thoughts and are free from thoughts which are subject to change [such as the existence of a permanent self (atman), etc.]. Since they have forsaken the rudimentary attachments derived from unwarranted speculation *(vikalpa)*, [their experience] is called enlightenment in appearance.

Bodhisattvas [who have come to the realization] of Dharmakaya become aware of the [temporarily] abiding state *(sthiti)* of thoughts and are not arrested by them.

Since they are free from their rudimentary [false] thoughts derived from the speculation [that the components of the world are real, their experience] is called approximate enlightenment.

Those Bodhisattvas who have completed the stages of a Bodhisattva and who have fulfilled the expedient means [needed to bring forth the original enlightenment to the fullest extent] will experience the oneness [with Suchness] in an instant; they will become aware of how the inceptions of [the deluded thoughts of] the mind arise (*jati*), and will be free from the rise of any [deluded] thought. Since they are far away even from subtle [deluded] thoughts, they are able to have an insight into the original nature of Mind. [The realization] that Mind is eternal is called the final enlightenment. It is, therefore, said in a sutra that if there is a man who is able to perceive that which is beyond thoughts he is advancing toward the Buddha wisdom.

Though it is said that there is [an inception of the rising of [deluded] thoughts in the mind, there is no inception as such that can be known [as being independent of the essence of Mind]. And yet to say that the inception [of the rising of deluded thoughts] is known means that it is known as [existing on the ground of] that which is beyond thoughts [i.e., the essence of Mind]. Accordingly, all ordinary people are said not to be enlightened because they have had a continuous stream of [deluded] thoughts and have never been freed from their thoughts; therefore, they are said to be in a beginingless ignorance. If a man gains [insight into] that which is free from thoughts, then he knows how those [thoughts] which characterize the mind [i.e., deluded thoughts] arise, abide, change, and cease to be, for he is identical with that which is free from thoughts. But, in reality, no difference exists in the process of the actualization of enlightenment, because the four states [of rising, abiding, etc.] exist simultaneously and each of them is not self-existent; they are originally of one and the same enlightenment [in that they are taking place on the ground of original enlightenment, as its phenomenal aspects].

And, again, original enlightenment, when analyzed in relation to the defiled state [in the phenomenal order], presents itself as having two attributes. One is the "Purity of Wisdom" and the other is the "Suprarational Functions."

(a) Purity of Wisdom. By virtue of the permeation (*vasana,* perfuming) of the influence of dharma [i.e., the essence of Mind or original enlightenment], a man comes to truly discipline himself and fulfills all expedient means [of unfolding enlightenment]; as a result, he breaks through the compound consciousness [i.e., the Storehouse Consciousness that contains both enlightenment and nonenlightenment], puts an end to the manifestation of the stream of [deluded] mind, and manifests the Dharmakaya [i.e., the essence of Mind], for his wisdom (*prajna*) becomes genuine and pure.

What is the meaning of this? All modes (*lakshana*) of mind and consciousness [under the state of nonenlightenment are [the products of] ignorance. Ignorance does not exist apart from enlightenment; therefore, it cannot be destroyed [because one cannot destroy something which does not really exist], and yet it cannot not be destroyed [in so far as it remains]. This is like the relationship that exists between the water of the ocean [i.e., enlightenment] and its waves [i.e., modes of mind] stirred by the wind [i.e., ignorance]. Water and wind are inseparable; but water is not mobile by nature, and if the wind stops the movement ceases. But the wet nature remains undestroyed. Likewise, man's Mind, pure in its own nature, is stirred by the wind of ignorance. Both Mind and ignorance have no particular forms of their own and they are inseparable. Yet Mind is not mobile by nature, and if ignorance ceases, then the continuity [of deluded activities] ceases. But the essential nature of wisdom [i.e., the essence of Mind, like the wet nature of the water] remains undestroyed.

(b) Suprarational Functions. [He who has fully uncovered the original enlightenment] is capable of creating all manner of excellent conditions because his wisdom is pure. The manifestation of his numberless excellent qualities is incessant; accommodating himself to the capacity of other men he responds spontaneously, reveals himself in manifold ways, and benefits them.

(3) The Characteristics of the Essence of Enlightenment: The characteristics of the essence of enlightenment have four great significances that are identical with those of empty space or that are analogous to those of a bright mirror.

First, [the essence of enlightenment is like] a mirror which is really empty [of images]. It is free from all marks of objects of the mind and it has nothing to reveal in itself, for it does not reflect any images.

Second, [it is, as it were] a mirror, influencing (vasana) [all men to advance toward enlightenment], serving as the primary cause [of their attaining enlightenment]. That is to say, it is truly nonempty; appearing in it are all the objects of the world which neither go out nor come in; which are neither lost nor destroyed. It is eternally abiding One Mind. [All things appear in it] because all things are real. And none of the defiled things are able to defile it, for the essence of wisdom [i.e., original enlightenment] is unaffected [by defilements], being furnished with an unsoiled quality and influencing all men [to advance toward enlightenment].

Third, [it is like] a mirror which is free from [defiled] objects [reflected in it]. This can be said because the nonempty state [of original enlightenment] is genuine, pure, and bright, being free from hindrances both affectional and intellectual, and transcending characteristics of that which is compounded [i.e., the Storehouse Consciousness].

Fourth, [it is like] a mirror influencing [a man to cultivate his capacity for goodness], serving as a coordinating cause [to encourage him in his endeavors]. Because [the essence of enlightenment] is free from [defiled] objects, it universally illumines the mind of man and induces him to cultivate his capacity for goodness, presenting itself in accordance with his desires [as a mirror presents his appearance].

b. THE ASPECT OF NONENLIGHTENMENT

Because of not truly realizing oneness with Suchness, there emerges an unenlightened mind and, consequently, its thoughts. These thoughts do not have any validity to be substantiated; therefore, they are not independent of the original enlightenment. It is like the case of a man who has lost his way: he is confused because of [his wrong sense of] direction. If he is freed from [the notion of] direction altogether, then there will be no such thing as going astray. It is the same with men: because of [the notion of] enlightenment, they are confused. But if they are freed from [the fixed notion of] enlightenment, then there will be no such thing as nonenlightenment. Because [there are men] of unenlightened, deluded mind, for them we speak of true enlightenment, knowing well what this [relative] term stands for. Independent of the unenlightened mind, there are no independent marks of true enlightenment itself that can be discussed.

Because of its nonenlightened state, [the deluded mind] produces three aspects which are bound to nonenlightenment and are inseparable from it.

First is the activity of ignorance. The agitation of mind because of its nonenlightened state is called activity. When enlightened, it is unagitated. When it is agitated, anxiety (duhkha) follows, for the result [i.e., anxiety] is not independent of the cause [i.e., the agitation contingent upon ignorance].

Second is the perceiving subject. Because of the agitation [that breaks the original unity with Suchness], there appears the perceiving subject. When unagitated, [the mind] is free from perceiving.

Third is the world of objects. Because of the perceiving subject, the world of objects erroneously appears. Apart from the perceiving, there will be no world of objects.

Conditioned by the [incorrectly conceived] world of objects, [the deluded mind] produces six aspects.

First is the aspect of the [discriminating] intellect. Depending on the [erroneously conceived] world of objects, the mind develops the discrimination between liking and disliking.

Second is the aspect of continuity. By virtue of [the discriminating function of] the intellect, the mind produces an awareness of pleasure and pain [with regard to things] in the world of objects. The mind, developing [deluded] thoughts and being bound to them, will continue uninterrupted.

Third is the aspect of attachment. Because of the continuity [of deluded thoughts], the mind, superimposing its deluded thoughts on the world of objects and holding fast to [the discriminations of liking and disliking] develops attachments [to what it likes].

Fourth is the aspect of the speculation (vikalpa) on names and letters [i.e., concepts]. On the basis of erroneous attachments, [the deluded mind] analyzes words which are provisional [and therefore devoid of validity].

Fifth is the aspect of giving rise to [evil] karma. Relying on names and letters [i.e., concepts which have no validity, the deluded mind] investigates names and words and becomes attached to them, and creates manifold types of evil karma.

Sixth is the aspect of anxiety attached to the [effects of evil] karma. Because of the [law of] karma, the deluded mind suffers the effects and will not be free.

It should be understood that ignorance is able to produce all types of defiled states; all defiled states are aspects of nonenlightenment.

C. THE RELATIONSHIPS BETWEEN ENLIGHTENMENT AND NONENLIGHTENMENT

Two relationships exist between the enlightened and nonenlightened states. They are "identity" and "nonidentity."

(1) Identity: Just as pieces of various kinds of pottery are of the same nature in that they are made of clay, so the various magic-like manifestations (maya) of both enlightenment (anasrava: nondefilement) and nonenlightenment (avidya) are aspects of the same essence, Suchness. For this reason, it is said in a sutra that "all sentient beings intrinsically abide in eternity and are entered into nirvana. The state of enlightenment is not something that is to be acquired by practice or to be created. In the end, it is unobtainable [for it is given from the beginning]." Also it has no corporeal aspect that can be perceived as such. Any corporeal aspects [such as the marks of the Buddha] that are visible are magic-like products [of Suchness manifested] in accordance with [the mentality of men in] defilement. It is not, however, that these corporeal aspects [which result from the suprarational functions] of wisdom are of the nature of nonemptiness [i.e., substantial]; for wisdom has no aspects that can be perceived.

(2) Nonidentity: just as various pieces of pottery differ from each other, so differences exist between the state of enlightenment and that of nonenlightenment, and between the magic-like manifestations [of Suchness manifested] in accordance with [the

mentality of men in] defilement, and those [of men of ignorance] who are defiled [i.e., blinded] as to the essential nature [of Suchness].

2. THE CAUSE AND CONDITIONS OF MAN'S BEING IN SAMSARA

That a man is in samsara results from the fact that his mind *(manas)* and consciousness *(vijnana)* develop on the ground of the Storehouse Consciousness *(citta).* This means that because of [the aspect of nonenlightenment of] the Storehouse Consciousness, he is said to be in possession of ignorance [and thus is bound to remain in samsara].

a. MIND

[The mentality] which emerges in the state of nonenlightenment, which [incorrectly] perceives and reproduces [the world of objects] and, conceiving that the [reproduced] world of objects is real, continues to develop [deluded] thoughts, is what we define as mind.

This mind has five different names. The first is called the "activating mind," for, without being aware of it, it breaks the equilibrium of mind by the force of ignorance.

The second is called the "evolving mind," for it emerges contingent upon the agitated mind as [the subject] that perceives [incorrectly].

The third is called the "reproducing mind," for it reproduces the entire world of objects as a bright mirror reproduces all material images. When confronted with the objects of the five senses, it reproduces them at once. It arises spontaneously at all times and exists forever [reproducing the world of objects] in front [of the subject].

The fourth is called the "analytical mind," for it differentiates what is defiled and what is undefiled.

The fifth is called the "continuing mind," for it is united with [deluded] thoughts and continues uninterrupted. It retains the entire karma, good and bad, accumulated in the immeasurable lives of the past, and does not permit any loss. It is also capable of bringing the results of the pain, pleasure, etc., of the present and the future to maturity; in doing so, it makes no mistakes. It can cause one to recollect suddenly the things of the present and the past and to have sudden and unexpected fantasies of the things to come.

The triple world, therefore, is unreal and is of mind only. Apart from it there are no objects of the five senses and of the mind. What does this mean? Since all things are, without exception, developed from the mind and produced under the condition of deluded thoughts, all differentiations are no other than the differentiations of one's mind itself. [Yet] the mind cannot perceive the mind itself; the mind has no marks of its own [that can be ascertained as a substantial entity as such]. It should be understood that [the conception of] the entire world of objects can be held only on the basis of man's deluded mind of ignorance. All things, therefore, are just like the images in a mirror which are devoid of any objectivity that one can get hold of; they are of the mind only and are unreal. When the [deluded] mind comes into being, then various conceptions (dharma) come to be; and when the [deluded] mind ceases to be, then these various conceptions cease to be.

b. CONSCIOUSNESS

What is called "consciousness *(vijnana)*" is the "continuing mind." Because of their deep-rooted attachment, ordinary men imagine that I and Mine are real and cling to them in their illusions. As soon as objects are presented, this consciousness rests on noughts], will be more and more liberated as they advance, and when they reach the stage of Tathagatahood," they will be completely liberated.

On "united." By the word "united" [appearing in the first three defilements] is meant that though difference [i.e., duality] exists between the mind (subject) and the atum of the mind (object), there is a simultaneous relation between them in that when he subject is defiled the object is also defiled, and when the subject is purified the object is also purified.

On "disunited." By the word "disunited" is meant that [the second three subtle and fundamental defilements are the aspects of] nonenlightenment on the part of the mind existing prior to the differentiation [into the subject and object relationship]; therefore, a simultaneous relation between the subject and object is not as yet established.

On the "defiled state of mind." It is called "the hindrance originating from defilements," for it obstructs any fundamental insight into Suchness.

On "ignorance." Ignorance is called the "hindrance originating from misconceptions of objects," for it obstructs the wisdom that functions spontaneously in the world.

Because of the defiled [state of] mind, there emerges the subject that perceives [incorrectly; i.e., the evolving mind] and that which reproduces [the reproducing mind] and thus one erroneously predicates the world of objects and causes oneself to deviate from the undifferentiated state [of Suchness]. Though all things are always in quiescence and devoid of any marks of rising, because of the nonenlightenment due to ignorance, one erroneously strays from the dharma [i.e., Suchness]; thus one fails to obtain the wisdom that functions spontaneously by adapting oneself to all circumstances in the world.

3. THE CHARACTERISTICS OF BEINGS IN SAMSARA

In analyzing the characteristics of beings in samsara, two categories may be distinguished. The one is "crude," for [those who belong to this category are] united with the [crude activities of the defiled] mind; the other is "subtle," for [those who belong to this category are] disunited from the [subtle activities of the defiled] mind. [Again, each category may in turn be subdivided into the cruder and the subtler]. The cruder of the crude belongs to the range of mental activity of ordinary men; the subtler of the crude and the cruder of the subtle belong to that of Bodhisattvas; and the subtler of the subtle belongs to that of Buddhas.

These two categories of beings in the phenomenal order come about because of the permeation of ignorance; that is to say, they come about because of the primary cause and the coordinating causes. By the primary cause, "nonenlightenment" is meant; and by the coordinating causes, "the erroneously represented world of objects."

When the primary cause ceases to be, then the coordinating causes will cease to be. Because of the cessation of the primary cause, the mind disunited [from the represented world of objects, etc.] will cease to be; and because of the cessation of the coordinating causes, the mind united [with the attachment to atman, etc.] will cease to be.

Question: If the mind ceases to be, what will become of its continuity? If there is continuity of mind, how can you explain its final cessation?

Answer: What we speak of as "cessation" is the cessation of the marks of [the deluded] mind only and not the cessation of its essence. It is like the case of the wind which, following the surface of the water, leaves the marks of its movement. If the water should cease to be, then the marks of the wind would be nullified and the wind would have no support [on which to display its movement]. But since the water does not cease to be, the marks of the wind may continue. Because only the wind ceases, the marks of

them and discriminates the objects of the five senses and of the mind. Th
"*vijnana* [i.e., the differentiating consciousness]" or the "separating cons
Or, again, it is called the "object-discriminating consciousness." [The pro
discrimination of] this consciousness will be intensified by both [the intel
filement of holding fast to perverse views and [the affectional] defilemei
gence in passion.

That the [deluded mind and] consciousness arise from the permeati
rance is something that ordinary men cannot understand. The follov
Hinayana, with their wisdom, likewise fail to realize this. Those Bodhisattvs
ing advanced from their first stage of correct faith by setting the mind [upo
ment] through practicing contemplation, have come to realize the Dharr
partially comprehend this. Yet even those who have reached the fin
Bodhisattvahood cannot fully comprehend this; only the Enlightened One
ough comprehension of it. Why? The Mind, though pure in its self nature
ginning, is accompanied by ignorance. Being defiled by ignorance, a defil
Mind comes into being. But, though defiled, the Mind itself is eternal and
Only the Enlightened Ones are able to understand what this means.

What is called the essential nature of Mind is always beyond thought:
fore, defined as "immutable." When the one World of Reality is yet to be
Mind [is mutable and] is not in perfect unity [with Suchness]. Suddenly,
thought arises; [this state] is called ignorance.

c. DEFILED STATES OF MIND

Six kinds of defiled states of mind [conditioned by ignorance] can be ider
The first is the defilement united with attachment [to atman], from
who have attained liberation in Hinayana and those [Bodhisattvas] at the
tablishment of faith" are free.

The second is the defilement united with the "continuing mind,"
those who are at the "stage of establishment of faith" and who are practici
means [to attain enlightenment] can gradually free themselves and fre
completely at the "stage of pure-heartedness."

The third is the defilement united with the discriminating "analytical
which those at the "stage of observing precepts" begin to be liberated and f
erated completely when they arrive at the "stage of expedient means witho

The fourth is the [subtle] defilement disunited from the represented
jects, from which those at the "stage of freedom from world of objects" c

The fifth is the [subtler] defilement disunited from the "[evolving] r
ceives" [i.e., the defilement existing prior to the act of perceiving], from v
the "stage of freedom from [evolving] mind" are freed.

The sixth [and most subtle] is the defilement disunited from the bas
mind," from which those Bodhisattvas who have passed the final stage a
into the stage of Tathagatahood" are freed.

d. COMMENTS ON THE TERMS USED IN THE FOREGOING DISCUSSION

On [the expression] "the one World of Reality is yet to be realized." F
those [Bodhisattvas] who have advanced from the "stage of the establish
to the "stage of pure-heartedness," after having completed and severed

its movement cease accordingly. This is not the cessation of water. So it is with ignorance; on the ground of the essence of Mind there is movement. If the essence of Mind were to cease, then people would be nullified and they would have no support. But since the essence does not cease to be, the mind may continue. Because only stupidity ceases to be, the marks of the [stupidity of the] mind cease accordingly. It is not that the wisdom [i.e., the essence] of Mind ceases.

Because of the four kinds of permeation, the defiled states and the pure state emerge and continue uninterrupted. They are (1) the pure state, which is called Suchness; (2) the cause of all defilements, which is called ignorance; (3) the deluded mind, which is called "activating mind"; (4) the erroneously conceived external world, which is called the "objects of the five senses and of mind."

The meaning of permeation. Clothes in the world certainly have no scent in themselves, but if man permeates them with perfumes, then they come to have a scent. It is just the same with the case we are speaking of. The pure state of Suchness certainly has no defilement, but if it is permeated by ignorance, then the marks of defilement appear on it. The defiled state of ignorance is indeed devoid of any purifying force, but if it is permeated by Suchness, then it will come to have a purifying influence.

a. PERMEATION OF IGNORANCE

How does the permeation [of ignorance] give rise to the defiled state and continue uninterrupted? It may be said that, on the ground of Suchness [i.e., the original enlightenment], ignorance [i.e., nonenlightenment] appears. Ignorance, the primary cause of the defiled state, permeates into Suchness. Because of this permeation a deluded mind results. Because of the deluded mind, [deluded thoughts further] permeate into ignorance. While the principle of Suchness is yet to be realized, [the deluded mind], developing thoughts [fashioned in the state] of nonenlightenment, predicates erroneously conceived objects of the senses and the mind. These erroneously conceived objects of the senses and the mind, the coordinating causes in [bringing about] the defiled state, permeate into the deluded mind and cause the deluded mind to attach itself to its thoughts, to create various [evil] karma, and to undergo all kinds of physical and mental suffering.

The permeation of the erroneously conceived objects of the senses and the mind is of two kinds. One is the permeation which accelerates [deluded] thoughts, and the other is the permeation which accelerates attachments.

The permeation of the deluded mind is of two kinds. One is the basic permeation by the "activating mind," which causes Arhats, Pratyeka-buddhas, and all Bodhisattvas to undergo the suffering of samsara, and the other is the permeation which accelerates [the activities of] the "object-discriminating consciousness" and which makes ordinary men suffer from the bondage of their karma.

The permeations of ignorance are of two kinds. One is the basic permeation, since it can put into operation the "activating mind," and the other is the permeation that develops perverse views and attachments, since it can put into operation the "object-discriminating consciousness."

b. PERMEATION OF SUCHNESS

How does the permeation [of Suchness] give rise to the pure state and continue uninterrupted? It may be said that there is the principle of Suchness, and it can permeate into ignorance. Through the force of this permeation, [Suchness] causes the deluded mind to loathe the suffering of samsara and to aspire for nirvana. Because this mind, though still deluded, is [now] possessed with loathing and aspiration, it permeates into Suchness [in that it induces Suchness to manifest itself]. Thus a man comes to believe in his essential nature, to know that what exists is the erroneous activity of the mind and that the world of objects in front of him is nonexistent, and to practice teachings to free himself [from the erroneously conceived world of objects]. He knows what is really so—that there is no world of objects in front of him—and therefore with various devices he practices courses by which to conform [himself to Suchness]. He will not attach himself to anything nor give rise to any [deluded] thoughts. Through the force of this permeation [of Suchness] over a long period of time, his ignorance ceases. Because of the cessation of ignorance, there will be no more rising of the [deluded activities of] mind. Because of the nonrising [of the deluded activities of mind], the world of objects [as previously conceived] ceases to be; because of the cessation of both the primary cause (ignorance) and the coordinating causes (objects), the marks of the [defiled] mind will all be nullified. This is called "gaining nirvana and accomplishing spontaneous acts."

The permeation [of Suchness] into the deluded mind is of two kinds. The first is the permeation into the "object-discriminating consciousness." [Because of this permeation], ordinary men and the Hinayanists come to loathe the suffering of samsara, and thereupon each, according to his capacity, gradually advances toward the highest enlightenment (Ch., *tao*). The second is the permeation into mind. [Because of this permeation], Bodhisattvas advance to nirvana rapidly and with aspiration and fortitude.

Two kinds of permeation of Suchness [into ignorance] can be identified. The first is the "permeation through manifestation of the essence [of Suchness], and the second is "the permeation through [external] influences."

(1) Permeation through Manifestation of the Essence of Suchness. [The essence of Suchness] is, from the beginningless beginning, endowed with the "perfect state of purity." It is provided with suprarational functions and the nature of manifesting itself. Because of these two reasons it permeates perpetually [into ignorance]. Through the force of [this permeation] it induces a man to loathe the suffering of samsara, to seek bliss in nirvana, and, believing that he has the principle of Suchness within himself, to make up his mind to exert himself.

Question: If this is so, then all sentient beings are endowed with Suchness and are equally permeated by it. Why is it that there are infinite varieties of believers and nonbelievers, and that there are some who believe sooner and some later? All of them should, knowing that they are endowed with the principle of Suchness, at once make an effort utilizing expedient means and should all equally attain nirvana.

Answer: Though Suchness is originally one, yet there are immeasurable and infinite [shades of] ignorance. From the very beginning ignorance is, because of its nature, characterized by diversity, and its degree of intensity is not uniform. Defilements, more numerous than the sands of the Ganges, come into being because of [the differences in intensity of] ignorance, and exist in manifold ways; defilements, such as the belief in the existence of atman and the indulgence in passion, develop because of ignorance and exist in different ways. All these defilements are brought about by ignorance, in an infinitely diversified manner in time. The Tathagatas alone know all about this.

In Buddhism there is [a teaching concerning] the primary cause and the coordinating causes. When the primary cause and the coordinating causes are sufficiently provided, there will be the perfection [of a result]. It is like the case of wood: though it possesses a [latent] fire nature which is the primary cause of its burning, it cannot be made to burn by itself unless men understand the situation and resort to means [of actualizing fire out of wood by kindling it]. In the same way a man, though he is in possession of the correct primary cause, [Suchness with] permeating force, cannot put an end to his defilements by himself alone and enter nirvana unless he is provided with coordinating causes, i.e., his encounters with the Buddhas, Bodhisattvas, or good spiritual friends. Even though coordinating causes from without may be sufficiently provided, if the pure principle [i.e., Suchness] within is lacking in the force of permeation, then a man cannot ultimately loathe the suffering of samsara and seek bliss in nirvana. However, if both the primary and the coordinating causes are sufficiently provided, then because of his possession of the force of permeation [of Suchness from within] and the compassionate protection of the Buddhas and Bodhisattvas [from without], he is able to develop a loathing for suffering, to believe that nirvana is real, and to cultivate his capacity for goodness. And when his cultivation of the capacity for goodness matures, he will as a result meet the Buddhas and Bodhisattvas and will be instructed, taught, benefitted, and given joy, and then he will be able to advance on the path to nirvana.

(2) Permeation through Influences. This is the force from without affecting men by providing coordinating causes. Such external coordinating causes have an infinite number of meanings. Briefly, they may be explained under two categories: namely, the specific and the general coordinating causes.

(a) The Specific Coordinating Causes. A man, from the time when he first aspires to seek enlightenment until he becomes an Enlightened One, sees or meditates on the Buddhas and Bodhisattvas [as they manifest themselves to him]; sometimes they appear as his family members, parents, or relatives, sometimes as servants, sometimes as close friends, or sometimes as enemies. Through all kinds of deeds and incalculable performances, such as the practice of the four acts of loving-kindness, etc., they exercise the force of permeation created by their great compassion, and are thus able to cause sentient beings to strengthen their capacity for goodness and are able to benefit them as they see or hear [about their needs]. This [specific] coordinating cause is of two kinds. One is immediate and enables a man to obtain deliverance quickly; and the other is remote and enables a man to obtain deliverance after a long time. The immediate and remote causes are again of two kinds: the causes which strengthen a man in his practices [of expedient means to help others], and those which enable him to obtain enlightenment (Ch., tao).

(b) The General Coordinating Causes. The Buddhas and Bodhisattvas all desire to liberate all men, spontaneously permeating them [with their spiritual influences] and never forsaking them. Through the power of the wisdom which is one [with Suchness], they manifest activities in response to [the needs of men] as they see and hear them. [Because of this indiscriminately permeating cause], men are all equally able, by means of concentration (samadhi), to see the Buddhas.

This permeation through the influence of the wisdom whose essence is one [with Suchness] is also divided into two categories [according to the types of recipients].

The one is yet to be united [with Suchness]. Ordinary men, the Hinayanists, and those Bodhisattvas who have just been initiated devote themselves to religious practices on the strength of their faith, being permeated by Suchness through their mind and consciousness. Not having obtained the indiscriminate mind, however, they are yet to be united with the essence [of Suchness], and not having obtained [the perfection of] the discipline of free acts, they are yet to be united with the influence [of Suchness].

The other is the already united [with Suchness]: Bodhisattvas who realize Dharmakaya have obtained undiscriminating mind [and are united with the essence of the Buddhas; they, having obtained free acts,] are united with the influence of the wisdom of the Buddhas. They singly devote themselves with spontaneity to their religious disciplines, on the strength of Suchness within; permeating into Suchness [so that Suchness will reclaim itself], they destroy ignorance.

Again, the defiled principle (dharma), from the beginningless beginning, continues perpetually to permeate until it perishes by the attainment of Buddhahood. But the permeation of the pure principle has no interruption and no ending. The reason is that the principle of Suchness is always permeating; therefore, when the deluded mind ceases to be, the Dharmakaya [i.e., Suchness, original enlightenment] will be manifest and will give rise to the permeation of the influence [of Suchness], and thus there will be no ending to it.

II. THE ESSENCE ITSELF AND THE ATTRIBUTES OF SUCHNESS, OR THE MEANINGS OF MAHA

A. THE GREATNESS OF THE ESSENCE OF SUCHNESS

[The essence of Suchness] knows no increase or decrease in ordinary men, the Hinayanists, the Bodhisattvas, or the Buddhas. It was not brought into existence in the beginning nor will it cease to be at the end of time; it is eternal through and through.

B. THE GREATNESS OF THE ATTRIBUTES OF SUCHNESS

From the beginning, Suchness in its nature is fully provided with all excellent qualities; namely, it is endowed with the light of great wisdom, [the qualities of] illuminating the entire universe, of true cognition and mind pure in its self-nature; of eternity, bliss, Self, and purity; of refreshing coolness, immutability, and freedom. It is endowed with [these excellent qualities], which outnumber the sands of the Ganges, which are not independent of, disjointed from, or different from [the essence of Suchness], and which are suprarational [attributes of] Buddhahood. Since it is endowed completely with all these, and is not lacking anything, it is called the *Tathagata-garbha* [when latent] and also the Dharmakaya of the Tathagata.

Question: It was explained before that the essence of Suchness is undifferentiated and devoid of all characteristics. Why is it, then, that you have described its essence as having these various excellent qualities?

Answer: Though it has, in reality, all these excellent qualities, it does not have any characteristics of differentiation; it retains its identity and is of one flavor; Suchness is solely one.

Question: What does this mean?

Answer: Since it is devoid of individuation, it is free from the characteristics of individuation; thus, it is one without any second.

Question: Then how can you speak of differentiation [i.e., the plurality of the characteristics of Suchness]?

Answer: In [contrast to] the characteristics of the phenomena of the "activating mind" [the characteristics of Suchness can] be inferred.

Question: How can they be inferred?

Answer: All things are originally of the mind only; they in fact transcend thoughts. Nevertheless, the deluded mind, in nonenlightenment, gives rise to [irrelevant] thoughts and predicates the world of objects. This being the case, we define [this mentality] as "the state of being destitute of wisdom (*avidya:* ignorance)." The essential nature of Mind is immutable [in that it does not give rise to any deluded thoughts, and, therefore, is the very opposite of ignorance]; hence, [it is spoken of as having the characteristic of] "the light of great wisdom."

When there is a particular perceiving act of the mind, objects [other than the objects being perceived] will remain unperceived. The essential nature of Mind is free from any partial perceiving; hence, [Suchness is spoken of as having the characteristic of] "illuminating the entire universe."

When the mind is in motion [stirred by ignorance], it is characterized by illusions and defilements, outnumbering the sands of the Ganges, such as lack of true cognition, absence of self-nature, impermanence, blisslessness, impurity, fever, anxiety, deterioration, mutation, and lack of freedom. By contrast to this, the essential nature of Mind, however, is motionless [i.e., undisturbed by ignorance]; therefore, it can be inferred that it must have various pure and excellent qualities, outnumbering the sands of the Ganges. But if the mind gives rise to [irrelevant thoughts] and further predicates the world of objects, it will continue to lack [these qualities]. All these numberless excellent qualities of the pure principle are none other than those of One Mind, and there is nothing to be sought after anew by thought. Thus, that which is fully endowed with them is called the Dharmakaya [when manifested] and the Tathagata-garbha [when latent].

c. The Greatness of the Influences of Suchness

The Buddha-Tathagatas, while in the stages of Bodhisattvahood, exercised great compassion, practiced *paramitas,* and accepted and transformed sentient beings. They took great vows, desiring to liberate all sentient beings through countless aeons until the end of future time, for they regarded all sentient beings as they regarded themselves. And yet, they never regarded them as [separate] sentient beings. Why? Because they truly knew that all sentient beings and they themselves were identical in Suchness and that there could be no distinction between them.

Because they possessed such great wisdom [which could be applied] to expedient means [in quest of enlightenment], they extinguished their ignorance and perceived the original Dharmakaya. Spontaneously performing incomprehensible activities, exercising manifold influences, they pervade everywhere in their identity with Suchness. Nevertheless, they reveal no marks of their influences that can be traced as such. Why? Because the Buddha-Tathagatas are no other than the Dharmakaya itself, and the embodiment of wisdom. [They belong to the realm of] the absolute truth, which transcends the world where the relative truth operates. They are free from any conventional activities. And yet, because of the fact that sentient beings receive benefit through seeing or hearing about them, their influences [i.e., of Suchness] can be spoken of [in relative terms].

The influences [of Suchness] are of two kinds. The first is that which is conceived by the mind of ordinary men and the followers of Hinayana [i.e., the influence of Suchness as reflected] in the "object-discriminating consciousness." This is called [the influence of Suchness in the form of] the "Transformation-body" (Nirmanakaya). Because they do not know that it is projected by the "evolving mind," they regard it as coming from without; they assume that it has a corporeal limitation because their understanding is limited.

The second is that which is conceived by the mind of the Bodhisattvas, from the first stage of aspiration to the highest stage, [i.e., the influence of Suchness as reflected] in the mentality which regards external objects as unreal. This is called [the influence of Suchness in the form of] the "Bliss-body" (Sambhogakaya). It has an infinite number of corporeal forms, each form has an infinite number of major marks, and each major mark has an infinite number of subtle marks. The land where it has its abode has innumerable adornments. It manifests itself without any bounds; [its manifestations are] inexhaustible and free from any limitations. It manifests itself in accordance with the needs [of sentient beings]; and yet it always remains firm without destroying or losing itself. These excellent qualities were perfected by the pure permeation acquired by the practice of *paramitas* and the suprarational permeation [of Suchness]. Since the influence is endowed with infinite attributes of bliss, it is spoken of as the "Bliss-body."

What is seen by ordinary men is only the coarse corporeal forms [of the manifestation of Suchness]. Depending upon where one is in the six transmigratory states, his vision of it will differ. [The visions of it conceived by] the unenlightened beings are not in a form of Bliss; this is the reason why it is called the "Transformation-body" [i.e., the body appearing in the likeness of the conceiver].

The Bodhisattvas in their first stage of aspiration and the others, because of their deep faith in Suchness, have a partial insight into [the nature of the influence of Suchness]. They know that the things [of the Bliss-body], such as its corporeal forms, major marks, adornments, etc., do not come from without or go away, that they are free from limitations, and that they are envisioned by mind alone and are not independent of Suchness. These Bodhisattvas, however, are not free from dualistic thinking, since they have yet to enter into the stage [where they gain complete realization] of the Dharmakaya. If they advance to the "stage of pure-heartedness," [the forms] they see will be subtler and the influences [of Suchness] will be more excellent than ever. When they leave the last stage of Bodhisattvahood, they will perfect their insight [into Suchness]. When they become free from the "activating mind" they will be free from the perceiving [of duality]. The Dharmakaya of the Buddhas knows no such thing as distinguishing this from that.

Question: If the Dharmakaya of the Buddhas is free from the manifestation of corporeal form, how can it appear in corporeal form?

Answer: Since the Dharmakaya is the essence of corporeal form, it is capable of appearing in corporeal form. The reason this is said is that from the beginning corporeal form and Mind have been nondual. Since the essential nature of corporeal form is identical with wisdom, the essence of corporeal form which has yet to be divided into tangible forms is called the "wisdom-body." Since the essential nature of wisdom is identical with corporeal form, [the essence of corporeal form which has yet to be divided into tangible forms] is called Dharmakaya pervading everywhere. Its manifested corporeal forms have no limitations. It can be freely manifested as an infinite number of Bodhisattvas, Buddhas of Bliss-body, and adornments in the ten quarters of the universe. Each of them has neither limitation nor interference. All of these are incomprehensible to the dualistic thinking of the [deluded] mind and consciousness, for they result from the free influence of Suchness.

III. FROM SAMSARA TO NIRVANA

Lastly, how to enter into the realm of Suchness from the realm of samsara will be revealed. Examining the five components, we find that they may be reduced to matter (object) and mind (subject). The objects of the five senses and of the mind are in the final analysis beyond what they are thought to be. And the mind itself is devoid of any form or mark and is, therefore, unobtainable as such, no matter where one may seek it. Just as a man, because he has lost his way, mistakes the east for the west, though the actual directions have not changed place, so people, because of their ignorance, assume Mind (Suchness) to be what they think it to be, though Mind in fact is unaffected [even if it is falsely predicated]. If a man is able to observe and understand that Mind is beyond what it is thought to be, then he will be able to conform to and enter the realm of Suchness.

CHAPTER TWO: THE CORRECTION OF EVIL ATTACHMENTS

All evil attachments originate from biased views; if a man is free from bias, he will be free from evil attachments. There are two kinds of biased view: one is the biased view held by those who are not free from the belief in atman [i.e., ordinary men]; the other is the biased view held by those who believe that the components of the world are real [i.e., the Hinayanists].

I. THE BIASED VIEWS HELD BY ORDINARY MEN

There are five kinds of biased views held by ordinary men which may be discussed.

Hearing that it is explained in the sutra that the Dharmakaya of the Tathagata is, in the final analysis, quiescent, like empty space, ordinary men think that the nature of the Tathagata is, indeed, the same as empty space, for they do not know [that the purpose of the sutra is] to uproot their adherence.

Question: How is this to be corrected?

Answer: [The way to correct this error is] to understand clearly that "empty space" is a delusive concept, the substance of which is nonexistent and unreal. It is merely predicated in relation to [its correlative] corporeal objects. If it is taken as a being [termed nonbeing, a negative being, then it should be discarded, because] it causes the mind to remain in samsara. In fact there are no external corporeal objects, because all objects are originally of the mind. And as long as there are no corporeal objects at all, "empty space" cannot be maintained. All objects are of the mind alone; but when illusions arise, [objects which are regarded as real] appear. When the mind is free from its deluded activities, then all objects [imagined as real] vanish of themselves. [What is real,] the one and true Mind, pervades everywhere. This is the final meaning of the Tathagata's great and comprehensive wisdom. [The Dharmakaya is, indeed,] unlike empty space."

Hearing that it is explained in the sutra that all things in the world, in the final analysis, are empty in their substance, and that nirvana or the principle of Suchness is also absolutely empty from the beginning and devoid of any characteristics, they, not knowing [that the purpose of the sutra is] to uproot their adherence, think that the essential nature of Suchness or nirvana is simply empty.

Question: How is this to be corrected?

Answer: [The way to correct this error is] to make clear that Suchness or the Dharmakaya is not empty, but is endowed with numberless excellent qualities.

Hearing that it is explained in the sutra that there is no increase or decrease in the *Tathagata-garbha* and that it is provided in its essence with all excellent qualities, they, not being able to understand this, think that in the *Tathagata-garbha* there is plurality of mind and matter.

Question: How is this to be corrected?

Answer: [They should be instructed that the statement in the sutra that "there is no increase or decrease in the *Tathagata-garbha*"] is made only in accordance with the [absolute] aspect of Suchness, and [the statement that "it is provided with all excellent qualities"] is made in accordance with [the pluralistic outlook held by the defiled minds in] samsara.

Hearing that it is explained in the sutra that all defiled states of samsara in the world exist on the ground of the *Tathagata-garbha* and that they are therefore not independent of Suchness, they, not understanding this, think that the *Tathagata-garbha* literally contains in itself all the defiled states of samsara in the world.

Question: How is this to be corrected?

[In order to correct this error it should be understood that] the *Tathagata-garbha*, from the beginning, contains only pure excellent qualities which, outnumbering the sands of the Ganges, are not independent of, severed from, or different from Suchness; that the soiled states of defilement which, outnumbering the sands of the Ganges, merely exist in illusion; are, from the beginning, nonexistent; and from the beginningless beginning have never been united with the *Tathagata-garbha*. It has never happened that the *Tathagata-garbha* contained deluded states in its essence and that it induced itself to realize [Suchness] in order to extinguish forever its deluded states.

Hearing that it is explained in the sutra that on the ground of the *Tathagata-garbha* there is samsara as well as the attainment of nirvana, they, without understanding this, think that there is a beginning for sentient beings. Since they suppose a beginning, they suppose also that the nirvana attained by the Tathagata has an end and that he will in turn become a sentient being.

Question: How is this to be corrected?

Answer: [The way to correct this error is to explain that] the *Tathagata-garbha* has no beginning, and that therefore ignorance has no beginning. If anyone asserts that sentient beings came into existence outside this triple world, he holds the view given in the scriptures of the heretics. Again, the *Tathagata-garbha* does not have an end; and the nirvana attained by the Buddhas, being one with it, likewise has no end.

II. The Biased Views Held by the Hinayanists

Because of their inferior capacity, the Tathagata preached to the Hinayanists only the doctrine of the nonexistence of atman and did not preach his doctrines in their entirety; as a result, the Hinayanists have come to believe that the five components, the constituents of samsaric existence, are real; being terrified at the thought of being subject to birth and death, they erroneously attach themselves to nirvana.

Question: How is this to be corrected?

Answer: [The way to correct this error is to make clear that] the five components are unborn in their essential nature and, therefore, are imperishable—that [what is made of the five components] is, from the beginning, in nirvana.

Finally, in order to be completely free from erroneous attachments, one should know that both the defiled and the pure states are relative and have no particular marks of their own-being that can be discussed. Thus, all things from the beginning are neither matter nor mind, neither wisdom nor consciousness, neither being nor non-being; they are ultimately inexplicable. And yet they are still spoken of. It should be understood that the Tathagatas, applying their expedient means, make use of conventional speech in a provisional manner in order to guide people, so that they can be free from their deluded thoughts and can return to Suchness; for if anyone thinks of anything [as real and absolute in its own right], he causes his mind to be [trapped] in samsara and consequently he cannot enter [the state filled with] true insight [i.e., enlightenment].

CHAPTER THREE: ANALYSIS OF THE TYPES OF ASPIRATION FOR ENLIGHTENMENT, OR THE MEANINGS OF YANA

All Bodhisattvas aspire to the enlightenment (*bodhi;* Ch., *tao*) realized by all the Buddhas, disciplining themselves to this end, and advancing toward it. Briefly, three types of aspiration for enlightenment can be distinguished. The first is the aspiration for enlightenment through the perfection of faith. The second is the aspiration for enlightenment through understanding and through deeds. The third is the aspiration for enlightenment through insight.

I. THE ASPIRATION FOR ENLIGHTENMENT THROUGH THE PERFECTION OF FAITH

Question: By whom and through what kind of discipline can faith be perfected so that the aspiration for enlightenment may be developed?

Answer: Among those who belong to the group of the undetermined, there are some who, by virtue of their excellent capacity for goodness developed through permeation, believe in the [law of] retribution of karma and observe the ten precepts. They loathe the suffering of samsara and wish to seek the supreme enlightenment. Having been able to meet the Buddhas, they serve them, honor them, and practice the faith. Their faith will be perfected after ten thousand aeons. Their aspiration for enlightenment will be developed either through the instruction of the Buddhas and the Bodhisattvas, or because of their great compassion [toward their suffering fellow beings], or from their desire to preserve the good teaching from extinction. Those who are thus able to develop their aspiration through the perfection of faith will enter the group of the determined and will never retrogress. They are called the ones who are united with the correct cause [for enlightenment] and who abide among those who belong to the Tathagata family.

There are, however, people [among those who belong to the group of the undetermined] whose capacity for goodness is slight and whose defilements, having accumulated from the far distant past, are deep-rooted. Though they may also meet the Buddhas and honor them, they will develop the potentiality merely to be born as men, as dwellers in heaven, or as followers of the Hinayana. Even if they should seek after the Mahayana, they would sometimes progress and sometimes regress because of the inconsistent nature of their capacity. And also there are some who honor the Buddhas and who, before ten thousand aeons have passed, will develop an aspiration because of some favorable circumstances. These circumstances may be the viewing of the Buddhas' corporeal forms, the honoring of monks, the receiving of instructions from the followers of the Hinayana, or the imitation of others' aspiration. But these types of aspiration are all inconsistent, for if the men who hold them meet with unfavorable circumstances, they will relapse and fall back into the stage of attainment of the followers of the Hinayana.

Now, in developing the aspiration for enlightenment through the perfection of faith, what kind of mind is to be cultivated? Briefly speaking, three kinds can be discussed. The first is the mind characterized by straightforwardness, for it correctly meditates on the principle of Suchness. The second is the mind of profoundness, for there is no limit to its joyful accumulation of all kinds of goodness. The third is the mind filled with great compassion, for it wishes to uproot the sufferings of all sentient beings.

Question: Earlier it has been explained that the World of Reality is one, and that the essence of the Buddhas has no duality. Why is it that people do not meditate [of their own accord] on Suchness alone, but must learn to practice good deeds?

Answer: Just as a precious gem is bright and pure in its essence but is marred by impurities, [so is a man.] Even if he meditates on his precious nature, unless he polishes it in various ways by expedient means, he will never be able to purify it. The principle of Suchness in men is absolutely pure in its essential nature, but is filled with immeasurable impurity of defilements. Even if a man meditates on Suchness, unless he makes an effort to be permeated by it in various ways by applying expedient means, he certainly cannot become pure. Since the state of impurity is limitless, pervading throughout all states of being, it is necessary to counteract and purify it by means of the practice of all kinds of good deeds. If a man does so, he will naturally return to the principle of Suchness.

As to the expedient means, there are, in short, four kinds: The first is the fundamental means to be practiced. That is to say, a man is to meditate on the fact that all things in their essential nature are unborn, divorcing himself from deluded views so that he does not abide in samsara. [At the same time] he is to meditate on the fact that all things are [the products of] the union of the primary and coordinating causes, and that the effect of karma will never be lost. [Accordingly] he is to cultivate great compassion, practice meritorious deeds, and accept and transform sentient beings equally without abiding in nirvana, for he is to conform himself to [the functions of] the essential nature of Reality (dharmata) which knows no fixation.

The second is the means of stopping [evils]. The practice of developing a sense of shame and repentance can stop all evils and prevent them from growing, for one is to conform oneself to the faultlessness of the essential nature of Reality.

The third is the means of increasing the capacity for goodness that has already been developed. That is to say, a man should diligently honor and pay homage to the Three Treasures, and should praise, rejoice in, and beseech the Buddhas. Because of the sincerity of his love and respect for the Three Treasures, his faith will be strengthened and he will be able to seek the unsurpassed enlightenment. Furthermore, being protected by the Buddha, the Dharma, and the Sangha, he will be able to wipe out the hindrances of evil karma. His capacity for goodness will not retrogress because he will be conforming himself to the essential nature of Reality, which is free from hindrances produced by stupidity.

The fourth is the means of the great vow of universal salvation. This is to take a vow that one will liberate all sentient beings, down to the last one, no matter how long it may take to cause them to attain the perfect nirvana, for one will be conforming one-self to the essential nature of Reality which is characterized by the absence of discontinuity. The essential nature of Reality is all-embracing, and pervades all sentient beings; it is everywhere the same and one without duality; it does not distinguish this from that, because it is, in the final analysis, in the state of quiescence.

When a Bodhisattva develops this aspiration for enlightenment [through faith], he will be able, to a certain extent, to realize the Dharmakaya. Because of this realization of the Dharmakaya, and because he is led by the force of the vow [that he made to liberate all sentient beings], he is able to present eight types of manifestation of himself for the benefit of all sentient beings. These are: the descent from the Tushita heaven; the entrance into a human womb; the stay in the womb; the birth; the renunciation; the attainment of enlightenment; the turning of the wheel of the Dharma (doctrine); and the entrance into nirvana. However, such a Bodhisattva cannot be said [to have perfectly realized] the Dharmakaya, for he has not yet completely destroyed the outflowing evil karma which has been accumulated from his numberless existences in the past. He must suffer some slight misery deriving from the state of his birth. However, this is due not to his being fettered by karma, but to his freely made decision to carry out the great vow [of universal salvation in order to understand the suffering of others].

It is said in a sutra that there are some [Bodhisattvas of this kind] who may regress and fall into evil states of existence, but this does not refer to a real regression. It says this merely in order to frighten and stir the heroism of the newly initiated Bodhisattvas who have not yet joined the group of the determined, and who may be indolent.

Furthermore, as soon as this aspiration has been aroused in the Bodhisattvas, they leave cowardice far behind them and are not afraid even of falling into the stage of the followers of the Hinayana. Even though they hear that they must suffer extreme hardship for innumerable aeons before they may attain nirvana, they do not feel any fear, for they believe and know that from the beginning all things are of themselves in nirvana.

II. THE ASPIRATION FOR ENLIGHTENMENT THROUGH UNDERSTANDING AND DEEDS

It should be understood that this type of aspiration is even more excellent than the former. Because the Bodhisattvas [who cherish this aspiration] are those who are about to finish the first term of the incalculable aeons since the time when they first had the correct faith, they have come to have a profound understanding of the principle of Suchness and to entertain no attachment to their attainments obtained through discipline.

Knowing that the essential nature of Reality is free from covetousness, they, in conformity to it, devote themselves to the perfection of charity. Knowing that the essential nature of Reality is free from the defilements which originate from the desires of the five senses, they, in conformity to it, devote themselves to the perfection of precepts. Knowing that the essential nature of Reality is without suffering and free from anger and anxiety, they, in conformity to it, devote themselves to the perfection of forbearance. Knowing that the essential nature of Reality does not have any distinction of body and mind and is free from indolence, they, in conformity to it, devote themselves to the perfection of zeal. Knowing that the essential nature of Reality is always calm and free from confusion in its essence, they, in conformity to it, devote themselves to the perfection of meditation. Knowing that the essential nature of Reality is always characterized by gnosis and is free from ignorance, they, in conformity to it, devote themselves to the perfection of wisdom.

III. THE ASPIRATION FOR ENLIGHTENMENT THROUGH INSIGHT

[As for the Bodhisattvas of this group, who range] from the "stage of pure-heartedness" to the "last stage of Bodhisattvahood," what object do they realize? They realize Suchness. We speak of it as an object because of the "evolving mind," but in fact there is no object in this realization [that can be stated in terms of a subject-object relationship]. There is only the insight into Suchness [transcending both the seer and the seen]; we call [this the experience of] the Dharmakaya.

The Bodhisattvas of this group can, in an instant of thought, go to all worlds of the universe, honor the Buddhas, and ask them to turn the wheel of the Dharma. In order to guide and benefit all men, they do not rely on words. Sometimes, for the sake of weak-willed men, they show how to attain perfect enlightenment quickly by skipping over the stages [of the Bodhisattva]. And sometimes, for the sake of indolent men, they say that men may attain enlightenment at the end of numberless aeons. Thus they can demonstrate innumerable expedient means and suprarational feats. But in reality all these Bodhisattvas are the same in that they are alike in their lineage, their capacity, their aspiration, and their realization [of Suchness]; therefore, there is no such thing as skipping over the stages, for all Bodhisattvas must pass through the three terms of innumerable aeons [before they can fully attain enlightenment]. However, because of the differences in the various worlds of beings, and in the objects of seeing and hearing, as well as in the capacity, desires, and nature of the various beings, there are also different ways of teaching them what to practice.

The characteristics of the aspiration for enlightenment entertained by a Bodhisattva belonging to this group can be identified in terms of the three subtle modes of mind. The first is the true mind, for it is free from [false intellectual] discrimination. The second is the mind [capable] of [applying] expedient means, for it pervades everywhere spontaneously and benefits sentient beings. The third is the mind [subject to the influence] of karma [operating] in subconsciousness, for it appears and disappears in the most subtle ways.

Again, a Bodhisattva of this group, when he brings his excellent qualities to perfection, manifests himself in the heaven of Akanishta as the highest physical being in the world. Through wisdom united with [original enlightenment or Suchness] in an instant of thought, he suddenly extinguishes ignorance. Then he is called [the one who has obtained] all-embracing knowledge. Performing suprarational acts spontaneously, he can manifest himself everywhere in the universe and benefit all sentient beings.

Question: Since space is infinite, worlds are infinite. Since worlds are infinite, beings are infinite. Since beings are infinite, the variety of their mentalities must also be infinite. The objects of the senses and the mind must therefore be limitless, and it is difficult to know and understand them all. If ignorance is destroyed, there will be no thoughts in the mind. How then can a comprehension [that has no content] be called "all-embracing knowledge"?

Answer: All objects are originally of One Mind and are beyond thought determination. Because unenlightened people perceive objects in their illusion, they impose

Prayer wheels in the Puning Temple, Chengde, Hebei Province. In Tibetan
Buddhism, prayer wheels are rotated to spread spiritual blessings to all beings
and invoke good karma in the next life. (*Forrest E. Baird*)

limitations in their mind. Since they erroneously develop these thought determinations,
which do not correspond to Reality *(dharmata)*, they are unable to reach any inclusive
comprehension. The Buddha-Tathagatas are free from all perverse views and thoughts
[that block correct vision; therefore,] there are no corners into which their comprehension does not penetrate. Their Mind is true and real; therefore, it is no other than the essential nature of all things. [The Buddhas], because of their very nature, can shed light
on all objects conceived in illusion. They are endowed with an influence of great wisdom [that functions as the application] of innumerable expedient means.
Accommodating themselves to the capacity of understanding of various sentient beings,
they can reveal to them the manifold meanings of the doctrine. This is the reason they
may be called those who have "all-embracing knowledge."

Question: If the Buddhas are able to perform spontaneous acts, to manifest themselves everywhere, and to benefit all sentient beings, then the sentient beings should all
be able, by seeing their physical forms, by witnessing their miracles, or by hearing their
preachings, to gain benefit. Why is it then that most people in this world have not been
able to see the Buddhas?

Answer: The Dharmakaya of all the Buddhas, being one and the same everywhere, is omnipresent. Since the Buddhas are free from any fixation of thought, their
acts are said to be "spontaneous." They reveal themselves in accordance with the mentalities of all the various sentient beings. The mind of the sentient being is like a mirror.

Just as a mirror cannot reflect images if it is coated with dirt, so the Dharmakaya cannot appear in the mind of the sentient being if it is coated with the dirt [of defilements].

PART FOUR: ON FAITH AND PRACTICE

Having already discussed interpretation, we will now present a discussion of faith and practice. This discussion is intended for those who have not yet joined the group of beings who are determined to attain enlightenment.

ON FOUR FAITHS

Question: What kind of faith [should a man have] and how should he practice it?

Answer: Briefly, there are four kinds of faith. The first is the faith in the *Ultimate Source*. Because [of this faith] a man comes to meditate with joy on the principle of Suchness. The second is the faith in the numberless excellent qualities of the *Buddhas*. Because [of this faith] a man comes to meditate on them always, to draw near to them in fellowship, to honor them, and to respect them, developing his capacity for goodness and seeking after the all-embracing knowledge. The third is the faith in the great benefits of the *Dharma* (Teaching). Because [of this faith] a man comes constantly to remember and practice various disciplines leading to enlightenment. The fourth is the faith in the *Sangha* (Buddhist Community) whose members are able to devote themselves to the practice of benefitting both themselves and others. Because [of this faith] a man comes to approach the assembly of Bodhisattvas constantly and with joy and to seek instruction from them in the correct practice.

ON FIVE PRACTICES

There are five ways of practice which will enable a man to perfect his faith. They are the practices of charity, [observance of] precepts, patience, zeal, and cessation [of illusions] and clear observation.

Question: How should a man practice charity?

Answer: If he sees anyone coming to him begging, he should give him the wealth and other things in his possession in so far as he is able; thus, while freeing himself from greed and avarice, he causes the beggar to be joyful. Or, if he sees one who is in hardship, in fear, or in grave danger, he should give him freedom from fear in so far as he is able. If a man comes to seek instruction in the teaching, he should, according to his ability and understanding, explain it by the use of expedient means. In doing so, however, he should not expect any fame, material gain, or respect, but he should think only of benefitting himself and others alike and of extending the merit [that he gains from the practice of charity] toward the attainment of enlightenment.

Question: How should he practice the [observance of] precepts?

Answer: He is not to kill, to steal, to commit adultery, to be double-tongued, to slander, to lie, or to utter exaggerated speech. He is to free himself from greed, jealousy, cheating, deceit, flattery, crookedness, anger, hatred, and perverse views. If he happens to be a monk [or nun] who has renounced family life, he should also, in order to cut off and suppress defilements, keep himself away from the hustle and bustle of the world and, always residing in solitude, should learn to be content with the least desire and should practice vigorous ascetic disciplines. He should be frightened and filled with awe by any slight fault and should feel shame and repent. He should not take lightly any of the Tathagata's precepts. He should guard himself from slander and from showing dislike so as not to rouse people in their delusion to commit any offense or sin.

Question: How should he practice patience?

Answer: He should be patient with the vexatious acts of others and should not harbor thoughts of vengeance, and he should also be patient in matters of gain or loss, honor or dishonor, praise or blame, suffering or joy, etc.

Question: How should he practice zeal?

Answer: He should not be sluggish in doing good, he should be firm in his resolution, and he should purge himself of cowardice. He should remember that from the far distant past he has been tormented in vain by all of the great sufferings of body and mind. Because of this he should diligently practice various meritorious acts, benefitting himself and others, and liberate himself quickly from suffering. Even if a man practices faith, because he is greatly hindered by the evil karma derived from the grave sins of previous lives, he may be troubled by the evil Tempter (Mara) and his demons, or entangled in all sorts of worldly affairs, or afflicted by the suffering of disease. There are a great many hindrances of this kind. He should, therefore, be courageous and zealous, and at the six four-hour intervals of the day and night should pay homage to the Buddhas, repent with sincere heart, beseech the Buddhas [for their guidance], rejoice in the happiness of others, and direct all the merits [thus acquired] to the attainment of enlightenment. If he never abandons these practices, he will be able to avoid the various hindrances as his capacity for goodness increases.

Question: How should he practice cessation and clear observation?

Answer: What is called "cessation" means to put a stop to all characteristics (*lakshana*) of the world [of sense objects and of the mind], because it means to follow the *shamatha* (tranquility) method of meditation. What is called "clear observation" means to perceive distinctly the characteristics of the causally conditioned phenomena (samsara), because it means to follow the *vipashyana* (discerning) method of meditation.

Question: How should he follow these?

Answer: He should step by step practice these two aspects and not separate one from the other, for only then will both be perfected.

THE PRACTICE OF CESSATION

Should there be a man who desires to practice "cessation," he should stay in a quiet place and sit erect in an even temper. [His attention should be focused] neither on breathing nor on any form or color, nor on empty space, earth, water, fire, wind, nor even on what has been seen, heard, remembered, or conceived. All thoughts, as soon as they are conjured up, are to be discarded, and even the thought of discarding them is to be put away, for all things are essentially [in the state of] transcending thoughts, and are not to be created from moment to moment nor to be extinguished from moment to moment; [thus one is to conform to the essential nature of Reality *(dharmata)* through this practice of cessation]. And it is not that he should first meditate on the objects of the senses in the external world and then negate them with his mind, the mind that has meditated on them. If the mind wanders away, it should be brought back and fixed in "correct thought." It should be understood that this "correct thought" is [the thought that] whatever is, is mind only and that there is no external world of objects [as conceived]; even this mind is devoid of any marks of its own [which would indicate its substantiality] and therefore is not substantially conceivable as such at any moment.

Even if he arises from his sitting position and engages in other activities, such as going, coming, advancing, or standing still, he should at all times be mindful [of the application] of expedient means [of perfecting "cessation"], conform [to the immobile principle of the essential nature of Reality], and observe and examine [the resulting experiences]. When this discipline is well mastered after a long period of practice, [the ideations of] his mind will be arrested. Because of this, his power of executing "cessation" will gradually be intensified and become highly effective, so that he will conform himself to, and be able to be absorbed into, the "concentration (samadhi) of Suchness." Then his defilements, deep though they may be, will be suppressed and his faith strengthened; he will quickly attain the state in which there will be no retrogression. But those who are skeptical, who lack faith, who speak ill [of the teaching of the Buddha], who have committed grave sins, who are hindered by their evil karma, or who are arrogant or indolent are to be excluded; these people are incapable of being absorbed into [the samadhi of Suchness].

Next, as a result of this samadhi, a man realizes the oneness of the World of Reality (dharmadhatu), i.e., the sameness everywhere and nonduality of the Dharmakaya of all the Buddhas and the bodies of sentient beings. This is called "the samadhi of one movement." It should be understood that [the samadhi of] Suchness is the foundation of [all other] samadhi. If a man keeps practicing it, then he will gradually be able to develop countless other kinds of samadhi.

If there is a man who lacks the capacity for goodness, he will be confused by the evil Tempter, by heretics and by demons. Sometimes these beings will appear in dreadful forms while he is sitting in meditation, and at other times they will manifest themselves in the shapes of handsome men and women. [In such a case] he should meditate on [the principle of] "mind only," and then these objects will vanish and will not trouble him any longer. Sometimes they may appear as the images of heavenly beings or Bodhisattvas, and assume also the figure of the Tathagata, furnished with all the major and minor marks; or they may expound the spells or preach charity, the precepts, patience, zeal, meditation, and wisdom; or they may discourse on how the true nirvana is the state of universal emptiness, of the nonexistence of characteristics, vows, hatreds, affections, causes, and effects; and of absolute nothingness. They may also teach him the knowledge of his own past and future states of existence, the method of reading other men's minds, and perfect mastery of speech, causing him to be covetous and attached to worldly fame and profit; or they may cause him to be frequently moved to joy and anger and thus to have unsteadiness of character, being at times very kind-hearted, very drowsy, very ill, or lazy-minded; or at other times becoming suddenly zealous, and then afterward lapsing into negligence; or developing a lack of faith, a great deal of doubt, and a great deal of anxiety; or abandoning his fundamental excellent practices [toward religious perfection] and devoting himself to miscellaneous religious acts, or being attached to worldly affairs which involve him in many ways; or sometimes they may cause him to experience a certain semblance of various kinds of samadhi, which are all the attainments of heretics and are not the true samadhi; or sometimes they may cause him to remain in samadhi for one, two, three, or up to seven days, feeling comfort in his body and joy in his mind, being neither hungry nor thirsty, partaking of natural, fragrant, and delicious drinks and foods, which induce him to increase his attachment to them; or at other times they may cause him to eat without any restraint, now a great deal, now only a little, so that the color of his face changes accordingly.

For these reasons, he who practices ["cessation"] should be discreet and observant, lest his mind fall into the net of evil [doctrine]. He should be diligent in abiding in "correct thought," neither grasping nor attaching himself to [anything]; if he does so, he will be able to keep himself far away from the hindrance of these evil influences.

He should know that the samadhi of the heretics are not free from perverse views, craving, and arrogance, for the heretics are covetously attached to fame, profit, and the respect of the world. The samadhi of Suchness is the samadhi in which one is not arrested by the activity of viewing [a subject] nor by the experiencing of objects [in the midst of meditation]; even after concentration one will be neither indolent nor arrogant and one's defilements will gradually decrease. There has never been a case in which an ordinary man, without having practiced this samadhi, was still able to join the group that is entitled to become Tathagatas. Those who practice the various types of dhyana (meditation) and samadhi which are popular in the world will develop much attachment to their flavors and will be bound to the triple world because of their perverse view that atman is real. They are therefore the same as heretics, for as they depart from the protection of their good spiritual friends, they turn to heretical views.

Next, he who practices this samadhi diligently and wholeheartedly will gain ten kinds of advantages in this life. First, he will always be protected by the Buddhas and the Bodhisattvas of the ten directions. Second, he will not be frightened by the Tempter and his evil demons. Third, he will not be deluded or confused by the ninety-five kinds of heretics and wicked spirits. Fourth, he will keep himself far away from slanders of the profound teaching [of the Buddha], and will gradually diminish the hindrances derived from grave sins. Fifth, he will destroy all doubts and wrong views on enlightenment. Sixth, his faith in the Realm of the Tathagata will grow. Seventh, he will be free from sorrow and remorse and in the midst of samsara will be full of vigor and undaunted. Eighth, having a gentle heart and forsaking arrogance, he will not be vexed by others. Ninth, even if he has not yet experienced samadhi, he will be able to decrease his defilements in all places and at all times, and he will not take pleasure in the world. Tenth, if he experiences samadhi, he will not be startled by any sound from without.

Now, if he practices "cessation" only, then his mind will be sunk [in self-complacency] and he will be slothful; he will not delight in performing good acts but will keep himself far away from the exercise of great compassion. It is, therefore, necessary to practice "clear observation" [as well].

THE PRACTICE OF CLEAR OBSERVATION

He who practices "clear observation" should observe that all conditioned phenomena in the world are unstationary and are subject to instantaneous transformation and destruction; that all activities of the mind arise and are extinguished from moment to moment; and that, therefore, all of these induce suffering. He should observe that all that had been conceived in the past was as hazy as a dream, that all that is being conceived in the present is like a flash of lightning, and that all that will be conceived in the future will be like clouds that rise up suddenly. He should also observe that the physical existences of all living beings in the world are impure and that among these various filthy things there is not a single one that can be sought after with joy.

He should reflect in the following way: all living beings, from the beginningless beginning, because they are permeated by ignorance, have allowed their mind to remain in samsara; they have already suffered all the great miseries of the body and mind, they are at present under incalculable pressure and constraint, and their sufferings in the future will likewise be limitless. These sufferings are difficult to forsake, difficult to shake off, and yet these beings are unaware [that they are in such a state]; for this, they are greatly to be pitied.

After reflecting in this way, he should pluck up his courage and make a great vow to this effect: may my mind be free from discriminations so that I may practice all of the various meritorious acts everywhere in the ten directions; may I, to the end of the future, by applying limitless expedient means, help all suffering sentient beings so that they may obtain the bliss of nirvana, the ultimate goal.

Having made such a vow, he must, in accordance with his capacity and without faltering, practice every kind of good at all times and at all places and not be slothful in his mind. Except when he sits in concentration in the practice of "cessation," he should at all times reflect upon what should be done and what should not be done.

Whether walking, standing, sitting, lying, or rising, he should practice both "cessation" and "clear observation" side by side. That is to say, he is to meditate upon the fact that things are unborn in their essential nature; but at the same time he is to meditate upon the fact that good and evil karma, produced by the combination of the primary cause and the coordinating causes, and the retributions [of karma] in terms of pleasure, pain, etc., are neither lost nor destroyed. Though he is to meditate on the retribution of good and evil karma produced by the primary and coordinating causes [i.e., he is to practice "clear observation"], he is also to meditate on the fact that the essential nature [of things] is unobtainable [by intellectual analysis]. The practice of "cessation" will enable ordinary men to cure themselves of their attachments to the world, and will enable the followers of the Hinayana to forsake their views, which derive from cowardice. The practice of "clear observation" will cure the followers of the Hinayana of the fault of having narrow and inferior minds which bring forth no great compassion, and will free ordinary men from their failure to cultivate the capacity for goodness. For these reasons, both "cessation" and "clear observation" are complementary and inseparable. If the two are not practiced together, then one cannot enter the path to enlightenment.

Next, suppose there is a man who learns this teaching for the first time and wishes to seek the correct faith but lacks courage and strength. Because he lives in this world of suffering, he fears that he will not always be able to meet the Buddhas and honor them personally, and that, faith being difficult to perfect, he will be inclined to fall back. He should know that the Tathagatas have an excellent expedient means by which they can protect his faith: that is, through the strength of wholehearted meditation on the Buddha, he will in fulfillment of his wishes be able to be born in the Buddhaland beyond, to see the Buddha always, and to be forever separated from the evil states of existence. It is as the sutra says: "If a man meditates wholly on Amitabha Buddha in the world of the Western Paradise and wishes to be born in that world, directing all the goodness he has cultivated [toward that goal], then he will be born there." Because he will see the Buddha at all times, he will never fall back. If he meditates on the Dharmakaya, the Suchness of the Buddha, and with diligence keeps practicing [the meditation], he will be able to be born there in the end because he abides in the correct samadhi.

PART FIVE: ENCOURAGEMENT OF PRACTICE AND THE BENEFITS THEREOF

As has already been explained in the preceding sections, the Mahayana is the secret treasury of the Buddhas. Should there be a man who wishes to obtain correct faith in the profound Realm of the Tathagata and to enter the path of Mahayana, putting far away from himself any slandering [of the teaching of Buddha], he should lay hold of this treatise, deliberate on it, and practice it; in the end he will be able to reach the unsurpassed enlightenment.

If a man, after having heard this teaching, does not feel any fear or weakness, it should be known that such a man is certain to carry on the lineage of the Buddha and to receive the prediction of the Buddha that he will obtain enlightenment. Even if a man were able to reform all living beings, throughout all the systems in the universe and to induce them to practice the ten precepts, he still would not be superior to a man who reflects correctly upon this teaching even for the time spent on a single meal, for the excellent, qualities which the latter is able to obtain are unspeakably superior to those which the former may obtain.

If a man takes hold of this treatise and reflects on and practices [the teachings given in it] only for one day and one night, the excellent qualities he will gain will be boundless and indescribable. Even if all the Buddhas of the ten directions were to praise these excellent qualities for incalculably long periods of time, they could never reach the end of their praise, for the excellent qualities of the Reality (*dharmata*) are infinite and the excellent qualities gained by this man will accordingly be boundless.

If, however, there is a man who slanders and does not believe in this treatise, for an incalculable number of aeons he will undergo immense suffering for his fault. Therefore all people should reverently believe in it and not slander it, [for slander and lack of faith] will gravely injure oneself as well as others and will lead to the destruction of the lineage of the Three Treasures.

Through this teaching all Tathagatas have gained nirvana, and through the practice of it all Bodhisattvas have obtained Buddha-wisdom. It should be known that it was by means of this teaching that the Bodhisattvas in the past were able to perfect their pure faith; that it is by means of this teaching that the Bodhisattvas of the present are perfecting their pure faith; and that it is by means of this teaching that the Bodhisattvas of the future will perfect their pure faith. Therefore men should diligently study and practice it.

Profound and comprehensive are the great principles of the Buddha,
    Which I have now summarized as faithfully as possible.
    May whatever excellent qualities I have gained from this endeavor
    In accordance with Reality be extended for the benefit of all beings.

FA-TSANG, TREATISE
ON THE GOLDEN LION

1. Clarifying the fact that things arise through causation

It means that gold has no nature of its own. As a result of the conditioning of the skillful craftsman, the character of the lion consequently arises. This arising is purely due to causes. Therefore it is called arising through causation.

2. Distinguishing matter and Emptiness

It means that the character of the lion is unreal; there is only real gold. The lion is not existent, but the substance of the gold is not nonexistent. Therefore they are [separately] called matter and Emptiness. Furthermore, Emptiness has no character of its own; it shows itself by means of matter. This does not obstruct its illusory existence. Therefore they are [separately] called matter and Emptiness.

3. Simply stating the Three Natures

The lion exists because of our feelings. This is called [the nature] arising from vast imagination. The lion seems to exist. This is called [the nature of] dependence on others (gold and craftsman) [for production]. The nature of the gold does not change. This is therefore called [the nature of] Perfect Reality.

4. Showing the nonexistence of characters

It means that as the gold takes in the lion in its totality, apart from the gold there is no character of the lion to be found. Therefore it is called the nonexistence of characters.

5. Explaining non–coming-into-existence

It means that the moment when we see the lion come into existence, it is only gold that comes into existence. There is nothing apart from the gold. Although the lion comes into existence and goes out of existence, the substance of the gold at bottom neither increases nor decreases. Therefore we say that [dharmas] do not come into existence [nor go out of existence].

6. Discussing the Five Doctrines

(1) Although the lion is a dharma produced through causation, and comes into and goes out of existence every moment, there is really no character of the lion to be found. This is called the Small Vehicle (Hinayana) Doctrine of Ordinary Disciples [that is, the Hinayana schools].

(2) These dharmas produced through causation are each without self-nature. It is absolutely Emptiness. This is called the Initial Doctrine of the Great Vehicle (Mahayana) [that is, the Three-Treatise and Conscious-Only Schools].

(3) Although there is absolutely only Emptiness, this does not prevent the illusory dharmas from being clearly what they are. The two characters of coming into existence through causation and dependent existence coexist. This is called the Final Doctrine of the Great Vehicle [that is, the T'ien-tai School].

(4) These two characters eliminate each other and both perish, and [consequently] neither [the products of] our feelings nor false existence remain. Neither of them has any more power, and both Emptiness and existence perish. Names and descriptions will be completely discarded and the mind will be at rest and have no more attachment. This is called the Great Vehicle's Doctrine of Sudden Enlightenment [that is, the Zen School].

(5) When the feelings have been eliminated and true substance revealed, all becomes an undifferentiated mass. Great function then arises in abundance, and whenever it does, there is surely Perfect Reality. All phenomena are in great profusion, and are interfused but not mixed (losing their own identity). The all is the one, for both are similar in being nonexistent in nature. And the one is the all, for [the relation between] cause and effect is perfectly clear. As the power [of the one] and the function [of the many] embraces each other, their expansion and contraction are free and at ease. This is called the Rounded (inclusive) Doctrine of the One [all-inclusive] Vehicle. [The Hua-yen School.]

7. Mastering the Ten Mysteries [Gates]

(1) The gold and the lion exist simultaneously, all-perfect and complete in their possession. This is called the gate of simultaneous completion and mutual correspondence.

(2) If the eye of the lion completely takes in the lion, then the all (the whole lion) is purely the eye (the one). If the ear completely takes in the lion, then the all is purely the ear. If all the sense organs simultaneously take in [the lion] and all are complete in their possession, then each of them is at the same time mixed (involving others) and pure (being itself), thus constituting the perfect storehouse. This is called the gate of full possession of the attributes of purity and mixture by the various storehouses.

(3) The gold and the lion are mutually compatible in their formation, the one and the many not obstructing each other. In this situation the principle (the one or the gold) and facts (the many or the lion) are each different, but whether the one or the many, each remains in its own position. This is called the gate of mutual compatibility and difference between the one and the many.

(4) Since the various organs and each and every hair of the lion completely take in the lion by means of the gold, each and every one of them penetrates the whole. The eye of the lion is its ear, its ear is its nose, its nose is its tongue, and its tongue is its body. They each exist freely and easily, one not hindering or obstructing the other. This is called the gate of mutual identification of all dharmas existing freely and easily.

(5) If we look at the lion [as lion], there is only the lion and no gold. This means that the lion is manifest while the gold is hidden. If we look at the gold, there is only the gold and no lion. This means that the gold is manifest while the lion is hidden. If we look at them both, then both are manifest and both hidden. Being hidden, they are secret, and being manifest, they are evident. This is called the gate of the completion of the secret, the hidden, and the manifest.

(6) The gold and the lion may be hidden or manifest, one or many, definitely pure or definitely mixed, powerful or powerless, the one or the other. The principal and the companion mutually shine. Principle and fact appear together and are completely compatible with each other. They do not obstruct each other's peaceful existence , and thus the subtle and the minute are accomplished. This is called the gate of the compatibility and peaceful existence of the subtle and the minute.

(7) In each of the lion's eyes, ears, limbs, joints, and in each and every hair, there is the golden lion. All the lions embraced by all the single hairs simultaneously and instantaneously enter a single hair. Thus in each and every hair there are an infinite number of lions, and in addition all the single hairs, together with their infinite number of

The Yonghe Lamasery in Beijing. This building in the complex houses an 18 meter-high statue of the Buddha, said to be made from a single piece of sandalwood. (*Forrest E. Baird*)

lions, in turn enter into a single hair. In this way the geometric progression is infinite, like the jewels of Celestial Lord Indra's net.* This is called the gate of the realm of Indra's net.

(8) The lion is spoken of in order to show the meaning of ignorance while its golden substance is spoken of in order to make sufficiently clear the true nature. And principle and fact are discussed together as a description of the storehouse consciousness so that correct understanding may be created. This is called the gate of relying on facts in order to explain dharmas and create understanding.

(9) The lion is a dharma produced from causes, coming into existence and going out of existence at every moment. Each of these instants is divided into three periods, that is, past, present, and future, and each of these periods contains past, present, and future. Altogether there are three times three units, thus forming nine ages, and these, grouped together, become the total gate [to truth]. Although there are nine ages, each separate from the other, yet, since they are formed because of one another, they are harmoniously merged and mutually penetrated without obstacle and together constitute one instant of time. This is called the gate of different formation of separate dharmas in ten ages (the nine ages separately and all of them together).

(10) The gold and the lion may be hidden or manifest, and may be one or many. Neither has self-nature. They are [always] turning and transforming in accordance with the mind. Whether spoken of as fact or principle, there is the way (the mind) by which

---

*Indra is the King of Heaven. His net is decorated with a bright jewel on each knot of the mesh. Each of these many jewels reflects all the other jewels.

they are formed and exist. This is called the gate of the excellent completion through the turning and transformation of the mind only.

8. Putting together the Six Characters

The lion represents the character of universality. The five sense organs, being various and different, represent the character of specialty. The fact that they all arise from one single cause represents the character of similarity. The fact that its eyes, ears, and so forth do not exceed their bounds represents the character of difference. Since the combination of the various organs becomes the lion, this is the character of integration. And as each of the several organs remains in its own position, this is the character of disintegration.

9. Achieving perfect wisdom (bodhi)

"Bodhi" means in Chinese the Way or enlightenment. It means that when we look at the lion, we see right away that all dharmas produced through causes, even before disintegration, are from the very beginning quiescent and extinct. By being free from attachment or renunciation one will flow right along this way into the sea of perfect knowledge. Therefore it is called the Way. One understands right away that from time immemorial all afflictions resulting from passions originally have no reality. This is called enlightenment. The ultimate possession of the wisdom that knows all is called the achievement of perfect wisdom.

10. Entering Nirvana

When we look at the lion and the gold, the two characters both perish and afflictions resulting from passions will no longer be produced. Although beauty and ugliness are displayed before the eye, the mind is as calm as the sea. Erroneous thoughts all cease, and there are no compulsions. One gets out of bondage and is free from hindrances, and forever cuts off the source of suffering. This is called entry into Nirvana.

HUI-NENG, THE PLATFORM SCRIPTURE (1–37)

The Platform Scripture Preached by the Sixth Patriarch, Hui-neng, in the Ta-fan Temple in Shao-chou, the Very Best Perfection of Great Wisdom Scripture on the Sudden Enlightenment Doctrine of the Southern School of Zen, one book, including the Giving of the Discipline that Frees One from the Attachment to Differentiated Characters for the Propagation of the Law. Gathered and recorded by disciple Fa-hai.

1. Great master Hui-neng ascended the high seat in the lecture hall of the Ta-fan Temple to preach the Law of the Perfection of Great Wisdom and to give the discipline that frees one from the attachment to differentiated characters. There were present more than ten thousand monks, nuns, disciples who had renounced their families, and lay-men. The prefect of Shao-chou, Wei ch'u, more than thirty government officials, and over thirty Confucian scholars jointly requested the Great Master to preach the Law of the Perfection of Great Wisdom. Thereupon the prefect ordered the disciple, Monk Fa-hai, to record the lecture so that it would prevail in future generations. It was to enable seekers of the Way to have something to rely on and to follow when they in turn transmitted and taught the Law according to this fundamental doctrine, that this *Platform Scripture* was spoken.

2. Great Master Hui-neng said: Good and learned friends, think of the Law of the Perfection of Great Wisdom with a pure mind.

Then the Great Master remained silent, concentrated in mind and tranquil in spirit. After a long while he said: Good and learned friends, listen quietly. My deeply loving father was originally a native of Fan-yang. After his demotion from office, he was banished to Ling-nan and became a citizen of Hsin-chou. My father passed away when I was very young. My aged mother and I, an orphan, moved to Nan-hai. We were poor and life was hard. I peddled firewood in the city. Once a customer bought some fuel and led me to a government store. The customer took the fuel-wood and I received the money. As I withdrew toward the door, I suddenly saw a customer reading the *Diamond Scripture.* As soon as I heard it, I understood and was immediately enlightened. Thereupon I asked the customer, "From what place did you bring this scripture?"

The customer answered, "I paid reverence to priest Hung-jen, the Fifth Patriarch, in the Feng-mu Mountain in the eastern part of Huang-mei district in Ch'i-chou. I found there more than a thousand disciples. There I heard the Great Master exhort both disciples who have renounced their families and laymen, saying that if they would only hold on to this one book, the *Diamond Scripture,* they would be able to see their own nature and immediately would be enlightened and become Buddhas." After I heard what he said and due to causes operating in my previous lives I begged leave of my mother and went to Feng-mu Mountain in Huang-mei to pay reverence to priest Hung-jen, the Fifth Patriarch.

3. Priest Hung-jen asked me, "Whence have you come to this mountain to pay reverence to me? What do you wish from me?"

The Platform Scripture, translated by Wing-tsit Chan (New York: St. John's University Press, 1963). Reprinted by permission.

I answered, "Your disciple is a native of Ling-nan, a citizen of Hsin-chou. I have purposely come a great distance to pay you reverence. I seek nothing other than to practice the Law of the Buddha."

The Great Master reproved me, saying, "You are from Ling-nan, and, furthermore, you are a barbarian. How can you become a Buddha?"

I answered, "Although people are distinguished as northerners and southerners, there is neither north nor south in the Buddha-nature. The physical body of the barbarian and [that of] the monk are different. But what difference is there in their Buddha-nature?"

The Great Master intended to argue with me further, but, seeing people around, said nothing more. He ordered me to attend to duties, among the rest. Then a lay attendant ordered me to the rice-pounding area to pound rice. This I did for more than eight months.

4. One day the Fifth Patriarch suddenly called his disciples to come to him. When we had already assembled, he said, "Let me say this to you: Life and death are serious matters. You disciples are engaged all day in making offerings, going after fields of blessings only, and you make no effort to achieve freedom from the bitter sea of life and death. If you are deluded in your own nature, how can blessings save you? Go to your rooms, all of you, and think for yourselves. Those who possess wisdom use the wisdom (*prajna*) inherent in their own nature. Each of you must write a verse and present it to me. After I see the verses, I will give the robe and the Law to the one who understands the basic idea and will appoint him to be the Sixth Patriarch. Hurry, hurry!"

5. After the disciples had received these instructions, they each retired to their own rooms. They said to each other, "There is no need to calm our minds and devote our attention to composing verses to present to the priest. Head Monk Shen-hsiu is an instructor of rituals; when he acquires the Law, we can of course follow and stay with him. We do not have to write verses." They were satisfied. None dared present a verse.

At that time there were three corridors in front of the hall of the Great Master. Offerings were made there. It was planned to paint there on the walls as records the pictures of the transfiguration of the assembly depicted in the *Scripture about the Buddha Entering into Lanka* and also pictures of the five Patriarchs transmitting the robe and the Law so that these stories might prevail in future generations. The artist Lu Chen had examined the wall. He was to begin work the next day.

6. Head Monk Shen-hsiu thought, "These people would not present verses to show their minds because I am an instructor. If I do not present a verse to show my mind, how can the Fifth Patriarch see whether my understanding is shallow or deep? I shall present the verse of my heart to the Fifth Patriarch to show him my ideas. It is good to seek the Law, but not good to seek the patriarchate. It would be similar to that of the ordinary people and I would be usurping the holy rank. If I do not present a verse to manifest my mind, I shall never acquire the Law." He thought for a long time but found it an extremely difficult matter. He then waited until midnight, and without allowing anyone to see him, went to the wall in the middle of the southern corridor and wrote a verse to manifest what was in his mind, thus wishing to seek the Law. "If the Fifth Patriarch sees the words of this verse—the words of this verse . . . If they are not acceptable, it is of course because the obstruction of my past deeds is so heavy that I am not qualified to obtain the Law. The Patriarch's holy opinion is difficult to guess but I shall be satisfied in my mind."

At midnight Head Monk Shen-hsiu, holding a candle, wrote a verse on the wall of the south corridor, without anyone knowing about it, which said:

The body is the tree of perfect wisdom (*bodhi*)
The mind is the stand of a bright mirror.
At all times diligently wipe it.
Do not allow it to become dusty.

7. After Head Monk Shen-hsiu had finished writing the verse, he returned to his room to retire without anyone seeing him. The next morning the Fifth Patriarch called court artist Lu to come to the south corridor to paint the pictures of the scripture about the Buddha entering into Lanka. Suddenly the Fifth Patriarch saw the verse. After reading it, he said to the court artist, "I will give you thirty thousand cash and will be much obliged to you for your coming from afar. But we will not paint the transfigurations. The *Diamond Scripture* says, 'All characters are unreal and imaginary.' It is better to keep this verse and let deluded people read it. If people practice according to it, they will not fall into the Three Evil Stages.* People who practice according to the Law will enjoy great benefits."

Thereupon the Great Master called all the disciples to come and burn incense before the verse so that everyone would see it and a sense of reverence would arise in all of them. "All of you read this. Only those who understand this verse will be able to see their own nature. Those who practice according to it will not fall."

The disciples all read the verse and a sense of reverence was aroused in them. They said, "Wonderful!"

Thereupon the Fifth Patriarch called Head Monk Shen-hsiu into the hall and asked, "Was this verse written by you? If you wrote it, you should receive my Law."

Head Monk Shen-hsiu said. "Please pardon me. In fact, I did write it. Yet I dare not seek the position of the patriarch. I hope Your Holiness will be compassionate and see if your disciple possesses a small amount of wisdom and understands the basic idea."

The Fifth Patriarch said, "The verse you wrote shows some but not complete understanding. You have arrived at the front door but you have not yet entered it. Ordinary people, by practicing in accordance with your verse, will not fail. But it is futile to seek the supreme perfect wisdom while holding to such a view. One must enter the door and see his own nature. Go away and come back after thinking a day or two. Write another verse and present it to me. If then you have entered the door and have seen your own nature, I will give you the robe and the Law." Head Monk Shen-hsiu went away and for several days could not produce another verse.

8. A boy was reciting this verse while passing by the rice-pounding area. As soon as I heard it, I knew that the author had not seen his own nature or understood the basic idea. I asked the boy, "What verse were you reciting a little while ago?" The boy answered, "Do you not know that the Great Master said that life and death are important matters? He wishes to transmit the robe and the Law to someone. He told the disciples to write and present a verse for him to see. He who understood the basic idea would be given the robe and the Law as testimony of making him the Sixth Patriarch. The head monk by the name of Shen-hsiu wrote in the south corridor a verse that frees one from the attachment to differentiated characters. The Fifth Patriarch told all the disciples to read it. Whoever understood this verse would immediately see his own nature, and those who practiced according to it would be emancipated."

I replied, "I have been pounding rice here for more than eight months and have not been to the front of the hall. Will you, sir, lead me to the south corridor so that I might see this verse and pay reverence to it. I also wish to recite it and to fulfill the conditions for birth in the Buddha-land in my next life."

---

*[Hell, hungry ghosts, and beasts.]

As the boy led me to the south corridor, I immediately paid reverence to the verse. As I did not know how to read, I asked someone to read it to me. After I heard it, I immediately understood the basic idea. I also composed a verse and asked a person who could read to write it on the wall of the western corridor to manifest what was in my own mind. It is useless to study the Law if one does not understand his own mind. Once a person understands his own mind and sees his own nature, he will immediately understand the basic idea. My verse says:

Fundamentally perfect wisdom has no tree.
Nor has the bright mirror any stand.
Buddha-nature is forever clear and pure.
Where is there any dust?

Another verse says:

The mind is the tree of perfect wisdom.
The body is the stand of a bright mirror.
The bright mirror is originally clear and pure.
Where has it been defiled by any dust?

Monks in the hall were all surprised at these verses. I, however, went back to the rice-pounding area. The Fifth Patriarch suddenly realized that I alone had the good knowledge and understanding of the basic idea but he was afraid lest the rest learn it. He therefore told them, "He does not understand perfectly after all."

9. The Fifth Patriarch waited till midnight, called me to come to the hall, and expounded the *Diamond Scripture*. As soon as I heard this, I understood. That night the Law was imparted to me without anyone knowing it, and thus the method of sudden enlightenment and the robe were transmitted to me. "You are now the Sixth Patriarch. This robe is the testimony of transmission from generation to generation. As to the Law, it is to be transmitted from mind to mind. Let people achieve enlightenment through their own effort."

The Fifth Patriarch said, "Hui-neng, from the very beginning, in the transmission of the Law one's life is as delicate as hanging by a thread. If you remain here, someone might harm you. You must leave quickly."

10. After I received the robe and the Law, I left at midnight. The Fifth Patriarch personally saw me off at the courier's station at Chiu-chiang. I then understood the instructions of the Patriarch. "Go and work hard. Carry the Law to the south. Do not preach for three years, for it is not easy for this Law to flourish. Later when you spread the Law and convert people, when you skillfully guide deluded people and open up their minds, you will not be different from me."

Having said goodbye, I started south.

11. In two months I reached the Ta-yu Mountain. I did not realize that there were several hundred people coming after me. They wanted to follow me and to snatch the robe and the Law. But half way they all withdrew, except one monk whose family name was Ch'en and whose private name was Hui-shun. He was formerly a general of the third rank. His nature and disposition were crude and evil. He got straightly to the peak, rushed forward and grabbed me. I immediately gave the robe of the Law to him but he refused to take it. "I purposely came this long way to seek the Law; I do not need the robe." Thereupon I transmitted the Law to him on the peak. As he heard what I said, his mind was opened. I told him to go to the north to convert the people there immediately.

12. Then I came and stayed in this place and associated with government officials, disciples who have renounced their families, and lay folk. This, after all, was due to

causes operating over many long periods of time. The doctrine has been handed down from past sages; it is not my own wisdom. Those who wish to hear the teachings of past sages must purify their hearts. Having heard them, they must vow to rid themselves of delusions and thereby to become enlightened, as the former sages. (This is the method described below.)

Great Master Hui-neng declared: Good and learned friends, perfect wisdom is inherent in all people. It is only because they are deluded in their minds that they cannot attain enlightenment by themselves. They must seek the help of good and learned friends of high standing to show them the way to see their own nature. Good and learned friends, as soon as one is enlightened, he attains wisdom.

13. Good and learned friends, calmness and wisdom are the foundations of my method. First of all, do not be deceived into thinking that the two are different. They are one substance and not two. Calmness is the substance of wisdom and wisdom is the function of calmness. Whenever wisdom is at work, calmness is within it. Whenever calmness is at work, wisdom is within it. Good and learned friends, the meaning here is that [calmness and] wisdom are identified. Seekers of the Way, arouse your minds. Do not say that wisdom follows calmness or vice versa, or that the two are different. To hold such a view would imply that the dharmas possess two different characters. In the case of those whose words are good but whose hearts are not good, wisdom and calmness are not identified. But in the case of those whose hearts and words are both good and in whom the internal and the external are one, calmness and wisdom are identified. Self-enlightenment and practice do not consist in argument. If one is concerned about which comes first, he is a [deluded] person. If he is not freed from the consideration of victory or defeat, he will produce the dharmas and the self. He cannot become free from the Four Characters.

14. Calmness in which one realizes that all dharmas are the same means to practice [attaining] a straightforward mind at all times, whether walking, standing, sitting, or reclining. *The Scripture Spoken by Vimalakirti* says, "The straightforward mind is the holy place. The straightforward mind is the Pure Land." Do not be crooked in the activities of your mind and merely talk about straightforwardness. One who merely talks about calmness in which one realizes that all dharmas are one and does not practice a straightforward mind is not a disciple of the Buddha. To practice a straightforward mind only and to be unattached to any dharma is called calmness in which one realizes that all dharmas are the same. Deluded people attached to the characters of dharmas hold that calmness, in which one realizes that all dharmas are the same, means simply to sit unperturbed and to remove erroneous thoughts without allowing others to arise in the mind; that to them is calmness in which one realizes that all dharmas are the same. If this were the case, this Law would [render us] equivalent to insentient beings and would be a cause of hindrance to the Way. The Way must be in operation. Why should it be impeded instead? When the mind is not attached to dharmas, then the Way is in operation. When it is attached then it is in bondage. If it were correct to sit without motion, Vimalakirti would not have reprimanded Shariputra for sitting silently in the forest.

Good and learned friends, I also know some who teach people to sit and look into the mind as well as to look at purity, so that the mind will not be perturbed and nothing will arise from it. Devoting their efforts to this, deluded people fail to become enlightened; consequently they are so attached to this method as to become insane. There have been several hundred such cases. Therefore I know that to teach people this way is a great mistake.

15. Good and learned friends, in what way are calmness and wisdom the same? They are like the lamp and its light. With the lamp there is light. Without the lamp there

is no light. The lamp is the substance of the light while the light is the function of the lamp. In name they are two but in substance they are not different. It is the same with calmness and wisdom.

16. Good and learned friends, in method there is no distinction between sudden enlightenment and gradual enlightenment. Among men, however, some are intelligent and others are stupid. Those who are deluded understand gradually, while the enlightened achieve understanding suddenly. But when they know their own minds, then they see their own nature, and there is no difference in their enlightenment. Without enlightenment, they remain forever bound in transmigration.

17. Good and learned friends, in this method of mine, from the very beginning, whether in the sudden-enlightenment or gradual-enlightenment tradition, absence-of-thought has been instituted as the main doctrine, absence-of-characters as the substance, and non-attachment as the foundation. What is meant by absence-of-characters? Absence-of-characters means to be free from characters while in the midst of them. Absence-of-thought means not to be carried away by thought in the process of thought. Non-attachment is man's original nature. Thought after thought goes on without remaining. Past, present, and future thought continue without termination. But if we cut off and terminate thought for one instant, the Law-body is freed from the physical body. At no time should a single instant of thought be attached to any dharma. If one single instant of thought is attached to anything, then every thought will be attached. This is bondage. But if in regard to dharmas no thought is attached to anything, that is freedom. This is the meaning of having non-attachment as the foundation.

Good and learned friends, to be free from all characters means the absence of characters. Only if we can be free from characters will the substance of our nature be pure. That is the meaning of taking absence-of-character as the substance. Absence-of-thought means not to be defiled by external objects. It is to free our thoughts from external objects and not to have thoughts arise over dharmas. But do not stop thinking about everything and eliminate all thought. As soon as thought stops, one dies and is reborn elsewhere. Take heed of this, followers of the Way. If one does not think over the meaning of the Law and becomes mistaken himself, that is excusable. How much worse is it to encourage others to be mistaken! Deluded, he does not realize that he is so, and he even blasphemes the scripture and the Law! That is the reason why absence-of-thought is instituted as the doctrine. Because people who are deluded have thoughts about external objects, perverse views arise in them, and all sorts of afflictions resulting from passions and erroneous thoughts are produced.

However, this school has instituted absence-of-thought as the doctrine. When people of the world are free from erroneous views, no thoughts will arise. If there are no thoughts, there will not even be an absence-of-thought. Absence means absence of what? Thought means thought of what? Absence-of-thought means freedom from the character of the duality [existence or non-existence of characters] and from all afflictions resulting from passions. [Thought means thought of the true nature of True Thusness.] True Thusness is the substance of thought and thought is the function of True Thusness. It is the self-nature that gives rise to thought. Therefore in spite of the functioning of seeing, hearing, sensing, and knowing, self-nature is not defiled by the many spheres of objects and always remains free and at ease. As the *Scripture Spoken by Vimalakirti* says, "Externally it skillfully differentiates the various dharma-characters while internally it abides immovably in the First Principle."

18. Good and learned friends, according to this method, sitting in meditation is at bottom neither looking at the mind nor looking at purity. Nor do we say that there should be imperturbability. Suppose we say to look at the mind. The mind is at bottom

false. Since being false is the same as being illusory, there is nothing to look at. Suppose we say to look at purity. Man's nature is originally pure. It is by false thoughts that True Thusness is obscured. Our original nature is pure as long as it is free from false thoughts. If one does not realize that his own nature is originally pure and makes up his mind to look at purity, he is creating a false purity. Such purity has no objective existence. Hence we know that what is looked at is false. Purity has neither physical form nor character, but some people set up characters of purity and say that this is the object of our task. People who take this view hinder their original nature and become bound by purity. If those who cultivate imperturbability would ignore people's mistakes and defects, their nature would not be perturbed. Deluded people may not be perturbed physically themselves, but whenever they speak, they criticize others and thus violate the Way. Thus looking at the mind or at purity causes a hindrance to the Way.

19. Now, this being the case, in this method, what is meant by sitting in meditation? In this method, to sit means to be free from all obstacles, and externally not to allow thoughts to rise from the mind over any sphere of objects. To meditate means to realize the imperturbability of one's original nature. What is meant by meditation and calmness? Meditation means to be free from all characters externally; calmness means to be unperturbed internally. If there are characters outside and the inner mind is not disturbed, one's original nature is naturally pure and calm. It is only because of the spheres of objects that there is contact, and contact leads to perturbation. There is calmness when one is free from characters and is not perturbed. There is meditation when

Shusi-wêng (Sotsu-ō). Hui-nêng (Enō) listening to the Diamond Sūtra. 13th–14th century. (*The New York Public Library Photographic Services/Art Resource.*)

one is externally free from characters, and there is calmness when one is internally undisturbed. Meditation and calmness mean that external meditation is attained and internal calmness is achieved. The *Scripture Spoken by Vimalakirti* says, "Immediately we become completely clear and recover our original mind." The *P'u-sa-chieh ching* (*Scripture of Disciplines for Bodhisattvahood*) says, "We are originally pure in our self-nature." Good and learned friends, realize that your self-nature is naturally pure. Cultivate and achieve for yourselves the Law-body of your self-nature. Follow the Way of the Buddha yourselves. Act and achieve Buddhahood for yourselves.

20. Good and learned friends, you must all go through the experience yourselves and receive the discipline that frees you from the attachment to differentiated characters. Follow me at the same time and repeat my slogans. They will enable you, good and learned friends, to see that the Three Bodies* of the Buddha are within you: "We take refuge in the pure Law-body of the Buddha with our own physical bodies. We take refuge in the Myriad Transformation-body with our own physical bodies. We take refuge in the Perfect Reward-body with our own physical bodies." (The above to be chanted three times.) The physical body is like an inn and cannot be spoken of as a refuge. It has always been the case that the Three Bodies lie in one's own nature. Everyone has them; yet because they are deluded they do not see, and they seek the Three Bodies of the Tathagata externally, without realizing that the Three Bodies are inherent in one's own physical body. Good and learned friends, listen to your good friend. If you, good and learned friends, now see in your own physical bodies the self-nature that involves the Three Bodies of the Buddha, these Three Bodies will arise from your nature.

What is meant by the Pure Law-body of the Buddha? Good and learned friends, our nature is originally pure. All dharmas lie in this self-nature. If we think of all kinds of evil deeds, we will practice evil. If we think of all kinds of good deeds, we will do good. Thus we know that all dharmas lie in one's self-nature. Self-nature is always pure, just as the sun and moon are always shining. It is only when they are obscured by clouds that there is brightness above but darkness below and the sun, the moon, and the stars cannot be seen. But when suddenly a gentle wind blows and scatters all clouds and fog, all phenomena are abundantly spread out before us, all appearing together. The purity of people's nature is comparable to the clear sky, their wisdom comparable to the sun, and sagacity comparable to the moon. Their sagacity and wisdom are always shining. It is only because externally people are attached to spheres of objects that erroneous thoughts, like floating clouds, cover the self-nature so that it is not clear. Therefore when they meet a good and learned friend who reveals to them the true method and scatters away delusions and falsehoods, then they are thoroughly illumined both internally and externally, and all dharmas reveal the free and easy character in their own nature. This is called the Pure Law-body. By taking refuge in the Pure Law-body we remove evil deeds. This is called taking refuge.

What is meant by the Myriad Transformation-body? When there is no thought, one's nature is empty of differentiated characters and is tranquil, but when there is thought, that is self-transformation. When one thinks of evil dharmas, the transformation becomes hell, but when one thinks of good dharmas, the transformation becomes Paradise. What is poisonous and harmful is transformed into beasts. What is compassionate is transformed into bodhisattvas. What is sagacious and wise is transformed into the higher realm. What is ignorant and deluded is transformed into the lower region.

---

*[Buddhism conceives a Buddha to have a threefold body: the Law-body or spiritual body, the Reward-body or Enjoyment body, and the Transformation-body or body of incarnation.]

The transformations of self-nature are many, but deluded people themselves do not know this. If one has a single good thought, sagacity and wisdom arise. This is called the Transformation-body of self-nature.

What is meant by the Perfect Reward-body? One light can illumine the darkness of a thousand years, and one bit of wisdom can destroy the ignorance of ten thousand years. Never mind looking back to the past; always consider the future, and always make future thoughts good. This is called the Reward-body. The reward of one evil thought will remove the good of a thousand years, and the reward of one good thought will destroy the evil of a thousand years. At all times make the next thought a good one. This is called the Reward-body. Thinking on the basis of the Law-body is the same as the Transformation-body, and making every thought good is the same as the Reward-body. Achieving enlightenment oneself and practicing the Law oneself is called taking refuge. Skin and flesh constitute the physical body. It is an inn and cannot be spoken of as a refuge. If a person understands the Three Bodies, he will recognize my basic idea.

21. Now that we have taken refuge in the Three Bodies of the Buddha, let me and you, good and learned friends, take the Four Very Great Vows. Good and learned friends, please all follow me and say at the same time:

> I vow to save an infinite number of beings.
> I vow to cut off an infinite number of afflictions resulting from passions.
> I vow to study an infinite number of gates to the Law.
> I vow to attain Supreme Buddhahood.

(This is to be chanted three times.)

Good and learned friends, when we make our vows to save an infinite number of living beings, it does not mean for me to save them. Good and learned friends, all living beings are in the mind; each must save itself in its own body and through its own nature. What is meant by saving oneself through one's own nature? In one's own physical body there are perverse views, afflictions resulting from passions, ignorance, delusion, and erroneous thoughts. Everyone possesses the nature of original enlightenment. Everyone can save himself with correct views. When there is understanding through correct views, wisdom will remove the ignorance, delusion, and error. Thus all beings can save themselves. When perversion comes, one saves himself through correctness. When delusion comes, one saves himself through understanding. When ignorance comes, one saves himself through wisdom. When evil comes, one saves himself through goodness. And when afflictions resulting from passion come, one saves himself through perfect wisdom. Salvation in this way is true salvation. By vowing to cut off an infinite number of afflictions resulting from passions is to remove illusions and erroneous thoughts in one's own mind. By vowing to study an infinite number of gates to the Law is meant to study the supremely correct Law. And by vowing to attain Supreme Buddhahood is meant always to behave humbly, to respect and reverence everything, to get far away from delusion, attachment, sensation, and knowledge, to cause wisdom to arise and to cut off delusions and erroneous thoughts. One will then achieve Buddhahood through self-enlightenment and will be practicing the power of vows.

22. Now that we have made the Four Very Great Vows, let me tell you, good and learned friends, about repentance that frees one from the attachment to differentiated characters in order to destroy the sins and obstructions of the past, the present, and the future.

The Great Master said: Good and learned friends, if a person does not allow a single thought, whether past, present, or future, to be contaminated by ignorance or delusion, and if he removes his previous evil deeds from his own nature all at once, that is repentance. Not to let any thought, whether past, present, or future, be contaminated by ignorance and delusion and to remove previous insincerity and dishonesty so that they are forever cut off is called repentance by one's own nature. Not to allow any thought, whether past, future, or present, to be contaminated by delusion and to remove previous jealousy so that jealousy is eliminated from one's nature is repentance. (The above to be chanted three times.)

Good and learned friends: What is repentance? To repent means never again to do evil in one's life time. To regret means to realize the evil of previous deeds and not to allow that realization ever to slip from the mind. It is useless merely to say so before the Buddhas. In my method, forever to cut off evil and never again to do it is called repentance.

23. Now that we have repented, let me give you, good and learned friends, the discipline of the Three Refuges that frees one from the attachment to differentiated characters.

The Great Master said: Good and learned friends. Take refuge in enlightenment, which is the Supreme Twofold Sufficiency. Take refuge in the correct doctrine, which is supreme freedom from desire. Take refuge in purity, which is supreme among the myriad things. From now on call the Enlightened One your teacher. Take no longer any refuge in various perverse people, deluded people, or heretics. Vow to testify with compassion to our own Three Treasures. Good and learned friends, I exhort you to take refuge in the Three Treasures—The Buddha, who is enlightenment; the Law, which is the correct doctrine, and the Order, which is purity. When your own minds take refuge in enlightenment, perversion and delusion will not arise. You will have few desires and will be contented, free from greed and lust. This is called the supreme twofold sufficiency. When your own minds take refuge in the correct doctrine, because every thought is free from perversion, there is no more craving or attachment. Because there is no more craving or attachment, it is called supreme freedom from desire. When your minds take refuge in purity, although afflictions resulting from passions and erroneous thoughts are present in your own nature, your own nature will not be contaminated. This is called being supreme among the myriad things. Ordinary people do not understand; yet they receive the discipline of the Three Refuges from morning to evening. If they say they take refuge in the Buddha, where is He? If the Buddha is not to be seen [outside], it means there cannot be any refuge. If there is no refuge, to say so would be erroneous. Good and learned friends, please examine this yourself and do not misdirect your attention. The scripture merely says to take refuge in the Buddha within the self; it does not say to take refuge in another Buddha. If we do not take refuge in our own nature, there is no place in which to take refuge.

24. Now that we have taken refuge in the Three Treasures ourselves, each of you please pay close attention. I shall speak to you, good and learned friends, about the method of salvation through great wisdom. Good and learned friends, although you recite the term, you do not understand. Let me explain. Everyone listen, each of you.

The word *mahaprajnaparamita* is Sanskrit and means in Chinese the great wisdom by which to reach the Other Shore. This Law must be put into practice and does not depend on its recitation. If we do not put it into practice, it amounts to an illusion and a phantom. If one practices it, his Law-body will be the same as that of the Buddha.

What does *maha* mean? It means great. The capacity of the mind is as great as that of empty space. If one sits with an empty mind, however, one will be attached to the emptiness characterized by indifference. Empty space can embrace the sun, the moon, stars, plants, the great earth, mountains, rivers, all trees and plants, good and evil people, good and evil dharmas, heavens and hells. They are all within this emptiness. The emptiness of human nature is the same.

25. The self-nature is great because it embraces all dharmas. All dharmas are nothing but the self-nature. It sees all men and all things other than men, good or evil, and good dharmas or evil dharmas, and it does not renounce any of them nor is it contaminated by them or attached to them. It is like empty space. This is called great and is what *maha* means. Deluded people recite the word with their mouths but wise people put it into practice with their minds. There are also deluded people who keep their minds empty without thought and call it great. That is also wrong. The capacity of the mind is great, but if it is not put into practice, it becomes small. Do not just talk about it and then fail to practice it. Such people are not my disciples.

26. What is meant by *prajna? Prajna* means wisdom. If at all times one is not ignorant but always acts wisely, that is practicing wisdom. One foolish thought will cut off wisdom, whereas one wise thought will produce it. People in the world are always ignorant in their mind and yet say to themselves that they practice wisdom. *Prajna* is without physical form or character. It is the nature of wisdom.

What does it mean by *paramita?* This is a Sanskrit word. In Chinese it is "to reach the Other Shore." It means to be free from birth and extinction. If one is attached to any sphere of objects, birth and extinction will arise, like waves in the sea. This means the shore on our side. If one is free from spheres of objects, there will be no birth or extinction. It is like water running forever. For this reason it is called reaching the Other Shore, or *paramita.* Deluded people recite the word with their mouths but wise people practice it with their minds. When they merely recite it they have erroneous thoughts. To have erroneous thoughts means not really to have it. If they practice it every moment, they will really have it. He who understands this method understands the method of wisdom and practices it. He who does not practice it is an ordinary man. He who practices it even for one moment is in his own body equal to the Buddha.

Good and learned friends, afflictions resulting from passions are the same as wisdom. To hold on to a previous deluded thought makes a person an ordinary man, but the next thought, if enlightened, makes one a Buddha. Good and learned friends, the *mahaprajnaparamita* is the most supreme, the highest, and the best. It neither remains, nor goes, nor comes. The Buddhas of the past, the present, and the future come from it; use this great wisdom to reach the Other Shore, and destroy the Five Aggregates* and the afflictions resulting from passions. The most supreme, the highest, and the best! Praise this very best method. If you practice it you will surely achieve Buddhahood. Being neither remaining, nor coming, nor going, this state is the same as calmness and wisdom, with no contamination by any dharma. The Buddhas of the past, the present, and the future come from it and change the Three Poisons** into discipline, calmness, and wisdom.

27. Good and learned friends, in this method of mine, one *prajna* produces 84,000 wisdoms. Why? Because there are in the world 84,000 afflictions resulting from passions. If there were no afflictions, wisdom would always be present and would not be separated from the self-nature. Those who understand this method will be without [erroneous] thoughts, recollection, or attachment. Dishonesty and erroneous thoughts will not arise. This is the nature of true Thusness. When all dharmas are examined in the light of wisdom and a person is neither attached to nor renounces them, he will see his own nature and will attain Buddhahood.

---

*[Matter, sensation, thought, disposition, and consciousness are the five elements that make up the self, which is but a temporary aggregate and therefore false.]

**[Greed, hatred, delusion.]

28. Good and learned friends, if you wish to enter deeply into the Realm of Law and the calmness of wisdom, you should forthwith practice the wisdom of salvation. If only you hold on to this one book, the *Diamond Scripture,* you will be able to see your own nature and will enter into the calmness of wisdom. You should realize that such a person has an infinite number of merits. The scripture clearly praises him. I cannot go into details.

This is the very best method and is intended for people of great wisdom and high intelligence. People of little wisdom or intelligence will not believe it when they hear it. Why? Suppose the great dragon causes a heavy rain to fall and the rain spreads over Jambudvipa. Cities, towns, and villages would be drifting in the flood as if they were drifting grass and leaves. But if the rain falls and spreads over the great ocean, the ocean is neither increased nor decreased by the rain. When followers of Great Vehicle hear the *Diamond Scripture,* their minds are opened up and enlightened. Therefore we know that one's own nature possesses wisdom. If we examine things in the light of wisdom, we do not depend on any writing. It is like the rain which does not really come from nothing. Originally the Dragon King himself draws this water from the ocean, thus enabling all people, and all plants, along with sentient or insentient beings to enjoy its benefit. When rivers and streams all flow into the great ocean, the vast ocean receives them and merges them into one body. The same is true of the wisdom inherent to the original nature of all people.

29. When people of little intelligence hear this doctrine of sudden enlightenment, they are like plants with weak roots. When such plants are soaked by a heavy rain, they collapse and can no longer grow. If is the same with people of little intelligence. People with the wisdom of *prajna* are not different from those with great wisdom. Why, then, do they not understand when they hear the Law? It is because they are completely obstructed by perverse views. Their roots of affliction are deep. It is like a thick cloud blocking the sun. Unless the wind blows the cloud away, the sun cannot be revealed.

Wisdom does not vary in degree with different persons. It is because people are deluded in their minds and are seeking Buddhahood by external practice, without understanding their own nature, that they are called people of small intelligence. When people hear the doctrine of sudden enlightenment and do not depend on external practice, but simply find correct views in their own nature, all these afflicted people are at once enlightened. It is like the great ocean receiving the rivers and streams. The big body of water and the small bodies of water merge to form one body. This is seeing [one's own] nature. If one is not attached either to the internal or the external, is free in coming and going, removes his attachment, and understands things without impediment—he who can do this will not differ from the *prajna* scripture.

30. All scriptures and writings, both the Great Vehicle and the Small Vehicle, and the twelve sections of the scripture are provided for men. It is because man possesses the nature of wisdom that these were instituted. If there were no men in the world, there would naturally not be any dharmas. We know, therefore, that dharmas exist because of man and that there are all these scriptures because there are people to preach them.

The reason is that among men some are wise and others are stupid. The stupid are inferior, whereas the wise are superior. The deluded consult the wise and the wise explain the Law to the stupid and enable them to understand and to open up their minds. When deluded people understand and open up their minds, they are no longer different from the superior and the wise. Hence we know that without enlightenment, a Buddha is no different from other living beings. With enlightenment, even in a single instant of thought, all living beings become the same as a Buddha. Hence we know that all dharmas are immanent in one's mind and person. Why not seek in one's own mind the sudden realization of the original nature of True Thusness? The *Scripture of Disciplines for*

Bodhisattvahood says, "We are originally pure in our self-nature. If we understand our minds and see our nature, we shall achieve Buddhahood ourselves." [The *Scripture Spoken by Vimalakirti* says], "Immediately we become completely clear and recover our original mind."

31. Good and learned friends, when I was at Priest Hung-jen's place, I understood immediately as soon as I heard him, and suddenly realized the original nature of True Thusness. For this reason I propagate this doctrine so that it will prevail among later generations and seekers of the Way will be able to achieve perfect wisdom through sudden enlightenment, each to see his own mind, and to become suddenly enlightened through his own original nature. If they are not able to enlighten themselves, they should seek good and learned friends of high standing to show them the way to see their nature.

What is meant by a good and learned friend of high standing? A good and learned friend of high standing is one who can explain to people the very best method and can directly show them the correct way. That is a good and learned friend of high standing. That is a great cause. That is to say, he will teach and direct people so they can see their own nature. For all good dharmas arise because of him. [The wisdom] of the past, present, and future Buddhas as well as the twelve sections of the scripture are all immanent in human nature. It originally possesses them to the fullest extent. Those who cannot enlighten themselves should have good and learned friends to show them the way to see their nature. Those who can enlighten themselves, however, need not depend on good and learned friends. If they seek outside for good and learned friends and hope for emancipation, they will get nowhere. Understanding coming from the good and learned friend inside a person's own mind, however, will lead him to emancipation. But if one's own mind is perverse and deluded, [full of] erroneous thoughts and perversions, even if good and learned friends from the outside offer instruction, no salvation can be attained. If you have not been able to enlighten yourselves, you should arouse your wisdom illuminatingly to examine [facts and principles]. Then in an instant all erroneous thoughts will vanish. This is your true and really good and learned friend, who as soon as he is enlightened immediately realizes Buddhahood.

When in your own nature and in your mind you use wisdom for an illuminating examination of things, you will become illumined within and without, and know your own mind. To know your own mind is to be emancipated. To be emancipated is wisdom. To have obtained wisdom means absence-of-thought.

What is meant by absence-of-thought? By the method of absence-of-thought is meant to see all dharmas but not to be attached to them, and [for the mind] to be everywhere but not to be attached anywhere. Let your own nature always remain pure, so that the Six Consciousnesses* in passing through the Six Gates** will neither be separated from nor be attached to the Six Qualities† produced by the objects and sense organs and will be able to come and go freely. That is wisdom. It is freedom and ease. It is emancipation. It is called the practice of absence-of-thought. If one does not think of anything in order to stop all thought, that is bondage by dharmas. That is called a one-sided view. Those who understand the method of absence-of-thought will penetrate all dharmas and will experience the spheres of all Buddhas. Those who understand the method of sudden enlightenment through absence-of-thought will reach the stage of the Buddha.

32. Good and learned friends, people in future generations who receive my method will always see my law-body by your side. Good and learned friends, those who

*[The five sense-consciousnesses and the sense-center consciousness.]
**[The five sense organs and the mind.]
†[Sight, sound, smell, taste, touch, mind (as intellection).]

apply this method of sudden enlightenment, who share similar views and similar practice, who take a vow of devotion as in serving the Buddha, and who devote their whole lives without retreating, will surely enter Nirvana. But when the Law has to be transmitted, they should transmit the Law silently handed down from one patriarch to another. They should transmit it to various people so long as they make a great vow not to retreat from seeking perfect wisdom. To people who do not share similar views and have no desire for it, do not foolishly publicize it at all. Else it will do them harm and will in the end be useless. If it should happen that they do not understand and if they should slander this method, they will go through hundreds of thousands of long periods of time and a hundred rebirths, and their seed of Buddha-nature will be annihilated.

33. The Great Master said: Good and learned friends, listen to me recite the verse that frees one from the attachment to differentiated characters. It enables you deluded people to destroy your sins. It is also called the verse that destroys sin. It says:

> Ignorant people cultivate blessing. Instead of cultivating the Way.
> They say that the cultivation of blessings is the way.
> Although merits for alms-giving and offerings are infinite,
> The Three Evils* are, after all, produced in the mind.
> If it is hoped that cultivating merit will destroy sin,
> Sin will still remain in future lives even if merits are obtained.
> If people understand that destruction of the cause of sin must be sought in their own minds,
> They will in their own nature truly repent.
> If they understand the true repentance of the Great Vehicle,
> They will remove the perverse, will practice the correct, and will thus be free from sin.
> If seekers of the Way examine themselves,
> They will be similar to the enlightened.
> The Great Master decrees that this doctrine of sudden enlightenment be transmitted.
> All who are willing to learn will form one body.
> If you wish to come and look for your law-body,
> You must remove the evil causes of the Three Poisons from your mind.
> Make vigorous efforts to cultivate the Way, without relaxation.
> Sudden relaxation means the end of a whole life.
> When you encounter the Great Vehicle doctrine of sudden enlightenment,
> Reverently put your palms together and seek it with all your heart.

When the Great Master had finished explaining the Law, the Imperial Delegate Wei, government officials, monks, disciples who had renounced their families, and lay folk all praised him endlessly, saying that they had never heard this before.

34. The imperial delegate paid reverence to the Master and said, 'The Law Your Holiness has expounded is really wonderful. Your disciple has, however, some doubts and wishes to consult Your Holiness. I beg Your Holiness, with your great compassion, for further explanation.'

The Great Master said, "If you have any doubts, please ask. Why hesitate?"

The imperial delegate asked, "Is not the Law the fundamental doctrine of the First Patriarch from the West, Bodhidharma?"

The Great Master said, "Yes."

The imperial delegate asked, "I have heard that when the Great Master Bodhidharma tried to convert Emperor Wu [reigned 502–549], the emperor asked him, 'During my entire life I have built temples, given alms, and made offerings. Is there any merit [achievement and virtue] for these deeds?'

*[The same as the Three Poisons: greed, hatred, and delusion.]

"Bodhidharma answered and said, 'No merit at all.'

"The emperor was disappointed and thereupon sent Bodhidharma out of his state. I do not understand Bodhidharma's words. I beg Your Holiness to explain."

The Sixth Patriarch said, "There is really no merit. Imperial Delegate, please do not doubt the words of Great Master Bodhidharma. Emperor Wu was attached to perverse ways and did not understand the correct doctrine."

The imperial delegate asked, "Why is there no merit?"

The priest said, "Building temples, giving alms, and making offerings are only cultivating blessings. Blessings should not be considered as merit. Merit lies in the law-body, not in the field of blessings. There is merit in one's own dharma-nature. Not to make any differentiation but to be straightforward is virtue. [Internally see] the Buddha-nature, and externally practice respect and reverence. If one looks down on others and does not get rid of the idea of the self, he will have no merit. If his self-nature is unreal and imaginary, his law-body will have no merit. One should practice virtue at every moment, entertain no differentiation and be straightforward in the mind; then his virtue will not be slight. Always practice reverence. To cultivate one's personal life is achievement, and to cultivate one's own mind is virtue. Merit is the product of one's own mind. Blessings are different from merit. Emperor Wu did not know the correct principle. The Great Patriarch was not mistaken."

35. The imperial delegate paid reverence and asked again, "I observe that monks, disciples who have renounced their families, and lay folk always recite the name of Amitabha with the hope of going to and being reborn in the Western Region [Pure Land, Paradise]. Will Your Holiness explain whether it is possible to be born there or not? Please remove my doubts."

The Great Master said, "Imperial Delegate, please listen. I will explain it to you. According to the scripture spoken by the World-honored One in Shravasti about leading people to the Western Region, it is quite clear that it is not far from here. It is said to be far away for the benefit of people of low intelligence, but it is said to be near for the benefit of people of high intelligence. People are of two kinds, but the Law is only one. Because men differ according as they are deluded or enlightened, some understand the Law quicker than others. Deluded people recite the name of the Buddha hoping to be born in the Pure Land, but the enlightened purifies his own mind, for, as the Buddha said, '"As a result of purity of mind, the Buddha Land becomes pure." Imperial Delegate, if people of the Eastern Region are pure in heart, they will be free from sin, and if people of the Western Region are not pure in heart, they are sinful. Deluded people want to be born in the Western Region, but the locations of the two regions do not differ. If the mind is absolutely pure, the Western Region is not far away. But if one's mind is not pure, it will be difficult to go and be born there through reciting the name of the Buddha. If one has removed the Ten Evils,* he will have traveled a hundred thousand miles, and if one is free from the Eight Perversions,** he will have traveled eight thousand miles. One has only to be straightforward in his actions and he will reach the Pure Land in a moment. All Your Honor should do is to practice the Ten Good Deeds.† What is the need for wanting to go and be born there? If one does not get rid of the Ten Evils from his mind, what Buddha will come to welcome him? If one understands the

---

*[Killing, stealing, adultery, lying, double-tongue, coarse language, filthy language, covetousness, anger, and perverted views.]

**[The perversion of the Noble Eightfold Path, namely, perverse views, perverse intention, perverse speech, perverse action, perverse livelihood, perverse effort, perverse mindfulness, and perverse concentration.]

†[The opposite of the Ten Evils.]

doctrine of sudden enlightenment leading to the ending of the cycle of birth and death, it takes only an instant to see the Western Region. If one does not understand the Great Vehicle doctrine of sudden enlightenment, the way to go and be born there through reciting the name of the Buddha is very far. How can one ever get there?"

The Sixth Patriarch further said, "Suppose Your Honor and I move to the Western Region. In an instant it will appear before our eyes. Do you wish to see it?"

The imperial delegate paid reverence and said, "If it can be seen here, what is the need of going to be born there? Will Your Holiness be compassionate and reveal the Western Region here? It will be perfect."

The Great Patriarch said, "No doubt you see the Western Region in the passage way." It immediately disappeared. The congregation were astonished, not knowing what was what.

The Great Master said, "Will all of you please be alert and listen. Our own physical body is a city. Our eyes, ears, nose, tongue, and body are the gates. There are five external gates. Inside there is the gate of the mind. The mind is the ground and the nature is the king. With the nature, there is king. Without the nature, there is no king. When the nature remains, our body and mind exist. When the nature is gone, our body and mind are destroyed. The Buddha is the product of one's own nature. Do not seek it outside of your body. If the self-nature is deluded, even a Buddha becomes an ordinary human being. If their self-nature is enlightened, all living beings are Buddhas. Compassion is the same as Avalokiteshvara.* Happiness in alms-giving is the same as Mahasthama. The ability to be pure is the same as Shakyamuni. And not to make differentiation but to be straight-forward is the same as Maitreya. The view that the self exists is the same as Mount Meru. A perverse mind is the same as a great ocean. Afflictions are the same as waves. A malicious mind is the same as an evil dragon. Afflictions are the same as fish and turtles. Falsehood and erroneous thoughts are the same as spiritual beings. The Three Poisons are the same as hell. Ignorance and delusions are the same as beasts. And the Ten Good Deeds are the same as Heaven. When there is no view of the self, Mount Meru will crumble of itself. When the perverse mind is eliminated, the waters of the ocean will be exhausted. When there are no afflictions, waves will be annihilated. And when poisonous harms are removed, fish and turtles will be extinct. The Tathagata of Enlightenment within the domain of our mind extends the light of His wisdom to shine through the Six Gates and purifies them. It shines and pierces its way through the Six Heavens of Desire. When the self-nature shines within, and when the Three Poisons are removed, hell disappears at once. When one is enlightened both within and without, his position is no different from that of the Western Region. If one does not practice this way, how can he reach there?"

When the congregation heard this, the sound of praise penetrated the heavens. No wonder deluded people understand thoroughly and immediately. The imperial delegate paid reverence and praised him, saying. "Excellent! Excellent! May all beings in the realm of dharmas hear this and understand at once."

36. The Great Master said, "Good and learned friends, if you wish to practice, you can do so at home, not necessarily in a monastery. Those in a monastery who do not practice are like people of the Western Region who are evil at heart. If one practices at home, he is like a person of the Eastern Region who practices the good. So long as one is willing to cultivate purity, that is the Western Region for him."

---

*[Avalokiteshvara is the most popular bodhisattva who works for the salvation of all; Mahasthama, Avalokiteshvara, and Amitabha are the Three Holy Ones of the Pure Land; Shakyamuni is the name of the historical Buddha; and Maitreya is the next Buddha, the Buddhist Messiah who will come to save the world.]

The imperial delegate asked, "Your Holiness, how does one practice at home? Please instruct us."

The Great Master said, "Good and learned friends, I have composed a verse that frees one from the attachment to differentiated characters for [officials], disciples who have renounced their families, and lay folk. Let us all recite it. Those who practice according to it will be the same as if they were with me all the time. The verse says:

> Both understanding gained from listening to teaching and understanding gained by the mind
> Are like the sun in empty space.
> Transmitting only the doctrine of sudden enlightenment,
> [The Buddhas] appear in the world to demolish the heretical schools.
> In doctrine there is neither sudden nor gradual enlightenment.
> Because of delusion or understanding, some attain enlightenment more quickly or more slowly than others.
> To study the method of the doctrine of sudden enlightenment
> Is beyond the comprehension of the ignorant.
> It is necessary to explain in ten thousand ways,
> But all of them, after all, are traced back to one principle.
> In the dark room of affliction,
> We should constantly bring forth the light of wisdom.
> Perverse views arrive because of afflictions.
> When correct views arrive, all afflictions are removed.
> When both perverse and correct views are discarded,
> Purity is absolute.
> Perfect wisdom is originally pure.
> To allow the mind [of distinctions] to rise is erroneous.
> Our pure nature lies in the erroneous mind.
> So long as the mind is correct, the Three Hindrances* are removed.
> If we practice the Way in this world,
> Nothing will hinder us.
> If we always see our own mistakes,
> We will always be in accord with the Way.
> The various species have their own ways of salvation.
> If one departs from one's own way to seek another way,
> He may keep seeking but he will not find it,
> And will have regret at the end.
> If one wishes to see the True Way,
> To practice correctly is the same as the Way.
> If one does not have the correct mind,
> Walking in the dark will not enable him to see the Way.
> One who truly practices the Way
> Will not find fault with the world.
> If one finds fault with the world,
> He is evidently at fault himself.
> When other people are wrong, I have committed a sin.
> When I am wrong, I am sinful myself.
> If only we can do away with the mind to find fault,
> All afflictions will be shattered to pieces.
> Those who wish to convert the ignorant
> Should have convenient means.
> Do not allow them to have any doubt,
> It means that perfect wisdom is realized.

*[Among the various sets of Three Hindrances are afflictions, evil deeds, and retribution.]

The Law is, after all, in the world,
The world should be transcended right in this world.
Do not depart from this world
To seek the transcendent world outside.
Perverse views are called worldly,
Correct views are called transcendent.
When correct and perverse views are both thrown away,
The nature of perfect wisdom becomes perfectly clear.
This alone is the doctrine of sudden enlightenment,
Also called the Great Vehicle.
Delusion may last for many infinitely long periods of time.
Enlightenment comes in an instant.

37. The Great Master said, "Good and learned friends, all of you recite this verse. If you practice according to this verse, even if you are a thousand *li** away from me, you will always be at my side. If you do not practice according to it, even when we are face to face, we will be a thousand *li* apart. Let each of you practice by himself. The Law waits for no one. You may disperse. I am going back to Ts'ao-hsi Mountain. If you have serious doubts, come to this mountain and ask me. I will remove your doubts. Together we will enter the Buddha world."

Officials, disciples who have renounced their families, and lay folk in the assembly paid reverence to the priest. All expressed their praise, "Excellent! We are greatly enlightened. We have heard something that we had never heard before. People in the Ling-nan region are blessed to have the Buddha born here. Anyone, no matter who, can attain wisdom." At once the assembly scattered.

*[A *li* is about one-third of a mile.]

NEO-CONFUCIAN SYNTHESES

Neo-Confucianism capped the synthesis prone middle period of Chinese philosophy (206 B.C.E.–1644 C.E.) by merging elements of Taoism and Buddhism with classical Confucianism. Confucian thinking itself had not advanced since the Han Dynasty (206 B.C.E.–220 C.E.). Neo-Confucianism revisited the teachings of Confucius and Mencius and expanded their limited vision into a complete worldview. To legitimate such a program, Neo-Confucianism adopted the Buddhist strategy of inventing an orthodox transmission dating from ancient times. It launched the theory that knowledge of the true Way had been passed regularly from the sage-kings of antiquity (third millennium B.C.E.) down to Confucius and Mencius, at which point the transmission lapsed for more than a thousand years until renewed in Neo-Confucianism. Inspiration for the new synthesis came from the metaphysical and religious appeal of Taoism and Buddhism, movements dominant in China after the Han. With one hand, Neo-Confucianism vigorously attacked these powerful rivals while freely borrowing from them with the other. It prevailed over them by incorporating their strengths into a system superior to both. This rich blend of philosophies was destined to become the main attraction in Chinese thought until the middle of the twentieth century.

The history of Neo-Confucianism, replete with famous names, can be summarized in five phases. In the first, the movement arose with the Five Masters of the Northern Sung Dynasty (960–1127): Shao Yung (Shao Yong, 1011–1077), Chou Tun-i (Zhou Dunyi, 1017–1073), Chang Tsai (Zhang Zai, 1020–1077), Ch'eng Hao (Cheng Hao, 1032–1085), and Ch'eng I (Cheng Yi, 1033–1107). The Ch'engs were brothers, Chang their uncle, and Chou their teacher. Second, the innovations of this circle fused brilliantly in the thought of Chu Hsi (1130–1200), with which the movement achieved its zenith. Chu was challenged in his own time by Lu Hsiang-shan (Lu Xiangshan, 1139–1193). Through public debates and correspondence between Chu and Lu, two major approaches within the movement hardened during the Southern Sung Dynasty (1127–1279). Chu's thought, however, triumphed as the established orthodoxy of the empire from the Yuan Dynasty (1279–1368) until the end of the Ch'ing Dynasty (1644–1911).

During the third phase, the approach developed by Lu Hsiang-shan reached its highest expression through Wang Yang-ming (1472–1529) during the Ming Dynasty (1368–1644). His thought enjoyed great popularity thereafter but never became the official viewpoint. Fourth, both schools had their detractors in the early Ch'ing. Some Confucians, Tai Chen (1723–1777) for example, objected to the infiltration of Taoist and Buddhist metaphysics and wished to purge those influences by returning to earlier forms of Confucianism. In the final fifth phase, both Chu's and Wang's philosophies survived the collapse of the dynastic system in 1911 and, despite harsh criticism, found advocates in the first half of the twentieth century who combined them with Western thought. Fung Yu-lan (1895–1990) and Hsiung Shih-li (1895–1968) were the leading Neo-Confucian reconstructionists of that time. During the second half of the twentieth century, Chinese communist ideologues initially attacked Neo-Confucianism but later (after 1978) came to treat it more even-handedly. Meanwhile, outside Mainland China, a remarkable revival of Neo-Confucianism has flourished, led by Chinese scholars such as Wing-tsit Chan (1901–1994), Chung-ying Cheng (b. 1935), and Tu Wei-ming (b. 1940). The following discussion is limited to Chu Hsi and Wang Yang-ming, the preeminent Neo-Confucians.

A variety of names for the philosophies of Chu and Wang appear in the secondary literature of Neo-Confucianism. These names attempt to identify each system descriptively. Since the names come in contrasting pairs, they also serve to sharply differentiate the two systems. This tendency of an older generation of scholars to juxtapose the two approaches has been replaced among contemporary scholars with a balanced view of differences and similarities. The first pair of names is "the Ch'eng-Chu School" and "the Lu-Wang School." These names point to the respective founders, linked with their predecessors. It is certainly true that Chu Hsi owed a huge debt to the Ch'eng brothers, Ch'eng I in particular. But current scholarship minimizes any real dependence of Wang on Lu Hsiang-shan. Wang never quoted Lu, claimed his thought came directly from Confucius and Mencius, and urged his associates to avoid the controversy, still active, between followers of Chu and Lu. It is better to regard the overlapping of ideas between Lu and Wang as coincidental. The second pair of names, "Sung Neo-Confucianism" and "Ming Neo-Confucianism," refers quite simply to the dynasties during which the two schools arose. "The School of Principle" and "the School of Mind," the third pair of names, aims to identify and distinguish the two viewpoints according to the central concept of each. This works only after deeper analysis, because both schools use the Principle and Mind concepts prominently. The final pair of names, "Rationalistic Neo-Confucianism" and "Idealistic Neo-Confucianism," strikes the difference between the two schools in terms of the method of self-cultivation each employs, a tactic that works also only with additional explanation, for the meaning of "rationalistic" and "idealistic" without more context is not self-evident. The appropriateness of the last two name pairs will become clear through discussion of Chu's and Wang's positions, to which we now turn, taking Chu first.

*   *   *

Chu Hsi (Zhu Xi) was the greatest of the Neo-Confucians and the most cele-brated figure in Chinese philosophy after Confucius, Mencius, Lao-tzu, and Chuang-tzu. As a proper Confucian Gentleman, he devoted his life to the cultiva-tion of virtue, observance of the rites (especially those honoring Confucius and other moral exemplars), the pursuit of learning, and public service. His public service record was modest, but his contributions to scholarship and education monumental. Though inclined toward the quiet career of a scholar-teacher, he oc-casionally accepted appointment to public office, limited to a few days at the court level and a few years at the local or regional level. Rather, he showed his lifelong concern for the welfare of the empire in a manner befitting an intellectual, by re-peatedly petitioning the emperor for moral leadership, the dismissal of corrupt of-ficials, and staunch resistance against the northern invaders. His outspokenness earned him enemies, who near the end of his life called for the banning of his teachings and even for his execution. Chu's renowned scholarship fills two mas-sive collections—his literary works in thirty-six volumes and his recorded sayings in forty. He also co-compiled *Reflections on Things at Hand,* the first Neo-Confucian anthology, containing excerpts with commentary from the works of the Five Northern Sung Masters, on which Chu himself drew heavily. His finest achievements, however, came in the field of education. Not only did he personally train the best scholar-teachers of the next generation, he also set the curriculum for public education in China that lasted hundreds of years. He established a list of core readings called the Four Books that surpassed the Five Classics as study material in Confucian academies throughout China. The Four Books are the *Analects* of Confucius, the *Great Learning,* the *Doctrine of the Mean,* and the *Mencius.* Chu decreed that all four contain the pure teaching of Confucius, the first directly and the other three later works through a filtering down process. Further, he wrote the definitive commentaries on these books, interpreting them to support his own philosophical viewpoint. The four plus his commentaries topped the official syllabus for the civil service exams in China from 1313 to 1905, thereby leaving an indelible mark on six centuries of Chinese education.

Chu Hsi's writings, though prolific and far ranging, lack a single text that cov-ers his complete system of thought. His works tend to be topical rather than com-prehensive, treating only one subject at a time, and this contributes to the main difficulty in interpreting his thinking. What he says about a topic in one context may seem incongruent with what he says about the same topic in another. Skillful commentators are nonetheless able to make sense out of Chu's philosophy, even without a master text to guide them and to arbitrate when plausible interpretations differ. The selection of his essays and sayings offered in this section is taken from Wing-tsit Chan's translation in *A Source Book in Chinese Philosophy.* Chan's arrangement, faithful to the order Chu himself preferred, moves topically from ethics to metaphysics, giving ethics the greater weight. In the discussion of his system here, however, that sequence is reversed, as it commonly is among his ex-positors. Metaphysics is addressed first, for an understanding of his metaphysics is assumed for his ethics.

Chu Hsi's metaphysics purports to explain in depth observable features of or-dinary things by means of special entities not open to observation. The following features of ordinary things, taken for granted by most people, piqued his curios-ity: Things exist, are many, fit together into a universe, possess specific natures, belong to classes sharing a common nature, display idiosyncrasies making them unique within a class, contain imperfections falling short of the class ideal, are good or bad relative to that ideal, have intrinsic value irrespective of goodness or badness, move, change, and are intelligible. Suppose there were nothing, or only one thing, or many chaotic things, or things that lacked natures and class membership, or things that were all identical within classes, or things that never moved or changed, or things that could not be fathomed, and so on. That a world with opposite features can be imagined underscores the relevance of explaining why our world is in fact the way it is. The special entities Chu invoked to explain these features are the Great Ultimate (*t'ai chi (taiji)*), Principle (*li*), and Material Force (*ch'i (qi)*). The first he took from Chou Tun-i and Shao Yung, the second from the Ch'eng brothers, and the third from Chang Tsai, demonstrating his indebtedness to all five of the Northern Sung masters. To weld these originally disjointed notions into a coherent theory, Chu had to reshape them. In so doing, he refined all three.

The Great Ultimate is the Absolute, the bedrock reality with nothing prior or beyond. It is the fountainhead of the cosmic flow, the cornucopia of perpetual creation, the one source from which the many issue and coalesce into a universe. It is without form, incognito, engulfed in wonder and mystery. It is both transcendent and immanent, eternally independent of the world it generates yet present within all temporal things as the reason for their existence, cohesiveness, and value. The fecundity of the Great Ultimate ensures that everything generated by it really exists, separate from its source and independent of perceiving minds. The unity of the Great Ultimate guarantees that the multitude of things emanating from it cohere into an organic whole, an insight of Hua-yen Buddhism too. And the perfection of the Great Ultimate makes certain that everything in which it resides has intrinsic value. Chu referred to it variously as the Way (Tao), Heaven, and Nature.

Principle is identical in essence with the Great Ultimate. The Great Ultimate is the supreme principle and the sum of all principles, while Principle is the ultimate beyond which there is nothing. Both are eternal, immaterial, immutable, indestructible, and perfect. Principle and the Great Ultimate, nevertheless, are usually assigned different functions, though not invariably so. In Chu's system, the Great Ultimate primarily explains the origin of things, while Principle commonly accounts for their nature and behavior. Principle means that which controls, regulates, determines, and defines the universe part and parcel. It has three modes—universal, particular, and normative. In its universal mode, Principle (alias Principle of Heaven, Principle of Nature) establishes the patterns or rules all natural and human processes obey, approximating the modern notion of "natural law." Here it is without form and prior to Material Force. This mode reflects the influence of Mencius (the Mean) and the Neo-Taoist Wang Pi (Tao = Principle). In its particular mode, Principle exists in each thing as its defining nature. Here it is equivalent to form and inseparable from Material Force, as the Hua-yen Buddhist Fa-tsang also held. In its normative mode, Principle sets the standards that measure correctness or deviancy, fulfillment or deficiency, goodness or badness, right or wrong, virtue or vice, in affairs human and natural. Chu, in sum, used Principle to explain the regularity of the universe (universal mode), the specific natures of things and their division into classes accordingly (particular mode), and the goodness of things that adhere closely to their ideal natures (normative mode). He also used the particular mode to account for the intelligibility of things. To comprehend anything is to discern from its nature and behavior what its controlling, defining Principle is. Principle plays the largest role in his metaphysics. His position is for that reason known as the School of Principle.

Material Force for Chu Hsi is the stuff that combines with Principle to produce particular things. If there were no Material Force, Principle would remain abstract and disembodied, lacking the substance necessary for actualization as concrete particulars. That is why it is called "material." Production, however, is not the work of an external agent. Material Force is itself dynamic, not static. That is why it is called "force." It fashions itself into particular things, using Principle as its pattern or plan. The process whereby things are produced is complex, according to Chu. From the principles of movement and rest within the Great Ultimate evolve the material forces of Yang and Yin, whose alternation produces the Five Agents (earth, metal, water, wood, fire), which in turn generate the myriad creatures of the world, each a compound of Principle and Material Force. The covert activity of Yin and Yang causes the manifoldness of things. As Yin and Yang alternate, Material Force contracts and expands, and on the contraction phase condenses around many points where particular things with Principle take form. The hidden activity of the Five Agents, endlessly engendering and conquering one another, accounts for the motion and transformation of things. Further, Material Force is not homogeneous. Any portion of it is by degree light/heavy, clear/opaque, pure/impure. The variability of Material Force explains in Chu's system the idiosyncrasies and imperfections of things. It also resolves the problem of evil. Things that happen to be endowed with impure Material Force cannot embody their Principles well and are hence prone to evil. Mention of evil prompts the transition from metaphysics to ethics.

Chu Hsi's ethics centers on a virtue known in Chinese as *jen* (*ren*), paramount to Confucius and Mencius also. There is no one word in English for *jen*. It has been translated as "benevolence," "kindness," "love," "loving kindness," "human-heartedness," "humanness," and, in the selections to follow, most frequently as "humanity." Confucians consider it the root from which all other virtues sprout and the hallmark of moral maturity in persons. The clue to grasping Chu's complex view of *jen* rests in his definition of it as both "the principle of love" and "the character of the mind." Principle and mind are distinguished in Chu's thought. Principle is the ruling, defining factor alone, apart from Material Force; it is not a particular thing, nor does it think or feel. Mind, on the other hand, is a particular thing (combining Principle and Material Force) that thinks and feels.

As the principle of love, *jen* also has the same three modes as Principle. In its universal mode, *jen* is the Principle of Nature or the Principle of Heaven (alias the mind of Heaven and Earth) that commands and controls the endless productivity of the universe. The law behind the constant outpouring of new creatures everywhere is the principle of love at the cosmic level. In its particular mode, *jen* is the nature of persons to be caring and giving. Human nature is structured by the virtues of humanity, righteousness, propriety, and wisdom (the Four Constant Virtues of Mencius), with the first (*jen*) the source of the rest. The natural inclination to benefit others, human and nonhuman, is the meaning of love at this level. In its normative mode, *jen* is the ideal or standard of unselfishness against which persons are judged moral or immoral.

Chu Hsi's stand on the classical Confucian debate over the moral condition of human nature deserves comment at this point. His position was something of a compromise between Mencius (human nature is originally good) and Hsun-tzu (human nature is originally evil) made possible by an ambivalence in Chu's concept of human nature. In its narrower sense as Principle alone, human nature is good, because Principle is inherently good. But in its broader sense as the full endowment of humans, including Material Force as well as Principle, human nature is mixed. The Principle component is good, but the Material Force component is evil in those humans where it is impure, good in those where it is pure. Material Force introduces the possibility of evil into human nature in its more inclusive sense.

Jen as the character of the mind extends into another equally important domain: moral feelings in contrast to moral principles. For the mind is a particular thing (composed of Principle and Material Force) that makes choices on the basis of what it thinks and feels. Moral feelings mediate between moral principles and moral actions. Without moral feelings, the moral agent is not motivated to act morally, even with full knowledge of moral principles. *Jen* in this regard is the mind characterized by the moral feelings of commiseration, shame, deference/compliance, and approval/disapproval. These are the so-called Four Beginnings touted by Mencius as the seeds innate in human nature that, with proper cultivation, blossom into the Four Constant Virtues of humanity, righteousness, propriety, and wisdom. Chu, departing from Mencius, saw commiseration as the epitome of the others, anchored the Four Beginnings in the mind rather than in human nature, and made the Four Virtues of human nature the basis for the Four Beginnings of the mind rather than the reverse. The situation inside the moral agent's mind, where moral feelings occur freely because of the moral nature, is complicated when selfish desires are aroused by impurities in the mind's Material Force. The struggle between selfish and unselfish motives poses a major challenge in the moral life. Moral rectification of the mind is the sustained endeavor to quell selfish feelings while encouraging unselfish ones. Chu linked *jen* as the principle of love and *jen* as the character of the mind by declaring the former the substance of *jen* and the latter its function. The substance-function distinction was a philosophical tool Chu used often and effectively.

The self-cultivation of *jen* lay for Chu Hsi at the heart of the moral life. Chu took his method of moral self-cultivation from the *Great Learning,* putting his own stamp on the eight progressive steps found there. Chu emphasized the first two steps of his method, since they together lay the foundation. The first step is the Investigation of Things—rational inquiry into the principles underlying the ordinary things of the external world. It does not renounce introspection or Ch'an Buddhist meditation, which intrigued Chu early on. Nor does it deny a role for reading and scholarship. But its gist is, in the spirit of science, the close observation of data and deep reflection on their meaning. Since this is a rational enterprise, Chu's school is called, among other names, Rationalistic Neo-Confucianism. The second step, the Extension of Knowledge, based on the investigation of things, is discovery of the factual and moral principles behind things and affairs. Third, the Sincerity of the Will is the firm resolve to abide by the moral principles uncovered in the extension of knowledge. Fourth, the Rectification of the Mind is the overmastering of selfish feelings by unselfish ones, making *jen* the character of the mind. Fifth, the Cultivation of the Self is actualizing in life human nature's innate virtues, enshrined within *jen* the principle of love. Sixth, the Regulation of the Family; Seventh, the Ordering of the State; and Eighth, Peace Throughout the World are social benefits that follow in turn when individuals successfully cultivate the virtues inherent in their nature. This program was intended to ensure a moral society operated by moral persons, a lofty ideal indeed.

*   *   *

Three centuries after Chu Hsi, Wang Yang-ming (Wang Yangming) rose to share with Chu top honors in the gallery of Neo-Confucian greats. Wang and his followers closed the middle period of Chinese philosophy with a flourish, amidst turbulent conditions. The once brilliant Ming Dynasty was in decline during Wang's lifetime (1472-1529), beset by hostile incursions from the north as well as by outlaws, rebels, and internal misrule. Wang's own career, strewn with reversals of fortune, reflected that turbulence. His father was a nobleman and high court official, and Wang grew up around the power elite of the central government. His interests during his student years included Chu Hsi's philosophy, Taoist techniques of immortality, and Ch'an Buddhist meditation. Degrees in hand, he commenced government service at age twenty-eight. He also began to formulate and teach a new direction in philosophy that was refreshingly different from Chu's. His deepest aspiration was to become a sage. In 1506, having angered an influential eunuch, he was flogged nearly to death and exiled for three years to a remote region. During that isolation, he added to his developing philosophy insights found through sudden enlightenment. Rehabilitated, he became a provincial magistrate and successfully resumed his political career. Soon he was promoted to various posts in the central government. During these years (1510–1517), his spreading fame as a philosopher attracted many students, including one of his superiors. After crushing several uprisings against the throne (1517–1519), including one led by a prince, he was rewarded with a title. Not long after, however, a charge of conspiracy, followed by ostracism at court, forced his retirement (1521–1527). With leisure, his circle of students swelled, and he wrote his major work. Recalled to military duty to quell another civil disturbance in 1527, he died two years later while on his way home. Chu Hsi supporters then attacked his teachings. His title was revoked but a higher one conferred some years later. His highest honor came fifty years after his death. The emperor inaugurated sacrifices to him in the Confucian temple. History finally confirmed the laurels that fluctuated during his lifetime.

Wang Yang-ming's philosophy is like a self-portrait. In a self-portrait, the artist alters the image of the self he or she encounters outwardly in a mirror or photo to make it expressive of the self he or she discovers inwardly through introspection. The upheavals of Wang's life drove him to search within for self-understanding. He articulated that self-understanding through ideas taken from Confucian masters. He appropriated from Confucius the idea of the sage, following the Way ordained by Heaven, cultivating virtue (*jen*), observing the rites, devoting oneself to learning, and serving in public office. From Mencius he borrowed the theory of the intrinsic goodness of human nature informed by moral knowledge and the inclination to live by that knowledge. Chang Tsai and Ch'eng Hao contributed the notion of the universe forming one body united by love. These teachings Wang creatively reinterpreted by projecting his own self-understanding on them. His largest debt was to Chu Hsi, his foil and antagonist. Wang developed his own views against a critique of Chu's. Wang, like Chu, spoke of principle, the Principle of Nature, the investigation of things and the extension of knowledge, and the original mind and its susceptibility to obstruction by selfish motives, but he revised these concepts to fit his own system. Later in life, Wang even attempted a makeover of Chu Hsi, arguing from Chu's writings that Chu had spotted and corrected the very errors of which Wang accused him. Wang's philosophy was, consequently, highly original in its reading of the Confucian masters. It was also highly idealistic, for in it Wang offered an ethical model for others to adopt. This prompted the labeling of his position as Idealistic Neo-Confucianism. It was highly inspirational as well, exerting great appeal from his day to the present.

Four points epitomize Wang's position. First, mind *is* principle. Wang's fundamental insight dawned on him during his exile in a flash of sudden enlightenment. It implies that the human mind, endowed by Heaven, comes ready-made with the moral principles necessary and sufficient for achieving sagehood. The idea parallels that of Mencius, but the wording has been modified. Mencius spoke of virtues innate in human nature, Wang of principles intrinsic to the human mind. Wang converted Chu Hsi's metaphysical term *principle* to mean moral principles. According to Wang, Chu was wrong about principles existing in things external and being known through objective investigation. After a week of intense study at age twenty, Wang had failed to fathom any metaphysical principle within the bamboo of his grandfather's garden. He concluded that such principles, if indeed any exist, do not matter. What matters are moral principles clearly comprehended by investigating one's own mind, where they reside exclusively. Wang's is thus appropriately designated the School of Mind.

Wang's second point is the unity of knowledge and action. Another spontaneous illumination in exile led Wang to invent this formulation, unprecedented among masters before him. Knowledge is the beginning and action the completion of one unified process. Genuine knowledge is the seed of correct action, and correct action the fruit of genuine knowledge. The bond between knowledge and action is organic. To know and not do is to not really know. Chu Hsi's purely theoretical knowledge does not automatically ripen into action, hence it lacks relevance for real life.

Third is extension of the innate knowledge of the good. Wang's most advanced proposal combined the first two by joining the notion of the extension of knowledge (construed as knowledge extending into action) from the *Great Learning* with the idea of the innate knowledge of the good found in Mencius. It underscores the kinetic character of genuine knowledge. The innate knowledge of the good motivates the knower to extend that knowledge into moral action. Wang equated the innate knowledge of the good with the original substance of mind and with the original goodness of human nature, erasing Chu's distinction between mind and nature in humans. He also equated such knowledge with the Principle of Nature—the latent sense of right and wrong that triggers action appropriate to the situation. When the sage has through personal cultivation eliminated selfishness, basic impulses may be trusted to prompt morally right action. Furthermore, the Principle of Nature is purely intuitive, unbounded by codified precepts such as the Ten Commandments. Controversy erupted over this point when some of Wang's followers used it to excuse conventionally questionable behavior. It was even blamed, implausibly, for the undoing of the Ming Dynasty.

The final point is forming one body with Heaven, Earth, and the myriad things. Wang used this phrase, adapted from Chang Tsai and Ch'eng Hao, to make explicit the ultimate extension of knowledge into action. All things animal, vegetable, and mineral comprise one cosmic ecosystem (echoes of Hua-yen Buddhism). To live in solidarity with all creatures as members of one community, one family, and one body is the essence of humanity (*jen*), according to Wang. It is to extend the intuitive knowledge of the good into the action of welcoming, respecting, caring for, and benefiting all the creatures of the universe as one does the limbs and organs of one's own body. In retrospect, these are not so much four different points as one point unfolding progressively.

Wang's chief philosophical writings are *Instructions for Practical Living* and *Inquiry on the Great Learning*. The former is a work of some length compiled by a disciple; it contains recorded conversations, letters, and short essays. Because the latter is a compact resume of Wang's mature philosophy (1527), it is presented here as the second selection of this section (translated by Wing-tsit Chan). The *Inquiry* is an ingenious commentary on the classical Confucian text known as the *Great Learning*. That text was originally an insignificant chapter in the *Book of Rites*, until elevated to prominence by Chu Hsi as one of his Four Books. For Wang, the title referred to the learning of the great person in contrast to the small person, the learning that brings sagehood. The work affirms all the points summarized earlier except the unity of knowledge and action, which is nonetheless implied. Of those four points, the emphasis falls on forming one body with Heaven, Earth, and the myriad things, a point condensing the others. The structure of the piece comes from what the commentaries call the "three major cords" and the "eight minor wires." These are two groups of main themes in the original *Great Learning*. The three major cords are "manifesting the clear character, loving the people, and abiding in the highest good." The eight minor wires are "investigating things, extending knowledge, making the will sincere, rectifying the mind, cultivating the personal life, regulating the family, ordering the state, and peace throughout the world." Wang bracketed the last three of these eight and dealt only with the first five. The fascination of Wang's commentary lies in the way he skillfully resolved into one the three major cords and the first five minor wires, giving the whole work a single thrust, that humanity (*jen*) is consolidating love, love that forms one body with all creatures without discrimination. The technique of reducing many to one was typical of Wang's style of philosophizing.

*   *   *

Neo-Confucianism has stimulated a large volume of quality research during the past half century, especially from Wm. Theodore de Bary and Wing-tsit Chan. That literature falls into four categories.

1. General studies of Neo-Confucianism, covering both the Sung (Chu Hsi) and Ming (Wang Yang-ming) periods: Carsun Chang, *The Development of Neo-Confucian Thought*, 2 vols. (New Haven, CT: College and University Press, 1963); Wm. Theodore de Bary and Irene Bloom, eds., *Principle and Practicality: Essays in Neo-Confucian Practicality* (New York: Columbia University Press, 1979); Wm. Theodore de Bary, *Neo-Confucian Orthodoxy and the Learning of Mind-and-Heart* (New York: Columbia University Press, 1981); Wm. Theodore de Bary, *The Message of the Mind in Neo-Confucianism* (New York: Columbia University Press, 1989); and Wm. Theodore de Bary, *Learning for One's Self: Essays on the Individual in Neo-Confucian Thought* (New York: Columbia University Press, 1991).

2. Studies of Chu Hsi in the setting of the Sung Dynasty: Wing-tsit Chan, ed., *Chu Hsi and Neo-Confucianism* (Honolulu: University of Hawaii Press, 1986); Wing-tsit Chan, *Chu Hsi: Life and Thought* (New York: St. Martin's Press, 1987);

Donald J. Monro, *Images of Human Nature: A Sung Portrait* (Princeton, NJ: Princeton University Press, 1988); Wing-tsit Chan, *Chu Hsi: New Studies* (Honolulu: University of Hawaii Press, 1989); and Daniel K. Gardner, *Learning to be a Sage* (Berkeley: University of California Press, 1990).

3. Studies of Wang Yang-ming in the setting of the Ming Dynasty: Carsun Chang, *Wang Yang-ming: The Idealist Philosopher of the Sixteenth-Century* (New York: St. John's University Press, 1962); Wm. Theodore de Bary, ed., *Self and Society in Ming Thought* (New York: Columbia University Press, 1970); Julia Ching, *To Acquire Wisdom: The Way of Wang Yang-ming* (New York: Columbia University Press, 1976); Tu Wei-ming, *Neo-Confucian Thought in Action: Wang Yang-ming's Youth, 1472–1509* (Berkeley: University of California Press, 1976); Antonio S. Cua, *The Unity of Knowledge and Action: A Study of Wang Yang-ming's Moral Psychology* (Honolulu: University of Hawaii Press, 1982); and Philip J. Ivanhoe, *Ethics in the Confucian Tradition: The Thought of Mengzi and Wang Yangming,* 2nd ed. (Indianapolis/Cambridge: Hackett, 2002).

4. Neo-Confucianism in post-Ming and contemporary perspectives: Wm. Theodore de Bary, ed., *The Unfolding of Neo-Confucianism* (New York: Columbia University Press, 1975); Wm. Theodore de Bary, *The Liberal Tradition in China* (New York: Columbia University Press, 1983); Chung-ying Cheng, *New Dimensions of Confucian and Neo-Confucian Philosophy* (Albany: SUNY Press, 1991); and John H. Berthrong, *Concerning Creativity: A Comparison of Chu Hsi, Whitehead, and Neville* (Albany: SUNY Press, 1998).

CHU HSI, TREATISES AND SAYINGS

A. TREATISES

1. A TREATISE ON *JEN*

"The mind of Heaven and Earth is to produce things." In the production of man and things, they receive the mind of Heaven and Earth as their mind. Therefore, with reference to the character of the mind, although it embraces and penetrates all and leaves nothing to be desired, nevertheless, one word will cover all of it, namely, *jen* (humanity). Let me try to explain fully.

The qualities of the mind of Heaven and Earth are four: origination, flourish, advantages, and firmness. And the principle of origination unites and controls them all. In their operation they constitute the course of the four seasons, and the vital force of spring permeates all. Therefore in the mind of man there are also four moral qualities—namely, *jen*, righteousness, propriety, and wisdom—and *jen* embraces them all. In their emanation and function, they constitute the feeling of love, respect, being right, and discrimination between right and wrong—and the feeling of commiseration pervades them all. Therefore in discussing the mind of Heaven and Earth, it is said, "Great is *ch'ien* (Heaven), the originator!" and "Great is *k'un* (Earth), the originator." Both substance and function of the four moral qualities are thus fully implied without enumerating them. In discussing the excellence of man's mind, it is said, "*Jen* is man's mind." Both substance and function of the four moral qualities are thus fully presented without mentioning them. For *jen* as constituting the Way (Tao) consists of the fact that the mind of Heaven and Earth to produce things is present in everything. Before feelings are aroused this substance is already existent in its completeness. After feelings are aroused, its function is infinite. If we can truly practice love and preserve it, then we have in it the spring of all virtues and the root of all good deeds. This is why in the teachings of the Confucian school, the student is always urged to exert anxious and unceasing effort in the pursuit of *jen*. In the teachings (of Confucius, it is said), "Master oneself and return to propriety." This means that if we can overcome and eliminate selfishness and return to the Principle of Nature (*T'ien-li*, Principle of Heaven), then the substance of this mind (that is, *jen*) will be present everywhere and its function will always be operative. It is also said, "Be respectful in private life, be serious in handling affairs, and be loyal in dealing with others." These are also ways to preserve this mind. Again, it is said, "Be filial in serving parents," "Be respectful in serving elder brothers," and "Be loving in dealing with all things." These are ways to put this mind into practice. It is again said, "They sought *jen* and found it," for (Po-i) declined a kingdom and left the country (in favor of his younger brother, Shu-ch'i) and they both remonstrated their superior against a punitive expedition and chose retirement and hunger, and in doing so, they prevented losing this mind. Again it is said, "Sacrifice life in order to realize *jen*." This means that we desire something more than life and hate something more than death, so as not to injure this mind. What mind is this? In Heaven and Earth it is the mind to produce things infinitely. In man it is the mind to love people gently and to benefit things. It includes the four virtues (of humanity, righteousness, propriety, and wisdom) and penetrates the Four Beginnings (of the sense of commiseration, the sense of shame, the sense of deference and compliance, and the sense of right and wrong).

Someone said: According to our explanation, is it not wrong for Master Ch'eng to say that love is feeling while *jen* is nature and that love should not be regarded as *jen?*

Answer: Not so. What Master Ch'eng criticized was the application of the term to the expression of love. What I maintain is that the term should be applied to the principle of love. For although the spheres of man's nature and feelings are different, their mutual penetration is like the blood system in which each part has its own relationship. When have they become sharply separated and been made to have nothing to do with each other? I was just now worrying about students' reciting Master Ch'eng's words without inquiring into their meaning, and thereby coming to talk about *jen* as clearly apart from love. I have therefore purposely talked about this to reveal the hidden meaning of Master Ch'eng's words, and you regard my ideas as different from his. Are you not mistaken?

Someone said: The followers of Master Ch'eng have given many explanations of *jen.* Some say that love is not *jen,* and regard the unity of all things and the self as the substance of *jen.* Others maintain that love is not *jen* but explain *jen* in terms of the possession of consciousness by the mind. If what you say is correct, are they all wrong?

Answer: From what they call the unity of all things and the self, it can be seen that *jen* involves love for all, but unity is not the reality which makes *jen* a substance. From what they call the mind's possession of consciousness, it can be seen that *jen* includes wisdom, but that is not the real reason why *jen* is so called. If you look up Confucius' answer to (his pupil) Tzu-kung's question whether conferring extensive benefit on the people and bringing salvation to all (will constitute *jen*) and also Master Ch'eng's statement that *jen* is not to be explained in terms of consciousness, you will see the point. How can you still explain *jen* in these terms?

Furthermore, to talk about *jen* in general terms of the unity of things and the self will lead people to be vague, confused, neglectful, and make no effort to be alert. The bad effect—and there has been—may be to consider other things as oneself. To talk about love in specific terms of consciousness will lead people to be nervous, irascible, and devoid of any quality of depth. The bad effect—and there has been—may be to consider desire as principle. In one case, (the mind) forgets (its objective). In the other (there is artificial effort to) help (it grow). Both are wrong. Furthermore, the explanation in terms of consciousness does not in any way approach the manner of (a man of *jen* who) "delights in mountains" (while a man of wisdom delights in water) or the idea that (*jen* alone) "can preserve" (what knowledge has attained), as taught his pupil by Confucius. How then can you still explain love in those terms? I hereby record what they said and write this treatise on *jen.*

2. A TREATISE ON CH'ENG MING-TAO'S DISCOURSE ON THE NATURE

Master Ch'eng Hao also said, "What is inborn is called nature. . . . They (nature and material force, *ch'i*) are both inborn." [His meaning is this]: What is imparted by Heaven (Nature) to all things is called destiny (*ming,* mandate, fate). What is received by them from Heaven is called nature. But in the carrying out of the Mandate of Heaven, there must first be the interaction, mutual influence, consolidation, and integration of the two material forces (yin and yang) and the Five Agents (of Metal, Wood,

Water, Fire, and Earth) before things can be produced. Man's nature and destiny exist before physical form [and are without it], while material force exists after physical form [and is with it]. What exists before physical form is the one principle harmonious and undifferentiated, and is invariably good. What exists after physical form, however, is confused and mixed, and good and evil are thereby differentiated. Therefore when man and things are produced, they have in them this material force, with the endowment of which they are produced. But the nature endowed by Heaven is therein preserved. This is how Master Ch'eng elucidated the doctrine of Kao Tzu that what is inborn is called nature, and expressed his own thought by saying that "One's nature is the same as material force and material force is the same as nature."

Master Ch'eng also said. "[According to principle, there are both good and evil] in the material force with which man is endowed at birth. . . . [Nature is of course good], but it cannot be said that evil is not nature." It is the principle of nature that the material force with which man is endowed necessarily has the difference of good and evil. For in the operation of material force, nature is the controlling factor. In accordance with its purity or impurity, material force is differentiated into good and evil. Therefore there are not two distinct things in nature opposing each other. Even the nature of evil material force is good, and therefore evil may not be said to be not a part of nature. The Master further said, "Good and evil in the world are both the Principle of Nature. What is called evil is not original evil. It becomes evil only because of deviation from the mean." For there is nothing in the world which is outside of one's nature. All things are originally good but degenerated into evil, that is all.

The Master further said, "For what is inborn is called one's nature. . . . The fact that whatever issues from the Way is good may be compared to water always flowing downward." Nature is simply nature. How can it be described in words? Therefore those who excel in talking about nature only do so in terms of the beginning of its emanation and manifestation, and what is involved in the concept of nature may then be understood in silence, as when Mencius spoke of the Four Beginnings (of humanity, righteousness, propriety, and wisdom). By observing the fact that water necessarily flows downward, we know the nature of water is to go downward. Similarly, by observing the fact that the emanation of nature is always good, we know that nature involves goodness.

The Master further said, "Water as such is the same in all cases. . . . Although they differ in being turbid or clear, we cannot say that the turbid water ceases to be water. . . . The original goodness of human nature is like the original clearness of water. Therefore it is not true that two distinct and opposing elements of good and evil exist in human nature and that each issues from it." This is again using the clearness and turbidity of water as an analogy. The clearness of water is comparable to the goodness of nature. Water flowing to the sea without getting dirty is similar to one whose material force with which he is endowed is pure and clear and who is good from childhood. In the case of a sage it is his nature to be so and he preserves his Heavenly endowment complete. Water that flows only a short distance and is already turbid is like one whose material endowment is extremely unbalanced and impure and is evil from childhood. Water that flows a long distance before becoming turbid is like one who, as he grows up, changes his character as he sees something novel and attractive to him, and loses his child's heart. That water may be turbid to a greater or smaller extent is similar to the fact that one's material force may be dark or clear and pure or impure in varying degrees. "We cannot say that the turbid water ceases to be water" means that it cannot be said that evil is not nature. Thus although man is darkened by material force and degenerates into evil, nature does not cease to be inherent in him. Only, if you call it nature, it is not the original nature, and if you say it is not nature, yet from the beginning it has never departed from it. Because of this, man must increase his effort at purification. If one can overcome material force through learning, he will know that this nature is harmonious and unified and from the beginning has never been destroyed. It is like the original water. Although the water is turbid, the clear water is nevertheless there, and therefore it is not that clear water has been substituted by turbid water. When it is clear, it is originally not turbid, and therefore it is not that turbid water has been taken out and laid in a corner. This being the case, the nature is originally good. How can there be two distinct, opposing, and parallel things existing in nature?

Master Ch'eng finally said, "This principle is the Mandate of Heaven. To obey and follow it is the Way. . . . One can neither augment nor diminish this function which corresponds to the Way. Such is the case of Shun who, [obeying and following the Way], possessed the empire as if it were nothing to him. The sentence "This principle is the Mandate of Heaven" includes the beginning and ending, and the fundament and the secondary. Although the cultivation of the Way is spoken of with reference to human affairs, what is cultivated is after all nothing but the Mandate of Heaven as it originally is and there is nothing man's selfishness or cunning can do about it. However, only the sage can completely fulfill it. Therefore the example of Shun is used to make the meaning clear.

$$* * *$$

4. A Treatise on the Examination of the Mind

Someone asked whether it is true that the Buddhists have a doctrine of the examination of the mind.

Answer: The mind is that with which man rules his body. It is one and not a duality, is subject and not object, and controls the external world instead of being controlled by it. Therefore, if we examine external objects with the mind, their principles will be apprehended. Now (in the Buddhist view), there is another thing to examine the mind. If this is true, then outside this mind there is another one which is capable of controlling it. But is what we call the mind a unity or a duality? Is it subject or object? Does it control the external world or is it controlled by the external world? We do not need to be taught to see the fallacy of the Buddhist doctrine.

Someone may say: In the light of what you have said, how are we to understand such expressions by sages and worthies as "absolute refinement and singleness (of mind)," "Hold it fast and you preserve it. Let it go and you lose it," "Exert the mind to the utmost and know one's nature. . . . Preserve one's mind and nourish one's nature," and "(Standing) let a man see (truthful words and serious action) in front of him, and (riding in a carriage), let him see them attached to the yoke."

Answer: These expressions and (the Buddhist doctrine) sound similar but are different, just like the difference between seedlings and weed, or between vermilion and purple, and the student should clearly distinguish them. What is meant by the precariousness of the human mind is the budding of human selfish desires, and what is meant by the subtlety of the moral mind is the all-embracing depth of the Principle of Heaven (Nature). The mind is one; it is called differently depending on whether or not it is rectified. The meaning of the saying, "Have absolute refinement and singleness (of mind)" is to abide by what is right and discern what is wrong, as well as to discard the wrong and restore the right. If we can do this, we shall indeed "hold fast the Mean," and avoid the partiality of too much or too little. The saying does not mean that the moral mind is one mind, the human mind another, and then still a third one to make them absolutely refined and single. By "holding it fast and preserving it" is not meant that one mind holds fast to another and so preserves it. Neither does "letting it go and losing it" mean that one mind lets go another and so loses it. It merely means that if the mind holds fast to itself, what might be lost will be saved, and if the mind does not hold fast but lets itself go, then what is preserved will be lost. "Holding it fast" is another way of saying that we should not allow our conduct during the day to fetter and destroy our innate mind characterized by humanity and righteousness. It does not mean that we should sit in a rigid position to preserve the obviously idle consciousness and declare that "This is holding it fast and preserving it!" As to the exerting of the mind to the utmost, it is to investigate things and study their principles to the utmost, to arrive at broad penetration, and thus to be able fully to realize the principle (li) embodied in the mind. By preserving the mind is meant "seriousness (ching) to straighten the internal life and righteousness to square the external life," a way of cultivation similar to what has just been called absolute refinement, singleness, holding fast, and preserving. Therefore one who has fully developed his mind can know his nature and know Heaven, because the substance of the mind is unbeclouded and he is equipped to search into principle in its natural state, and one who has preserved the mind can nourish his nature and serve Heaven, because the substance of the mind is not lost and he is equipped to follow principle in its natural state. Is this the same as using one mind fully to develop another, or one mind to preserve another, like two things holding on to each other and refusing to let go?

The expressions "in front of him" and "attached to the yoke" are intended to teach loyalty, faithfulness, earnestness, and seriousness, as if saying that if these moral qualities are always borne in mind, we will see them no matter where we may go. But it does not mean that we observe the mind. Furthermore, suppose the body is here while the mind is in the front beholding it, and the body is in the carriage while the mind is attached to its yoke. Is that not absurd? Generally speaking, the doctrine of the sage is to base one's mind on investigating principle to the utmost and to respond to things by following it. It is like the body using the arm and the arm using the finger. The road will be level and open, the abiding place will be broad and easy, and the principle concrete and its operation natural.

According to the doctrine of the Buddhists, one seeks the mind with the mind, one employs the mind with the mind, like the mouth gnawing the mouth or the eye seeing the eye. Such an operation is precarious and oppressive, the road dangerous and obstructed, and the principle empty and running against its own course. If their doctrine seems to have something similar (to the Confucian), in reality it is different like this. But unless one is a superior man who thinks accurately and sifts clearly, how can he avoid being deluded in this matter?

B. THE COMPLETE WORKS OF CHU HSI

1. MORAL CULTIVATION

a. HOW TO STUDY

1. *Question:* Does what is called the fundamental task consist only in preserving the mind, nourishing the nature, and cultivating and controlling them?

Answer: Both the effort of preserving and nourishing and that of the investigation of principle to the utmost must be thorough. However, the effort of investigating principle to the utmost is already found within that of preserving and nourishing, and the effort of preserving and nourishing is already found within that of the investigation of principle to the utmost. To investigate principle to the utmost is the same as investigating to the utmost what is preserved, and to preserve and nourish is the same as nourishing what has been investigated. (*Complete Works*, 1:18b–19a)

2. Now there is nothing for the student to do except to examine all principles with his mind. Principle is what is possessed by the mind. Always preserve this mind to examine all principles. These are the only things to do. (1:19a)

3. Although literature cannot be abolished, nevertheless the cultivation of the essential and the examination of the difference between the Principle of Nature (*T'ien-li*, Principle of Heaven) and human selfish desires are things that must not be interrupted for a single moment in the course of our daily activities and movement and rest. If one understands this point clearly, he will naturally not get to the point where he will drift into the popular ways of success and profit and expedient schemes. I myself did not really see the point until recently. Although my past defect of emphasizing fragmentary and isolated details showed different symptoms from these ways of life, yet the faults of forgetting the self, chasing after material things, leaving the internal empty, and greedily desiring the external remain the same. Master Ch'eng said, "One must not allow the myriad things in the world to disturb him. When the self is established, one will naturally understand the myriad things in the world." When one does not even know where to anchor his body and mind, he talks about the kingly way and the despotic way, and discusses and studies the task of putting the world in order as if it were a trick. Is that not mistaken? (1:30a–b)

4. I have heard the sayings of Master Ch'eng I, "Self-cultivation requires seriousness. The pursuit of learning depends on the extension of knowledge." These two sayings are really the essentials for the student to advance in establishing himself in life. And the two efforts have never failed to develop each other. However, when Master Ch'eng taught people to hold fast to seriousness, he meant nothing more than the primary importance of being orderly in clothing and appearance, and by the extension of knowledge he meant no more than to find out, in reading books and history and in dealing with things, where their principles are. The teachings are nothing like the absurd, wild, and unreasonable theories of recent times. (1:37b–38a)

b. PRESERVING THE MIND AND NOURISHING THE NATURE

5. If one can in his daily life and at leisurely moments decidedly collect his mind right here, that is the equilibrium before the feelings of pleasure, anger, sorrow, and joy are aroused, and is the undifferentiated Principle of Nature. As things and affairs approach, the mind can clearly see which is right and which is wrong accordingly. What is right is the Principle of Nature, and what is wrong is in violation of the Principle of Nature. If one can always collect the mind like this, it would be as if he holds the scale and balance to measure things. (2:2a)

6. The mind embraces all principles and all principles are complete in this single entity, the mind. If one is not able to preserve the mind, he will be unable to investigate principle to the utmost. If he is unable to investigate principle to the utmost, he will be unable to exert his mind to the utmost. (2:4b)

7. *Someone asked:* How about guarding against depravity and concentrating on one thing? *Answer:* Concentrating on one thing is similar to "holding the will firm," and guarding against depravity is similar to "never doing violence to the vital force." To guard against depravity merely means to prevent depraved forces from entering [the

mind], whereas in concentrating on one thing one protects it from the inside. Neither should be unbalanced in any way. This is the way the internal and the external mutually cultivate each other. (2:8b)

c. HOLDING FAST TO SERIOUSNESS (CHING)

8. The task of seriousness is the first principle of the Confucian School. From the beginning to the end, it must not be interrupted for a single moment. (2:21b)

9. Seriousness merely means the mind being its own master. (2:22a)

10. If one succeeds in preserving seriousness, his mind will be tranquil and the Principle of Nature will be perfectly clear to him. At no point is the slightest effort exerted, and at no point is the slightest effort not exerted. (2:22a)

11. To be serious does not mean to sit still like a blockhead, with the ear hearing nothing, the eye seeing nothing, and the mind thinking of nothing, and only then it can be called seriousness. It is merely to be apprehensive and careful and dare not give free rein to oneself. In this way both body and mind will be collected and concentrated as if one is apprehensive of something. If one can always be like this, his dispositions will naturally be changed. Only when one has succeeded in preserving this mind can he engage in study. (2:22a)

12. It is not necessary to talk much about the doctrine of holding fast to seriousness. One has only to brood over thoroughly these sayings [of Ch'eng I], "Be orderly and dignified," "Be grave and austere," "Be correct in movement and appearance and be orderly in thoughts and deliberations," and "Be correct in your dress and dignified in your gaze," and make real effort. Then what [Ch'eng] called straightening the internal life and concentrating on one thing will naturally need no manipulation, one's body and mind will be serious, and the internal and external will be unified. (2:22a–b)

d. TRANQUILLITY

13. In the human body there is only a [combination of] activity and tranquillity. Tranquillity nourishes the root of activity and activity is to put tranquillity into action. There is tranquillity in activity. For example, when the feelings are aroused and all attain due measure and degree, that is tranquillity in activity. (2:38a)

14. About response to things. Things and the principle [inherent] in my mind are fundamentally one. Neither is deficient in any degree. What is necessary is for me to respond to things. Things and the mind share the same principle. To be calm is to be tranquil. To respond is to be active. (2:38b)

15. Ch'eng I sometimes also taught people sitting in meditation. But from Confucius and Mencius upward, there was no such doctrine. We must search and investigate on a higher plane and see that sitting in meditation and the examination of principle do not interfere with each other, and then it will be correct. (2:44a–b)

e. THE EXAMINATION OF THE SELF AND THINGS

16. There is dead seriousness and there is living seriousness. If one merely adheres to seriousness in concentrating on one thing and, when things happen, does not support it with righteousness to distinguish between right and wrong, it will not be living seriousness. When one becomes at home with it, then wherever there is seriousness, there is righteousness, and wherever there is righteousness, there is seriousness. When tranquil, one examines himself as to whether one is serious or not, and when active, one

examines himself as to whether he is righteous or not. Take, for example, the cases of "going abroad and behaving to everyone as if you were receiving a guest and employing the people as if you were assisting at a great sacrifice." What would happen if you were not serious? Or the cases of "sitting as if one is impersonating an ancestor, and standing as if one is sacrificing." What would happen if you were not serious? Righteousness and seriousness must support each other, one following the other without beginning or end, and then both internal and external life will be thoroughly penetrated by them. (3:1b–2a)

17. If the Principle of Nature exists in the human mind, human selfish desires will not, but if human selfish desires win, the Principle of Nature will be destroyed. There has never been a case where both the Principle of Nature and human selfish desires are interwoven and mixed. This is where the student must realize and examine for himself. (3:3a)

18. "Thinking alone can check passionate desires." What do you think of the saying? *Answer:* Thinking is the same as examining. It means that when one is angry, if one can directly forget his anger and examine the right and wrong according to principle, then right and wrong will be clearly seen and desires will naturally be unable to persist. (3:3b)

19. To say that one must examine at the point where the feelings are about to be aroused means to be careful when thoughts and deliberations are just beginning, and to say that one must examine after the feelings have been aroused means that one must examine one's words and actions after they have taken place. One must of course be careful about thoughts and deliberations when they begin, but one must not fail to examine his words and action after they have taken place. (3:7a)

f. KNOWLEDGE AND ACTION

20. Knowledge and action always require each other. It is like a person who cannot walk without legs although he has eyes, and who cannot see without eyes although he has legs. With respect to order, knowledge comes first, and with respect to importance, action is more important. (3:8a)

21. The efforts of both knowledge and action must be exerted to the utmost. As one knows more clearly, he acts more earnestly, and as he acts more earnestly, he knows more clearly. Neither of the two should be unbalanced or discarded. It is like a person's two legs. If they take turn to walk, one will be able gradually to arrive at the destination. If one leg is weak and soft, then not even one forward step can be taken. However, we must first know before we can act. This is why the *Great Learning* first talks about the extension of knowledge, the *Doctrine of the Mean* puts wisdom ahead of humanity and courage, and Confucius first of all spoke of knowledge being sufficient to attain its objective. But none of extensive study, accurate inquiry, careful thinking, clear sifting, and vigorous practice can be omitted. (3:8b)

22. When one knows something but has not yet acted on it, his knowledge is still shallow. After he has experienced it, his knowledge will be increasingly clear, and its character will be different from what it was before. (3:12b)

23. Generally speaking, in any matter there is only one right or wrong. When the right or wrong is determined, one should choose the right and keep acting on it. How can one expect that by wavering he can win approval from everyone? Whether a thing is right or wrong will eventually become definite of itself. For the moment what is important is that one is satisfied within himself, so that looking up, he has no occasion for shame, and looking down, he has no occasion to blush. Never mind whether other people say they like it or not. (3:12b–13a)

24. Throughout a person's handling of affairs and dealing with things, there is no point at which moral principles are not present. Although one cannot know all of them, in all likelihood he has heard the great essentials. The important point is to put into action vigorously what he has already known and make efforts to go beyond it. In this way he can go from the near to the far and from the coarse to the refined, methodically and in an orderly manner, and observable effect can be achieved every day. (3:22b–23a)

g. THE EXTENSION OF KNOWLEDGE

25. What sages and worthies call extensive learning means to study everything. From the most essential and most fundamental about oneself to every single thing or affair in the world, even the meaning of one word or half a word, everything should be investigated to the utmost, and none of it is unworthy of attention. Although we cannot investigate all, still we have to keep on devoting our attention to them in accordance with our intelligence and ability, and in time there will necessarily be some accomplishment. Is this not better than not to pay attention at all? If we absolutely pay no attention, even ignoring things passing before us whose names are unknown to us, is that the way to investigate things to the utmost? (3:26a)

26. Ch'i-yuan asked: In investigating the principles of things and affairs to the utmost, should one investigate exhaustively the point where all principles converge? What do you think? *Answer:* There is no need to talk about the converging point. All that is before our eyes is things and affairs. Just investigate one item after another somehow until the utmost is reached. As more and more is done, one will naturally achieve a far and wide penetration. That which serves as the converging point is the mind. (3:26a–b)

27. Moral principles are quite inexhaustible. No matter what past scholars have said, they have not necessarily exhausted the subject. We must examine them this way and that way ourselves. The more deeply we go into them, the more we shall discover. (3:27a)

28. Pay no attention to names. We must investigate into the reason things are as they are. (3:27b)

29. There is no other way to investigate principle to the utmost than to pay attention to everything in our daily reading of books and handling of affairs. Although there may not seem to be substantial progress, nevertheless after a long period of accumulation, without knowing it one will be saturated [with principle] and achieve an extensive harmony and penetration. Truly, one cannot succeed if one wants to hurry. (3:33b)

30. To investigate principle to the utmost means to seek to know the reason for which things and affairs are as they are and the reason according to which they should be, that is all. If we know why they are as they are, our will will not be perplexed. and if we know what they should be, our action will not be wrong. It does not mean to take the principle of something and put it in another. (3:34a)

2. THE RELATION BETWEEN THE NATURE
OF MAN AND THINGS AND THEIR DESTINY

31. *Question:* About the distinction between Heaven (Nature), destiny *(ming,* fate), nature, and principle. Heaven refers to what is self-existent; destiny refers to that which operates and is endowed in all things; nature refers to the total substance and that by which all things attain their being; and principle refers to the laws underlying all things and events. Taken together, Heaven is principle, destiny is nature, and nature is principle. Is this correct?

Answer: Yes. Nowadays, it is maintained that Heaven does not refer to the blue sky. In my view it cannot be left out of account. (42:1a–b)

32. Principle is the substance of Heaven, while destiny is the function of principle. One's nature is what is endowed in man. And one's feelings are the function of one's nature. (42:1b)

33. I-ch'uan (Ch'eng I) said that destiny is that which is endowed by Heaven and nature is what things have received from Heaven. Principle is one. As endowed by Heaven in all things it is called destiny. As received by creatures from Heaven, it is called nature. The difference lies really in the different points of view. (42:2b)

34. On being asked about (Chang Tsai's) section on moral character failing to overcome material force, (Chu Hsi) said: Master Chang Tsai merely said that both man's nature and material force flow down from above. If my moral character is not adequate to overcome material force, then there is nothing to do but to submit to material force as endowed by Heaven. If my moral character is adequate to overcome material force, however, then what I receive from the endowment is all moral character. Therefore if I investigate principle to the utmost and fully develop my nature, then what I have received is wholly Heaven's moral character, and what Heaven has endowed in me is wholly Heaven's principle. The cases in which material force cannot be altered are life, death, longevity and brevity of life, for these, and poverty and wealth, and honor and humble station, all depend on material force. On the other hand, the practice of righteousness between the ruler and his ministers and the exercise of humanity between father and son, are what we call matters of fate. But there is also man's nature. The superior man does not say they are matters of fate. They must proceed from myself, not from fate. (42:3a–b)

35. *Question:* [Chang Tsai said,] "If one investigates principle to the utmost and fully develops his nature, then his nature will be in accord with the character of Heaven and his destiny will be in accord with the Principle of Heaven." How are nature and destiny to be distinguished?

Answer: Nature refers to what is stabilized whereas destiny refers to what is operating. Destiny, for example, refers to water flowing, while nature refers to water contained in a bowl. A big bowl contains more water, whereas a small one contains less. The water in a clean bowl will be clear, whereas that in a dirty bowl will be turbid. (42:3b)

36. *Question:* Destiny is what Heaven endows in man and things and nature is what they receive from Heaven. But nature and destiny each has two aspects. From the point of view of their principle, the principle that is destined in man and things by Heaven is called destiny, and the principle received by them from Heaven is called their nature. From the point of view of material force, the material force that is destined in man and things by Heaven is also called destiny and the material force received by them from Heaven is also called their nature. Is this correct?

Answer: Material force cannot be called the nature or destiny. They exist because of it, that is all. When the nature of Heaven and Earth is spoken of, it refers to principle only; when the physical nature is spoken of, it refers to principle and material force combined. Material force is not to be referred to as nature or destiny. (42:4b)

37. "Heaven produces the teeming multitude. As there are things, there are their specific principles." This means that at the very time when a person is born, Heaven has already given him his nature. Man's nature is nothing but principle. It is called nature because it is endowed in man. It is not a concrete entity by itself which is to be destined as nature and which neither comes into nor goes out of existence. As I once illustrated, destiny (mandate) is like an appointment to office by the throne, and nature is like the office retained by the officer. This is why Master I-ch'uan (Ch'eng I) said, "Destiny is what is endowed by Heaven and nature is what things receive." The reason is very clear.

Therefore when ancient sages and worthies spoke of nature and destiny, they always spoke of them in relation to actual living. For example, when they spoke of the full development of human nature, they mean the complete realization of the moral principles of the Three Bonds (between ruler and minister, father and son, and husband and wife) and the Five Constant Virtues (that is, righteousness on the part of the father, love on the part of the mother, brotherliness on the part of the elder brother, respect on the part of the younger brother, and filial piety on the part of the son), covering the relationships between the ruler and ministers and between father and son. When they spoke of nourishing our nature, they mean that we should nourish these moral principles without doing them any harm. This central truth runs through the most subtle principles and the most obvious facts, with nothing left uncovered. These are not empty words. (42:5a)

3. THE NATURE OF MAN AND THINGS

38. The Way (Tao, Moral Law) is identical with the nature of man and things and the nature is identical with the Way. They are one and the same but we must understand in what connection it is called the nature and in what connection it is called the Way. (42:6a)

Scholar Steles in the Confucius Temple, Beijing. These 198 stone tablets record the names of the 51,624 Jinshi, scholars from the Yuan, Ming and Ch'ing (Qing) dynasties who passed the Neo-Confucian imperial examinations. To pass the examination, a scholar had to endure being locked in a small cubicle for three days answering questions about Confucian classics. (*Forrest E. Baird*)

39. [Ch'eng I said,] "The nature is the same as principle." In relation to the mind, it is called the nature. In relation to events, it is called principle. (42:6a)

40. The principle of life is called the nature. (42:6b)

41. The nature consists of innumerable principles created by Heaven. (42:6b)

42. The nature consists of concrete principle, complete with humanity, righteousness, propriety, and wisdom. (42:6b)

43. After reading some essays by Hsun and others on nature, the Teacher said that in discussing nature it is important to know first of all what kind of entity it really is. (At bottom nature has neither physical form nor shadow. It is merely the moral principle possessed by the mind.) Master Ch'eng I put it best when he said that "nature is the same as principle." Now if we regard it as principle, then surely it has neither physical form nor shadow. It is nothing but this very principle. In man, humanity, righteousness, propriety and wisdom are his nature, but what physical form or shape have they? All they have are the principles of humanity, righteousness, propriety, and wisdom. As they possess these principles, many deeds are carried out, and man is enabled to have the feelings of commiseration, shame, deference and compliance, and right and wrong. Take for example the nature of drugs, such as their property of increasing or decreasing heat (vigor, strength, vitality). There is no external form of this nature to be found in the drugs. Only after the drug is taken, heat or cold is produced—this is their nature. In man, nature is merely humanity, righteousness, propriety, and wisdom. According to Mencius, humanity, righteousness, propriety, and wisdom are rooted in the mind. When, for example, he speaks of the mind of commiseration, he attributes feeling to the mind.

The Teacher further said: Shao Yao-fu (Shao Yung, 1011–1077) said that "nature is the concrete embodiment of the Way and the mind is the enclosure of the nature." This theory is very good. For the Way itself has no physical form or body; it finds it only in man's nature. But if there were no mind, where could nature be? There must be mind before nature can be gotten hold of and put forth into operation, for the principles contained in man's nature are humanity, righteousness, propriety, and wisdom, and these are concrete principles. We Confucianists regard nature as real, whereas Buddhists regard it as unreal. However, it is incorrect to equate mind with nature. Nowadays people often explain nature in terms of mind. They should first understand before they talk. (If they consider consciousness as nature, they are only talking about the mind.) For example, wherever there is the nature as endowed by Heaven, there is also the physical nature. If we regard the nature endowed by Heaven as rooted in the mind, then where will you place the physical nature? When, for example, it is said that "the human mind is precarious (liable to make mistakes), the moral mind is subtle (the mind that follows Tao, the Moral Law)," the word "mind" is used in both cases. It is incorrect to say that the mind following the Moral Law is mind whereas the mind of the natural man is not mind. (42:6b–7a)

44. The Teacher asked how the nature is concrete embodiment of the Way. Ch'un replied: The Way is principle inherent in the nature. The Teacher said: The term Way is used with reference to a universal order, whereas the term nature is used with reference to an individual self. How do we know that the Way operates in the world? Simply by putting it into operation in one's own experience. Wherever nature is, there is the Way. The Way is the principle inherent in things, whereas nature is the principle inherent in the self. But the principle in all things is also in the principle inherent in the self. One's nature is the framework of the Way. (42:9b)

45. Chi-sui, adhering to the doctrine of his family, said that nature cannot be spoken of as good, for the goodness that is originally so has no opposite. As soon as you describe nature as good, you are already contrasting it with evil, and when you speak

of it in terms of the opposites of good and evil, it is no longer the original nature you are talking about. Original nature is transcendent, absolute, and beyond comparison, whereas goodness applies to the mundane world. The moment you say it is good, you are contrasting it with evil and you are no longer talking about original nature. When Mencius said that nature is good, he did not mean that nature is morally good, but simply used the language of admiration, like saying "How fine the nature!" just as the Buddha exclaimed, "Excellent is the Path!"

I have criticized this theory and said that it is true that original nature is an all-pervading perfection not contrasted with evil. This is true of what Heaven has endowed in the self. But when it operates in man, there is the differentiation between good and evil. When man acts in accord with it, there is goodness. When man acts out of accord with it, there is evil. How can it be said that the good is not the original nature? It is in its operation in man that the distinction between good and evil arises, but conduct in accord with the original nature is due to the original nature. If, as they say, there is the goodness that is originally so and there is another goodness contrasted with evil, there must be two natures. Now what is received from Heaven is the same nature as that in accordance with which goodness ensues, except that as soon as good appears, evil, by implication, also appears. Therefore good and evil must be spoken of as contrast. But it is not true that there is originally an evil existing out there, waiting for the appearance of good to oppose it. We fall into evil only when our actions are not in accordance with the original nature. (42:9b–10a)

46. Again, referring to Master Shao's saying, "Man's nature is the concrete embodiment of the Way," the Teacher said: The Way exists everywhere, but how are we to find it? Simply by returning to the self and discovering it within one's nature and function. From the fact that we possess the principles of humanity, righteousness, propriety, and wisdom, we know that others also possess them. Of the thousands and tens of thousands of human beings and of all things, there is none independent of these moral principles. Even if extended to include all existence, you will find none to be independent of them. He put it very well when he said that "The nature is the concrete embodiment of the Way." (42:13a–b)

47. It is said that the word "good" in the expression "Nature is good" is different from the good as contrasted with evil. On that theory I hold that the good traced to the source of our being and the good in the process of life involving both good and evil are not two different things. They merely refer to two different states before and after it has emanated into activity. But it is the same good whether before it has emanated or afterward when it becomes contrasted with evil. Only after its emanation is it intermingled with evil. But the good in this state is the same good that emanates from the source of our being. (42:13b–14a)

48. In your (Ho Shu-ching's) letter you say that you do not know whence comes human desire. This is a very important question. In my opinion, what is called human desire is the exact opposite of the Principle of Nature. It is permissible to say that human desire exists because of the Principle of Nature, but it is wrong to say that human desire is the same as the Principle of Nature. For in its original state the Principle of Nature is free from human desire. It is from the deviation in the operation of the Principle of Nature that human desire arises. Master Ch'eng Hao says that "Good and evil in the world are both the Principle of Nature. What is called evil is not originally evil. It becomes evil only because of deviation from the mean." Your quotation, "But it cannot be said that evil is not nature," expresses the same idea. (42: 14b–15a)

49. Before material force exists, there is already nature. There is a time when material force does not exist, but nature is eternal. Although it is implanted in material

force, yet material force is still material force and nature is still nature, the two not being confused. As to nature being inherent in all things and existing everywhere, there is no material force, whether refined or coarse, without principle. It is incorrect to regard the more refined part of material force as nature and the coarser part of nature as material force. (42:18b)

50. It is true that nature cannot be without activity, but its all-inclusiveness is not due to its inevitable activity. Even if it were without activity, is there anything wanting in its all-inclusiveness? The fallacy of the Buddhists lies in their erroneously regarding the heavenly and earthly aspects of the soul *(hun-p'o)* as nature and not in their ignorance of the fact that nature does not become all-inclusive through activity. (42:19a)

51. Master Ch'eng I said that nature is the same as principle and Master Shao Yung said that nature is the concrete embodiment of the Way. These two sayings explain each other. But in your (Chiang Shu-ch'uan's) deliberation you consider one better than the other. In this, you not only have failed to grasp Master Shao's idea, but I fear you also have not reached the depth of Master Ch'eng's expression. When Mr. Fang Pin-wang says that "the Way is Heaven as the self-existent and that nature is what Heaven has endowed in all things and what they have received from Heaven," he is transmitting the old doctrines of past scholars. While in reality nature and the Way are not two different things, yet there is a difference in the two terms which must be distinguished. Furthermore, in the passage that [immediately] follows, he says, "Although nature is received from Heaven, it is no more or less as compared with Heaven as such." This clearly shows that he does not cut them into pieces. However, he says, "The substance of the Way has no activity, whereas the human mind does have activity." This means, that nature (which is the concrete embodiment of the Way) and the mind operate in two different spheres, a theory hardly tenable. Master Shao is nearer to the truth when he says that "The mind is the enclosure of nature." However, the meaning of such an expression is much too unrefined. We must know that the mind is the master of the body, and nature is the moral principle inherent in the mind, and then we will not be wrong. (42:19b–20a)

52. "Nature is the same as principle." If you regard it as the source of the ten thousand principles, it would seem to be a different thing. Master K'ang-chieh (Shao Yung) said, "Man's nature is the concrete embodiment of the Way." His statement seems to the point. He also said, "Although the nature remains tranquil, but if we do not know how to preserve it, it will not attain the mean." Now, the nature should necessarily attain the Mean, just as water should necessarily be cold and fire be hot. But the Mean is sometimes not attained because man loses his original nature and beclouds it by habits engendered by material force. It is not that nature fails to attain the Mean. (42:21b)

53. "Nature is the concrete embodiment of the Way" is a sentence in (Shao Yung's) preface to his *Chi-jang ko* (Striking Earthen Musical Instruments; A Collection of Poems). Its meaning is that nature is the concrete substance of what man receives from Heaven while the Way is the principle by which things are as they are. The principle of things is, of course, inherent in their nature, but when it is spoken of as the Way, it means something indefinite, boundless, and different in infinite variety, where concreteness is not to be seen. Only when we look into nature—and nowhere else—do we find the Way in its concreteness. When the *Doctrine of the Mean* says "To follow human nature is called the Way," it means this. (42:21b–22a)

54. "Nature is the concrete embodiment of the Way." When it is spoken of as the Way, it means something to spread over all things, with no clue for us to find it. But if we look for it in the mind, we shall find that all the principles inherent in it have definite substance and are unchangeable. These principles inherent in the mind are what we call nature. Therefore Master Shao goes on to say, "The mind is the endowment of na-

ture." If you examine the matter in this way, the truth or error of what you (Fang Pin-wang) say can readily be seen. (42:22a)

4. The Nature of Man and the Nature of Things Compared

55. *Question:* Do all the Five Agents (Metal, Wood, Water, Fire, and Earth) possess the Great Ultimate?

Answer: They all do.

Question: Does man embody all the Five Agents while things embody only one of them?

Answer: Things also embody all the Five Agents, except that they embody them partially. (42:25a)

56. *Question:* Man and things are all endowed with the principle of the universe as their nature, and receive the material force of the universe as their physical form. The difference in personality is of course due to the various degrees of purity and strength of the material force. But in the case of things, are they as they are because of the incompleteness of the principle with which they are endowed or because of the impurity and beclouding character of the material force endowed in them?

Answer: The principle received by things is precisely in the same degree as the material force received by them. For example, the physical constitution of dogs and horses being what it is, they know how to do only certain things.

Further question: If each individual thing possesses its own Great Ultimate in its completeness, then principle can never be incomplete. [In this case, how is it that things possess principle only to a limited degree?]

Answer: You may consider it complete or you may consider it partial. From the point of view of principle, it is always complete, but from the point of view of material force, it cannot help being partial. This is why Lu Ta-lin (Lu Yu-shu, 1044–1090) said that in certain cases the nature of things approximates to the nature of man and in some cases the nature of man approximates that of things. (42:26b–27a)

57. *Question:* Physical nature differs in the degree of purity. Does the nature bestowed by Heaven differ in the degree of its completeness?

Answer: No, there is no difference in the degree of its completeness. It is like the light of the sun and moon. In a clear, open field, it is seen in its entirety. Under a mat-shed, however, some of it is hidden and obstructed so that part of it is visible and part of it is not. What is impure is due to the impurity of material force. The obstruction is due to the self, like the mat-shed obstructing itself. However, man possesses the principle that can penetrate this obstruction, whereas in birds and animals, though they also possess this nature, it is nevertheless restricted by their physical structure, which creates such a degree of obstruction as to be impenetrable. In the case of love, for example, in tigers and wolves, or in the sacrificial rites in the wolf and otter, or in the righteousness in bees and ants, only the obstruction to a particular part of their nature is penetrated, just as light penetrates only a crack. As to the monkey, whose bodily form resembles that of man, it is the most intelligent among other creatures except that it cannot talk. (42:27a–b)

58. Chi submitted to the Teacher the following statement concerning a problem in which he was still in doubt: The nature of man and the nature of things are in some respects the same and in other respects different. Only after we know wherein they are similar and wherein they are different can we discuss nature. Now, as the Great Ultimate begins its activity, the two material forces (yin and yang, passive and active cosmic

forces) assume physical form, and as they assume physical form, the myriad transformations of things are produced. Both man and things have their origin here. This is where they are similar. But the two material forces and the Five Agents, in their fusion and intermingling, and in their interaction and mutual influence, produce innumerable changes and inequalities. This is where they are different. They are similar in regard to principle, but different in respect to material force. There must be principle before there can be that which constitutes the nature of man and things. Consequently, what makes them similar cannot make them different. There must be material force before there can be that which constitutes their physical form. Consequently, what makes them different cannot make them similar. For this reason, in your *Ta-hsueh huo-wen* (Questions and Answers on the Great Learning), you said, "From the point of view of principle, all things have one source, and of course man and things cannot be distinguished as higher and lower creatures. From the point of view of material force, that which receives it in its perfection and is unimpeded becomes man, while those that receive it partially and are obstructed become things. Because of this, they cannot be equal, but some are higher and others are lower." However, while in respect to material force they are unequal, they both possess it as the stuff of life, and while in respect to principle they are similar, in receiving it to constitute his nature, man alone differs from other things. This consciousness and movement proceed from material force while humanity, righteousness, propriety, and wisdom proceed from principle. Both man and things are capable of consciousness and movement, but though things possess humanity, righteousness, propriety, and wisdom, they cannot have them completely. Now Kao Tzu (c.420–c.350 B.C.E.) pointed to material force and neglected principle. He was confined to what is similar and ignorant of what is different, and was therefore attacked by Mencius. In your *[Meng Tzu] chi-chu* (Collected Commentaries on the *Book of Mencius*) you maintain that "in respect to material force, man and things do not seem to differ in consciousness and movement, but in respect to principle, the endowment of humanity, righteousness, propriety, and wisdom are necessarily imperfect in things." Here you say that man and things are similar in respect to material force but different in respect to principle, in order to show that man is higher and cannot be equaled by things. In the *Ta-hsueh huo-wen,* you say that man and things are similar in respect to principle but different in respect to material force, in order to show that the Great Ultimate is not deficient in anything and cannot be interfered with by any individual. Looked at this way, there should not be any question. When someone was puzzled by the discrepancies in the *Ta-hsueh huo-wen* and the *chi-chu, I* explained it in this way. Is this correct?

The Teacher commented: On this subject you have discussed very clearly. It happened that last evening a friend talked about this matter and I briefly explained it to him, but not as systematically as you have done in this statement. (42:27b–29a)

59. *Question:* How is it that dry and withered things also possess the nature?

Answer: Because from the very beginning they possess this nature. This is why we say so. There is not a single thing in the universe that is outside nature.

Thereupon the Teacher walked up the step and said: The bricks of these steps have in them the principle of bricks. Then he sat down and said: A bamboo chair has in it the principle of the bamboo chair. It is correct to say that dry and withered things have no spirit of life, but it is incorrect to say that they have no principle of life. For example, rotten wood is useless except as fuel—there is in it no spirit of life. But when a particular kind of wood is burned, a particular kind of force is produced, each different from the other. This is so because of the principle originally inherent in it. (42:29b–30a)

60. *Question:* Principle is what is received from Heaven by both man and things. Do things without feelings also possess principle?

Answer: They of course have principle. For example, a ship can go only on water while a cart can go only on land. (42:30a)

61. *Question:* Man and birds and animals all have consciousness, although with varying degrees of penetration or impediment. Do plants also have consciousness?

Answer: Yes, they also have. Take a pot of flowers, for example. When watered, they flourish gloriously, but if broken off, they will wither and droop. Can they be said to be without consciousness? Chou Mao-shu (Chou Tun-i) did not cut the grass growing outside his window and said that he felt toward the grass as he felt toward himself. This shows that plants have consciousness [in so far as it has the spirit of life]. But the consciousness of animals is inferior to that of man, and that of plants is inferior to that of animals. Take also the example of the drug rhubarb, which, when taken, acts as a purgative, and the drug aconite, which, when taken, produces heat (vitality and strength). In these cases, the consciousness acts in one direction only.

When asked further whether decayed things also have consciousness, the Teacher said: They also have, as when burned into ashes, made into broth, and drunk, they will be caustic or bitter. (42:31b–32a)

5. PHYSICAL NATURE

62. Nature is principle only. However, without the material force and concrete stuff of the universe, principle would have nothing in which to inhere. When material force is received in its state of clearness, there will be no obscurity or obstruction and principle will express itself freely. If there is obscurity or obstruction, then in its operation of principle, the Principle of Heaven will dominate if the obstruction is small and human selfish desire will dominate if the obstruction is great. From this we know that original nature is perfectly good. This is the nature described by Mencius as "good," by Master Chou Tun-i as "pure and perfectly good," and by Master Ch'eng I as "the fundamental character of our nature" and "the nature traced to the source of our being." However, it will be obstructed if physical nature contains impurity. Hence, [as Chang Tsai said] "In physical nature there is that which the superior man denies to be his original nature," and "If one learns to return to the original nature endowed by Heaven and Earth, then it will be preserved." In our discussion of nature, we must include physical nature before the discussion can be complete. (43:2b–3a)

63. When we speak of the nature of Heaven and Earth, we refer to principle alone. When we speak of the physical nature, we refer to principle and material force combined. Before material force existed, basic nature was already in existence. Material force does not always exist, but nature is eternal. Although nature is implanted in material force, yet material force is still material force and nature is still nature, without being confused or mixed up. As to its immanence in things and universal existence, regardless of whether material force is refined or coarse, there is nothing without its principle. (43:3a–b)

64. The physical nature is no different from the nature of Heaven and Earth. The point is that the nature of Heaven and Earth runs through the physical nature. For example, the good nature is like water. The physical nature is as though you sprinkled some sauce and salt in it and it then acquired a peculiar flavor. (43:4a)

65. The nature of all men is good, and yet there are those who are good from their birth and those who are evil from their birth. This is because of the difference in material force with which they are endowed. The revolutions of the universe consist of countless variety and are endless. But these may be seen: If the sun and moon are clear

and bright, and the climate temperate and reasonable, the man born at such a time and endowed with such material force, which is clear, bright, well-blended, and strong, should be a good man. But if the sun and moon are darkened and gloomy, and the temperature abnormal, all this is evidence of violent material force. There is no doubt that if a man is endowed with such material force, he will be a bad man. The objective of learning is to transform this material endowment. (43:4b)

66. Nature is like water. If it flows in a clean channel, it is clear, if it flows in a dirty channel, it becomes turbid. When physical nature that is clear and balanced is received, it will be preserved in its completeness. This is true of man. When physical nature that is turbid and unbalanced is received, it will be obscured. This is true of animals. Material force may be clear or turbid. That received by men is clear and that received by animals is turbid. Men mostly have clear material force; hence the difference between them and animals. However, there are some whose material force is turbid, and they are not far removed from animals. (43:7a–b)

67. Someone asked about the inequality in the clearness of the material endowment. The Teacher said: The differences in the material endowment are not limited to one kind and are not described only in terms of clearness and turbidity. There are men who are so bright that they know everything. Their material force is clear, but what they do may not all be in accord with principle. The reason is that their material force is not pure. There are others who are respectful, generous, loyal, and faithful. Their material force is pure, but in their knowledge they do not always penetrate principle. The reason is that their material force is not clear. From this you can deduce the rest. (42:8a)

68. Although nature is the same in all men, it is inevitable that [in most cases] the various elements in their material endowment are unbalanced. In some men the material force of Wood predominates. In such cases, the feeling of commiseration is generally uppermost, but the feeling of shame, of deference and compliance, and of right and wrong are impeded by the predominating force and do not emanate into action. In others, the material force of Metal predominates. In such cases, the feeling of shame is generally uppermost, but the other feelings are impeded and do not emanate into action. So with the material forces of Water and Fire. It is only when yin and yang are harmonized and the five moral natures (of humanity, righteousness, propriety, wisdom, and good faith) are all complete that a man has the qualities of the Mean and correctness and becomes a sage. (43:8a–b)

69. *Question:* Men often differ in the degree of clearness and purity. These are of course due to material endowment. By necessity their minds differ depending on their material endowment. Now, the mouth, the ear, and the eye, as well as the mind are all organs. Why is it that Heaven, in imparting the physical nature, invests the qualities of clearness and turbidity and purity and impurity only in the mind but not in the mouth, ear, or eye? . . . *Answer:* The mouth, ear, and eye also differ in clearness and turbidity and in purity and impurity. For example, people like I-ya (famous cook of the seventh century B.C.E.), the musicmaster Kuang (music-master shortly before Confucius), and Li-lou (legendary figure famous for power of vision) preserved clearness in the highest degree. It is the same with the mind. (43:17a–b)

70. Question about man's nature and destiny. *Answer:* If those born wise are completely and perfectly good, material force is there as material force and principle is there as principle, without any connection between each other. In such cases, there is no need to speak of the physical nature. But in the cases of men inferior to those born wise [those who learn through study to be wise, those who learn through hard work, and those who work hard but still do not learn], even the Principle of Nature is not deficient. Nevertheless it is tied up with material force. When material force is clear, principle will

be obvious. When material force is turbid, principle will be obscured. The two—material force and principle—always go together, and therefore we designate this state as physical nature. It means that principle advances or retards depending on material force, and not to consider physical nature as the nature and destiny.

Answer: In the cases of those who are born wise, material force is extremely clear and principle is not obstructed. In the cases of those who learn to be wise and those below them, the clearness or turbidity of material force varies in degree. Whether principle is complete or incomplete depends on this. (43:18a)

*   *   *

7. THE MIND

75. The principle of the mind is the Great Ultimate. The activity and tranquillity of the mind are the yin and yang. (44:1b)

76. Mind alone has no opposite. (44:1b)

77. *Question:* Is consciousness what it is because of the intelligence of the mind or is it because of the activity of material force?

Answer: Not material force alone. [Before material force existed], there was already the principle of consciousness. But principle at this stage does not give rise to consciousness. Only when it comes into union with material force is consciousness possible. Take, for example, the flame of this candle. It is because it has received this rich fat that there is so much light.

Question: Is that which emanates from the mind material force?

Answer: No, that is simply consciousness. (44:2a)

78. *Question:* Mind is consciousness and the nature is principle. How do the mind and principle pervade each other and become one?

Answer: They need not move to pervade each other. From the very start they pervade each other.

Question: How do they pervade each other from the very start?

Answer: Without the mind, principle would have nothing in which to inhere. (44:2a)

79. *Question:* Mind as an entity embraces all principles. The good that emanates of course proceeds from the mind. But the evil that emanates is all due to selfish material desires endowed by material force. Does it also proceed from the mind?

Answer: It is certainly not the original substance of the mind, but it also emanates from the mind.

Further question: Is this what is called the human mind?

Answer: Yes.

Thereupon Ch'ien Tzu-sheng asked: Does the human mind include both good and evil?

Answer: Both are included. (44:2b–3a)

80. Master Chang Tsai said that "in the unity of the nature and consciousness, there is the mind." I am afraid this idea is not free from error, as though there was a consciousness outside our nature. (44:5a)

81. *Question:* The mind is essentially an active thing. It is not clear to me whether before (feelings) are aroused the mind is completely quiet and tranquil or whether its tranquillity contains within it a tendency toward activity.

Answer: It is not that tranquillity contains within it a tendency toward activity. Master Chou Tun-i said that "when tranquil, it is in the state of non-being. When active, it is in the state of being." Tranquillity is not non-being as such. Because it has not assumed physical form, we call it non-being. It is not because of activity that there is being. Because (activity makes) it visible, we call it being. Heng-ch'u's (Chang Tsai's) theory that "the mind commands man's nature and feelings" is excellent. The nature is tranquil while feelings are active, and the mind involves both tranquillity and activity. Whether these refer to its substance or its function depends on one's point of view. While it is in the state of tranquillity, the principle of activity is already present. Ch'eng I said that in the state of equilibrium (before the feelings are aroused), "Although the ear hears nothing and the eye sees nothing, nevertheless the principles of hearing and seeing must be already there before hearing and seeing are possible." When activity takes place, it is the same tranquillity that becomes active. (44:6b–7a)

82. In the passage, "By enlarging one's mind, one can enter into all things in the world," the expression "enter into" is like saying that humanity enters into all events and is all-pervasive. It means that the operation of the principle of the mind penetrates all as blood circulates and reaches the entire body. If there is a single thing not yet entered, the reaching is not yet complete and there are still things not yet embraced. This shows that the mind still excludes something. For selfishness separates and obstructs, and consequently one and others stand in opposition. This being the case, even those dearest to us may be excluded. "Therefore the mind that leaves something outside is not capable of uniting itself with the mind of Heaven." (44:12b)

83. *Question:* How can the mind by means of moral principles (Tao) penetrate all things without any limit?

Answer: The mind is not like a side door which can be enlarged by force. We must eliminate the obstructions of selfish desires, and then it will be pure and clear and able to know all. When the principles of things and events are investigated to the utmost, penetration will come as a sudden release. Heng-ch'u (Chang Tsai) said, "Do not allow what is seen or heard to fetter the mind." "By enlarging one's mind one can enter into all things in the world." This means that if penetration is achieved through moral principles, there will be penetration like a sudden release. If we confine (the mind) to what is heard and what is seen, naturally our understanding will be narrow. (44:13a–b)

84. "The mind is the principle of production. . . . The feeling of commiseration is the principle of production in man." This is because man is born with the mind of Heaven. The mind of Heaven is to produce things. (44:14a)

8. THE MIND, THE NATURE, AND THE FEELINGS

85. The nature is comparable to the Great Ultimate, and the mind to yin and yang. The Great Ultimate exists only in the yin and yang, and cannot be separated from them. In the final analysis, however, the Great Ultimate is the Great Ultimate and yin and yang are yin and yang. So it is with nature and mind. They are one and yet two, two and yet one, so to speak. Philosopher Han Yu (768–824) described nature as humanity, righteousness, propriety, wisdom, and faithfulness and the feelings as pleasure, anger, sorrow, and joy. This is an advance over other philosophers on the problem of human nature. As to his division of human nature into three grades (superior, medium, and inferior), he has only explained material force but not nature. (45:1a)

86. Although nature is a vacuity, it consists of concrete principles. Although the mind is a distinct entity, it is vacuous, and therefore embraces all principles. This truth will be apprehended only when people examine it for themselves. (45:2a)

87. Nature consists of principles embraced in the mind, and the mind is where these principles are united. (45:2a)

88. Nature is principle. The mind is its embracement and reservoir, and issues it forth into operation. (45:2a)

89. Some time ago I read statements by Wu-feng (Hu Hung, 1100–1155) in which he spoke of the mind only in contrast to nature, leaving the feelings unaccounted for. Later when I read Heng-ch'u's (Chang Tsai's) doctrine that "the mind commands man's nature and feelings," I realized that it was a great contribution. Only then did I find a satisfactory account of the feelings. His doctrine agrees with that of Mencius. In the words of Mencius, "the feeling of commiseration is the beginning of humanity." Now humanity is nature, and commiseration is feeling. In this, the mind can be seen through the feelings. He further said, "Humanity, righteousness, propriety, and wisdom are rooted in the mind." In this, the mind is seen through nature. For the mind embraces both nature and the feelings. Nature is substance and feelings are function. (45:3a–b)

90. Nature is the state before activity begins, the feelings are the state when activity has started, and the mind includes both of these states. For nature is the mind before it is aroused, while feelings are the mind after it is aroused, as is expressed in [Chang Tsai's] saying, "The mind commands man's nature and feelings." Desire emanates from feelings. The mind is comparable to water, nature is comparable to the tranquillity of still water, feeling is comparable to the flow of water, and desire is comparable to its waves. Just as there are good and bad waves, so there are good desires, such as when "I want humanity," and bad desires which rush out like wild and violent waves. When bad desires are substantial, they will destroy the Principle of Heaven, as water bursts a dam and damages everything. When Mencius said that "feelings enable people to do good," he meant that the correct feelings flowing from our nature are originally all good. (45:4a)

91. The mind means master. It is master whether in the state of activity or in the state of tranquillity. It is not true that in the state of tranquillity there is no need of a master and there is a master only when the state becomes one of activity. By master is meant an all-pervading control and command existing in the mind by itself. The mind unites and apprehends nature and the feelings, but it is not united with them as a vague entity without any distinction. (45:4a–b)

92. In his reply to Heng-ch'u's dictum that "nature in the state of calmness cannot be without activity," Ming-tao's (Ch'eng Hao's) idea is that we should not hate things and events nor chase after them. Nowadays people who hate things avoid them completely, and who chase after them are continuously lured away by them. The best thing is neither to shun away from things nor to drift with them, but to face and respond to them in various ways. For Heng-ch'u's idea was to cut ourselves from the external world and achieve calmness internally, whereas Ming-tao's idea was that the internal and the external must be harmonized and unified. If (as Ming-tao said) that nature is calm "whether it is in a state of activity or in a state of tranquillity," then in our response to things we will naturally not be bound by them. If nature can be calmed only in a state of tranquillity, I am afraid that in time of activity it will be tempted and carried away by external things. (45:11b–12a)

93. *Question:* Is it correct to suppose that sages never show any anger?

Answer: How can they never show anger? When they ought to be angry, they will show it in their countenances. But if one has to punish someone for his crime and purposely smiles, that would be wrong.

Question: In that case, does it not show some feeling of wrath?

Answer: When Heaven is angry, thunder is also aroused. When sage-emperor Shun executed the four cruel criminals, he must have been angry at that time. When one becomes angry at the right time, he will be acting in the proper degree. When the matter is over, anger disappears, and none of it will be retained. (45:14b–15a)

94. *Question:* "How can desires be checked? Simply by thought. In learning there is nothing more important than thought. Only thought can check desires." Someone said that if thought is not correct, it will not be adequate to check desires. Instead, it will create trouble. How about "having no depraved thoughts"?

Answer: Thoughts that are not correct are merely desires. If we think through the right and wrong, and the ought and ought-not of a thing, in accordance with its principle, then our thought will surely be correct. (45:19b)

9. JEN

95. Whenever and wherever humanity *(jen)* flows and operates, righteousness will fully be righteousness and propriety and wisdom will fully be propriety and wisdom. It is like the ten thousand things being stored and preserved. There is not a moment of cessation in such an operation for in all of these things there is the spirit of life. Take for example such things as seeds of grain or the peach and apricot kernels. When sown, they will grow. They are not dead things. For this reason they are called *jen* (the word *jen* meaning both kernel and humanity). This shows that *jen* implies the spirit of life. (47:3a)

96. *Jen is* spontaneous, altruism *(shu)* is cultivated. *Jen is* natural, altruism is by effort. *Jen is* uncalculating and has nothing in view, altruism is calculating and has an object in view. (47:6a–b)

97. *Jen is* the principle of love, and impartiality is the principle of *jen.* Therefore, if there is impartiality, there is *jen,* and if there is *jen,* there is love. (47:6b)

98. *Question:* Master Ch'eng Hao said, "'Seriousness is to straighten the internal life and righteousness is to square the external life.' This means *jen.*" How can these be sufficient to be regarded as *jen?*

Answer: These two are *jen.* Wherever selfish desires can be entirely eliminated and the Principle of Nature freely operates, there is *jen.* For example, if one can "study extensively," be "steadfast in one's purpose," "inquire earnestly," and "reflect on things at hand (that is, what one can put into practice)," then "humanity *(jen)* consists in these." "To master oneself and return to propriety" is also *jen.* "When you go abroad, behave to everyone as if you were receiving a great guest. Employ the people as if you were assisting at a great sacrifice"—this is also *jen.* To "be respectful in private life, be serious in handling affairs, and be loyal in dealing with others"—these are also *jen.* All these depend on what path you follow. Once you have entered that path, exert effort until the limit is reached—all this is *jen.* (47:14b)

99. "When one makes impartiality the substance of his person, that is *jen.*" *Jen* is the principle originally inherent in man's mind. With impartiality, there is *jen.* With partiality, there is no *jen.* But impartiality as such should not be equated with *jen.* It must be made man's substance before it becomes *jen.* Impartiality, altruism, and love are all descriptions of *jen.* Impartiality is antecedent to *jen;* altruism and love are subsequent. This is so because impartiality makes *jen* possible, and *jen* makes love and altruism possible. (47:19b–20a)

10. PRINCIPLE (*LI*) AND MATERIAL FORCE (*CH'I*)

100. In the universe there has never been any material force *(ch'i)* without principle *(li)* or principle without material force. (49:1a)

101. *Question:* Which exists first, principle or material force?

Answer: Principle has never been separated from material force. However, principle "exists before physical form [and is therefore without it]" whereas material force "exists after physical form [and is therefore with it]." Hence when spoken of as being before or after physical form, is there not the difference of priority and posteriority? Principle has no physical form, but material force is coarse and contains impurities. (49:1a–b)

102. Fundamentally principle and material force cannot be spoken of as prior or posterior. But if we must trace their origin, we are obliged to say that principle is prior. However, principle is not a separate entity. It exists right in material force. Without material force, principle would have nothing to adhere to. As material force there are the Agents (or Elements) of Metal, Wood, Water, and Fire. As principle, there are humanity, righteousness, propriety, and wisdom (49:1b)

103. Question about the relation between principle and material force.

Answer: I-ch'uan (Ch'eng I) expressed it very well when he said that principle is one but its manifestations are many. When heaven, earth, and the myriad things are spoken of together, there is only one principle. As applied to man, however, there is in each individual a particular principle. (49:1b)

104. *Question:* What are the evidences that principle is in material force?

Answer: For example, there is order in the complicated interfusion of the yin and the yang and the Five Agents. Principle is there. If material force does not consolidate and integrate, principle would have nothing to attach itself to. (49:2b)

105. *Question:* May we say that before heaven and earth existed there was first of all principle?

Answer: Before Heaven and earth existed, there was after all only principle. As there is this principle, therefore there are heaven and earth. If there were no principle, there would also be no heaven and earth, no man, no things, and in fact, no containing or sustaining (of things by heaven and earth) to speak of. As there is principle, there is therefore material force to operate everywhere and nourish and develop all things.

Question: Is it principle that nourishes and develops all things?

Answer: As there is this principle, therefore there is this material force operating, nourishing, and developing. Principle itself has neither physical form nor body. (49:3a–b)

106. K'o-chi asked: When the creative process disposes of things, is it the end once a thing is gone, or is there a principle by which a thing that is gone may return?

Answer: It is the end once a thing is gone. How can there be material force that has disintegrated and yet integrates once more? (49:3b–4a)

107. *Question:* "The Lord on High has conferred even on the inferior people a moral sense." "When Heaven is about to confer a great responsibility on any man . . ." "Heaven, to protect the common people, made for them rulers." "Heaven, in the production of things, is sure to be bountiful to them, according to their qualities." "On the good-doer, the Lord on High sends down all blessings, and on the evil-doer, He sends down all miseries." "When Heaven is about to send calamities to the world, it will always produce abnormal people as a measure of their magnitude." In passages like these, does it mean that Heaven has no personal consciousness and the passages are merely deductions from principle?

Answer: These passages have the same meaning. It is simply that principle operates this way. (49:4a)

108. Principle attaches to material force and thus operates. (49:4b)

109. Throughout the universe there are both principle and material force. Principle refers to the Way, which exists before physical form [and is without it] and is the root

from which all things are produced. Material force refers to material objects, which exists after physical form [and is with it]; it is the instrument by which things are produced. Therefore in the production of man and things, they must be endowed with principle before they have their nature, and they must be endowed with material force before they have physical form. (49:5b)

110. What are called principle and material force are certainly two different entities. But considered from the standpoint of things, the two entities are merged one with the other and cannot be separated with each in a different place. However, this does not destroy the fact that the two entities are each an entity in itself. When considered from the standpoint of principle, before things existed, their principles of being had already existed. Only their principles existed, however, but not yet the things themselves. Whenever one studies these aspects, one should clearly recognize and distinguish them, and consider both principle and material force from the beginning to the end, and then one will be free from error. (49:5b–6a)

111. There is principle before there can be material force. But it is only when there is material force that principle finds a place to settle. This is the process by which all things are produced, whether large as heaven and earth or small as ants. Why should we worry that in the creative process of Heaven and Earth, endowment may be wanting? Fundamentally, principle cannot be interpreted in the senses of existence or nonexistence. Before Heaven and Earth came into being, it already was as it is. (49:6a)

112. Considering the fact that all things come from one source, we see that their principle is the same but their material force different. Looking at their various substances, we see that their material force is similar but their principle utterly different. The difference in material force is due to the inequality of its purity or impurity, whereas the difference in principle is due to its completeness or partiality. If you will please examine thoroughly, there shall be no further doubt. (49:7a)

113. The nature of man and things is nothing but principle and cannot be spoken of in terms of integration and disintegration. That which integrates to produce life and disintegrates to produce death is only material force. What we call the spirit, the heavenly and earthly aspects of the soul (hun-p'o), and consciousness are all effects of the material force. Therefore when material force is integrated, there are these effects. When it is disintegrated, there are no more. As to principle, fundamentally it does not exist or cease to exist because of such integration or disintegration. As there is a certain principle, there is the material force corresponding to it, and as this material force integrates in a particular instance, its principle is also endowed in that instance. (49:8a)

11. THE GREAT ULTIMATE

114. The Great Ultimate is nothing other than principle. (49:8b)

115. *Question:* The Great Ultimate is not a thing existing in a chaotic state before the formation of heaven and earth, but a general name for the principles of heaven and earth and the myriad things. Is that correct?

Answer: The Great Ultimate is merely the principle of heaven and earth and the myriad things. With respect to heaven and earth, there is the Great Ultimate in them. With respect to the myriad things, there is the Great Ultimate in each and every one of them. Before heaven and earth existed, there was assuredly this principle. It is the principle that "through movement generates the yang." It is also this principle that "through tranquillity generates the yin." (49:8b–9a)

116. *Question:* [In your commentary on Chou Tun-i's *T'ung shu*], you said: "Principle is a single, concrete entity, and the myriad things partake it as their substance. Hence each of the myriad things possesses in it a Great Ultimate." According to this theory, does the Great Ultimate not split up into parts?

Answer: Fundamentally there is only one Great Ultimate, yet each of the myriad things has been endowed with it and each in itself possesses the Great Ultimate in its entirety. This is similar to the fact that there is only one moon in the sky but when its light is scattered upon rivers and lakes, it can be seen everywhere. It cannot be said that the moon has been split. (49:10b–11a)

117. The Great Ultimate has neither spatial restriction nor physical form or body. There is no spot where it may be placed. When it is considered in the state before activity begins, this state is nothing but tranquillity. Now activity, tranquillity, yin and yang all exist only after physical form [and are with it]. However, activity is after all the activity of the Great Ultimate and tranquillity is also its tranquillity, although activity and tranquillity themselves are not the Great Ultimate. This is why Master Chou Tun-i spoke only of that state as Non-ultimate. While the state before activity begins cannot be spoken of as the Great Ultimate, nevertheless the principles of pleasure, anger, sorrow, and joy are already inherent in it. Pleasure and joy belong to yang and anger and sorrow belong to yin. In the initial stage the four are not manifested, but their principles are already there. As contrasted with the state after activity begins, it may be called the Great Ultimate. But still it is difficult to say. All this is but a vague description. The truth must be personally realized by each individual himself. (49:11a–b)

118. Someone asked about the Great Ultimate. *Reply:* The Great Ultimate is simply the principle of the highest good. Each and every person has in him the Great Ultimate and each and every thing has in it the Great Ultimate. What Master Chou called the Great Ultimate is a name to express all the virtues and the highest good in Heaven and Earth, man, and things. (49:11b)

119. The Great Ultimate is similar to the top of a house or the zenith of the sky, beyond which point there is no more. It is the ultimate of principle. Yang is active and yin is tranquil. In these it is not the Great Ultimate that acts or remains tranquil. It is simply that there are the principles of activity and tranquillity. Principle is not visible; it becomes visible through yin and yang. Principle attaches itself to yin and yang as a man sits astride a horse. As soon as yin and yang produce the Five Agents, they are confined and fixed by physical nature and are thus differentiated into individual things each with its nature. But the Great Ultimate is in all of them. (49:14a)

120. The Great Ultimate contains all principles of the Five Agents and, yin and yang. It is not an empty thing. If it were a void, it would approach the Buddhist theory of dharma-nature (which maintains that the nature of dharmas, that is, elements of existence, are void). (49:14a)

121. *Question:* Is the Great Ultimate the highest principle of the human mind?

Answer: There is an ultimate in every thing or event. That is the ultimate of principle.

Someone asked: Like humanity on the part of the ruler and respect on the part of ministers. These are ultimates.

Answer: These are ultimates of a particular thing or event. When all principles of heaven and earth and the myriad things are put together, that is the Great Ultimate. The Great Ultimate originally has no such name. It is merely a name to express its character. (49:14b–15a)

122. There is no other event in the universe except yin and yang succeeding each other in an unceasing cycle. This is called Change. However, for these activity and

tranquillity, there must be the principles which make them possible. This is the Great Ultimate. (49:16a)

12. HEAVEN AND EARTH

123. In the beginning of the universe there was only material force consisting of yin and yang. This force moved and circulated, turning this way and that. As this movement gained speed, a mass of sediment was compressed (pushed together), and since there is no outlet for this, it consolidated to form the earth in the center of the universe. The clear part of material force formed the sky, the sun, and moon, and the stars and zodiacal spaces. It is only on the outside that the encircling movement perpetually goes on. The earth exists motionless in the center of the system, not at the bottom. (49:19a)

124. In the beginning of the universe, when it was still in a state of undifferentiated chaos, I imagine there were only water and fire. The sediment from water formed the earth. If today we climb the high mountains and look around, we will see ranges of mountains in the shape of waves. This is because the water formed them like this, though we do not know in what period they solidified. The solidification was at first very soft, but in time it became hard.

Question: I imagine it is like the tide rushing upon and making waves in the sand.

Answer: Yes. The most turbid water formed the earth and the purest fire became wind, thunder, lightning, the stars, and the like. (49:19b–20a)

125. *Question:* From the beginning of the universe to this day, it has not yet been ten thousand years. I do not know how things looked before then.

Answer: The past is to be understood in the same way.

Further question: Can the universe be destroyed?

Answer: It is indestructible. But in time man will lose all moral principles and everything will be thrown together in a chaos. Man and things will all die out, and then there will be a new beginning.

Further question: How was the first man created?

Answer: Through the transformation of material force. When the essence of yin and yang and the Five Agents are united, man's physical form is established. This is what the Buddhists call production by transformation. There are many such productions today, such as lice. (49:20a)

126. *Question:* With reference to the mind of Heaven and Earth and the Principle of Heaven and Earth. Principle is moral principle. Is mind the will of a master?

Answer: The mind is the will of a master, it is true, but what is called master is precisely principle itself. It is not true that outside of the mind there is principle, or that outside of principle there is a mind. (49:23a)

127. Heaven and Earth have no other business except to have the mind to produce things. The material force of one origin (the Great Ultimate including principle and material force) revolves and circulates without a moment of rest, doing nothing except creating the myriad things.

Question: Master Ch'eng I said, "Heaven and Earth create and transform without having any mind of their own. The sage has a mind of his own but does not take any [unnatural] action."

Answer: That shows where Heaven and Earth have no mind of their own. It is like this: The four seasons run their course and the various things flourish. When do Heaven and Earth entertain any mind of their own? As to the sage, he only follows principle. What action does he need to take? This is the reason why Ming-tao (Ch'eng

Hao) said, "The constant principle of Heaven and Earth is that their mind is in all things and yet they have no mind of their own. The constant principle of the sage is that his feelings are in accord with all creation, and yet he has no feelings of his own." This is extremely well said.

Question: Does having their mind in all things not mean to pervade all things with their mind without any selfishness?

Answer: Heaven and Earth reach all things with this mind. When man receives it, it then becomes the human mind. When things receive it, it becomes the mind of things (in general). And when grass, trees, birds, animals receive it, it becomes the mind of grass, trees, birds, and animals (in particular). All of these are simply the one mind of Heaven and Earth. Thus we must understand in what sense Heaven and Earth have mind and in what sense they have no mind. We cannot be inflexible. (49:23b–24a)

128. When the myriad things are born and grow, that is the time when Heaven and Earth have no mind. When dried and withered things desire life, that is the time when Heaven and Earth have mind. (49:24a)

129. The Lord (*Ti*) is principle acting as master. (49:25a)

13. Spiritual Beings and Spiritual Forces (Kuei-Shen)

130. Someone asked whether there are spiritual beings *(kuei-shen)*?

Answer: How can this matter be quickly explained? Even if it could, would you believe it? You must look into all principles of things and gradually understand, and then this puzzling problem will be solved by itself. When Fan Ch'ih asked about wisdom, Confucius said, "Devote oneself earnestly to the duties due to men, and respect spiritual beings but keep them at a distance. This may be called wisdom." Let us attend to those things that should be attended to. Those that cannot be attended to, let us set aside. By the time we have attended thoroughly to ordinary daily matters, the principles governing spiritual beings will naturally be understood. This is the way to wisdom. [When Confucius said], "If we are not yet able to serve man, how can we serve spiritual beings?" he expresses the same idea. (51:2a)

131. Is expansion positive spiritual force *(shen)* and contraction negative spiritual force *(kuei)*?

The Teacher drew a circle on the desk with his hand and pointed to its center and said: Principle is like a circle. Within it there is differentiation like this. All cases of material force which is coming forth belong to yang and are positive spiritual force. All cases of material force which is returning to its origin belong to yin and are the negative spiritual force. In the day, forenoon is the positive spiritual force, afternoon is the negative spiritual force. In the month, from the third day onward is the positive spiritual force; after the sixteenth day, it is the negative spiritual force.

T'ung Po-yu *asked:* Is it correct when speaking of the sun and moon as opposites, to say that the sun is the positive spiritual force and the moon is the negative spiritual force?

Answer: Yes, it is. Plants growing are the positive spiritual force, plants declining are the negative spiritual force. A person from childhood to maturity is the positive spiritual force, while a man in his declining years and old age is the negative spiritual force. In breathing, breath going out is the positive spiritual force, breath coming in is the negative spiritual force. (51:6b)

132. The positive and negative spiritual forces are so called with respect to function. Spirit is so-called with respect to the wonderful functioning. In the cases of positive and

negative spiritual forces, like yin and yang, contraction and expansion, going and coming, and diminution and augmentation, there are rough traces that can be seen. In the case of spirit which is so-called because of the mysterious functioning, it happens all of a sudden and is unfathomable. It suddenly comes, suddenly goes; it is suddenly here, suddenly there. (51:7b)

133. Question about the principles of life and death and spiritual beings. (*Question:* Although we know that spiritual beings and life and death are governed by one and the same principle, we do not understand the exact point. *Answer:* "Essence and material force are combined to be things. The wandering away of the spirit becomes change." This is the principle of life and death. The questioner did not understand. *Further remark:* Essence and material force consolidate to become man, and as they disintegrate, they become a spiritual being.

Further question: When essence and material force consolidate, is this principle attached to material force?)

Answer: As the Way of Heaven operates, the myriad things develop and grow. There is (logically) principle first and then material force. Although they coexist at the same time, in the final analysis principle is basic. Man receives it and thus possesses life. (But material force may be clear or turbid.) The clear part of material force becomes his vital force *(ch'i)*, while the turbid part becomes his physical nature. (The clear part belongs to yang while the turbid part belongs to yin.) Consciousness and movement are due to yang, while physical form and body (bones and flesh, skin and hair) are due to yin. The vital force belongs to the heavenly aspect of the soul *(hun)* and the body is governed by the earthly aspect of the soul *(p'o)*. In his commentary on the *Huai-nan Tzu*, Kao Yu (fl. 205) said, "*Hun* is the spirit of yang and *p'o* is the spirit of yin." By spirit is meant the master of the body and the vital force. Man is born as a result of integration of essence and material force. He possesses this material force only in a certain amount, which in time necessarily becomes exhausted. (This is what is meant by physicians when they say that yin or yang no longer rises or falls.) When exhaustion takes place, the heavenly aspect of the soul and the vital force return to Heaven, and the earthly aspect of the soul and the body return to the Earth, and the man dies. When a man is about to die, the warm material force leaves him and rises. This is called the *hun* rising. The lower part of his body gradually becomes cold. This is called the *p'o* falling. Thus as there is life, there is necessarily death, and as there is beginning, there must be an end. What integrates and disintegrates is material force. As to principle, it merely attaches itself to material force, but from the beginning it does not consolidate into a separate thing by itself. However, whatever in one's functioning that is correct is principle. It need not be spoken of in terms of integration and disintegration. When a man dies, his material force necessarily disintegrates. However, it does not disintegrate completely at once. Therefore in religious sacrifices we have the principle of spiritual influence and response. Whether the material force (or vital force) of ancestors of many generations ago is still there or not cannot be known. Nevertheless, since those who perform the sacrificial rites are their descendants, the material force between them is after all the same. Hence there is the principle by which they can penetrate and respond. But the material force that has disintegrated cannot again be integrated. And yet the Buddhists say that man after death becomes a spiritual being and the spiritual being again becomes a man. If so, then in the universe there would always be the same number of people coming and going, with no need of the creative process of production and reproduction. This is decidedly absurd. (51:18b–19b)

WANG YANG-MING, INQUIRY ON THE GREAT LEARNING

Question: The *Great Learning* was considered by a former scholar [Chu Hsi] as the learning of the great man. I venture to ask why the learning of the great man should consist in "manifesting the clear character."

Master Wang said: The great man regards Heaven, Earth, and the myriad things as one body. He regards the world as one family and the country as one person. As to those who make a cleavage between objects and distinguish between the self and others, they are small men. That the great man can regard Heaven, Earth, and the myriad things as one body is not because he deliberately wants to do so, but because it is natural to the humane nature of his mind that he do so. Forming one body with Heaven, Earth, and the myriad things is not only true of the great man. Even the mind of the small man is no different. Only he himself makes it small. Therefore when he sees a child about to fall into a well, he cannot help a feeling of alarm and commiseration. This shows that his humanity (*jen*) forms one body with the child. It may be objected that the child belongs to the same species. Again, when he observes the pitiful cries and frightened appearance of birds and animals about to be slaughtered, he cannot help feeling an "inability to bear" their suffering. This shows that his humanity forms one body with birds and animals. It may be objected that birds and animals are sentient beings as he is. But when he sees plants broken and destroyed, he cannot help a feeling of pity. This shows that his humanity forms one body with plants. It may be said that plants are living things as he is. Yet, even when he sees tiles and stones shattered and crushed, he cannot help a feeling of regret. This shows that his humanity forms one body with tiles and stones. This means that even the mind of the small man necessarily has the humanity that forms one body with all. Such a mind is rooted in his Heaven-endowed nature, and is naturally intelligent, clear, and not beclouded. For this reason it is called the "clear character." Although the mind of the small man is divided and narrow, yet his humanity that forms one body can remain free from darkness to this degree. This is due to the fact that his mind has not yet been aroused by desires and obscured by selfishness. When it is aroused by desires and obscured by selfishness, compelled by greed for gain and fear of harm, and stirred by anger, he will destroy things, kill members of his own species, and will do everything. In extreme cases he will even slaughter his own brothers, and the humanity that forms one body will disappear completely. Hence, if it is not obscured by selfish desires, even the mind of the small man has the humanity that forms one body with all as does the mind of the great man. As soon as it is obscured by selfish desires, even the mind of the great man will be divided and narrow like that of the small man. Thus the learning of the great man consists entirely in getting rid of the obscuration of selfish desires in order by his own efforts to make manifest his clear character, so as to restore the condition of forming one body with Heaven, Earth, and the myriad things, a condition that is originally so, that is all. It is not that outside of the original substance something can be added.

Question: Why, then, does the learning of the great man consist in loving the people?

Answer: To manifest the clear character is to bring about the substance of the state of forming one body with Heaven, Earth, and the myriad things, whereas loving the people is to put into universal operation the function of the state of forming one body. Hence manifesting the clear character consists in loving the people, and loving the people is the way to manifest the clear character. Therefore, only when I love my father, the fathers of others, and the fathers of all men can my humanity really form one body with my father, the fathers of others, and the fathers of all men. When it truly forms one body with them, then the clear character of filial piety will be manifested. Only when I love my brother, the brothers of others, and the brothers of all men can my humanity really form one body with my brother, the brothers of others, and the brothers of all men. When it truly forms one body with them, then the clear character of brotherly respect will be manifested. Everything from ruler, minister, husband, wife, and friends to mountains, rivers, spiritual beings, birds, animals, and plants should be truly loved in order to realize my humanity that forms one body with them, and then my clear character will be completely manifested, and I will really form one body with Heaven, Earth, and the myriad things. This is what is meant by "manifesting the clear character throughout the empire." This is what is meant by "regulation of the family," "ordering the state," and "bringing peace to the world." This is what is meant by "full development of one's nature."

Question: Then why does the learning of the great man consist in "abiding in the highest good"?

Answer: The highest good is the ultimate principle of manifesting character and loving people. The nature endowed in us by Heaven is pure and perfect. The fact that it is intelligent, clear, and not beclouded is evidence of the emanation and revelation of the highest good. It is the original substance of the clear character which is called innate knowledge of the good. As the highest good emanates and reveals itself, we will consider right as right and wrong as wrong. Things of greater or less importance and situations of grave or light character will be responded to as they act upon us. In all our changes and movements, we will stick to no particular point, but possess in ourselves the Mean that is perfectly natural. This is the ultimate of the normal nature of man and the principle of things. There can be no consideration of adding to or subtracting from it. If there is any, it means selfish ideas and shallow cunning, and cannot be said to be the highest good. Naturally, how can anyone who does not watch over himself carefully when alone, and who has no refinement and singleness of mind, attain to such a state of perfection? Later generations fail to realize that the highest good is inherent in their own minds, but exercise their selfish ideas and cunning and grope for it outside their minds, believing that every event and every object has its own peculiar definite principle. For this reason the law of right and wrong is obscured; the mind becomes concerned with fragmentary and isolated details and broken pieces; the selfish desires of man become rampant and the Principle of Nature is at an end. And thus the learning of manifesting character and loving people is everywhere thrown into confusion. In the past there have, of course, been people who wanted to manifest their clear character. But simply because they did not know how to abide in the highest good, but instead drove their own minds toward something too lofty, they thereby lost them in illusions, emptiness, and quietness, having nothing to do with the work of the family, the state, and the world. Such are the followers of Buddhism and Taoism. There have, of course, been those who wanted to love their people. Yet simply because they did not know how to abide in the highest good, but instead sank their own minds in base and trifling things, they thereby lost them in scheming strategy and cunning techniques, having neither the sincerity of humanity nor that of commiseration. Such are the followers of the

*These despots were: Duke Huan of Ch'i (r. 685–643 B.C.E.), Duke Wen of Chin (r. 636–628 B.C.E.), Duke Mu of Ch'in (r. 659–619 B.C.E.), King Chuang of Ch'u (r. 613–589 B.C.E.), and Duke Hsiang of Sung (r. 650–635 B.C.E.).

Five Despots* and the pursuers of success and profit. All of these defects are due to a failure to know how to abide in the highest good. Therefore abiding in the highest good is to manifesting character and loving people as the carpenter's square and compass are to the square and the circle, or rule and measure to length, or balances and scales to weight. If the square and the circle do not abide by the compass and the carpenter's square, their standard will be wrong; if length does not abide by the rule and measure, its adjustment will be lost; if weight does not abide by the balances, its exactness will be gone; and if manifesting clear character and loving people do not abide by the highest good, their foundation will disappear. Therefore, abiding in the highest good so as to love people and manifest the clear character is what is meant by the learning of the great man.

Question: "Only after knowing what to abide in can one be calm. Only after having been calm can one be tranquil. Only after having achieved tranquillity can one have peaceful repose. Only after having peaceful repose can one begin to deliberate. Only after deliberation can the end be attained." How do you explain this?

Answer: People fail to realize that the highest good is in their minds and seek it outside. As they believe that everything or every event has its own definite principle, they search for the highest good in individual things. Consequently, the mind becomes fragmentary, isolated, broken into pieces; mixed and confused, it has no definite direction. Once it is realized that the highest good is in the mind and does not depend on any

The Shengong Shengde Stele Pavilion, Sacred Way, Ming Tombs, outside Beijing. Marking the entrance to the tombs of the emperors from Ming Dynasty, this pavilion houses a 50-ton tortoise carrying a stone tablet. (*Forrest E. Baird*)

search outside, then the mind will have definite direction and there will be no danger of its becoming fragmentary, isolated, broken into pieces, mixed, or confused. When there is no such danger, the mind will not be erroneously perturbed but will be tranquil. Not being erroneously perturbed but being tranquil, it will be leisurely and at ease in its daily functioning and will attain peaceful repose. Being in peaceful repose, whenever a thought arises or an event acts upon it, the mind with its innate knowledge will thoroughly sift and carefully examine whether or not the thought or event is in accord with the highest good, and thus the mind can deliberate. With deliberation, every decision will be excellent and every act will be proper, and in this way the highest good will be attained.

Question: "Things have their roots and their branches." A former scholar [Chu Hsi] considered manifesting the clear character as the root (or fundamental) and renovating the people as the branch (or secondary), and thought that they are two things opposing each other as internal and external. "Affairs have their beginnings and their ends." The former scholar considered knowing what to abide in as the beginning and the attainment of the highest good as the end, both being one thing in harmonious continuity. According to you, "renovating the people" (*hsin-min*) should be read as "loving the people" (*ch'in-min*). If so, isn't the theory of root and branches in some respect incorrect?

Answer: The theory of beginnings and ends is in general right. Even if we read "renovating the people" as "loving the people" and say that manifesting the character is the root and loving the people is the branches, it is not incorrect. The main thing is that root and branches should not be distinguished as two different things. The trunk of the tree is called the root (or essential part), and the twigs are called the branches. It is precisely because the tree is one that its parts can be called root and branches. If they are said to be two different things, then since they are two distinct objects, how can we speak of them as root and branches of the same thing? Since the idea of renovating the people is different from that of loving the people, obviously the task of manifesting the character and that of loving the people are two different things. If it is realized that manifesting the clear character is to love the people and loving the people is to manifest the clear character, how can they be split in two? What the former scholar said is due to his failure to realize that manifesting the character and loving the people are basically one thing. Instead, he believed them to be two different things and consequently, although he knew that root and branches should be one, yet he could not help splitting them in two.

Question: The passage from the phrase, "The ancients who wished to manifest their clear character throughout the world" to the clause, "first [order their state . . . regulate their families . . .] cultivate their personal lives," can be understood by your theory of manifesting the character and loving the people. May I ask what task, what procedure, and what effort are involved in the passage from "Those who wished to cultivate their personal lives would first rectify their minds . . . make their will sincere . . . extend their knowledge" to the clause, "the extension of knowledge consists in the investigation of things?"

Answer: This passage fully explains the task of manifesting the character, loving the people, and abiding in the highest good. The person, the mind, the will, knowledge, and things constitute the order followed in the task. While each of them has its own place, they are really one thing. Investigating, extending, being sincere, rectifying, and cultivating are the task performed in the procedure. Although each has its own name, they are really one affair. What is it that is called the person? It is the physical functioning of the mind. What is it that is called the mind? It is the clear and intelligent master of the person. What is meant by cultivating the personal life? It means to do good and get rid of evil. Can the body by itself do good and get rid of evil? The clear and intelligent master must desire to do good and get rid of evil before the body that functions physically can do so. Therefore he who wishes to cultivate his personal life must first rectify his mind.

Now the original substance of the mind is man's nature. Human nature being universally good, the original substance of the mind is correct. How is it that any effort is required to rectify the mind? The reason is that, while the original substance of the mind is originally correct, incorrectness enters when one's thoughts and will are in operation. Therefore he who wishes to rectify his mind must rectify it in connection with the operation of his thoughts and will. If, whenever a good thought arises, he really loves it as he loves beautiful colors, and whenever an evil thought arises, he really hates it as he hates bad odors, then his will will always be sincere and his mind can be rectified.

However, what arises from the will may be good or evil, and unless there is a way to make clear the distinction between good and evil, there will be a confusion of truth and untruth. In that case, even if one wants to make his will sincere, he cannot do so. Therefore he who wishes to make his will sincere must extend his knowledge. By extension is meant to reach the limit. The word "extension" is the same as that used in the saying, "Mourning is to be carried to the utmost degree of grief." In the *Book of Changes* it is said: "Knowing the utmost, one should reach it." "Knowing the utmost" means knowledge and "reaching it" means extension. The extension of knowledge is not what later scholars understand as enriching and widening knowledge. It is simply extending one's innate knowledge of the good to the utmost. This innate knowledge of the good is what Mencius meant when he said, "The sense of right and wrong is common to all men." The sense of right and wrong requires no deliberation to know, nor does it depend on learning to function. This is why it is called innate knowledge. It is my nature endowed by Heaven, the original substance of my mind, naturally intelligent, shining, clear, and understanding.

Whenever a thought or a wish arises, my mind's faculty of innate knowledge itself is always conscious of it. Whether it is good or evil, my mind's innate knowing faculty itself also knows it. It has nothing to do with others. Therefore, although an inferior man may have done all manner of evil, when he sees a superior man he will surely try to disguise this fact, concealing what is evil and displaying what is good in himself. This shows that innate knowledge of the good does not permit any self-deception. Now the only way to distinguish good and evil in order to make the will sincere is to extend to the utmost the knowledge of the innate faculty. Why is this? When [a good] thought or wish arises, the innate faculty of my mind already knows it to be good. Suppose I do not sincerely love it but instead turn away from it. I would then be regarding good as evil and obscuring my innate faculty which knows the good. When [an evil] thought or wish arises, the innate faculty of my mind already knows it to be evil. If I did not sincerely hate it but instead carried it out, I would be regarding evil as good and obscuring my innate faculty which knows evil. In such cases what is supposed to be knowledge is really ignorance. How then can the will be made sincere? If what the innate faculty knows to be good or evil is sincerely loved or hated, one's innate knowing faculty is not deceived and the will can be made sincere.

Now, when one sets out to extend his innate knowledge to the utmost, does this mean something illusory, hazy, in a vacuum, and unreal? No, it means something real. Therefore, the extension of knowledge must consist in the investigation of things. A thing is an event. For every emanation of the will there must be an event corresponding to it. The event to which the will is directed is a thing. To investigate is to rectify. It is to rectify that which is incorrect so it can return to its original correctness. To rectify that which is not correct is to get rid of evil, and to return to correctness is to do good.

This is what is meant by investigation. The *Book of History* says, "He [Emperor Yao] investigated (*ko*) heaven above and earth below"; "[Emperor Shun] investigated (*ko*) in the temple of illustrious ancestors"; and "[The ruler] rectifies (*ko*) the evil of his heart." The word "investigation" (*ko*) in the phrase "the investigation of things" combines the two meanings.

If one sincerely loves the good known by the innate faculty but does not in reality do the good as he comes into contact with the thing to which the will is directed, it means that the thing has not been investigated and that the will to love the good is not yet sincere. If one sincerely hates the evil known by the innate faculty but does not in reality get rid of the evil as he comes into contact with the thing to which the will is directed, it means that the thing has not been investigated and that the will to hate evil is not sincere. If as we come into contact with the thing to which the will is directed, we really do the good and get rid of the evil to the utmost which is known by the innate faculty, then everything will be investigated and what is known by our innate faculty will not be deficient or obscured but will be extended to the utmost. Then the mind will be joyous in itself, happy and without regret, the functioning of the will will carry with it no self-deception, and sincerity may be said to have been attained. Therefore it is said, "When things are investigated, knowledge is extended; when knowledge is extended, the will becomes sincere; when the will is sincere, the mind is rectified; and when the mind is rectified, the personal life is cultivated." While the order of the tasks involves a sequence of first and last, in substance they are one and cannot be so separated. At the same time, while the order and the tasks cannot be separated into first and last, their function must be so refined as not to be wanting in the slightest degree. This is why the doctrine of investigation, extension, being sincere, and rectification is a correct exposition of the true heritage of Sage-Emperors Yao and Shun and why it coincides with Confucius' own ideas.

WESTERN ENCOUNTERS— CHINA

Western influence characterizes the modern period of Chinese philosophy (1644–present). Contacts between China and the West began during the T'ang Dynasty (618–907), when Christians, Jews, and Muslims settled in China but made no deep impression. The Franciscan mission during the Yuan Dynasty (1279–1368) also passed without much trace. It was not until the "Jesuit century" (1600–1700) that Western thought really penetrated Chinese society. Christian theology has had a continuing role ever since. The learned Jesuit monks also disseminated Western science and technology. The nineteenth century saw Protestant groups from Europe and North America intensify the campaign to Christianize the Chinese. Concurrently, Western governments used military superiority to force acceptance of unfair commercial agreements, subjecting China to colonial practices for the first time. During the twentieth century, trade, educational and cultural exchanges, an Allied presence in World War II, and modern media communications made a tremendous Western impact on Chinese awareness. Communist ideology from the Soviet Union began to infiltrate in 1917, leading to a communist victory and the establishment of the People's Republic of China in 1949. After a period of political isolation (1949–1979), China reopened to the world and today is speeding toward globalization. A philosophical exchange between China and the West has occurred during much of the last century. Chinese philosophy has embraced its Western counterpart. The West is now reciprocating.

Each of the outstanding developments in Chinese philosophy over the past 350 years exhibits Western influence. The revolt against Neo-Confucianism in the early Ch'ing Dynasty (1644–1911) was spearheaded by thinkers who had absorbed the Jesuit spirit of scientific objectivity. The materialist Wang Fu-chih

(Wang Fuzhi, 1619–1692) and the reactionary Confucianist Tai Chen (Dai Zhen, 1723–1777) faulted the theories of Chu Hsi and Wang Yang-ming for lack of hard evidence. Both varieties of Neo-Confucianism were too abstract and speculative for their tastes.

The full introduction of Western philosophy into China in the early decades of the twentieth century received an enormous boost from the lecture tours (1919–1921) of Bertrand Russell and John Dewey, two of the leading Western philosophers of that time. Chinese intellectuals responded in three ways. Some stood by the superiority of Chinese thinking over the Western. Others turned from their native tradition to some brand of Western thought, as did Hu Shih (Hu Shi, 1891–1962), an advocate of Dewey's pragmatism, and Chang Tung-sun (Zhang Dongsun, 1886–1973), who built his thinking on that of Kant. Yet others attempted to blend the two traditions creatively.

The revival of Neo-Confucianism in the middle of the twentieth century exemplifies the third response. It featured the work of Fung Yu-lan (1895–1990) and Hsiung Shih-li (1885–1968). Fung reconstructed Chu Hsi's thought into a logical deductive system based on the Western model. Hsiung's revision of Idealistic Neo-Confucianism has been compared to the thinking of Bergson and Whitehead.

The triumph of Chinese Marxism over the entire profession of Chinese philosophy since 1949 has been complete. Philosophers in China have been expected to uphold that position as their personal philosophy and to bring it to bear in their teaching and research. Chinese Marxism is, of course, a variation of a Western philosophy. Establishing that position as official has limited freedom of philosophical thought to some extent; it has also stimulated careful study of European philosophy, especially the period from Kant through Hegel and Marx to Lenin.

The introduction of Chinese philosophy into the West created a vital frontier for both Chinese and Western philosophers during the closing decades of the twentieth century. Fung Yu-lan's histories of Chinese philosophy and Wing-tsit Chan's translations of Chinese texts have been instrumental. One key aspect of the movement is the new Neo-Confucianism. Contemporary Chinese philosophers working outside Mainland China in either Taiwan or the West have continued the project started in China at mid-century to bring Confucianism into dialogue with current Western philosophy. Chung-ying Cheng (b. 1935) and Tu Wei-ming (b. 1940) stand at the forefront of this development. Both were born in China, educated in Taiwan, came to the United States for graduate studies, and now teach at American universities. This pattern is typical of a growing group busy making what Cheng calls "overseas Chinese philosophy." In the discussion that follows, Mao Tse-tung and Lin Yutang represent the last two movements mentioned.

*   *   *

Mao Tse-tung (1893–1976) was the master strategist of the Chinese revolution, a victorious general, and the nearly omnipotent ruler of the most populous nation in the world for twenty-seven years. Born of southern peasant stock, in his youth Mao studied the history and philosophy of both his motherland and the West. The May Fourth Movement (1919), a push for reform sparked by student demonstrations, kindled his revolutionary zeal and inclined him toward Marxism. He was a charter member of the Chinese Communist Party at its founding in 1921 and by 1935 its acknowledged leader. He commanded a Red Army first against Chiang Kai-shek's Nationalists in the mid-1930s, then with them against a common

Japanese enemy (1937–1945), and ultimately to victory over them in 1949. As "Chairman Mao," he engineered the construction of the People's Republic of China. In a decade, a poor, weak, divided country, long subject to feudalism under emperors and warlords and to imperialism under Western powers, reversed itself and started on the road to international prominence. Mao's disastrous mistakes were the Great Leap Forward (forced collectivization of farming in 1958) and the Cultural Revolution (drastic purging of "reactionary and counter-revolutionary" elements within society and the Party, 1966–1976). Once idolized by the masses, he fell from grace in their eyes after his death in 1976. He remains, nevertheless, the major change agent of China during a revolutionary era in its history and one of the giant figures of the twentieth century.

Mao was the primary architect of Chinese Marxism, a philosophy with roots in both Western and Chinese thought. Mao espoused the standard doctrines of the German and Soviet socialist philosophers before him (Marx, Engels, Lenin, Stalin), such as dialectical materialism, class struggle, and the dictatorship of the proletariat. But he seasoned their teachings with ideas taken from his Chinese heritage and geared to the Chinese situation. Early on, he condemned prerevolutionary Chinese philosophy wholesale, finding in it only abstract metaphysical speculation not certified scientific fact, idealism rather than materialism, and escape into the private self instead of exaltation of the social self. After 1938, however, he moved beyond this simplistic critique and identified with everything in the Chinese philosophical tradition that could enrich dialectical materialism. Especially meaningful to him in this regard were the unity of knowledge and action ("conscious action" he called it) and subjective factors (such as conviction and will power) that figure crucially in the human shaping of events. In formulating his position, Mao was guided by four criteria of an authentic revolutionary philosophy. First, it must be practical. It must generate concrete improvements in the conditions under which the people actually live and work together. Second, it must be scientific. It must be grounded in objective fact and verified experientially in the practice of economic production, revolutionary struggle, and controlled experiment. Third, it must be democratic. Under the dictatorship of the proletariat, it must serve the people by building mutual respect, equality, cooperation, solidarity, participatory governance, and the total renovation of society. Last of all, it must be popular. Simple folk must be able to understand it and make it work in their lives. Mao wanted a philosophy that was down to earth and socially conscious, as well as specifically focused.

Mao's two most important philosophical writings are "On Practice" and "On Contradiction" (offered here, translator anonymous). "On Practice" sets forth Mao's theory of knowledge and "On Contradiction" his theory of dialectic—two pillars of his philosophy. That both theories were intertwined in his thinking can be inferred from the fact that these works appeared in the same year (1937). The problem of knowledge for Mao amounted to a single two-part question: "What do I need to know, and how can I acquire that knowledge?" Since Mao was a down-to-earth, socially conscious, specifically focused philosopher, that question had to include time, place, and situation references. It thus became "What do I as a twentieth-century Chinese need to know about my immediate socioeconomic situation, and how can I acquire that knowledge?" Being a practical, scientific philosopher, Mao needed to worry only about the immediate socioeconomic situation (social relations, working conditions) in China, because that was all that he could see and touch. Metaphysics and religion are about what cannot be seen and touched, hence of no concern. Mao could see that the immediate socioeconomic situation in China during the twentieth century was changing rapidly and that human beings were both objects of change and agents of change. So his question became "How are human beings changed by and changing the socioeconomic situation of twentieth-century China, and how can I come by that knowledge?"

This brought to his awareness the phenomenon of contradiction—the clash between two groups of human beings with opposing views on some issue. The crucial problems facing humans anywhere anytime, he held, are contradictions. He could see that the Chinese were changing their immediate socioeconomic situation by participating in clashes and being changed by those clashes whether or not they were direct participants. On examination, he came to believe that the dynamic whereby contradictions changed situations for people was dialectical, that is, like a dialogue. In a dialogue or debate, one side advances a position; then the other side attacks that position and makes a counter-proposal; then the first side modifies its position in light of the attack and counterproposal; then the other side attacks that modification with another counterproposal; and so forth until some mutually satisfactory resolution of the issue is finally reached. The dynamics of socioeconomic change in history follow the same dialectical pattern, Mao the Marxist thought. Change comes as two groups struggle against each other, learn from their successes and failures, modify their approaches, and exchange the lead back and forth until one side ultimately wins. What was new in Mao's vision of the dialectical process in history was his Chinese conviction that the two opposing sides in every contradiction were also dependent on each other, like dancing partners. The perception of the underlying unity of opposites required taking a larger view.

This led Mao to inquire into what contradictions were troubling the socioeconomic situation of China in his time. One was the clash between the Chinese and the neo-colonial Japanese (1937–1945). Another was the collision between the Communists and the neo-feudal Nationalists (1930s and 1940s). Another was the conflict between proletariat (workers, peasants, soldiers) and bourgeoisie (landowners, merchants, managers, intellectuals) within Chinese society (after 1949). Another was the tension between the workers and the peasants within the proletariat (1950s). Yet another was the argument between the progressives and the reactionaries within the Chinese Communist Party (1960s). The last was the perennial struggle between society and Nature for human survival. These Mao identified as the principal contradictions facing him as a twentieth-century Chinese. The lead question needed once again to be redefined: "What do I need to know about these contradictions, and how can I acquire that knowledge?"

Mao concluded that he needed to know what made each contradiction qualitatively unique and what qualitatively different methods would resolve each one. He also needed to know what priority to place upon each (which to tackle first, which second, etc.) and on which side of each contradiction to apply his efforts as a revolutionary change agent. It is the core of his theory of knowledge that by practice only could he acquire the knowledge sought. For Mao, practice in this context meant participating in the contradiction, joining one side or the other actively and energetically, and as a participant bringing about potentially constructive change. Only as a situation changes does it reveal vital information about the qualitative nature of some contradiction. Out of that information, a theory can be formulated by means of rational reflection. That theory can then be verified or falsified by putting it to work in the struggle between opposing sides, to see if improvements emerge. When further change has been brought about, fresh information is made available; better theory can be devised; further application of theory to situation can be made along with more change, new data, and further revision of theory; with progress all along the way and no end in sight.

Mao thought that some contradictions were antagonistic (between enemies) and could be resolved only by suppression, coercion, or force. Others were nonantagonistic (between friends) and could be handled through discussion, persuasion, and education. Mao advanced this idea in a famous speech entitled "On the Correct Handling of Contradiction Among the People" (1957). The contradictions between China and Japan and between the Chinese Communists and Nationalists, for example, were antagonistic and had to be dealt with through revolutionary war. Of these two contradictions, the problem with the Japanese was more pressing. So Mao's Red Army joined with the Nationalists in the War of Resistance Against the Japanese, the national revolution won in 1945 with help from the Allies. That struggle behind, the next priority was defeating the Nationalists in the War of Liberation, the democratic revolution won in 1949. The contradiction between the proletariat and the bourgeoisie (the Reds and the Blacks, respectively) within Chinese society after Liberation could best be met through socialist revolution (class struggle), in which the masses would overthrow the middle class and establish the dictatorship of the proletariat. The contradiction between the workers (industry) and the peasants (agriculture) could be settled through the mechanization and collectivization of farming, a revolution in China's methods of material production. The contradiction between progressive and reactionary factions within the Communist Party could be overcome through criticism and self-criticism when possible and by suppression when necessary. Last of all, the contradiction between society and Nature for survival of the race could be won for humankind by building up the productive forces of agriculture and industry. In each case, the correct method of handling a certain contradiction is a specific kind of revolution.

What did Mao need to know, and how could he acquire that knowledge? He needed to understand the nature of these contradictions and the correct revolutionary methods he as the change agent in charge must apply toward resolving them. That knowledge was available to him only through practice. This is the gist of Mao's key philosophical essays and of his philosophy at large. It all boils down to contradiction and revolution understood through practice.

*   *   *

Lin Yutang (1895-1976) deserves recognition as perhaps the foremost ambassador of cultural exchange between China and the West in his time. During the first half of his life, while living in China and writing in Chinese, he brought his own people an enriched understanding of Western literature, philosophy, and religion. Then during the second half, after 1935, as a resident of the United States writing in English, he, more than any other figure of that period, provided Westerners with a vivid impression of ancient Chinese wisdom, making that wisdom relevant to their lifestyle. He was one of the most outstanding Chinese men of letters of the twentieth century, with a large volume of literary output in many genres to his credit. He was nominated in 1975 for the Nobel Prize in literature. His ability to transmit culture both ways was the result of a dual education. His early training in China was acquired in Christian, Western-oriented schools; his family was devoutly Christian and his father a Chinese Presbyterian minister. He then earned a master's degree from Harvard (1920) and a doctorate from Leipzig in Germany (1923). He returned to China and busied himself with editing literary journals, teaching in universities, and his own writing. Then, in 1935, at the urging of the American writer Pearl Buck, he immigrated to the United States. His self-administered second education in Chinese culture, from which he had been shielded in his youth, had begun long before his American sojourn, in his early twenties, however. As the nourishment he drew from Chinese spirituality increased, his Christian faith paled. He came to describe himself as a "pagan," by which he meant one with no specific religious identification, immersed in the wonder of the universe and the love of life. In his later years, however, after what he called his "grand detour," he returned to a simple faith in Jesus, shorn of dogma and ritual. All this he recounts in his spiritual autobiography, *From Pagan to Christian* (1959). His most popular renditions of Chinese thought for Western readers are *My Country and My People* (1935), *The Importance of Living* (1937), and his translations of ancient Chinese classics, *The Wisdom of Confucius* (1938) and *The Wisdom of Laotse* (1948). These writings earned him his American reputation as a modern Chinese sage, one accomplished in the art of living. He spent the last decade of his life in Taiwan, where he wrote once again in Chinese for the Chinese audience, and died in Hong Kong at the age of 81.

The Importance of Living, selections from which are included later in this section, was a best seller in the United States throughout the World War II era, and in China once the ban on it was lifted in the 1980s. It is regarded in both countries as Lin Yutang's most thoughtful and thought-provoking work. Lin calls the philosophy of life he sets forth in this book "Chinese humanism" and represents it as the "wise and merry" perennial philosophy of the Chinese scholar class of old. He makes it out to be the composite of Confucian, Taoist, and Buddhist wisdom of life favored by the Chinese intelligentsia over the centuries. Buddhism plays a slender role in the mix, and the main flavor is Taoist, especially the Neo-Taoism of the *Lieh-tzu* (fourth century C.E.) with its emphasis on pleasure. Lin proposes that the enjoyment of life is the sensible answer to the question of the meaning of life. Cultivation of the capacity for the full appreciation of leisure ("loafing"), family, friendship, the beauties of Nature, the fascinations of travel, the fine arts, and, oh yes, good food and drink—this is what life is all about. Lin advocates a childlike delight in the pleasures of life. But since we adults have outgrown our childish ways, we must cultivate the art of living afresh. Lin knows about evolution. We humans are, he says, monkeys on the rise, with an animal past and a more human future. Our animal instincts are to be trusted, though cautiously, for they have an evolutionary rationale. The human spirit, which urges us to transcend our animal past, is integral with the human body and a part of our evolutionary endowment. True religion is the simple sense of wonder at the mysteries of a universe issuing from some indefinable Creative Force. Science will one day explain it all. Formal religions are bogged down in dogma and worries about eternity. Paganism is the natural religious response of reverence before the marvels of life and Nature, builds an adult attitude of human self-reliance, and avoids pointless arguments with science by keeping to what our senses and minds can be sure of. It has been debated to what extent Lin's book is an actual report of the consensual wisdom of China over the ages, and to what extent it is a personal distillation of his own cultural Chinese and Western past. It is undeniable, however, that for a generation Lin's book shaped the impression curious Americans held of oriental wisdom. It played a meaningful role in the transmission of Chinese thought to the West, and it poses to modern Americans a philosophy of life worth considering.

*   *   *

For further reading in twentieth-century Chinese philosophy, see O. Briere, *Fifty Years of Chinese Philosophy, 1898–1950,* tr. Laurence G. Thompson (London: George Allen & Unwin, 1956); Chung-ying Cheng and Nicholas Bunnin, eds., *Contemporary Chinese Philosophy* (Boston/Oxford: Blackwell, 2002); and relevant articles in Antonio S. Cua, ed., *Encyclopedia of Chinese Philosophy* (New York/London: Routledge, 2003). For works specifically on Chinese Marxism and the philosophy of Mao Tse-tung, consult Bill Brugger and David Kelly, *Chinese Marxism in the Post-Mao Era* (Stanford, CA: Stanford University Press, 1990); Shiping Hua, *Scientism and Humanism: Two Cultures in Post-Mao China (1978–1989)* (Albany: SUNY Press, 1995); Nick Knight, *Mao Zedong on Dialectical Materialism: Writings on Philosophy, 1937* (Armonk, NY: Sharpe, 1990); Donald J. Monro, *The Concept of Man in Contemporary China* (Ann Arbor: University of Michigan Press, 1977); Stuart R. Schram, *The Thought of Mao Tse-tung* (Cambridge, Eng.: Cambridge University Press, 1989); and Francis Y.K. Soo, *Mao Tse-tung's Theory of Dialectic* (Dordrecht, Holland: D. Reidel, 1968). For Contemporary Confucianism, see Chung-ying Cheng, *New Dimensions of Confucian/Neo-Confucian Philosophy* (Albany: SUNY Press, 1991); Tu Wei-ming, *Humanity and Self-Cultivation: Essays in Confucian Philosophy* (Berkeley, CA: Asian Humanities, 1979); and Tu Wei-ming, *Confucian Thought: Selfhood as Creative Transformation* (Albany: SUNY Press, 1985).

MAO TSE-TUNG, ON PRACTICE

ON THE RELATION BETWEEN KNOWLEDGE AND PRACTICE, BETWEEN KNOWING AND DOING

JULY 1937

INTRODUCTION:

There used to be a number of comrades in our Party who were dogmatists and who for a long period rejected the experience of the Chinese revolution, denying the truth that "Marxism is not a dogma but a guide to action" and overawing people with words and phrases from Marxist works, torn out of context. There were also a number of comrades who were empiricists and who for a long period restricted themselves to their own fragmentary experience and did not understand the importance of theory for revolutionary practice or see the revolution as a whole, but worked blindly though industriously. The erroneous ideas of these two types of comrades, and particularly of the dogmatists, caused enormous losses to the Chinese revolution during 1931–34, and yet the dogmatists, cloaking themselves as Marxists, confused a great many comrades. "On Practice" was written in order to expose the subjectivist errors of dogmatism and empiricism in the Party, and especially the error of dogmatism, from the standpoint of the Marxist theory of knowledge. It was entitled "On Practice" because its stress was on exposing the dogmatist kind of subjectivism, which belittles practice. The ideas contained in this essay were presented by Comrade Mao Tse-tung in a lecture at the Anti-Japanese Military and Political College in Yenan.

Before Marx, materialism examined the problem of knowledge apart from the social nature of man and apart from his historical development, and was therefore incapable of understanding the dependence of knowledge on social practice, that is, the dependence of knowledge on production and the class struggle.

Above all, Marxists regard man's activity in production as the most fundamental practical activity, the determinant of all his other activities. Man's knowledge depends mainly on his activity in material production, through which he comes gradually to understand the phenomena, the properties and the laws of nature, and the relations between himself and nature; and through his activity in production he also gradually comes to understand, in varying degrees, certain relations that exist between man and man. None of this knowledge can be acquired apart from activity in production. In a classless society every person, as a member of society, joins in common effort with the other members, enters into definite relations of production with them and engages in production to meet man's material needs. In all class societies, the members of the different social classes also enter, in different ways, into definite relations of production

Reprinted by permission from Committee for the Publication of the Selected Works of Mao Tse-tung, Central Committee of the Communist Party of China, *Selected Works of Mao Tse-Tung* (Foreign Language Press, Peking, 1965).

and engage in production to meet their material needs. This is the primary source from which human knowledge develops.

Man's social practice is not confined to activity in production, but takes many other forms—class struggle, political life, scientific and artistic pursuits; in short, as a social being, man participates in all spheres of the practical life of society. Thus man, in varying degrees, comes to know the different relations between man and man, not only through his material life but also through his political and cultural life (both of which are intimately bound up with material life). Of these other types of social practice, class struggle in particular, in all its various forms, exerts a profound influence on the development of man's knowledge. In class society everyone lives as a member of a particular class, and every kind of thinking, without exception, is stamped with the brand of a class.

Marxists hold that in human society activity in production develops step by step from a lower to a higher level and that consequently man's knowledge, whether of nature or of society, also develops step by step from a lower to a higher level, that is, from the shallower to the deeper, from the one-sided to the many-sided. For a very long period in history, men were necessarily confined to a one-sided understanding of the history of society because, for one thing, the bias of the exploiting classes always distorted history and, for another, the small scale of production limited man's outlook. It was not until the modern proletariat emerged along with immense forces of production (large-scale industry) that man was able to acquire a comprehensive, historical understanding of the development of society and turn this knowledge into a science, the science of Marxism.

Marxists hold that man's social practice alone is the criterion of the truth of his knowledge of the external world. What actually happens is that man's knowledge is verified only when he achieves the anticipated results in the process of social practice (material production, class struggle or scientific experiment). If a man wants to succeed in his work, that is, to achieve the anticipated results, he must bring his ideas into correspondence with the laws of the objective external world; if they do not correspond, he will fail in his practice. After he fails, he draws his lessons, corrects his ideas to make them correspond to the laws of the external world, and can thus turn failure into success; this is what is meant by "failure is the mother of success" and "a fall into the pit, a gain in your wit." The dialectical-materialist theory of knowledge places practice in the primary position, holding that human knowledge can in no way be separated from practice and repudiating all the erroneous theories which deny the importance of practice or separate knowledge from practice. Thus Lenin said, "*Practice is higher than (theoretical) knowledge,* for it has not only the dignity of universality, but also of immediate actuality." The Marxist philosophy of dialectical materialism has two outstanding characteristics. One is its class nature: it openly avows that dialectical materialism is in the service of the proletariat. The other is its practicality: it emphasizes the dependence of theory on practice, emphasizes that theory is based on practice and in turn serves practice. The truth of any knowledge or theory is determined not by subjective feelings, but by objective results in social practice. Only social practice can be the criterion of truth. The standpoint of practice is the primary and basic standpoint in the dialectical-materialist theory of knowledge.

But how then does human knowledge arise from practice and in turn serve practice? This will become clear if we look at the process of development of knowledge.

In the process of practice, man at first sees only the phenomenal side, the separate aspects, the external relations of things. For instance, some people from outside come to Yenan on a tour of observation. In the first day or two, they see its topography, streets and houses; they meet many people, attend banquets, evening parties and mass meetings, hear talk of various kinds and read various documents, all these being the phenomena, the separate aspects and the external relations of things. This is called the perceptual stage of cognition, namely, the stage of sense perceptions and impressions. That is, these particular things in Yenan act on the sense organs of the members of the observation group, evoke sense perceptions and give rise in their brains to many impressions together with a rough sketch of the external relations among these impressions: this is the first stage of cognition. At this stage, man cannot as yet form concepts, which are deeper, or draw logical conclusions.

As social practice continues, things that give rise to man's sense perceptions and impressions in the course of his practice are repeated many times; then a sudden change (leap) takes place in the brain in the process of cognition, and concepts are formed. Concepts are no longer the phenomena, the separate aspects and the external relations of things; they grasp the essence, the totality and the internal relations of things. Between concepts and sense perceptions there is not only a quantitative but also a qualitative difference. Proceeding further, by means of judgement and inference one is able to draw logical conclusions. The expression in *San Kuo Yen Yi,** "knit the brows and a stratagem comes to mind," or in everyday language, "let me think it over," refers to man's use of concepts in the brain to form judgements and inferences. This is the second stage of cognition. When the members of the observation group have collected various data and, what is more, have "thought them over," they are able to arrive at the judgement that "the Communist Party's policy of the National United Front Against Japan is thorough, sincere and genuine." Having made this judgement, they can, if they too are genuine about uniting to save the nation, go a step further and draw the following conclusion, "The National United Front Against Japan can succeed." This stage of conception, judgement and inference is the more important stage in the entire process of knowing a thing; it is the stage of rational knowledge. The real task of knowing is, through perception, to arrive at thought, to arrive step by step at the comprehension of the internal contradictions of objective things, of their laws and of the internal relations between one process and another, that is, to arrive at logical knowledge. To repeat, logical knowledge differs from perceptual knowledge in that perceptual knowledge pertains to the separate aspects, the phenomena and the external relations of things, whereas logical knowledge takes a big stride forward to reach the totality, the essence and the internal relations of things and discloses the inner contradictions in the surrounding world. Therefore, logical knowledge is capable of grasping the development of the surrounding world in its totality, in the internal relations of all its aspects.

This dialectical-materialist theory of the process of development of knowledge, basing itself on practice and proceeding from the shallower to the deeper, was never worked out by anybody before the rise of Marxism. Marxist materialism solved this problem correctly for the first time, pointing out both materialistically and dialectically the deepening movement of cognition, the movement by which man in society progresses from perceptual knowledge to logical knowledge in his complex, constantly recurring practice of production and class struggle. Lenin said, "The abstraction of *matter,* of a *law* of nature, the abstraction of *value,* etc., in short, *all* scientific (correct, serious, not absurd) abstractions reflect nature more deeply, truly and *completely.*" Marxism-Leninism holds that each of the two stages in the process of cognition has its own characteristics, with knowledge manifesting itself as perceptual at the lower stage and

*[San Kuo Yen Yi (Tales of the Three Kingdoms) is a famous Chinese historical novel by Lo Kuan-chung (late 14th and early 15th century).]

logical at the higher stage, but that both are stages in an integrated process of cognition. The perceptual and the rational are qualitatively different, but are not divorced from each other; they are unified on the basis of practice. Our practice proves that what is perceived cannot at once be comprehended and that only what is comprehended can be more deeply perceived. Perception only solves the problem of phenomena; theory alone can solve the problem of essence. The solving of both these problems is not separable in the slightest degree from practice. Whoever wants to know a thing has no way of doing so except by coming into contact with it, that is, by living (practising) in its environment. In feudal society it was impossible to know the laws of capitalist society in advance because capitalism had not yet emerged, the relevant practice was lacking. Marxism could be the product only of capitalist society. Marx, in the era of laissez-faire capitalism, could not concretely know certain laws peculiar to the era of imperialism beforehand, because imperialism, the last stage of capitalism, had not yet emerged and the relevant practice was lacking; only Lenin and Stalin could undertake this task. Leaving aside their genius, the reason why Marx, Engels, Lenin and Stalin could work out their theories was mainly that they personally took part in the practice of the class struggle and the scientific experimentation of their time; lacking this condition, no genius could have succeeded. The saying, "without stepping outside his gate the scholar knows all the wide world's affairs," was mere empty talk in past times when technology was undeveloped. Even though this saying can be valid in the present age of developed technology, the people with real personal knowledge are those engaged in practice the wide world over. And it is only when these people have come to "know" through their practice and when their knowledge has reached him through writing and technical media that the "scholar" can indirectly "know all the wide world's affairs." If you want to know a certain thing or a certain class of things directly, you must personally participate in the practical struggle to change reality, to change that thing or class of things, for only thus can you come into contact with them as phenomena; only through personal participation in the practical struggle to change reality can you uncover the essence of that thing or class of things and comprehend them. This is the path to knowledge which every man actually travels, though some people, deliberately distorting matters, argue to the contrary. The most ridiculous person in the world is the "know-all" who picks up a smattering of hearsay knowledge and proclaims himself "the world's Number One authority"; this merely shows that he has not taken a proper measure of himself. Knowledge is a matter of science, and no dishonesty or conceit whatsoever is permissible. What is required is definitely the reverse—honesty and modesty. If you want knowledge, you must take part in the practice of changing reality. If you want to know the taste of a pear, you must change the pear by eating it yourself. If you want to know the structure and properties of the atom, you must make physical and chemical experiments to change the state of the atom. If you want to know the theory and methods of revolution, you must take part in revolution. All genuine knowledge originates in direct experience. But one cannot have direct experience of everything; as a matter of fact, most of our knowledge comes from indirect experience, for example, all knowledge from past times and foreign lands. To our ancestors and to foreigners, such knowledge was—or is—a matter of direct experience, and this knowledge is reliable if in the course of their direct experience the requirement of "scientific abstraction," spoken of by Lenin, was—or is—fulfilled and objective reality scientifically reflected; otherwise it is not reliable. Hence a man's knowledge consists only of two parts, that which comes from direct experience and that which comes from indirect experience. Moreover, what is indirect experience for me is direct experience for other people. Consequently, considered as a whole, knowledge of any kind is inseparable from direct experience. All knowledge originates in perception of the objective external world through man's physical sense organs. Anyone who denies such perception, denies direct experience, or denies personal participation in the practice that changes reality, is not a materialist. That is why the "know-all" is ridiculous. There is an old Chinese saying, "How can you catch tiger cubs without entering the tiger's lair?" This saying holds true for man's practice and it also holds true for the theory of knowledge. There can be no knowledge apart from practice.

To make clear the dialectical-materialist movement of cognition arising on the basis of the practice which changes reality—to make clear the gradually deepening movement of cognition—a few additional concrete examples are given below.

In its knowledge of capitalist society, the proletariat was only in the perceptual stage of cognition in the first period of its practice, the period of machine-smashing and spontaneous struggle; it knew only some of the aspects and the external relations of the phenomena of capitalism. The proletariat was then still a "class-in-itself." But when it reached the second period of its practice, the period of conscious and organized economic and political struggles, the proletariat was able to comprehend the essence of capitalist society, the relations of exploitation between social classes and its own historical task; and it was able to do so because of its own practice and because of its experience

Tiananmen (Gate of Heavenly Peace), Beijing. Built in 1417, this is the front entrance to the Forbidden City and the site where Mao Tse-tung (Zedong) proclaimed the Peoples Republic in 1949. The slogans on each side of Mao's portrait proclaim, "Long Live the People's Republic of China" and "Long Live the Unity of the Peoples of the World." (*Forrest E. Baird*)

of prolonged struggle, which Marx and Engels scientifically summed up in all its variety to create the theory of Marxism for the education of the proletariat. It was then that the proletariat became a "class-for-itself."

Similarly with the Chinese people's knowledge of imperialism. The first stage was one of superficial, perceptual knowledge, as shown in the indiscriminate anti-foreign struggles of the Movement of the Taiping Heavenly Kingdom, the Yi Ho Tuan Movement, and so on. It was only in the second stage that the Chinese people reached the stage of rational knowledge, saw the internal and external contradictions of imperialism and saw the essential truth that imperialism had allied itself with China's comprador and feudal classes to oppress and exploit the great masses of the Chinese people. This knowledge began about the time of the May 4th Movement of 1919.

Next, let us consider war. If those who lead a war lack experience of war, then at the initial stage they will not understand the profound laws pertaining to the directing of a specific war (such as our Agrarian Revolutionary War of the past decade). At the initial stage they will merely experience a good deal of fighting and, what is more, suffer many defeats. But this experience (the experience of battles won and especially of battles lost) enables them to comprehend the inner thread of the whole war, namely, the laws of that specific war, to understand its strategy and tactics, and consequently to direct the war with confidence. If, at such a moment, the command is turned over to an inexperienced person, then he too will have to suffer a number of defeats (gain experience) before he can comprehend the true laws of the war.

"I am not sure I can handle it." We often hear this remark when a comrade hesitates to accept an assignment. Why is he unsure of himself? Because he has no systematic understanding of the content and circumstances of the assignment, or because he has had little or no contact with such work, and so the laws governing it are beyond him. After a detailed analysis of the nature and circumstances of the assignment, he will feel more sure of himself and do it willingly. If he spends some time at the job and gains experience and if he is a person who is willing to look into matters with an open mind and not one who approaches problems subjectively, one-sidedly and superficially, then he can draw conclusions for himself as to how to go about the job and do it with much more courage. Only those who are subjective, one-sided and superficial in their approach to problems will smugly issue orders or directives the moment they arrive on the scene, without considering the circumstances, without viewing things in their totality (their history and their present state as a whole) and without getting to the essence of things (their nature and the internal relations between one thing and another). Such people are bound to trip and fall.

Thus it can be seen that the first step in the process of cognition is contact with the objects of the external world; this belongs to the stage of perception. The second step is to synthesize the data of perception by arranging and reconstructing them; this belongs to the stage of conception, judgement and inference. It is only when the data of perception are very rich (not fragmentary) and correspond to reality (are not illusory) that they can be the basis for forming correct concepts and theories.

Here two important points must be emphasized. The first, which has been stated before but should be repeated here, is the dependence of rational knowledge upon perceptual knowledge. Anyone who thinks that rational knowledge need not be derived from perceptual knowledge is an idealist. In the history of philosophy there is the "rationalist" school that admits the reality only of reason and not of experience, believing that reason alone is reliable while perceptual experience is not; this school errs by turning things upside down. The rational is reliable precisely because it has its source in sense perceptions, otherwise it would be like water without a source, a tree without roots, subjective, self-engendered and unreliable. As to the sequence in the process of cognition, perceptual experience comes first; we stress the significance of social practice in the process of cognition precisely because social practice alone can give rise to human knowledge and it alone can start man on the acquisition of perceptual experience from the objective world. For a person who shuts his eyes, stops his ears and totally cuts himself off from the objective world there can be no such thing as knowledge. Knowledge begins with experience—this is the materialism of the theory of knowledge.

The second point is that knowledge needs to be deepened, that the perceptual stage of knowledge needs to be developed to the rational stage—this is the dialectics of the theory of knowledge. To think that knowledge can stop at the lower, perceptual stage and that perceptual knowledge alone is reliable while rational knowledge is not, would be to repeat the historical error of "empiricism." This theory errs in failing to understand that, although the data of perception reflect certain realities in the objective world (I am not speaking here of idealist empiricism which confines experience to so-called introspection), they are merely one-sided and superficial, reflecting things incompletely and not reflecting their essence. Fully to reflect a thing in its totality, to reflect its essence, to reflect its inherent laws, it is necessary through the exercise of thought to reconstruct the rich data of sense perception, discarding the dross and selecting the essential, eliminating the false and retaining the true, proceeding from the one to the other and from the outside to the inside, in order to form a system of concepts and theories—it is necessary to make a leap from perceptual to rational knowledge. Such reconstructed knowledge is not more empty or more unreliable; on the contrary, whatever has been scientifically reconstructed in the process of cognition, on the basis of practice, reflects objective reality, as Lenin said, more deeply, more truly, more fully. As against this, vulgar "practical men" respect experience but despise theory, and therefore cannot have a comprehensive view of an entire objective process, lack clear direction and long-range perspective, and are complacent over occasional successes and glimpses of the truth. If such persons direct a revolution, they will lead it up a blind alley.

Rational knowledge depends upon perceptual knowledge and perceptual knowledge remains to be developed into rational knowledge—this is the dialectical-materialist theory of knowledge. In philosophy, neither "rationalism" nor "empiricism" understands the historical or the dialectical nature of knowledge, and although each of these schools contains one aspect of the truth (here I am referring to materialist, not to idealist, rationalism and empiricism), both are wrong on the theory of knowledge as a whole. The dialectical-materialist movement of knowledge from the perceptual to the rational holds true for a minor process of cognition (for instance, knowing a single thing or task) as well as for a major process of cognition (for instance, knowing a whole society or a revolution).

But the movement of knowledge does not end here. If the dialectical-materialist movement of knowledge were to stop at rational knowledge, only half the problem would be dealt with. And as far as Marxist philosophy is concerned, only the less important half at that. Marxist philosophy holds that the most important problem does not lie in understanding the laws of the objective world and thus being able to explain it, but in applying the knowledge of these laws actively to change the world. From the Marxist viewpoint, theory is important, and its importance is fully expressed in Lenin's statement, "Without revolutionary theory there can be no revolutionary movement." But Marxism emphasizes the importance of theory precisely and only because it can guide action. If we have a correct theory but merely prate about it, pigeonhole it and do not put it into practice, then that theory, however good, is of no significance. Knowledge begins with practice, and theoretical knowledge is acquired through practice and must then return to practice. The active function of knowledge manifests itself not only in the active leap from perceptual to rational knowledge, but—and this is more important—it must manifest itself in the leap from rational knowledge to revolutionary practice. The knowledge which grasps the laws of the world, must be redirected to the practice of changing the world, must be applied anew in the practice of production, in the practice of revolutionary class struggle and revolutionary national struggle and in the practice of scientific experiment. This is the process of testing and developing theory, the continuation of the whole process of cognition. The problem of whether theory corresponds to objective reality is not, and cannot be, completely solved in the movement of knowledge from the perceptual to the rational, mentioned above. The only way to solve this problem completely is to redirect rational knowledge to social practice, apply theory to practice and see whether it can achieve the objectives one has in mind. Many theories of natural science are held to be true not only because they were so considered when natural scientists originated them, but because they have been verified in subsequent scientific practice. Similarly, Marxism-Leninism is held to be true not only because it was so considered when it was scientifically formulated by Marx, Engels, Lenin and Stalin but because it has been verified in the subsequent practice of revolutionary class struggle and revolutionary national struggle. Dialectical materialism is universally true because it is impossible for anyone to escape from its domain in his practice. The history of human knowledge tells us that the truth of many theories is incomplete and that this incompleteness is remedied through the test of practice. Many theories are erroneous and it is through the test of practice that their errors are corrected. That is why practice is the criterion of truth and why "the standpoint of life, of practice, should be first and fundamental in the theory of knowledge." Stalin has well said, "Theory becomes purposeless if it is not connected with revolutionary practice, just as practice gropes in the dark if its path is not illuminated by revolutionary theory."

When we get to this point, is the movement of knowledge completed? Our answer is: it is and yet it is not. When men in society throw themselves into the practice of changing a certain objective process (whether natural or social) at a certain stage of its development, they can, as a result of the reflection of the objective process in their brains and the exercise of their subjective activity, advance their knowledge from the perceptual to the rational, and create ideas, theories, plans or programmes which correspond in general to the laws of that objective process. They then apply these ideas, theories, plans or programmes in practice in the same objective process. And if they can realize the aims they have in mind, that is, if in that same process of practice they can translate, or on the whole translate, those previously formulated ideas, theories, plans or programmes into fact, then the movement of knowledge may be considered completed with regard to this particular process. In the process of changing nature, take for example the fulfilment of an engineering plan, the verification of a scientific hypothesis, the manufacture of an implement or the reaping of a crop; or in the process of changing society, take for example the victory of a strike, victory in a war or the fulfilment of an educational plan. All these may be considered the realization of aims one has in mind. But generally speaking, whether in the practice of changing nature or of changing society, men's original ideas, theories, plans or programmes are seldom realized without any alteration. This is because people engaged in changing reality are usually subject to numerous limitations; they are limited not only by existing scientific and technological conditions but also by the development of the objective process itself and the degree to which this process has become manifest (the aspects and the essence of the objective process have not yet been fully revealed). In such a situation, ideas, theories, plans or programmes are usually altered partially and sometimes even wholly, because of the discovery of unforeseen circumstances in the course of practice. That is to say, it does happen that the original ideas, theories, plans or programmes fail to correspond with reality either in whole or in part and are wholly or partially incorrect. In many instances, failures have to be repeated many times before errors in knowledge can be corrected and correspondence with the laws of the objective process achieved, and consequently before the subjective can be transformed into the objective, or in other words, before the anticipated results can be achieved in practice. But when that point is reached, no matter how, the movement of human knowledge regarding a certain objective process at a certain stage of its development may be considered completed.

However, so far as the progression of the process is concerned, the movement of human knowledge is not completed. Every process, whether in the realm of nature or of society, progresses and develops by reason of its internal contradiction and struggle, and the movement of human knowledge should also progress and develop along with it. As far as social movements are concerned, true revolutionary leaders must not only be good at correcting their ideas, theories, plans or programmes when errors are discovered, as has been indicated above; but when a certain objective process has already progressed and changed from one stage of development to another, they must also be good at making themselves and all their fellow-revolutionaries progress and change in their subjective knowledge along with it, that is to say, they must ensure that the proposed new revolutionary tasks and new working programmes correspond to the new changes in the situation. In a revolutionary period the situation changes very rapidly; if the knowledge of revolutionaries does not change rapidly in accordance with the changed situation, they will be unable to lead the revolution to victory.

It often happens, however, that thinking lags behind reality; this is because man's cognition is limited by numerous social conditions. We are opposed to die-hards in the revolutionary ranks whose thinking fails to advance with changing objective circumstances and has manifested itself historically as Right opportunism. These people fail to see that the struggle of opposites has already pushed the objective process forward while their knowledge has stopped at the old stage. This is characteristic of the thinking of all die-hards. Their thinking is divorced from social practice, and they cannot march ahead to guide the chariot of society; they simply trail behind, grumbling that it goes too fast and trying to drag it back or turn it in the opposite direction.

We are also opposed to "Left" phrase-mongering. The thinking of "Leftists" outstrips a given stage of development of the objective process; some regard their fantasies as truth, while others strain to realize in the present an ideal which can only be realized in the future. They alienate themselves from the current practice of the majority of the people and from the realities of the day, and show themselves adventurist in their actions.

Idealism and mechanical materialism, opportunism and adventurism, are all characterized by the breach between the subjective and the objective, by the separation of knowledge from practice. The Marxist-Leninist theory of knowledge, characterized as it is by scientific social practice, cannot but resolutely oppose these wrong ideologies. Marxists recognize that in the absolute and general process of development of the universe, the development of each particular process is relative, and that hence, in the endless flow of absolute truth, man's knowledge of a particular process at any given stage of development is only relative truth. The sum total of innumerable relative truths constitutes absolute truth. The development of an objective process is full of contradictions and struggles, and so is the development of the movement of human knowledge. All the dialectical movements of the objective world can sooner or later be reflected in human knowledge. In social practice, the process of coming into being, developing and passing away is infinite, and so is the process of coming into being, developing and passing away in human knowledge. As man's practice which changes objective reality in accordance with given ideas, theories, plans or programmes, advances further and further, his knowledge of objective reality likewise becomes deeper and deeper. The movement of change in the world of objective reality is never-ending and so is man's cognition of truth through practice. Marxism-Leninism has in no way exhausted truth but ceaselessly opens up roads to the knowledge of truth in the course of practice. Our conclusion is the concrete, historical unity of the subjective and the objective, of theory and practice, of knowing and doing, and we are opposed to all erroneous ideologies, whether "Left" or Right, which depart from concrete history.

In the present epoch of the development of society, the responsibility of correctly knowing and changing the world has been placed by history upon the shoulders of the proletariat and its party. This process, the practice of changing the world, which is determined in accordance with scientific knowledge, has already reached a historic moment in the world and in China, a great moment unprecedented in human history, that is, the moment for completely banishing darkness from the world and from China and for changing the world into a world of light such as never previously existed. The struggle of the proletariat and the revolutionary people to change the world comprises the fulfilment of the following tasks: to change the objective world and, at the same time, their own subjective world—to change their cognitive ability and change the relations between the subjective and the objective world. Such a change has already come about in one part of the globe, in the Soviet Union. There the people are pushing forward this process of change. The people of China and the rest of the world either are going through, or will go through, such a process. And the objective world which is to be changed also includes all the opponents of change, who, in order to be changed, must go through a stage of compulsion before they can enter the stage of voluntary, conscious change. The epoch of world communism will be reached when all mankind voluntarily and consciously changes itself and the world.

Discover the truth through practice, and again through practice verify and develop the truth. Start from perceptual knowledge and actively develop it into rational knowledge; then start from rational knowledge and actively guide revolutionary practice to change both the subjective and the objective world. Practice, knowledge, again practice, and again knowledge. This form repeats itself in endless cycles, and with each cycle the content of practice and knowledge rises to a higher level. Such is the whole of the dialectical-materialist theory of knowledge, and such is the dialectical-materialist theory of the unity of knowing and doing.

MAO TSE-TUNG, ON CONTRADICTION*

AUGUST 1937

The law of contradiction in things, that is, the law of the unity of opposites, is the basic law of materialist dialectics. Lenin said, "Dialectics in the proper sense is the study of contradiction in the *very essence of objects.*"** Lenin often called this law the essence of dialectics; he also called it the kernel of dialectics.[†] In studying this law, therefore, we cannot but touch upon a variety of questions, upon a number of philosophical problems. If we can become clear on all these problems, we shall arrive at a fundamental understanding of materialist dialectics. The problems are: the two world outlooks, the universality of contradiction, the particularity of contradiction, the principal contradiction and the principal aspect of a contradiction, the identity and struggle of the aspects of a contradiction, and the place of antagonism in contradiction.

The criticism to which the idealism of the Deborin school has been subjected in Soviet philosophical circles in recent years has aroused great interest among us. Deborin's idealism has exerted a very bad influence in the Chinese Communist Party, and it cannot be said that the dogmatist thinking in our Party is unrelated to the approach of that school. Our present study of philosophy should therefore have the eradication of dogmatist thinking as its main objective.

I. THE TWO WORLD OUTLOOKS

Throughout the history of human knowledge, there have been two conceptions concerning the law of development of the universe, the metaphysical conception and the dialectical conception, which form two opposing world outlooks. Lenin said:

> The two basic (or two possible? or two historically observable?) conceptions of development (evolution) are: development as decrease and increase, as repetition, *and* development as a

Reprinted by permission from Committee for the Publication of the Selected Works of Mao Tse-tung, Central Committee of the Communist Party of China, *Selected Works of Mao Tse-Tung* (Foreign Language Press, Peking, 1965).

*This essay on philosophy was written by Comrade Mao Tse-tung after his essay "On Practice" and with the same object of overcoming the serious error of dogmatist thinking to be found in the Party at the time. Originally delivered as lectures at the Anti-Japanese Military and Political College in Yenan, it was revised by the author on its inclusion in his *Selected Works*.

**V.I. Lenin, "Conspectus of Hegel's *Lectures on the History of Philosophy*," *Collected Works*, Russ. ed., Moscow, 1958, Vol. XXXVIII, p. 249.

[†] In his essay "On the Question of Dialectics," Lenin said, "The splitting in two of a single whole and the cognition of its contradictory parts (see the quotation from Philo on Heraclitus at the beginning of Section 3 'On Cognition' in Lassalle's book on Heraclitus) is the *essence* (one of the 'essentials,' one of the principal, if not the principal, characteristics or features) of dialectics." (*Collected Works*, Russ. ed., Moscow, 1958, Vol. XXXVIII, p. 357.) In his "Conspectus of Hegel's *The Science of Logic*," he said, "In brief, dialectics can be defined as the doctrine of the unity of opposites. This grasps the kernel of dialectics, but it requires explanations and development." (*Ibid.*, p. 215.)

unity of opposites (the division of a unity into mutually exclusive opposites and their recipro-cal relation).*

Here Lenin was referring to these two different world outlooks.

In China another name for metaphysics is *hsuan-hsueh*. For a long period in his-tory whether in China or in Europe, this way of thinking, which is part and parcel of the idealist world outlook, occupied a dominant position in human thought. In Europe, the materialism of the bourgeoisie in its early days was also metaphysical. As the social economy of many European countries advanced to the stage of highly developed capi-talism, as the forces of production, the class struggle and the sciences developed to a level unprecedented in history, and as the industrial proletariat became the greatest mo-tive force in historical development, there arose the Marxist world outlook of material-ist dialectics. Then, in addition to open and barefaced reactionary idealism, vulgar evolutionism emerged among the bourgeoisie to oppose materialist dialectics.

The metaphysical or vulgar evolutionist world outlook sees things as isolated, static and one-sided. It regards all things in the universe, their forms and their species, as eternally isolated from one another and immutable. Such change as there is can only be an increase or decrease in quantity or a change of place. Moreover, the cause of such an increase or decrease or change of place is not inside things but outside them, that is, the motive force is external. Metaphysicians hold that all the different kinds of things in the universe and all their characteristics have been the same ever since they first came into being. All subsequent changes have simply been increases or decreases in quantity. They contend that a thing can only keep on repeating itself as the same kind of thing and cannot change into anything different. In their opinion, capitalist exploitation, cap-italist competition, the individualist ideology of capitalist society, and so on, can all be found in ancient slave society, or even in primitive society, and will exist for ever un-changed. They ascribe the causes of social development to factors external to society, such as geography and climate. They search in an over-simplified way outside a thing for the causes of its development, and they deny the theory of materialist dialectics which holds that development arises from the contradictions inside a thing. Consequently they can explain neither the qualitative diversity of things, nor the phe-nomenon of one quality changing into another. In Europe, this mode of thinking existed as mechanical materialism in the 17th and 18th centuries and as vulgar evolutionism at the end of the 19th and the beginning of the 20th centuries. In China, there was the metaphysical thinking exemplified in the saying "Heaven changeth not, likewise the Tao changeth not,"** and it was supported by the decadent feudal ruling classes for a long time. Mechanical materialism and vulgar evolutionism, which were imported from Europe in the last hundred years, are supported by the bourgeoisie.

As opposed to the metaphysical world outlook, the world outlook of materialist dialectics holds that in order to understand the development of a thing we should study it internally and in its relations with other things; in other words, the development of things should be seen as their internal and necessary self-movement, while each thing in its movement is interrelated with and interacts on the things around it. The funda-mental cause of the development of a thing is not external but internal; it lies in the con-tradictoriness within the thing. There is internal contradiction in every single thing,

---

*V.I. Lenin, "On the Question of Dialectics," *Collected Works*, Russ. ed., Moscow, 1958, Vol. XXXVIII, p. 358.

**A saying of Tung Chung-shu (179–104 B.C.E.), a well-known exponent of Confucianism in the Han Dynasty.

hence its motion and development. Contradictoriness within a thing is the fundamental cause of its development, while its interrelations and interactions with other things are secondary causes. Thus materialist dialectics effectively combats the theory of external causes, or of an external motive force, advanced by metaphysical mechanical materialism and vulgar evolutionism. It is evident that purely external causes can only give rise to mechanical motion, that is, to changes in scale or quantity, but cannot explain why things differ qualitatively in thousands of ways and why one thing changes into another. As a matter of fact, even mechanical motion under external force occurs through the internal contradictoriness of things. Simple growth in plants and animals, their quantitative development, is likewise chiefly the result of their internal contradictions. Similarly, social development is due chiefly not to external but to internal causes. Countries with almost the same geographical and climatic conditions display great diversity and unevenness in their development. Moreover, great social changes may take place in one and the same country although its geography and climate remain unchanged. Imperialist Russia changed into the socialist Soviet Union, and feudal Japan, which had locked its doors against the world, changed into imperialist Japan, although no change occurred in the geography and climate of either country. Long dominated by feudalism, China has undergone great changes in the last hundred years and is now changing in the direction of a new China, liberated and free, and yet no change has occurred in her geography and climate. Changes do take place in the geography and climate of the earth as a whole and in every part of it, but they are insignificant when compared with changes in society; geographical and climatic changes manifest themselves in terms of tens of thousands of years, while social changes manifest themselves in thousands, hundreds or tens of years, and even in a few years or months in times of revolution. According to materialist dialectics, changes in nature are due chiefly to the development of the internal contradictions in nature. Changes in society are due chiefly to the development of the internal contradictions in society, that is, the contradiction between the productive forces and the relations of production, the contradiction between classes and the contradiction between the old and the new; it is the development of these contradictions that pushes society forward and gives the impetus for the supersession of the old society by the new. Does materialist dialectics exclude external causes? Not at all. It holds that external causes are the condition of change and internal causes are the basis of change, and that external causes become operative through internal causes. In a suitable temperature an egg changes into a chicken, but no temperature can change a stone into a chicken, because each has a different basis. There is constant interaction between the peoples of different countries. In the era of capitalism, and especially in the era of imperialism and proletarian revolution, the interaction and mutual impact of different countries in the political, economic and cultural spheres are extremely great. The October Socialist Revolution ushered in a new epoch in world history as well as in Russian history. It exerted influence on internal changes in the other countries in the world and, similarly and in a particularly profound way, on internal changes in China. These changes, however, were effected through the inner laws of development of these countries, China included. In battle, one army is victorious and the other is defeated; both the victory and the defeat are determined by internal causes. The one is victorious either because it is strong or because of its competent generalship, the other is vanquished either because it is weak or because of its incompetent generalship; it is through internal causes that external causes become operative. In China in 1927, the defeat of the proletariat by the big bourgeoisie came about through the opportunism then to be found within the Chinese proletariat itself (inside the Chinese Communist Party). When we liquidated this opportunism, the Chinese revolution resumed its advance. Later, the

Chinese revolution again suffered severe setbacks at the hands of the enemy, because adventurism had risen within our Party. When we liquidated this adventurism, our cause advanced once again. Thus it can be seen that to lead the revolution to victory, a political party must depend on the correctness of its own political line and the solidity of its own organization.

The dialectical world outlook emerged in ancient times both in China and in Europe. Ancient dialectics, however, had a somewhat spontaneous and naive character; in the social and historical conditions then prevailing, it was not yet able to form a theoretical system, hence it could not fully explain the world and was supplanted by metaphysics. The famous German philosopher Hegel, who lived in the late 18th and early 19th centuries, made most important contributions to dialectics, but his dialectics was idealist. It was not until Marx and Engels, the great protagonists of the proletarian movement, had synthesized the positive achievements in the history of human knowledge and, in particular, critically absorbed the rational elements of Hegelian dialectics and created the great theory of dialectical and historical materialism that an unprecedented revolution occurred in the history of human knowledge. This theory was further developed by Lenin and Stalin. As soon as it spread to China, it wrought tremendous changes in the world of Chinese thought.

This dialectical world outlook teaches us primarily how to observe and analyse the movement of opposites in different things and, on the basis of such analysis, to indicate the methods for resolving contradictions. It is therefore most important for us to understand the law of contradiction in things in a concrete way.

II. THE UNIVERSALITY OF CONTRADICTION

For convenience of exposition, I shall deal first with the universality of contradiction and then proceed to the particularity of contradiction. The reason is that the universality of contradiction can be explained more briefly, for it has been widely recognized ever since the materialist-dialectical world outlook was discovered and materialist dialectics applied with outstanding success to analysing many aspects of human history and natural history and to changing many aspects of society and nature (as in the Soviet Union) by the great creators and continuers of Marxism—Marx, Engels, Lenin and Stalin; whereas the particularity of contradiction is still not clearly understood by many comrades, and especially by the dogmatists. They do not understand that it is precisely in the particularity of contradiction that the universality of contradiction resides. Nor do they understand how important is the study of the particularity of contradiction in the concrete things confronting us for guiding the course of revolutionary practice. Therefore, it is necessary to stress the study of the particularity of contradiction and to explain it at adequate length. For this reason, in our analysis of the law of contradiction in things, we shall first analyse the universality of contradiction, then place special stress on analysing the particularity of contradiction, and finally return to the universality of contradiction.

The universality or absoluteness of contradiction has a twofold meaning. One is that contradiction exists in the process of development of all things, and the other is that in the process of development of each thing a movement of opposites exists from beginning to end.

Engels said, "Motion itself is a contradiction."* Lenin defined the law of the unity of opposites as "the recognition (discovery) of the contradictory, *mutually exclusive, opposite* tendencies in *all* phenomena and processes of nature (*including* mind and society)."** Are these ideas correct? Yes, they are. The interdependence of the contradictory aspects present in all things and the struggle between these aspects determine the life of all things and push their development forward. There is nothing that does not contain contradiction; without contradiction nothing would exist.

Contradiction is the basis of the simple forms of motion (for instance, mechanical motion) and still more so of the complex forms of motion.

Engels explained the universality of contradiction as follows:

> If simple mechanical change of place contains a contradiction, this is even more true of the higher forms of motion of matter, and especially of organic life and its development. . . . life consists precisely and primarily in this—that a being is at each moment itself and yet something else. Life is therefore also a contradiction which is present in things and processes themselves, and which constantly originates and resolves itself; and as soon as the contradiction ceases, life, too, comes to an end, and death steps in. We likewise saw that also in the sphere of thought we could not escape contradictions, and that for example the contradiction between man's inherently unlimited capacity for knowledge and its actual presence only in men who are externally limited and possess limited cognition finds its solution in what is—at least practically, for us—an endless succession of generations, in infinite progress.
>
> . . . one of the basic principles of higher mathematics is the contradiction that in certain circumstances straight lines and curves may be the same. . . .
>
> But even lower mathematics teems with contradictions.[†]

Lenin illustrated the universality of contradiction as follows:

In mathematics: + and −. Differential and integral.
In mechanics: action and reaction.
In physics: positive and negative electricity.
In chemistry: the combination and dissociation of atoms.
In social science: the class struggle.[††]

In war, offence and defence, advance and retreat, victory and defeat are all mutually contradictory phenomena. One cannot exist without the other. The two aspects are at once in conflict and in interdependence, and this constitutes the totality of a war, pushes its development forward and solves its problems.

Every difference in men's concepts should be regarded as reflecting an objective contradiction. Objective contradictions are reflected in subjective thinking, and this process constitutes the contradictory movement of concepts, pushes forward the development of thought, and ceaselessly solves problems in man's thinking.

Opposition and struggle between ideas of different kinds constantly occur within the Party; this is a reflection within the Party of contradictions between classes and between the new and the old in society. If there were no contradictions in the Party and no ideological struggles to resolve them, the Party's life would come to an end.

*Frederick Engels, "Dialectics. Quantity and Quality," *Anti-Dühring,* Eng. ed., FLPH, Moscow, 1959, p. 166.

**V.I. Lenin, "On the Question of Dialectics," *Collected Works,* Russ. ed., Moscow, 1958, Vol. XXXVIII, pp. 357–58.

[†]Frederick Engels, *op. cit.,* pp. 166–67.

[††]V.I. Lenin, "On the Question of Dialectics," *Collected Works,* Russ. ed., Moscow, 1958, Vol. XXXVIII, p. 357.

Thus it is already clear that contradiction exists universally and in all processes, whether in the simple or in the complex forms of motion, whether in objective phenomena or ideological phenomena. But does contradiction also exist at the initial stage of each process? Is there a movement of opposites from beginning to end in the process of development of every single thing?

As can be seen from the articles written by Soviet philosophers criticizing it, the Deborin school maintains that contradiction appears not at the inception of a process but only when it has developed to a certain stage. If this were the case, then the cause of the development of the process before that stage would be external and not internal. Deborin thus reverts to the metaphysical theories of external causality and of mechanism. Applying this view in the analysis of concrete problems, the Deborin school sees only differences but not contradictions between the kulaks and the peasants in general under existing conditions in the Soviet Union, thus entirely agreeing with Bukharin. In analysing the French Revolution, it holds that before the Revolution there were likewise only differences but not contradictions within the Third Estate, which was composed of the workers, the peasants and the bourgeoisie. These views of the Deborin school are anti-Marxist. This school does not understand that each and every difference already contains contradiction and that difference itself is contradiction. Labour and capital have been in contradiction ever since the two classes came into being, only at first the contradiction had not yet become intense. Even under the social conditions existing in the Soviet Union, there is a difference between workers and peasants and this very difference is a contradiction, although, unlike the contradiction between labour and capital, it will not become intensified into antagonism or assume the form of class struggle; the workers and the peasants have established a firm alliance in the course of socialist construction and are gradually resolving this contradiction in the course of the advance from socialism to communism. The question is one of different kinds of contradiction, not of the presence or absence of contradiction. Contradiction is universal and absolute, it is present in the process of development of all things and permeates every process from beginning to end.

What is meant by the emergence of a new process? The old unity with its constituent opposites yields to a new unity with its constituent opposites, whereupon a new process emerges to replace the old. The old process ends and the new one begins. The new process contains new contradictions and begins its own history of the development of contradictions.

As Lenin pointed out, Marx in his *Capital* gave a model analysis of this movement of opposites which runs through the process of development of things from beginning to end. This is the method that must be employed in studying the development of all things. Lenin, too, employed this method correctly and adhered to it in all his writings.

> In his *Capital*, Marx first analyses the simplest, most ordinary and fundamental, most common and everyday *relation* of bourgeois (commodity) society, a relation encountered billions of times, viz. the exchange of commodities. In this very simple phenomenon (in this "cell" of bourgeois society) analysis reveals *all* the contradictions (or the germs of *all* the contradictions) of modern society. The subsequent exposition shows us the development (*both* growth *and* movement) of these contradictions and of this society in the Σ [summation] of its individual parts, from its beginning to its end.

Lenin added, "Such must also be the method of exposition (or study) of dialectics in general."*

*Ibid., pp. 358–59.

Chinese Communists must learn this method; only then will they be able correctly to analyse the history and the present state of the Chinese revolution and infer its future.

III. THE PARTICULARITY OF CONTRADICTION

Contradiction is present in the process of development of all things; it permeates the process of development of each thing from beginning to end. This is the universality and absoluteness of contradiction which we have discussed above. Now let us discuss the particularity and relativity of contradiction.

This problem should be studied on several levels.

First, the contradiction in each form of motion of matter has its particularity. Man's knowledge of matter is knowledge of its forms of motion, because there is nothing in this world except matter in motion and this motion must assume certain forms. In considering each form of motion of matter, we must observe the points which it has in common with other forms of motion. But what is especially important and necessary, constituting as it does the foundation of our knowledge of a thing, is to observe what is particular to this form of motion of matter, namely, to observe the qualitative difference between this form of motion and other forms. Only when we have done so can we distinguish between things. Every form of motion contains within itself its own particular contradiction. This particular contradiction constitutes the particular essence which distinguishes one thing from another. It is the internal cause or, as it may be called, the basis for the immense variety of things in the world. There are many forms of motion in nature, mechanical motion, sound, light, heat, electricity, dissociation, combination, and so on. All these forms are interdependent, but in its essence each is different from the others. The particular essence of each form of motion is determined by its own particular contradiction. This holds true not only for nature but also for social and ideological phenomena. Every form of society, every form of ideology, has its own particular contradiction and particular essence.

The sciences are differentiated precisely on the basis of the particular contradictions inherent in their respective objects of study. Thus the contradiction peculiar to a certain field of phenomena constitutes the object of study for a specific branch of science. For example, positive and negative numbers in mathematics; action and reaction in mechanics; positive and negative electricity in physics; dissociation and combination in chemistry; forces of production and relations of production, classes and class struggle, in social science; offence and defence in military science; idealism and materialism, the metaphysical outlook and the dialectical outlook, in philosophy; and so on—all these are the objects of study of different branches of science precisely because each branch has its own particular contradiction and particular essence. Of course, unless we understand the universality of contradiction, we have no way of discovering the universal cause or universal basis for the movement or development of things; however, unless we study the particularity of contradiction, we have no way of determining the particular essence of a thing which differentiates it from other things, no way of discovering the particular cause or particular basis for the movement or development of a thing, and no way of distinguishing one thing from another or of demarcating the fields of science.

As regards the sequence in the movement of man's knowledge, there is always a gradual growth from the knowledge of individual and particular things to the knowledge of things in general. Only after man knows the particular essence of many different things can he proceed to generalization and know the common essence of things. When man attains the knowledge of this common essence, he uses it as a guide and proceeds to study various concrete things which have not yet been studied, or studied thoroughly, and to discover the particular essence of each; only thus is he able to supplement, enrich and develop his knowledge of their common essence and prevent such knowledge from withering or petrifying. These are the two processes of cognition: one, from the particular to the general, and the other, from the general to the particular. Thus cognition always moves in cycles and (so long as scientific method is strictly adhered to) each cycle advances human knowledge a step higher and so makes it more and more profound. Where our dogmatists err on this question is that, on the one hand, they do not understand that we have to study the particularity of contradiction and know the particular essence of individual things before we can adequately know the universality of contradiction and the common essence of things, and that, on the other hand, they do not understand that after knowing the common essence of things, we must go further and study the concrete things that have not yet been thoroughly studied or have only just emerged. Our dogmatists are lazy-bones. They refuse to undertake any painstaking study of concrete things, they regard general truths as emerging out of the void, they turn them into purely abstract unfathomable formulas, and thereby completely deny and reverse the normal sequence by which man comes to know truth. Nor do they understand the interconnection of the two processes in cognition—from the particular to the general and then from the general to the particular. They understand nothing of the Marxist theory of knowledge.

It is necessary not only to study the particular contradiction and the essence determined thereby of every great system of the forms of motion of matter, but also to study the particular contradiction and the essence of each process in the long course of development of each form of motion of matter. In every form of motion, each process of development which is real (and not imaginary) is qualitatively different. Our study must emphasize and start from this point.

Qualitatively different contradictions can only be resolved by qualitatively different methods. For instance, the contradiction between the proletariat and the bourgeoisie is resolved by the method of socialist revolution; the contradiction between the great masses of the people and the feudal system is resolved by the method of democratic revolution; the contradiction between the colonies and imperialism is resolved by the method of national revolutionary war; the contradiction between the working class and the peasant class in socialist society is resolved by the method of collectivization and mechanization in agriculture; contradiction within the Communist Party is resolved by the method of criticism and self-criticism; the contradiction between society and nature is resolved by the method of developing the productive forces. Processes change, old processes and old contradictions disappear, new processes and new contradictions emerge, and the methods of resolving contradictions differ accordingly. In Russia, there was a fundamental difference between the contradiction resolved by the February Revolution and the contradiction resolved by the October Revolution, as well as between the methods used to resolve them. The principle of using different methods to resolve different contradictions is one which Marxist-Leninists must strictly observe. The dogmatists do not observe this principle; they do not understand that conditions differ in different kinds of revolution and so do not understand that different methods should be used to resolve different contradictions; on the contrary, they invariably adopt what they imagine to be an unalterable formula and arbitrarily apply it everywhere, which only causes setbacks to the revolution or makes a sorry mess of what was originally well done.

Portrait of Mao Tse-tung (Zedong) in the Underground City, Beijing. During a conflict with the Soviet Union, Mao ordered the construction of a complex of interconnected bomb shelters that is said to cover an area of 850,000 square meters. This portrait, along with many slogans on the walls of the tunnels, reflects the adulation of Mao during the Cultural Revolution (1966–1976) (*Forrest E. Baird*)

In order to reveal the particularity of the contradictions in any process in the development of a thing, in their totality or interconnections, that is, in order to reveal the essence of the process, it is necessary to reveal the particularity of the two aspects of each of the contradictions in that process; otherwise it will be impossible to discover the essence of the process. This likewise requires the utmost attention in our study.

There are many contradictions in the course of development of any major thing. For instance, in the course of China's bourgeois-democratic revolution, where the conditions are exceedingly complex, there exist the contradiction between all the oppressed classes in Chinese society and imperialism, the contradiction between the great masses of the people and feudalism, the contradiction between the proletariat and the bourgeoisie, the contradiction between the peasantry and the urban petty bourgeoisie on the one hand and the bourgeoisie on the other, the contradiction between the various reactionary ruling groups, and so on. These contradictions cannot be treated in the same way since each has its own particularity; moreover, the two aspects of each contradiction cannot be treated in the same way since each aspect has its own characteristics. We who are engaged in the Chinese revolution should not only understand the particularity of these contradictions in their totality, that is, in their interconnections, but should also study the two aspects of each contradiction as the only means of understanding the totality. When we speak of understanding each aspect of a contradiction, we mean understanding what specific position each aspect occupies, what concrete forms it assumes in its interdependence and in its contradiction with its opposite, and what concrete methods are employed in the struggle with its opposite, when the two are both interdependent and in contradiction, and also after the interdependence breaks down. It is of great importance to study these problems. Lenin meant just this when he said that the most essential thing in Marxism, the living soul of Marxism, is the concrete analysis of concrete conditions. Our dogmatists have violated Lenin's teachings; they never use their brains to analyse anything concretely, and in their writings and speeches they always use stereotypes devoid of content, thereby creating a very bad style of work in our Party.

In studying a problem, we must shun subjectivity, one-sidedness and superficiality. To be subjective means not to look at problems objectively, that is, not to use the materialist viewpoint in looking at problems. I have discussed this in my essay "On Practice." To be one-sided means not to look at problems all-sidedly, for example, to understand only China but not Japan, only the Communist Party but not the Kuomintang, only the proletariat but not the bourgeoisie, only the peasants but not the landlords, only the favourable conditions but not the difficult ones, only the past but not the future, only individual parts but not the whole, only the defects but not the achievements, only the plaintiff's case but not the defendant's, only underground revolutionary work but not open revolutionary work, and so on. In a word, it means not to understand the characteristics of both aspects of a contradiction. This is what we mean by looking at a problem one-sidedly. Or it may be called seeing the part but not the whole, seeing the trees but not the forest. That way it is impossible to find the method for resolving a contradiction, it is impossible to accomplish the tasks of the revolution, to carry out assignments well or to develop inner-Party ideological struggle correctly. When Sun Wu Tzu said in discussing military science, "Know the enemy and know yourself, and you can fight a hundred battles with no danger of defeat,"* he was referring to the two sides in a battle. Wei Cheng* of the Tang Dynasty also understood the error of one-sidedness when he said, "Listen to both sides and you will be enlightened, heed only one side and you will be benighted." But our comrades often look at problems one-sidedly, and so they often run into snags. In the novel *Shui Hu Chuan*, Sung Chiang thrice attacked Chu Village.** Twice he was defeated because he was ignorant of the local conditions and used the wrong method. Later he changed his method; first he investigated the situation, and he familiarized himself with the maze of roads, then he broke up the alliance between the Li, Hu and Chu Villages and sent his men in disguise into the enemy camp to lie in wait, using a stratagem similar to that of the Trojan Horse in the foreign story. And on the third occasion he won. There are many examples of materialist dialectics in *Shui Hu Chuan,* of which the episode of the three attacks on Chu Village is one of the best. Lenin said:

> ... in order really to know an object we must embrace, study, all its sides, all connections and "mediations." We shall never achieve this completely, but the demand for all-sidedness is a safeguard against mistakes and rigidity.[†]

We should remember his words. To be superficial means to consider neither the characteristics of a contradiction in its totality nor the characteristics of each of its aspects; it means to deny the necessity for probing deeply into a thing and minutely studying the characteristics of its contradiction, but instead merely to look from afar and,

---

*Sun Wu Tzu, or Sun Wu, also known as Sun Tzu, was a famous Chinese soldier and military scientist of the 5th century B.C.E., who wrote *Sun Tzu*, a treatise on war containing thirteen chapters. This quotation is from Chapter 3, "The Strategy of Attack".

*Wei Cheng (580–643 C.E.) was a statesman and historian of the Tang Dynasty.

**Shui Hu Chuan (Heroes of the Marshes)*, a famous 14th century Chinese novel, describes a peasant war towards the end of the Northern Sung Dynasty. Chu Village was in the vicinity of Liangshanpo, where Sung Chiang, leader of the peasant uprising and hero of the novel, established his base. Chu Chao-feng, the head of this village, was a despotic landlord.

[†]V.I. Lenin, "Once Again on the Trade Unions, the Present Situation and the Mistakes of Trotsky and Bukharin," *Selected Works,* Eng. ed., International Publishers, New York, 1943, Vol. IX, p. 66.

after glimpsing the rough outline, immediately to try to resolve the contradiction (to answer a question, settle a dispute, handle work, or direct a military operation). This way of doing things is bound to lead to trouble. The reason the dogmatist and empiricist comrades in China have made mistakes lies precisely in their subjectivist, one sided and superficial way of looking at things. To be one-sided and superficial is at the same time to be subjective. For all objective things are actually interconnected and are governed by inner laws, but instead of undertaking the task of reflecting things as they really are some people only look at things one-sidedly or superficially and know neither their interconnections nor their inner laws, and so their method is subjectivist.

Not only does the whole process of the movement of opposites in the development of a thing, both in their interconnections and in each of the aspects, have particular features to which we must give attention, but each stage in the process has its particular features to which we must give attention too.

The fundamental contradiction in the process of development of a thing and the essence of the process determined by this fundamental contradiction will not disappear until the process is completed; but in a lengthy process the conditions usually differ at each stage. The reason is that, although the nature of the fundamental contradiction in the process of development of a thing and the essence of the process remain unchanged, the fundamental contradiction becomes more and more intensified as it passes from one stage to another in the lengthy process. In addition, among the numerous major and minor contradictions which are determined or influenced by the fundamental contradiction, some become intensified, some are temporarily or partially resolved or mitigated, and some new ones emerge; hence the process is marked by stages. If people do not pay attention to the stages in the process of development of a thing, they cannot deal with its contradictions properly.

For instance, when the capitalism of the era of free competition developed into imperialism, there was no change in the class nature of the two classes in fundamental contradiction, namely, the proletariat and the bourgeoisie, or in the capitalist essence of society; however, the contradiction between these two classes became intensified, the contradiction between monopoly and non-monopoly capital emerged, the contradiction between the colonial powers and the colonies became intensified, the contradiction among the capitalist countries resulting from their uneven development manifested itself with particular sharpness, and thus there arose the special stage of capitalism, the stage of imperialism. Leninism is the Marxism of the era of imperialism and proletarian revolution precisely because Lenin and Stalin have correctly explained these contradictions and correctly formulated the theory and tactics of the proletarian revolution for their resolution.

Take the process of China's bourgeois-democratic revolution, which began with the Revolution of 1911; it, too, has several distinct stages. In particular, the revolution in its period of bourgeois leadership and the revolution in its period of proletarian leadership represent two vastly different historical stages. In other words, proletarian leadership has fundamentally changed the whole face of the revolution, has brought about a new alignment of classes, given rise to a tremendous upsurge in the peasant revolution, imparted thoroughness to the revolution against imperialism and feudalism, created the possibility of the transition from the democratic revolution to the socialist revolution, and so on. None of these was possible in the period when the revolution was under bourgeois leadership. Although no change has taken place in the nature of the fundamental contradiction in the process as a whole, *i.e.,* in the anti-imperialist, anti-feudal, democratic-revolutionary nature of the process (the opposite of which is its semi-colonial and semi-feudal nature), nonetheless this process has passed through several stages of development in the course of more than twenty years; during this time many great events have taken place—the failure of the Revolution of 1911 and the establishment of the regime of the Northern warlords, the formation of the first national united front and the revolution of 1924–27, the break-up of the united front and the desertion of the bourgeoisie to the side of the counter-revolution, the wars among the new warlords, the Agrarian Revolutionary War, the establishment of the second national united front and the War of Resistance Against Japan. These stages are marked by particular features such as the intensification of certain contradictions (*e.g.,* the Agrarian Revolutionary War and the Japanese invasion of the four northeastern provinces), the partial or temporary resolution of other contradictions (*e.g.,* the destruction of the Northern warlords and our confiscation of the land of the landlords), and the emergence of yet other contradictions (*e.g.,* the conflicts among the new warlords, and the landlords' recapture of the land after the loss of our revolutionary base areas in the south).

In studying the particularities of the contradictions at each stage in the process of development of a thing, we must not only observe them in their interconnections or their totality, we must also examine the two aspects of each contradiction.

For instance, consider the Kuomintang and the Communist Party. Take one aspect, the Kuomintang. In the period of the first united front, the Kuomintang carried out Sun Yat-sen's Three Great Policies of alliance with Russia, co-operation with the Communist Party, and assistance to the peasants and workers; hence it was revolutionary and vigorous, it was an alliance of various classes for the democratic revolution. After 1927, however, the Kuomintang changed into its opposite and became a reactionary bloc of the landlords and big bourgeoisie. After the Sian Incident in December 1936, it began another change in the direction of ending the civil war and co-operating with the Communist Party for joint opposition to Japanese imperialism. Such have been the particular features of the Kuomintang in the three stages. Of course, these features have arisen from a variety of causes. Now take the other aspect, the Chinese Communist Party. In the period of the first united front, the Chinese Communist Party was in its infancy; it courageously led the revolution of 1924–27 but revealed its immaturity in its understanding of the character, the tasks and the methods of the revolution, and consequently it became possible for Chen Tu-hsiuism, which appeared during the latter part of this revolution, to assert itself and bring about the defeat of the revolution. After 1927, the Communist Party courageously led the Agrarian Revolutionary War and created the revolutionary army and revolutionary base areas; however, it committed adventurist errors which brought about very great losses both to the army and to the base areas. Since 1935 the Party has corrected these errors and has been leading the new united front for resistance to Japan; this great struggle is now developing. At the present stage, the Communist Party is a Party that has gone through the test of two revolutions and acquired a wealth of experience. Such have been the particular features of the Chinese Communist Party in the three stages. These features, too, have arisen from a variety of causes. Without studying both these sets of features we cannot understand the particular relations between the two parties during the various stages of their development, namely, the establishment of a united front, the break-up of the united front, and the establishment of another united front. What is even more fundamental for the study of the particular features of the two parties is the examination of the class basis of the two parties and the resultant contradictions which have arisen between each party and other forces at different periods. For instance, in the period of its first cooperation with the Communist Party, the Kuomintang stood in contradiction to foreign imperialism and was therefore anti-imperialist; on the other hand, it stood in contradiction to the great masses of the people within the country—although in words it promised many benefits to the working people, in fact it gave them little or nothing. In the period when it carried on the anti-Communist war, the Kuomintang collaborated with imperialism and feudalism against the great masses of the people and wiped out all the gains they had won in the revolution, and thereby intensified its contradictions with them. In the present period of the anti-Japanese war, the Kuomintang stands in contradiction to Japanese imperialism and wants co-operation with the Communist Party, without how-ever relaxing its struggle against the Communist Party and the people or its oppression of them. As for the Communist Party, it has always, in every period, stood with the great masses of the people against imperialism and feudalism, but in the present period of the anti-Japanese war, it has adopted a moderate policy towards the Kuomintang and the domestic feudal forces because the Kuomintang has expressed itself in favour of resist-ing Japan. The above circumstances have resulted now in alliance between the two par-ties and now in struggle between them, and even during the periods of alliance there has been a complicated state of simultaneous alliance and struggle. If we do not study the particular features of both aspects of the contradiction, we shall fail to understand not only the relations of each party with the other forces, but also the relations between the two parties.

It can thus be seen that in studying the particularity of any kind of contradiction—the contradiction in each form of motion of matter, the contradiction in each of its processes of development, the two aspects of the contradiction in each process, the con-tradiction at each stage of a process, and the two aspects of the contradiction at each stage—in studying the particularity of all these contradictions, we must not be subjec-tive and arbitrary but must analyse it concretely. Without concrete analysis there can be no knowledge of the particularity of any contradiction. We must always remember Lenin's words, the concrete analysis of concrete conditions.

Marx and Engels were the first to provide us with excellent models of such con-crete analysis.

When Marx and Engels applied the law of contradiction in things to the study of the socio-historical process, they discovered the contradiction between the productive forces and the relations of production, they discovered the contradiction between the exploiting and exploited classes and also the resultant contradiction between the eco-nomic base and its superstructure (politics, ideology, etc.), and they discovered how these contradictions inevitably lead to different kinds of social revolution in different kinds of class society.

When Marx applied this law to the study of the economic structure of capitalist society, he discovered that the basic contradiction of this society is the contradiction be-tween the social character of production and the private character of ownership. This contradiction manifests itself in the contradiction between the organized character of production in individual enterprises and the anarchic character of production in society as a whole. In terms of class relations, it manifests itself in the contradiction between the bourgeoisie and the proletariat.

Because the range of things is vast and there is no limit to their development, what is universal in one context becomes particular in another. Conversely, what is particular in one context becomes universal in another. The contradiction in the cap-italist system between the social character of production and the private ownership of the means of production is common to all countries where capitalism exists and de-velops; as far as capitalism is concerned, this constitutes the universality of contra-diction. But this contradiction of capitalism belongs only to a certain historical stage in the general development of class society; as far as the contradiction between the productive forces and the relations of production in class society as a whole is concerned, it constitutes the particularity of contradiction. However, in the course of dissecting the particularity of all these contradictions in capitalist society, Marx gave a still more profound, more adequate and more complete elucidation of the universality of the contradiction between the productive forces and the relations of production in class society in general.

Since the particular is united with the universal and since the universality as well as the particularity of contradiction is inherent in everything, universality residing in particularity, we should, when studying an object, try to discover both the particular and the universal and their interconnection, to discover both particularity and universality and also their interconnection within the object itself, and to discover the interconnections of this object with the many objects outside it. When Stalin explained the historical roots of Leninism in his famous work, *The Foundations of Leninism,* he analysed the international situation in which Leninism arose, analysed those contradictions of capitalism which reached their culmination under imperialism, and showed how these contradictions made proletarian revolution a matter for immediate action and created favourable conditions for a direct onslaught on capitalism. What is more, he analysed the reasons why Russia became the cradle of Leninism, why tsarist Russia became the focus of all the contradictions of imperialism, and why it was possible for the Russian proletariat to become the vanguard of the international revolutionary proletariat. Thus, Stalin analysed the universality of contradiction in imperialism, showing why Leninism is the Marxism of the era of imperialism and proletarian revolution, and at the same time analysed the particularity of tsarist Russian imperialism within this general contradiction, showing why Russia became the birthplace of the theory and tactics of proletarian revolution and how the universality of contradiction is contained in this particularity. Stalin's analysis provides us with a model for understanding the particularity and the universality of contradiction and their interconnection.

On the question of using dialectics in the study of objective phenomena, Marx and Engels, and likewise Lenin and Stalin, always enjoin people not to be in any way subjective and arbitrary but, from the concrete conditions in the actual objective movement of these phenomena, to discover their concrete contradictions, the concrete position of each aspect of every contradiction and the concrete interrelations of the contradictions. Our dogmatists do not have this attitude in study and therefore can never get anything right. We must take warning from their failure and learn to acquire this attitude, which is the only correct one in study.

The relationship between the universality and the particularity of contradiction is the relationship between the general character and the individual character of contradiction. By the former we mean that contradiction exists in and runs through all processes from beginning to end; motion, things, processes, thinking—all are contradictions. To deny contradiction is to deny everything. This is a universal truth for all times and all countries, which admits of no exception. Hence the general character, the absoluteness of contradiction. But this general character is contained in every individual character; without individual character there can be no general character. If all individual character were removed, what general character would remain? It is because each contradiction is particular that individual character arises. All individual character exists conditionally and temporarily, and hence is relative.

This truth concerning general and individual character, concerning absoluteness and relativity, is the quintessence of the problem of contradiction in things; failure to understand it is tantamount to abandoning dialectics.

IV. THE PRINCIPAL CONTRADICTION
AND THE PRINCIPAL ASPECT OF A CONTRADICTION

There are still two points in the problem of the particularity of contradiction which must be singled out for analysis, namely, the principal contradiction and the principal aspect of a contradiction.

There are many contradictions in the process of development of a complex thing, and one of them is necessarily the principal contradiction whose existence and development determine or influence the existence and development of the other contradictions.

For instance, in capitalist society the two forces in contradiction, the proletariat and the bourgeoisie, form the principal contradiction. The other contradictions, such as those between the remnant feudal class and the bourgeoisie, between the peasant petty bourgeoisie and the bourgeoisie, between the proletariat and the peasant petty bourgeoisie, between the non-monopoly capitalists and the monopoly capitalists, between bourgeois democracy and bourgeois fascism, among the capitalist countries and between imperialism and the colonies, are all determined or influenced by this principal contradiction.

In a semi-colonial country such as China, the relationship between the principal contradiction and the non-principal contradictions presents a complicated picture.

When imperialism launches a war of aggression against such a country, all its various classes, except for some traitors, can temporarily unite in a national war against imperialism. At such a time, the contradiction between imperialism and the country concerned becomes the principal contradiction, while all the contradictions among the various classes within the country (including what was the principal contradiction, between the feudal system and the great masses of the people) are temporarily relegated to a secondary and subordinate position. So it was in China in the Opium War of 1840, the Sino-Japanese War of 1894 and the Yi Ho Tuan War of 1900, and so it is now in the present Sino-Japanese War.

But in another situation, the contradictions change position. When imperialism carries on its oppression not by war, but by milder means—political, economic and cultural—the ruling classes in semi-colonial countries capitulate to imperialism, and the two form an alliance for the joint oppression of the masses of the people. At such a time, the masses often resort to civil war against the alliance of imperialism and the feudal classes, while imperialism often employs indirect methods rather than direct action in helping the reactionaries in the semi-colonial countries to oppress the people, and thus the internal contradictions become particularly sharp. This is what happened in China in the Revolutionary War of 1911, the Revolutionary War of 1924–27, and the ten years of Agrarian Revolutionary War after 1927. Wars among the various reactionary ruling groups in the semi-colonial countries, *e.g.*, the wars among the warlords in China, fall into the same category.

When a revolutionary civil war develops to the point of threatening the very existence of imperialism and its running dogs, the domestic reactionaries, imperialism often adopts other methods in order to maintain its rule; it either tries to split the revolutionary front from within or sends armed forces to help the domestic reactionaries directly. At such a time, foreign imperialism and domestic reaction stand quite openly at one pole while the masses of the people stand at the other pole, thus forming the principal contradiction which determines or influences the development of the other contradictions. The assistance given by various capitalist countries to the Russian reactionaries after the October Revolution is an example of armed intervention. Chiang Kai-shek's betrayal in 1927 is an example of splitting the revolutionary front.

But whatever happens, there is no doubt at all that at every stage in the development of a process, there is only one principal contradiction which plays the leading role.

Hence, if in any process there are a number of contradictions, one of them must be the principal contradiction playing the leading and decisive role, while the rest occupy a secondary and subordinate position. Therefore, in studying any complex process in which there are two or more contradictions, we must devote every effort to finding its principal contradiction. Once this principal contradiction is grasped, all problems can be readily solved. This is the method Marx taught us in his study of capitalist society. Likewise Lenin and Stalin taught us this method when they studied imperialism and the general crisis of capitalism and when they studied the Soviet economy. There are thousands of scholars and men of action who do not understand it, and the result is that, lost in a fog, they are unable to get to the heart of a problem and naturally cannot find a way to resolve its contradictions.

As we have said, one must not treat all the contradictions in a process as being equal but must distinguish between the principal and the secondary contradictions, and pay special attention to grasping the principal one. But, in any given contradiction, whether principal or secondary, should the two contradictory aspects be treated as equal? Again, no. In any contradiction the development of the contradictory aspects is uneven. Sometimes they seem to be in equilibrium, which is however only temporary and relative, while unevenness is basic. Of the two contradictory aspects, one must be principal and the other secondary. The principal aspect is the one playing the leading role in the contradiction. The nature of a thing is determined mainly by the principal aspect of a contradiction, the aspect which has gained the dominant position.

But this situation is not static; the principal and the non-principal aspects of a contradiction transform themselves into each other and the nature of the thing changes accordingly. In a given process or at a given stage in the development of a contradiction, A is the principal aspect and B is the non-principal aspect; at another stage or in another process the roles are reversed—a change determined by the extent of the increase or decrease in the force of each aspect in its struggle against the other in the course of the development of a thing.

We often speak of "the new superseding the old." The supersession of the old by the new is a general, eternal and inviolable law of the universe. The transformation of one thing into another, through leaps of different forms in accordance with its essence and external conditions—this is the process of the new superseding the old. In each thing there is contradiction between its new and its old aspects, and this gives rise to a series of struggles with many twists and turns. As a result of these struggles, the new aspect changes from being minor to being major and rises to predominance, while the old aspect changes from being major to being minor and gradually dies out. And the moment the new aspect gains dominance over the old, the old thing changes qualitatively into a new thing. It can thus be seen that the nature of a thing is mainly determined by the principal aspect of the contradiction, the aspect which has gained predominance. When the principal aspect which has gained predominance changes, the nature of a thing changes accordingly.

In capitalist society, capitalism has changed its position from being a subordinate force in the old feudal era to being the dominant force, and the nature of society has accordingly changed from feudal to capitalist. In the new, capitalist era, the feudal forces changed from their former dominant position to a subordinate one, gradually dying out. Such was the case, for example, in Britain and France. With the development of the productive forces, the bourgeoisie changes from being a new class playing a progressive role to being an old class playing a reactionary role, until it is finally overthrown by the proletariat and becomes a class deprived of privately owned means of production and stripped of power, when it, too, gradually dies out. The proletariat, which is much more numerous than the bourgeoisie and grows simultaneously with it but under its rule, is a new force which, initially subordinate to the bourgeoisie, gradually gains strength, becomes an independent class playing the leading role in history, and finally seizes political power and becomes the ruling class. Thereupon the nature of society changes and the old capitalist society becomes the new socialist society. This is the path already taken by the Soviet Union, a path that all other countries will inevitably take.

Look at China, for instance. Imperialism occupies the principal position in the contradiction in which China has been reduced to a semi-colony, it oppresses the Chinese people, and China has been changed from an independent country into a semi-colonial one. But this state of affairs will inevitably change; in the struggle between the two sides, the power of the Chinese people which is growing under the leadership of the proletariat will inevitably change China from a semi-colony into an independent country, whereas imperialism will be overthrown and old China will inevitably change into New China.

The change of old China into New China also involves a change in the relation between the old feudal forces and the new popular forces within the country. The old feudal landlord class will be overthrown, and from being the ruler it will change into being the ruled; and this class, too, will gradually die out. From being the ruled the people, led by the proletariat, will become the rulers. Thereupon, the nature of Chinese society will change and the old, semi-colonial and semi-feudal society will change into a new democratic society.

Instances of such reciprocal transformation are found in our past experience. The Ching Dynasty which ruled China for nearly three hundred years was overthrown in the Revolution of 1911, and the revolutionary *Tung Meng Hui* under Sun Yat-sen's leadership was victorious for a time. In the Revolutionary War of 1924–27, the revolutionary forces of the Communist-Kuomintang alliance in the south changed from being weak to being strong and won victory in the Northern Expedition, while the Northern warlords who once ruled the roost were overthrown. In 1927, the people's forces led by the Communist Party were greatly reduced numerically under the attacks of Kuomintang reaction, but with the elimination of opportunism within their ranks they gradually grew again. In the revolutionary base areas under Communist leadership, the peasants have been transformed from being the ruled to being the rulers, while the landlords have undergone a reverse transformation. It is always so in the world, the new displacing the old, the old being superseded by the new, the old being eliminated to make way for the new, and the new emerging out of the old.

At certain times in the revolutionary struggle, the difficulties outweigh the favourable conditions and so constitute the principal aspect of the contradiction and the favourable conditions constitute the secondary aspect. But through their efforts the revolutionaries can overcome the difficulties step by step and open up a favourable new situation; thus a difficult situation yields place to a favourable one. This is what happened after the failure of the revolution in China in 1927 and during the Long March of the Chinese Red Army. In the present Sino-Japanese War, China is again in a difficult position, but we can change this and fundamentally transform the situation as between China and Japan. Conversely, favourable conditions can be transformed into difficulty if the revolutionaries make mistakes. Thus the victory of the revolution of 1924–27 turned into defeat. The revolutionary base areas which grew up in the southern provinces after had all suffered defeat by 1934.

When we engage in study, the same holds good for the contradiction in the passage from ignorance to knowledge. At the very beginning of our study of Marxism, our ignorance of or scanty acquaintance with Marxism stands in contradiction to knowledge of Marxism. But by assiduous study, ignorance can be transformed into knowledge, scanty knowledge into substantial knowledge, and blindness in the application of Marxism into mastery of its application.

Some people think that this is not true of certain contradictions. For instance, in the contradiction between the productive forces and the relations of production, the productive forces are the principal aspect; in the contradiction between theory and practice, practice is the principal aspect; in the contradiction between the economic base and the superstructure, the economic base is the principal aspect; and there is no change in their respective positions. This is the mechanical materialist conception, not the dialectical materialist conception. True, the productive forces, practice and the economic base generally play the principal and decisive role; whoever denies this is not a materialist. But it must also be admitted that in certain conditions, such aspects as the relations of production, theory and the superstructure in turn manifest themselves in the principal and decisive role. When it is impossible for the productive forces to develop without a change in the relations of production, then the change in the relations of production plays the principal and decisive role. The creation and advocacy of revolutionary theory plays the principal and decisive role in those times of which Lenin said, "Without revolutionary theory there can be no revolutionary movement."* When a task, no matter which, has to be performed, but there is as yet no guiding line, method, plan or policy, the principal and decisive thing is to decide on a guiding line, method, plan or policy. When the superstructure (politics, culture, etc.) obstructs the development of the economic base, political and cultural changes become principal and decisive. Are we going against materialism when we say this? No. The reason is that while we recognize that in the general development of history the material determines the mental and social being determines social consciousness, we also—and indeed must—recognize the reaction of mental on material things, of social consciousness on social being and of the superstructure on the economic base. This does not go against materialism; on the contrary, it avoids mechanical materialism and firmly upholds dialectical materialism.

In studying the particularity of contradiction, unless we examine these two facets—the principal and the non-principal contradictions in a process, and the principal and the non-principal aspects of a contradiction—that is, unless we examine the distinctive character of these two facets of contradiction, we shall get bogged down in abstractions, be unable to understand contradiction concretely and consequently be unable to find the correct method of resolving it. The distinctive character or particularity of these two facets of contradiction represents the unevenness of the forces that are in contradiction. Nothing in this world develops absolutely evenly; we must oppose the theory of even development or the theory of equilibrium. Moreover, it is these concrete features of a contradiction and the changes in the principal and non-principal aspects of a contradiction in the course of its development that manifest the force of the new superseding the old. The study of the various states of unevenness in contradictions, of the principal and non-principal contradictions and of the principal and the non-principal aspects of a contradiction constitutes an essential method by which a revolutionary political party correctly determines its strategic and tactical policies both in political and in military affairs. All Communists must give it attention.

---

*V.I. Lenin, "What Is to Be Done?," *Collected Works,* Eng. ed., FLPH, Moscow, 1961, Vol. V, p. 369.

V. THE IDENTITY AND STRUGGLE
OF THE ASPECTS OF A CONTRADICTION

When we understand the universality and the particularity of contradiction, we must proceed to study the problem of the identity and struggle of the aspects of a contradiction.

Identity, unity, coincidence, interpenetration, interpermeation, interdependence (or mutual dependence for existence), interconnection or mutual co-operation—all these different terms mean the same thing and refer to the following two points: first, the existence of each of the two aspects of a contradiction in the process of the development of a thing presupposes the existence of the other aspect, and both aspects coexist in a single entity; second, in given conditions, each of the two contradictory aspects transforms itself into its opposite. This is the meaning of identity.

Lenin said:

> *Dialectics* is the teaching which shows how *opposites* can be and how they happen to be (how they become) identical—under what conditions they are *identical*, transforming themselves into one another,—why the human mind should take these *opposites* not as dead, rigid, but as living, conditional, mobile, transforming themselves into one another.*

What does this passage mean?

The contradictory aspects in every process exclude each other, struggle with each other and are in opposition to each other. Without exception, they are contained in the process of development of all things and in all human thought. A simple process contains only a single pair of opposites, while a complex process contains more. And in turn, the pairs of opposites are in contradiction to one another. That is how all things in the objective world and all human thought are constituted and how they are set in motion.

This being so, there is an utter lack of identity or unity. How then can one speak of identity or unity?

The fact is that no contradictory aspect can exist in isolation. Without its opposite aspect, each loses the condition for its existence. Just think, can any one contradictory aspect of a thing or of a concept in the human mind exist independently? Without life, there would be no death; without death, there would be no life. Without "above," there would be no "below"; without "below," there would be no "above." Without misfortune, there would be no good fortune; without good fortune, there would be no misfortune. Without facility, there would be no difficulty; without difficulty, there would be no facility. Without landlords, there would be no tenant-peasants; without tenant-peasants, there would be no landlords. Without the bourgeoisie, there would be no proletariat; without the proletariat, there would be no bourgeoisie. Without imperialist oppression of nations, there would be no colonies or semi-colonies; without colonies or semi-colonies, there would be no imperialist oppression of nations. It is so with all opposites; in given conditions, on the one hand they are opposed to each other, and on the other they are interconnected, interpenetrating, interpermeating and interdependent, and this character is described as identity. In given conditions, all contradictory aspects possess the character of non-identity and hence are described as being in contradiction. But they also possess the character of identity and hence are interconnected. This is what Lenin

*V.I. Lenin, "Conspectus of Hegel's *The Science of Logic*," *Collected Works*, Russ. ed., Moscow, 1958, Vol. XXXVIII, pp. 97–98.

means when he says that dialectics studies "how *opposites* can be . . . *identical.*" How then can they be identical? Because each is the condition for the other's existence. This is the first meaning of identity.

But is it enough to say merely that each of the contradictory aspects is the condition for the other's existence, that there is identity between them and that consequently they can coexist in a single entity? No, it is not. The matter does not end with their dependence on each other for their existence; what is more important is their transformation into each other. That is to say, in given conditions, each of the contradictory aspects within a thing transforms itself into its opposite, changes its position to that of its opposite. This is the second meaning of the identity of contradiction.

Why is there identity here, too? You see, by means of revolution the proletariat, at one time the ruled, is transformed into the ruler, while the bourgeoisie, the erstwhile ruler, is transformed into the ruled and changes its position to that originally occupied by its opposite. This has already taken place in the Soviet Union, as it will take place throughout the world. If there were no interconnection and identity of opposites in given conditions, how could such a change take place?

The Kuomintang, which played a certain positive role at a certain stage in modern Chinese history, became a counter-revolutionary party after 1927 because of its inherent class nature and because of imperialist blandishments (these being the conditions); but it has been compelled to agree to resist Japan because of the sharpening of the contradiction between China and Japan and because of the Communist Party's policy of the united front (these being the conditions). Things in contradiction change into one another, and herein lies a definite identity.

Our agrarian revolution has been a process in which the landlord class owning the land is transformed into a class that has lost its land, while the peasants who once lost their land are transformed into small holders who have acquired land, and it will be such a process once again. In given conditions having and not having, acquiring and losing, are interconnected; there is identity of the two sides. Under socialism, private peasant ownership is transformed into the public ownership of socialist agriculture; this has already taken place in the Soviet Union, as it will take place everywhere else. There is a bridge leading from private property to public property, which in philosophy is called identity, or transformation into each other, or interpenetration.

To consolidate the dictatorship of the proletariat or the dictatorship of the people is in fact to prepare the conditions for abolishing this dictatorship and advancing to the higher stage when all state systems are eliminated. To establish and build the Communist Party is in fact to prepare the conditions for the elimination of the Communist Party and all political parties. To build a revolutionary army under the leadership of the Communist Party and to carry on revolutionary war is in fact to prepare the conditions for the permanent elimination of war. These opposites are at the same time complementary.

War and peace, as everybody knows, transform themselves into each other. War is transformed into peace; for instance, the First World War was transformed into the post-war peace, and the civil war in China has now stopped, giving place to internal peace. Peace is transformed into war; for instance, the Kuomintang-Communist cooperation was transformed into war in 1927, and today's situation of world peace may be transformed into a second world war. Why is this so? Because in class society such contradictory things as war and peace have an identity in given conditions.

All contradictory things are interconnected; not only do they coexist in a single entity in given conditions, but in other given conditions, they also transform themselves into each other. This is the full meaning of the identity of opposites. This is what Lenin meant when he discussed "how they happen to be (how they become) *identical*—under what conditions they are identical, transforming themselves into one another."

Why is it that "the human mind should take these opposites not as dead, rigid, but as living, conditional, mobile, transforming themselves into one another"? Because that is just how things are in objective reality. The fact is that the unity or identity of opposites in objective things is not dead or rigid, but is living, conditional, mobile, temporary and relative; in given conditions, every contradictory aspect transforms itself into its opposite. Reflected in man's thinking, this becomes the Marxist world outlook of materialist dialectics. It is only the reactionary ruling classes of the past and present and the metaphysicians in their service who regard opposites not as living, conditional, mobile and transforming themselves into one another, but as dead and rigid, and they propagate this fallacy everywhere to delude the masses of the people, thus seeking to perpetuate their rule. The task of Communists is to expose the fallacies of the reactionaries and metaphysicians, to propagate the dialectics inherent in things, and so accelerate the transformation of things and achieve the goal of revolution.

In speaking of the identity of opposites in given conditions, what we are referring to is real and concrete opposites and the real and concrete transformations of opposites into one another. There are innumerable transformations in mythology, for instance, Kua Fu's race with the sun in *Shan Hai Ching*,* Yi's shooting down of nine suns in *Huai Nan Tzu*,** the Monkey King's seventy-two metamorphoses in *Hsi Yu Chi*,† the numerous episodes of ghosts and foxes metamorphosed into human beings in the *Strange Tales of Liao Chai*,†† etc. But these legendary transformations of opposites are not concrete changes reflecting concrete contradictions. They are naive, imaginary, subjectively conceived transformations conjured up in men's minds by innumerable real and complex transformations of opposites into one another. Marx said, "All mythology masters and dominates and shapes the forces of nature in and through the imagination; hence it disappears as soon as man gains mastery over the forces of nature."§ The myriads of changes in mythology (and also in nursery tales) delight people because they imaginatively picture man's conquest of the forces of nature, and the best myths possess "eternal charm," as Marx put it; but myths are not built out of the concrete contradictions existing in given conditions and therefore are not a scientific reflection of reality. That is to say, in myths or nursery tales the aspects constituting a contradiction have only an imaginary identity, not a concrete identity. The scientific reflection of the identity in real transformations is Marxist dialectics.

Why can an egg but not a stone be transformed into a chicken? Why is there identity between war and peace and none between war and a stone? Why can human beings

---

*Shan Hai Ching (*Book of Mountains and Seas*) was written in the era of the Warring States (403–221 B.C.E.). In one of its fables Kua Fu, a superman, pursued and overtook the sun. But he died of thirst, whereupon his staff was transformed into the forest of Teng.

**Yi is one of the legendary heroes of ancient China, famous for his archery. According to a legend in *Huai Nan Tzu*, compiled in the 2nd century B.C.E., there were ten suns in the sky in the days of Emperor Yao. To put an end to the damage to vegetation caused by these scorching suns, Emperor Yao ordered Yi to shoot them down. In another legend recorded by Wang Yi (2nd century C.E.), the archer is said to have shot down nine of the ten suns.

†*Hsi Yu Chi* (*Pilgrimage to the West*) is a 16th century novel, the hero of which is the monkey god Sun Wu-kung. He could miraculously change at will into seventy-two different shapes, such as a bird, a tree and a stone.

††*The Strange Tales of Liao Chai*, written by Pu Sung-ling in the 17th century, is a well-known collection of 431 tales, mostly about ghosts and fox spirits.

§Karl Marx, "Introduction to the Critique of Political Economy," *A Contribution to the Critique of Political Economy*, Eng. ed., Chicago, 1904, pp. 310–11.

give birth only to human beings and not to anything else? The sole reason is that the identity of opposites exists only in necessary given conditions. Without these necessary given conditions there can be no identity whatsoever.

Why is it that in Russia in 1917 the bourgeois-democratic February Revolution was directly linked with the proletarian socialist October Revolution, while in France the bourgeois revolution was not directly linked with a socialist revolution and the Paris Commune of 1871 ended in failure? Why is it, on the other hand, that the nomadic system of Mongolia and Central Asia has been directly linked with socialism? Why is it that the Chinese revolution can avoid a capitalist future and be directly linked with socialism without taking the old historical road of the Western countries, without passing through a period of bourgeois dictatorship? The sole reason is the concrete conditions of the time. When certain necessary conditions are present, certain contradictions arise in the process of development of things and, moreover, the opposites contained in them are interdependent and become transformed into one another; otherwise none of this would be possible.

Such is the problem of identity. What then is struggle? And what is the relation between identity and struggle?

Lenin said:

> The unity (coincidence, identity, equal action) of opposites is conditional, temporary, transitory, relative. The struggle of mutually exclusive opposites is absolute, just as development and motion are absolute.*

What does this passage mean?

All processes have a beginning and an end, all processes transform themselves into their opposites. The constancy of all processes is relative, but the mutability manifested in the transformation of one process into another is absolute.

There are two states of motion in all things, that of relative rest and that of conspicuous change. Both are caused by the struggle between the two contradictory elements contained in a thing. When the thing is in the first state of motion, it is undergoing only quantitative and not qualitative change and consequently presents the outward appearance of being at rest. When the thing is in the second state of motion, the quantitative change of the first state has already reached a culminating point and gives rise to the dissolution of the thing as an entity and thereupon a qualitative change ensues, hence the appearance of a conspicuous change. Such unity, solidarity, combination, harmony, balance, stalemate, deadlock, rest, constancy, equilibrium, solidity, attraction, etc., as we see in daily life, are all the appearances of things in the state of quantitative change. On the other hand, the dissolution of unity, that is, the destruction of this solidarity, combination, harmony, balance, stalemate, deadlock, rest, constancy, equilibrium, solidity and attraction, and the change of each into its opposite are all the appearances of things in the state of qualitative change, the transformation of one process into another. Things are constantly transforming themselves from the first into the second state of motion; the struggle of opposites goes on in both states but the contradiction is resolved through the second state. That is why we say that the unity of opposites is conditional, temporary and relative, while the struggle of mutually exclusive opposites is absolute.

---

*V.I. Lenin, "On the Question of Dialectics," *Collected Works*, Russ. ed., Moscow, 1958, Vol. XXXVIII, p. 358.

When we said above that two opposite things can coexist in a single entity and can transform themselves into each other because there is identity between them, we were speaking of conditionality, that is to say, in given conditions two contradictory things can be united and can transform themselves into each other, but in the absence of these conditions, they cannot constitute a contradiction, cannot coexist in the same entity and cannot transform themselves into one another. It is because the identity of opposites obtains only in given conditions that we have said identity is conditional and relative. We may add that the struggle between opposites permeates a process from beginning to end and makes one process transform itself into another, that it is ubiquitous, and that struggle is therefore unconditional and absolute.

The combination of conditional, relative identity and unconditional, absolute struggle constitutes the movement of opposites in all things.

We Chinese often say, "Things that oppose each other also complement each other."* That is, things opposed to each other have identity. This saying is dialectical and contrary to metaphysics. "Oppose each other" refers to the mutual exclusion or the struggle of two contradictory aspects. "Complement each other" means that in given conditions the two contradictory aspects unite and achieve identity. Yet struggle is inherent in identity and without struggle there can be no identity.

In identity there is struggle, in particularity there is universality, and in individuality there is generality. To quote Lenin, ". . . there *is* an absolute *in* the relative."**

VI. THE PLACE OF ANTAGONISM IN CONTRADICTION

The question of the struggle of opposites includes the question of what is antagonism. Our answer is that antagonism is one form, but not the only form, of the struggle of opposites.

In human history, antagonism between classes exists as a particular manifestation of the struggle of opposites. Consider the contradiction between the exploiting and the exploited classes. Such contradictory classes coexist for a long time in the same society, be it slave society, feudal society or capitalist society, and they struggle with each other; but it is not until the contradiction between the two classes develops to a certain stage that it assumes the form of open antagonism and develops into revolution. The same holds for the transformation of peace into war in class society.

Before it explodes, a bomb is a single entity in which opposites coexist in given conditions. The explosion takes place only when a new condition, ignition, is present. An analogous situation arises in all those natural phenomena which finally assume the form of open conflict to resolve old contradictions and produce new things.

It is highly important to grasp this fact. It enables us to understand that revolutions and revolutionary wars are inevitable in class society and that without them, it is impossible to accomplish any leap in social development and to overthrow the reactionary ruling classes and therefore impossible for the people to win political power. Communists must expose the deceitful propaganda of the reactionaries, such as the assertion that social revolution is unnecessary and impossible. They must firmly uphold

---

*The saying "Things that oppose each other also complement each other" first appeared in the *History of the Earlier Han Dynasty* by Pan Ku, a celebrated historian in the 1st century C.E. It has long been a popular saying.

**V.I. Lenin, "On the Question of Dialectics," *Collected Works,* Russ. ed., Moscow, 1958, Vol. XXXVIII, p. 358.

the Marxist-Leninist theory of social revolution and enable the people to understand that social revolution is not only entirely necessary but also entirely practicable, and that the whole history of mankind and the triumph of the Soviet Union have confirmed this scientific truth.

However, we must make a concrete study of the circumstances of each specific struggle of opposites and should not arbitrarily apply the formula discussed above to everything. Contradiction and struggle are universal and absolute, but the methods of resolving contradictions, that is, the forms of struggle, differ according to the differences in the nature of the contradictions. Some contradictions are characterized by open antagonism, others are not. In accordance with the concrete development of things, some contradictions which were originally non-antagonistic develop into antagonistic ones, while others which were originally antagonistic develop into nonantagonistic ones.

As already mentioned, so long as classes exist, contradictions between correct and incorrect ideas in the Communist Party are reflections within the Party of class contradictions. At first, with regard to certain issues, such contradictions may not manifest themselves as antagonistic. But with the development of the class struggle, they may grow and become antagonistic. The history of the Communist Party of the Soviet Union shows us that the contradictions between the correct thinking of Lenin and Stalin and the fallacious thinking of Trotsky, Bukharin and others did not at first manifest themselves in an antagonistic form, but that later they did develop into antagonism. There

Monument to the Heroes of the Revolution with the Mao Tse-tung (Zedong) Memorial Hall in the background, Tiananmen Square, Beijing. Mao's body lies in state inside the Memorial Hall. (*Forrest E. Baird*)

are similar cases in the history of the Chinese Communist Party. At first the contradictions between the correct thinking of many of our Party comrades and the fallacious thinking of Chen Tu-hsiu, Chang Kuo-tao and others also did not manifest themselves in an antagonistic form, but later they did develop into antagonism. At present the contradiction between correct and incorrect thinking in our Party does not manifest itself in an antagonistic form, and if comrades who have committed mistakes can correct them, it will not develop into antagonism. Therefore, the Party must on the one hand wage a serious struggle against erroneous thinking, and on the other give the comrades who have committed errors ample opportunity to wake up. This being the case, excessive struggle is obviously inappropriate. But if the people who have committed errors persist in them and aggravate them, there is the possibility that this contradiction will develop into antagonism.

Economically, the contradiction between town and country is an extremely antagonistic one both in capitalist society, where under the rule of the bourgeoisie the towns ruthlessly plunder the countryside, and in the Kuomintang areas in China, where under the rule of foreign imperialism and the Chinese big comprador bourgeoisie the towns most rapaciously plunder the countryside. But in a socialist country and in our revolutionary base areas, this antagonistic contradiction has changed into one that is non-antagonistic; and when communist society is reached it will be abolished.

Lenin said, "Antagonism and contradiction are not at all one and the same. Under socialism, the first will disappear, the second will remain."* That is to say, antagonism is one form, but not the only form, of the struggle of opposites; the formula of antagonism cannot be arbitrarily applied everywhere.

VII. CONCLUSION

We may now say a few words to sum up. The law of contradiction in things, that is, the law of the unity of opposites, is the fundamental law of nature and of society and therefore also the fundamental law of thought. It stands opposed to the metaphysical world outlook. It represents a great revolution in the history of human knowledge. According to dialectical materialism, contradiction is present in all processes of objectively existing things and of subjective thought and permeates all these processes from beginning to end; this is the universality and absoluteness of contradiction. Each contradiction and each of its aspects have their respective characteristics; this is the particularity and relativity of contradiction. In given conditions, opposites possess identity, and consequently can coexist in a single entity and can transform themselves into each other; this again is the particularity and relativity of contradiction. But the struggle of opposites is ceaseless, it goes on both when the opposites are coexisting and when they are transforming themselves into each other, and becomes especially conspicuous when they are transforming themselves into one another; this again is the universality and absoluteness of contradiction. In studying the particularity and relativity of contradiction, we must give attention to the distinction between the principal contradiction and the non-principal contradictions and to the distinction between the principal aspect and the non-principal aspect of a contradiction; in studying the universality of contradiction and the

*V.I. Lenin, "Remarks on N.I. Bukharin's *Economics of the Transitional Period,*" *Selected Works,* Russ. ed., Moscow-Leningrad, 1931, Vol. XI, p. 357.

struggle of opposites in contradiction, we must give attention to the distinction between the different forms of struggle. Otherwise we shall make mistakes. If, through study, we achieve a real understanding of the essentials explained above, we shall be able to demolish dogmatist ideas which are contrary to the basic principles of Marxism-Leninism and detrimental to our revolutionary cause, and our comrades with practical experience will be able to organize their experience into principles and avoid repeating empiricist errors. These are a few simple conclusions from our study of the law of contradiction.

LIN YUTANG, THE IMPORTANCE OF LIVING (IN PART)

CHAPTER 1: THE AWAKENING

I. APPROACH TO LIFE

In what follows I am presenting the Chinese point of view, because I cannot help myself. I am interested only in presenting a view of life and of things as the best and wisest Chinese minds have seen it and expressed it in their folk wisdom and their literature. It is an idle philosophy born of an idle life, evolved in a different age, I am quite aware. But I cannot help feeling that this view of life is essentially true, and since we are alike under the skin, what touches the human heart in one country touches all. I shall have to present a view of life as Chinese poets and scholars evaluated it with their common sense, their realism and their sense of poetry. I shall attempt to reveal some of the beauty of the pagan world, a sense of the pathos and beauty and terror and comedy of life, viewed by a people who have a strong feeling of the limitations of our existence, and yet somehow retain a sense of the dignity of human life.

The Chinese philosopher is one who dreams with one eye open, who views life with love and sweet irony, who mixes his cynicism with a kindly tolerance, and who alternately wakes up from life's dream and then nods again, feeling more alive when he is dreaming than when he is awake, thereby investing his waking life with a dream-world quality. He sees with one eye closed and with one eye opened the futility of much that goes on around him and of his own endeavors, but barely retains enough sense of reality to determine to go through with it. He is seldom disillusioned because he has no illusions, and seldom disappointed because he never had extravagant hopes. In this way his spirit is emancipated.

For, after surveying the field of Chinese literature and philosophy, I come to the conclusion that the highest ideal of Chinese culture has always been a man with a sense of *detachment (takuan)* toward life based on a sense of wise disenchantment. From this detachment comes *high-mindedness (k'uanghuai),* a high-mindedness which enables one to go through life with tolerant irony and escape the temptations of fame and wealth and achievement, and eventually makes him take what comes. And from this detachment arise also his sense of freedom, his love of vagabondage and his pride and nonchalance. It is only with this sense of freedom and nonchalance that one eventually arrives at the keen and intense joy of living.

It is useless for me to say whether my philosophy is valid or not for the Westerner. To understand Western life, one would have to look at it as a Westerner born, with his own temperament, his bodily attitudes and his own set of nerves. I have no doubt that American nerves can stand a good many things that Chinese nerves cannot stand, and *vice versa.* It is good that it should be so—that we should all be born different. And yet it is all a question of relativity. I am quite sure that amidst the hustle and bustle of American life, there is a great deal of wistfulness, of the divine desire to lie on a plot of grass under tall beautiful trees of an idle afternoon and *just do nothing.* The necessity for such common cries as "Wake up and live" is to me a good sign that a wise portion

Lin Yutang, *The Importance of Living* (New York: John Day, 1937). Reprinted by permission.

of American humanity prefer to dream the hours away. The American is after all not as bad as all that. It is only a question whether he will have more or less of that sort of thing, and how he will arrange to make it possible. Perhaps the American is merely ashamed of the word "loafing" in a world where everybody is doing something, but somehow, as sure as I know he is also an animal, he likes sometimes to have his muscles relaxed, to stretch on the sand, or to lie still with one leg comfortably curled up and one arm placed below his head as his pillow. If so, he cannot be very different from Yen Huei, who had exactly that virtue and whom Confucius desperately admired among all his disciples. The only thing I desire to see is that he be honest about it, and that he proclaim to the world that he likes it when he likes it, that it is not when he is working in the office but when he is lying idly on the sand that his soul utters, "Life is beautiful."

We are, therefore, about to see a philosophy and art of living as the mind of the Chinese people as a whole has understood it. I am inclined to think that, in a good or bad sense, there is nothing like it in the world. For here we come to an entirely new way of looking at life by an entirely different type of mind. It is a truism to say that the culture of any nation is the product of its mind. Consequently, where there is a national mind so racially different and historically isolated from the Western cultural world, we have the right to expect new answers to the problems of life, or what is better, new methods of approach, or, still better, a new posing of the problems themselves. We know some of the virtues and deficiencies of that mind, at least as revealed to us in the historical past. It has a glorious art and a contemptible science, a magnificent common sense and an infantile logic, a fine womanish chatter about life and no scholastic philosophy. It is generally known that the Chinese mind is an intensely practical, hardheaded one, and it is also known to some lovers of Chinese art that it is a profoundly sensitive mind; by a still smaller proportion of people, it is accepted as also a profoundly poetic and philosophical mind. At least the Chinese are noted for taking things philosophically, which is saying more than the statement that the Chinese have a great philosophy or have a few great philosophers. For a nation to have a few philosophers is not so unusual, but for a nation to take things philosophically is terrific. It is evident anyway that the Chinese as a nation are more philosophic than efficient, and that if it were otherwise, no nation could have survived the high blood pressure of an efficient life for four thousand years. Four thousand years of efficient living would ruin any nation. An important consequence is that, while in the West, the insane are so many that they are put in an asylum, in China the insane are so unusual that we worship them, as anybody who has a knowledge of Chinese literature will testify. And that, after all, is what I am driving at. Yes, the Chinese have a light, an almost gay, philosophy, and the best proof of their philosophic temper is to be found in this wise and merry philosophy of living.

II. A Pseudo-Scientific Formula

*   *   *

Gifted with this realism, and with a profound distrust of logic and of the intellect itself, philosophy for the Chinese becomes a matter of direct and intimate feeling of life itself, and refuses to be encased in any system. For there is a robust sense of reality, a sheer animal sense, a spirit of reasonableness which crushes reason itself and makes the rise of any hard and fast philosophic system impossible. There are the three religions of China, Confucianism, Taoism and Buddhism, all magnificent systems in themselves, and yet robust common sense dilutes them all and reduces them all into the common problem of the pursuit of a happy human life. The mature Chinese is always a person who refuses to think too hard or to believe in any single idea or faith or school of philosophy whole-heartedly. When a friend of Confucius told him that he always thought three times before he acted, Confucius wittily replied, "To think twice is quite enough." A follower of a school of philosophy is but a student of philosophy, but a man is a student, or perhaps a master, of life.

The final product of this culture and philosophy is this: in China, as compared with the West, man lives a life closer to nature and closer to childhood, a life in which the instincts and the emotions are given free play and emphasized against the life of the intellect, with a strange combination of devotion to the flesh and arrogance of the spirit, of profound wisdom and foolish gaiety, of high sophistication and childish naivete. I would say, therefore, that this philosophy is characterized by: first, a gift for seeing life whole in art; secondly, a conscious return to simplicity in philosophy; and thirdly, an ideal of reasonableness in living. The end product is, strange to say, a worship of the poet, the peasant and the vagabond.

III. THE SCAMP AS IDEAL

To me, spiritually a child of the East and the West, man's dignity consists in the following facts which distinguish man from animals. First, that he has a playful curiosity and a natural genius for exploring knowledge; second, that he has dreams and a lofty idealism (often vague, or confused, or cocky, it is true, but nevertheless worthwhile); third, and still more important, that he is able to correct his dreams by a sense of humor, and thus restrain his idealism by a more robust and healthy realism; and finally, that he does not react to surroundings mechanically and uniformly as animals do, but possesses the ability and the freedom to determine his own reactions and to change surroundings at his will. This last is the same as saying that human personality is the last thing to be reduced to mechanical laws; somehow the human mind is forever elusive, uncatchable and unpredictable, and manages to wriggle out of mechanistic laws or a materialistic dialectic that crazy psychologists and unmarried economists are trying to impose upon him. Man, therefore, is a curious, dreamy, humorous and wayward creature.

In short, my faith in human dignity consists in the belief that man is the greatest scamp on earth. Human dignity must be associated with the idea of a scamp and not with that of an obedient, disciplined and regimented soldier. The scamp is probably the most glorious type of human being, as the soldier is the lowest type, according to this conception. It seems in my last book, *My Country and My People,* the net impression of readers was that I was trying to glorify the "old rogue." It is my hope that the net impression of the present one will be that I am doing my best to glorify the scamp or vagabond. I hope I shall succeed. For things are not so simple as they sometimes seem. In this present age of threats to democracy and individual liberty, probably only the scamp and the spirit of the scamp alone will save us from becoming lost as serially numbered units in the masses of disciplined, obedient, regimented and uniformed coolies. The scamp will be the last and most formidable enemy of dictatorships. He will be the champion of human dignity and individual freedom, and will be the last to be conquered. All modern civilization depends entirely upon him.

Probably the Creator knew well that, when He created man upon this earth, He was producing a scamp, a brilliant scamp, it is true, but a scamp nonetheless. The scamp-like qualities of man are, after all, his most hopeful qualities. This scamp that the Creator has produced is undoubtedly a brilliant chap. He is still a very unruly and awkward adolescent, thinking himself greater and wiser than he really is, still full of mischief and naughtiness and love of a free-for-all. Nevertheless, there is so much good in him that the Creator might still be willing to pin on him His hopes, as a father sometimes pins his hopes on a brilliant but somewhat erratic son of twenty. Would He be willing some day to retire and turn over the management of this universe to this erratic son of His? I wonder. . . .

Speaking as a Chinese, I do not think that any civilization can be called complete until it has progressed from sophistication to unsophistication, and made a conscious return to simplicity of thinking and living, and I call no man wise until he has made the progress from the wisdom of knowledge to the wisdom of foolishness, and become a laughing philosopher, feeling first life's tragedy and then life's comedy. For we must weep before we can laugh. Out of sadness comes the awakening and out of the awakening comes the laughter of the philosopher, with kindliness and tolerance to boot.

The world, I believe, is far too serious, and being far too serious, it has need of a wise and merry philosophy. The philosophy of the Chinese art of living can certainly be called the "gay science," if anything can be called by that phrase used by Nietzsche. After all, only a gay philosophy is profound philosophy; the serious philosophies of the West haven't even begun to understand what life is. To me personally, the only function of philosophy is to teach us to take life more lightly and gayly than the average business man does, for no business man who does not retire at fifty, if he can, is in my eyes a philosopher. This is not merely a casual thought, but is a fundamental point of view with me. The world can be made a more peaceful and more reasonable place to live in only when men have imbued themselves in the light gaiety of this spirit. The modern man takes life far too seriously, and because he is too serious, the world is full of troubles. We ought, therefore, to take time to examine the origin of that attitude which will make possible a wholehearted enjoyment of this life and a more reasonable, more peaceful and less hot-headed temperament.

I am perhaps entitled to call this the philosophy of the Chinese people rather than of any one school. It is a philosophy that is greater than Confucius and greater than Laotse, for it transcends these and other ancient philosophers; it draws from these fountain springs of thought and harmonizes them into a whole, and from the abstract outlines of their wisdom, it has created an art of living in the flesh, visible, palpable and understandable by the common man. Surveying Chinese literature, art and philosophy as a whole, it has become quite clear to me that the philosophy of a wise disenchantment and a hearty enjoyment of life is their common message and teaching—the most constant, most characteristic and most persistent refrain of Chinese thought.

CHAPTER 2: VIEWS OF MANKIND

*   *   *

II. EARTH-BOUND

The situation then is this: man wants to live, but he still must live upon this earth. All questions of living in heaven must be brushed aside. Let not the spirit take wings and soar to the abode of the gods and forget the earth. Are we not mortals, condemned to die? The span of life vouchsafed us, threescore and ten, is short enough, if the spirit gets too haughty and wants to live forever, but on the other hand, it is also long enough, if the spirit is a little humble. One can learn such a lot and enjoy such a lot in seventy years, and three generations is a long, long time to see human follies and acquire human wisdom. Anyone who is wise and has lived long enough to witness the changes of fashion and morals and politics through the rise and fall of three generations should be perfectly satisfied to rise from his seat and go away saying, "It was a good show," when the curtain falls.

For we are of the earth, earth-born and earth-bound. There is nothing to be unhappy about the fact that we are, as it were, delivered upon this beautiful earth as its transient guests. Even if it were a dark dungeon, we still would have to make the best of it; it would be ungrateful of us not to do so when we have, instead of a dungeon, such a beautiful earth to live on for a good part of a century. Sometimes we get too ambitious and disdain the humble and yet generous earth. Yet a sentiment for this Mother Earth, a feeling of true affection and attachment, one must have for this temporary abode of our body and spirit, if we are to have a sense of spiritual harmony.

We have to have, therefore, a kind of animal skepticism as well as animal faith, taking this earthly life largely as it is. And we have to retain the wholeness of nature that we see in Thoreau who felt himself kin to the sod and partook largely of its dull patience, in winter expecting the sun of spring, who in his cheapest moments was apt to think that it was not his business to be "seeking the spirit," but as much the spirit's business to seek him, and whose happiness, as he described it, was a good deal like that of the woodchucks. The earth, after all is real, as the heaven is unreal: how fortunate is man that he is born between the real earth and the unreal heaven!

Any good practical philosophy must start out with the recognition of our having a body. It is high time that some among us made the straight admission that we are animals, an admission which is inevitable since the establishment of the basic truth of the Darwinian theory and the great progress of biology, especially bio-chemistry. It was very unfortunate that our teachers and philosophers belonged to the so-called intellectual class, with a characteristic professional pride of intellect. The men of the spirit were as proud of the spirit as the shoemaker is proud of leather. Sometimes even the spirit was not sufficiently remote and abstract and they had to use the words, "essence" or "soul" or "idea," writing them with capital letters to frighten us. The human body was distilled in this scholastic machine into a spirit, and the spirit was further concentrated into a kind of essence, forgetting that even alcoholic drinks must have a "body"—mixed with plain water—if they are to be palatable at all. And we poor laymen were supposed to drink that concentrated quintessence of spirit. This over-emphasis on the spirit was fatal. It made us war with our natural instincts, and my chief criticism is that it made a whole and rounded view of human nature impossible. It proceeded also from an inadequate knowledge of biology and psychology, and of the place of the senses, emotions and, above all, instincts in our life. Man is made of flesh and spirit both, and it should be philosophy's business to see that the mind and body live harmoniously together, that there be a reconciliation between the two.

* * *

CHAPTER 6: THE FEAST OF LIFE

I. THE PROBLEM OF HAPPINESS

The enjoyment of life covers many things: the enjoyment of ourselves, of home life, of trees, flowers, clouds, winding rivers and falling cataracts and the myriad things in Nature, and then the enjoyment of poetry, art, contemplation, friendship, conversation, and reading, which are all some form or other of the communion of spirits. There are obvious things like the enjoyment of food, a gay party or family reunion, an outing on a beautiful spring day; and less obvious things like the enjoyment of poetry, art and contemplation. I have found it impossible to call these two classes of enjoyment material and spiritual, first because I do not believe in this distinction, and secondly because I am puzzled whenever I proceed to make this classification. How can I say, when I see a gay picnic party of men and women and old people and children, what part of their pleasures is material and what part spiritual? I see a child romping about on the grass plot, another child making daisy chains, their mother holding a piece of sandwich, the uncle of the family biting a juicy, red apple, the father sprawling on the ground looking at the sailing clouds, and the grandfather holding a pipe in his mouth. Probably somebody is playing a gramophone, and from the distance there come the sound of music and the distant roar of the waves. Which of these pleasures is material and which spiritual? Is it so easy to draw a distinction between the enjoyment of a sandwich and the enjoyment of the surrounding landscape, which we call poetry? Is it possible to regard the enjoyment of music which we call art, as decidedly a higher type of pleasure than the smoking of a pipe, which we call material? This classification between material and spiritual pleasures is therefore confusing, unintelligible and untrue for me. It proceeds, I suspect, from a false philosophy, sharply dividing the spirit from the flesh, and not supported by a closer direct scrutiny of our real pleasures.

Or have I perhaps assumed too much and begged the question of the proper end of human life? I have always assumed that the end of living is the true enjoyment of it. It is so simply because it is so. I rather hesitate at the word "end" or "purpose." Such an end or purpose of life, consisting in its true enjoyment, is not so much a conscious purpose, as a natural attitude toward human life. The word "purpose" suggests too much contriving and endeavor. The question that faces every man born into this world is not what should be his purpose, which he should set about to achieve, but just what to do with life, a life which is given him for a period of on the average fifty or sixty years? The answer that he should order his life so that he can find the greatest happiness in it is more a practical question, similar to that of how a man should spend his weekend, than a metaphysical proposition as to what is the mystic purpose of his life in the scheme of the universe.

On the contrary, I rather think that philosophers who start out to solve the problem of the purpose of life beg the question by assuming that life must have a purpose. This question, so much pushed to the fore among Western thinkers, is undoubtedly given that importance through the influence of theology. I think we assume too much design and purpose altogether. And the very fact that people try to answer this question and quarrel over it and are puzzled by it serves to show it up as quite vain and uncalled for. Had there been a purpose or design in life, it should not have been so puzzling and vague and difficult to find out.

The question may be divided into two: either that of a divine purpose, which God has set for humanity, or that of a human purpose, a purpose that mankind should set for itself. As far as the first is concerned, I do not propose to enter into the question, because everything that we think God has in mind necessarily proceeds from our own mind; it is what we imagine to be in God's mind, and it is really difficult for human intelligence to guess at a divine intelligence. What we usually end up with by this sort of reasoning is to make God the color-sergeant of our army and to make Him as chauvinistic as ourselves; He cannot, so we conceive, possibly have a "divine purpose" and "destiny" for the world, or for Europe, but only for our beloved Fatherland. I am quite sure the Nazis can't conceive of God without a swastika arm-band. This *Gott* is always *mit uns* and cannot possibly be *mit ihnen.* But the Germans are not the only people who think this way.

As far as the second question is concerned, the point of dispute is not what *is,* but what *should be,* the purpose of human life, and it is therefore a practical, and not a metaphysical question. Into this question of what should be the purpose of human life, every man projects his own conceptions and his own scale of values. It is for this reason that we quarrel over the question, because our scales of values differ from one another. For myself, I am content to be less philosophical and more practical. I should not presume that there must be necessarily a purpose, a meaning of human existence. As Walt Whitman says, "I am sufficient as I am." It is sufficient that I live—and am probably going to live for another few decades—and that human life exists. Viewed that way, the problem becomes amazingly simple and admits of no two answers. What can be the end of human life except the enjoyment of it?

It is strange that this problem of happiness, which is the great question occupying the minds of all pagan philosophers, has been entirely neglected by Christian thinkers. The great question that bothers theological minds is not human happiness, but human "salvation"—a tragic word. The word has a bad flavor for me, because in China I hear everyday some one talking about our "national salvation." Everybody is trying to "save" China. It suggests the feeling of people on a sinking ship, a feeling of ultimate doom and the best method of getting away alive. Christianity, which has been described as "the last sigh of two expiring worlds" (Greek and Roman), still retains something of that characteristic today in its preoccupation with the question of salvation. The question of living is forgotten in the question of getting away alive from this world. Why should man bother himself so much about salvation, unless he has a feeling of being doomed? Theological minds are so much occupied with salvation, and so little with happiness, that all they can tell us about the future is that there will be a vague heaven, and when questioned about what we are going to do there and how we are going to be happy in heaven, they have only ideas of the vaguest sort, such as singing hymns and wearing white robes. Mohammed at least painted a picture of future happiness with rich wine and juicy fruits and black-haired, big-eyed, passionate maidens that we laymen can understand. Unless heaven is made much more vivid and convincing for us, there is no reason why one should strive to go there, at the cost of neglecting this earthly existence. As some one says, "An egg today is better than a hen tomorrow." At least, when we're planning a summer vacation, we take the trouble to find out some details about the place we are going to. If the tourist bureau is entirely vague on the question, I am not interested; I remain where I am. Are we going to strive and endeavor in heaven, as I am quite sure the believers in progress and endeavor must assume? But how can we strive and make progress when we are already perfect? Or are we going merely to loaf and do nothing and not worry? In that case, would it not be better for us to learn to loaf while on this earth as a preparation for our eternal life?

If we must have a view of the universe, let us forget ourselves and not confine it to human life. Let us stretch it a little and include in our view the purpose of the entire creation—the rocks, the trees and the animals. There is a scheme of things (although "scheme" is another word, like "end" and "purpose," which I strongly distrust)—I mean there is a pattern of things in the creation, and we can arrive at some sort of opinion, however lacking in finality, about this entire universe, and then take our place in it. This view of nature and our place in it must be natural, since we are a vital part of it in our life and go back to it when we die. Astronomy, geology, biology and history all provide pretty good material to help us form a fairly good view if we don't attempt too much and jump at conclusions. It doesn't matter if, in this bigger view of the purpose of the creation, man's place recedes a little in importance. It is enough that he has a place, and by living in harmony with nature around him, he will be able to form a workable and reasonable outlook on human life itself.

*   *   *

V. How About Mental Pleasures?

Let us take the supposedly higher pleasures of the mind and the spirit, and see to what extent they are vitally connected with our senses, rather than with our intellect. What are those higher spiritual pleasures that we distinguish from those of the lower senses? Are they not parts of the same thing, taking root and ending up in the senses, and inseparable from them? As we go over these higher pleasures of the mind—literature, art, music, religion and philosophy—we see what a minor role the intellect plays in comparison with the senses and feelings. What does a painting do except to give us a landscape or a portrait and recall in us the sensuous pleasures of seeing a real landscape or a beautiful face? And what does literature do except to recreate a picture of life, to give us the atmosphere and color, the fragrant smell of the pastures or the stench of city gutters? We all say that a novel approaches the standard of true literature in proportion as it gives us real people and real emotions. The book which takes us away from this human life, or merely coldly dissects it, is not literature and the more humanly true a book is, the better literature we consider it. What novel ever appeals to a reader if it contains only a cold analysis, if it fails to give us the salt and tang and flavor of life?

As for the other things, poetry is but truth colored with emotion, music is sentiment without words, and religion is but wisdom expressed in fancy. As painting is based on the sense of color and vision, so poetry is based on the sense of sound and tone and rhythm, in addition to its emotional truth. Music is pure sentiment itself, dispensing entirely with the language of words with which alone the intellect can operate. Music can portray for us the sounds of cowbells and fishmarkets and the battlefield; it can portray for us even the delicacy of the flowers, the undulating motion of the waves, or the sweet serenity of the moonlight; but the moment it steps outside the limit of the senses and tries to portray for us a philosophic idea, it must be considered decadent and the product of a decadent world.

And did not the degeneration of religion begin with reason itself? As Santayana says, the process of degeneration of religion was due to too much reasoning: "This religion unhappily long ago ceased to be wisdom expressed in fancy in order to become superstition overlaid with reasoning." The decay of religion is due to the pedantic spirit, in the invention of creeds, formulas, articles of faith, doctrines and apologies. We become increasingly less pious as we increasingly justify and rationalize our beliefs and become so sure that we are right. That is why every religion becomes a narrow sect, which believes itself to have discovered the only truth. The consequence is that the more we justify our beliefs, the more narrow-minded we become, as is evident in all religious sects. This has made it possible for religion to be associated with the worst forms of bigotry, narrow-mindedness and even pure selfishness in personal life. Such a religion nourishes a man's selfishness not only by making it impossible for him to be broad-minded toward other sects, but also by turning the practice of religion into a private bargain between God and himself, in which the party of the first part is glorified by the party of the second part, singing hymns and calling upon His name on every conceivable occasion, and in return the party of the first part is to bless the party of the second part, bless particularly himself more than any other person and his own family more than any other family. That is why we find selfishness of nature goes so well with some of the most "religious" and regularly church-going old women. In the end, the sense of self-justification, of having discovered the only truth, displaces all the finer emotions from which religion took its rise.

I can see no other reason for the existence of art and poetry and religion except as they tend to restore in us a freshness of vision and a more emotional glamour and more vital sense of life. For as we grow older in life, our senses become gradually benumbed, our emotions become more callous to suffering and injustice and cruelty, and our vision of life is warped by too much preoccupation with cold, trivial realities. Fortunately, we have a few poets and artists who have not lost that sharpened sensibility, that fine emotional response and that freshness of vision, and whose duties are therefore to be our moral conscience, to hold up a mirror to our blunted vision, to tone up our withered nerves. Art should be a satire and a warning against our paralyzed emotions, our devitalized thinking and our denaturalized living. It teaches us unsophistication in a sophisticated world. It should restore to us health and sanity of living and enable us to recover from the fever and delirium caused by too much mental activity. It should sharpen our senses, re-establish the connection between our reason and our human nature, and assemble the ruined parts of a dislocated life again into a whole, by restoring our original nature. Miserable indeed is a world in which we have knowledge without understanding, criticism without appreciation, beauty without love, truth without passion, righteousness without mercy, and courtesy without a warm heart!

As for philosophy, which is the exercise of the spirit *par excellence,* the danger is even greater that we lose the feeling of life itself. I can understand that such mental delights include the solution of a long mathematical equation, or the perception of a grand order in the universe. This perception of order is probably the purest of all our mental pleasures and yet I would exchange it for a well prepared meal. In the first place, it is in itself almost a freak, a by-product of our mental occupations, enjoyable because it is gratuitous, but not in any case as imperative for us as other vital processes. That intellectual delight is, after all, similar to the delight of solving a crossword puzzle successfully. In the second place, the philosopher at this moment more often than not is likely to cheat himself, to fall in love with this abstract perfection, and to conceive a greater logical perfection in the world than is really warranted by reality itself. It is as much a false picture of things as when we paint a star with five points—a reduction to formula, an artificial stylizing, an over-simplification. So long as we do not overdo it, this delight in perfection is good, but let us remind ourselves that millions of people can be happy without discovering this simple unity of design. We really can afford to live without it. I prefer talking with a colored maid to talking with a mathematician; her words are more concrete, her laughter is more energetic, and I generally gain more in knowledge of human nature by talking with her. I am such a materialist that at any time I would prefer pork to poetry, and would waive a piece of philosophy for a piece of filet, brown and crisp and garnished with good sauce.

Only by placing living above thinking can we get away from this heat and the re-breathed air of philosophy and recapture some of the freshness and naturalness of true insight of the child. Any true philosopher ought to be ashamed of himself when he sees a child, or even a lion cub in a cage. How perfectly nature has fashioned him with his paws, his muscles, his beautiful coat of fur, his pricking ears, his bright round eyes, his agility and his sense of fun! The philosopher ought to be ashamed that God-made perfection has sometimes become man-made imperfection, ashamed that he wears spectacles, has no appetite, is often distressed in mind and heart, and is entirely unconscious of the fun in life. From this type of philosopher nothing is to be gained, for nothing that he says can be of importance to us. That philosophy alone can be of use to us which joins hands merrily with poetry and establishes for us a truer vision, first of nature and then of human nature.

Any adequate philosophy of life must be based on the harmony of our given instincts. The philosopher who is too idealistic is soon tripped up by nature herself. The highest conception of human dignity, according to the Chinese Confucianists, is when man reaches ultimately his greatest height, an equal of heaven and earth, by living in accordance with nature. This is the doctrine given in *The Golden Mean*, written by the grandson of Confucius.

> What is God-given is called nature; to follow nature is called *Tao* (the Way); to cultivate the Way is called culture. Before joy, anger, sadness and happiness are expressed, they are called the inner self; when they are expressed to the proper degree, they are called harmony. The inner self is the correct foundation of the world, and harmony is the illustrious Way. When a man has achieved the inner self and harmony, the heaven and earth are orderly and the myriad things are nourished and grow thereby.
>
> To arrive at understanding from being one's true self is called nature, and to arrive at being one's true self from understanding is called culture; he who is his true self has thereby understanding, and he who has understanding finds thereby his true self. Only those who are their absolute selves in the world can fulfil their own nature; only those who fulfil their own nature can fulfil the nature of others; only those who fulfil the nature of others can fulfil the nature of things; those who fulfil the nature of things are worthy to help Mother Nature in growing and sustaining life; and those who are worthy to help Mother Nature in growing and sustaining life are the equals of heaven and earth.